13-Digit ISBN: 978-1-64643-003-1

10-Digit ISBN: 1-64643-003-4

This book may be ordered by mail from the publisher. Please include $5.99 for
postage and handling. Please support your local bookseller first!
Books published by Cider Mill Press Book Publishers are available at special
discounts for bulk purchases in the United States by corporations, institutions,
and other organizations. For more information, please contact the publisher.

Cider Mill Press Book Publishers
"Where good books are ready for press"
501 Nelson Place
Nashville, Tennessee 37214
cidermillpress.com

Typography: Adobe Garamond, Brandon Grotesque, Lastra, Sackers English Script
Front cover image: Margherita, see page 237
Back cover image: Margherita with Panfried Zucchini, see page 396
Front endpaper image: Pear & Ricotta Focaccia, see page 600
Back endpaper image: Thick-Crust Pizza with Onions, see page 316

Printed in Malaysia
23 24 25 26 27 COS 10 9 8 7 6

PIZZA

The Ultimate Cookbook

BARBARA CARACCIOLO

CIDER MILL PRESS

BOOK PUBLISHERS

CONTENTS

Introduction 9

History of Focaccia 19

History of Pizza 55

The Perfect Pizza Pie 65

Master Doughs 81

Traditional Focaccia Recipes 127

Traditional Pizza Recipes 233

Global Pizza 281

Pizza Today 335

Focaccia Today 595

Salads and Sides 641

Desserts 679

Industry Insiders 709

Glossary 783

Index 794

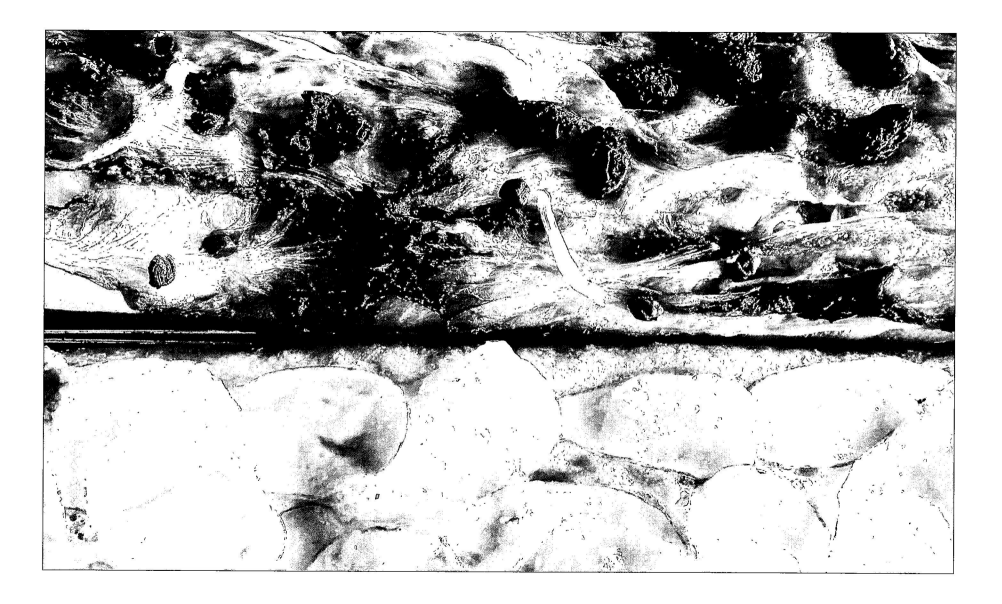

INTRODUCTION

$\mathscr{D}$o I remember the first time I ate pizza? Can I remember the first time I savored this special moist and flavored bread that melts in your mouth like no other bread?

Having been born in Rome in the 1970s, my first experience of pizza must have been paired with a good sip of baby formula. But I don't recall a singular first bite, just countless pizza-flavored childhood memories that blend together. The most vivid ones include the round, soft, and greasy Roman *pizza rossa*, eaten at the beach with a loud jukebox playing in the background; my mother's *pizza bianca e fichi*, salty white focaccia filled with Parma ham and fresh figs eaten on the way to the beach; the *pizza al taglio* I munched on so many times during epic traffic jams or mixed with tears after a vaccination shot; the round *pizza al piatto* delivered by a waiter at the restaurant when the whole family dined out with friends; and above all the little, fried *pizzelle* with tomato sauce that my Neapolitan neighbor's mom once made for us after a local fair.

As a young adult, I also had the chance to get to know the traditional ways of pizza and focaccia in other parts of Italy, from my Ligurian maternal grandmother's classic *focaccia Genovese*, *focaccia di Recco*, and *farinata*, to the pillowy yet substantial *sfincione* and *fugazz* dear to my paternal grandparents, who hailed from the southern reaches of Italy. And, of course, there were stops in Naples to taste the authentic Neapolitan pizza, the thin, chewy crust, which completely blended with its toppings to create a singular melting-in-the-mouth taste experience.

More recently, through my marriage to an American and my many trips overseas, I've been lucky to experience the latest developments of American pizza making and have learned to appreciate the regional variations, including the ever-changing gourmet pizza scene that has contributed immensely to the lively and, at times, unorthodox styles of pizza found across the continents today.

Finally, life brought me to Northern Europe, where I've had the chance to put some of my pizza and focaccia know-how to practice and share some of my love for this type of bread with my bakers and customers at Spigamadre, the Italian bakery I started in Stockholm.

My background is in health sciences, but the subject that has always made my heart beat stronger is food—baking in particular. That

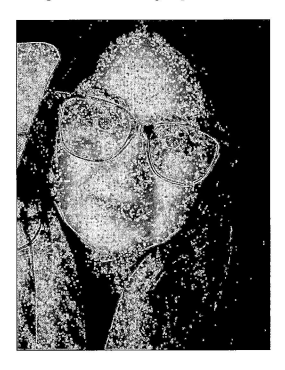

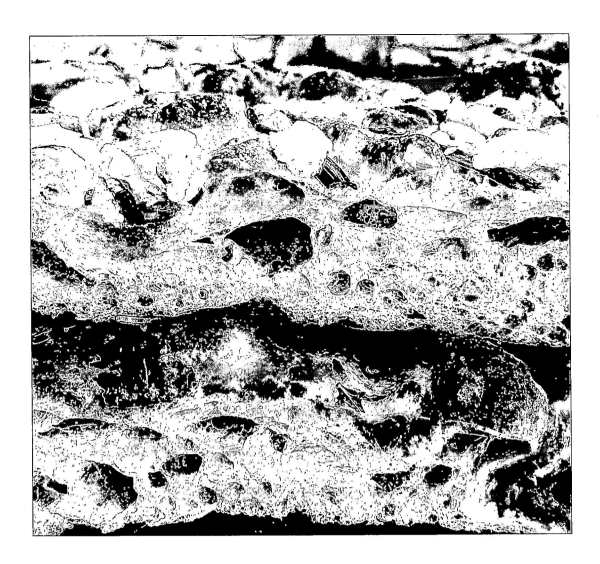

is why I am so grateful to have this opportunity to share my lifelong experience with one of the world's most popular foods in *Pizza: The Ultimate Cookbook*. I have so enjoyed fully immersing myself in my favorite subject once again, hoping that my deep love and admiration spreads to readers.

Pizza aims to cover the very broad topic of Italian flatbreads, including all sorts of traditional regional focaccias and pizzas. You will find an in-depth account of the history of focaccia and pizza in Italy and the world, from pre-Roman focaccias baked on an open fire to contemporary American styles and wild fusions.

I also present some of the foundational elements to make both focaccia and pizza, including various types of doughs that not only create different styles of these finished products, but also suit daily schedules and baking preferences.

Going through the traditional focaccia recipes, you will not only learn about the origins of pizza as we know it today, you will also be able to recreate, in your own kitchen, authentic regional Italian focaccias, many of which are rare and difficult to find today, even in Italy.

The pizza recipes cover a comprehensive selection of traditional Neapolitan and Italian toppings together with an even wider selection of modern American and international toppings. There are toppings galore here, with something for every palate, from vegetarian to meat lover, subtle to wildly spicy.

Two general notes about all of the focaccia and pizza recipes that follow:

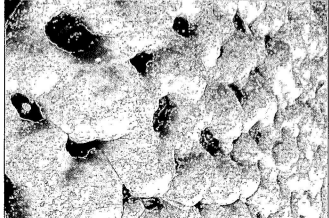

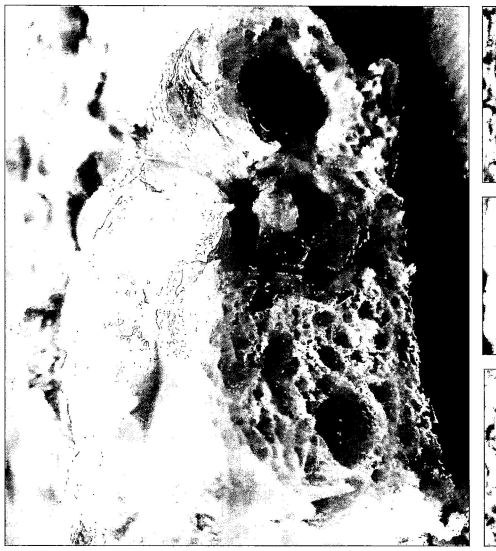

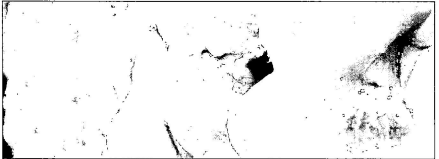
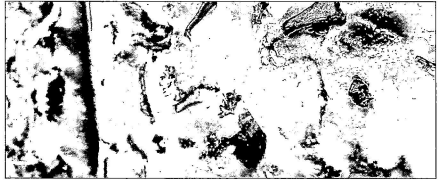

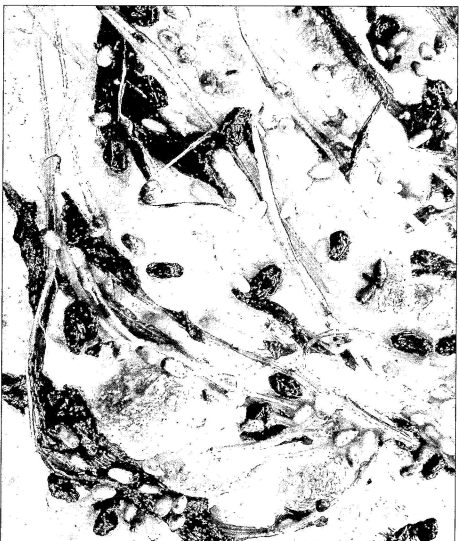

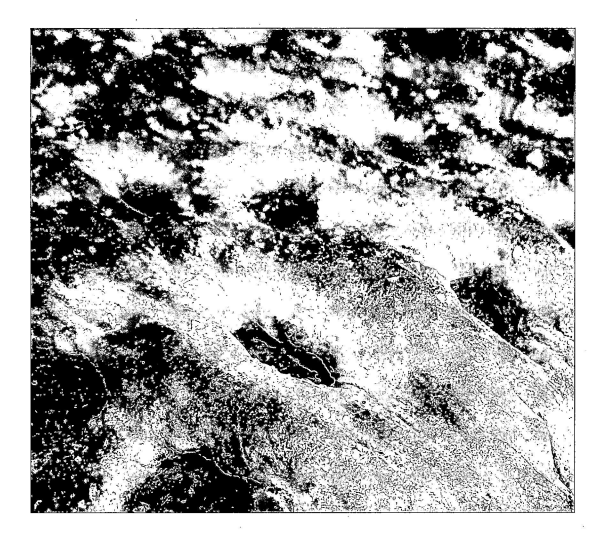

1. Different flours, particularly whole-wheat flours, can be used to make any of the crusts described in this book. I offer the simplest method possible, but experimentation with specialty flours is encouraged.

2. No matter where you live, all ovens are different. How long you allow your oven to preheat, how it holds heat, and whether or not a pizza stone or steel is being used will make a difference in cooking times. The recipes provide estimated cooking times that reflect how these focaccias and pizzas cook in my home oven when I make them. You'll want to watch what you're making and judge for yourself, using the recipe's timing as a guideline. There is also personal preference to take into account here, too, as some people like their crust crispier or their cheese more browned than others.

I hope this book will stay with you for a long time and feed your interest and love for focaccia and pizza, while feeding you and yours with a food that is not only scrumptious and soulful, but also wholesome and nourishing if baked, at home or commercially, by someone dedicated to this craft. When the dough is allowed to rise long enough and the toppings are carefully sourced, focaccia and pizza can in fact return to be the staples they once were— foods that are not only a joy to eat, but feed our bodies and make the best of ingrdients to create a whole meal in one sustaining slice.

Buon appetito!

Barbara

HISTORY OF FOCACCIA

When humans first started to understand that wild grains from the ripe grasses found in the fields surrounding their villages could be mashed, mixed with water, made into patties, and cooked on some type of pan over a fire, they may not have known it, but they had a close ancestor to what became focaccia. When talking of focaccia, in fact, we trace the development of this ancestral flatbread over the course of more than 2,500 years in Italy.

We know that, at some point in history, flatbread made out of a simple mixture of flour and water started to be flavored with wild herbs, and eventually this evolved to be leavened and cooked in an oven. But, originally, this Italian flatbread was simply cooked on the hearth.

The word *focaccia*, in fact, derives from the Latin *focàcia*, which literally means "baked on the ashes of a fireplace." In contemporary Italian dictionaries, focaccia is still defined as a flattened piece of dough that is cooked on the hearth or in an oven.

From the origins of the word, we have proof that the unleavened form of focaccia must have been the earliest form of bread in Italy.

THE FIRST FOCACCIA

According to legend, Aeneas was the progenitor of the people who came to inhabit Rome. The hero of Virgil's *Aeneid*, Aeneas arrived on the shores of Latium from his native Troy. Troy, its territory roughly corresponding to that of modern-day Turkey, was a bustling center of civilization for millennia until it was destroyed in a war with the ancient Greeks. Although the figure of Aeneas is legendary, it is possible that central Italy received eastern Mediterranean influence just before Rome's foundation in the sixth century BCE, and it is also possible that through this influence the first flatbreads—aka the precursors of focaccia—made their way to the shores of Italy.

Aeneas, handsome Iulus, and the foremost leaders, settled their limbs under the branches of a tall tree, and spread a meal: *they set wheat cakes for a base under the food (as Jupiter himself inspired them) and added wild fruits to these plates [mensa] of Ceres.*

When the poor fare drove them to set their teeth into the thin discs, the rest being eaten, and to break the fateful circles of bread boldly with hands and jaws, not sparing the quartered cakes, Iulus, jokingly, said: *"Ha! Are we eating the plates [mensa] too?"*

That voice on first being heard brought them to the end of their labors, and his father, as the words fell from the speaker's lips, caught them up and stopped him, awestruck at the divine will.

Immediately he said: "Hail, land destined to me by fate, and hail to you, O faithful gods of Troy: here is our home, here is our country. For my father Anchises (now I remember) left this secret of fate with me: *'Son, when you're carried to an unknown shore, food is lacking, and you're forced to eat the plates [mensa].'*"

—*Virgil,* Aeneid *(VII.107–147),*
translated by A. S. Kline

From this passage, we learn that this hardened flatbread called *mensa,* which meant "table" or "plate," was not eaten by the higher classes but instead served as a base for other food, particularly juicy meats, to rest upon. The servants would then eat the leftover flatbread, which had been softened and flavored by the meats they could not afford. This fits with the very humble role that focaccia assumed in Italian cuisine: an unsophisticated food, eaten by common people, often serving as a worker's lunch thanks to its affordability and portability.

So perhaps the first Italian focaccia was not Roman in origin, but Mediterranean. Or maybe it was Greek, considering that Greek colonies were established in southern Italy long before the Romans settled in central Italy.

Another possibility is that the first focaccia was Italic rather than Roman, Mediterranean, or Greek. We know that cereals such as barley and emmer were the staple of the Sabini and Etruscans, the Italic populations that were settled near Rome and its surrounding regions before the advent of Roman civilization. Among those populations, cereals were eaten as a porridge consisting of ground flour, cooked whole in soups, or rudimentarily baked into flat cakes.

A round, focaccia-like cake was indeed part of a complex ritual devoted to the Italic goddess Juno. The two surviving descriptions of this ritual mention a young virgin carrying a cake as an offering to a dragon-snake.

Etruscans were also known to bake a focaccia that has survived to modern times, the *focaccia al testo*, typical to the formerly Etruscan region of Umbria, which sits northeast of Rome. The focaccia al testo, also known as *torta al testo*, is nowadays cooked on a hot cast-iron plate, but originally, it was cooked on earthenware. The focaccia al testo was unleavened and probably unsalted, and it is easy to imagine it being filled with savory foods after cooking, just as it is nowadays.

We know of a similarly small, round focaccia made with emmer existing in Rome's early period. Known as *offa*, it was used as an offering in religious rituals.

Further evidence of proto-focaccia existing during the rise of Rome was found on a vase recovered from the ruins of Pompeii (79 BCE), on which a snake is represented beside a round flatbread.

THE FOCACCIA OF THE ROMANS

The Romans became master bakers thanks to four major innovations. First, wheat started to be imported to Latium's shores, quickly becoming *the* cereal of Rome. Second, the Romans learned how to leaven bread via the Greeks (a technique the Greeks had learned from the Egyptians) and the Romans then perfected what they'd learned. Third, the Romans invented water mills, which are still in use today. These precursors to windmills allowed for the production of much finer flours, resulting in breads that were much lighter than those previously known. This light, feathery quality remains a trademark of Italian breads and focaccias to this day. Fourth, the Romans perfected the bread oven, inventing wood-fired ovens that were very similar to the wood-fired pizza ovens in use today.

We know of many types of breads available to the Romans, but besides the name—*focàcia,* or the Latin *panis focàcius* that later transferred to Italian—there is no known mention of focaccia in Roman texts.

Some scholars think *placenta* was a type of focaccia, and of this preparation we have a recipe dated circa 160 BCE, appearing in the treatise *De Agri Cultura* by Cato the Elder:

Make *placenta* in this way. Two pounds of wheat flour, from which you make the base, four pounds of flour and two pounds of best emmer for the *tracta* (strips of pastry). Soak the emmer in water.

When it is well-softened, place in a clean mortar and drain well. Then knead with your hands. When it will have been well kneaded, add four pounds of flour gradually. Make both into *tracta*. Arrange them in a wicker basket, where they may dry.

The recipe goes on to describe how to alternate the dried strips of dough with cheese and honey, producing something that sounds similar to a lasagna.

In the same text, we also find a recipe for *libum*, which is more similar to the focaccia we know today:

In a mortar, mince 1 kg of sheep's cheese; after having chopped it well, add 500 [grams] of flour or, if you want it to be softer, only 250 [grams] of flour; you will add an egg and mix well. Then you will form the bread; put some bay leaves under the bread; you will cook it slowly on a hot fire, covering it with a lid.

We now know that *libum* was a rich flatbread used as an offering in religious rituals; it was not eaten on a daily basis by common people.

Panis focàcius, on the other hand, was not known by the Roman elite, as the fine bakeries in Rome and other affluent centers of the empire turned out much more sophisticated loaves.

No, the delicious humble flatbread we know as focaccia was with all certainty baked in the home, upon the *focus*—as the hearth in plebeian homes was known. Similar to later wood-fired stoves, the *focus* was often located at the rear of these small dwellings, so that these unrefined kitchens would remain out of sight. In Latin, *focus* means "center of the home," and the derived Italian word, *focolare*, is indeed used as a synonym for home.

Panis focàcius, then, was likely the only bread that could be baked in these rudimentary kitchens. As the etymology of the word focàcius tells us, focaccia was baked upon the ashes that collected in the base of this wood-fired stove rather than on the stove itself. This simple bread was most likely what laborers took with them to eat as their *prandium*, or lunch.

It is also possible that a version of pa*nis focàcius* was turned out by bakeries and sold as a cheap street food. Indeed, we know that in Rome a simple focaccia seasoned with olive oil and salt, known as *pizza bianca*, has been a staple of the city's life for what seems like forever.

A SENSE OF PLACE:
THE FOCACCIA OF THE ITALIANS

When talking about focaccia, we should not think that there is a prototypical Italian focaccia. There is nothing of the sort. There are as many focaccias as there are regions in Italy and, if we went deep enough, we would find some regions that have as many focaccias as there are villages.

After the fall of the Roman Empire, the availability of cereals in Italy was reduced considerably. Wheat was no longer grown or imported through the once-affluent harbor of Ostia. During the lower Middle Ages, focaccia survived, but was made with lower-quality grains—whatever was locally available in those austere, uncertain times.

Concerning this era, there is once again a paucity of focaccia-related evidence. But we can imagine that the wide diversity of Italian focaccias arose in these times where regions, cities, and villages were isolated from each other.

Even with the obvious differences between these regional variants, it is indisputable that they hold the Roman origin in common—despite the fact that Italy wasn't politically or linguistically united for centuries.

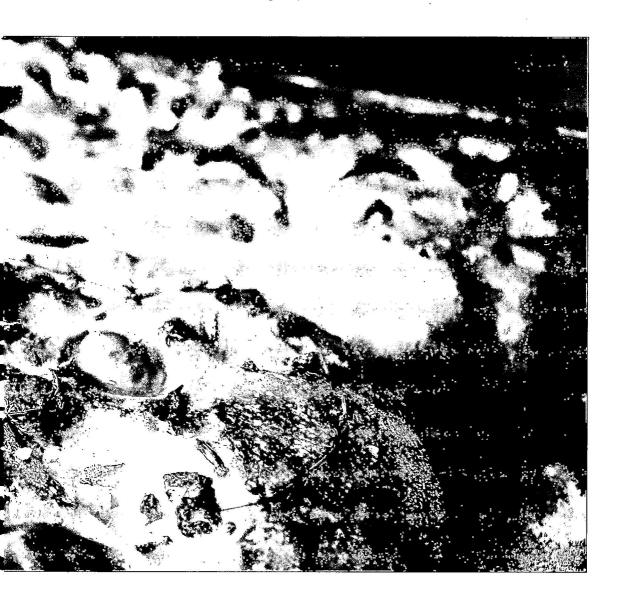

A REGIONAL FOCACCIA ENCYCLOPEDIA

*T*his collection of the best-known styles of focaccia is organized by region. So many more focaccias are to be found in local contexts, and many other variations have disappeared. I have tried to be as comprehensive as possible, but as it is an inexhaustible topic, someone's beloved variety of this flatbread is bound to be overlooked.

Focaccia, although used in several regions, is not the only name used to define this flatbread. *Schiacciata, stiacciata, pinza, pinzone*, and *pizza* are other popular terms, and many other lesser-known appellations exist.

TRENTINO ALTO ADIGE &
FRIULI VENEZIA GIULIA

The most northeastern regions of Italy lack a strong focaccia tradition due to their weather and geography, which are not optimal for growing wheat (grapes for wine do much better).

SMACAFAM

This is the closest dish the northeastern regions have to a focaccia. It comes from Trentino Alto Adige and is enriched with eggs and sausage and eaten in slices. Its roots are in the Christian carnival celebrated in February, but it is now eaten year round.

VENETO

Just below Friuli Venezia Giulia, in Veneto *focaccia* means "cake," and, confusingly, we can find panettone-like cakes referred to as focaccia there. The savory and flat focaccia we know is called *pinza* in the region, and a few variations exist within its borders.

PINZA ONTA POLESANA

From Polesine, a town close to the city of Rovigo, this focaccia is enriched with lard and milk and can include pieces of fried pork (*ciccioli*); it is often enjoyed with one of the local cured meats.

SCHIZOTO

Moving closer to Padova, we find a focaccia that is similar to pinza onta polesana, but thinner because it is unleavened. It seems every family has its own version, but it is common to include goose lard and grappa in the dough.

PINZA MUNARA

It is only appropriate that legend cites this Po River Valley focaccia as being created by a miller whose mill was on the river. One day, the river was so high that the miller was stuck in the mill with no food, and his family couldn't bring him anything. So he used the only ingredients he had at hand: flour and grease from his lantern. Thus pinza munara, with its unique multilayered appearance, was born. Today, it is best to recreate it with better ingredients—in particular, lard or olive oil in place of the lantern grease.

LOMBARDY

In Lombardy, local focaccias have survived mostly in the countryside, while the cities have been overrun by imported versions. If one goes to Italy's fashion and business capital, Milan—which is also the biggest city in Lombardy—most focaccias are actually pizzas that originated in other parts of the country.

BRUSADELA

The small village of Romagnese, which has a population of fewer than 1,000, holds an annual festival dedicated to this focaccia, the name of which means "a little burned" in local dialect; it is a reference to how these little round focaccia pies are baked directly on the stone of a wood-fired oven. Extremely simple but nonetheless delicious when done right, brusadela is made by flattening pieces of leavened dough that were originally used to test the temperature of an oven.

TIRÒT

In the town of Felonica, near Mantua, we find a focaccia that comprises a thin layer of soft dough covered with an abundance of local onions. The name derives from how the dough is stretched to make it fit in a baking pan (from *tirare,* "to stretch"). The onion variety is a delicate, golden one harvested during the summer, meaning this focaccia was once a seasonal treat— but now you can savor it year-round in the town.

FOCACCIA FIORETTO

Hailing from the mountains of Valchiavenna, in Sondrio Province, this sweet focaccia is characterized by the use of wild anise, known as *fioretto* in the region. Traditionally baked at home, this focaccia originated by combining leftover bread dough with eggs, butter, and sugar. Once out of the oven, focaccia fioretto is topped with the aforementioned chopped wild anise; anise seeds are a good substitute for wild anise if the latter is not available near you.

PIEDMONT

In Piedmont, the northern Italian region bordered by France and Switzerland, traditional focaccia primarily survives in its sweet version, and only in a few small outposts. In Turin, Piedmont's capital, there is a predominance of southern focaccias and pizzas that became popular thanks to the immigrants that arrived after World War II. The most popular of them all is *pizza al padellino*, a savory focaccia baked in a round cast-iron skillet, like the Apulian *focaccia barese*, but topped like Neapolitan pizza—a real fusion of Italian traditions.

FUGASCINA DI MERGOZZO

Also called *figascina*, it was traditionally baked for the celebration of Saint Elizabeth in Mergozzo and nearby villages. Today, local bakeries carry it year-round; it is made of a dough enriched with butter, sugar, and eggs, rolled thin, and cut into squares to be baked on a baking sheet.

FOCACCIA DI SUSA

Coming from the mountainous area of Valle di Susa, this focaccia is rounder and taller than fugascina di mergozzo, though also made with a dough featuring butter, sugar, and eggs. Originally made to celebrate Christmas and New Year, it is now found year-round in local bakeries.

FOCACCIA DI GIAVENO

A variation on focaccia di susa hailing from the beautiful mountain town of Giaveno, the dough is enriched by orange zest and vanilla and shaped into small, fluffy focaccia that are absolutely delectable.

MIACCIA

This focaccia is typical of the Valsesia area of Piedmont, an alpine valley close to the Swiss border, but it is also found in villages nearby. Made with wheat flour or a combination of wheat flour and cornmeal, it is enriched with milk or cream and eggs. It is a very thin focaccia, almost like a French crepe, and it is cooked over an open fire or on a stove using a specialty cast-iron pan known as *ferro delle miacce*, which has to be extremely hot before the batter gets poured onto it. Miaccia can be eaten plain, filled with local soft cheeses, or made into a sweet treat with blueberry jam.

AOSTA VALLEY

In this beautiful Alpine region, corn is the grain that dominates the focaccia scene.

MIASSA

This is a close relative of Piedmont's miaccia, as it is cooked and filled in the same way. But the dough is based upon cornmeal, and traditionally it would only use cornmeal and water; later versions that have been enriched with butter, eggs, and milk are common. Miassa is baked on extremely hot and thin square cast-iron pans that are placed directly over an open fire. Miassa vendors are commonly found at local fairs, where they fill these focaccia with soft local cheeses, cold cuts, or jam.

LIGURIA

Liguria is one of the most important regions for focaccia. In fact, this thin stretch of land between the Mediterranean and the northern Apennine Mountains has such a strong tradition that focaccia is often mistakenly thought of as Ligurian rather than Italian.

Indeed, the focaccia drought that followed the fall of Rome never took hold in Liguria, especially in the Genoa area. Here, focaccia remains the daily bread. It is eaten at breakfast, dipped in *caffè latte,* and serves as a quick lunch when there is no time to stop for a full meal; it is also frequently served with a cocktail in the late afternoon. Focaccia is the most traditional afternoon snack, or *merenda,* for kids as well.

So, what is the secret of focaccia remaining so popular in Liguria for so long? One reason may be the consistent availability of wheat, particularly in the large port of Genoa. The landscape of Liguria is also favorable for the cultivation of wheat, although harvests were probably not sufficient to cover the needs of the local population. However, when there was no wheat to harvest or trade, Ligurians still held dearly to their focaccia, using chickpea flour to make a delicious variation called *farinata.*

Another reason for the endurance of Liguria's focaccia tradition is the abundance of the other main ingredient of the focaccias found along the Italian coastline: olive oil. It is often argued that Ligurian olive oil is the best in the country. While there are, of course, different schools of thought about this, with several other regions vying for the title, it is universally agreed that the olives growing in this sun-kissed, hilly soil are of the highest quality.

FOCACCIA GENOVESE

This is the classical white and oily flatbread with the "holes" that many assume to be a ubiquitous characteristic of focaccia. *Fugàssa,* as it is called locally, is typical of Genoa. It used to be eaten on street corners as well as in church, and was particularly popular among the *camalli,* workers who loaded and unloaded cargo in the large harbor.

Focaccia genovese is baked in oven trays, so it has a square rather than round shape. It is taller than average but not towering, rising about ¾ inch high. The focaccia has deep indents put there by the baker's fingers, and these are then filled with olive oil. The only other ingredient is time. This focaccia, more than others, needs to

be given enough time to rise in order to achieve that perfect amount of chewiness in the crumb and slightly crunchy crust.

FUGÀSSA CO A CIÒULA

"Focaccia with onions," this was popular in the working-class neighborhoods of Genoa and a big favorite among the *camalli*.

FOCACCIA DI VOLTRI

A thinner version of focaccia genovese which is not baked in oven trays but is instead loaded directly on the bak-ing stone, a special technique that makes it stretch considerably inside the oven. While focaccia Genovese can be made very easily at home, focaccia di Voltri is typically a specialty product turned out by bakeries.

FOCACCIA CON LE OLIVE

Moving west along the Ligurian coast, we find this "olive focaccia." The addition of this delicious ingredient can be attributed to the many olive-processing facilities in this area, creating a need for a method to use olives that were a bit damaged, as this defect precluded them from being made into quality olive oil. There is also a version that uses the leftover olives from the first processing of the oil, which, after being boiled, make for an amazing focaccia.

PISSALANDREA

In Imperia, at the western end of the Ligurian coast, we find the pissalandrea. The origin of the name is uncertain. Some attribute it to Andrea Doria, a famous admiral; others believe that the name derives from the French *pissaladière*. Pissalandrea, also known as *piscialandrea* or *pizza all'Andrea*, was originally topped with anchovies, garlic, and olives; later, when tomatoes were imported to Europe from the New World, tomato sauce was added. Pissalandrea does evoke pizza napoletana, both for the presence of tomato sauce and its round shape; even the name evokes the close relationship. However, this focaccia is thicker than pizza napoletana and is baked in a pan, not directly on a stone. At best, this ancient focaccia is a great-grandmother of pizza as we know it. A very similar version of can be found in Apricale, where it is called *machetusa*. In the beautiful town of Sanremo, this focaccia is enriched by capers and called *sardenaira*.

KIZOA

In the inland of La Spezia, close to the border with Tuscany, we find a peculiar focaccia that features *salsiccia*, an Italian sausage, enclosed between two thin layers of bread. This special focaccia was traditionally baked on November 2, All Souls' Day, the Catholic day of remembrance.

FARINATA

Going back to the Genoa coast, this ancient focaccia is made with chickpea flour, *farinata* or *fainâ* in Ligurian, instead of wheat flour. There are many stories speculating about its origin, including one that credits Roman soldiers; another story posits that the recipe was accidentally created during a battle between Genoa and Pisa. This focaccia is made from chickpea flour, water, and olive oil, and seasoned with salt and rosemary. It is generally eaten as is, delicious in its simplicity.

REVZORA

In the hilly inland of Genoa, Campo Ligure in Valle Stura, wheat was not always readily available, and so we find this focaccia that was originally made with wheat bran. The name derives from the local word for "bran," *ravezö*, as the region's peasants could not afford wheat flour and had access only to the leftovers from the milling and sifting process—the wheat bran, which was not considered nutritious prior to the modern era. Today, these small, round focaccia are baked in oven dishes and made with a mix of cornmeal and wheat flour.

FOCACCIA DI RECCO

One of the most celebrated Ligurian specialties, and with good reason. Together with piadina romagnola, it is the rare Italian focaccia with an IGP mark (Protected Geographical Designation). It consists of two thin layers of focaccia dough wrapped around a rich layer of local soft cheese that melts wonderfully when baked. It is possible to recreate something similar to focaccia di Recco at home, but as the IGP mark states, tasting the real thing requires a trip to Recco, which is not too far from Genoa.

EMILIA ROMAGNA

This is where Parmesan cheese, Parma ham, tortellini, and ragù were born, a rather wide region culturally divided in two parts: Emilia, where the cities of Piacenza, Parma, Reggio Emilia, Modena, Ferrara, and Bologna are located; and Romagna, home to Cesena, Faenza, Forlì, Imola, Ravenna, and Rimini. Unsurprisingly, the focaccia tradition follows this division—a good reason to explore both sides of this culinary wonderland. On one side, there is Romagna's trademark, the piadina, an unleavened focaccia similar to Umbria's torta al testo. In Emilia, unique, leavened focaccias called crescentine can be found.

PIADINA

The name derives from the Byzantine term for "plate," which refers to piadina or *piada* being cooked on an earthenware plate. Piadina can also be baked in a cast-iron pan. This thin, unleavened focaccia is an extremely popular street food on the coasts of Romagna, the locals' daily bread now as it was millennia ago. It is often filled with cured meats and cheese and enjoyed hot.

CRESCENTA

In Emilia, particularly in Bologna, "focaccia" is a synonym of crescenta. This focaccia is leavened (*crescere* means "to grow"), and bears a close resemblance to focaccia Genovese, though the "crescenta" is often taller and softer.

CRESCENTINE O TIGELLE

Crescentine means "little crescent," and indeed these focaccia are a smaller version of the leavened focaccia that is classic in the region. They are also called *tigelle*, from the name of the double-earthenware plates originally used to cook them. Now they are mostly cooked on aluminum or cast-iron pans. They are popular in the mountainside towns of Emilia, but are also eaten in the cities as a street food, especially during festivals and fairs. When made in the designated tigelle pans, these soft flatbreads commonly feature unique floral patterns.

PINZONE FERRARESE

In Ferrara it was traditional to bake small focaccia shaped like a diamond, with slits on the top; variations include ham or onion fillings. One thing that never changes: lard is always one of the ingredients.

CHISOLA PIACENTINA

In the Emilian town of Val Tidone, it is traditional to make a leavened focaccia enriched with pieces of ciccioli (see torta coi ciccioli, page 38). According to legend, this leavened focaccia dates back to 1155, when King Frederick Barbarossa of Germany passed through the town with his troops. The king and his troops were supposedly given heaps of chisola, an offering they found so satisfying that no locals were harmed.

TUSCANY

Tuscany, just south of Liguria, is part of the territory that was once occupied by the Etruscans, among the earliest makers of focaccia in Italy. The tradition of focaccia in the region, popularly known as *schiaccia* or *schiacciata*, remains strong.

CECINA

This chickpea-based focaccia is called *cecina* in Pisa and Lucca, and *torta di ceci* in the town of Livorno. There is a fascinating legend linked to its origin, revolving around a heroine that saved Pisa from the attack of the *saraceni* (the Arabs) circa 1000 CE. According to the legend a young woman, Kinzica de' Sismondi, sounded the alarm as the invaders approached. Among the many items thrown at the invaders from the barricaded city were chickpeas and oil. The story says that the two mixed and the sun cooked them in the street, resulting in a discovery that the combination was delicious.

CIACCINO SENESE

A focaccia filled with leftovers from the processing of pork. Originally, this was made in the countryside. Today, the best-known version is made in Siena, where it is filled with ham and mozzarella cheese. A properly made ciaccino senese should be crunchy on the outside and very soft on the inside.

FOCACCIA LEVA DI GALLICANO

In the northern inland of Tuscany, in a beautiful

mountainous area called Garfagnana, it is still common to find focaccia made just as it was in antiquity by the Etruscans and Romans, in a *testo*. The *testo* is a two-sided, heavy metal pan with long handles that can be placed directly over a fire and easily flipped, allowing one to produce perfect focaccia. The focaccia made in Gallicano is *leva* ("leavened"), and contains potatoes, shortening, and milk; it is typically filled with local cured meats or cheese.

FOCACCETTE DI AULLA

In Lunigiana, on the border with Liguria, these small, leavened focaccias are made with corn and wheat. Typically, they are baked in miniature, earthenware *testo* pans that are placed directly on an open fire, but it is also possible to make focaccette di aulla in a regular oven.

SCHIACCIA

In Tuscany, the most common terms for focaccia are *schiacciata, schiaccia*, and *ciaccia*; they all mean "flattened," referring to the process of flattening the dough before baking it. Tuscan schiaccia has rural origins; it was made in the wood-fired ovens found on every farm, big or small, and baked once a week along with the other breads. This type of focaccia was cooked directly on the stone before the bread, helping to determine if the oven was ready to bake the more substantial loaves. It is a focaccia similar to the Genovese iteration, but thinner and crunchier. Another characteristic of Tuscan schiaccia is that the most common versions do not include much salt—this focaccia was originally made from the same dough as bread, which in Tuscany is unsalted.

SCHIACCIA CON L'UVA

This popular variation of schiaccia adds fresh black grapes; it used to be seasonal, made during the harvest of the juicy Tuscan grapes. Like the regular schiaccia, it was made with an unsalted dough, rolled into two thin layers, and filled with grapes before the final rise and baking. Simple and absolutely toothsome.

UMBRIA

This beautiful region borders Tuscany and is part of the territory once inhabited by the Etruscans. Here focaccia is usually cooked in *testo* pans, though there are also *schiacciate*—focaccias traditionally baked on the stone of a wood-fired oven.

SCHIACCIATA CON CIPOLLA E SALVIA

One of the tastiest Umbrian schiacciate is flavored with onions and sage. Like Tuscan schiaccia, it's made with a simple bread dough containing little or no salt. It is generally shaped into a round disk and covered with finely sliced onions and sage leaves before going into the oven.

TORTA AL TESTO

The most typical Umbrian focaccia is not called focaccia but *torta*, which means "cake" in Italian. Torta al testo is a rather thin and dry disk cooked in a *testo* pan. The original recipe is unsalted and unleavened, but baking soda is frequently added today.

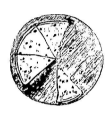

TORTA COI CICCIOLI

Umbria, a hilly region known for pig farming, produces some of the best Italian cured meats. Ciccioli is a by-product of making lard. In the name of using every part of a slaughtered pig, pieces of ciccioli are worked directly into the dough for this thin, unleavened focaccia, making it a meal in itself.

MARCHE

This region runs along Italy's eastern coastline before heading up into the hills inland.

CRESCIA SFOGLIATA

Close to the border with Romagna, in the UNESCO World Heritage Site of Urbino, we find a focaccia very similar to piadina. Disregard the fact that the name evokes leavening (remember, *crescere* means "to grow"), this focaccia is unleavened and cooked in a *testo*. Another peculiarity of this flatbread lies in the *sfogliata* component, which means "layered." The dough is layered with lard, flattened, and baked, giving this focaccia a flaky lightness that piadina doesn't have. It is typically eaten filled with a soft cheese and ham.

CHICHIRIPIENO

In the ancient town of Offida we find a leavened focaccia filled with a won-derfully Mediterranean blend of flavors, such as tuna, anchovies, paprika, and capers. Every first Sunday of August, Offida hosts a fair dedicated solely to this scrumptious focaccia.

CACCIANNANZE

The name of this rustic focaccia roughly translates to "taken out of the oven before the bread," mean-ing that it was used to test the temperature of the oven before the primary baking could be done. Like many other focaccias of this type, cacciannanze is made with the same dough used for the bread and flattened. In this case, that dough gets topped with salt, olive oil, rosemary, and garlic.

LAZIO

Lazio, the region surrounding Rome, where 2,000 years ago bakers brought the craft of breadmaking to unprecedented levels of sophistication. Here, focaccia is mainly urban, coming from the minds and hands of professional bakers since antiquity, rather than being a product of the land, as is generally the case with focaccia in Italy. The more recent innovations made by this gifted bunch will be covered in depth in the pizza section.

PIZZA BIANCA ROMANA

As in the south-central regions of Italy, in Rome focaccia is known as *pizza*.

Today, there are plenty of versions of Roman pizza, but the only authentically ancient version is pizza bianca. Compared with focaccia Genovese, pizza bianca romana is thinner, featuring a more alveolate crumb, visible bubbles on the surface, and a crispy crust. It is often cut in the middle and filled with cured ham or mortadella. In the summer, a (very Roman) filling of fresh figs is added. Created in bakeries, this focaccia is slid right off a baker's peel into the oven. It was traditionally baked after bread, because it needs more time to ferment. Typically ready around 11 a.m., it was, and still is, a great *spezzafame* ("midday snack"), an important option in a busy and chaotic city like Rome. Different from most focaccias, pizza bianca is never baked at home—but it is possible, of course, and a worthy experiment for those unable to travel to Rome.

FALIA DI PRIVERNO

This peculiar focaccia comes from the rural rather than the urban tradition.

Thick and oval, it is made from dough that has been enriched with lard and olive oil; it is slightly reminiscent of French *fougasse*. Often filled with sautéed baby broccoli, it was the staple food of local shepherds. Today it is hard to find; your best bet is in early March, during the festival dedicated to this broccoli-based food in Priverno: Sagra della Falia e Broccoletti.

ABRUZZI

Perched on the Adriatic coastline and in the Apennine Mountains, in Abruzzi focaccias are called *pizze*.

PIZZ'ONTA

This thin, round, and large focaccia was traditionally fried in big pans filled with sizzling lard; that preparation is still very typical at local fairs. It is generally paired with roasted meat skewers in its salted version. There is also a sweet version that gets coated with sugar instead of sprinkled with salt.

PIZZA CON LE SFRIGOLE

Another focaccia that includes the leftovers of lard processing, called *sfrigole* in Abruzzi. These are the fibrous parts that remain after rendering a pig's fat. In Abruzzi, as in other rural, hilly Italian regions, it was very common for families to raise pigs to be slaughtered in late fall. Eating meat was a luxury in these rural areas, and because of this scarcity, nothing could be wasted. Pizza con le sfrigole employs a leavened dough that is rolled quite thin and baked in an oven, typically on a baking sheet.

PIZZA SCIMA

The name literally means "stupid pizza," which is probably a reference to the extreme simplicity of this unleavened focaccia. Its taste is not dull, however, thanks to the higher than usual amount of olive oil added to the dough. The traditional way of cooking it is also noteworthy: the disk of dough is scored in a crosshatch pattern and then placed directly on the stone in a fireplace under a cone-shaped lid called a *coppo*, which is then covered with embers.

MOLISE

Just south of Abruzzi, the rural inland region of Molise has a strong tradition of both leavened and unleavened focaccias that utilize the best local ingredients.

PIZZA DI GRANOTURCO

In many areas of Italy starting in the 1600s, maize (*granoturco* in Italian) became a staple cereal. It is likely that this focaccia was being made before then, with other cereals commonly used by peasants, such as millet or semolina. The traditional pizza di granoturco includes equal parts coarse durum flour and cornmeal. It is baked in the same fashion as Abruzzi's pizza scima (see page 41). It is typical to serve this focaccia with a soup featuring wild local greens.

PIZZA ASSETTATA

Another unleavened focaccia. The name means "seated pizza," and it consists of a thin disk made from a mix of soft wheat and durum flours and flavored with fennel seeds and chili flakes. It is typically baked in a wood-fired oven.

KRESE

Found in the town of San Felice only, this focaccia owes its name to a colony of Slavic people that occupied this area in the 1600s. It is leavened and topped with onions and anchovies. Typically made on the occasion of Saint Joseph's Day in March, it was traditionally baked on a large baking sheet or shaped into small, round focaccias.

CAMPANIA

Focaccia in Campania is mostly influenced by the tradition of its main city, Naples. The most celebrated treat hailing from this region, Neapolitan pizza, will be described in depth in the next section.

PANUOZZO

From the hills around Gragnano, not far from the breathtaking destinations of Amalfi and Ravello, comes this scrumptious filled focaccia. Panuozzo is made with the same dough used for Neapolitan pizza, but is shaped into long, ciabatta-type loaves, baked, and then cut in the middle; it is then filled with everything from cheese and sausage to broccoli rabe and baked again, allowing the fillings to influence the flavor and lending the crust a delightful crunch.

PARIGINA

Like panuozzo, the base of this filled focaccia is Neapolitan pizza dough. The dough is placed in a deep

dish and then topped with tomato sauce, ham, and cheese, covered with a layer of puff pastry, and then brushed with a wash of heavy cream and egg yolk. The name *parigina*, "from Paris," is a reference to the French origin of puff pastry. It is generally a midday snack served by cafes and take-away restaurants, but it is also possible to make a delicious version at home.

MONTANARE

These miniature focaccia are also called *pizzelle* and are fried pieces of highly hydrated or overproofed pizza dough, topped with marinara sauce and pecorino cheese. The origin is uncertain. Some sources say they are older than Neapolitan pizza and that they came to Naples via people who emigrated from the mountains (*montanare* means "from the mountains"); other sources say that they were first made in the homes of local bakers. According to this version, the bakers were allowed to take leftover pizza dough home, where their wives would fry it, rather than baking it, simply because they did not have an oven. In this version of the story, the name would have derived from the toppings, which were the simple ingredients mountain people filled their sandwiches with. No matter how it came about, montanare is a must-try; not only is it tasty, you don't even need an oven.

CALABRIA

The southernmost region of mainland Italy has some very special focaccias that have survived in the small and isolated towns in the countryside.

LESTOPITTA

Bova Superiore, a magnificent hamlet on the hilly side of the most southern part of Calabria, is considered the center of the small community of Calabrian people who still speak Greek; they are direct descendants of the region's ancient Greek colonies. The name of this focaccia is of clear Greek origin, from *leptòs*, "thin," and *pita*, "flatbread." This round focaccia is made with local durum wheat flour and little else, and it is fried in olive oil instead of baked. Absolutely scrumptious and crunchy when hot, it becomes pliable when cool and can be rolled around various fillings.

GRUPARIATA

From the in the little town of Luzzi, comes a colorful focaccia made red by the chili powder and tomatoes in its dough; it is fluffy and tall, and topped with anchovies or sardines, tomatoes, oregano, and garlic. Grupariata is an explosion of southern Italian flavors. Its name means "pitted," due to the indentations made to accommodate the toppings. It was traditionally made for religious festivities but is now enjoyed year round.

BASILICATA

This southern, inland region of Italy is characterized by fertile plains enclosed by mountains. Its rich cuisine, including its focaccias, is a result of ancient traditions.

FUCUAZZA

Hailing from the ancient Avigliano, this leavened, sheet-pan focaccia is rolled quite thin and seasoned with tomato sauce, olive oil, and oregano; the tomato sauce is a more recent development, likely added in the mid-1800s.

STRAZZATA

Something between a bread and a focaccia, *strazzata* means "torn apart," which alludes to the way it is supposed to be eaten. Originally served on festive occasions, particularly weddings, this flatbread has a hole in the center and a spicy kick. The very simple dough is made with sourdough and a mixture of wheat flours and then spiced up with abundant pepper. It is baked on a hot stone and eaten as is or filled with meats, savory cheeses, or grilled sweet peppers. The town of Stagliuozzo, which counts no more than 250 residents, holds a strazzata festival every August.

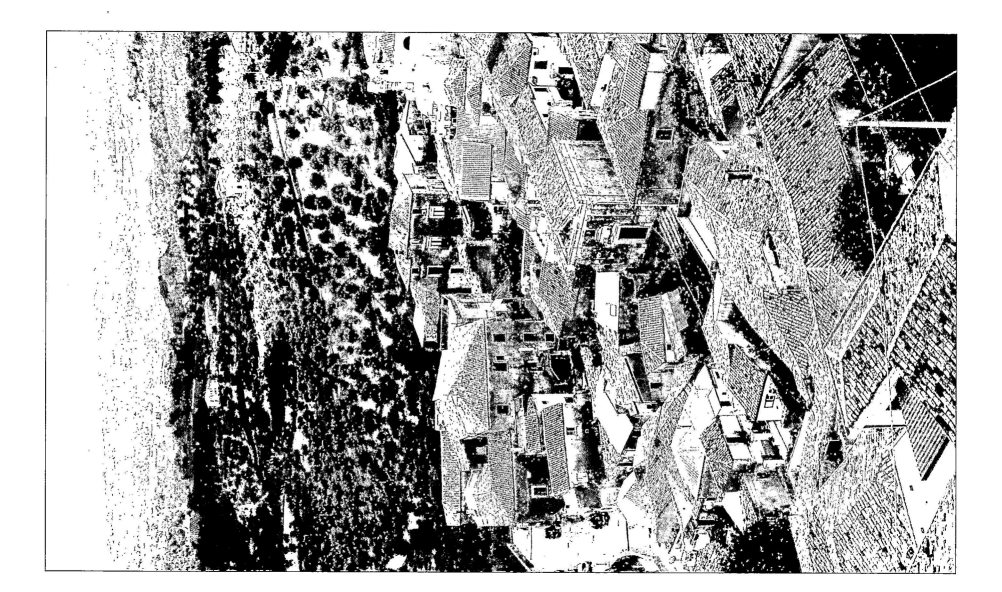

APULIA

Along with Sicily, Apulia has the strongest focaccia tradition in southern Italy. Found between the Apennine Mountains and a beautiful, long coastline, Apulia is characterized by a fertile inland marked by olive trees and durum wheat fields, and coastal cities with bustling ports, making the region a bridge between the East and West since antiquity. Focaccia was traditionally made at home, and every household had its own version. Nowadays dozens of different Apulian focaccias still survive; these are the most common ones.

FOCACCIA BARESE

In the busy city of Bari, focaccia is eaten straight out of the oven, savored while walking down the streets by stylish locals who are unconcerned about the prospect of staining their outfits. Often consumed for breakfast, lunch, or a midday snack, focaccia barese is perfect for a long hot day on the beach, and it is even better with an aperitif. The popularity of this focaccia has extended well beyond Apulia; in northern Italy, several chains have made it a standard treat in Milan and Turin. The trademark of focaccia barese, which in Bari is called *fucazz,* is to be baked in a round, ovenproof skillet, ideally a cast-iron one, a method that reaches back to a time when focaccia was made at home with less sophisticated heat sources than modern ovens. The typical fucazz is tall and soft and includes potatoes in the dough, another allusion to a past when resources were limited. It is topped with cherry tomatoes and oregano, as well as black olives and an abundance of olive oil.

FOCACCIA DI ALTAMURA

Altamura, considered by many the capital of Apulia's bread tradition, is home to the world-famous durum wheat *pane di Altamura,* which is often imitated but never replicated outside the town. The main characteristic of barese-type focaccia is its being made with 100 percent finely ground durum wheat

flour, or *semola rimacinata.* A fucazz topped with onions is also typical in the area, often paired either with olives or cherry tomatoes—and sometimes with both. Focaccia tradition is so consolidated in Altamura that an American fast-food chain opened in the town not too long ago and quickly went out of business, as locals had no desire to replace focaccia with burgers and fries. (This story garnered international attention and inspired a movie, *Focaccia Blues,* which I highly recommend to my fellow focaccia lovers).

PUDDICA SALENTINA

In the southernmost part of Apulia—the beautiful Salento Peninsula that looks like a heel on a map—we find a focaccia that is similar to barese but made without semolina or potato. Another characteristic that sets puddica salentina apart is the addition of capers to the classic tomato-and-oregano topping. This focaccia is extremely popular in the city of Brindisi.

SCEBLASTI

This focaccia is found in the deep inland of Salento, in the little town of Zollino. *Sceblasti* is a word from the Greek dialect still spoken locally, meaning "without shape." The name refers to the fact that the dough does not hold its shape because of the onions, cherry tomatoes, tomato

sauce, pitted black olives, zucchini, hot peppers, and butternut squash that get kneaded into the dough after the initial rise. Sceblasti is a real feast, and it is celebrated with an annual fair held in the beginning of August. In the nearby city of Lecce, there is a version called *pizzo* that does not include butternut squash.

loaves of bread. Originally made with the overproofed scraps of bread dough left in the kneading trough, the dough was formed into rolls and then stretched into 8- to 12-inch-long focaccia (20 to 30 centimeters) before being placed on the baking stone. Paposcia is generally filled with local cheeses and vegetables.

PAPOSCIA DEL GARGANO

In the northern part of Apulia there is a little peninsula called Gargano, which is gifted with ample natural beauty. Here, specifically in Vico del Gargano, we find paposcia, something between bread and focaccia. It likely inspired the famous ciabatta, made popular in the 1980s by entrepreneurs from the northern part of the country. Paposcia means "slipper," just like ciabatta, due to its elongated and flat shape. Paposcia has been used for centuries to test the temperature of the ovens before baking

CALZONE PUGLIESE

In Taranto, on the western side of Apulia, it is very common to make focaccia pies, here called *calzoni*. Apulian calzoni are made with two rolled disks of focaccia dough that enclose a filling. The filling can vary; in Taranto it is typical to use a scallion-based filling enriched by tomatoes, anchovies, black olives, and capers. This focaccia may be the one that ultimately inspired Chicago's deepdish pizza.

SICILY

The history of focaccia in Sicily is so rich that it deserves a full treatise. The strong tradition is not surprising, considering that Sicily was the granary of the Roman Empire and of the Greeks before that. The largest island in the Mediterranean is ideal for the cultivation of wheat, particularly durum. Even when wheat farming ceased to be practiced on a large scale, wheat kept being cultivated by Sicilian families that owned a small piece of land and needed wheat for their own subsistence. Before the 1950s, nearly every garden had a stone oven and every household made its own breads and focaccias.

SFINCIONE PALERMITANO

This focaccia is native to Palermo, the capital of Sicily, a busy and lively city known for its dynamic street food tradition. Sfincione is a tall, soft, and airy focaccia with a rich topping. The name comes either from the Greek-Latin word *spongia,* which means "sponge," or from the name of a sweet Arabic focaccia, *isfang.* Possibly first developed by the nuns of the local San Vito monastery, it was originally used for religious festivities.

Only later did *sfincione* become street food, sold by vendors on every corner. It is made from a mixture of wheat and durum flours, in different proportions according to different recipes. It is a soft dough with a high percentage of water, topped with tomato sauce, sardines, local cheese (tuma, caciocavallo, or pecorino), sliced white onions, oregano, bread crumbs, and grated cheese. As you can imagine from that rundown, it is a complete meal and was indeed the standard lunch for laborers in the surrounding farmlands. In the nearby town of Baghera, it is also possible to eat a

sfincione bianco, which only differs in its lack of tomato sauce.

FACCIA DI VECCHIA
This looks very much like Neapolitan pizza and owes its name to the bubbles that form on the surface when it makes contact with a hot baking stone. The bubbles tend to deflate when the focaccia cools down, giving it a wrinkly appearance, hence the name, *facc'i viacchia* in local dialect, which means "old lady's face." Faccia di vecchia is typical both of San Martino delle Scale and of Torretta. Just like Apulian paposcia (see page 49), this focaccia is a result of using the scraps from the kneading trough, which patient old ladies shaped into irregular focaccias to be seasoned and baked before the bread. The dough, made with either finely ground durum wheat or a combination of flours, is shaped into rounds and then flattened and baked. The toppings are typical of the focaccias in the region: tomato sauce, local

cheese, sardines, sliced white onions, and a mixture of bread crumbs and oregano. The result is a crunchier version of the Neapolitan pizza, with all the flavors of a sfincione.

FOCACCIA MESSINESE
In Messina, the port that connects Sicily to mainland Italy, it is common to eat this sheet-pan focaccia topped with escarole, local hard cheeses, tomatoes, oregano, and anchovies. The base is made with a mixture of durum and soft wheat flour, as is often the case in Sicilian focaccias.

RIANATA TRAPANESE
In Trapani and western Sicily, focaccia is synonymous with rianata. The name refers to the abundant oregano-based topping, paired with tomatoes, pecorino cheese, and anchovies, creating the

same flavors of the *pani cunzato*, a popular sandwich in the area. The dough is generally made with durum flour, shaped into an oval, topped, and baked directly on a hot stone. As in the case of faccia di vecchia, rianata has a peasant origin and derives from the need to use up leftover scraps of dough.

by the addition of eggs. The recipe dates back to the Middle Ages, apparently created in the monastery of San Michele Arcangelo, and from there it spread out to the nearby households. Troina still hosts an annual vastedda festival in early June, coinciding with the time the elderflowers are in full bloom.

VASTEDDA CON SAMBUCO

This unique focaccia consists of two fluffy layers of leavened dough that enclose a filling of cheese and salami. Typical of Troina, a town in the island's hilly northern inland, vastedda is flavored with elderflowers and is built around soft wheat flour instead of durum, unlike most Sicilian focaccias. The use of soft wheat flour is due to Troina being about 1 kilometer (3,280 feet) above sea level, a perfect climate for the Sicilian wheat variety known as *maiorca*. Vastedda is cooked in a round pan and is made even softer

SCACCIA RAGUSANA

Scaccia is a filled focaccia that is typical of the cities of Ragusa and Modica. It consists of a thin layer of dough made with finely ground semolina flour, topped with various items, and then folded on itself, baked, and sliced. Common fillings are fried eggplants, caciocavallo cheese, and/or sautéed onions, all of which go on a tomato sauce base. Versions *in bianco* (without tomato sauce) can also be found, like the scrumptious *scacce* with ricotta and sausage, or broccoli rabe and sausage.

SARDINIA

Sardinia is the second-largest island in the Mediterranean, and possesses a long heritage of wheat cultivation and bread baking. The Sardinian diet, which includes a large amount of wheat-based products, has been studied in depth as Sardinia, a so-called Blue Zone, has one of the world's highest rates of centenarians.

FOCACCIA PORTOSCUSESE

Similar to Sicilian faccia di vecchia, this focaccia is typical of Portoscuso on the southwestern coast. The dough, which includes potatoes and durum wheat flour, is shaped in rounds and then flattened before being baked directly on a hot stone. The toppings echo Sicilian ones, with tomato sauce, pecorino cheese, and sliced onions being common, though these are cooked beforehand rather than put on raw.

MUSTAZZEDDU

In Sulcis-Iglesiente, also in the southwestern part of this island, mustazzeddu is the name for this focaccia, which is known by different names in other parts of the island, such as *sa pratzida*, *pani cun tamatiga*, and *prazzira de tamatta*. No matter the name, it looks very much like a fruit-filled galette, with the edges of the dough folded over the filling without completely covering it. Unlike a galette, mustazzeddu is made from a leavened, durum flour dough, filled with fresh tomatoes, and simply seasoned with salt, garlic, and olive oil. Different fillings, such as eggplant, are also used.

Genoa. A holdover from that era is a local version of farinata, the chickpea focaccia, called fainè. There are several versions, the simplest being seasoned only with olive oil and salt, and more elaborate iterations enriched by onions or mushrooms.

FAINÈ
In the Middle Ages, the northern city of Sassari was under the influence of

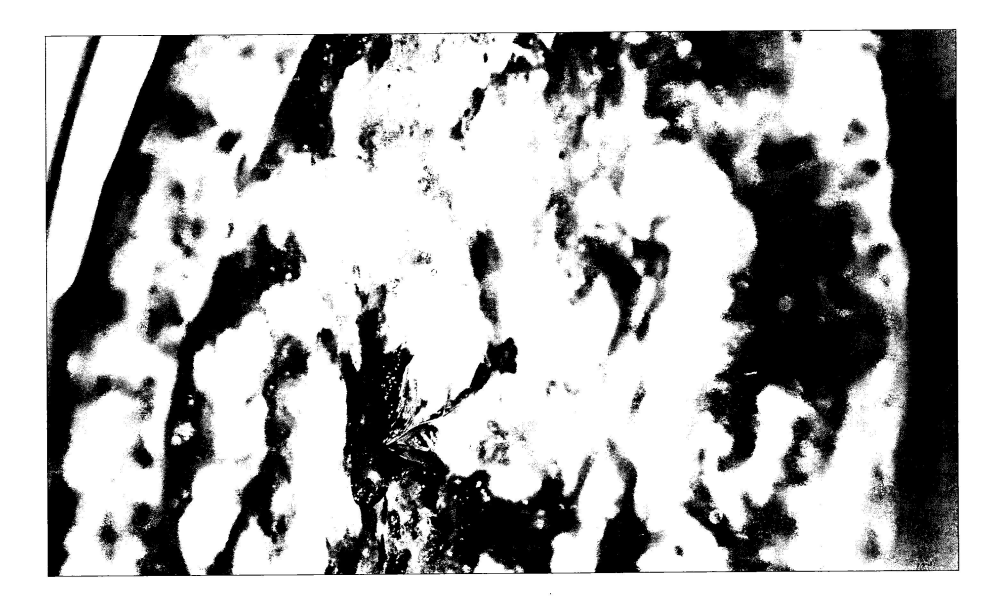

HISTORY OF PIZZA

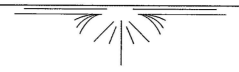

HISTORY OF NEAPOLITAN PIZZA

When we mention pizza, no matter where in the world we might be, everyone seems to know what we are referring to. But if we ask what pizza is, things change. And indeed, do we really know the answer?

Is pizza a bread, a flatbread, a focaccia? Or rather something wholly distinctive? The answer is both enticing and something of a cop-out: all of the above.

Even the etymological origin of the word is controversial. Without question, pizza is a newer word than focaccia, which is of Roman origin. The first mention of pizza appears in the Middle Ages manuscript *Codex Diplomaticus Caietanus*. The word is most likely not of Latin origin, and either derived from the Greek name for bread, *pita*, or from the proto-Germanic *bizzo-pizzo*, meaning both "bite of food" and "piece of bread."

After the fall of the Roman Empire, Italy endured several conquests, and in some regions the Latin word *focaccia* was replaced by the foreign term *pizza*. But we should not be fooled by this name change. In these instances, pizza was nothing more than another word for the traditional focaccia: a flattened piece of dough, enriched by whatever was readily available at the moment, baked or cooked with the most convenient source of heat.

When pizza is mentioned nowadays, most think of a specific type of pizza, the one that first developed in Naples in the 1800s and became world famous thanks to the incredible developments it experienced in the United States over the course of the 20th century.

THE FOCACCIA OF THE NEAPOLITANS

The history of Neapolitan pizza starts in the 1700s, when it was common practice among Neapolitan bakers to use flattened rounds of dough to test an oven's temperature before baking bread. These test doughs were usually discarded, but soon they became a go-to dish for the city's poor because they were quick to make and, consequently, considered less valuable.

These simple small focaccia were called *pizza*, the common name for focaccia in Naples and surrounding regions. Early Neapolitan pizzas were topped with a white sauce rather than the tomato sauce common today. They rose to prominence in the most crowded and least sophisticated neighborhoods of Naples and, within a short time, became extremely popular. Soon the white sauce was replaced with bacon, lard, cheese, tomatoes, or fish, a development described by the legendary French writer Alexandre Dumas, who visited the city in 1843. As recounted by Dumas, pizza was the food of the *lazzaroni*, the people who inhabited the streets and performed menial jobs or did not work at all. The topping depended on what was most abundant at a particular time of the year. If fishing hauls had been bountiful, then plenty of fish-topped pizza was sold; if butchers had lots of leftover lard, then pizzas freighted with that surplus were offered up.

By the early 1820s, bakeries that specialized in pizza-making, pizzerias, started to pop up all over the city. They soon become popular to the point that King Ferdinand I of the Two Sicilies would disguise himself in humble clothing in order to visit his favorite pizzeria, where Antonio Testa turned out pies. Ferdinand, always very close to the people and to the *lazzaroni* in particular, discovered that only the freshest-baked pizza would satisfy his craving, and so he violated court etiquette. This story epitomizes a characteristic of Neapolitan pizza: it pleases every palate, from the least to the most sophisticated, uniting social classes with its irresistible *scioglievolezza*—"melting in the mouth"—feeling.

King Ferdinand was responsible for having a royal decree banishing pizza from the court lifted, which only increased the food's popularity among the elite. After Piedmont's elites took over Italy, a special pizza was dedicated to the new queen, Margherita di Savoia. When she visited Naples, the *pizza margherita* was made as a tribute to her and the Italian flag: red from the tomato sauce, white represented by the mozzarella cheese on top, and basil leaves symbolizing the green band.

NEAPOLITAN PIZZA IMMIGRATES TO AMERICA

At the end of the 1800s, an economic crisis forced many Italians to search out better fortunes overseas. The immigrants were predominately from the southern part of the country, which suffered the most under the newly united Italy's dysfunctional government; the unification was heavily inclined toward the interests of the north (Piedmont in particular).

Many of these immigrants chose the United States as their destination and, once processed through New York's Ellis Island, they settled in that city or headed for places like Boston, Philadelphia, and Chicago.

Soon after the first Neapolitans reached New York, shops selling pizza started to appear. Italian immigrants from other cities and regions brought their own focaccia traditions, too, but Neapolitan Americans were the first to realize that instead of baking their regional specialties at home, it was possible to turn them into a successful business. Following that revelation, the popularity of pizza began to spread across the nation; eventually, it became ubiquitous. Ironically, the main reason for the mass exodus of Italians from Italy, and the subsequent Americanization of Neapolitan pizza, was the administration of the royal class for whom pizza margherita had been created.

THE FIRST AMERICAN PIZZERIAS

Until very recently, it was thought that the very first American pizzeria was Lombardi's on Spring Street in lower Manhattan. The family that has owned the business for over a century claims that their grandfather, the Neapolitan immigrant Gennaro Lombardi, brought pizza to America; according to family lore, Lombardi founded the Spring Street pizza joint in 1905. But historian Peter Regas has questioned this oft-repeated story. His reconstruction, which is based on historical documents, shows that the first pizzerias in New York were founded by another Neapolitan, Filippo Milone. Milone had opened several pizzerias by the end of the 1800s and then sold them off a few years later, including the one on Spring Street that was later acquired by Lombardi. Milone is also behind another iconic New York slice joint, John's on Bleecker Street; Milone opened that location in 1915, calling it Pizzeria Port'Alba.

Initially, pizzerias were mostly frequented by Italian immigrants. It was only after World War II that pizza entered the American mainstream.

THE POST-WAR PIZZA BOOM

After World War II, many of the American soldiers who had occupied Italy returned home with a love of focaccia and pizza. Their hunger for the gooey, savory Italian bread they'd grown accustomed to created a much bigger market for pizza than ever before. With this, the American pizza pie at last crossed the boundaries of the country's Italian American communities and became the national treasure we know today.

The economic boom of the '50s enabled the newborn craze to grow exponentially. Now that people had the resources to afford eating at restaurants, aspiring entrepreneurs could feel confident in their plans. It also helped that opening a pizza place was relatively cheap and undemanding compared to the other options in the restaurant industry. In the early 1900s, pizza parlors used coal-fired ovens, which are difficult to both install and operate. After World War II, easy and affordable commercial gas ovens became widely available, and inexpensive, secondhand military surplus mixers arrived on the market as well. Pizza parlors did not need to have lots of seating, because pizza could be taken home and eaten. The final thrust in pizza's ascent to becoming the most-loved American takeout was the innovation of home delivery. Now the melt-in-your-mouth, savory pies could be enjoyed without even having to step outside your door—an unimaginable luxury for the time.

By the early 1960s, the first wave of American pizza chains were gaining steam: Pizza Hut in Kansas (1958), and Little Caesars (1959) and Domino's (1960) in Michigan. Each of the three started as a stand-alone pizza place that eventually leveraged its success into a replicable model, growing from a few pizza parlors to thousands of them. And it all started with third-class Neapolitan immigrants who, though looking to start a new life, could not let go of one cherished piece of the old country.

THE QUEST FOR AUTHENTIC NEAPOLITAN PIZZA

After the family-friendly boom of the 1960s and 1970s, there was a counter-reaction: the quest for authentic or artisan Neapolitan pizza. When Alice Waters opened Chez Panisse in Berkeley, California, in 1980, and installed a wood-fired pizza oven, she set off a trend that would eventually conquer the country. Wolfgang Puck opened Spago in Los Angeles in 1982, with Ed LaDou as the pizza chef; LaDou would create hundreds of wood-fired, California-inspired pizzas for Puck before going on to create the first menu for California Pizza Kitchen, which remains a hugely popular chain worldwide. In major cities throughout America, wood-fired pizza ovens appeared, facilitating the creation of top-notch, Neapolitan-style crusts topped with carefully sourced and high-quality ingredients, both traditional and completely unorthodox (though delicious).

Thanks to the use of wood-fired ovens, these so-called gourmet pizzas started to change the concept of pizza as a cheap and unhealthy comfort food. Having one of these ovens in the kitchen quickly became a hallmark of a quality restaurant that offered pizza as a real meal to be savored in a pleasant atmosphere.

A special place in the authentic Neapolitan pizza renaissance is reserved for New York native Chris Bianco, who started the small but superb Pizzeria Bianco in 1988 after relocating to Phoenix, Arizona. His attention to original ingredients took him as far as making his own mozzarella cheese and going to Naples to learn directly from the local masters. Bianco has been widely recognized as a driving force in the artisan pizza movement.

Less known than Bianco, but possibly even more relevant to the history of pizza in the US and beyond, is LaDou, Puck's right-hand man. Through incessant attention to his crusts and to the quality of his pizza toppings, Ladou managed to turn Neapolitan pizza into haute cuisine, opening the door to all of the high-end pizzaioli to come.

Together with the gourmet pizza movement that originated out West, another boon to the revival of Neapolitan pizza has been the renaissance of quality pizza in Naples, which started around the time of the gourmet trend in the US. In Italy, the movement was guided by a group of Neapolitan pizza masters that were not keen to accept the mediocrity to which expansion had dragged their art.

NEAPOLITAN PIZZA TODAY

The demand for pizza continued to grow in Naples until the beginning of the 1900s. During World War I, pizzerias suffered due to overall economic stagnancy, and the situation only became worse during World War II. During the postwar period in Italy, there was a considerable uptick in the production of pizza accompanied by a reduction in quality, which paralleled what was happening in the United States and indeed was related to it.

The postwar economic boom and the subsequent industrial development in the US resulted in the proliferation of cheap ingredients such as vegetable oils and processed cheese. These inferior ingredients invaded the Italian market and changed the face of Neapolitan pizza for decades to come. Ironically, it was during this period that Neapolitan pizza finally gained a foothold in the rest of Italy, becoming popular from Rome to Milan and Turin, and even in regions with deeply rooted focaccia traditions like Liguria, Apulia, and Sicily.

So it came to be during the '60s, '70s, and early '80s that in Italy Neapolitan pizza was thought of as a cheap, easy option. With processed ingredients, quick fermentations featuring premade flour blends, and less-than-fresh toppings, the offerings from pizza's birthplace became divorced from the delicious wonders Italian immigrants had carried across the Atlantic.

Things started to change drastically in the mid-1980s. In 1984, the *Associazione Verace Pizza Napoletana* (AVPN) was founded by Antonio Pace, owner of the pizzeria Ciro a Santa Brigida, and a collection of several other old-school Neapolitan pizza masters. The AVPN regulations for the authentic Neapolitan pizza received approval by the Italian Chamber of Commerce and started to spread around the world. Today, close to a thousand restaurants worldwide are proudly following AVPN guidelines.

Even when not part of this network, the quest for quality pizza has left its mark, and a new generation of enlightened pizza makers, such as Enzo Coccia, Gino Sorbillo, and Franco Pepe have changed the pizza landscape in Naples and Italy, bringing Neapolitan pizza to artisan heights not known before.

HISTORY OF ROMAN PIZZA

In Rome, as in Naples, focaccia has been known as pizza for quite some time, probably since the late Middle Ages. However, the habit of eating slices of focaccia while walking the streets of the Eternal City is much older than the term *pizza*.

Focaccia by the slice is in fact likely to date back to the ancient Romans, who were so obsessed with bread in all forms that they classified bakers as elite workers. Since then, Roman bakers have developed the habit of putting a bit of bread dough to the side, and then enriching that reserved dough with olive oil and abundant salt to make it a stand-alone bread, excellent on its own or when topped with modest and fresh ingredients.

With this rich history in mind, it is safe to say that Roman pizza did not change much over the next two millennia. Pizza bianca has always just been pizza bianca (see page 181), focaccia without sauce, and apparently no local baker has ever felt the need to reinterpret it. It is only

since World War II that other types of pizza have emerged in Rome. Before the war, there had been attempts to bring Neapolitan pizza to the capital, but they all failed. It was only in the mid-1950s that the Neapolitan variety gained a foothold in the capital, as economic growth created a need for a wider variety of ready-to-eat food. As this burgeoning market was not addressed by bakeries, take-away shops, known as *rosticcerie*, arose to meet the demand.

PIZZA AL TAGLIO

 Rome would not be Rome without its *pizza al taglio* ("pizza to go"), cut with scissors and sold by the slice. As ubiquitous in the city as its ancient ruins, pizza by the slice has become a trademark of Italy's capital, to the point that one would be justified in thinking these greasy pizza joints have always been around. Surprisingly, pizza al taglio originated in the 1950s and took until the 1970s to really take off in the "City of Seven Hills." Initially, pizza al taglio was made in the *rosticcerie*. These take-away shops had no seating, very simple kitchens, and lacked proper bread ovens. The dough was baked in *teglie*, shallow, rimmed sheet pans that could fit inside the small deck ovens that were a feature of these establishments. The combination of all these factors resulted in a pizza that was thicker and softer than the classic pizza bianca. Another factor was the amount of water used in the dough, as a higher amount was required in order to produce a moist and light product that would not dry out while sitting on the counter, waiting for customers to come past. As for toppings, inspiration came from the other homey dishes served by the *rosticcerie*. All of the seasonal vegetables dear to Roman cuisine are served over a pillowy square of pizza, as are local cured meats and, occasionally, seafood. The possible combinations of toppings for pizza al taglio are seemingly endless, but always dictated by what is locally and seasonally available, which is the essence of this pizza's authenticity.

Recently, pizza al taglio has been revamped by a chef-turned-pizza maker named Gabriele Bonci, who should be considered Rome's answer to American innovator Ed LaDou. Bonci, with his Pizzarium, has successfully made Rome's most beloved fast food trendy again as well as internationally respected. This elevated status is the result of Bonci's insistence on high-quality ingredients for his doughs as well as for his toppings, which are always extremely rich and luscious.

PIZZA ALLA PALA

 After the emergence of pizza al taglio, Roman bakeries started offering variations on pizza bianca. Initially, the alternatives were pizza with tomato sauce and pizza with sliced potatoes. The techniques used to make Rome's bakery-made pizza, *pizza del fornaio*, have inspired *pizza alla pala*, which literally means "loaded with a baker's peel." Pizza bianca is traditionally loaded onto the baking stone via a long, oval peel, which is why these types of pizza are long tongues of crunchy crust.

While pizza bianca and *pizza rossa* ("with tomato sauce") were humble by-products of breadmaking, pizza alla pala is a hybrid between the two cornerstones of Rome's pizza traditions: pizza bianca and pizza al taglio. It has the shape and the crust of pizza bianca with the toppings of pizza al taglio. Pizzerias that specialize in pizza alla pala generally offer a higher-quality product compared to the classic pizza al taglio joints: the emphasis is on a long fermentation of the dough and the best available toppings. In the last 20 years, several pizza alla pala restaurants and parlors have flourished, to the point that they now lead the scene. The success has caused some bakeries, including the legendary Antico Forno Roscioli, to modernize their offerings, producing gourmet versions of the classic pizza bianca.

PINZA ROMANA

A special subset of pizza alla pala is pinza romana. Created in 2001 by culinary expert Corrado Di Marco, pinza is the antithesis of the artisan movement behind pizza alla pala. Pinza flour is a blend of three flours, in fact—wheat, soy, and rice—and has been falsely marketed as the original ancient Roman pizza. This said, pinza is a delicious, lighter version of pizza alla pala and worth trying if you come across it in Italy or elsewhere.

PIZZA AL PIATTO ROMANA

Neapolitan-style pizza has become a real institution in Rome: generally served for dinner in dedicated pizza restaurants, *pizza al piatto* ("pizza served on a plate") has become one of the capital's most common meals when dining out. To fully adapt to the taste of Romans, this version of Neapolitan pizza has a smaller border and a lighter, crunchier crust than what is traditional. This is due to differences in the dough and in the baking techniques employed for centuries in Rome.

THE AMERICAN PIZZA PIE

Pizza is now part of the United States's cultural heritage, and not the adopted stepchild of any European cousin. The United States has advanced the development and the popularity of pizza well beyond any expectations of years ago. The Americanization of pizza should not proceed like a carnival sideshow, but should step up to the standards of industry and craft that [are] the basis of our way of life and heritage.
   —*Ed LaDou, Founder of Caioti Pizza Café*

Once pizza reached America's shores, it continued to evolve, consistently generating new styles and new flavor combinations, as well as different crusts. The main styles that developed in the States are unique due to their adaptation to the locals' taste buds, and by use of the ingredients that were readily available. Although several of the classic American styles can be traced back to their Italian roots—Neapolitan in New York, Sicilian in Detroit, and Apulian in Chicago—there is in each of them an indisputable American touch that makes them true originals.

A common denominator is the presence of low-moisture cheese, mostly mozzarella, which became widely available and incredibly cheap after World War II. Even today, processed offerings drive cheese production thanks to the happy and long-lasting marriage between Italian-inspired pizza crust with the all-American gooey topping. Exceptions are New Haven pizza and the revolutionary gourmet pizza that began in California—a development that shifted how pizza is viewed around the world, including in Japan and India.

NEW YORK PIZZA

The quintessential American pizza pie is surely the one that originated in New York City: a thin crust, rising slightly at the edge, with a center that is softer so that the slice can be folded and eaten on the go. The particular consistency of a New York–style crust is often attributed to the chemical composition of the city's water (most of which comes from the Delaware River Basin that sits about 125 miles north of the city); the same reason is also cited for the unique quality of Neapolitan crusts. And, as in Naples, in New York the toppings are often simple: marinara sauce and grated low-moisture mozzarella cheese.

What really set New York pizza apart from its Italian cousin is the amount of cheese used. A New York pie is loaded with grated cheese, which is so abundant that it entirely covers the tomato sauce. Various toppings are also added, often in excessive amounts, especially compared to the Neapolitan variety. Initially, pizza in New York was baked in coal-fired ovens, but, as they were soon banned, electric deck ovens became the most common method for cooking pies, which resulted in a less crunchy, lighter-colored crust devoid of char.

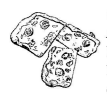

NEW HAVEN PIZZA

About 80 miles north of New York City, pizza in New Haven, Connecticut, took a slightly different turn. In 1925, Frank Pepe opened Pizzeria Napoletana. Originally from the town of Maiori on the Amalfi coast, Pepe used his former local dialect and branded his product *apizza*. Pepe's pizza had a more rustic and artisan touch compared to the pizza being made down the coast in the Big Apple. The pies are not round but slightly oval and irregularly shaped; the crust is crunchy and light, blistered with char, and imbued with a slight smokiness thanks to both coal and gas ovens.

The biggest difference when compared to New York pizza is the omission of low-moisture mozzarella cheese. The best New Haven pizzas let the sauce shine, so much in fact that they are often called *tomato pie*. In New Haven, mozzarella is considered a topping rather than a key component.

Pepe also invented a special seafood pizza, which is white—without tomato sauce—and topped with littleneck clams, garlic, oregano, olive oil, and grated pecorino. In other words, a gourmet pizza created long before anyone thought that term could apply within the pizza universe.

Sally's Apizza is another long-standing New Haven favorite that was started in 1938 by Salvatore Consiglio.

CHICAGO DEEP-DISH PIZZA

The origin of Chicago's deep-dish pizza is disputed. The most commonly accepted story is that in 1943 Ike Sewell opened the flagship location of Pizzeria Uno at the corner of Ohio Street and Wabash Avenue, offering a pizza in an entirely new form, which soon became the city's signature.

As the name suggests, Chicago deep dish is baked in a deep dish, a choice that results in a high, buttery crust that gets filled much like a dessert pie.

By the mid-20th century, Chicago was home to many Italian immigrants, and it is likely that Sewell was familiar with the pizza and focaccia traditions of numerous Italian regions. Deep-dish pizza does looks like a hybrid between the crust of an Apulian calzoni and a Neapolitan pizza. Apulian calzoni is indeed a savory focaccia filled with seasonal vegetables and baked in a round dish with high edges; the focaccia is generally covered with a layer of dough. In Chicago deep dish, a Neapolitan-style tomato sauce and mozzarella cheese replace the vegetables. This heavy, over-stuffed pizza has been a big hit since it was first served. Before Pizzeria Uno became a popular international chain, the original Chicago establishment was so popular that Sewell opened Pizzeria Due in 1955.

Another popular, but unconfirmed, story about the inventor of deep dish involves bartender Rudy Malnati Sr. Malnati did in fact work at Pizzeria Uno, as well as at other restaurants owned by Sewell and his partners. His family claims he helped develop the idea for the deep-dish crust, but there is no hard evidence to back up this claim. Researchers and pizza fanatics have searched for a conclusive answer and have come up empty-handed. One thing is for certain, however: Pizzeria Uno popularized this delicious style of American pizza.

DETROIT PIZZA

The story behind Detroit-style pizza is well known. In 1946, bar owner Gus Guerra wanted a dish to revamp his menu. His wife, Anna, had a recipe for Sicilian focaccia, which was Americanized by smothering it with tomato sauce and low-moisture mozzarella cheese. The pizza became extremely popular and the bar became Buddy's Pizza, which now has locations all over Michigan.

Like its Chicago cousin, Detroit pizza relies on an abundance of sauce, cheese, and toppings. But that's where the similarity ends. Detroit pizza is rectangular and is not dominated by a tall crust. This development is actually a direct result of the city's famed auto industry; the original pizza pans were actually metal containers that had held small mechanical parts before being discarded by the factories. The flavor hinges on the thick, moist, and well-risen focaccia-like crust. This pizza pie has been a local delicacy since its first appearance in the 1940s and only recently has it become available nationwide, to the joy of many.

ST. LOUIS PIZZA

Like so many regional pizzas in the United States, St. Louis pizza dates back to the 1940s—1945, to be precise. That's when Amedeo Fiore opened the Melrose Pizzeria, a full-service Italian restaurant with a menu that featured pizza made on an unleavened, cracker-thin crust. Another defining trait of this pizza is the cheese; originally Fiore used provolone, which inspired a local processed mix known as Provel to be created. This is sold as a blend of cheddar, Swiss, and provolone, but in reality it's really all about melting like American cheese, thanks to extra fat, moisture, and chemical salts. Provel, an acquired taste, is now the go-to cheese used in St. Louis–style pizza parlors. In

terms of toppings, anything goes, really, and the fattier the better. Fancy a pie with double bacon? Head to St. Louis.

If you've never tasted this style of pizza, food writer J. Kenji Lopez-Alt sums it up masterfully: "Don't think of St. Louis–style pizza as pizza, think of it as a big, pizza-flavored nacho."

CALIFORNIA PIZZA

In 1980, Californian cuisine began to take shape, spurring radical innovation throughout the country, reviving Old World common sense with its emphasis on eating seasonally and locally and making sure not to waste what, today, are understood to be precious resources. Two restaurants started to offer a new type of pizza that would soon be defined as gourmet. At Berkeley's Chez Panisse, Alice Waters had a wood-fired oven built to marry traditional Neapolitan pizza with West Coast whimsy. Soon after, Ed LaDou was baking in the same type of oven at Spago in Los Angeles, where he applied endless creativity in selecting fresh ingredients to top carefully crafted and leavened pizza crusts. The late LaDou, gone prematurely before his contribution to American pizza received its due, was known for generating original and extremely well-matched pizza toppings in no time whatsoever. Without a doubt, LaDou's creativity has influenced generations of pizza chefs, and will continue to do so.

Thanks to these two pioneers, gourmet pizza soon popped up all over the United States and throughout the rest of the world. California-style pizza, however, has become a specific style rather than a generic gourmet one. It has a well-leavened and properly baked Neapolitan-style crust, and toppings centered around local produce. Seasonal, and often foraged, herbs, vegetables, mushrooms, and fruit are popular toppings, along with goat cheese and runny eggs.

THE PERFECT PIZZA PIE

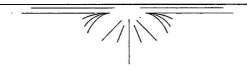

NOT ONLY ONE DOUGH

Pizza making is part of a transmission; it's almost spiritual.

Dough is a living thing; it has a life cycle that goes from birth to consumption, with stages in between like childhood and adulthood.

A good pizza maker has to honor this. The process possesses a kind of potential centeredness; it's almost Zen-like.

—*Ed LaDou, cited by Peter Rehinard in* American Pie

When talking about pizza, people often sound as if they are referring to one specific type of flatbread. As the previous sections make clear, pizza is not one, but many. From the tall or thinner sheet-pan focaccias to the gooey or crunchy pizzas baked on a baking stone, from the fried pizzas to the unleavened focaccias cooked on the stovetop, there are myriad variations. And each of these different types of pizza starts from a different type of dough, which then serves as the base for a seemingly limitless number of toppings. Add both together, and you've got a potentially infinite number of pizza combinations.

So many possibilities are exciting, but they can also be daunting. That's why it's important to first familiarize yourself with the fundamentals of pizza making and the tools needed to create the essential doughs in your own kitchen.

INGREDIENTS
Different pizza doughs will require different ingredients. But there are basic ingredients that

most pizzas and focaccias share, such as flour, water, salt, fat, and yeast.

Flour
Not all flours are the same—not even all wheat flour is the same—and this must be kept in mind when setting out to make pizza or focaccia. One important aspect to consider is how extensible and elastic the dough needs to be for a particular style of pizza. A weaker flour may provide plenty of stretch, but it is generally not elastic, meaning that the resulting dough will not spring back when spread out. Another factor that is important is the amount of time the dough is supposed to ferment. Stronger flours will withstand long fermentation times, while doughs made with weaker flours will lose their structure in the process. Based on these considerations—stretchiness vs. elasticity and fermentation time—we can choose the strength we want in our flour for each type of pizza. An easy way to have an approximate idea of the flour strength is to look at its protein in the chart on the next page.

Protein Content (%) | Strength

Protein Content (%)	Strength
<10	weak
10.5 to 11	medium
11.5 to 12.5	medium-strong
>12.5	strong

Gluten is formed by two proteins contained in flour, glutenin and gliadin, and therefore protein content is a good proxy of how much gluten will be developed when combining a specific flour with water. We have to be aware, however, that this is just an approximation. More precise measures exist but are not readily available to the home baker.

Focaccias & Pan Pizzas

Focaccia is extremely varied, and therefore it is difficult to generalize about "ideals." It will be important to follow the recommendations indicated in each specific recipe regarding what type of flour is best. As a rule of thumb, however, most focaccias and pan pizzas require a moderately strong flour, one that can produce a dough that has the strength to bear the weight of the toppings without releasing the carbon dioxide created by fermentation while also being extensible enough not to spring back too energetically once it has been stretched. In other words, we need a flour with a protein content between 10.5 and 11 percent. A good all-purpose flour could do the job, but if the protein content is too low, it will be good to blend it with a stronger flour, such as a common bread flour. Several focaccias require the use of durum flour, alone or in combination with soft wheat flour. In these instances, the optimal durum wheat flour is *semola rimacinata*, i.e., extra-fine semolina flour.

Neapolitan Pizza

For this pizza, there is a consensus that a very fine soft wheat flour, such as the Italian "00" flour, is ideal. However, the term "00" says nothing about the strength of the flour, which can be anything from 7 to 14 percent. If looking into popular Italian "00" flours, the protein content tends to be higher than an all-purpose flour, between 11.5 and 12.5 percent—the same level commonly found in bread flour. Such proportions of gluten proteins should enable the dough to be stretchable but also elastic, since a Neapolitan pizza dough does need to spring back quite energetically when it is spread out. You can buy the specialty pizza flours, but be aware that you can achieve acceptable results with even a common bread flour.

Roman Pizza

The trademark of Roman pizza is the dough's long fermentation, whether it be the pizza bianca, al taglio, alla pala, or al piatto that you are looking to master. All of these require a dough that has fermented for a minimum of several hours, and often days. This extended fermentation is what gives Roman pizza its lightness and digestibility, both of which are further bolstered by the longer baking times compared to Neapolitan pizza. Considering the lengthy fermentation time and extended period in the oven, a strong flour is best, one with a protein content between 12.5 and 14 percent. This will allow the gluten net to retain its structure during the fermentation. Again, an ordinary bread flour can do the job, but if you can find a particularly strong bread flour or, even better, a flour intended for long fermentation, you may achieve even better results.

American Regional Pizza

There is no general rule of thumb when it comes to the optimal flour to use for American pizza pies, as, like the various Italian focaccias, they differ quite a bit from one another. American pizzas, however, do share the common characteristic of not requiring an extremely long fermentation. Thus, a very strong flour is completely unnecessary. Any medium-strength flour should yield good results for most regional American pizzas, with the exception of Detroit-style pizza. For that one a medium-strong flour may be best.

Gourmet Pizza

With its emphasis on quality, wholesome ingredients, and continual looking toward Neapolitan pizza for inspiration, a medium-strong flour is advisable for gourmet pizzas. Today, however, many gourmet pizzas are inspired by the long fermentation approach of Roman pizza, in which case a strong flour is recommended. Furthermore, although buying organic flour is always advisable, this is even more relevant for gourmet pizza. Recently, stone-ground and artisan whole wheat flours have become part of this line of pizza baking, with interesting results.

Water

In both Naples and New York City, there is much discussion about how the unique properties of the local water effects the pizza dough produced. Although this is more myth than reality, there are characteristics in water that will wield influence over any dough, anywhere. In particular, it is worth checking the amount of minerals in the water you are using, a measure classified as the "hardness" of water. Medium-hard water, with a pH around 7, is ideal for pizza dough. If you live in an area with soft water—a pH lower than 6—add more salt to the dough. If you have hard water—a pH of 8 or above—reduce the amount of salt. Too much chlorine is also not ideal; if your tap water is highly chlorinated, use purified water.

Another characteristic relevant to pizza making is the temperature of the water. Use nearly ice-cold water when making dough during hot weather conditions and when you are making a dough with high hydration content.

Salt

In baking, salt is not only used for taste; it serves several functions that influence the chemistry and development of a dough. For pizza, salt is generally used in higher percentages as compared to other baking preparations. This is done to increase the tenacity of the dough, which, especially in Neapolitan pizza, needs enough elasticity to spring back once spread out. It is important to avoid adding the salt at the same time as the yeast, because salt can inhibit the activity of the yeast. The proper time to add salt depends on how tenacious and elastic we want the dough to be. For a round pizza, like a Neapolitan-style one, the salt is added quite close to the beginning. For focaccia and pan pizza, it is better to add the salt toward the end of the kneading process, because this type of dough needs to be more extensible than elastic. Regarding the type of salt, any type works, as the differences in results between table, kosher, and the other varieties of salt are truly minimal.

Yeast

There are several types of yeasts available, and they will all do the job. But instant yeast is by far the easiest to manage. Unlike fresh yeast, instant yeast can be stored for a long amount of time (up to two months when opened and refrigerated), but, like fresh yeast and unlike active dry yeast, it does not need to be activated. Instant yeast can be difficult to find in regular supermarkets, though it is widely available online.

As I mentioned, any pizza dough can be made with any of the three main types of yeast. There will be some discrepancy in how much is required of each. No matter the type of yeast you use, pizza dough tastes best when it has time to develop.

The table below shows how the same degree of leavening power is achieved by different amounts of fresh yeast, instant yeast, and active dry yeast.

Type of Yeast	Amount
Fresh Yeast	1 tablespoon	9.4 grams
Instant Yeast	1 teaspoon	3.2 grams
Active Dry Yeast	1¼ teaspoons	3.6 grams

Old Dough & Pre-Ferments

Pre-ferment simply means a mixture of flour and water that a leavening agent has been added to and left to ferment, from a few hours to a few days, and then added to new dough. In pizza making, it is common to use pre-ferments both with yeast and on their own.

The easiest pre-ferment you can use is a piece of dough from a previous bake. Old dough, *pasta di riporto* in Italian, can keep in the fridge up to five days, and it simply needs to be taken out and added to your dough, lending complexity to the flavor of your crusts. For the occasional home baker, it will be difficult to have old dough on hand, so a pre-ferment will have to be created for the occasion. This is achieved by combining a small amount of yeast with water and flour and letting the mixture rest at room temperature for several hours.

Sourdough

Sourdough is rarely used for pizza or focaccia. In rural contexts, sourdough was surely used for focaccia, but over the last two centuries yeast has become by far the most common leavening agent for pizza and focaccia. Contrary to commonly held belief, brewer's yeast was available long before the later part of the 1800s, which is when its chemistry was deciphered. Long before then, brewer's yeast for baking was so popular in France that its wholesomeness was at the center of a lively official debate during much of the 1700s. As history tends to repeat itself, yeast's health benefits have again been questioned during the last two decades. As a result, many home bakers, and a limited number of professional bakers, have embraced sourdough for pizza. And good results can be obtained when utilizing a wild yeast, particularly when making gourmet pizza.

Fats

The fat of election for most focaccias and for almost every pizza is olive oil. For baking, it

is advisable to use extra virgin olive oil. One exception to olive oil's supremacy is the focaccia tradition of northern Italy—excepting Liguria—where butter, whole milk, and lard are the go-to options; some deep-dish pizza recipes will also call for butter.

Sauces

Tomatoes are not native to Europe and only became popular in Italy in the 1800s. One can therefore find a large number of focaccia and pizza recipes that do not include tomato sauce. For all the recipes that do include tomato sauce, like the famed Neapolitan pizza, it is important to know that the best sauce for pizza is uncooked. When putting an already-cooked tomato sauce on pizza dough, the result will be a sauce that is overdone, if not burned, and does no justice to the original taste of the tomatoes. The best tomatoes for sauce are peeled, whole, canned tomatoes, ideally the San Marzano vari-

ety. There is truly no need to use dedicated pizza sauces. The practice of using precooked tomato sauce over pizza is likely a result of the low quality of the canned tomatoes available in the past in the US. This led to people correcting the taste with vinegar, sugar, and seasonings. When using high-quality canned tomatoes, however, little adulteration is required. The sauce should leave the tomato as untouched as possible in an effort to preserve the original flavor. To make a perfect sauce, simply crush the peeled tomatoes, add salt and olive oil, and, voilà, the sauce is ready.

The sauce will be cooked to perfection in the oven. If using fresh tomatoes, peeling will be required, as will a brief sautéing. In any case, make sure you do not use hot tomato sauce over the uncooked pizza dough. A cold tomato sauce will also be detrimental to the optimal rise in the oven. The best option is to always have your tomato sauce at room temperature before applying it to pizza dough.

BASIC METHODS

The creation of both focaccia and pizza doughs share some basic methods. The following is a brief introduction to these fundamental techniques, which will be expanded upon further in specific recipes.

MIXING

There are three main methods to making a pizza or focaccia dough. You may feel more comfortable with a specific one or alternate between them based on your mood, the amount of time and energy available, or a specific outcome you have in mind.

Hand Mixing

When mixing by hand, it is important to start by combining the flour and water, followed by any other ingredients; depending on the recipe, the additional ingredients can be incorporated later in a large bowl. The use of a mixing bowl will minimize the mess that is inevitably created when mixing by hand. Once the flour is combined with the water to form a dough, it can be transferred to a flour-dusted work surface and kneaded. One exception are doughs with high levels of hydration, which can be kneaded in the same bowl they were mixed in.

There are several kneading techniques, but a method that is quite easy to follow is to work the dough for only a few minutes at a time before covering it with a damp kitchen towel and letting it rest for a bit before kneading for another few minutes, repeating the process until the dough feels smooth and springs back when pulled from one corner.

Keep in mind that kneading by hand is a rather intuitive process. It is best to let your hands inform your brain as to when the dough is ready, a feel that will be developed with practice.

To check whether a dough has been worked enough, it is common to perform the "windowpane" test. This simply means taking a piece of dough and stretching it between your fingers: if it can be stretched to where you can almost see through it and it does not tear, the dough is ready.

Machine Mixing

When using a stand mixer to mix pizza or focaccia dough, it is necessary to start at low speed

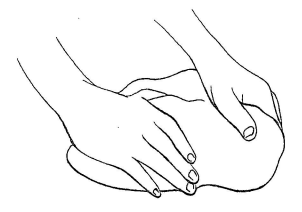

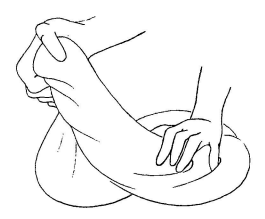

TIPS ON MIXING BY HAND

There is not one way to produce a dough, but many. The best method is whichever gives you the best feel for the dough and the confidence to work it energetically. But, for a moment, think about the original bakers: as bread was the main staple, it needed to be good, meaning that everyone needed to learn quickly. The best way to do this is to mix the dough by hand. Don't be nervous, just imagine your ancestors and follow your "dough instinct"—I bet you'll be surprised.

SIMPLE KNEADING: After combining the flour, water, and yeast in a bowl, turn the dough out onto a flour-dusted work surface and work it with the palms of your hands until the mass comes together. Add the salt and any other ingredients and keep working the dough with your palms until they are thoroughly incorporated. At this point, you can start stretching the dough—pulling it toward you with one hand, pushing it away with the other, and then folding it over itself. Continue to stretch and fold the dough until the dough is well developed, smooth, and extensible (you are able to extend it without tearing it).

STRETCHING AND FOLDING IN THE BOWL: When the water-to-flour ratio is high (over 70 percent hydration with a flour of average strength), it is possible to knead the dough directly in the bowl you used to combine the flour, water, and yeast in. After combining them, let the dough rest for a minimum of 15 minutes and a maximum of 30 minutes (the optimal amount of time will depend on the amount of yeast included in the recipe). The salt is then worked into the dough until thoroughly incorporated. Over the next hour, stretch and fold the dough, pulling up one side with both hands, folding it back on itself, and letting it rest for 15 to 20 minutes before repeating the stretch-and-fold two more times. When the dough is well developed, it is then left to rest to complete bulk fermentation.

SLAP AND FOLD: This is a modern technique developed by Richard Bertinet, the renowned French baker, and it works best with highly hydrated doughs. This method involves turning your mixed dough out on your countertop, picking it up with one hand on each side, slapping the dough down on the working surface, and folding the upper part of the dough over the bottom. The dough is then turned 90 degrees and the movement is repeated until the dough appears smooth and well developed.

TIPS ON MIXING BY MACHINE

When using a stand mixer, always start by setting the machine at one of the slowest settings. If mixing very small batches of dough, it is best to add the water first, then the flour and yeast. If mixing larger batches of dough, proceed as usual, adding the flour first, then the water and yeast.

It is generally best to add the salt and any fats at a later stage, allowing the water to hydrate the flour and start changing its structure without any interference. Generally, an interval of 15 to 20 minutes before adding salt and fats is sufficient.

Overall, machine mixing should not last more than 15 active minutes, combined with a minimum of 15 minutes of rest in between intervals of active mixing.

The first interval of active mixing is done at low speed, with the aim of incorporating the water into the flour. This stage should not last more than 5 minutes. The dough is then left to rest, covered, for about 10 to 15 minutes. After this rest, salt and fats can be added and the dough is worked at low speed for another 5 minutes. If additional water is required, this stage is a good time to incorporate it. Let the dough rest for another 15 minutes before commencing the final stage, which should be done at a higher speed to achieve ideal gluten development. When the dough is well developed, it should adhere to the dough hook attachment and should not break when pulled away from one side.

in order to give the dough time to take shape and develop the gluten net. It is also useful to let the dough rest between intervals, which keeps it from getting too warm and aids in the formation of gluten through autolysis, a series of biochemical reactions that occur when mixing a dough.

Mixing times are dependent on the flour that is being used. A weak flour requires less energetic mixing for a shorter period of time, while a strong flour will require more work to achieve optimal development. Depending on the flour, one may need to conclude the mixing at high speed.

No-Knead Mixing

This technique involves mixing ingredients by hand or machine just enough to combine them—which generally takes only a few minutes—and then letting the dough rest in a covered bowl for an extended amount of time. This technique is particularly effective with wet doughs featuring high hydration. These types of doughs can be helped by simply stretching the mass and folding it on itself a few times during the first hours of fermentation. The dough is developed mostly through autolysis, where time allows the dough to catalyze its own transformation.

FERMENTATION

The beauty of pizza and focaccia is that they are fermented by living organisms. Of course, unleavened versions do exist, like St. Louis–style pizza and the Italian piadina, but they are exceptions. Pizza and focaccia are mostly living doughs, meaning doughs that ferment through the interaction of the myriad microorganisms living in them. It is therefore useful to understand fermentation techniques, which will help considerably in your attempt to master the recipes in this book.

Direct and Indirect Method

With this we distinguish between doughs fermented directly, by simply adding yeast to the mix, and doughs that are instead fermented indirectly with a starter, the so-called pre-ferment.

Pre-Ferments

There are several types of starters that can be fermented ahead of time and added to the mix when creating a dough.

Biga: Originally from Italy, this is a stiff pre-ferment based on yeast and made with half as much water as flour.

Poolish: Originally from Poland, this is a pre-ferment based on yeast and made with equal amounts of water and flour.

Sourdough: This pre-ferment relies on wild yeasts and lactic acid rather than commercial yeast; sourdough cultures can thrive with various water-to-flour ratios.

Old Dough: The simplest pre-ferment is a piece of old dough from a previous batch. This constitutes an already fermented pre-ferment that can be added directly to the new dough, helping to leaven it while at the same time enhancing the flavor's complexity.

First Fermentation (Bulk)

The fermentation process is started the moment the leavening agent, either yeast or a pre-ferment, is added to the dough. Every dough requires a period of rest after mixing, which allows the fermentation to proceed undisturbed and the carbon dioxide generated by the yeast—and lactic acid in sourdough—to foment, a process that makes the dough grow visibly. This period of development before shaping is called bulk fermentation. It is helpful to have a few large bowls (or containers) with lids for this specific part of pizza and focaccia making.

Second Fermentation (Proofing)

After the first fermentation, when the dough has expanded to 1½ to 2 times its original size, it needs to be shaped according to the specific recipe. The period of rest generally given to a dough after the

TIPS ON SHAPING FOCACCIA

After the first rise, the leavened focaccia dough generally needs to complete its second rise directly on the baking sheet or skillet that it will be cooked upon.

First, the baking sheet or skillet should always be greased before the dough is placed upon it.

Place the focaccia dough in the center of the pan and drizzle olive oil over it. The spreading of the focaccia should happen in a very deliberate fashion, rather than all at once. This will allow the dough to slowly relax and become more extensible. Spreading the dough too quickly will result in deflating it excessively, producing a tough focaccia, rather than the soft and light version that is ideal.

To stretch the focaccia, shape the dough into an oval by spreading it with the palms of your hands, pushing each hand in opposite directions.

Let the dough rest for 15 to 20 minutes, and then proceed to a new round of stretching. It will be very useful to keep the surface of the dough moist by adding olive oil, or an emulsion of olive oil and water, after each interval.

After three to four stages of stretching, the focaccia should have extended to cover the entire pan without having lost its volume. A final period of rest, lasting at least 30 minutes, will be required before putting the toppings on the focaccia and baking it.

Depending on the toppings and of the amount of yeast used, the focaccia can benefit from an extra period of rest after the toppings are applied before going in the oven.

TIPS ON SHAPING PIZZA

There are numerous ways to shape a pizza and, with time, you will develop your own style.

As a rule of thumb, pizza does not require the use of a rolling pin. Exceptions are specific regional varieties (like St. Louis–style pizza) that require a crust that departs from the classical Neapolitan style.

One method relies on gravity. The trick is to slightly flatten the ball of pizza dough, then grab the top edge with both hands and lift it, allowing the bottom edge of the dough to come in contact with the work surface underneath. The hands need to keep shifting around the dough in a clockwise fashion, allowing the dough to slowly stretch on all sides. If done properly, this technique will provide a perfectly shaped disk of dough that will be thinner in the center and thicker on the edges.

An alternative method involves placing the dough on a work surface that has been dusted with semolina or cornmeal and gently stretching the dough by pressing in opposite directions with each hand. The dough is rotated on the surface while being stretched until the desired shape is achieved.

Whatever approach is used, the most important thing when shaping pizza dough is making sure the dough is thicker around the edge.

Lastly, when getting acquainted with pizza making it is essential to learn how to master the loading of the pizza on the peel and into the oven without altering the pizza's shape or losing the toppings. One way is to heavily dust a peel (or a flat baking sheet) with semolina or cornmeal and place the dough on the peel before distributing the toppings. Another method consists of stretching the dough directly on a piece of semolina-dusted parchment paper. This final method will ensure that the transfer to the heated baking implement in the oven is uneventful.

shaping stage is called the second fermentation, or proofing. During this stage, the dough continues to expand while the microorganisms in it keep "eating" the sugars present in the flour.

It is important to end the second fermentation before all of the sugars have been consumed, so that there is room for a final expansion. This final expansion happens at high temperature during the first stages of baking, and is commonly referred to as "oven spring." When a proofing stage has exceeded optimal fermentation and all of the sugars have been exhausted, the dough is defined as "overproofed." This will generally result in harder and flatter crusts, owing to the loss of the gluten network that traps the carbon dioxide inside the dough, allowing it to become soft and voluminous.

To prevent overproofing, you need to keep a close eye on the dough and observe when it is losing its elasticity. A common way to monitor the fermentation process is by simply poking the dough with a finger. Simply press the dough with your index finger and then observe how fast or slow the dough springs back to its original shape. If the dough does not spring back at all, the dough is overproofed. The refrigerator is a great ally in controlling fermentation, as is altering the amount of leavening agent used initially.

Short vs. Long Fermentation

Although it is important to avoid overproofing, pizza and focaccia do benefit from extended fermentation times. While there are "cheat" recipes with short leavening times, in most cases it's better not to expedite the process by overloading the dough with excessive amounts of yeast.

Besides producing clearly inferior taste and structure, a fermentation of less than four hours will result in products that are less digestible. This is particularly true for Neapolitan pizza, which requires a very short baking time of just a few minutes. During the fermentation process, wheat starches and proteins are pre-digested by the microorganisms present in yeasts, and by wild yeasts and lactic acid in sourdough. These microorganisms transform the complex carbohydrates and proteins present in cereal flours, which are otherwise indigestible, into a proper food for our body. A further transformation of the starches occurs during baking, particularly during prolonged baking. A quick fermentation paired with a short time in the oven makes for a pizza with mediocre flavor and texture, and adverse effects on your digestive system.

Conversely, pizza and focaccia fermented for an extended amount of time, sometimes even days, results in an extremely light crust that will melt in your mouth and also agrees with your stomach. The good news about long fermentation is that it does not require much effort, just a bit of planning ahead. Time is in fact the most important ingredient in a tasty and digestible crust.

BAKING EQUIPMENT

Different types of focaccia and pizza require different equipment. The kitchen utensils and cookware listed below will be of great help when attempting the recipes in this book.

FOCACCIA

Baking focaccia at home is generally easier than baking pizza, for the simple reason that focaccia was created in home kitchens, while pizza was developed in a commercial setting. The chapter Traditional Focaccia Recipes (see page 127) features 70 different traditional focaccias, and a discussion of what you will need to master the majority of them follows (some focaccias require more specific equipment, which will be detailed in those recipes).

COOKWARE

Most focaccias are baked on baking sheets, but some are supposed to be baked directly on a baking stone (see Other Tools, page 79), or in a skillet (either in the oven or on the stovetop). Basically, you can manage the vast majority of focaccias with only three pans.

Shallow Skillet

This type of pan is essential in cooking focaccias that are not baked, particularly those that are fried like pizzelle or unleavened like piadina romagnola. Some of these focaccias require a special type of skillet, but the standard-issue shallow one you are familiar with will work for most preparations.

Cast-Iron Skillet or Cast-Iron Pizza Pan

A round cast-iron skillet with a medium-to-high edge is essential for baresestyle focaccias. Other oven-safe skillets will work, too, but a cast-iron skillet will distribute the heat better and retain it during the baking process, ensuring optimal rise.

Baking Sheet

Focaccias of medium height fit perfectly in a baking sheet, and it's a good idea to have a few different sizes to account for the different amounts of dough you may want to bake. The typical baking sheet is aluminum, and, although health concerns have been raised about this material, there is no consensus regarding its toxicity. There are quality baking sheets that are made with different materials, but aluminum is a better heat conductor than most of these other materials, and will help you produce a great focaccia. If you have reservations about using aluminum, one option is to use parchment paper to prevent the metal from coming into direct contact with the dough. Even better, it is possible to find sheet pans made of anodized aluminum, which has some nonstick qualities and will not release anything into the food.

HEAT SOURCES

Most focaccias will need nothing more than your standard oven or stove. Focaccia is not meant to be baked at the high temperatures pizza is, so there is no need to fret over ways to make your oven strain for temperatures commonly held to be beyond its grasp.

PIZZA

COOKWARE

Unlike the majority of focaccias, pizza is most often baked directly on a hot surface. Exceptions are Chicago deep dish, Detroit-style pizza, and Rome's pizza al taglio. In these cases, the pans recommended for focaccia will suffice. Below follows a description of the essential tools needed for classic pizza crusts, and for those focaccias that share the same baking techniques as pizza.

Baking Stone/Steel

Owning a baking stone or a baking steel is essential when making pizza in a home oven. For one, where would you load your pizza? But

these surfaces are also important for how they hold heat. Steel will actually cook pizza about 30 percent faster than stone, which results in a crisper crust. A baking steel is also more or less indestructible; a stone will crack over time, or if dropped. Both steel and stone need to be pre-seasoned before using and both should only be cleaned with warm water. (Because stone is porous, you never want to use soap when cleaning it.) If you are planning on cooking multiple pizzas one after another, it is worth investing in both a baking stone and steel and using them in tandem, placing the steel on top of the stone. In doing this, the stone becomes a heat sink, allowing the steel to hold heat better between removing a cooked pizza and firing an uncooked one. And since these tools can in fact be used for more than pizza, it is wise to use rectangular ones. No matter the material you choose, preheating a baking stone and/or steel for as long as possible will improve the end result.

Baking Peel

It is very difficult to load a pizza and all its toppings on a baking stone or steel without a baking peel. Make sure to find one that fits the size of your oven.

HEAT SOURCES

This is possibly the trickiest part of baking pizza at home, especially Neapolitan-style pizza, which some will tell you is impossible to repro-

duce at a temperature below 700°F. This is true only to a certain extent.

Home Oven: With a regular oven, the crust will never be exactly the same as what a good pizzeria can produce. But it can still be very good, especially if you employ a few tricks. You want to place your baking stone or steel on the highest rack in your oven and then set your broiler to high so the stone becomes extremely hot. Once you have preheated the stone with the

broiler, shut it off and preheat the oven to the highest temperature it can achieve. When it reaches that temperature, the oven is ready to produce a quality pizza.

Grill: An outdoor grill can be a surprisingly great ally in making a perfect pizza crust. With the right accessories, you can even achieve that wood-fired touch that is so in demand today. What you'll need are a grill lid and a baking stone or steel. The lid will retain the steam from the cooking pizza and will also help to keep the temperature high. The stone/steel will allow the temperature of the grill to be maximized and not dispersed. If you are thinking of using the grill to make pizza, be sure to buy a stone/steel that will fit on your grill.

Electric Pizza Ovens: There are several electric pizza ovens made for home use that promise to reach high temperatures and are often relatively affordable. Be sure to research this option thoroughly before purchasing, as the technology hasn't necessarily followed through on the promise.

Outdoor Gas and Wood-Fired Ovens: For the committed pizza baker with enough room and resources, an outdoor pizza oven is probably the safest bet. There are several models to choose from, and most are reliable in terms of performance. Fire is what pizza likes most, so one will surely have the best results with wood-fired ovens, and the second-best with gas ovens. Cooking times are massively reduced with wood-fired ovens, and heat is not always evenly distributed, so be aware that you will need some practice before achieving optimal results.

OTHER TOOLS

Both pizza and focaccia are easier to make with the following tools at the ready. While they are categorized as "Other Tools," I'd go so far as to say they are essential.

Scale
No matter what type of focaccia or pizza you are baking, a scale will make life a whole lot easier. There are plenty of inexpensive scales on the market, and learning to measure ingredients when making a dough is the only way to really master the craft. By weighing ingredients, it is also easier to calculate percentages and scale ingredients for different sized batches. As most of the ingredients in this book are listed by weight, a scale will come in very handy.

Stand Mixer
A stand mixer makes the preparation of pizza and focaccia dough a much less messy concern, as ingredients are just mixed in a bowl rather than flying all over the kitchen while you knead them by hand. Mixing with a machine not only saves you energy and time, it also ensures more consistent results when it comes to dough development and strength.

Bench Scraper
This inexpensive tool can be used to divide dough and remove it from the work surface without deflating it.

MASTER DOUGHS

*T*he doughs featured in this chapter will help you craft a wide variety of focaccias and pizzas, using some of the most widely used techniques available to home and commercial bakers alike. Always keep in mind that a recipe is just a *canovaccio,* a thread around which to build your own method, and this is even more true when it comes to leavened goods. Every recipe needs to be adapted to your own skills, tools, flours, baking conditions, and taste and texture preferences. Note that ingredients are mostly given as weights rather than volumes (see page 793 for a conversion chart). Also, doughs behave differently according to the initial temperature of the ingredients, final temperature of the dough, room or refrigerator temperature, etc. The times provided should be used as estimates. The best tip is to learn to recognize when your doughs are ready to be used, which will come with practice and a little bit of passion. Finally, when you are ready to use one of these doughs to make a focaccia or pizza, be sure to let the dough rest at room temperature for at least 2 hours before starting to follow a recipe's steps.

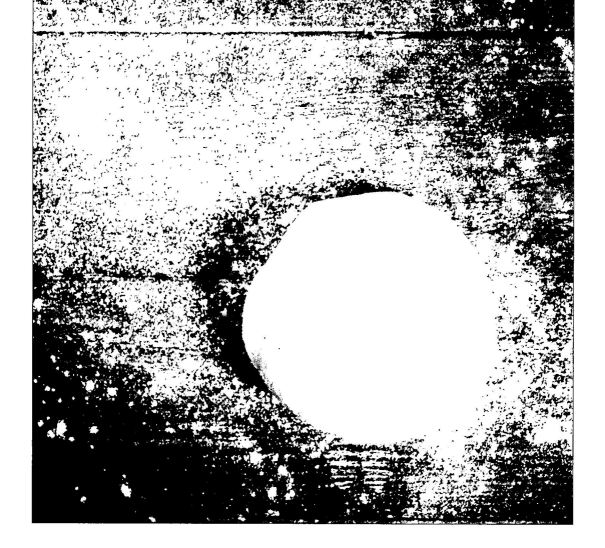

MASTER
FOCACCIA DOUGHS

QUICK FOCACCIA DOUGH

YIELD: 1 LARGE FOCACCIA / **ACTIVE TIME:** 15 MINUTES / **TOTAL TIME:** 2 HOURS

The simplest and quickest focaccia dough in my repertoire, providing a wonderfully soft dough in just a couple of hours.

1. If using active dry yeast, dissolve the yeast in the water and let the mixture rest for 5 to 10 minutes. Instant yeast does not need to be proofed.

2. In a large bowl, combine the flours, sugar, yeast, and water and work the mixture until it just holds together. If kneading by hand, transfer the dough to a flour-dusted work surface. Work it until it is compact, smooth, and elastic. For further instructions on kneading and mixing dough see page 71.

3. Add the olive oil and salt and knead until the dough is developed, elastic, and extensible, about 5 minutes. Form the dough into a ball and place it in an airtight container that has been greased with olive oil. Let rest in a naturally warm spot (in the oven with the light on is a good option) until it has doubled in size, about 1 hour.

4. After 1 hour, the dough can be spread and flavored as desired. It will need another 30 minutes to 1 hour for the second rise before baking.

INGREDIENTS:

4⅕ TEASPOONS | 12 GRAMS ACTIVE DRY YEAST OR 3⅓ TEASPOONS | 10 GRAMS INSTANT YEAST

16 OZ. | 450 GRAMS WARM WATER (105°F | 40°C)

12.3 OZ. | 350 GRAMS BREAD FLOUR OR TYPE 00 FLOUR

12.3 OZ. | 350 GRAMS ALL-PURPOSE FLOUR, PLUS MORE AS NEEDED

2 TEASPOONS | 8 GRAMS GRANULATED SUGAR

2.4 OZ. | 70 GRAMS OLIVE OIL, PLUS MORE AS NEEDED

3 TEASPOONS | 17 GRAMS TABLE SALT

BASIC FOCACCIA DOUGH

YIELD: 1 LARGE FOCACCIA / **ACTIVE TIME:** 30 MINUTES / **TOTAL TIME:** 5 HOURS

This dough will give you a soft focaccia with a nice, complex texture. It takes several hours to make, but keep in mind that most of it is rising time, during which you can attend to other activities (my favorite is napping). This dough is extremely versatile and can be used in most of the focaccia recipes in this book.

1. If using active dry yeast, warm 3½ tablespoons (1.75 oz./50 grams) of the water until it is about 105°F (40°C). Add the water and the yeast to a bowl and gently stir. Let sit for 5 to 10 minutes. Instant yeast does not need to be proofed.

2. In a large bowl, combine the flours, yeast, and water. Work the mixture until it just holds together. If kneading by hand, transfer the dough to a flour-dusted surface. Work it until it is smooth and elastic. The stretch-and-fold and slap-and-fold techniques are particularly effective for wet doughs. For further instructions on kneading and mixing see page 71.

3. Add the olive oil and salt and work the dough until it is developed, elastic, and extensible, about 5 minutes. Form the dough into a ball, place it in an airtight container that is at least three times bigger than the ball, and let it rest at room temperature until it has doubled in size, 3 to 4 hours. The time for this first fermentation can be reduced if you place the dough in a naturally warm spot. In the oven with the light on is a good option if you're going to go this route.

4. Stretch and flavor the dough as desired. It will need about 2 hours for the second rise before baking. The additional rising time will only benefit the dough, as the relatively low amount of yeast means the risk of overproofing is small.

INGREDIENTS:

1¼ TEASPOONS | 3.6 GRAMS ACTIVE DRY YEAST OR 1 TEASPOON | 3 GRAMS INSTANT YEAST

17.3 OZ. | 490 GRAMS WATER

15.9 OZ. | 450 GRAMS BREAD FLOUR OR TYPE 00 FLOUR

8.8 OZ. | 250 GRAMS ALL-PURPOSE FLOUR, PLUS MORE AS NEEDED

1 TABLESPOON | 13.3 GRAMS OLIVE OIL, PLUS MORE AS NEEDED

3 TEASPOONS | 17 GRAMS TABLE SALT

24-HOUR FOCACCIA DOUGH

A 24-hour focaccia will put time and temperature to work for you so that you will not have to continuously babysit the dough.

Below I present different versions that include different water-to-flour ratios and will therefore give you different types of dough.

As a rule of thumb, the higher the hydration, the softer the dough and the more pillowy the focaccia.

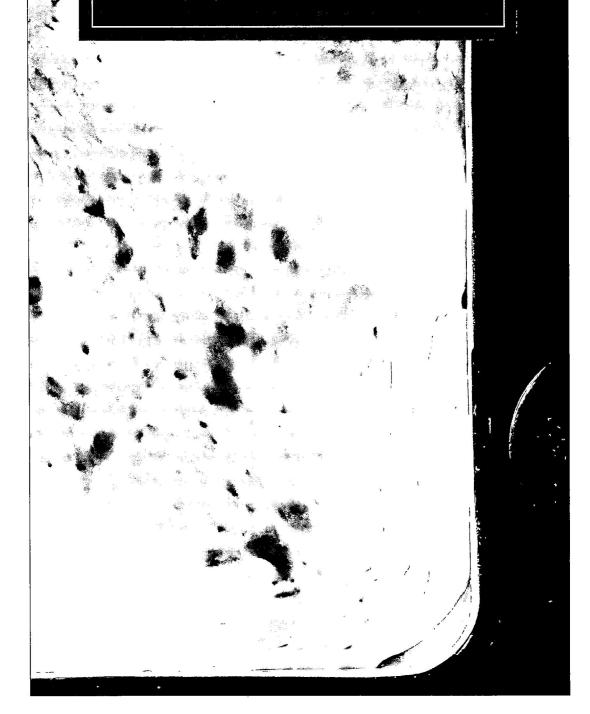

24-HOUR FOCACCIA WITH 60 PERCENT HYDRATION

YIELD: 1 LARGE FOCACCIA / **ACTIVE TIME:** 30 MINUTES / **TOTAL TIME:** 24 HOURS

This dough is rather dry for a focaccia, making it perfect for recipes that need a rather thin and substantial focaccia base. You can use this dough with several of the traditional Italian focaccia recipes, such as many of the focaccias from Northern and Central Italy, which are often less hydrated than ones from southern regions.

INGREDIENTS:

1½ TEASPOONS | 4.2 GRAMS ACTIVE DRY YEAST OR 1¹⁄₁₀ TEASPOONS | 3.5 GRAMS INSTANT YEAST

13 OZ. | 360 GRAMS WATER

10.6 OZ. | 300 GRAMS BREAD FLOUR OR "00" FLOUR

10.6 OZ. | 300 GRAMS ALL-PURPOSE FLOUR, PLUS MORE AS NEEDED

2⅔ TEASPOONS | 15 GRAMS TABLE SALT

1 OZ. | 30 GRAMS OLIVE OIL

1. If using active dry yeast, warm 3½ tablespoons (1.75 oz./50 grams) of the water until it is about 105°F (40°C). Add the water and the yeast to a bowl and gently stir. Let sit for 5 to 10 minutes. Instant yeast does not need to be proofed.

2. In a large bowl, combine the flour, yeast, and water. Work the mixture until it just holds together. If kneading by hand, transfer the dough to a flour-dusted work surface. Work it until it is compact, smooth, and elastic. For further instructions on kneading and mixing dough see page 71.

3. Add the salt and olive oil and knead until the dough is developed, elastic, and extensible, about 5 minutes. Form the dough into a ball, place it in an airtight container that is at least three times bigger, cover, and let rest at room temperature for 1 hour. After the 1-hour interval, refrigerate the dough in its container for a minimum of 20 hours.

4. Remove the dough from the refrigerator and let it warm to room temperature. Stretch and flavor the dough as desired. It will need another 2 to 3 hours for the second rise before baking.

24-HOUR FOCACCIA WITH 70 PERCENT HYDRATION

YIELD: 1 LARGE FOCACCIA / **ACTIVE TIME:** 30 MINUTES / **TOTAL TIME:** 24 HOURS

This dough is rather wet, but not "liquid," like the more hydrated focaccia doughs. It is perfect for a Focaccia Genovese (see page 140) and for focaccias that need to be thick without being overly pillowy.

1. If using active dry yeast, warm 3½ tablespoons (1.75 oz./50 grams) of the water until it is about 105°F (40°C). Add the water and the yeast to a bowl and gently stir. Let sit for 5 to 10 minutes. Instant yeast does not need to be proofed.

2. In a large bowl, combine the flour, yeast, and water. Work the mixture until it just holds together. If kneading by hand, transfer the dough to a flour-dusted surface. Work it until it is smooth and elastic. The stretch-and-fold and slap-and-fold techniques are particularly effective for wet doughs. For further instructions on kneading and mixing see page 71.

3. Add the salt and olive oil and knead the dough, until it is developed, elastic, and extensible, about 5 minutes. Form the dough into a ball, place it in an airtight container that is at least three times bigger, cover, and let rest at room temperature for 1 hour. After the 1-hour interval, refrigerate the dough in its container for a minimum of 20 hours.

4. Remove the dough from the refrigerator and let it warm to room temperature. Stretch and flavor the dough as desired. It will need another 2 to 3 hours for the second rise before baking.

INGREDIENTS:

1⅔ TEASPOONS | 4.8 GRAMS ACTIVE DRY YEAST OR 1¼ TEASPOONS | 4 GRAMS INSTANT YEAST

17.3 OZ. | 490 GRAMS WATER

1.1 LBS. | 500 GRAMS BREAD FLOUR OR "00" FLOUR

7 OZ. | 200 GRAMS ALL-PURPOSE FLOUR, PLUS MORE AS NEEDED

1 TABLESPOON | 17 GRAMS TABLE SALT

1 OZ. | 30 GRAMS OLIVE OIL

24-HOUR FOCACCIA WITH 80 PERCENT HYDRATION

YIELD: 1 LARGE FOCACCIA / **ACTIVE TIME:** 30 MINUTES / **TOTAL TIME:** 24 HOURS

This dough makes for the ultimate tall and fluffy focaccia. I recommend using a strong flour that will support the high water-to-flour ratio. Another important factor is working the dough long enough to develop the gluten effectively.

INGREDIENTS:

1⅔ TEASPOONS | 4.8 GRAMS ACTIVE DRY YEAST OR 1¼ TEASPOONS | 4 GRAMS INSTANT YEAST

19.75 OZ. | 560 GRAMS WATER

1.5 LBS. | 700 GRAMS BREAD FLOUR OR STRONG "00" FLOUR, PLUS MORE AS NEEDED

1 TABLESPOON (SCANT) | 17 GRAMS TABLE SALT

1 OZ. | 30 GRAMS OLIVE OIL

1. If using active dry yeast, warm 3½ tablespoons (1.75 oz./50 grams) of the water until it is about 105°F (40°C). Add the water and the yeast to a bowl and gently stir. Let sit for 5 to 10 minutes. Instant yeast does not need to be proofed.

2. In a large bowl, combine the flour, yeast, and two-thirds of the water. Work the mixture until it just holds together. If kneading by hand, transfer the dough to a flour-dusted work surface. Work it until it is compact, smooth, and elastic. The stretch-and-fold and slap-and-fold techniques are particularly effective for wet doughs. For further instructions on kneading and mixing dough see page 71.

3. Add the salt and knead the dough, gradually incorporating the remaining water, until the dough is developed, elastic, and extensible, about 5 minutes. Add the olive oil and work the dough until it has been incorporated. Form the dough into a ball, place it in an airtight container that is at least three times bigger, cover, and let rest at room temperature for 1 hour. After the 1-hour interval, refrigerate the dough in its container for a minimum of 20 hours.

4. Remove the dough from the refrigerator and let it warm to room temperature. Stretch and flavor the dough as desired. It will need another 2 to 3 hours for the second rise before baking.

48-HOUR FOCACCIA DOUGH

YIELD: 1 LARGE FOCACCIA / **ACTIVE TIME:** 45 MINUTES / **TOTAL TIME:** 48 HOURS

This dough is very similar to the 24-Hour Focaccia with 70 Percent Hydration on page 88, but it includes less yeast and therefore is suitable to even longer cold fermentation (up to 5 days). The result is a very soft focaccia with a complex taste and a lovely structure. Just keep in mind: this dough requires a strong flour with a high protein content that can manage the long fermentation.

1. If using active dry yeast, warm 3½ tablespoons (1.75 oz./50 grams) of the water until it is about 105°F (40°C). Add the water and the yeast to a bowl and gently stir. Let sit for 5 to 10 minutes. Instant yeast does not need to be proofed.

2. In a large bowl, combine the flour, yeast, and water. Work the mixture until it just holds together. If kneading by hand, transfer the dough to a flour-dusted surface. Work it until it is smooth and elastic. The stretch-and-fold and slap-and-fold techniques are particularly effective for wet doughs. For further instructions on kneading and mixing see page 71.

3. Add the salt and olive oil and work the dough, until the dough is developed, elastic, and extensible, about 5 minutes. Form the dough into a ball, place it in an airtight container that is at least three times bigger, cover, and let rest at room temperature for 30 minutes. After the 30-minute interval, refrigerate the dough in its container for a minimum of 40 to 44 hours.

4. Remove the dough from the refrigerator and let it warm to room temperature. Stretch and flavor the dough as desired. It will need another 2 hours or so for the second rise before baking.

INGREDIENTS:

1 TEASPOON | 3.1 GRAMS ACTIVE DRY YEAST OR 1 TEASPOON (SCANT) | 2.5 GRAMS INSTANT YEAST

17.3 OZ. | 490 GRAMS WATER

1.5 LBS. | 700 GRAMS BREAD FLOUR, STRONG "00" FLOUR, OR LONG-FERMENTATION FLOUR, PLUS MORE AS NEEDED

1 TABLESPOON (SCANT) | 17 GRAMS TABLE SALT

1 OZ. | 30 GRAMS OLIVE OIL

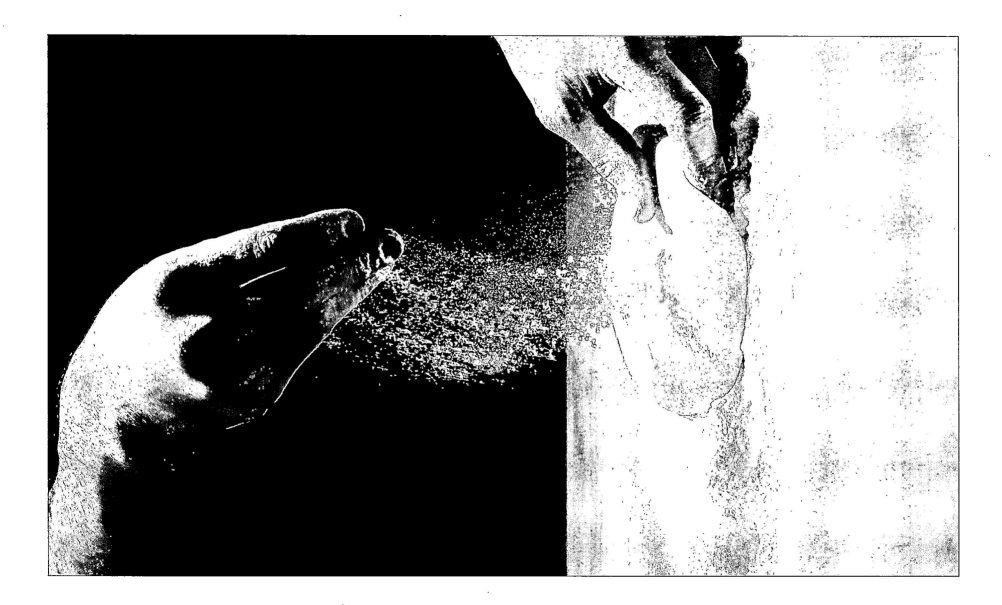

NO-KNEAD FOCACCIA DOUGH

YIELD: 1 LARGE FOCACCIA / **ACTIVE TIME:** 15 MINUTES / **TOTAL TIME:** 12 TO 16 HOURS

A focaccia dough is forgiving in terms of being overproofed. Therefore, a long fermentation at room temperature is a good and easy way to let the yeast do its job, and reduces any need to knead the dough. This dough can be fermented overnight, or prepared in the morning and used that evening. In terms of digestibility, a long fermentation with very little yeast is beneficial, so this dough is both healthful and low maintenance.

1. If using active dry yeast, warm 3½ tablespoons (1.75 oz./50 grams) of the water until it is about 105°F (40°C). Add the water and the yeast to a bowl and gently stir. Let sit for 5 to 10 minutes. Instant yeast does not need to be proofed.

2. In a large bowl, combine the flour, yeast, and water. Work the mixture until it just holds together. Add the salt and olive oil and work them into the dough.

3. Cover the bowl with plastic wrap and let the dough rest at room temperature for 12 to16 hours.

4. Grease an 18 x 13–inch baking sheet generously with olive oil and place the dough on it. Let the dough spread to the edges of the pan, helping it along by gently stretching on occasion, being careful not to deflate the dough. Let the dough rest in the pan for 1 hour and then flavor as desired.

INGREDIENTS:

⅖ TEASPOON | 1.2 GRAMS ACTIVE DRY YEAST OR ⅓ TEASPOON | 1 GRAM INSTANT YEAST

18.7 OZ. | 530 GRAMS WATER

1.5 LBS. | 700 GRAMS BREAD FLOUR, STRONG "00" FLOUR, OR LONG-FERMENTATION FLOUR, PLUS MORE AS NEEDED

1 TABLESPOON | 17 GRAMS TABLE SALT

1 OZ. | 30 GRAMS OLIVE OIL, PLUS MORE AS NEEDED

FOCACCIA DOUGH WITH BIGA

YIELD: 1 LARGE FOCACCIA / **ACTIVE TIME:** 30 MINUTES / **TOTAL TIME:** 27 HOURS

In Italy, the most common pre-ferment for focaccia is called *biga*. Stiff and yeast-based, biga should be prepared 12 to 16 hours before the final dough, so do plan ahead.

1. If using active dry yeast, warm 3½ tablespoons (1.75 oz./50 grams) of the water until it is about 105°F (40°C). Add the water and the yeast to a bowl and gently stir. Let sit for 5 to 10 minutes. Instant yeast does not need to be proofed.

2. In a large bowl, combine the biga, flours, yeast, and water. Work the mixture until it just holds together.

3. If kneading by hand, transfer the dough to a flour-dusted surface. Work it until it is smooth and elastic. The stretch-and-fold as well as the slap-and-fold techniques are particularly effective for wet doughs. For further instructions on kneading and mixing see page 71.

4. Add the olive oil and salt and work the dough until it is developed, elastic, and extensible, about 5 minutes. Form the dough into a ball and place it in an airtight container that is at least three times bigger.

5. Let the dough rest 1 hour at room temperature. After the 1-hour interval, refrigerate the dough in its container for a minimum of 20 hours.

6. Remove the dough from the refrigerator and let it warm to room temperature. Stretch and flavor the dough as desired. It will need another 2 to 3 hours for the second rise before baking.

BIGA FOR FOCACCIA

1. Combine all of the ingredients in a mixing bowl and work the mixture until it is a sticky dough.

2. Place the biga in a greased bowl, cover with plastic wrap, place it in a naturally cool spot, and let it sit until it has tripled in size, about 18 hours. Use immediately or store in the refrigerator for up to 5 days.

INGREDIENTS:

¼ TEASPOON PLUS 1 PINCH | 1.15 GRAMS ACTIVE DRY YEAST OR ¼ TEASPOON | 1 GRAM INSTANT YEAST

16 OZ. | 450 GRAMS WATER

150 GRAMS BIGA FOR FOCACCIA (SEE RECIPE)

14 OZ. | 400 GRAMS BREAD FLOUR OR "00" FLOUR

8.8 OZ. | 250 GRAMS ALL-PURPOSE FLOUR, PLUS MORE AS NEEDED

1 OZ. | 30 GRAMS OLIVE OIL

3½ TEASPOON | 20 GRAMS TABLE SALT

BIGA FOR FOCACCIA

2.8 OZ. | 100 GRAMS BREAD FLOUR OR STRONG PIZZA FLOUR

1.4 OZ. | 50 GRAMS WATER

⅛ TEASPOON | 0.4 GRAMS INSTANT YEAST OR ⅛ TEASPOON PLUS 1 PINCH | 0.5 GRAMS ACTIVE DRY YEAST

FOCACCIA DOUGH WITH A PRE-FERMENT

Using an already fermented mix of water and flour, a pre-ferment, to ferment your dough can add complexity and help develop the texture of your focaccia. Here are some suggestions on how to utilize this option.

FOCACCIA WITH OLD DOUGH

YIELD: 1 LARGE FOCACCIA / **ACTIVE TIME:** 30 MINUTES / **TOTAL TIME:** 27 HOURS

In the rural Italian countryside, a piece of leftover dough from a previous batch of bread was always the starter for a new batch. In the modern Italian bakery, this old dough is called *pasta di riporto*, and it can be used to leaven focaccia as well as bread and pizza. If kept in the fridge, the old dough will keep its leavening powers for up to 5 days, and it can be used right out of the refrigerator.

1. If using active dry yeast, warm 3½ tablespoons (1.75 oz./50 grams) of the water until it is about 105°F (40°C). Add the water and the yeast to a bowl and gently stir. Let sit for 5 to 10 minutes. Instant yeast does not need to be proofed.

2. In a large bowl, combine the flour, water, old dough, and yeast. Work the mixture until it just holds together.

3. If kneading by hand, transfer the dough to a flour-dusted surface. Work it until it is smooth and elastic. The stretch-and-fold as well as the slap-and-fold techniques are particularly effective for wet doughs. For further instructions on kneading and mixing see page 71.

4. Add the olive oil and salt and work the dough until it is developed, elastic, and extensible, about 5 minutes. Form the dough into a ball and place it in an airtight container that is at least three times bigger.

5. Let the dough rest 1 hour at room temperature. After the 1-hour interval, refrigerate the dough in its container for a minimum of 20 hours.

6. Remove the dough from the refrigerator and let it warm to room temperature. Stretch and flavor the dough as desired. It will need another 2 to 3 hours for the second rise before baking.

INGREDIENTS:

¼ TEASPOON PLUS 1 PINCH | 1.15 GRAMS ACTIVE DRY YEAST OR ¼ TEASPOON | 1 GRAM INSTANT YEAST

16 OZ. | 450 GRAMS WATER

14 OZ. | 400 GRAMS BREAD FLOUR OR "00" FLOUR

8.8 OZ. | 250 GRAMS ALL-PURPOSE FLOUR, PLUS MORE AS NEEDED

5.3 OZ. | 150 GRAMS OLD FOCACCIA DOUGH

1 OZ. | 30 GRAMS OLIVE OIL, PLUS MORE AS NEEDED

3½ TEASPOONS | 20 GRAMS TABLE SALT

SOURDOUGH FOCACCIA DOUGH

YIELD: 1 LARGE FOCACCIA / **ACTIVE TIME:** 30 MINUTES / **TOTAL TIME:** 27 HOURS

If you have a sourdough starter, you can of course use it to make focaccia. The result will be a more substantial and less pillowy, but still delicious, dough.

1. In a large bowl, combine the levain, flour, and water. Just make sure your levain is very active. Work the mixture until it just holds together. If kneading by hand, transfer the dough to a flour-dusted surface. Work it until it is smooth and elastic. The stretch-and-fold and slap-and-fold techniques are particularly effective for wet doughs. For further instructions on kneading and mixing see page 71.

2. Add the olive oil and salt and work the dough until it is developed, elastic, and extensible, about 5 minutes. Form the dough into a ball and place it in an airtight container that is at least three times bigger.

3. Let the dough rest for 2 hours at room temperature. After the 2-hour interval, refrigerate the dough in its container for a minimum of 20 hours.

4. Remove the dough from the refrigerator and let it warm to room temperature. Stretch and flavor the dough as desired. It will need another 2 to 3 hours for the second rise before baking.

INGREDIENTS:

LEVAIN FOR FOCACCIA (SEE RECIPE)

14 OZ. | 400 GRAMS BREAD FLOUR OR "00" FLOUR

8.8 OZ. | 250 GRAMS ALL-PURPOSE FLOUR, PLUS MORE AS NEEDED

16 OZ. | 450 GRAMS WATER

2 TABLESPOONS | 30 GRAMS OLIVE OIL, PLUS MORE AS NEEDED

3½ TEASPOONS | 20 GRAMS TABLE SALT

LEVAIN FOR FOCACCIA

2 OZ. | 60 GRAMS SOURDOUGH STARTER (SEE RECIPE)

2 OZ. | 60 GRAMS WATER

2.8 OZ. | 80 GRAMS BREAD FLOUR OR STRONG "00" FLOUR

SOURDOUGH STARTER

0.9 OZ. | 25 GRAMS ORGANIC RYE FLOUR

2.6 OZ. | 75 GRAMS ORGANIC BREAD FLOUR

3.5 OZ. | 100 GRAMS WATER

LEVAIN FOR FOCACCIA

1. About 8 to 12 hours before preparing the focaccia dough, add all of the ingredients to a mixing bowl and stir to combine. Store at room temperature.

SOURDOUGH STARTER

1. Combine the rye flour, bread flour, and water in a large mason jar. Place it in a dark, naturally warm place and let stand for 24 hours.

2. The next day, discard three-quarters of the mixture. Add 1.75 oz. (50 grams) water and bread flour to the mason jar and stir until thoroughly combined. Let stand for 24 hours.

3. The following day, combine 1.75 oz. (50 grams) of the starter with equivalent amounts of bread flour and water.

4. Repeat Step 3 until the mixture starts to bubble (around day 5). At this point you should start to feed the starter twice a day, with equal amounts of water and flour (1:1:1 ratio).

5. After 1 week the starter can be placed in the fridge after feeding; when kept in the refrigerator, the starter needs to be fed once a week.

6. To reactivate the starter, feed it a couple of times at 12-hour intervals, at room temperature, before use.

RAW PIZZA SAUCE

YIELD: 1¼ CUPS / **ACTIVE TIME:** 5 MINUTES / **TOTAL TIME:** 5 MINUTES

The most authentic Neapolitan and Italian sauce for pizza simply consists of crushed peeled whole tomatoes—preferably canned—salt, and olive oil. Oregano is sometimes added to the mix, but not always; I tend to omit this ingredient so as to have a versatile base that goes well with most toppings. What truly matters is the quality of the tomatoes. Ideally, unflavored canned San Marzano tomatoes, or tomatoes of similar quality, will be used. I recommend avoiding already salted and flavored tomatoes, as this provides you with more control and versatility.

1. Crush the tomatoes by hand, with a fork, or with a food processor and place them in a bowl. If you use a food processor, make sure to not overprocess the tomatoes; you want them to have a chunky texture.

2. Add the olive oil, stir until it has been emulsified, and season with salt. If your chosen pizza topping agrees with it, feel free to stir in some oregano as well. Store at room temperature if making pizza within 2 hours, or refrigerate and then return to room temperature before using.

INGREDIENTS:

14 OZ. | 400 GRAMS PEELED WHOLE CANNED TOMATOES, WITH THEIR JUICE

1½ TABLESPOONS | 20 GRAMS OLIVE OIL

SALT, TO TASTE

DRIED OREGANO, TO TASTE (OPTIONAL)

MARINARA SAUCE

YIELD: 1¾ CUPS / **ACTIVE TIME:** 15 MINUTES / **TOTAL TIME:** 40 MINUTES

This is a rather classic marinara sauce that fits traditional American pizza, but is not recommended for the overwhelming majority of the recipes in this book.

1. Coat the bottom of a skillet with olive oil and warm over medium-high heat. When the oil starts to shimmer, add the onion and garlic and sauté until the onion has softened, about 8 minutes.

2. Crush the tomatoes by hand or with a fork. Add them and the remaining ingredients to the skillet, reduce the heat, and simmer the sauce until the flavor has developed to your liking, about 20 minutes. Transfer the sauce to a food processor or blender and puree until smooth.

INGREDIENTS:

1 TABLESPOON | 13.3 GRAMS OLIVE OIL, PLUS MORE AS NEEDED

½ SMALL WHITE ONION, MINCED

3 GARLIC CLOVES, MINCED

14 OZ. | 400 GRAMS WHOLE CANNED TOMATOES, WITH THEIR JUICE

2 TEASPOONS | 11 GRAMS TOMATO PASTE

1½ TEASPOONS | 7.7 GRAMS RED WINE VINEGAR

½ TEASPOON | 0.5 GRAMS DRIED OREGANO

½ TEASPOON | 0.5 GRAMS DRIED BASIL

RED PEPPER FLAKES, TO TASTE

SALT AND PEPPER, TO TASTE

MASTER PIZZA DOUGHS

QUICK PIZZA DOUGH

YIELD: 4 BALLS OF DOUGH / **ACTIVE TIME:** 20 MINUTES / **TOTAL TIME:** 2 HOURS

A simple and relatively quick pizza dough recipe that can accommodate any topping of your choice.

1. If using active dry yeast, warm 3½ tablespoons (1.75 oz./50 grams) of the water until it is about 105°F (40°C). Add the water and the yeast to a bowl and gently stir. Let sit for 5 to 10 minutes. Instant yeast does not need to be proofed.

2. In a large bowl, combine the flour, yeast, and water and work the mixture until it just holds together.

3. If kneading by hand, transfer the dough to a flour-dusted surface. Work it until it is smooth and elastic. For further instructions on kneading and mixing see page 71.

4. Add the salt and knead until the dough is developed, elastic, and extensible, about 5 minutes. Form the dough into a ball and place it in a lightly greased airtight container that is at least three times bigger. Let rest in a naturally warm spot (in the oven with the light on is a good option) until it has doubled in size, about 1 hour.

5. Transfer the dough to a floured work surface, divide it into four pieces, and shape them into balls. Place the rounds in a greased baking dish with high edges, leaving enough space between rounds so that they won't touch when fully risen. Cover with greased plastic wrap and let rest for 40 minutes to 1 hour before using to make pizza.

INGREDIENTS:

3⅓ TEASPOONS | 9.6 GRAMS ACTIVE DRY YEAST OR 2½ TEASPOONS | 8 GRAMS INSTANT YEAST

15.5 OZ. | 440 GRAMS WATER

23.2 OZ. | 660 GRAMS BREAD FLOUR OR "00" FLOUR, PLUS MORE AS NEEDED

1 TABLESPOON | 17 GRAMS TABLE SALT

OLIVE OIL, AS NEEDED

NEAPOLITAN PIZZA DOUGH

YIELD: 4 BALLS OF DOUGH / **ACTIVE TIME:** 30 MINUTES / **TOTAL TIME:** 8 TO 12 HOURS

This dough is inspired by the classic Neapolitan pizza dough as described by the collective trademark "Verace Pizza Napoletana" (Real Neapolitan Pizza). The original Neapolitan pizza includes neither fats nor sugar and uses only a pinch of yeast, letting time do all the work. The fundamentals are a good flour and proper technique when working the dough. This dough can be started in the morning and baked the evening of the same day.

1. If using active dry yeast, warm 3½ tablespoons (1.75 oz./50 grams) of the water until it is about 105°F (40°C). Add the water and the yeast to a bowl and gently stir. Let sit for 5 to 10 minutes. Instant yeast does not need to be proofed.

2. In a large bowl, combine the flour, yeast, and water. Work the mixture until it just holds together. If kneading by hand, transfer the dough to a flour-dusted surface. Work it until it is smooth and elastic. For further instructions on kneading and mixing see page 71.

3. Add the salt and knead until the dough is developed and elastic. A Neapolitan-style pizza dough needs to be very well developed, which means the gluten in the dough should be at maximum strength. The resulting dough needs to be both extensible and elastic, meaning it needs to be easy to spread out thin but it also needs to spring back quite energetically, in order not to lose its shape. Transfer the dough to an airtight container, and let rest for 3 to 4 hours at room temperature. For a classic Neapolitan dough, room temperature should be 73°F (23°C). If your kitchen is colder, let the dough rest longer before shaping it into rounds.

4. Divide the dough into four pieces and shape them into very tight rounds. It is important to create tension in the outer layer of the dough (see sidebar). Place the rounds in greased baking dish with high edges, leaving enough space between rounds that they won't touch when fully risen. Cover with greased plastic wrap and let rest for 6 to 8 hours, depending on the temperature in the room.

INGREDIENTS:

⅛ TEASPOON PLUS 1 PINCH| 0.5 GRAMS ACTIVE DRY YEAST OR ⅛ TEASPOON | 0.4 GRAMS INSTANT YEAST

14.8 OZ. | 420 GRAMS WATER

23.9 OZ. | 680 GRAMS BREAD FLOUR OR "00" FLOUR, PLUS MORE AS NEEDED

1 TABLESPOON | 17 GRAMS TABLE SALT

OLIVE OIL, AS NEEDED

FORMING A PIZZA ROUND

There are several ways to create a tight "skin" around the ball of dough, so that it will better retain gasses from fermentation even when pressed to form the pizza disk.

   One way is to pull all the sides of a piece of dough toward the bottom of the dough, pinching them together.

   Alternatively, the piece of dough can be slightly flattened and folded in on itself from different angles a few times until it looks like a ball.

   Either way, the final step is to roll the resulting ball over an unfloured counter, cupping your hand over the ball and moving it in circular motion, counterclockwise.

24-HOUR PIZZA DOUGHS

An easy adaptation of the traditional Neapolitan pizza dough, which is fermented at room temperature, is to use cold fermentation for the final part of the process. This way, you can prepare the dough the evening before, let it rest at room temperature for a few hours, and then place it in the refrigerator until you're ready to make pizza. The following versions feature several water-to-flour ratios, each of which will give you a slightly different result. After 48 hours, the gluten in the dough will start to deteriorate and the quality of the pizza with it, so it is optimal to use the dough at some point within that window. However, if you love a very light crust, longer cold proofing times are possible, when using the proper flour.

24-HOUR PIZZA DOUGH
WITH 62 PERCENT HYDRATION

YIELD: 4 BALLS OF DOUGH / **ACTIVE TIME:** 30 MINUTES / **TOTAL TIME:** 24 HOURS

This recipe represents a twist on the classic Neapolitan pizza dough. By performing only the first stage of fermentation at room temperature and the rest in the refrigerator it is easy to make the dough in the evening and have the pizza balls ready for dinner the following night. Like a classic Neapolitan pizza, this dough is relatively dry, so it can withstand a more energetic stretch when shaping it into pizza disks and can also be made into a thinner disk, as compared to doughs with a higher hydration.

1. If using active dry yeast, warm 3½ tablespoons (1.75 oz./50 grams) of the water until it is about 105°F (40°C). Add the water and the yeast to a bowl and gently stir. Let sit for 5 to 10 minutes. Instant yeast does not need to be proofed.

2. In a large bowl, combine the flour, yeast, and water. Work the mixture until it just holds together. If kneading by hand, transfer the dough to a flour-dusted surface. Work it until it is smooth and elastic. For further instructions on kneading and mixing see page 71.

3. Add the salt and knead until the dough is developed, elastic, and extensible, about 5 minutes. Form the dough into a ball, transfer to an airtight container, and let it rest at room temperature until it has doubled in size, 3 to 4 hours. The time for this first fermentation can be reduced if you place the dough in a naturally warm spot. In the oven with the light on is a good option if you're going to go this route.

4. Divide the dough into four pieces and shape them into very tight rounds. It is important to create tension in the outer layer of the dough (see page 109). Place the rounds in greased baking dish with high edges, leaving enough space between rounds that they won't touch when fully risen. Cover with greased plastic wrap and refrigerate for a minimum of 20 hours. Let sit at room temperature for 1 to 2 hours before making pizza.

INGREDIENTS:

1¼ TEASPOONS | 3.6 GRAMS ACTIVE DRY YEAST OR 1 TEASPOON | 3 GRAMS INSTANT YEAST

14.8 OZ. | 420 GRAMS WATER

23.9 OZ. | 680 GRAMS BREAD FLOUR OR "00" FLOUR, PLUS MORE AS NEEDED

1 TABLESPOON | 17 GRAMS TABLE SALT

OLIVE OIL, AS NEEDED

24-HOUR PIZZA DOUGH
WITH 67 PERCENT HYDRATION

YIELD: 4 BALLS OF DOUGH / **ACTIVE TIME:** 30 MINUTES / **TOTAL TIME:** 24 HOURS

With a 67 percent hydration this dough will appear soft but not overly sticky and it will be easy to handle. This level of hydration works with most styles of pizza.

---

1. If using active dry yeast, warm 3½ tablespoons (1.75 oz./50 grams) of the water until it is about 105°F (40°C). Add the water and the yeast to a bowl and gently stir. Let sit for 5 to 10 minutes. Instant yeast does not need to be proofed.

2. In a large bowl, combine the flour, yeast, and water. Work the mixture until it just holds together. If kneading by hand, transfer the dough to a flour-dusted surface. Work it until it is smooth and elastic. For further instructions on kneading and mixing see page 71.

3. Add the salt and knead until the dough is developed, elastic, and extensible, about 5 minutes. Form the dough into a ball, transfer to an airtight container, and let it rest at room temperature until it has doubled in size, 3 to 4 hours. The time for this first fermentation can be reduced if you place the dough in a naturally warm spot. In the oven with the light on is a good option if you're going to go this route.

4. Divide the dough into four pieces and shape them into very tight rounds. It is important to create tension in the outer layer of the dough (see page 109). Place the rounds in greased baking dish with high edges, leaving enough space between rounds that they won't touch when fully risen. Cover with greased plastic wrap and refrigerate for a minimum of 20 hours. Let sit at room temperature for 1 to 2 hours before making pizza.

INGREDIENTS:

1¼ TEASPOONS | 3.6 GRAMS ACTIVE DRY YEAST OR 1 TEASPOON | 3 GRAMS INSTANT YEAST

15.5 OZ. | 440 GRAMS WATER

23.3 OZ. | 660 GRAMS BREAD FLOUR OR "00" FLOUR, PLUS MORE AS NEEDED

1 TABLESPOON | 17 GRAMS TABLE SALT

OLIVE OIL, AS NEEDED

24-HOUR PIZZA DOUGH
WITH 72 PERCENT HYDRATION

YIELD: 4 BALLS OF DOUGH / **ACTIVE TIME:** 30 MINUTES / **TOTAL TIME:** 24 HOURS

This dough has the highest water-to-flour ratio in this book. The mass will be slightly sticky in the initial stages but not as liquid as more hydrated doughs (not recommended for pizza). This level of hydration is good for a pizza with a thick crust.

1. If using active dry yeast, warm 3½ tablespoons (1.75 oz./50 grams) of the water until it is about 105°F (40°C). Add the water and the yeast to a bowl and gently stir. Let sit for 5 to 10 minutes. Instant yeast does not need to be proofed.

2. In a large bowl, combine the flour, yeast, and water. Work the mixture until it just holds together. If kneading by hand, transfer the dough to a flour-dusted surface. Work it until it is smooth and elastic. For further instructions on kneading and mixing see page 71.

3. Add the salt and knead until the dough is developed, elastic, and extensible, about 5 minutes. Form the dough into a ball, transfer to an airtight container, and let it rest at room temperature until it has doubled in size, 3 to 4 hours. The time for this first fermentation can be reduced if you place the dough in a naturally warm spot. In the oven with the light on is a good option if you're going to go this route.

4. Divide the dough into four pieces and shape them into very tight rounds. It is important to create tension in the outer layer of the dough (see page 109). Place the rounds in greased baking dish with high edges, leaving enough space between rounds that they won't touch when fully risen. Cover with greased plastic wrap and refrigerate for a minimum of 20 hours. Let sit at room temperature for 1 to 2 hours before making pizza.

INGREDIENTS:

1¼ TEASPOONS | 3.6 GRAMS ACTIVE DRY YEAST OR 1 TEASPOON | 3 GRAMS INSTANT YEAST

16.2 OZ. | 460 GRAMS WATER

22.6 OZ. | 640 GRAMS BREAD FLOUR OR "00" FLOUR, PLUS MORE AS NEEDED

1 TABLESPOON | 17 GRAMS TABLE SALT

OLIVE OIL, AS NEEDED

NO-KNEAD PIZZA DOUGH

YIELD: 4 BALLS OF DOUGH / **ACTIVE TIME:** 10 MINUTES / **TOTAL TIME:** 10 HOURS

The easiest pizza dough is one that is not kneaded. Kneading is fundamental in a proper Neapolitan-style pizza, but if you're just shooting for a "good enough" crust, a no-knead approach will surely get you there.

1. If using active dry yeast, warm 3½ tablespoons (1.75 oz./50 grams) of the water until it is about 105°F (40°C). Add the water and the yeast to a bowl and gently stir. Let sit for 5 to 10 minutes. Instant yeast does not need to be proofed.

2. In a large bowl, combine the flour, yeast, water, and salt. Work the mixture until there are no more lumps. Cover the bowl with plastic wrap and let it rest until it has doubled in size, 8 to 12 hours.

3. Divide the dough into four pieces and shape them into tight rounds. Place the rounds in a greased baking dish with high edges, leaving enough space between rounds so that they won't touch when fully risen. Cover with a damp kitchen towel, or greased plastic wrap, and let rest for 1 hour before making pizza.

INGREDIENTS:

⅛ TEASPOON PLUS 1 PINCH | 0.5 GRAMS ACTIVE DRY YEAST OR ⅛ TEASPOON | 0.4 GRAMS INSTANT YEAST

16.2 OZ. | 460 GRAMS WATER

22.6 OZ. | 640 GRAMS BREAD FLOUR OR "00" FLOUR, PLUS MORE AS NEEDED

1 TABLESPOON | 17 GRAMS TABLE SALT

PIZZA DOUGH WITH
A PRE-FERMENT

Using an already fermented mixture of water and flour, aka a pre-ferment, to prepare your dough can add complexity and texture to your pizza crust. The following are a few options if you choose to go this route.

PIZZA DOUGH WITH BIGA

YIELD: 4 BALLS OF DOUGH / **ACTIVE TIME:** 40 MINUTES / **TOTAL TIME:** 24 HOURS

Bakers in Italy turn to their biga day after day. If you're lucky enough to have enjoyed their results, you have a good idea of how delicious this pizza dough will be.

1. If using active dry yeast, warm 3½ tablespoons (1.75 oz./50 grams) of the water until it is about 105°F (40°C). Add the water and the yeast to a bowl and gently stir. Let sit for 5 to 10 minutes. Instant yeast does not need to be proofed.

2. In a large bowl, combine the flour, yeast, water, and biga. Work the mixture until it just holds together. If kneading by hand, transfer the dough to a flour-dusted work surface. Work it until it is compact, smooth, and elastic. For further instructions on kneading and mixing see page 71.

3. Add the salt and knead until the dough is developed, elastic, and extensible, about 5 minutes. Form the dough into a ball, transfer to an airtight container, and let it rest at room temperature until it has doubled in size, 2 to 3 hours. The time for this first fermentation can be reduced if you place the dough in a naturally warm spot. In the oven with the light on is a good option if you're going to go this route.

4. Divide the dough into four pieces and shape them into very tight rounds. It is important to create tension in the outer layer of the dough (see page 109). Place the rounds in greased baking dish with high edges, leaving enough space between rounds so that they won't touch when fully risen. Cover with greased plastic wrap and refrigerate for at least 20 hours. Let sit at room temperature for 1 to 2 hours before making pizza.

INGREDIENTS:

¼ TEASPOON | 1 GRAM INSTANT YEAST OR ¼ TEASPOON PLUS 1 PINCH | 1.15 GRAMS ACTIVE DRY YEAST

13.4 OZ. | 380 GRAMS WATER

20.1 OZ. | 570 GRAMS BREAD FLOUR OR "00" FLOUR

150 GRAMS BIGA FOR PIZZA DOUGH (SEE RECIPE)

3½ TEASPOONS | 20 GRAMS TABLE SALT

BIGA FOR PIZZA DOUGH

3.5 OZ. | 100 GRAMS BREAD FLOUR OR STRONG "00" FLOUR

1.8 OZ. | 50 GRAMS WATER

⅛ TEASPOON | 0.4 GRAMS INSTANT YEAST OR ⅛ TEASPOON PLUS 1 PINCH | 0.5 GRAMS ACTIVE DRY YEAST

BIGA FOR PIZZA DOUGH

1. Combine all of the ingredients in a mixing bowl and work the mixture until it is a sticky dough.

2. Place the biga in a greased bowl, cover with plastic wrap, place it in a naturally cool spot, and let it sit until it has tripled in size, about 18 hours. Use immediately or store in the refrigerator for up to 5 days.

PIZZA WITH OLD DOUGH

YIELD: 4 BALLS OF DOUGH / **ACTIVE TIME:** 40 MINUTES / **TOTAL TIME:** 24 HOURS

If you don't have a biga ready to go but happen to have some already fermented pizza dough from a previous bake, this method will come in handy. If refrigerated, old dough—or *pasta di riporto* in Italian, and criscito o crescente in southern Italy's dialects—can be used up to one week after it first has been made, and it is good to go straight out of the fridge.

1. If using active dry yeast, warm 3½ tablespoons (1.75 oz./50 grams) of the water until it is about 105°F (40°C). Add the water and the yeast to a bowl and gently stir. Let sit for 5 to 10 minutes. Instant yeast does not need to be proofed.

2. In a large bowl, combine the old dough, flour, yeast, and water. Work the mixture until it just holds together. If kneading by hand, transfer the dough to a flour-dusted work surface. Work it until it is compact, smooth, and elastic. For further instructions on kneading and mixing see page 71.

3. Add the salt and knead until the dough is developed, elastic, and extensible, about 5 minutes. Form the dough into a ball, transfer to an airtight container, and let it rest at room temperature until it has doubled in size, 2 to 3 hours. The time for this first fermentation can be reduced if you place the dough in a naturally warm spot. In the oven with the light on is a good option if you're going to go this route.

4. Divide the dough into four pieces and shape them into very tight rounds. It is important to create tension in the outer layer of the dough (see page 109). Place the rounds in greased baking dish with high edges, leaving enough space between rounds that they won't touch when fully risen. Cover with greased plastic wrap and refrigerate for at least 20 hours. Let sit at room temperature for 1 to 2 hours before making pizza.

INGREDIENTS:

¼ TEASPOON | 1 GRAM INSTANT YEAST OR ¼ TEASPOON PLUS 1 PINCH | 1.15 GRAMS ACTIVE DRY YEAST

13.4 OZ. | 380 GRAMS WATER

5.3 OZ. | 150 GRAMS OLD DOUGH (FROM A PREVIOUS BATCH)

20.1 OZ. | 570 GRAMS BREAD FLOUR OR "00" FLOUR

1 TABLESPOON | 17 GRAMS TABLE SALT

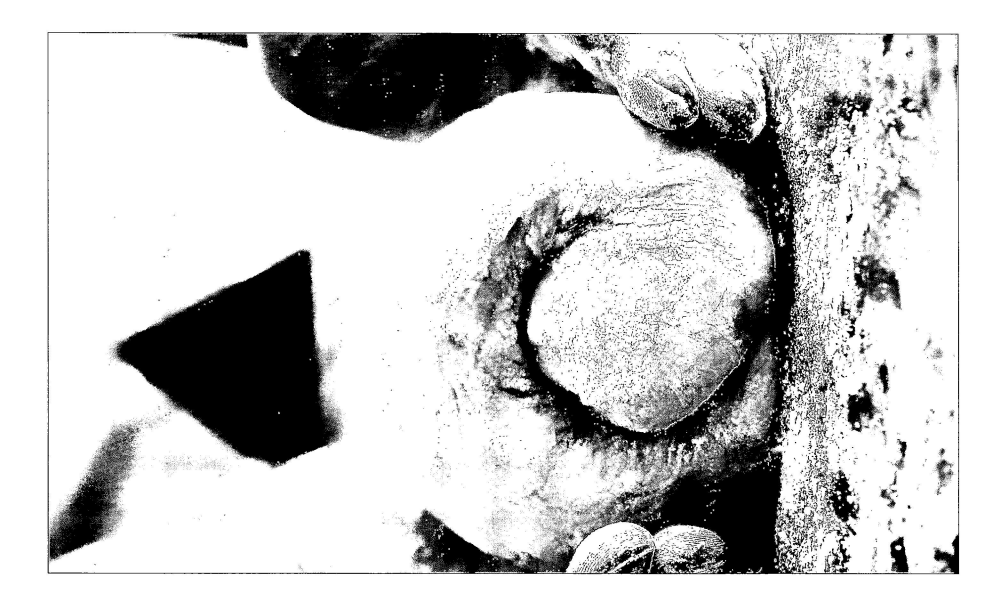

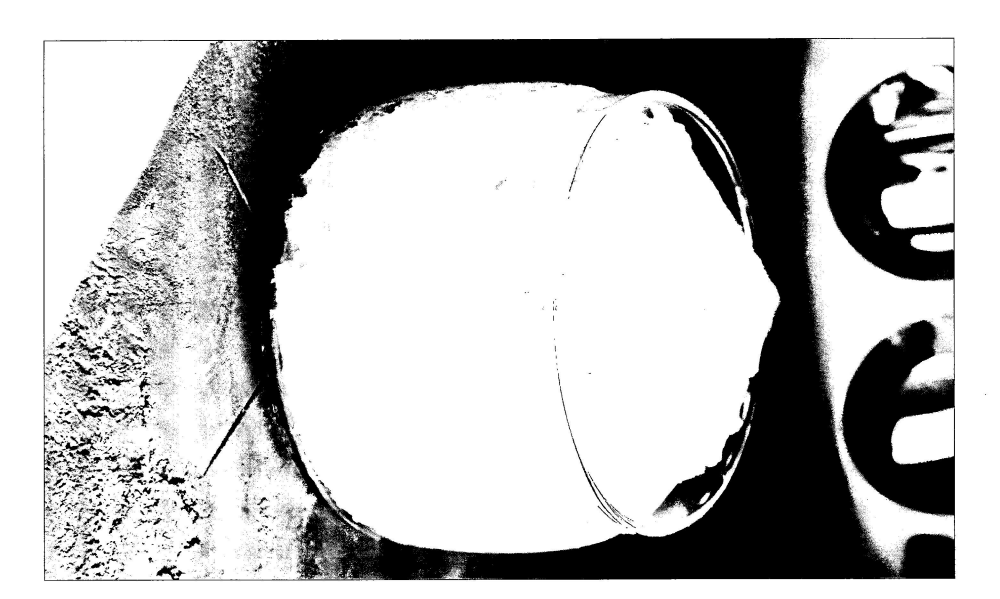

SOURDOUGH PIZZA DOUGH

YIELD: 4 BALLS OF DOUGH / **ACTIVE TIME:** 40 MINUTES / **TOTAL TIME:** 24 HOURS

For all the fans of sourdough pizza, here is a simple method that combines cold and room-temperature fermentation. When using sourdough, it is important to have a very lively starter. A sourdough crust can equal and even surpass a yeast-based one in terms of texture and flavor.

1. In a large bowl, combine the levain, flour, and water. Just make sure your levain is very active. Work the mixture until it just holds together. Transfer it to a flour-dusted work surface and knead the dough until it is compact, smooth, and elastic. For further instructions on kneading dough see page 71.

2. Add the salt and knead until the dough is developed, elastic, and extensible, about 5 minutes. Form the dough into a ball and place it in an airtight container. Let rest at room temperature for 2 hours.

3. Divide the dough into four pieces and shape them into rounds. Place the rounds in greased baking dish with high edges, leaving enough space between rounds that they won't touch when fully risen. Cover with greased plastic wrap and refrigerate for a minimum of 20 hours. Let sit at room temperature for 1 to 2 hours before making pizza.

LEVAIN FOR PIZZA

1. About 8 to 12 hours before preparing the pizza dough, add all of the ingredients to a mixing bowl and stir to combine. Store at room temperature.

INGREDIENTS:

150 GRAMS LEVAIN FOR PIZZA (SEE RECIPE)

20.1 OZ. | 570 GRAMS BREAD FLOUR OR "00" FLOUR

13.4 OZ. | 380 GRAMS WATER

1 TABLESPOON | 17 GRAMS TABLE SALT

LEVAIN FOR PIZZA

1.4 OZ. | 40 GRAMS SOURDOUGH STARTER (SEE PAGE 101)

1.4 OZ. | 40 GRAMS WATER

2.1 OZ. | 60 GRAMS BREAD FLOUR OR STRONG "00" FLOUR

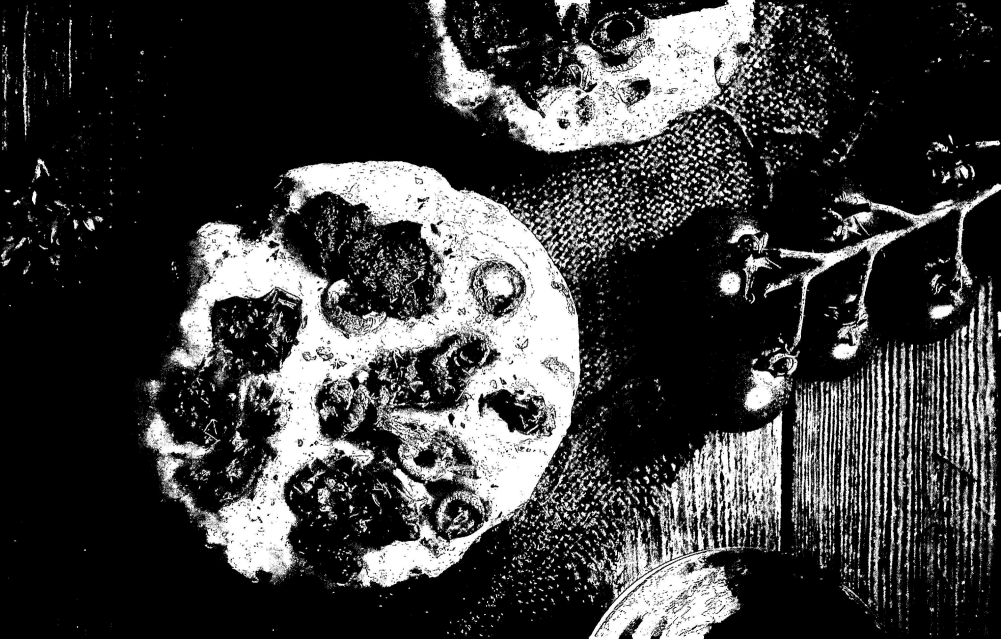

TRADITIONAL FOCACCIA RECIPES

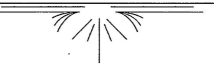

A chef laying claims of invention is a rejection of inspiration,
of influence, of history.
—*Chris Bianco*

From the Alps to the Mediterranean Sea, there is almost no Italian region without its local focaccia. Here is a selection of my favorite regional recipes, a sampling of one of the most humble, yet most beloved Italian foods.

NORTHERN
ITALY

SMACAFAM

The name of this dish means "keep away the hunger," *scaccia fame* in Italian. Something between a focaccia and a quiche, smacafam is served in bite-sized pieces. A common version substitutes wheat flour with buckwheat flour.

1. Preheat the oven to 360°F (185°C) and grease a 9 × 13–inch baking pan with butter. Add all of the ingredients, except for 3 oz. (85 grams) of the sausage, to a mixing bowl and stir until the batter looks smooth. Pour the batter into the pan and sprinkle the remaining sausage over the top.

2. Place the focaccia in the oven and bake for 30 to 40 minutes, until the edges are golden brown. Remove and let cool briefly before serving.

INGREDIENTS:

UNSALTED BUTTER, AS NEEDED

14 OZ. | 400 GRAMS ALL-PURPOSE FLOUR, PLUS MORE AS NEEDED

18 OZ. | 510 GRAMS WHOLE MILK

2 EGGS

8 OZ. | 225 GRAMS ITALIAN SAUSAGE, CHOPPED

2 TEASPOONS | 12 GRAMS TABLE SALT

2 PINCHES BLACK PEPPER

PINZA ONTA POLESANA

YIELD: 1 LARGE FOCACCIA / **ACTIVE TIME:** 40 MINUTES / **TOTAL TIME:** 4 HOURS

Most versions of this recipe include ciccioli, a type of processed pork that pancetta or bacon can be substituted for; the meat can also be removed altogether. This focaccia is traditionally made with lard, but feel free to use butter or margarine if you prefer.

1. Place half of the pancetta or bacon in a skillet and cook over medium heat until the fat has rendered, about 4 minutes. Transfer the bacon to a paper towel–lined plate to cool.

2. If using active dry yeast, warm 3½ tablespoons (1.75 oz./50 grams) of the water until it is about 105°F (40°C). Add the water and the yeast to a bowl and gently stir. Let sit for 5 to 10 minutes. Instant yeast does not need to be proofed.

3. In a large bowl, combine the flour, milk, half of the lard or butter, yeast, and water and work the mixture until it just holds together. If kneading by hand, transfer dough to a flour-dusted work surface. Work it until it is compact, smooth, and elastic. For further instructions on kneading and mixing dough see page 71.

4. Add the salt, pepper, and the cooled bacon and work the dough until it is developed, elastic, and extensible, about 5 minutes. Let the dough rest in a warm spot until it has doubled in size, about 2 hours. A good option is your oven with the light on and the door cracked open slightly. You can also place a pot of simmering water on the bottom of the oven.

INGREDIENTS:

7 OZ. | 200 GRAMS PANCETTA OR BACON, DICED

2 TEASPOONS | 6 GRAMS ACTIVE DRY YEAST OR 1½ TEASPOONS | 5 GRAMS INSTANT YEAST

4.6 OZ. | 130 GRAMS WATER

21.1 OZ. | 600 GRAMS ALL-PURPOSE FLOUR

7 OZ. | 200 GRAMS WHOLE MILK

4.2 OZ. | 120 GRAMS LARD OR BUTTER, AT ROOM TEMPERATURE AND CHOPPED, PLUS MORE AS NEEDED

2 TEASPOONS | 12 GRAMS TABLE SALT

2 PINCHES BLACK PEPPER

BREAD CRUMBS, AS NEEDED

COARSE SEA SALT, AS NEEDED

5. Grease an 18 × 13–inch baking pan with some lard or butter and sprinkle a light coating of bread crumbs over the pan to prevent the focaccia from sticking to the pan. Place the dough on the pan and stretch it into a thick rectangle, making sure not to go all the way to the edges of the pan. Cover with plastic wrap and let rest at room temperature for 1 hour.

6. Gently stretch the dough until it covers the entire pan. Let rest for another 30 minutes. Preheat the oven to 410°F (210°C).

7. Sprinkle the coarse salt over the focaccia and top with the remaining lard or butter. Place in the oven and bake for 30 to 35 minutes, until crispy and golden brown. Remove and let cool briefly before serving.

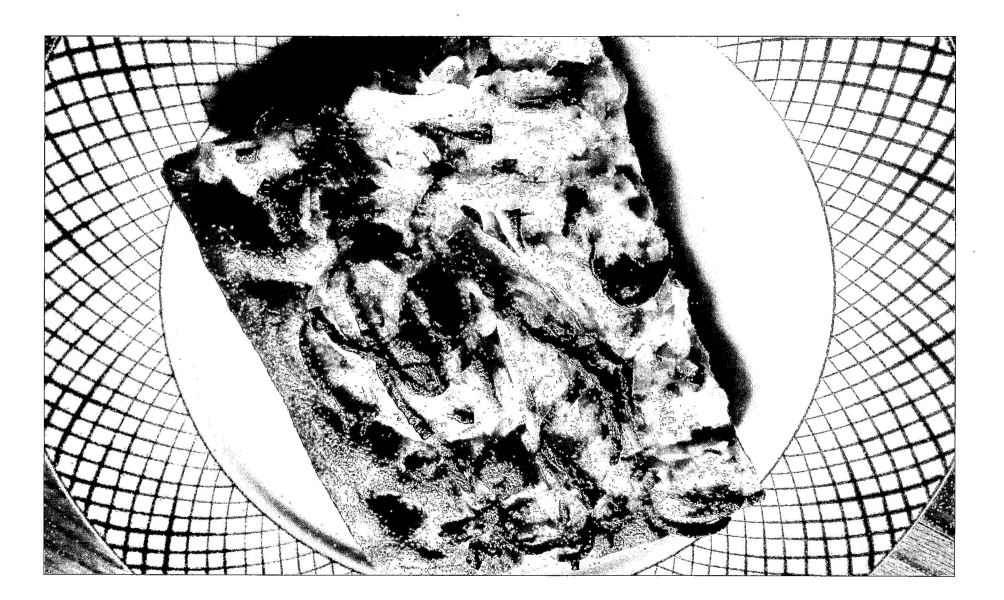

TIROT

YIELD: 1 LARGE FOCACCIA / **ACTIVE TIME:** 40 MINUTES / **TOTAL TIME:** 4 HOURS AND 45 MINUTES

Typical of Lombardy, the region surrounding Milan, this focaccia is enriched with yellow onions that confer a sweet note and provide a contrast to the crunchy crust.

1. If using active dry yeast, warm 3½ tablespoons (1.75 oz./50 grams) of the water until it is about 105°F (40°C). Add the water and the yeast to a bowl and gently stir. Let sit for 5 to 10 minutes. Instant yeast does not need to be proofed.

2. In a large bowl, combine the flour, two-thirds of the lard or butter, yeast, and water and work the mixture until it just holds together. If kneading by hand, transfer the dough to a flour-dusted work surface. Work it until it is compact, smooth, and elastic. For further instructions on kneading and mixing dough see page 71.

3. Add the onions and salt and work the dough until the onions are well incorporated. Shape the dough into a ball and let rest in a warm spot until it has doubled in size, about 2 hours. A good option is your oven with the light on and the door cracked open slightly. You can also place a pot of simmering water on the bottom of the oven.

4. Grease an 18 × 13–inch baking pan with lard or butter and sprinkle a light coating of bread crumbs on top to prevent the focaccia from sticking to the pan. Place the dough on a flour-dusted work surface and press it out into a thick rectangle that is smaller than the pan. Place the dough on the pan, brush the surface with olive oil, and cover with a kitchen towel. Let rest for 30 minutes.

5. Gently stretch the dough until it covers the whole pan. Let rest for another hour. Preheat the oven to 390°F (200°C).

6. Season the focaccia with salt and top with the remaining lard or butter. Place in the oven and bake for 30 to 35 minutes, until golden brown and crispy. Remove from the oven and briefly let cool before serving.

INGREDIENTS:

2 TEASPOONS | 6 GRAMS ACTIVE DRY YEAST OR 1½ TEASPOONS | 5 GRAMS INSTANT YEAST

13 OZ. | 360 GRAMS WATER

21.1 OZ. | 600 GRAMS ALL-PURPOSE FLOUR, PLUS MORE AS NEEDED

5.3 OZ. | 150 GRAMS LARD OR BUTTER, CHOPPED AND AT ROOM TEMPERATURE, PLUS MORE AS NEEDED

1 LB. | 450 GRAMS YELLOW ONIONS, SLICED THIN

2 TEASPOONS | 12 GRAMS TABLE SALT, PLUS MORE AS NEEDED

BREAD CRUMBS, AS NEEDED

OLIVE OIL, AS NEEDED

SCHIZOTO

YIELD: 1 LARGE FOCACCIA / **ACTIVE TIME:** 15 MINUTES / **TOTAL TIME:** 1 HOUR AND 30 MINUTES

A very simple, unleavened focaccia, which means it can be prepared relatively quickly. The use of lard makes it crispy and light even in the absence of yeast.

1. Preheat the oven to 375°F (190°C) and line an 18 × 13–inch baking pan with parchment paper. In a large bowl, combine all of the ingredients and work the mixture until it is smooth and elastic. Cover with plastic wrap and let rest at room temperature for 30 minutes.

2. Place the dough on a flour-dusted work surface and flatten it into a 1-inch-thick disk (3 centimeters). Place the disk on the pan and score the surface in a crosshatch pattern.

3. Place in the oven and bake for 30 to 40 minutes, until the focaccia is a light golden brown. Remove from the oven, brush with water, and let cool briefly.

INGREDIENTS:

21.1 OZ. | 600 GRAMS ALL-PURPOSE FLOUR, PLUS MORE AS NEEDED

8.8 OZ. | 250 GRAMS WATER, PLUS MORE AS NEEDED

5.3 OZ. | 150 GRAMS LARD OR BUTTER

2 TEASPOONS | 12 GRAMS TABLE SALT

FUGASCINA DI MERGOZZO

YIELD: 1 LARGE FOCACCIA / **ACTIVE TIME:** 10 MINUTES / **TOTAL TIME:** 1 HOUR AND 30 MINUTES

This sweet and crispy focaccia is typical of the dreamy lakeside town of Mergozzo. It pairs really well with a good grappa or a sweet wine but is also great with coffee or tea.

1. Preheat the oven to 340°F (170°C) and grease an 18 × 13–inch baking pan with butter. Combine all of the ingredients in a large bowl and work the mixture until a smooth dough forms. Form the dough into a ball, envelop it in plastic wrap, and refrigerate for 1 hour.

2. Place the dough on a flour-dusted work surface and use a rolling pin to roll it out so that it fits in the baking pan and is approximately ¼ inch thick (5 millimeters). Place the dough in the pan and make deep cuts, as though you were dividing it into squares, making sure not to cut all the way through.

3. Place in the oven and bake for 20 minutes, until golden brown. Remove, cut the focaccia into squares, and let cool completely. The squares can be stored in an airtight container and enjoyed for several days after being baked.

INGREDIENTS:

7 OZ. | 200 GRAMS BUTTER, MELTED, PLUS MORE AS NEEDED

21.1 OZ. | 600 GRAMS ALL-PURPOSE FLOUR, PLUS MORE AS NEEDED

10.5 OZ. | 300 GRAMS SUGAR

3.5 OZ. | 100 GRAMS GRAPPA OR BRANDY

5 EGG YOLKS

2 PINCHES TABLE SALT

ZEST OF 1 LEMON

FOCACCIA DI GIAVENO

YIELD: 1 LARGE FOCACCIA / **ACTIVE TIME:** 30 MINUTES / **TOTAL TIME:** 4 HOURS

The north of Italy is characterized by several versions of sweet focaccia. The one from Giaveno, a beautiful town in Piedmont, is very soft and utterly delicious, due in large part to the citrus zests.

1. If using active dry yeast, add the yeast and 3½ tablespoons (1.75 oz./50 grams) of 105°F water (40°C) to a bowl and gently stir. Let sit for 5 to 10 minutes. Instant yeast does not need to be proofed.

2. In a large bowl, combine the flours. Add the milk and yeast and work the mixture until it just holds together. If kneading by hand, transfer dough to a flour-dusted work surface. Work it until it is compact, smooth, and elastic. For further instructions on kneading and mixing dough see page 71.

3. Incorporate all of the remaining ingredients, except for the butter, into the dough one at a time. When incorporated, work the dough until it is developed, elastic, and extensible, about 5 minutes. Gradually incorporate the butter and work the dough until it does not feel sticky. Let the dough rest in a warm spot until it has doubled in size, about 2 hours. A good option is your oven with the light on and the door cracked open slightly. You can also place a pot of simmering water on the bottom of the oven.

4. Grease an 18 × 13–inch baking pan with butter. Place the dough on the sheet and gently flatten it into an approximately ¾-inch-thick disk (2 centimeters). There is no need to cover the whole pan with the dough. Cover with a kitchen towel and let the focaccia rest at room temperature for 1 hour. Preheat the oven to 430°F (220°C).

5. Dip your fingers in butter and press down on the dough to make deep indentations in it. Sprinkle sugar generously over the top, place in the oven, and bake for 15 to 20 minutes, until the focaccia is a light golden brown. Remove from the oven, sprinkle with more sugar, and let cool briefly before serving.

INGREDIENTS:

2½ TEASPOONS | 7.5 GRAMS ACTIVE DRY YEAST OR 2 TEASPOONS | 6 GRAMS INSTANT YEAST

WATER, AS NEEDED

7 OZ. | 200 GRAMS ALL-PURPOSE FLOUR, PLUS MORE AS NEEDED

17.6 OZ. | 500 GRAMS BREAD FLOUR

15.5 OZ. | 400 GRAMS WHOLE MILK

2.6 OZ. | 75 GRAMS SUGAR, PLUS MORE TO TASTE

3 EGG YOLKS

ZEST OF ½ LEMON

ZEST OF ½ ORANGE

1 TEASPOON | 6 GRAMS TABLE SALT

½ TEASPOON | 2.1 GRAMS PURE VANILLA EXTRACT

3.5 OZ. | 100 GRAMS UNSALTED BUTTER, CHOPPED, PLUS MORE AS NEEDED

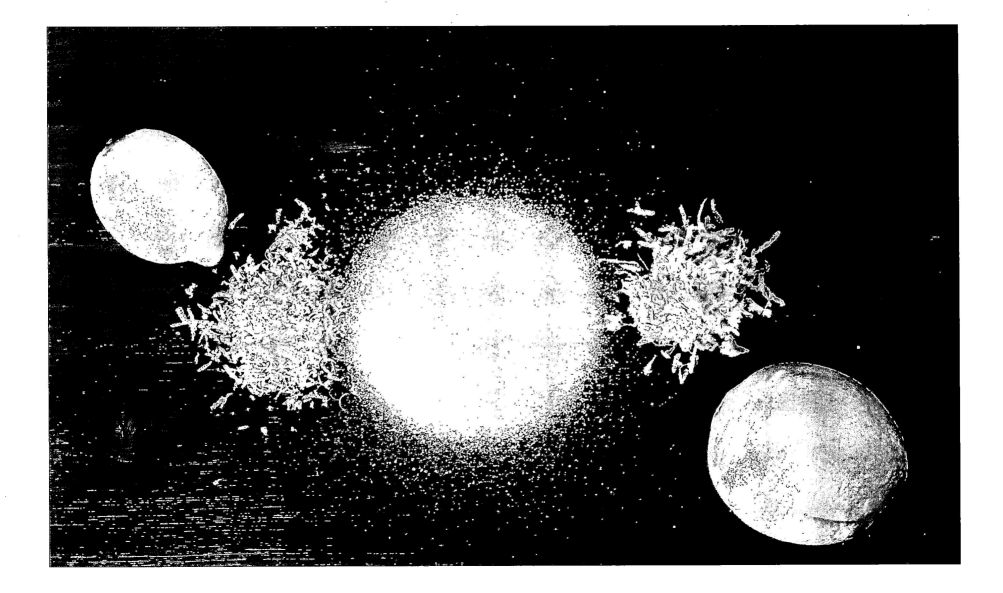

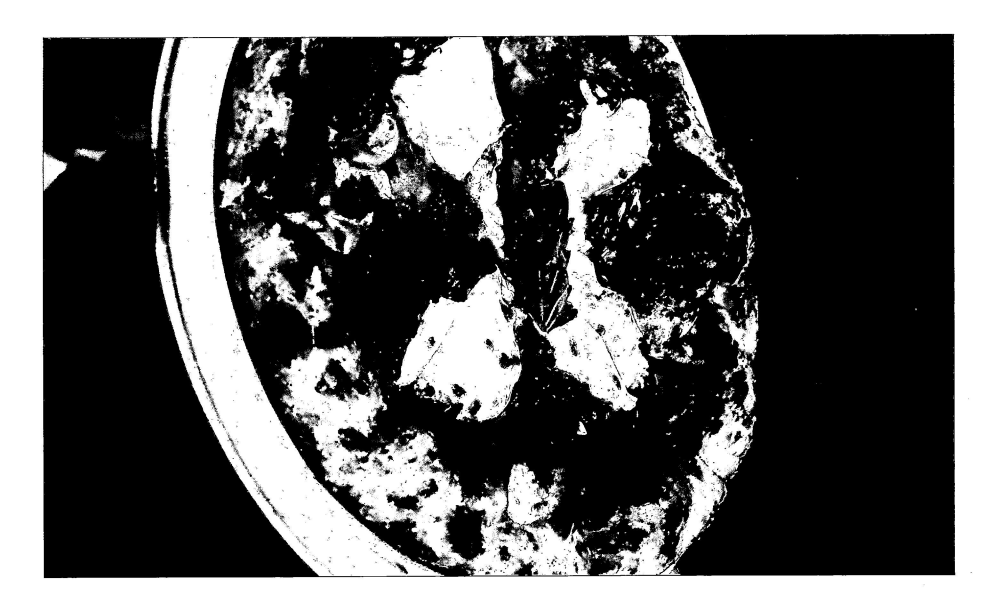

PIZZA AL PADELLINO

YIELD: 1 9-INCH FOCACCIA / **ACTIVE TIME:** 15 MINUTES / **TOTAL TIME:** 3 HOURS

This delicious focaccia baked in a cast-iron pan is also called *pizza al tegamino*, and it is a popular street food in Turin. Although nowadays it is considered a local delicacy, pizza al padellino does not have a centuries-old tradition like most local focaccias. Instead, it is a relative newcomer, brought by immigrants from the south of Italy.

1. Place the dough in a greased 10-inch cast-iron skillet and gently spread it to the edge of the pan, being careful not to deflate the dough. Brush with olive oil, cover the skillet with plastic wrap, and let rest at room temperature for 30 minutes.

2. Preheat the oven to 480°F (280°C). Place the tomatoes, salt, dried oregano, and olive oil in a mixing bowl and stir to combine. Spread the sauce over the focaccia, season with salt, if desired, and generously drizzle olive oil over the top.

3. Place in the oven and bake for about 10 minutes, until the focaccia is a light golden brown. Take the focaccia out, top with the mozzarella, and return it to the oven. Bake until the mozzarella is melted and the edges of the focaccia are golden brown, about 5 minutes. Remove and let cool briefly before serving.

INGREDIENTS:

1 BALL 24-HOUR FOCACCIA WITH 70 PERCENT HYDRATION (SEE PAGE 88)

1 TABLESPOON | 13.3 GRAMS OLIVE OIL, PLUS MORE TO TASTE

8.8 OZ. | 250 GRAMS CANNED TOMATOES, CRUSHED

½ TEASPOON (SCANT) | 2.5 GRAMS TABLE SALT, PLUS MORE TO TASTE

2 PINCHES DRIED OREGANO

7 OZ. | 200 GRAMS FRESH MOZZARELLA CHEESE, SLICED

FOCACCIA GENOVESE

YIELD: 1 LARGE FOCACCIA / **ACTIVE TIME:** 20 MINUTES / **TOTAL TIME:** 3 HOURS AND 30 MINUTES

The quintessential focaccia hails, without a doubt, from Genoa. This focaccia is generally of medium height, salty, and soft. Producing a high-quality version of this at home can be challenging, but it is achievable after a few attempts.

1. Place the dough on a flour-dusted work surface and form it into a loose ball, making sure not to compress the core of the dough and deflate it. Grease an 18 ×13–inch baking pan with olive oil, place the dough on the pan, and gently flatten the dough into an oval. Cover with a kitchen towel and let rest at room temperature for 30 minutes to 1 hour.

2. Stretch the dough toward the edges of the baking pan. If the dough does not want to extend to the edges of the pan right away, let it rest for 15 to 20 minutes before trying again. Cover with the kitchen towel and let rest for another 30 minutes to 1 hour.

3. Place the oil, water, and salt in a mixing bowl and stir to combine. Set the mixture aside.

4. Lightly dust the focaccia with flour and press down on the dough with two fingers to make deep indentations. Cover the focaccia with half of the olive oil mixture and let it rest for another 30 minutes. Preheat the oven to 445°F (230°C).

5. Cover the focaccia with the remaining olive oil mixture and sprinkle the coarse sea salt over the top. Place in the oven and bake for 15 to 20 minutes, until the focaccia is a light golden brown. As this focaccia is supposed to be soft, it's far better to remove it too early as opposed to too late. Remove and let cool briefly before serving.

INGREDIENTS:

FOCACCIA DOUGH WITH BIGA (SEE PAGE 96)

ALL-PURPOSE FLOUR, AS NEEDED

1.75 OZ. | 50 GRAMS OLIVE OIL, PLUS MORE AS NEEDED

5.3 OZ. | 150 GRAMS WATER

1 TEASPOON | 6 GRAMS TABLE SALT

COARSE SEA SALT, TO TASTE

FUGÀSSA CO A ÇIÒULA

YIELD: 1 LARGE FOCACCIA / **ACTIVE TIME:** 20 MINUTES / **TOTAL TIME:** 3 HOURS AND 30 MINUTES

Don't be turned off by the amount of onions, as they will caramelize in the oven and add a sweetness that contrasts wonderfully with the savory dough.

1. Place the dough on a flour-dusted work surface and form it into a loose ball, making sure not to compress the core of the dough. Grease an 18 × 13–inch baking pan with olive oil, place the dough on the pan, and gently flatten the dough into an oval. Cover with plastic wrap and let rest at room temperature for 1 hour.

2. Stretch the dough toward the edges of the baking pan. If the dough does not want to extend to the edges of the pan right away, let it rest for 15 to 20 minutes before trying again.

3. Add the olive oil, water, and salt to a mixing bowl and stir to combine. Cover the focaccia with half of the mixture, cover with plastic wrap, and let it rest for another hour.

4. Preheat the oven to 445°F (230°C). Distribute the onions over the focaccia and drizzle the rest of the olive oil mixture over the onions.

5. Place in the oven and bake for 20 to 25 minutes, until the onions look slightly charred and the focaccia is a deep golden brown. Remove from the oven and let cool slightly before serving.

INGREDIENTS:

24-HOUR FOCACCIA WITH 60 PERCENT HYDRATION (SEE PAGE 87)

ALL-PURPOSE FLOUR, AS NEEDED

1.75 OZ. | 50 GRAMS OLIVE OIL, PLUS MORE AS NEEDED

5.3 OZ. | 150 GRAMS WATER

1 TEASPOON | 6 GRAMS TABLE SALT

2 LARGE WHITE ONIONS, SLICED THIN

FOCACCIA CON LE OLIVE

YIELD: 1 LARGE FOCACCIA / **ACTIVE TIME:** 20 MINUTES / **TOTAL TIME:** 3 HOURS AND 30 MINUTES

This is a typical Ligurian focaccia, but similar versions exist in other regions. You can use any type of olives, but Ligurian *taggiasche* olives are a great choice.

1. Place the dough on a flour-dusted work surface and form it into a loose ball, making sure not to press down too hard on the core of the dough and deflate it. Grease an 18 × 13–inch baking pan with olive oil, place the dough on the pan, and gently flatten the dough into an oval. Cover with a kitchen towel and let rest at room temperature for 1 hour.

2. Stretch the dough toward the edges of the baking pan. If the dough does not want to extend to the edges of the pan right away, let it rest for 15 to 20 minutes before trying again. Cover with the kitchen towel and let rest for another 30 minutes.

3. Add the olive oil, water, and salt to a mixing bowl and stir to combine. Cover the focaccia with half of the mixture and let rest for another hour.

4. Preheat the oven to 445°F (230°C). Distribute the olives over the focaccia, pressing each of them into the dough until they don't bounce back. Brush the focaccia with the remaining olive oil mixture.

5. Place in the oven and bake for 15 minutes, until the focaccia is golden brown. Remove from the oven and let cool briefly before serving.

INGREDIENTS:

24-HOUR FOCACCIA WITH 60 PERCENT HYDRATION (SEE PAGE 87)

ALL-PURPOSE FLOUR, AS NEEDED

1.75 OZ. | 50 GRAMS OLIVE OIL, PLUS MORE AS NEEDED

5.3 OZ. | 150 GRAMS WATER

1 TEASPOON | 6 GRAMS TABLE SALT

10.6 OZ. | 300 GRAMS GREEN OLIVES, PITTED

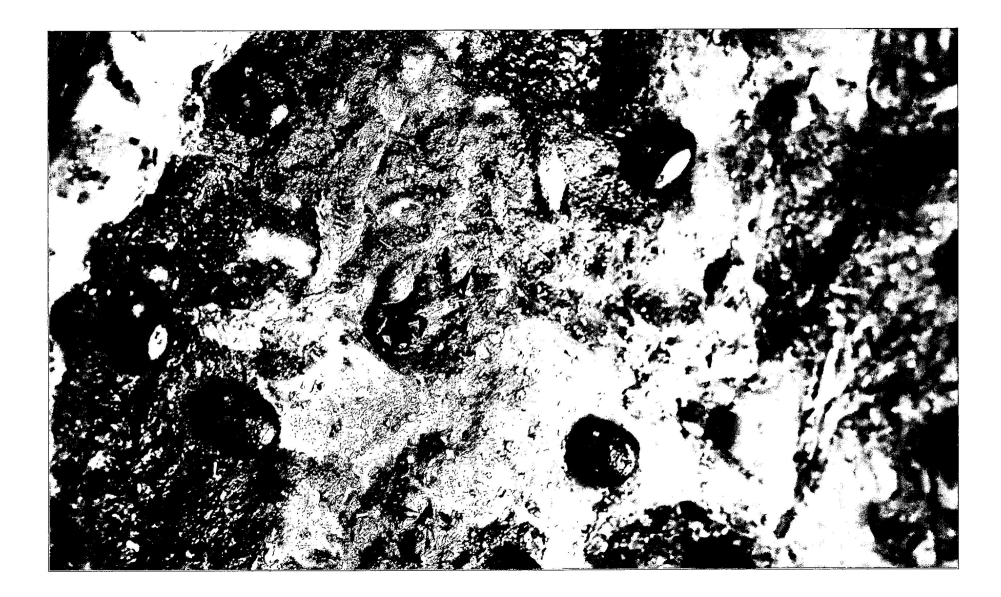

PISSALANDREA

YIELD: 1 10-INCH FOCACCIA / **ACTIVE TIME:** 45 MINUTES / **TOTAL TIME:** 3 HOURS AND 30 MINUTES

Often referred to as the Ligurian take on Neapolitan pizza, this actually dates back to long before the famous pie became popular in Naples. While it does have tomato sauce, a spongy crust, olives, and anchovies put pissalandrea in a world all its own.

INGREDIENTS:

½ BATCH 24-HOUR FOCACCIA WITH 70 PERCENT HYDRATION (SEE PAGE 88)

3 OZ. | 85 GRAMS OLIVE OIL, PLUS MORE AS NEEDED

1 ONION, SLICED THIN

21.1 OZ. | 600 GRAMS CANNED TOMATOES, CRUSHED AND WITH THEIR LIQUID

¾ TEASPOON | 4.5 GRAMS TABLE SALT, PLUS MORE TO TASTE

2 PINCHES DRIED OREGANO

2.1 OZ. | 60 GRAMS CANNED ANCHOVIES, DRAINED AND CHOPPED

8.8 OZ. | 250 GRAMS BLACK OLIVES (IDEALLY TAGGIASCHE), PITTED

9 GARLIC CLOVES, UNPEELED (OPTIONAL)

1 TABLESPOON | 8.6 GRAMS CAPERS (OPTIONAL)

1. Grease a round, 10-inch cake pan with olive oil, place the dough in the pan, and flatten the dough slightly. Cover with a kitchen towel and let it rest at room temperature for 1 hour.

2. Place the onion and the olive oil in a saucepan and sauté over medium-high heat until the onion starts to soften, about 5 minutes. Add the tomatoes, salt, and oregano and simmer until the flavor is to your liking, about 30 minutes. Remove from heat and let the sauce cool completely.

3. Gently stretch the dough toward the edge of the pan. If the dough does not want to extend to the edges of the pan right away, let it rest for 15 to 20 minutes before trying again. When the dough is covering the pan, brush it with olive oil, cover with the kitchen towel, and let it rest until it looks completely risen, about 45 minutes.

4. Preheat the oven to 430°F (220°C). Spread the tomato sauce over the focaccia, taking care not to press down too hard and deflate it. Top with the anchovies, olives, and, if desired, the cloves of garlic and capers. Season with salt, if desired, and drizzle olive oil over the focaccia.

5. Place in the oven and bake for 20 to 30 minutes, until golden brown. Remove and let cool briefly before serving.

FARINATA

YIELD: 1 LARGE FOCACCIA / **ACTIVE TIME:** 20 MINUTES / **TOTAL TIME:** 3 TO 24 HOURS

B orn during a time when wheat was scarce, farinata is a true poor man's focaccia. Though, believe me, it lacks nothing for flavor.

1. In a large bowl, combine the chickpea flour and the salt. While whisking constantly, gradually add the water. If possible, use a handheld mixer or an immersion blender, as you do not want lumps to form in the dough. When all of the water has been incorporated, cover the batter with a kitchen towel and let rest at room temperature for 2 to 3 hours. If time allows, let the batter rest overnight.

2. Preheat the oven to 480°F (250°C). Remove the foam that has gathered on the surface of the batter and discard. Stir the olive oil and, if desired, the rosemary into the batter.

3. Grease an 18 × 13–inch baking pan with olive oil, pour the batter into the pan, and use a rubber spatula to even the surface. Drizzle olive oil over the top.

4. Place the focaccia on the top rack in the oven and bake for 10 to 15 minutes, until the focaccia is set and lightly brown. Remove and let cool briefly before seasoning with pepper and cutting into squares.

INGREDIENTS:

14 OZ. | 400 GRAMS CHICKPEA FLOUR

2 TEASPOONS | 12 GRAMS TABLE SALT

42.3 OZ. | 1200 GRAMS WATER

3.5 OZ. | 100 GRAMS OLIVE OIL, PLUS MORE AS NEEDED

LEAVES FROM 3 SPRIGS FRESH ROSEMARY (OPTIONAL)

BLACK PEPPER, TO TASTE

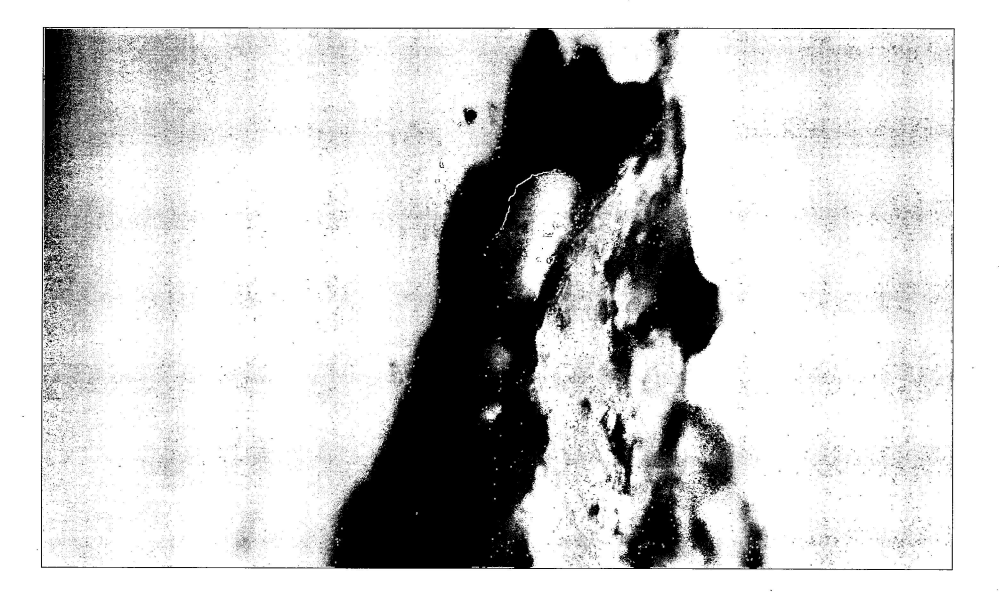

FOCACCIA DI RECCO

YIELD: 1 MEDIUM FOCACCIA / **ACTIVE TIME:** 45 MINUTES / **TOTAL TIME:** 1 HOUR AND 20 MINUTES

A beloved focaccia from the town of Recco in Liguria. It is stuffed with fresh, local cheeses, and the surprising contrast created by the thin, mildly flavored, crispy outside and the slightly sour, melted cheese on the inside can raise goosebumps. The cheeses used in Recco, stracchino and crescenza, may be difficult to find outside of Italy, so feel free to use Taleggio cheese in their place.

1. In a large bowl, combine the flour with the salt. Add the water and work the mixture until it just holds together. If kneading by hand, transfer dough to a flour-dusted work surface and work it for at least 10 minutes. You want it to be very smooth and elastic. For further instructions on kneading and mixing dough see page 71. Form the dough into two balls, place them in an airtight container, and let rest at room temperature for 30 minutes.

2. Grease a 9 × 13–inch baking pan with olive oil. Transfer one of the balls to a flour-dusted work surface and roll it into a rectangle that will fit in the pan. Stretching the dough with your hands until it is about ⅒₅ inch thick (1 millimeter), taking great care not to tear the dough.

3. Preheat the oven to the maximum temperature. With the help of a flat flour-dusted baking sheet or peel, transfer the rolled and stretched dough onto the baking sheet and cover with the cheese. Roll and stretch the other piece of dough to the same thickness and place it over the cheese. Remove any excess dough with a sharp knife and crimp the edges to seal. Make a few holes in different parts of the focaccia by pinching the surface with your fingers until it breaks.

4. Drizzle olive oil over the focaccia and season with salt. Place on the top rack of the oven and bake until dark spots begin to appear on the surface, about 10 minutes. Remove from the oven and let cool briefly before serving.

INGREDIENTS:

14 OZ. | 400 GRAMS BREAD FLOUR, PLUS MORE AS NEEDED

½ TEASPOON (SCANT) | 2.5 GRAMS TABLE SALT, PLUS MORE TO TASTE

7.8 OZ. | 220 GRAMS WATER

OLIVE OIL, AS NEEDED

28.2 OZ. | 800 GRAMS STRACCHINO, CRESCENZA, OR TALEGGIO CHEESE, TORN

PIADINA

YIELD: 4 SMALL FOCACCIA / **ACTIVE TIME:** 30 MINUTES / **TOTAL TIME:** 1 HOUR

This small, round, and flat focaccia from the Romagna side of the Emilia Romagna region is more reminiscent of pita bread than its Italian relatives. Unleavened and cooked on the stove, piadina used to be made with cereals that were not optimal for bread baking. It is delicious filled with creamy cheese and ham, but innumerable other fillings can be used.

1. Combine the water and salt and stir until the salt has dissolved. In a large mixing bowl, combine the flour and the baking soda. Add the lard or olive oil and the salted water and work the mixture until it just holds together. If kneading by hand, transfer dough to a flour-dusted work surface. Work it until it is compact, smooth, and elastic, about 10 minutes. For further instructions on kneading and mixing dough see page 71. Grease an airtight container with lard or olive oil, form the dough into a ball, place it in the container, cover with plastic wrap, and let it rest at room temperature for 30 minutes.

2. Place the dough on a flour-dusted work surface and divide it into four pieces. Form the pieces into balls and roll each one until it is an approximately ⅛-inch-thick disk (4 millimeters).

3. Warm a dry skillet over medium-high heat. When the skillet is hot, cook one piadina at a time until dark brown spots appear on both sides, about 5 minutes per side. Pop any big bubbles with a fork as the piadina cooks.

INGREDIENTS:

4.8 OZ. | 170 GRAMS LUKEWARM WATER (90°F | 32.2°C)

2 TEASPOONS | 12 GRAMS TABLE SALT

18 OZ. | 510 GRAMS ALL-PURPOSE FLOUR, PLUS MORE AS NEEDED

1½ TEASPOONS | 9 GRAMS BAKING SODA

3.5 OZ. | 100 GRAMS LARD OR OLIVE OIL, PLUS MORE AS NEEDED

CRESCENTA BOLOGNESE

YIELD: 1 LARGE FOCACCIA / **ACTIVE TIME:** 45 MINUTES / **TOTAL TIME:** 5 HOURS

Hailing from the city of Bologna, crescenta is a tall and fluffy focaccia enriched with prosciutto and pancetta. It was once the breakfast of the city's bakers, who made this focaccia using leftover dough from their morning preparations and scraps of cured meat from nearby butchers.

1. If using active dry yeast, warm 3½ tablespoons (1.75 oz./50 grams) of the water until it is about 105°F (40°C). Add the water and the yeast to a bowl and gently stir. Let sit for 5 to 10 minutes. Instant yeast does not need to be proofed.

2. Place the prosciutto and pancetta in a food processor and blitz until very fine.

3. In a large bowl, combine the flour, lard or olive oil, biga, sugar, yeast, and water and work the mixture until it just holds together. If kneading by hand, transfer the dough to a flour-dusted work surface. Work it until it is compact, smooth, and elastic. For further instructions on kneading and mixing dough see page 71.

4. Add the salt, prosciutto, and pancetta and work the dough until it is developed, elastic, and extensible, about 5 minutes. Grease an airtight container, shape the dough into a ball, place it in the container, and let it rest in a warm spot until it has doubled in size, about 2 hours. A good option is your oven with the light on and the door cracked open slightly. You can also place a pot of simmering water on the bottom of the oven.

INGREDIENTS:

⅔ TEASPOON | 1.9 GRAMS ACTIVE DRY YEAST OR ½ TEASPOON | 1.5 GRAMS INSTANT YEAST

11 OZ. | 310 GRAMS WATER

8 OZ. | 225 GRAMS PROSCIUTTO

8 OZ. | 225 GRAMS PANCETTA

1.5 LBS. | 700 GRAMS BREAD FLOUR, PLUS MORE AS NEEDED

2.4 OZ. | 70 GRAMS LARD OR OLIVE OIL, PLUS MORE AS NEEDED

8 OZ. | 230 GRAMS BIGA FOR FOCACCIA (SEE PAGE 96)

1 TABLESPOON | 12 GRAMS SUGAR

2⅔ TEASPOONS | 14 GRAMS TABLE SALT

5. Place the dough on a flour-dusted work surface and form it into a ball. Grease an 18 × 13–inch baking pan with lard or olive oil and place the dough in the center. Brush lard or olive oil onto the surface of the dough and gently press it into an oval. Cover and let rest for 1 hour.

6. Stretch the dough toward the edges of the baking sheet. If the dough does not want to extend to the edges of the pan right away, let it rest for 15 to 20 minutes before trying again. Cover with a kitchen towel or greased plastic wrap and let rest until fully risen, about 1 hour. You may need to stretch the dough again halfway through this final rise to get the desired results.

7. Preheat the oven to 430°F (220°C) and place a rack in the middle position. Brush the focaccia with lard or olive oil, place it in the oven, and bake for 25 to 30 minutes, until golden brown. Remove from the oven and let cool slightly before serving.

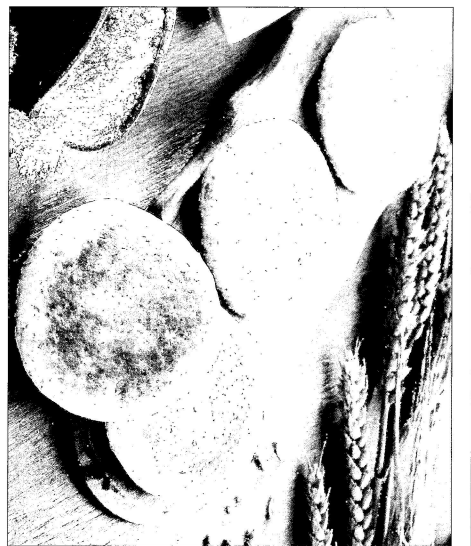
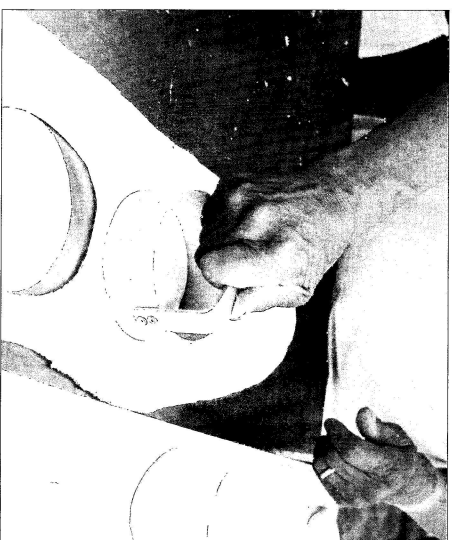

TIGELLE

YIELD: 20 TO 30 SMALL FOCACCIA / **ACTIVE TIME:** 30 MINUTES / **TOTAL TIME:** 3 HOURS AND 30 MINUTES

A yeasted version of piadina (see page 152), these small, round focaccia are traditionally cooked in a specific double cast-iron pan with built-in molds, but a standard skillet with a lid will work just fine.

1. If using active dry yeast, warm 3½ tablespoons (1.75 oz./50 grams) of the water until it is about 105°F (40°C). Add the water and the yeast to a bowl and gently stir. Let sit until it starts to foam. Instant yeast does not need to be proofed.

2. In a large bowl, combine the flour, milk, lard, yeast, and water and work the mixture until it just holds together. If kneading by hand, transfer the dough to a flour-dusted work surface. Work it until it is compact, smooth, and elastic. For further instructions on kneading and mixing dough see page 71.

3. Add the salt and work the dough until it is developed, elastic, and extensible, about 5 minutes. Grease an airtight container, shape the dough into a ball, place it in the container, and let rest at room temperature until it has doubled in size, about 2 hours.

4. Place the dough on a flour-dusted work surface and roll it out until it is approximately ¼ inch thick (5 millimeters). Using a water glass or a round cookie cutter, cut 20 to 30 rounds out of the dough. Place the rounds on a parchment-lined baking sheet, dust with flour, cover with the kitchen towel, and let rest at room temperature for 1 hour.

5. Lightly grease a 10-inch skillet with lard and warm over medium heat. Working in batches, cook the focaccia for 5 to 6 minutes per side in a covered skillet. You want the tigelle to remain flat; if necessary, place a weight on them during the last minute of cooking. Cut the warm tigelle open and eat as is or fill with whatever your heart desires.

INGREDIENTS:

1¾ TEASPOONS | 5 GRAMS ACTIVE DRY YEAST OR 1⅓ TEASPOONS | 4 GRAMS INSTANT YEAST

4.6 OZ. | 130 GRAMS WATER

17.6 OZ. | 500 GRAMS ALL-PURPOSE FLOUR, PLUS MORE AS NEEDED

4.6 OZ. | 130 GRAMS WHOLE MILK

1.4 OZ. | 40 GRAMS LARD, PLUS MORE AS NEEDED

1½ TEASPOONS | 10 GRAMS TABLE SALT

CHISOLA PIACENTINA

YIELD: 1 10-INCH FOCACCIA / **ACTIVE TIME:** 40 MINUTES / **TOTAL TIME:** 4 HOURS

In Piacenza, like in other parts of the Emilia Romagna region, focaccia is enriched with different types of cured pork and lard. A tremendous treat to enjoy once in a while.

1. Place the pancetta and the lard or olive oil in a skillet and cook over medium heat until the pancetta is browned, about 6 to 8 minutes. Transfer to a bowl, making sure to reserve the rendered fat and oil as well.

2. If using active dry yeast, warm 3½ tablespoons (1.75 oz./50 grams) of the water until it is about 105°F (40°C). Add the water and the yeast to a bowl and gently stir. Let sit until it starts to foam. Instant yeast does not need to be proofed.

3. In a large bowl, combine the flour, wine, yeast, and water and work the mixture until it just holds together. If kneading by hand, transfer the dough to a flour-dusted work surface. Work it until it is compact, smooth, and elastic. For further instructions on kneading and mixing dough see page 71.

4. Add the salt, the pancetta, and the rendered fat and oil and work the dough until they have been incorporated and the dough is developed, elastic, and extensible, about 5 minutes. Grease an airtight container, shape the dough into a ball, place it in the container, and let rest at room temperature until it has doubled in size, about 2 hours.

5. Place the dough on a flour-dusted work surface and roll it out until it is an approximately ⅓-inch-thick disk (1 centimeter). Grease a round 10-inch cake pan with lard or oil and place the focaccia in the pan. Brush the focaccia with lard or oil, cover with a kitchen towel, and let rest for 1 hour.

6. Preheat the oven to 390°F (200°C). Top the focaccia with more lard or olive oil. Place in the oven and bake for about 30 minutes, until it is golden brown. Remove and let cool briefly before serving.

INGREDIENTS:

7 OZ. | 200 GRAMS PANCETTA

1.75 OZ. | 50 GRAMS LARD OR OLIVE OIL, PLUS MORE AS NEEDED

1¾ TEASPOONS | 5 GRAMS ACTIVE DRY YEAST OR 1⅓ TEASPOONS | 4 GRAMS INSTANT YEAST

5.3 OZ. | 150 GRAMS WATER

10.6 OZ. | 300 GRAMS BREAD FLOUR

10.6 OZ. | 300 GRAMS ALL-PURPOSE FLOUR, PLUS MORE AS NEEDED

3.5 OZ. | 100 GRAMS WHITE WINE

1½ TEASPOONS | 10 GRAMS TABLE SALT

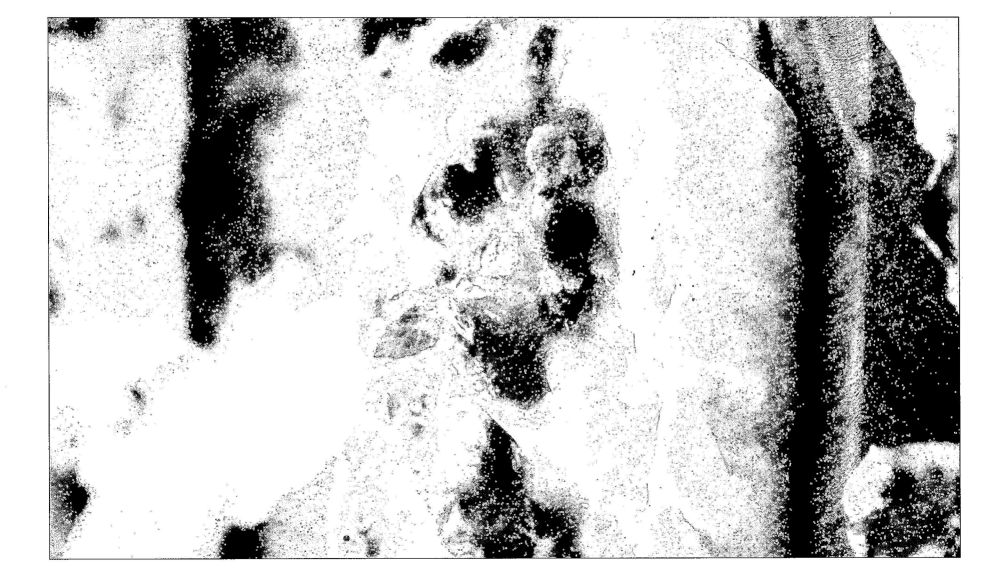

CENTRAL
ITALY

FOCACCETTE DI AULLA

YIELD: 16 SMALL FOCACCIA / **ACTIVE TIME:** 30 MINUTES / **TOTAL TIME:** 4 HOURS

These miniature focaccia are really fragrant due to the presence of cornmeal. Focaccette di Aulla are traditionally baked in special pans called *testi*, which are placed directly over an open fire. Here you find a recipe developed for the standard kitchen oven. Focaccette are delicious when cut open while still warm and filled with fresh cheese and cold cuts.

1. If using active dry yeast, warm 3½ tablespoons (1.75 oz./50 grams) of the water until it is about 105°F (40°C). Add the water and the yeast to a bowl and gently stir. Let sit for 5 to 10 minutes. Instant yeast does not need to be proofed.

2. In a large bowl, combine the flour and cornmeal and then incorporate the yeast and water. Work the mixture until it just holds together. If kneading by hand, transfer the dough to a flour-dusted work surface. Work it until it is compact, smooth, and elastic. For further instructions on kneading and mixing dough see page 71.

3. Add the salt and knead until the dough is developed, elastic, and extensible, about 5 minutes. Form the dough into a ball and place it in an airtight container that has been greased with olive oil. Let rest at room temperature until it has doubled in size, about 2 hours.

4. Divide the dough into 16 pieces and shape each piece into a ball. Cover with plastic wrap and let rest for another hour.

5. Preheat the oven to 390°F (200°C) and place a rack in the middle position. Place a baking stone or steel in the oven as it warms up. Flatten the balls until they are approximately ½ inch thick (1.5 centimeters).

6. Using a peel or a flat baking sheet, transfer the focaccia onto the heated baking implement and bake for 15 to 20 minutes, until golden brown. Remove and let cool before serving.

INGREDIENTS:

1¾ TEASPOONS | 5 GRAMS ACTIVE DRY YEAST OR 1⅓ TEASPOONS | 4 GRAMS INSTANT YEAST

10.6 OZ. | 300 GRAMS WATER

8.8 OZ. | 250 GRAMS ALL-PURPOSE FLOUR, PLUS MORE FOR DUSTING

8.8 OZ. | 250 GRAMS FINELY GROUND CORNMEAL

1¾ TEASPOONS | 10 GRAMS TABLE SALT

OLIVE OIL, AS NEEDED

SCHIACCIA TOSCANA

YIELD: 1 LARGE FOCACCIA / **ACTIVE TIME:** 30 MINUTES / **TOTAL TIME:** 4 HOURS AND 30 MINUTES

This focaccia is rather thin and crunchy, making it the perfect bread to pair with an aperitif.

1. If using active dry yeast, warm 3½ tablespoons (1.75 oz./50 grams) of the water until it is about 105°F (40°C). Add the water and the yeast to a bowl and gently stir. Let sit for 5 to 10 minutes. Instant yeast does not need to be proofed.

2. In a large bowl, combine the flour, wine, milk, sugar, yeast, and water. Work the mixture until it just holds together. If kneading by hand, transfer the dough to a flour-dusted work surface and knead the dough until it is compact, smooth, and elastic. For further instructions on kneading and mixing dough see page 71.

3. Add the salt and work the dough until it is developed, elastic, and extensible, about 5 minutes. Grease an airtight container, shape the dough into a ball, place it in the container, and let it rest at room temperature until it has doubled in size, about 2 hours.

4. Generously grease an 18 × 13–inch baking pan with olive oil, place the dough in the center of the pan, and gently flatten it into an oval. Brush the dough with olive oil, cover with plastic wrap, and let rest for 30 minutes.

5. Use your hands to flatten the dough and spread it toward the edges of the baking pan. If the dough does not want to extend to the edges of the pan right away, let it rest for 15 to 20 minutes before trying again.

6. Brush the focaccia with more olive oil and use your fingers to make indentations in the dough. Cover with plastic wrap and let rest for another 30 minutes. Preheat the oven to 480°F (250°C).

7. Brush the dough with more olive oil and season with salt. Place in the oven and bake for 15 minutes, until the "valleys" between the bubbles are a deep golden brown. As this focaccia is supposed to be slightly crunchy, you want the bottom to be golden brown as well. Remove and let cool briefly before serving.

INGREDIENTS:

1¾ TEASPOONS | 5 GRAMS ACTIVE DRY YEAST OR 1⅓ TEASPOONS | 4 GRAMS INSTANT YEAST

7 OZ. | 200 GRAMS WATER

17.6 OZ. | 500 GRAMS ALL-PURPOSE FLOUR, PLUS MORE FOR DUSTING

1.75 OZ. | 50 GRAMS WHITE WINE

1.75 OZ. | 50 GRAMS MILK

1 TABLESPOON | 12.5 GRAMS SUGAR

1 TEASPOON | 6 GRAMS TABLE SALT, PLUS MORE TO TASTE

OLIVE OIL, AS NEEDED

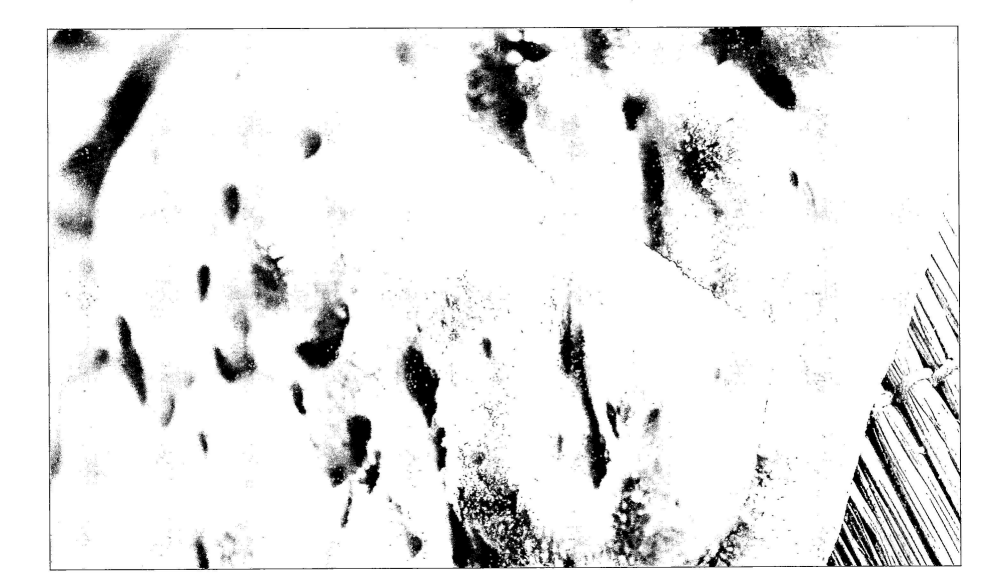

SCHIACCIA ALL'UVA

YIELD: 1 LARGE FOCACCIA / **ACTIVE TIME:** 40 MINUTES / **TOTAL TIME:** 3 HOURS

Popular in Tuscany since the days of the Etruscans, this grape-enriched focaccia was linked to the rituals of the *vendemmia*, the local wine grape harvest, and made with the unsalted bread dough that is traditional in the region.

1. If using active dry yeast, warm 3½ tablespoons (1.75 oz./50 grams) of the water until it is about 105°F (40°C). Add the water and the yeast to a bowl and gently stir. Let sit until it starts to foam. Instant yeast does not need to be proofed.

2. In a large bowl, combine the flour, honey, yeast, and water. Work the mixture until it just holds together. If kneading by hand, transfer the dough to a flour-dusted work surface. Work it until it is compact, smooth, and elastic. For further instructions on kneading and mixing dough see page 71. Grease an airtight container, shape the dough into a ball, place it in the container, and let it rest at room temperature until it has doubled in size, about 2 hours.

3. Preheat the oven to 360°F (180°C). Working the mixture with your hands, incorporate the granulated sugar and the oil. Divide the dough in two and roll each piece into a rectangle that is approximately the size of an 18 × 13–inch baking sheet.

4. Grease the baking sheet and place one piece of dough on it. Place half of the grapes on top of the dough and gently press down on them. Sprinkle caster sugar and drizzle olive oil over the grapes.

5. Cover with the second piece of dough and crimp the edges to seal. Place the remaining grapes on top of the second sheet of dough, and gently press down on them. Sprinkle caster sugar and drizzle olive oil over the grapes.

6. Place the focaccia in the oven and bake for 40 minutes, until golden brown. Remove from the oven and let cool briefly before serving.

INGREDIENTS:

1 TABLESPOON | 9 GRAMS ACTIVE DRY YEAST OR 2½ TEASPOONS | 7.5 GRAMS INSTANT YEAST

18.3 OZ. | 520 GRAMS WATER

31.75 OZ. | 900 GRAMS ALL-PURPOSE FLOUR, PLUS MORE AS NEEDED

2 TEASPOONS | 14 GRAMS HONEY

4 OZ. | 113.4 GRAMS GRANULATED SUGAR

2.8 OZ. | 80 GRAMS OLIVE OIL, PLUS MORE AS NEEDED

2.8 LBS. | 1.3 KILOGRAMS PURPLE GRAPES

CASTER SUGAR, TO TASTE

SCHIACCIATA CON CIPOLLA & SALVIA

YIELD: 1 LARGE FOCACCIA / **ACTIVE TIME:** 40 MINUTES / **TOTAL TIME:** 4 HOURS AND 30 MINUTES

In Umbria, it is very typical to eat a thin focaccia flavored with golden onions and sage, a delicious combination that can provide warmth on a cold winter day.

INGREDIENTS:

1¾ TEASPOONS | 5 GRAMS ACTIVE DRY YEAST OR 1⅓ TEASPOONS | 4 GRAMS INSTANT YEAST

10.6 OZ. | 300 GRAMS WATER

17.6 OZ. | 500 GRAMS ALL-PURPOSE FLOUR, PLUS MORE AS NEEDED

2½ TEASPOONS | 10 GRAMS SUGAR

1 TEASPOON | 6 GRAMS TABLE SALT, PLUS MORE TO TASTE

30 FRESH SAGE LEAVES, FINELY CHOPPED

OLIVE OIL, AS NEEDED

4 LARGE YELLOW ONIONS, SLICED THIN

1. If using active dry yeast, warm 3½ tablespoons (1.75 oz./50 grams) of the water until it is about 105°F (40°C). Add the water and the yeast to a bowl and gently stir. Let sit until it starts to foam. Instant yeast does not need to be proofed.

2. In a large bowl, combine the flour, sugar, yeast, and water. Work the mixture until it just holds together. If kneading by hand, transfer the dough to a flour-dusted work surface. Work it until it is compact, smooth, and elastic. For further instructions on kneading and mixing dough see page 71.

3. Add the salt and half of the sage leaves and knead until they have been incorporated and the dough appears smooth and elastic again. Grease an airtight container, shape the dough into a ball, place it in the container, and let rest at room temperature until it has doubled in size, about 2 hours.

4. Place the onions on parchment paper, sprinkle salt over them, and let them dry.

5. Generously grease a 18 × 13–inch pan with olive oil, place the dough in the center of the pan, and gently flatten into an oval. Generously brush the dough with olive oil, cover with a kitchen towel or greased plastic wrap, and let rest for 30 minutes.

6. Use your hands to flatten the dough and stretch it toward the edges of the baking pan. If the dough does not want to extend to the edges of the pan right away, let rest for 15 to 20 minutes before trying again.

Continued . . .

7. Brush the focaccia with more olive oil and use your fingers to make indentations in the dough. Cover with plastic wrap and let rest for another 30 minutes. Preheat the oven to 390°F (200°C).

8. Distribute the onions and remaining sage leaves over the focaccia. Drizzle with olive oil and season with just a bit of salt, keeping in mind that the onions are salted.

9. Place in the oven and bake for 30 to 35 minutes, until the edges are golden brown. Remove and let cool briefly before serving.

TORTA AL TESTO CON I CICCIOLI

YIELD: 2 9-INCH FOCACCIA / **ACTIVE TIME:** 25 MINUTES / **TOTAL TIME:** 1 HOUR AND 15 MINUTES

This classic version of torta al testo includes small bites of a rustic cured pork known as ciccioli. In the absence of ciccioli, cubed pancetta or bacon will do.

1. Place the pancetta or bacon in a skillet and cook over medium heat until the fat has rendered and it starts to turn crispy, about 6 minutes. Transfer to a plate and let cool.

2. In a large bowl, combine the flour, salt, and baking soda. Incorporate the water gradually and work the mixture until it holds together. Add the pancetta or bacon. If kneading by hand, transfer the dough to a flour-dusted work surface. Work it until it is compact, smooth, and elastic. For further instructions on kneading and mixing dough, see page 71. Divide the dough in two and shape each piece into a ball. Envelop the balls in plastic wrap and let rest at room temperature for 30 minutes.

3. Warm a 10-inch skillet over medium heat. Using a rolling pin, flatten each ball until it is approximately ¼ inch thick (6 millimeters). Use a fork to poke holes in the disks.

4. Working with one disk at a time, place it in the pan and cook until golden brown all over, about 6 minutes per side.

5. Cut the cooked focaccia into wedges that can be filled with cold cuts, cheese, or sautéed vegetables.

INGREDIENTS:

5.3 OZ. | 150 GRAMS PANCETTA OR BACON, CUBED

17.6 OZ. | 500 GRAMS ALL-PURPOSE FLOUR, PLUS MORE FOR DUSTING

1 TEASPOON | 6 GRAMS TABLE SALT

1 TEASPOON | 4 GRAMS BAKING SODA

8.8 OZ. | 250 GRAMS WATER

TORTA AL TESTO

YIELD: 2 9-INCH FOCACCIA / **ACTIVE TIME:** 25 MINUTES / **TOTAL TIME:** 1 HOUR

One of the many unleavened focaccias from Central Italy that have survived the test of time. Popular in Etruscan times (approximately 2,500 years ago), torta al testo is faster to make than a regular focaccia. It is traditionally cooked in a specific pan called a *testo*, but still tastes delicious if cooked in a cast-iron or nonstick skillet.

1. In a large bowl, combine the flour, salt, and baking soda. Incorporate the water gradually and work the mixture until it holds together. If kneading by hand, transfer the dough to a flour-dusted work surface. Work it until it is compact, smooth, and elastic. For further instructions on kneading and mixing dough see page 71. Divide the dough in two and shape each piece into a ball. Envelop the balls in plastic wrap and let rest at room temperature for 30 minutes.

2. Warm a 10-inch skillet over medium heat. Using a rolling pin, flatten the balls of dough until they are approximately ¼ inch thick (6 millimeters). Use a fork to poke holes in the disks.

3. Working with one disk at a time, place it in the pan and cook until golden brown all over, about 6 minutes per side.

4. Cut the cooked focaccia into wedges that can be filled with cold cuts, cheese, or sautéed vegetables.

INGREDIENTS:

17.6 OZ. | 500 GRAMS ALL-PURPOSE FLOUR, PLUS MORE AS NEEDED

1 TEASPOON | 6 GRAMS TABLE SALT

1 TEASPOON | 4 GRAMS BAKING SODA

8.8 OZ. | 250 GRAMS WATER

TORTA AL TESTO CON FARINA DI MAIS

YIELD: 2 9-INCH FOCACCIA / **ACTIVE TIME:** 25 MINUTES / **TOTAL TIME:** 1 HOUR

A popular version of the Umbrian torta al testo uses cornmeal. Here's an easy version made for the modern home.

INGREDIENTS:

8.8 OZ. | 250 GRAMS ALL-PURPOSE FLOUR, PLUS MORE AS NEEDED

8.8 OZ. | 250 GRAMS CORNMEAL

1 TEASPOON | 6 GRAMS TABLE SALT

1 TEASPOON | 4 GRAMS BAKING SODA

8.8 OZ. | 250 GRAMS WATER

1. In a large bowl, combine the flour, cornmeal, salt, and baking soda. Incorporate the water gradually and work the mixture until it holds together. If kneading by hand, transfer the dough to a flour-dusted work surface. Work it until it is compact, smooth, and elastic. For further instructions on kneading and mixing dough see page 71. Divide the dough in two and shape each piece into a ball. Envelop the balls in plastic wrap and let rest at room temperature for 30 minutes.

2. Warm a 10-inch skillet over medium heat. Using a rolling pin, flatten each ball until it is approximately ⅓ inch thick (8 millimeters). Use a fork to poke holes in the disks.

3. Working with one disk at a time, place it in the pan and cook until golden brown all over, about 6 minutes per side.

4. Cut the cooked focaccia into wedges that can be filled with cold cuts, cheese, or sautéed vegetables.

CRESCIA SFOGLIATA

YIELD: 6 SMALL FOCACCIA / **ACTIVE TIME:** 45 MINUTES / **TOTAL TIME:** 2 HOURS

As one would expect of the stylish city of Urbino in the Marche region, this focaccia is a luxurious take on the piadina. Crescia sfogliata is rumored to have been born during the Renaissance, specifically in the kitchen of the duke of Urbino. It is wonderful on its own but is at its best if accompanied by Italian soft cheeses like crescenza or stracchino and vegetables or cold cuts.

1. In a large bowl, combine the flour, water, lard, eggs, salt, and pepper and work the mixture until it just holds together. If kneading by hand, transfer the dough to a flour-dusted work surface. Work it until it is compact, smooth, and elastic. For further instructions on kneading and mixing dough see page 71. Divide the dough in two and shape each piece into a ball. Form the dough into a ball, envelop with plastic wrap, and let rest at room temperature for 30 minutes.

2. Divide the dough into six pieces and form them into balls. Flatten each ball, brush with lard, and roll the disks up as tightly as possible. Twist the rolls into spirals, transfer to a parchment-lined baking sheet, and cover with plastic wrap. Refrigerate for 30 minutes to 1 hour.

3. Remove the spirals from the refrigerator and flatten them out to approximately ⅛ inch thick (3 millimeters).

4. Warm a 10-inch skillet over medium heat. Working with one disk at a time, cook until dark spots appear all over, about 5 minutes per side. Remove from the oven and let cool briefly before serving.

INGREDIENTS:

17.6 OZ. | 500 GRAMS ALL-PURPOSE FLOUR

7 OZ. | 200 GRAMS WATER

3.5 OZ. | 100 GRAMS LARD, PLUS MORE AS NEEDED

2 EGGS

1¾ TEASPOONS | 10 GRAMS TABLE SALT

2 PINCHES BLACK PEPPER

CHICHIRIPIENO

YIELD: 1 LARGE FOCACCIA / **ACTIVE TIME:** 45 MINUTES / **TOTAL TIME:** 3 HOURS

From the Marche region comes this scrumptious flatbread, the name of which is the local term for "filled focaccia." Originally made with leftover bread dough, this focaccia was traditionally filled with what was locally available. *Chichiripieno* stands as a perfect picnic food, with every slice standing as a meal in itself.

1. If using active dry yeast, warm 3½ tablespoons (1.75 oz./50 grams) of the water until it is about 105°F (40°C). Add the water and the yeast to a bowl and gently stir. Let sit until it starts to foam. Instant yeast does not need to be proofed.

2. In a large bowl, combine the flour, honey, yeast, and water and work the mixture until it just holds together. If kneading by hand, transfer the dough to a flour-dusted work surface. Work it until it is compact, smooth, and elastic. For further instructions on kneading and mixing dough see page 71.

3. Add the salt and work the dough until it is incorporated and the dough is smooth, elastic, and extensible. Divide the dough in two and shape each piece into a ball. Place them on a parchment-lined baking sheet, cover with plastic wrap, and let rest at room temperature until they have doubled in size, about 2 hours.

4. Preheat the oven to 390°F (200°C). Roll out both balls of dough until they are approximately the size of an 18 × 13–inch baking pan. Generously grease the pan with olive oil and place one piece of dough on the pan.

5. Add all of the remaining ingredients to a mixing bowl and stir to combine. Cover the sheet of dough in the pan with the mixture and place the second sheet of dough on top. Cut away any excess dough with a sharp knife and crimp the edge to seal. Brush the focaccia with oil, season with salt, and use a fork to poke several holes in the surface.

6. Place in the oven and bake for 20 to 25 minutes, until golden brown. Remove and let cool briefly before serving.

INGREDIENTS:

1 TABLESPOON | 9 GRAMS ACTIVE DRY YEAST OR 2½ TEASPOONS | 7.5 GRAMS INSTANT YEAST

18.3 OZ. | 520 GRAMS WATER

2 LBS. | 900 GRAMS ALL-PURPOSE FLOUR

2½ TEASPOONS | 7 GRAMS HONEY

1½ TEASPOONS | 8 GRAMS TABLE SALT, PLUS MORE AS NEEDED

OLIVE OIL, AS NEEDED

1 LB. | 450 GRAMS SMOKED PAPRIKA

6 OZ. | 170 GRAMS ANCHOVY FILLETS IN OLIVE OIL, DRAINED

3.2 OZ. | 90 GRAMS CAPERS

10 OZ. | 285 GRAMS GREEN OLIVES

10 OZ. | 285 GRAMS ARTICHOKES IN OLIVE OIL, DRAINED AND CHOPPED

14 OZ. | 400 GRAMS TUNA IN OLIVE OIL, DRAINED

CACCIANNANZE

YIELD: 1 LARGE FOCACCIA / **ACTIVE TIME:** 30 MINUTES / **TOTAL TIME:** 3 HOURS

A very simple and easy focaccia from the rural portion of the Marche region, cacciannanze is great as an appetizer but can also work as a side for dinner.

1. Place the dough on a flour-dusted work surface and form it into a loose ball, making sure not to press down too hard on the core of the mass and deflate it. Grease an 18 × 13–inch baking sheet with olive oil, place the dough in the center, and gently flatten it into an oval. Brush the dough with olive oil, cover it with plastic wrap, and let rest at room temperature for 1 hour.

2. Place the rosemary, garlic, and a few pinches of salt in a mixing bowl and stir to combine. Use your hands to flatten the dough and stretch it toward the edges of the baking sheet. If the dough does not want to extend to the edges of the pan right away, let it rest for 15 to 20 minutes before trying again.

3. Brush the dough with olive oil, sprinkle the garlic-and-rosemary mixture over the top, and let the focaccia rest at room temperature for another 30 minutes. If desired, you can also sprinkle chunks of lard over the focaccia. Preheat the oven to 390°F (200°C).

4. Place in the oven and bake for 15 to 20 minutes, until the focaccia is golden brown and slightly crispy on the edges. Remove from the oven and let cool briefly before serving.

INGREDIENTS:

BASIC FOCACCIA DOUGH (SEE PAGE 84)

ALL-PURPOSE FLOUR, AS NEEDED

OLIVE OIL, AS NEEDED

LEAVES FROM 6 SPRIGS FRESH ROSEMARY

3 GARLIC CLOVES, SLICED THIN

SALT, TO TASTE

LARD (OPTIONAL), AS NEEDED

PIZZA BIANCA ROMANA

YIELD: 2 9-INCH FOCACCIA / **ACTIVE TIME:** 30 MINUTES / **TOTAL TIME:** 7 HOURS

In Rome, focaccia is referred to as *pizza bianca*, which can be found in virtually every bakery. Compared to other regional focaccias, this is probably the most alveolated one due to the long fermentation time, the strong flour used, and the relatively high water content. It is scrumptious filled with cold cuts—ideally mortadella or Parma ham—and fresh figs, but there are countless possible fillings.

1. If using active dry yeast, warm 3½ tablespoons (1.75 oz./50 grams) of the water until it is about 105°F (40°C). Add the water and the yeast to a bowl and gently stir. Let sit for 5 to 10 minutes. Instant yeast does not need to be proofed.

2. In a large bowl, combine the flour and three-quarters of the water. Add the yeast, malt, and sugar and work the mixture until it just holds together. Using your hands or a stand mixer, work the dough until compact, smooth, and elastic, 10 to 15 minutes. For further instructions on kneading and mixing dough see page 71.

3. Add the salt and the remaining water and knead the dough until it passes the windowpane test (see page 70). Place the dough in an airtight container and let rest at room temperature until it has risen and is full of bubbles, about 5 hours.

4. Preheat the oven to 480°F (250°C). Invert the dough onto a flour-dusted work surface and divide it in two. Place each piece of dough on a flat tray or sheet pan covered with flour-dusted parchment paper. Flatten each piece into an oval and let rest for 2 to 3 hours in a warm spot, ideally the oven with the light on, stretching the dough lengthwise every 30 minutes, being careful not to deflate excessively. After the last stretch, generously drizzle olive oil and sprinkle crushed sea salt over the whole surface.

5. Using a peel or a flat baking sheet, transfer one of the focaccia and its parchment paper onto the heated baking implement. Bake for 10 to 15 minutes, until golden brown. Remove from the oven and brush with olive oil. Repeat with the remaining focaccia.

INGREDIENTS:

1 TEASPOON | 3 GRAMS INSTANT YEAST OR 1¼ TEASPOONS | 3.6 GRAMS ACTIVE DRY YEAST

18.5 OZ. | 525 GRAMS WATER

24.7 OZ. | 700 GRAMS BREAD FLOUR OR "00" PIZZA FLOUR, PLUS MORE AS NEEDED

2 TEASPOONS | 7 GRAMS DIASTATIC MALT

1¾ TEASPOONS | 7 GRAMS SUGAR

1.4 OZ. | 40 GRAMS OLIVE OIL, PLUS MORE AS NEEDED

1 TABLESPOON | 17 GRAMS TABLE SALT, PLUS MORE TO TASTE

FALIA DI PRIVERNO

YIELD: 2 MEDIUM FOCACCIA / **ACTIVE TIME:** 1 HOUR / **TOTAL TIME:** 5 HOURS AND 30 MINUTES

Latio is not a big region for local variations on focaccia, because it has long been dominated by Roman pizza. But this is an exception, and it is still baked in the small town of Priverno. It is traditionally made with sourdough, but biga can also be used. If you can get ahold of baby broccoli, sauté it and use as a filling.

1. In a large bowl, combine all of the ingredients, except for the salt, and work the mixture with your hands or a stand mixer until the dough holds together.. This will take about 20 minutes, with a few intervals of rest.

2. Add the table salt and work the dough until it has been incorporated and the dough is smooth and elastic. Place the dough in an airtight container and let it rest for 3 to 4 hours, until it has doubled in size. The time will vary depending on the temperature of the room.

3. Preheat the oven to 450°F (230°C) and place a baking stone or steel in the oven as it warms. Place the dough on a flour-dusted work surface and divide it in two. Place the pieces on two flour-dusted sheets of parchment paper. Stretch the focaccia lengthwise, being careful not to deflate them excessively. They should have a rough oval shape.

4. Place the focaccia and their associated parchment paper sheets on a peel or a flat baking sheet. Before loading into the oven, generously drizzle olive oil over the focaccias, sprinkle the salt on top, and make three, deep lengthwise cuts in each focaccia. Slide the focaccia onto the heated baking implement (bake one at a time if your oven is small). Bake for 20 minutes, until they are golden brown. Remove from the oven, brush with olive oil, and let cool slightly. When they are cool enough to handle, slice the focaccia open and fill with whatever your heart desires (sautéed baby broccoli and Italian sausage are best).

INGREDIENTS:

180 GRAMS BIGA (SEE RECIPE), OR 180 GRAM STIFF SOURDOUGH

17.6 OZ. | 500 GRAMS BREAD FLOUR OR "00" PIZZA FLOUR, PLUS MORE AS NEEDED

13.2 OZ. | 375 GRAMS WATER

1 TEASPOON | 3.5 GRAMS DIASTATIC MALT OR SUGAR

1 TABLESPOON | 15 GRAMS OLIVE OIL, PLUS MORE AS NEEDED

2 TEASPOONS | 12 GRAMS TABLE SALT

COARSE SEA SALT, AS NEEDED

BIGA FOR FALIA DI PRIVERNO

4.2 OZ | 120 GRAMS BREAD FLOUR

2.1 OZ. | 60 GRAMS WATER

⅙ TEASPOON | 0.5 GRAMS INSTANT YEAST

BIGA FOR FALIA DI PRIVERNO

1. In a large mixing bowl, add all of the ingredients and work the mixture until combined. Cover with plastic wrap and let rest at room temperature until it triples in size, about 18 hours.

CIACCINO SENESE

YIELD: 1 LARGE FOCACCIA / **ACTIVE TIME:** 30 MINUTES / **TOTAL TIME:** 4 HOURS

Typical of the town of Siena in Tuscany, ciaccino is just too good to be true. Here you can savor steamy ham and cheese baked directly inside a flaky focaccia, a must-try for all lovers of ham-and-cheese sandwiches.

1. If using active dry yeast, warm 3½ tablespoons (1.75 oz./50 grams) of the water 105°F (40°C). Add the water and yeast to a bowl and gently stir. Let sit for 5 to 10 minutes. Instant yeast does not need to be proofed.

2. In a large bowl, combine the flour, yeast, sugar, and water and work the mixture until the dough just holds together. If kneading by hand, transfer the dough to a flour-dusted work surface. Work it until it is compact, smooth, and elastic. For further instructions on kneading and mixing dough see page 71.

3. Add the olive oil and salt and work the dough until it is developed, elastic, and extensible, about 5 minutes. Form the dough into a ball and place it in an airtight container that has been greased with olive oil. Let rest at room temperature until it has doubled in size, about 2 hours.

4. Transfer the dough to a flour-dusted surface and divide it in two. Roll each piece of dough into a rectangle that is approximately 1⁄16 inch thick (3 millimeters).

5. Grease an 18 × 13–inch baking pan with olive oil and place one of the rectangles on it. Distribute the slices of ham and mozzarella over the dough. Cover with the second sheet of dough and crimp the edge to seal. Let rest at room temperature for 1 hour.

6. Preheat the oven to 390°F (200°C). Use a fork to poke holes in the top of the focaccia. Brush with olive oil and season with salt.

7. Place in the oven and bake for 20 minutes, until the top is golden brown and crispy. Remove and let cool briefly before serving.

INGREDIENTS:

2½ TEASPOONS | 7.5 GRAMS ACTIVE DRY YEAST OR 2 TEASPOONS | 6 GRAMS INSTANT YEAST

13.2 OZ. | 375 GRAMS WATER

26.4 OZ. | 750 GRAMS ALL-PURPOSE FLOUR, PLUS MORE FOR DUSTING

3.7 OZ. | 100 GRAMS OLIVE OIL, PLUS MORE AS NEEDED

2 TEASPOONS | 8 GRAMS SUGAR

2½ TEASPOONS | 14 GRAMS TABLE SALT, PLUS MORE TO TASTE

11 OZ. | 312 GRAMS SLICED HAM (PROSCIUTTO COTTO PREFERRED)

13.2 OZ. | 375 GRAMS FRESH MOZZARELLA CHEESE, DRAINED AND SLICED

SOUTHERN
ITALY

PIZZA DI GRANOTURCO

YIELD: 8 SMALL FOCACCIA / **ACTIVE TIME:** 10 MINUTES / **TOTAL TIME:** 45 MINUTES

Pizza di granoturco was traditionally made from cornmeal and cooked among the embers of a fireplace or a wood-fired stove. Serve with sautéed vegetables, such as broccoli rabe.

INGREDIENTS:

17.6 OZ. | 500 GRAMS CORNMEAL, PLUS MORE AS NEEDED

1 TEASPOON | 6 GRAMS TABLE SALT

31.75 OZ. | 900 GRAMS BOILING WATER

1. Preheat the oven to 430°F (220°C) and place a baking stone or steel in the oven as it warms. In a large bowl, combine the cornmeal and salt. Using a wooden spoon, gradually incorporate the boiling water and work the mixture until the dough is just holding together. Transfer the dough to a cornmeal-dusted work surface and knead it until smooth. Divide the dough into eight pieces, form them into rounds and flatten them into rather thick disks.

2. Place the disks directly on the heated baking implement and bake for about 25 minutes, until the top is crispy. Remove from the oven and let cool slightly before serving.

PIZZ'ONTA

YIELD: 12 SMALL FOCACCIA / **ACTIVE TIME:** 30 MINUTES / **TOTAL TIME:** 3 HOURS

In Abruzzi it is very common to eat a fried crunchy focaccia called *pizz'onta*, or "greasy pizza." This focaccia is very easy to make at home, and it is out-of-this-world scrumptious, perfect beside cheese and cold cuts or grilled steak tips.

1. If using active dry yeast, warm 3½ tablespoons (1.75 oz./50 grams) of the water until it is about 105°F (40°C). Add the water and the yeast to a bowl and gently stir. Let sit for 5 to 10 minutes. Instant yeast does not need to be proofed.

2. In a large bowl, combine the flour, water, yeast, and sugar. Work the mixture until it just holds together. If kneading by hand, transfer the dough to a flour-dusted work surface. Work it until it is compact, smooth, and elastic. For further instructions on kneading and mixing dough see page 71.

3. Add the salt and olive oil and work the dough until it is developed, elastic, and extensible, about 5 minutes. Form the dough into a ball and place it in an airtight container that has been greased with olive oil. Let rest at room temperature until it has doubled in size, about 2 hours.

4. Divide the dough into 12 pieces and form them into rounds, taking care not to overwork the dough. Cover with a kitchen towel or greased plastic wrap and let rest for 30 minutes.

5. Add vegetable oil to a Dutch oven until it is approximately 2 inches deep and warm it to 350°F (175°C). Flatten the rounds and, working in batches, fry them until golden brown on both sides, about 4 minutes. Transfer to a paper towel–lined plate to drain and sprinkle with salt before serving.

INGREDIENTS:

1¼ TEASPOONS | 3.6 GRAMS ACTIVE DRY YEAST OR 1 TEASPOON | 3 GRAMS INSTANT YEAST

8.5 OZ. | 240 GRAMS WATER

14 OZ. | 400 GRAMS BREAD FLOUR, PLUS MORE AS NEEDED

2 TEASPOONS | 8 GRAMS SUGAR

1 OZ. | 30 GRAMS OLIVE OIL, PLUS MORE AS NEEDED

1 TEASPOON | 6 GRAMS TABLE SALT, PLUS MORE TO TASTE

VEGETABLE OIL, AS NEEDED

PIZZA SCIMA

YIELD: 1 LARGE FOCACCIA / **ACTIVE TIME:** 25 MINUTES / **TOTAL TIME:** 1 HOUR AND 15 MINUTES

Notwithstanding the name, which implies that it is "dull," this focaccia carries a distinctive flavor and crunchiness, both which are provided by the high amount of olive oil in the dough. The "dull," then, refers to it being unleavened, as was typical in the Jewish communities that traditionally inhabited parts of Abruzzi.

1. In a large bowl, combine the flours with the baking soda and the salt. Incorporate the olive oil, wine, and water gradually and work the mixture until it just holds together. Transfer the dough to a flour-dusted work surface and knead until it is compact, smooth, and elastic. Form the dough into a ball, envelop it in plastic wrap, and let rest at room temperature for 30 minutes. Preheat the oven to 430°F (220°C) and place a baking stone or steel in the oven as it warms.

2. Using a rolling pin, roll the dough out until it is approximately ¾ inch thick (2 centimeters). Place the dough on a piece of parchment paper and make deep cuts in it in a crosshatch pattern, taking care not to cut all the way through. Using a peel or a flat baking sheet, transfer the dough onto the heated baking implement and bake for 20 to 30 minutes, until golden brown. Remove from the oven and let cool slightly before serving.

INGREDIENTS:

17.6 OZ. | 500 GRAMS BREAD FLOUR

7 OZ. | 200 GRAMS ALL-PURPOSE FLOUR, PLUS MORE AS NEEDED

¼ TEASPOON | 1.5 GRAMS BAKING SODA

2 TEASPOONS | 12 GRAMS TABLE SALT

2.8 OZ. | 80 GRAMS OLIVE OIL

2.8 OZ. | 80 GRAMS WHITE WINE

6.3 OZ. | 180 GRAMS WATER

PIZZA ASSETTATA

YIELD: 1 LARGE FOCACCIA / **ACTIVE TIME:** 25 MINUTES / **TOTAL TIME:** 1 HOUR AND 15 MINUTES

This unleavened focaccia is made with a mix of semolina and bread flour and flavored with fennel seeds and red pepper flakes. As it is unleavened, it is among the quickest, easiest focaccias to make.

1. Preheat the oven to 430°F (220°C). In a large bowl, combine the flours and table salt. Gradually incorporate the water and work the mixture with your hands until it just holds together. Add the olive oil, fennel seeds, and red pepper flakes and work the dough until they have been incorporated.

2. If kneading by hand, transfer the dough to a flour-dusted work surface. Work it until it is smooth, compact, and elastic, about 10 minutes. For further instructions on kneading and mixing see page 71. Form the dough into a ball, envelop it in plastic wrap, and let rest at room temperature for 30 minutes. Preheat the oven to 430°F (220°C).

3. Grease an 18 × 13–inch baking pan with olive oil, roll the dough out into a rectangle that will fit within the pan, and place the dough in the pan. Drizzle olive oil over the dough and sprinkle the coarse salt on top. Place in the oven and bake for 20 to 25 minutes, until it is a light golden brown. Remove and let cool slightly before serving.

INGREDIENTS:

12.3 OZ. | 350 GRAMS BREAD FLOUR, PLUS MORE AS NEEDED

12.3 OZ. | 350 GRAMS FINE SEMOLINA FLOUR

2 TEASPOONS | 12 GRAMS TABLE SALT

16.6 OZ. | 470 GRAMS WARM WATER (110°F | 43.3°C)

1.75 OZ. | 50 GRAMS OLIVE OIL, PLUS MORE AS NEEDED

1 TABLESPOON | 5.8 GRAMS FENNEL SEEDS

1 TEASPOON | 2 GRAMS RED PEPPER FLAKES

COARSE SEA SALT, TO TASTE

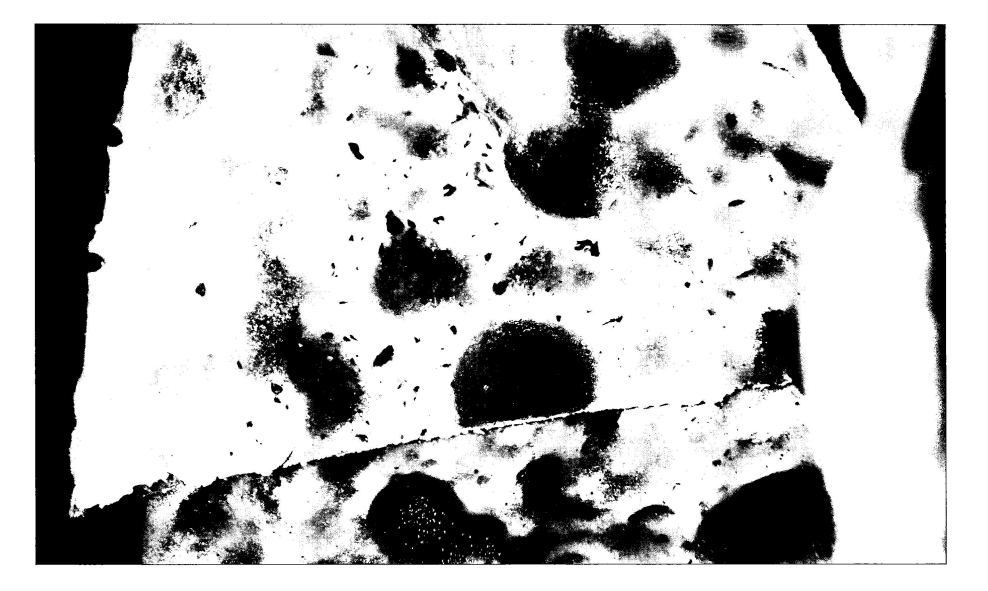

PANUOZZO

YIELD: 6 SMALL FOCACCIA / **ACTIVE TIME:** 20 MINUTES / **TOTAL TIME:** 3 HOURS AND 30 MINUTES

A focaccia traditionally made with pizza dough, what is truly special about Panuozzo is that it is baked twice: first to cook the bread, and then to incorporate the fillings. The most typical fillings are thin slices of pancetta or bacon with mozzarella, but the sky is the limit in this scrumptious flatbread.

1. Place the dough on a flour-dusted work surface and cut it into six pieces. Stretch the pieces of dough into 8- to 10-inch-long ovals (20 to 25 centimeters), place them on pieces of flour-dusted parchment paper, and cover with kitchen towels or greased plastic wrap. Let rest in a warm spot for 2 to 3 hours.

2. Preheat the oven to 410°F (210°C) and place a baking stone or steel in the oven as it warms. Using a peel or a flat baking sheet, slide the focaccia onto the heated baking implement and bake for 15 to 20 minutes, until the crust is set. Remove and let cool before cutting a slit along the equator of each focaccia. Fill each focaccia with an equal amount of the pancetta or bacon, mozzarella, tomato, and lettuce. Sprinkle red pepper flakes and salt over the filling and drizzle with olive oil.

3. Return the focaccia to the oven and bake for about 10 minutes, until the pancetta or bacon looks cooked and the mozzarella has melted. Remove from the oven and let cool briefly before serving.

INGREDIENTS:

48-HOUR FOCACCIA DOUGH (SEE PAGE 92)

ALL-PURPOSE FLOUR, AS NEEDED

12.7 OZ. | 360 GRAMS PANCETTA OR BACON, SLICED THIN

26.4 OZ. | 750 GRAMS FRESH MOZZARELLA, DRAINED AND SLICED

2 TOMATOES, SLICED

12 LETTUCE LEAVES

RED PEPPER FLAKES, TO TASTE

SALT, TO TASTE

OLIVE OIL, TO TASTE

PARIGINA

YIELD: 1 LARGE FOCACCIA / **ACTIVE TIME:** 20 MINUTES / **TOTAL TIME:** 3 HOURS AND 30 MINUTES

If you are walking the streets of Naples during the day you will probably stumble into this beloved street food. Decadent and delicious, parigina typically features multiple layers of toppings, such as tomato sauce, ham, cheese, puff pastry, and heavy cream.

1. Grease an 18 × 13-inch baking pan with olive oil, place the dough on it, and stretch it toward the edges of the pan, taking care not to tear it. Cover the dough with greased plastic wrap and let rest at room temperature for 2 hours. As the dough rests, stretch it toward the edges of the pan every 20 minutes until it covers the entire pan.

2. Preheat the oven to 390°F (200°C). Place the tomatoes in a bowl, mash them, and season with salt. Spread the tomatoes over the dough, making sure to leave a 1-inch (2.5-centimeter) border of dough at the edges. Cover with a layer of ham and top this with a layer of cheese. Cover the focaccia with the puff pastry, beat the egg and cream together until combined, and brush the pastry with the egg wash.

3. Place in the oven and bake for 30 to 35 minutes, until golden brown. Remove from the oven and let cool slightly before cutting into squares.

INGREDIENTS:

OLIVE OIL, AS NEEDED

24-HOUR FOCACCIA DOUGH WITH 60 PERCENT HYDRATION (SEE PAGE 87)

22.9 OZ. | 650 GRAMS CANNED TOMATOES, DRAINED

SALT, TO TASTE

7 OZ. | 200 GRAMS HAM, SLICED

14 OZ. | 400 GRAMS CACIOCAVALLO CHEESE OR LOW-HYDRATION MOZZARELLA CHEESE, SLICED THIN

1 SHEET FROZEN PUFF PASTRY, THAWED

2 EGG YOLKS

2 OZ. | 56.6 GRAMS HEAVY CREAM

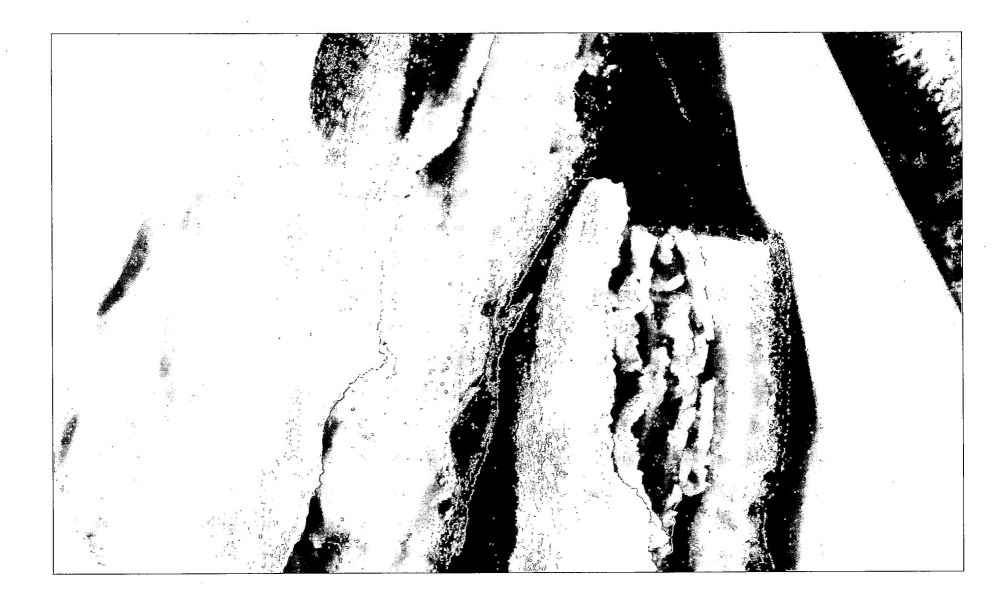

MONTANARE

YIELD: 20 MINIATURE FOCACCIA / **ACTIVE TIME:** 45 MINUTES / **TOTAL TIME:** 2 HOURS AND 45 MINUTES

A recipe that dates back to a time when people living in cities didn't have a kitchen large enough to accommodate an oven, and so focaccia was fried rather than baked. These miniature focaccia are a real treat, particularly beloved by children. A good way to use up leftover dough.

1. Place the dough on a flour-dusted work surface, divide it into 20 pieces, and shape each piece into a ball. Cover with greased plastic wrap and let sit at room temperature until they have doubled in size, about 2 hours.

2. Add olive oil to a deep skillet until it is about 1 inch deep and warm to 350°F (175°C). Flatten the balls of dough. Working in batches of three, add them to the oil and cook until golden brown, turning them frequently, about 5 minutes. Place the cooked focaccia on paper towel–lined plates to drain.

3. When all of the focaccia have been cooked, top with the Marinara Sauce, pecorino, basil, and, if desired, the mozzarella. Drizzle olive oil over the top and serve.

INGREDIENTS:

½ BATCH QUICK PIZZA DOUGH (SEE PAGE 107)

ALL-PURPOSE FLOUR, AS NEEDED

OLIVE OIL, AS NEEDED

26.4 OZ. | 750 GRAMS MARINARA SAUCE (SEE PAGE 104), WARMED

PECORINO CHEESE, GRATED, TO TASTE

FRESH BASIL LEAVES, TO TASTE

MOZZARELLA CHEESE, SLICED, TO TASTE (OPTIONAL)

LESTOPITTA

YIELD: 8 SMALL FOCACCIA / **ACTIVE TIME:** 45 MINUTES / **TOTAL TIME:** 2 HOURS AND 45 MINUTES

This fried focaccia is similar to the one that is popular in Abruzzi. It is not leavened, and although it is crunchy when hot it becomes soft as it cools. It is usually wrapped around a savory filling when eaten soft.

1. Combine the flour, water, and olive oil and work the mixture until it is smooth and elastic. Cover with plastic wrap and let rest at room temperature for 1 hour.

2. Divide the dough into eight pieces, form them into balls, and cover with greased plastic wrap. Let rest at room temperature for 1 hour.

3. Add olive oil to a deep skillet until it is about 1 inch deep and warm to 350°F (175°C). Flatten the balls of dough. Working in batches of three, add them to the oil and cook until golden brown, turning them frequently, about 5 minutes. Place the cooked focaccia on paper towel–lined plates to drain. Eat warm or wait until they have cooled and fill with anything you desire.

INGREDIENTS:

14 OZ. | 400 GRAMS FINE SEMOLINA FLOUR

7 OZ. | 200 GRAMS WATER

1 OZ. | 30 GRAMS OLIVE OIL, PLUS MORE AS NEEDED

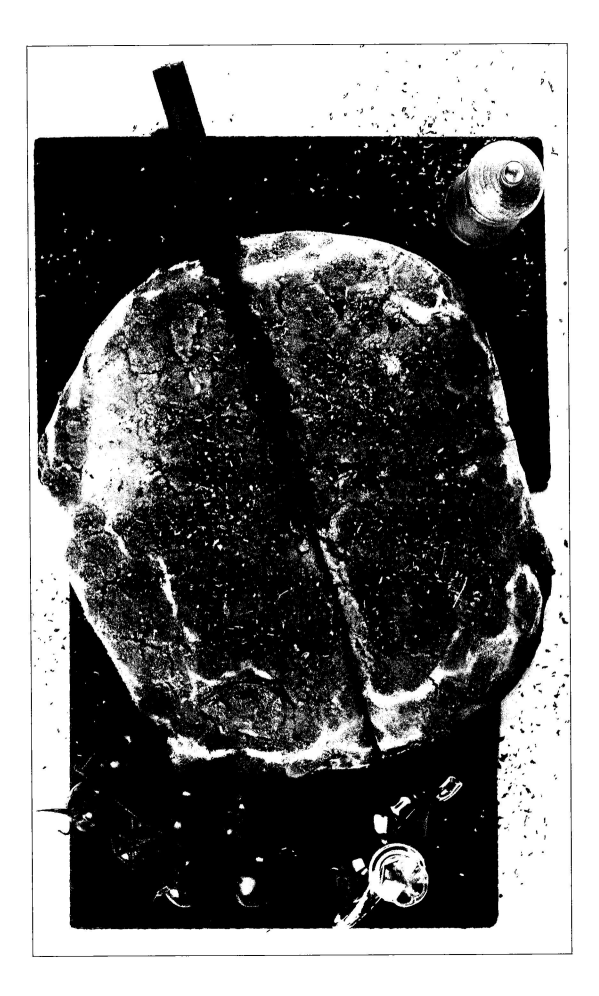

GRUPARIATA

YIELD: 1 13-INCH FOCACCIA / **ACTIVE TIME:** 30 MINUTES / **TOTAL TIME:** 3 HOURS AND 30 MINUTES

Hailing from Calabria, this is a very tall and fluffy focaccia with a pleasantly red crumb that is due to the presence of tomatoes and chili powder in the dough.

1. Line a deep, round 13-inch cake pan with parchment paper and grease it with olive oil. If using active dry yeast, warm 3½ tablespoons (1.75 oz./50 grams) of the water until it is about 105°F (40°C). Add the water and the yeast to a bowl and gently stir. Let sit for 5 to 10 minutes. Instant yeast does not need to be proofed.

2. In a large bowl, combine the flours, canned tomatoes, chili powder, olive oil, salt, yeast, and water and work the mixture until the dough is thoroughly combined. Incorporate the garlic and a few pinches of fresh oregano and transfer the dough into the cake pan. Cover with a kitchen towel and let the dough rest at room temperature until it has doubled in size, about 2½ hours.

3. Preheat the oven to 390°F (200°C). Cover the focaccia with the anchovies and the fresh tomato slices, pressing down on them so that they are embedded deep within the dough. Sprinkle more oregano and salt over the dough, and add the rosemary, if desired. Drizzle olive oil over the top, place in the oven, and bake for 30 to 35 minutes, until golden brown. Remove from the oven and let cool slightly before serving.

INGREDIENTS:

1.2 OZ. | 35 GRAMS OLIVE OIL, PLUS MORE AS NEEDED

2½ TEASPOONS | 7 GRAMS ACTIVE DRY YEAST OR 2 TEASPOONS (SCANT) | 5.8 GRAMS INSTANT YEAST

14 OZ. | 400 GRAMS WATER

17.6 OZ. | 500 GRAMS BREAD FLOUR

10.6 OZ. | 300 GRAMS "00" FLOUR

1 LB. | 450 GRAMS CANNED WHOLE PEELED TOMATOES, PARTLY DRAINED AND CHOPPED

2 TABLESPOONS | 16 GRAMS CHILI POWDER

2½ TEASPOONS | 14 GRAMS TABLE SALT, PLUS MORE TO TASTE

2 GARLIC CLOVES, MINCED

FRESH OREGANO, FINELY CHOPPED, TO TASTE

ANCHOVIES, DRAINED AND TORN, TO TASTE

1 FRESH TOMATO, SLICED

FRESH ROSEMARY, TO TASTE (OPTIONAL)

FOCACCIA BARESE

YIELD: 2 10-INCH FOCACCIA / **ACTIVE TIME:** 30 MINUTES / **TOTAL TIME:** 4 HOURS

B ari is the birthplace of one of the most prototypical Italian focaccia, the barese. This is the most typical version—round and topped with fresh tomatoes and olives—but many variations can be found.

1. If using active dry yeast, warm 3½ tablespoons (1.75 oz./50 grams) of the water until it is about 105°F (40°C). Add the water and the yeast to a bowl and gently stir. Let sit for 5 to 10 minutes. Instant yeast does not need to be proofed.

2. In a large bowl, combine the flours, potato, yeast, and water. Work the mixture until it just holds together. If kneading by hand, transfer the dough to a flour-dusted work surface. Work it until it is compact, smooth, and elastic. For further instructions on kneading and mixing dough see page 71.

3. Add the salt and work the dough until it is developed, elastic, and extensible, about 5 minutes. Form the dough into a ball and place it in an airtight container that has been greased with olive oil. Let rest at room temperature until it has doubled in size, about 2 hours.

4. Generously grease two 10-inch cast-iron skillets or round cake pans with olive oil. Place the dough on a flour-dusted work surface and divide it in two. Place the dough in the pans and spread it to the edge of each, making sure not to press down too hard and deflate the focaccia. Let rest in a warm spot for 1 hour.

5. Preheat the oven to its maximum temperature and place a rack in the middle position. Top the focaccia with the tomatoes, olives, and oregano, season with salt, and drizzle olive oil over everything. Place the pans directly on the bottom of the oven and bake for 10 minutes.

6. Transfer the pans to the middle rack and bake until the edges look brown and crunchy, 5 to 7 more minutes. Remove and let cool slightly before serving.

INGREDIENTS:

2 TEASPOONS | 6 GRAMS ACTIVE DRY YEAST OR 1⅓ TEASPOONS | 5 GRAMS INSTANT YEAST

14 OZ. | 400 GRAMS WATER

14 OZ. | 400 GRAMS BREAD FLOUR, PLUS MORE AS NEEDED

7 OZ. | 200 GRAMS FINE SEMOLINA FLOUR

1 POTATO, BOILED, PEELED, AND MASHED

2½ TEASPOONS | 14 GRAMS TABLE SALT, PLUS MORE TO TASTE

OLIVE OIL, AS NEEDED

2 VERY RIPE TOMATOES, CHOPPED

GREEN OLIVES, PITTED AND CHOPPED, TO TASTE

FRESH OREGANO, FINELY CHOPPED, TO TASTE

FOCACCIA DI ALTAMURA

YIELD: 2 10-INCH FOCACCIA / **ACTIVE TIME:** 30 MINUTES / **TOTAL TIME:** 4 HOURS

n Altamura, focaccia is made from 100 percent durum wheat flour and features a topping of onions and fresh tomatoes.

1. If using active dry yeast, warm 3½ tablespoons (1.75 oz./50 grams) of the water until it is about 105°F (40°C). Add the water and the yeast to a bowl and gently stir. Let sit for 5 to 10 minutes. Instant yeast does not need to be proofed.

2. In a large bowl, combine the flour, yeast, and water and work the mixture until it just holds together. If kneading by hand, transfer the dough to a flour-dusted work surface. Work it until it is compact, smooth, and elastic. For further instructions on kneading and mixing dough see page 71.

3. Add the salt and work the dough until it is developed, elastic, and extensible, about 5 minutes. Form the dough into a ball and place it in an airtight container that has been greased with olive oil. Let rest at room temperature until it has doubled in size, about 2 hours.

4. Generously grease two 10-inch cast-iron skillets or round cake pans with olive oil. Place the dough on a flour-dusted work surface and divide it in two. Place a piece of dough in each pan and spread it to the edge, making sure not to press down too hard and deflate it. Let rest at room temperature for 1 hour.

5. Preheat the oven to its maximum temperature and place a rack in the middle position. Top the focaccia with the onions, press the tomatoes into the dough, season with salt and oregano, and drizzle olive oil over the top. Place the pans directly on the bottom of the oven and bake for 10 minutes.

6. Transfer the pans to the middle rack and bake until the edges look brown and crunchy, 5 to 7 more minutes. Remove and let cool slightly before serving.

INGREDIENTS:

2 TEASPOONS | 6 GRAMS ACTIVE DRY YEAST OR 1⅗ TEASPOONS | 5 GRAMS INSTANT YEAST

14 OZ. | 400 GRAMS WATER

21.1 OZ. | 600 GRAMS FINE SEMOLINA FLOUR, PLUS MORE AS NEEDED

2½ TEASPOONS | 14 GRAMS TABLE SALT, PLUS MORE TO TASTE

OLIVE OIL, AS NEEDED

1 LARGE ONION, SLICED

2 VERY RIPE TOMATOES, SLICED

FRESH OREGANO, FINELY CHOPPED, TO TASTE

PUDDICA SALENTINA

YIELD: 2 10-INCH FOCACCIA / **ACTIVE TIME:** 30 MINUTES / **TOTAL TIME:** 4 HOURS

In Salento, particularly in the city of Brindisi, Apulian focaccia is made without durum flour and with capers in place of olives as a topping.

INGREDIENTS:

2 TEASPOONS | 6 GRAMS ACTIVE DRY YEAST OR 1⅔ TEASPOONS | 5 GRAMS INSTANT YEAST

14 OZ. | 400 GRAMS WATER

14 OZ. | 400 GRAMS BREAD FLOUR

7 OZ. | 200 GRAMS ALL-PURPOSE FLOUR, PLUS MORE AS NEEDED

2½ TEASPOONS | 14 GRAMS TABLE SALT, PLUS MORE TO TASTE

OLIVE OIL, AS NEEDED

2 VERY RIPE TOMATOES, CHOPPED

CAPERS, DRAINED, TO TASTE

FRESH OREGANO, FINELY CHOPPED, TO TASTE

1. If using active dry yeast, warm 3½ tablespoons (1.75 oz./50 grams) of the water until it is about 105°F (40°C). Add the water and the yeast to a bowl and gently stir. Let sit for 5 to 10 minutes. Instant yeast does not need to be proofed.

2. In a large bowl, combine the flours, yeast, and water and work the mixture until it just holds together. If kneading by hand, transfer the dough to a flour-dusted work surface. Work it until it is compact, smooth, and elastic. For further instructions on kneading and mixing dough see page 71.

3. Add the salt and work the dough until it is developed, elastic, and extensible, about 5 minutes. Form the dough into a ball and place it in an airtight container that has been greased with olive oil. Let rest at room temperature until it has doubled in size, about 2 hours.

4. Generously grease two 10-inch cast-iron skillets or round cake pans with olive oil. Place the dough on a flour-dusted work surface and divide it in two. Place a piece of dough in each of the pans and spread it to the edge, making sure not to press down too hard and deflate it. Let rest at room temperature for 1 hour.

5. Preheat the oven to its maximum temperature and place a rack in the middle position. Top the focaccia with the capers, press the tomatoes into the dough, season with salt and oregano, and drizzle olive oil over the top. Place the pans directly on the bottom of the oven and bake for 10 minutes.

6. Transfer the pans to the middle rack and bake until the edges look brown and crunchy, 5 to 7 more minutes. Remove and let cool slightly before serving.

SCEBLASTI & PIZZO LECCESE

YIELD: 30 MINIATURE FOCACCIA / **ACTIVE TIME:** 45 MINUTES / **TOTAL TIME:** 3 HOURS

Deep in the Apulian inland, one can still find a focaccia that dates back to Greek times. It is rich with healthy, yummy vegetables and makes a great way to present them to your family. There are two main variations: in Zollino this focaccia is called *sceblasti*, a Greek word that means "without shape" because the dough is more like a batter. It includes a blend of different vegetables, richer than the version that we find in Lecce. Here is a method for both versions.

1. If using active dry yeast, warm 3½ tablespoons (1.75 oz./50 grams) of the water until it is about 105°F (40°C). Add the water and the yeast to a bowl and gently stir. Let sit for 5 to 10 minutes. Instant yeast does not need to be proofed.

2. In a large bowl, combine the flour, water, and yeast and work the mixture until it just holds together. Transfer it to a flour-dusted work surface and knead the dough until it is compact, smooth, and elastic. For further instructions on kneading dough see page 71.

3. Add the salt and knead until the dough is smooth, elastic, and extensible. Form the dough into a ball and place it in an airtight container that has been greased with olive oil. Let rest at room temperature until it has doubled in size, about 2 hours.

4. Preheat the oven to the maximum temperature and place a baking stone or steel in the oven as it warms. While the dough is rising, clean and mince all the vegetables and combine with the tomato sauce, olive oil, salt, oregano, and red pepper flakes (if using).

5. Flatten the dough and spread the vegetables over it, folding the dough over the vegetables and pressing with your hands to incorporate them into the dough. Place the dough on a peel or flat baking sheet and transfer it to the heated baking implement. Bake until golden brown, about 20 minutes. Remove from the oven and let cool briefly before serving.

INGREDIENTS:

2 TEASPOONS | 6 GRAMS ACTIVE DRY YEAST OR 1⅗ TEASPOONS | 5 GRAMS INSTANT YEAST

14.8 OZ. | 420 GRAMS WATER

21.1 OZ. | 600 GRAMS ALL-PURPOSE FLOUR

2½ TEASPOONS | 15 GRAMS TABLE SALT, PLUS MORE TO TASTE

2 MEDIUM ONIONS, SLICED

7 OZ. | 200 GRAMS CHERRY TOMATOES

1 ZUCCHINI (OMIT IF MAKING PIZZO LECCESE)

7 OZ. | 200 GRAMS FRESH PUMPKIN (OMIT IF MAKING PIZZO LECCESE)

3.5 OZ. | 100 GRAMS RAW PIZZA SAUCE (SEE PAGE 103)

7 OZ. | 200 GRAMS PITTED BLACK OLIVES

2.8 OZ. | 80 GRAMS OLIVE OIL

FRESH OREGANO, FINELY CHOPPED, TO TASTE

RED PEPPER FLAKES, TO TASTE (OPTIONAL)

PAPOSCIA DEL GARGANO

YIELD: 5 MEDIUM FOCACCIA / **ACTIVE TIME:** 30 MINUTES / **TOTAL TIME:** 9 HOURS AND 30 MINUTES

From the beautiful Gargano region of Apulia, this focaccia is possibly the original version of ciabatta. Traditionally baked in wood-fired ovens out of scraps of leftover dough, it can be made at home—with some adjustments—and it is surely worth trying, as it also makes a delicious bread for sandwiches.

1. If using active dry yeast, warm 3½ tablespoons (1.75 oz./50 grams) of the water until it is about 105°F (40°C). Add the water and the yeast to a bowl and gently stir. Let sit for 5 to 10 minutes. Instant yeast does not need to be proofed.

2. In a large bowl, combine the bread flour, yeast, and water and work the mixture until the dough just holds together. If kneading by hand, transfer the dough to a work surface dusted with bread flour. Work it until it is compact, smooth, and elastic. For further instructions on kneading and mixing dough see page 71.

3. Add the salt and work the dough until it is developed, elastic, and extensible, about 5 minutes. Divide the dough into five pieces, shape them into balls, and place them in an airtight container that has been greased with olive oil. Let rest at room temperature for at least 8 hours.

4. Preheat the oven to the maximum temperature and place a baking stone or steel in the oven as it warms.

5. Dust a peel or a flat baking sheet with semolina flour. Place 2 to 3 focaccia on it at a time and stretch them into long ovals. Use the peel to transfer them to the heated baking implement and bake for about 10 minutes, until golden brown and crispy. Remove and let cool slightly before serving.

INGREDIENTS:

⅚ TEASPOON | 2.4 GRAMS ACTIVE DRY YEAST OR ⅔ TEASPOON | 2 GRAMS INSTANT YEAST

14.8 OZ. | 420 GRAMS WATER

22.9 OZ. | 700 GRAMS BREAD FLOUR, PLUS MORE AS NEEDED

2½ TEASPOONS | 14 GRAMS TABLE SALT

OLIVE OIL, AS NEEDED

SEMOLINA FLOUR, AS NEEDED

CALZONE PUGLIESE

YIELD: 1 10-INCH FOCACCIA / **ACTIVE TIME:** 45 MINUTES / **TOTAL TIME:** 4 HOURS

Although the name *calzone* evokes the popular Neapolitan pizza pockets, in Apulia it refers to a round pie made from two layers of focaccia dough.

1. If using active dry yeast, warm 3½ tablespoons (1.75 oz./50 grams) of the water until it is about 105°F (40°C). Add the water and the yeast to a bowl and gently stir. Let sit for 5 to 10 minutes. Instant yeast does not need to be proofed.

2. In a large bowl, combine the flour, yeast, and water and work the mixture until the dough holds together. If kneading by hand, transfer the dough to a flour-dusted work surface. Work it until it is compact, smooth, and elastic. For further instructions on kneading and mixing dough see page 71.

3. Add the salt and work the dough until it is developed, elastic, and extensible, about 5 minutes. Form the dough into a ball and place it in an airtight container that has been greased with olive oil. Let rest at room temperature until it has doubled in size, about 2 hours.

4. Coat the bottom of a skillet with olive oil and warm over medium-high heat. Add the onions and sauté until translucent, about 3 minutes. Add the cherry tomatoes and cook until they start to collapse, about 10 minutes. Remove from heat and let cool completely.

5. Grease a 10-inch cast-iron skillet or round cake pan with olive oil. Transfer the dough to a flour-dusted surface and divide into two pieces, making sure one piece is slightly bigger than the other. Roll out one piece into a disk that is slightly larger than the pan. Place the disk in the pan, top with the onion and tomato mixture, and distribute the olives, anchovies, and capers over the mixture. Roll out the second piece of dough so that it will fit within the pan, place it over the filling, and crimp the edge to seal the focaccia. Brush the top of the focaccia with olive oil and use a fork to poke holes in it. Cover with greased plastic wrap and let rest for 1 hour.

INGREDIENTS:

2 TEASPOONS | 6 GRAMS ACTIVE DRY YEAST OR 1⅔ TEASPOONS | 5 GRAMS INSTANT YEAST

8.8 OZ. | 250 GRAMS WATER

17.6 OZ. | 500 GRAMS ALL-PURPOSE FLOUR, PLUS MORE AS NEEDED

1½ TEASPOONS | 10 GRAMS TABLE SALT, PLUS MORE TO TASTE

OLIVE OIL, AS NEEDED

3 ONIONS, SLICED

5.3 OZ. | 150 GRAMS CHERRY TOMATOES

5.3 OZ. | 150 GRAMS PITTED BLACK OLIVES

1 OZ. | 30 GRAMS ANCHOVIES, DRAINED

2 TABLESPOONS | 17.2 GRAMS CAPERS

6. Preheat the oven to 430°F (220°C). Place the focaccia in the oven and bake for 20 minutes. Lower the temperature to 350°F (175°C) and bake for another 20 to 25 minutes, until golden brown both on top and on the bottom. Remove and let cool slightly before serving.

CAVICIONE

I n Ischitella, the typical Apulian calzone is filled with sautéed spring onions, which give it a very special flavor.

1. If using active dry yeast, warm 3½ tablespoons (1.75 oz./50 grams) of the water until it is about 105°F (40°C). Add the water and the yeast to a bowl and gently stir. Let sit for 5 to 10 minutes. Instant yeast does not need to be proofed.

2. In a large bowl, combine the flour, yeast, and water until the dough holds together. If kneading by hand, transfer the dough to a flour-dusted work surface. Work it until it is compact, smooth, and elastic. For further instructions on kneading and mixing dough see page 71.

3. Add the salt and knead until the dough is developed, elastic, and extensible, about 5 minutes. Form the dough into a ball and place it in an airtight container that has been greased with olive oil. Let rest at room temperature until it has doubled in size, about 2 hours.

4. Coat the bottom of a skillet with olive oil and warm over medium-high heat. When the oil starts to shimmer, add the spring onions and about 1 tablespoon of water and cook until the onions are tender and all of the liquid has evaporated, about 10 minutes. Remove from heat and let cool completely.

5. Grease a 10-inch cast-iron skillet or round cake pan with olive oil. Transfer the dough to a flour-dusted surface and divide into two pieces, making sure one piece is slightly bigger. Roll out one piece into a disk that is slightly larger than the pan. Place it in the pan, top with the onions, and distribute the olives and anchovies over the onions. Roll out the second piece of dough so that it will fit within the pan, place it over the filling, and crimp the edge to seal the focaccia. Brush the focaccia with olive oil and poke holes in it. Cover with greased plastic wrap and let rest for 1 hour.

6. Preheat the oven to 430°F (220°C). Place the focaccia in the oven and bake for 20 minutes. Lower the temperature to 350°F (175°C) and bake for another 20 to 25 minutes, until golden brown both on top and on the bottom. Remove and let cool slightly before serving.

INGREDIENTS:

2 TEASPOONS | 6 GRAMS ACTIVE DRY YEAST OR 1⅔ TEASPOONS | 5 GRAMS INSTANT YEAST

8.8 OZ. | 250 GRAMS WATER, PLUS MORE AS NEEDED

17.6 OZ. | 500 GRAMS ALL-PURPOSE FLOUR, PLUS MORE AS NEEDED

1½ TEASPOONS | 10 GRAMS SALT, PLUS MORE TO TASTE

OLIVE OIL, AS NEEDED

17.6 OZ. | 500 GRAMS SPRING ONIONS, CHOPPED

5.3 OZ. | 150 GRAMS PITTED BLACK OLIVES

4.2 OZ. | 120 GRAMS ANCHOVIES, DRAINED

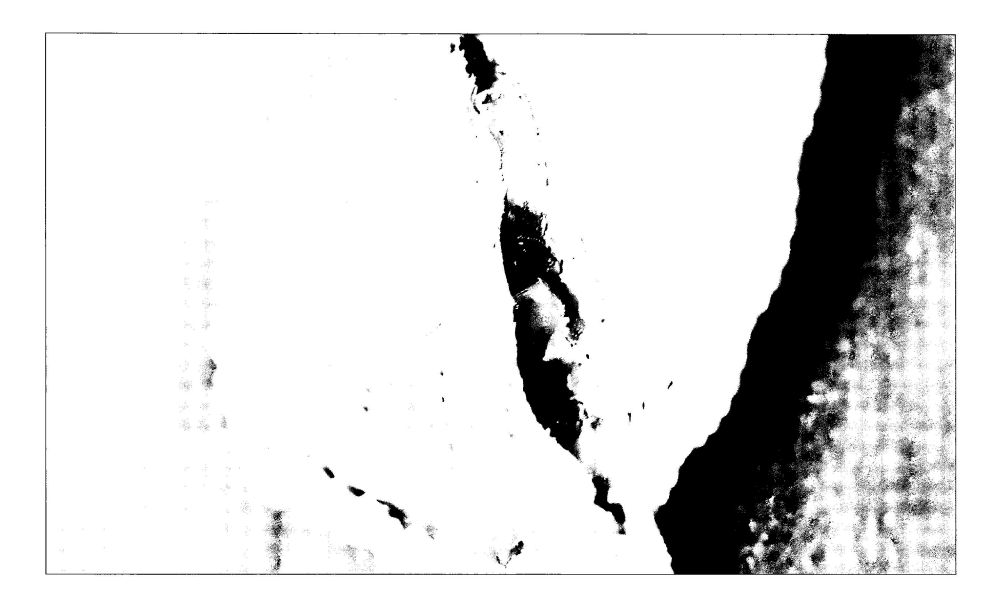

FOCACCIA DI CARNEVALE SALENTINA

YIELD: 1 10-INCH FOCACCIA / **ACTIVE TIME:** 45 MINUTES / **TOTAL TIME:** 4 HOURS

This rich and delicious Apulian calzone is typical of the region of Salento, where it is presented during the Carnival.

1. If using active dry yeast, warm 3½ tablespoons (1.75 oz./50 grams) of the water until it is about 105°F (40°C). Add the water and the yeast to a bowl and gently stir. Let sit for 5 to 10 minutes. Instant yeast does not need to be proofed.

2. In a large bowl, combine the flour, yeast, and water until the dough holds together. If kneading by hand, transfer the dough to a flour-dusted work surface. Work it until it is compact, smooth, and elastic. For further instructions on kneading and mixing dough see page 71.

3. Add the salt and work the dough until it is developed, elastic, and extensible, about 5 minutes. Form the dough into a ball and place it in an airtight container that has been greased with olive oil. Let rest at room temperature until it has doubled in size, about 2 hours.

4. Coat the bottom of a skillet with olive oil and warm over medium-high heat. When the oil starts to shimmer, add the onion and sausage, season with salt and pepper, and sauté until the sausage is browned and the onion is soft, about 10 minutes. Remove from heat and let cool.

5. Grease a 10-inch cast-iron skillet or round cake pan with olive oil. Transfer the dough to a flour-dusted surface and divide into two pieces, with one piece slightly bigger than the other. Roll out one piece into a disk that is slightly larger than the pan. Place it in the pan, top with the onion-and-sausage mixture and distribute the tomatoes, pecorino, and mozzarella over the mixture. Roll out the second piece of dough so that it will fit within the pan, place it over the filling, and crimp the edge to seal the focaccia. Brush the top of the focaccia with olive oil and use a fork to poke holes in it. Cover with greased plastic wrap and let rest for 1 hour.

INGREDIENTS:

2 TEASPOONS | 6 GRAMS ACTIVE DRY YEAST OR 1⅔ TEASPOONS | 5 GRAMS INSTANT YEAST

8.8 OZ. | 250 GRAMS WATER

17.6 OZ. | 500 GRAMS ALL-PURPOSE FLOUR, PLUS MORE AS NEEDED

1½ TEASPOONS | 10 GRAMS TABLE SALT, PLUS MORE TO TASTE

OLIVE OIL, AS NEEDED

1 ONION, SLICED

14 OZ. | 400 GRAMS ITALIAN SAUSAGE, CHOPPED

BLACK PEPPER, TO TASTE

3 TO 4 SMALL TOMATOES, PEELED, SEEDED, AND SLICED

2.4 OZ. | 70 GRAMS PECORINO CHEESE, GRATED

9.9 OZ. | 280 GRAMS FRESH MOZZARELLA CHEESE, TORN

6. Preheat the oven to 430°F (220°C). Place the focaccia in the oven and bake for 20 minutes. Lower the temperature to 350°F (175°C) and bake for another 20 to 25 minutes, until golden brown both on top and on the bottom. Remove and let cool slightly before serving.

SFINCIONE PALERMITANO

YIELD: 1 LARGE FOCACCIA / **ACTIVE TIME:** 1 HOUR / **TOTAL TIME:** 4 HOURS AND 30 MINUTES

Although I really love all focaccias and focaccia traditions, I have to admit that I am very partial to Sicilian sfincione. I love the soft and spongy consistency of the crumb as well the bold toppings, so rich that eating sfincione makes me feel like I had a complete meal rather than a snack. This is a seriously delicious food, and if you have never had the chance to visit Sicily, here you find a version that is very close to the original.

1. If using active dry yeast, warm 3½ tablespoons (1.75 oz./50 grams) of the water until it is about 105°F (40°C). Add the water and the yeast to a bowl and gently stir. Let sit for 5 to 10 minutes. Instant yeast does not need to be proofed.

2. In a large bowl, combine the flours, yeast, and water until the dough holds together. If kneading by hand, transfer the dough to a flour-dusted work surface. Work it until it is compact, smooth, and elastic. For further instructions on kneading and mixing dough see page 71.

3. Add the salt and work the dough until it is developed, elastic, and extensible, about 5 minutes. Form the dough into a ball and cover the bowl with a damp kitchen towel. Let rest at room temperature until it has doubled in size, about 2 hours.

4. Coat the bottom of a skillet with olive oil and warm over medium-low heat. When the oil starts to shimmer, add the onions and sauté until they are soft, about 12 minutes. Add the tomatoes and three of the anchovies, cover the skillet, reduce the heat, and simmer until the flavor is to your liking, 20 to 30 minutes. Season with salt and pepper and let cool completely.

5. Grease an 18 × 13–inch baking pan with olive oil, place the dough on the pan, and gently stretch it until it covers the entire pan. Cover with plastic wrap and let rest for 1 hour.

INGREDIENTS:

2½ TEASPOONS | 7 GRAMS ACTIVE DRY YEAST OR 2 TEASPOONS | 6 GRAMS INSTANT YEAST

22.5 OZ. | 640 GRAMS WATER

19.75 OZ. | 560 GRAMS BREAD FLOUR, PLUS MORE AS NEEDED

8.4 OZ. | 240 GRAMS FINE SEMOLINA FLOUR

1 TABLESPOON | 17 GRAMS TABLE SALT, PLUS MORE TO TASTE

1.4 OZ. | 40 GRAMS OLIVE OIL, PLUS MORE AS NEEDED

2 ONIONS, SLICED

22.9 OZ. | 650 GRAMS CANNED WHOLE PEELED TOMATOES WITH THEIR SAUCE, MASHED

11 TO 14 ANCHOVIES, DRAINED AND TORN

BLACK PEPPER, TO TASTE

10.6 OZ. | 300 GRAMS CACIOCAVALLO CHEESE, CUBED

FRESH OREGANO, FINELY CHOPPED, TO TASTE

5.3 OZ. | 150 GRAMS CACIOCAVALLO CHEESE, GRATED

BREAD CRUMBS, TO TASTE

6. Preheat the oven to 430°F (220°C). Top the focaccia with the cubed caciocavallo and the remaining anchovies and press down on them until they are embedded in the dough. Cover with the tomato sauce, generously sprinkle oregano over the sauce, and drizzle with olive oil. Sprinkle the grated caciocavallo and a generous handful of bread crumbs over the focaccia.

7. Place in the oven and bake for 20 minutes. Lower the temperature to 180°F (75°C) and bake for another 15 to 20 minutes, until the focaccia is golden brown both on the edges and on the bottom.

FACCIA DI VECCHIA

YIELD: 6 MEDIUM FOCACCIA / **ACTIVE TIME:** 1 HOUR / **TOTAL TIME:** 4 HOURS

The toppings here are the same as the ones used in sfincione, but the smaller focaccia are baked directly on the stone, as a Neapolitan pizza would be. Some versions omit both the cheese and the anchovies from the topping, so if that sounds more to your taste, don't hesitate to go that route.

1. If using active dry yeast, warm 3½ tablespoons (1.75 oz./50 grams) of the water until it is about 105°F (40°C). Add the water and the yeast to a bowl and gently stir. Let sit for 5 to 10 minutes. Instant yeast does not need to be proofed.

2. In a large bowl, combine the flours, yeast, and water until the dough holds together. If kneading by hand, transfer the dough to a flour-dusted work surface. Work it until it is compact, smooth, and elastic. For further instructions on kneading and mixing dough see page 71.

3. Add the salt and knead until the dough is developed, elastic, and extensible, about 5 minutes. Form the dough into a ball and cover the bowl with a damp kitchen towel. Let rest at room temperature until it has doubled in size, about 2 hours.

4. Coat the bottom of a skillet with olive oil and warm over medium-low heat. When the oil starts to shimmer, add the onions and sauté until they are soft, about 12 minutes. Add the tomatoes and three of the anchovies, cover the skillet, reduce the heat, and simmer until the flavor is to your liking, 20 to 30 minutes. Season with salt and pepper and let cool completely.

5. Place the dough on a flour-dusted work surface and divide it into six pieces. Shape the pieces into balls, cover with greased plastic wrap, and let rest for 1 hour.

6. Preheat the oven to its maximum temperature and place a baking stone or steel in the oven as it warms. Gently flatten the balls of dough and cover with the tomato sauce. Top with the cubed caciocavallo or tuma, the remaining anchovies, a generous amount of the oregano, olive oil, grated caciocavallo, and bread crumbs.

7. Using a peel or a flat baking sheet, transfer the focaccia onto the heated baking implement and bake for about 30 minutes, until the edges are golden brown. Remove from the oven and let cool slightly before serving.

INGREDIENTS:

2½ TEASPOONS | 7 GRAMS ACTIVE DRY YEAST OR 2 TEASPOONS | 6 GRAMS INSTANT YEAST

19.4 OZ. | 550 GRAMS WATER

19.75 OZ. | 560 GRAMS BREAD FLOUR, PLUS MORE AS NEEDED

8.4 OZ. | 240 GRAMS FINE SEMOLINA FLOUR

1 TABLESPOON | 17 GRAMS TABLE SALT, PLUS MORE TO TASTE

OLIVE OIL, AS NEEDED

2 ONIONS, SLICED

22.9 OZ. | 650 GRAMS CANNED WHOLE PEELED TOMATOES WITH THEIR SAUCE, MASHED

11 TO 14 ANCHOVIES, DRAINED

BLACK PEPPER, TO TASTE

10.6 OZ. | 300 GRAMS CACIOCAVALLO OR TUMA CHEESE, CUBED

FRESH OREGANO, FINELY CHOPPED, TO TASTE

7 OZ. | 200 GRAMS CACIOCAVALLO CHEESE, GRATED

BREAD CRUMBS, TO TASTE

FOCACCIA MESSINESE

YIELD: 1 LARGE FOCACCIA / **ACTIVE TIME:** 40 MINUTES / **TOTAL TIME:** 4 HOURS AND 30 MINUTES

This delicious focaccia reigns in Messina, where escarole is queen. If you're searching for some way to make salad look and taste amazing, look no further.

1. If using active dry yeast, warm 3½ tablespoons (1.75 oz./50 grams) of the water until it is about 105°F (40°C). Add the water and the yeast to a bowl and gently stir. Let sit for 5 to 10 minutes. Instant yeast does not need to be proofed.

2. In a large bowl, combine the flours, olive oil, yeast, and water until the dough holds together. If kneading by hand, transfer to a flour-dusted work surface. Work until until it is compact, smooth, and elastic. For further instructions on kneading dough see page 71.

3. Add the salt and work the dough until it is developed, elastic, and extensible, about 5 minutes. Form the dough into a ball and place it in an airtight container that has been greased with olive oil. Let rest at room temperature until it has doubled in size, about 2 hours.

4. Grease an 18 × 13–inch baking pan with olive oil, place the dough on it, and brush the dough with more olive oil. Cover with a kitchen towel and let rest for 30 minutes.

5. Gently stretch the dough until it covers the entire pan. Let rest for another hour.

6. Preheat the oven to 390°F (200°C). Press the anchovies and the cubes of caciocavallo into the dough and top with the escarole and tomatoes. Season with the oregano, salt, and pepper and drizzle olive oil over the focaccia.

7. Place in the oven and bake for 20 to 30 minutes, until golden brown and crisp on the edges and the bottom.

INGREDIENTS:

2½ TEASPOONS | 7 GRAMS ACTIVE DRY YEAST OR 2 TEASPOONS | 6 GRAMS INSTANT YEAST

14.8 OZ. | 420 GRAMS WATER

1 LB. | 450 GRAMS BREAD FLOUR, PLUS MORE AS NEEDED

8.8 OZ. | 250 GRAMS FINE SEMOLINA FLOUR

0.7 OZ. | 20 GRAMS OLIVE OIL, PLUS MORE AS NEEDED

1 TABLESPOON | 17 GRAMS TABLE SALT, PLUS MORE TO TASTE

12 CANNED ANCHOVIES, DRAINED AND TORN

21.1 OZ. | 600 GRAMS CACIOCAVALLO CHEESE, CUBED

14 OZ. | 400 GRAMS ESCAROLE, CHOPPED

3 TOMATOES, CHOPPED

FRESH OREGANO, FINELY CHOPPED, TO TASTE

BLACK PEPPER, TO TASTE

RIANATA

YIELD: 1 LARGE FOCACCIA / **ACTIVE TIME:** 40 MINUTES / **TOTAL TIME:** 4 HOURS AND 45 MINUTES

A simple and scrumptious focaccia loaded with tomatoes and oregano. Don't hesitate to be extravagant with the latter, as *rianata* means "with oregano."

1. If using active dry yeast, warm 3½ tablespoons (1.75 oz./50 grams) of the water until it is about 105°F (40°C). Add the water and the yeast to a bowl and gently stir. Let sit until it starts to foam. Instant yeast does not need to be proofed.

2. In a large bowl, combine the flours, olive oil, yeast, and water until the dough holds together. Transfer it to a flour-dusted work surface and knead the dough until it is compact, smooth, and elastic. For further instructions on kneading dough see page 71.

3. Add the salt and knead until the dough is developed, elastic, and extensible, about 5 minutes. Form the dough into a ball and place it in an airtight container that has been greased with olive oil. Let rest at room temperature until it has doubled in size, about 2 hours.

4. Grease an 18 × 13–inch baking pan with olive oil, place the dough on it, and brush the dough with more olive oil. Cover with a kitchen towel and let rest for 30 minutes.

5. Gently stretch the dough until it covers the entire pan. Let rest for another hour.

6. Preheat the oven to 430°F (220°C). Press the anchovies and the tomatoes into the dough, sprinkle the pecorino over the focaccia, season with salt and the oregano, and drizzle olive oil over everything.

7. Place in the oven and bake for 20 to 30 minutes, until the focaccia is golden brown and crisp on the edges and the bottom. Remove and let cool slightly before serving.

INGREDIENTS:

2½ TEASPOONS | 7 GRAMS ACTIVE DRY YEAST OR 2 TEASPOONS | 6 GRAMS INSTANT YEAST

14.8 OZ. | 420 GRAMS WATER

1 LB. | 450 GRAMS BREAD FLOUR, PLUS MORE AS NEEDED

8.8 OZ. | 250 GRAMS FINE SEMOLINA FLOUR

0.7 OZ. | 20 GRAMS OLIVE OIL, PLUS MORE AS NEEDED

1 TABLESPOON | 17 GRAMS TABLE SALT, PLUS MORE TO TASTE

7 TO 8 ANCHOVIES, DRAINED

30 CHERRY TOMATOES, HALVED

8.8 OZ. | 250 GRAMS PECORINO CHEESE, GRATED

FRESH OREGANO, FINELY CHOPPED, TO TASTE

VASTEDDA CON SAMBUCO

YIELD: 1 10-INCH FOCACCIA / ACTIVE TIME: 30 MINUTES / TOTAL TIME: 4 HOURS AND 30 MINUTES

A focaccia enriched with eggs, flavored with elderflowers, and filled with salami and cheese. Delicious and really different.

INGREDIENTS:

2½ TEASPOONS | 7 GRAMS ACTIVE DRY YEAST OR 2 TEASPOONS | 6 GRAMS INSTANT YEAST

12.3 OZ. | 350 GRAMS WATER

21.1 OZ. | 600 GRAMS ALL-PURPOSE FLOUR, PLUS MORE AS NEEDED

3.5 OZ. | 100 GRAMS LARD OR BUTTER

ELDERFLOWERS, FRESH OR DRIED, TO TASTE

1½ TEASPOONS | 10 GRAMS TABLE SALT

5 EGGS

OLIVE OIL, AS NEEDED

17.6 OZ. | 500 GRAMS SLICED SALAMI

17.6 OZ. | 500 GRAMS CACIOCAVALLO OR TUMA

1. If using active dry yeast, warm 3½ tablespoons (1.75 oz./50 grams) of the water until it is about 105°F (40°C). Add the water and the yeast to a bowl and gently stir. Let sit for 5 to 10 minutes. Instant yeast does not need to be proofed.

2. In a large bowl, combine the flour, lard or butter, a handful of the elderflowers, yeast, and water until the dough holds together. If kneading by hand, transfer the dough to a flour-dusted work surface. Work it until it is compact, smooth, and elastic. For further instructions on kneading and mixing dough see page 71.

3. Add the salt and the eggs and work the dough until it is developed, elastic, and extensible, about 5 minutes. Form the dough into a ball and place it in an airtight container that has been greased with olive oil. Let rest at room temperature until it has doubled in size, about 2 hours.

4. Grease a 10-inch cast-iron skillet or round cake pan with olive oil. Transfer the dough to a flour-dusted surface and divide it in two. Roll out one piece into a disk that is the size of the pan. Place it in the pan and layer the salami and cheese on top. Roll out the second piece of dough so that it will fit within the pan, place it over the filling, and crimp the edge to seal the focaccia. Brush the top of the focaccia with olive oil, cover with greased plastic wrap, and let rest in a warm spot for 1 to 2 hours.

5. Preheat the oven to 390°F (200°C). Sprinkle elderflowers over the focaccia and drizzle olive oil over them. Place the focaccia in the oven and bake for 30 to 35 minutes, until it is golden brown and crispy. Remove from the oven and let cool slightly before serving.

SCACCIA RAGUSANA

YIELD: 3 MEDIUM FOCACCIA / **ACTIVE TIME:** 1 HOUR AND 15 MINUTES / **TOTAL TIME:** 3 HOURS AND 20 MINUTES

This layered focaccia from Ragusa and Modica is a beloved street food and comes in many variations. Popular fillings are eggplant with tomato sauce and broccoli with salsiccia. Here is a typical filling with tomato sauce, onions and caciocavallo cheese.

1. If using active dry yeast, warm 3½ tablespoons (1.75 oz./50 grams) of the water until it is about 105°F (40°C). Add the water and the yeast to a bowl and gently stir. Let sit for 5 to 10 minutes. Instant yeast does not need to be proofed.

2. In a large bowl, combine the flours, yeast, and water until the dough holds together. If kneading by hand, transfer the dough to a flour-dusted work surface. Work it until it is compact, smooth, and elastic. For further instructions on kneading and mixing dough see page 71.

3. Add the salt and work the dough until it is developed, elastic, and extensible, about 5 minutes. Form the dough into a ball and place it in an airtight container that has been greased with olive oil. Let rest at room temperature until it has doubled in size, about 2 hours.

4. Coat the bottom of a skillet with olive oil and warm over medium-low heat. When the oil starts to shimmer, add the onions and sauté until they are soft, about 12 minutes. Add the tomatoes, cover the skillet, reduce the heat, and simmer until the flavor is to your liking, 20 to 30 minutes. Season with salt and let cool completely.

INGREDIENTS:

2 TEASPOONS | 6 GRAMS ACTIVE DRY YEAST OR 1⅔ TEASPOONS | 5 GRAMS INSTANT YEAST

11.8 OZ. | 335 GRAMS WATER

21.1 OZ. | 600 GRAMS FINE SEMOLINA FLOUR, PLUS MORE AS NEEDED

1½ TEASPOONS | 10 GRAMS TABLE SALT, PLUS MORE TO TASTE

OLIVE OIL, AS NEEDED

21.1 OZ. | 600 GRAMS ONIONS, SLICED THIN

21.1 OZ. | 600 GRAMS CANNED WHOLE PEELED TOMATOES, MASHED

10.6 OZ. | 300 GRAMS CACIOCAVALLO CHEESE, GRATED

5. Preheat the oven to 430°F (220°C). Place the dough on a flour-dusted work surface, divide it into three pieces, and shape them into balls. Roll each ball into a thin rectangle. Cover with some of the tomato sauce and a generous sprinkle of the grated cheese, leaving a 1-inch border of dough (2 to 3 centimeters) around the edges. Fold the ends of the rectangles toward the center, lengthwise. Cover the rectangles with more tomato sauce and grated cheese, leaving more space near the edges. Again, fold both ends of the rectangles toward the center, lengthwise. Cover the folded dough with more sauce and grated cheese, and fold the rectangles in half.

6. Place the focaccia on a parchment-lined baking sheet, brush with olive oil, and poke holes in them with a fork. Place in the oven and bake for 25 to 30 minutes, until crispy and golden brown. Remove and let cool slightly before serving.

FOCACCIA PORTOSCUSESE

YIELD: 4 MEDIUM FOCACCIA / **ACTIVE TIME:** 40 MINUTES / **TOTAL TIME:** 3 HOURS AND 45 MINUTES

A traditional Sardinian focaccia that looks like a Neapolitan pizza but has a special dough that contains more potato than flour. A must try!

1. If using active dry yeast, warm 3½ tablespoons (1.75 oz./50 grams) of the milk until it is about 105°F (40°C). Add the milk and the yeast to a bowl and gently stir. Let sit for 5 to 10 minutes. Instant yeast does not need to be proofed.

2. In a large bowl, combine the flour, potatoes, and yeast until a soft and not too sticky dough forms. If needed, gradually add the remaining milk; how much you need depends on how watery the potatoes are.

3. Work the salt into the dough, transfer it to a flour-dusted work surface, and work the dough until it is smooth. For further instructions on kneading and mixing dough see page 71. Place the dough in an airtight container that has been greased with olive oil. Let rest at room temperature until it has increased in size, about 2 hours.

4. Coat the bottom of a skillet with olive oil and warm over medium-low heat. When the oil starts to shimmer, add the onions and sauté until they are soft, about 12 minutes. Add the tomatoes, cover the skillet, reduce the heat, and simmer until the flavor is to your liking, 20 to 30 minutes. Season with salt and let cool completely.

5. Place the dough on a flour-dusted work surface and divide it into four pieces. Shape the pieces into balls, cover with greased plastic wrap, and let rest for 1 hour.

6. Preheat the oven to 390°F (200°C) and place a baking stone or steel in the oven as it warms. Gently flatten the balls of dough and cover with the tomato sauce. Sprinkle the pecorino on top and drizzle with olive oil. Use a peel to transfer the focaccia onto the heated cooking surface and bake for about 20 to 25 minutes, until the edges and bottom are golden brown.

INGREDIENTS:

2 TEASPOONS | 6 GRAMS ACTIVE DRY YEAST OR 1⅔ TEASPOONS | 5 GRAMS INSTANT YEAST

5.3 OZ. | 150 GRAMS MILK

10.6 OZ. | 300 GRAMS BREAD FLOUR, PLUS MORE AS NEEDED

28.2 OZ. | 800 GRAMS POTATOES, BOILED, PEELED, AND MASHED

1½ TEASPOONS | 10 GRAMS TABLE SALT, PLUS MORE TO TASTE

OLIVE OIL, AS NEEDED

14 OZ. | 400 GRAMS ONIONS, SLICED THIN

14 OZ. | 400 GRAMS CANNED WHOLE PEELED TOMATOES, MASHED

7 OZ. | 200 GRAMS PECORINO CHEESE, GRATED

MUSTAZZEDDU

YIELD: 1 LARGE FOCACCIA / **ACTIVE TIME:** 40 MINUTES / **TOTAL TIME:** 4 HOURS AND 30 MINUTES

Traditionally, this was the sustenance food of the Sardinian women who baked for their community; they used to make this focaccia to feed themselves during the day-long process of making large batches of bread.

1. Place the tomatoes, garlic, basil leaves, and a generous amount of olive oil in a bowl, season with salt, and stir to combine. Let the mixture sit for 2 hours, drain it in a colander, and let drain further for 1 hour.

2. If using active dry yeast, warm 3½ tablespoons (1.75 oz./50 grams) of the water until it is about 105°F (40°C). Add the water and the yeast to a bowl and gently stir. Let sit for 5 to 10 minutes. Instant yeast does not need to be proofed.

3. In a large bowl, combine the flours, the olive oil, yeast, and water until the dough holds together. Add the salt and work the dough until it is compact, smooth, and elastic. For further instructions on kneading and mixing dough see page 71. Cover the bowl with a damp kitchen towel and let rest at room temperature until it has doubled in size, about 2 hours.

4. Place the dough on a flour-dusted work surface and roll it out until it is an approximately ¾-inch-thick disk (2 centimeters). Place it on a parchment-lined baking sheet, cover with the kitchen towel, and let rest for another hour.

5. Preheat the oven to 430°F (220°C) and place a rack in the middle position. Place the tomato mixture on the focaccia, making sure to leave some dough at the edge. Season with salt and pepper and fold the dough over the filling. You can leave the filling exposed or cover it completely; both are traditional in Sardinia.

6. Brush the dough with olive oil, place the pan directly on the bottom of the oven, and bake for 10 minutes. Lower the temperature to 390°F (200°C), transfer the focaccia to the middle rack, and bake for 30 to 40 minutes, until golden brown on the edges and on the bottom. Remove and let cool slightly before serving.

INGREDIENTS:

28.2 OZ. | 800 GRAMS CHERRY TOMATOES, CHOPPED

2 GARLIC CLOVES, CHOPPED

3 TO 4 BASIL LEAVES

1 TABLESPOON | 13.3 GRAMS OLIVE OIL, PLUS MORE AS NEEDED

1½ TEASPOONS | 10 GRAMS TABLE SALT, PLUS MORE TO TASTE

2 TEASPOONS | 6 GRAMS ACTIVE DRY YEAST OR 1⅔ TEASPOONS | 5 GRAMS INSTANT YEAST

11.6 OZ. | 330 GRAMS WATER

12.3 OZ. | 350 GRAMS FINE SEMOLINA FLOUR (SEMOLA RIMACINATA)

5.3 OZ. | 150 GRAMS BREAD FLOUR, PLUS MORE AS NEEDED

BLACK PEPPER, TO TASTE

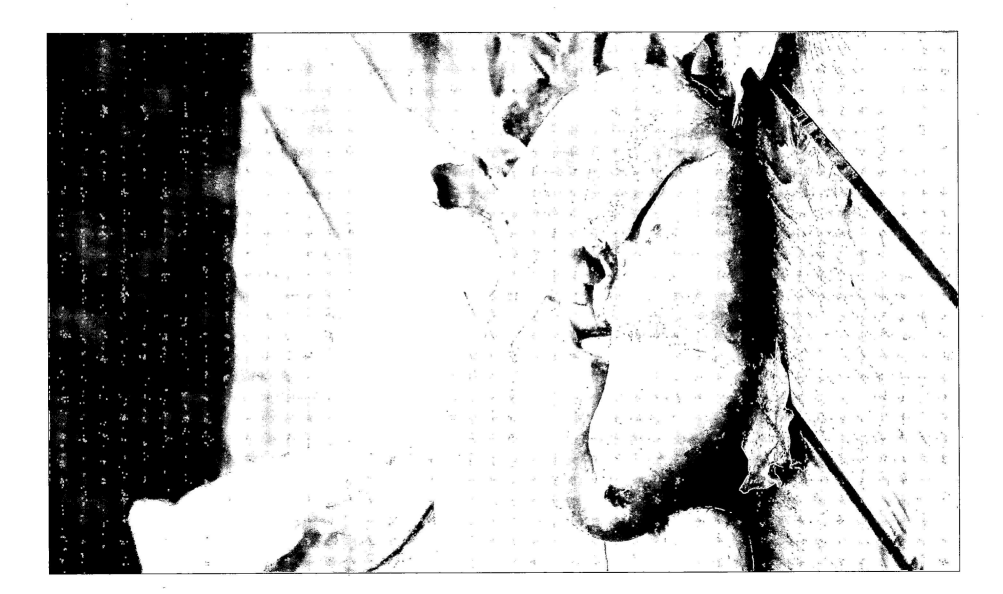

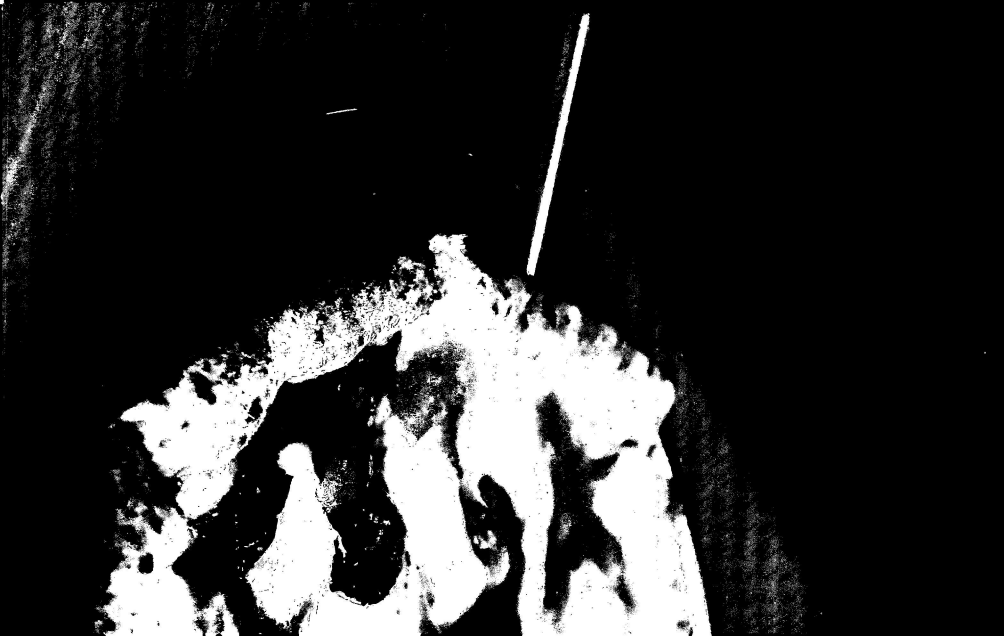

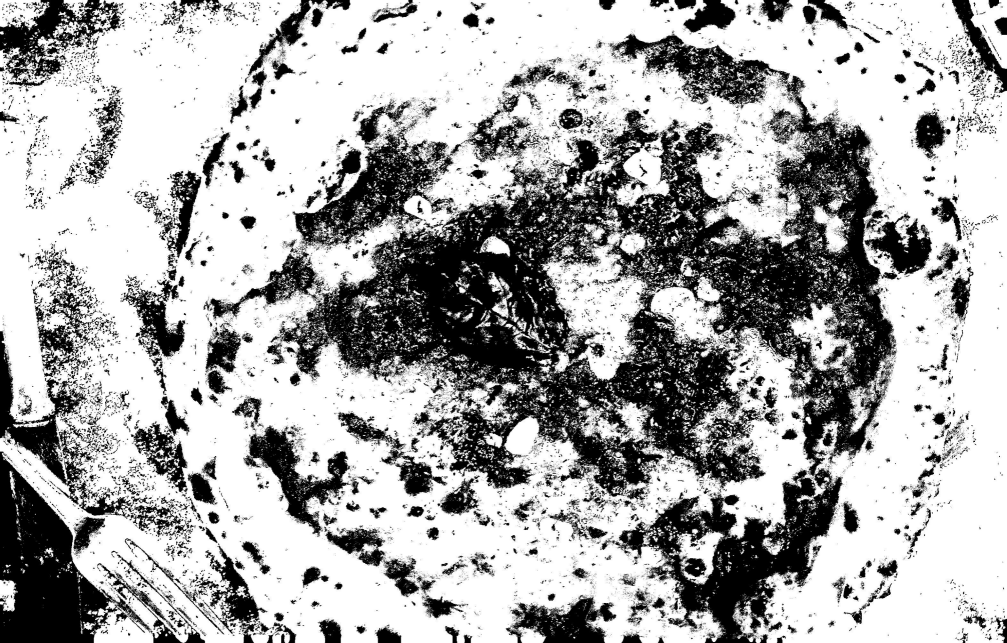

TRADITIONAL
PIZZA RECIPES

*T*he original Neapolitan pizza toppings were the essence of simplicity: tomato sauce, garlic, oregano, mozzarella, basil. As pizza evolved into a food eaten off plates in restaurants, the range of toppings expanded, inspired by the produce available around Naples. These are now the classic versions of pizza found on most pizzerias' menus all over the world.

Note: for all of these recipes, make sure the dough you are using is ready by pressing it with a finger; an indent should remain in the dough if it is ready to be shaped.

PIZZA MARINARA

YIELD: 1 PIZZA / **ACTIVE TIME:** 15 MINUTES / **TOTAL TIME:** 30 MINUTES

According to the European Union, there are only two authentic Neapolitan pizzas that deserve the TSG (Traditional Speciality Guaranteed) appellation: this and pizza margherita. Pizza marinara is possibly the oldest variety of Neapolitan pizza still popular today, and it is surprising in its simplicity. The key to making a good version of this pizza at home is to use top-notch ingredients, as that is the only way to do justice to this simple topping.

1. Place a baking stone or steel on the middle rack of the oven and preheat the oven to the maximum temperature. Dust a work surface with semolina flour, place the dough on the surface, and gently stretch it into a round. For more detailed instructions on properly stretching a ball of pizza dough see page 73.

2. Cover the dough with the sauce and top with the garlic. Season the pizza with salt and dried oregano and drizzle olive oil over the top.

3. Using a peel or a flat baking sheet, transfer the pizza to the heated baking implement in the oven. Bake for 5 to 12 minutes, depending on your oven, until the crust is golden brown and starting to char. Remove and let cool slightly before slicing and serving.

INGREDIENTS

SEMOLINA FLOUR, AS NEEDED

1 BALL PIZZA DOUGH

5.3 OZ. | 150 GRAMS RAW PIZZA SAUCE (SEE PAGE 103)

1 GARLIC CLOVE, SLICED THIN

SALT, TO TASTE

DRIED OREGANO, TO TASTE

OLIVE OIL, TO TASTE

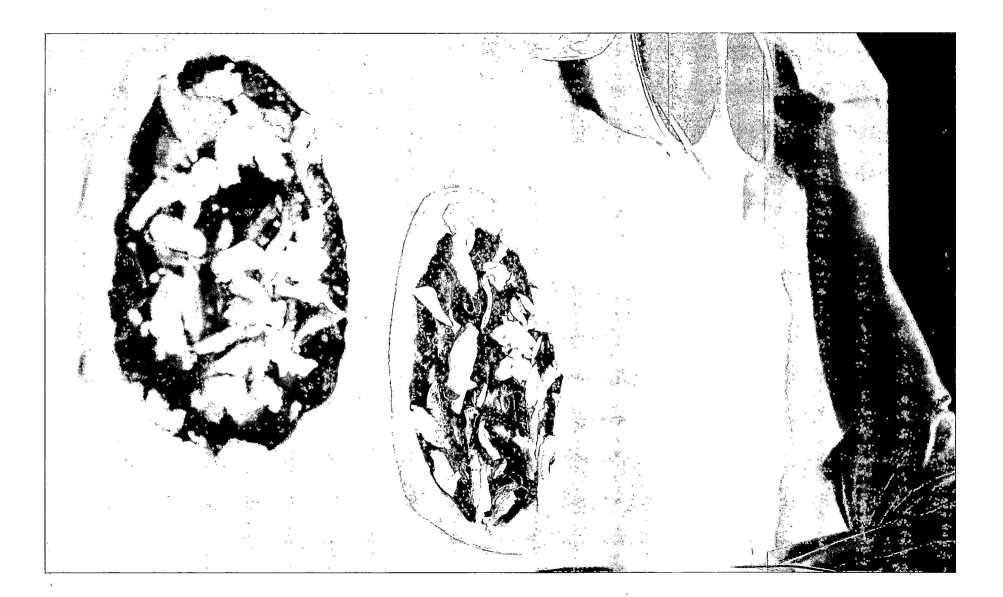

MARGHERITA

YIELD: 1 PIZZA / **ACTIVE TIME:** 15 MINUTES / **TOTAL TIME:** 30 MINUTES

For most, both in Italy and abroad, this is the true original Neapolitan pizza: gooey mozzarella and a tomato sauce base. *Buon appetito.*

1. Place a baking stone or steel on the middle rack of the oven and preheat the oven to the maximum temperature. Dust a work surface with semolina flour, place the dough on the surface, and gently stretch it into a round. For more detailed instructions on properly stretching a ball of pizza dough see page 73.

2. Cover the dough with the sauce and top with the mozzarella and basil leaves. Season the pizza with salt and drizzle olive oil over the top.

3. Using a peel or a flat baking sheet, transfer the pizza to the heated baking implement in the oven. Bake for 5 to 12 minutes, depending on your oven, until the crust is golden brown and starting to char. Remove and let cool slightly before slicing and serving.

INGREDIENTS:

SEMOLINA FLOUR, AS NEEDED

1 BALL PIZZA DOUGH

3.5 OZ. | 100 GRAMS RAW PIZZA SAUCE (SEE PAGE 103)

3.5 OZ. | 100 GRAMS FRESH MOZZARELLA CHEESE (FIOR DI LATTE OR BUFFALO), DRAINED AND CUT INTO SHORT STRIPS

FRESH BASIL LEAVES, TO TASTE

SALT, TO TASTE

OLIVE OIL, TO TASTE

ROMANA

YIELD: 1 PIZZA / **ACTIVE TIME:** 15 MINUTES / **TOTAL TIME:** 30 MINUTES

There are two different versions of this pizza: with or without mozzarella. It also has two names: it is *Romana* to the Neapolitans, who created the topping, and *Napoli* for everyone else. What never changes in this pizza is the presence of tomato sauce, anchovies, capers, and oregano.

1. Place a baking stone or steel on the middle rack of the oven and preheat the oven to the maximum temperature. Dust a work surface with semolina flour, place the dough on the surface, and gently stretch it into a round. For more detailed instructions on properly stretching a ball of pizza dough see page 73.

2. Cover the dough with the sauce and top with the mozzarella, anchovies, and capers. Season the pizza with salt and oregano and drizzle olive oil over the top.

3. Using a peel or a flat baking sheet, transfer the pizza to the heated baking implement in the oven. Bake for 5 to 12 minutes, depending on your oven, until the crust is golden brown and starting to char. Remove and let cool slightly before slicing and serving.

INGREDIENTS:

3.5 OZ | 100 GRAMS FRESH MOZZARELLA CHEESE (FIORDILATTE OR BUFFALO), DRAINED AND CUT INTO SHORT STRIPS (OPTIONAL)

4 TO 5 ANCHOVIES, TORN

1 TABLESPOON | 8.6 GRAMS CAPERS

SALT, TO TASTE

DRIED OREGANO, TO TASTE

OLIVE OIL, TO TASTE

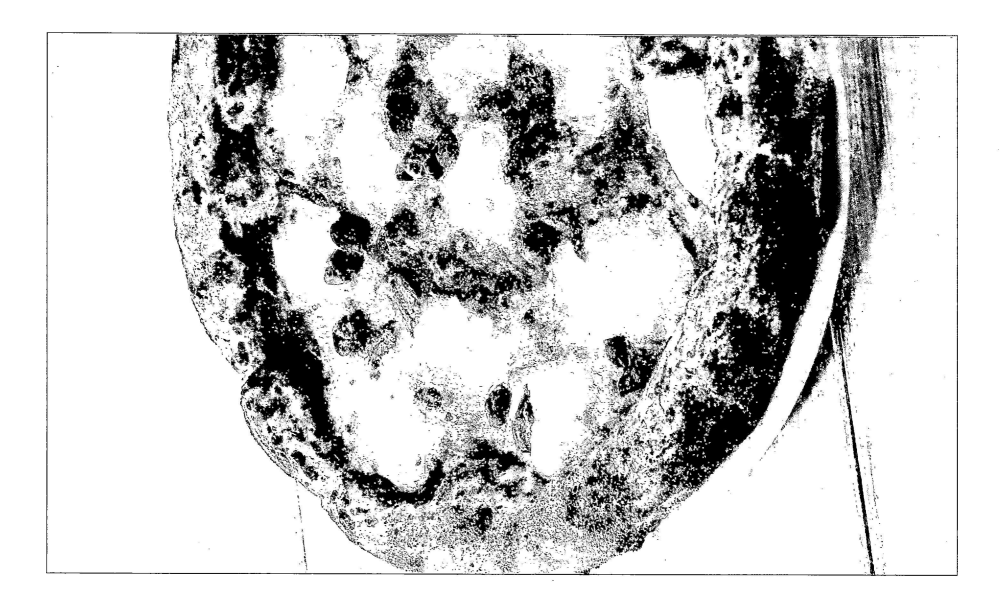

CAPRICCIOSA

YIELD: 1 PIZZA / **ACTIVE TIME:** 15 MINUTES / **TOTAL TIME:** 30 MINUTES

*C*apricciosa means "capricious" in Italian, and in Neapolitan pizza jargon this means a topping that, as it cannot make a simple decision, simply overdoes it.

1. Place a baking stone or steel on the middle rack of the oven and preheat the oven to the maximum temperature. Dust a work surface with semolina flour, place the dough on the surface, and gently stretch it into a round. For more detailed instructions on properly stretching a ball of pizza dough see page 73.

2. Cover the dough with the sauce and top with the artichokes and mushrooms. Season the pizza with salt and drizzle olive oil over the top.

3. Using a peel or a flat baking sheet, transfer the pizza to the heated baking implement in the oven. Bake for about 5 minutes, until the crust starts to brown. Remove the pizza, distribute the mozzarella, prosciutto, and olives over the top, and return the pizza to the oven. Bake for about 10 minutes, until the crust is golden brown and starting to char. Remove from the oven and let cool slightly before slicing and serving.

INGREDIENTS:

SEMOLINA FLOUR, AS NEEDED

1 BALL PIZZA DOUGH

2.8 OZ. | 80 GRAMS RAW PIZZA SAUCE (SEE PAGE 103)

2 ARTICHOKE HEARTS IN OLIVE OIL, CUT INTO WEDGES

1.4 OZ. | 40 GRAMS MUSHROOMS, SLICED

SALT, TO TASTE

OLIVE OIL, TO TASTE

3.1 OZ. | 90 GRAMS FRESH MOZZARELLA CHEESE, DRAINED AND CUT INTO SHORT STRIPS

2 SLICES PROSCIUTTO, TORN

1 SMALL HANDFUL PITTED BLACK OLIVES

FRESH BASIL LEAVES, TO TASTE

BOSCAIOLA

YIELD: 1 PIZZA / **ACTIVE TIME:** 25 MINUTES / **TOTAL TIME:** 40 MINUTES

*B*oscaiola means "from the woods" in Italian, referring to mushrooms and game. Here, the game component is just humble sausage, but the pizza retains its earthy and substantial promise.

1. Place a baking stone or steel on the middle rack of the oven and preheat the oven to the maximum temperature. Coat the bottom of a skillet with olive oil and warm over medium high heat. When the oil starts to shimmer, add the sausage and cook until it starts to brown, about 6 minutes. Remove from heat and set aside.

2. Dust a work surface with semolina flour, place the dough on the surface, and gently stretch it into a round. For more detailed instructions on properly stretching a ball of pizza dough see page 73.

3. Cover the dough with the sauce and top with the mushrooms and sausage. Season the pizza with salt and drizzle olive oil over the top.

4. Using a peel or a flat baking sheet, transfer the pizza to the heated baking implement in the oven. Bake for about 5 minutes, until the crust starts to brown. Remove the pizza, distribute the mozzarella over the top, and return the pizza to the oven. Bake for about 10 minutes, until the crust is golden brown and starting to char. Remove and let cool slightly before slicing and serving.

INGREDIENTS:

2.8 OZ. | 80 GRAMS RAW PIZZA SAUCE
(SEE PAGE 103)

2.1 OZ. | 60 GRAMS MUSHROOMS, SLICED

SALT, TO TASTE

3.1 OZ. | 90 GRAMS FRESH MOZZARELLA
CHEESE, DRAINED AND CUT INTO SHORT
STRIPS

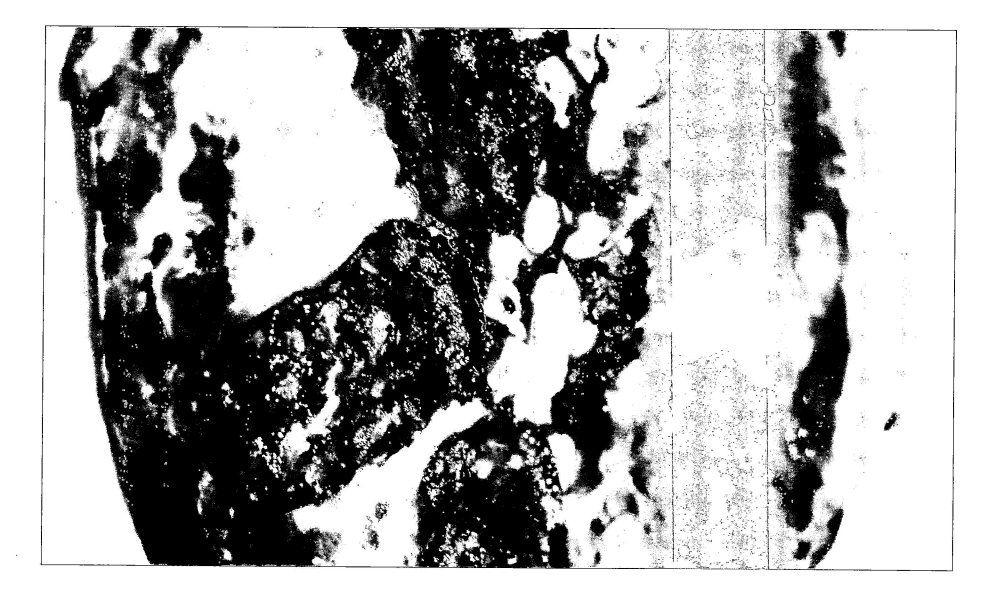

DIAVOLA

YIELD: 1 PIZZA / **ACTIVE TIME:** 15 MINUTES / **TOTAL TIME:** 30 MINUTES

This pizza "from hell" refers to its hot and spicy bite. This is the topping that inspired the pepperoni pizza that became classic in America.

1. Place a baking stone or steel on the middle rack of the oven and preheat the oven to the maximum temperature. Combine the olive oil and red pepper flakes in a small bowl and set aside.

2. Dust a work surface with semolina flour, place the dough on the surface, and gently stretch it into a round. For more detailed instructions on properly stretching a ball of pizza dough see page 73.

3. Cover the dough with the sauce and top with the cheese and salami. Season the pizza with salt and oregano.

4. Using a peel or a flat baking sheet, transfer the pizza to the heated baking implement in the oven. Bake for about 10 minutes, until the crust is golden brown and starting to char. Remove and let cool slightly before slicing and serving.

INGREDIENTS:

1 OZ. | 30 GRAMS OLIVE OIL, PLUS MORE TO TASTE

RED PEPPER FLAKES, TO TASTE

SEMOLINA FLOUR, AS NEEDED

1 BALL PIZZA DOUGH

2.8 OZ. | 80 GRAMS RAW PIZZA SAUCE (SEE PAGE 103)

2.4 OZ. | 70 GRAMS CACIOCAVALLO OR PROVOLA CHEESE, CUBED

4 TO 5 SLICES SPICY SALAMI

SALT, TO TASTE

DRIED OREGANO, TO TASTE

CARRETTIERA

YIELD: 1 PIZZA / **ACTIVE TIME:** 30 MINUTES / **TOTAL TIME:** 45 MINUTES

The name refers to a sandwich filling popular with the Neapolitan *carrettieri*, who spent the day pushing around goods in a wooden trolley. Substantial and extremely tasty, this is a must, assuming one can get hold of broccoli rabe.

1. Place a baking stone or steel on the middle rack of the oven and preheat the oven to the maximum temperature. Coat the bottom of a skillet with olive oil and warm over medium high heat. When the oil starts to shimmer, add the garlic and broccoli rabe and sauté until the broccoli rabe is soft, about 8 minutes. Season with salt and pepper, add the sausage, and cook until the sausage is browned, about 6 minutes. Remove from heat and let cool.

2. Dust a work surface with semolina flour, place the dough on the surface, and gently stretch it into a round. For more detailed instructions on properly stretching a ball of pizza dough see page 73.

3. Cover the dough with the sautéed broccoli rabe and sausage and top with the mozzarella. Drizzle olive oil over the pizza.

4. Using a peel or a flat baking sheet, transfer the pizza to the heated baking implement in the oven. Bake for about 10 minutes, until the crust is golden brown and starting to char. Remove and let cool slightly before slicing and serving.

INGREDIENTS:

½ LINK ITALIAN SAUSAGE, CHOPPED

SEMOLINA FLOUR, AS NEEDED

1 BALL PIZZA DOUGH

2.8 OZ. | 80 GRAMS FRESH MOZZARELLA CHEESE, DRAINED AND CUT INTO SHORT STRIPS

QUATTRO STAGIONI

YIELD: 1 PIZZA / ACTIVE TIME: 15 MINUTES / TOTAL TIME: 30 MINUTES

Meaning "four seasons" in Italian, the name here refers to the topping being divided into four sections, each one featuring a different ingredient. The toppings here are the same used in pizza capricciosa, the difference being that here they are separated.

1. Place a baking stone or steel on the middle rack of the oven and preheat the oven to the maximum temperature. Dust a work surface with semolina flour, place the dough on the surface, and gently stretch it into a round. For more detailed instructions on properly stretching a ball of pizza dough see page 73.

2. Cover the dough with the sauce and the mozzarella. Place each of the artichokes, prosciutto, mushrooms, and olives on their own section of the pizza. Season the pizza with salt and drizzle olive oil over the top.

3. Using a peel or a flat baking sheet, transfer the pizza to the heated baking implement in the oven. Bake for about 10 minutes, until the crust is golden brown and starting to char. Remove and let cool slightly before slicing and serving.

NOTE: If your oven is not very hot, it is recommended that you wait to add the olives and the prosciutto a few minutes before the pizza is fully baked, so as not to dry out the prosciutto or burn the olives.

INGREDIENTS:

SEMOLINA FLOUR, AS NEEDED

1 BALL PIZZA DOUGH

2.8 OZ. | 80 GRAMS RAW PIZZA SAUCE (SEE PAGE 103)

3.1 OZ. | 90 GRAMS FRESH MOZZARELLA CHEESE, DRAINED AND CUT INTO SHORT STRIPS

2 ARTICHOKE HEARTS IN OLIVE OIL, CUT INTO WEDGES

2 SLICES PROSCIUTTO, TORN

1.4 OZ. | 40 GRAMS MUSHROOMS, SLICED

1 SMALL HANDFUL PITTED BLACK OLIVES

SALT, TO TASTE

OLIVE OIL, TO TASTE

QUATTRO FORMAGGI

YIELD: 1 PIZZA / ACTIVE TIME: 15 MINUTES / TOTAL TIME: 30 MINUTES

That's right: "four cheeses." As you might expect, this is the most gooey traditional Italian pizza, and a must-have for cheese lovers.

1. Place a baking stone or steel on the middle rack of the oven and preheat the oven to the maximum temperature. Dust a work surface with semolina flour, place the dough on the surface, and gently stretch it into a round. For more detailed instructions on properly stretching a ball of pizza dough see page 73.

2. Cover the dough with the cheeses. Season the pizza with salt and pepper and drizzle olive oil over the top.

3. Using a peel or a flat baking sheet, transfer the pizza to the heated baking implement in the oven. Bake for about 10 minutes, until the crust is golden brown and starting to char. Remove and let cool slightly before slicing and serving.

INGREDIENTS:

SEMOLINA FLOUR, AS NEEDED

... OZ. | 50 GRAMS FONTINA OR PROVOLONE CHEESE, SHREDDED

1.75 OZ. | 50 GRAMS GORGONZOLA CHEESE, CRUMBLED

1.75 OZ. | 50 GRAMS PECORINO OR PARMESAN CHEESE, GRATED

SALT AND PEPPER, TO TASTE

OLIVE OIL, TO TASTE

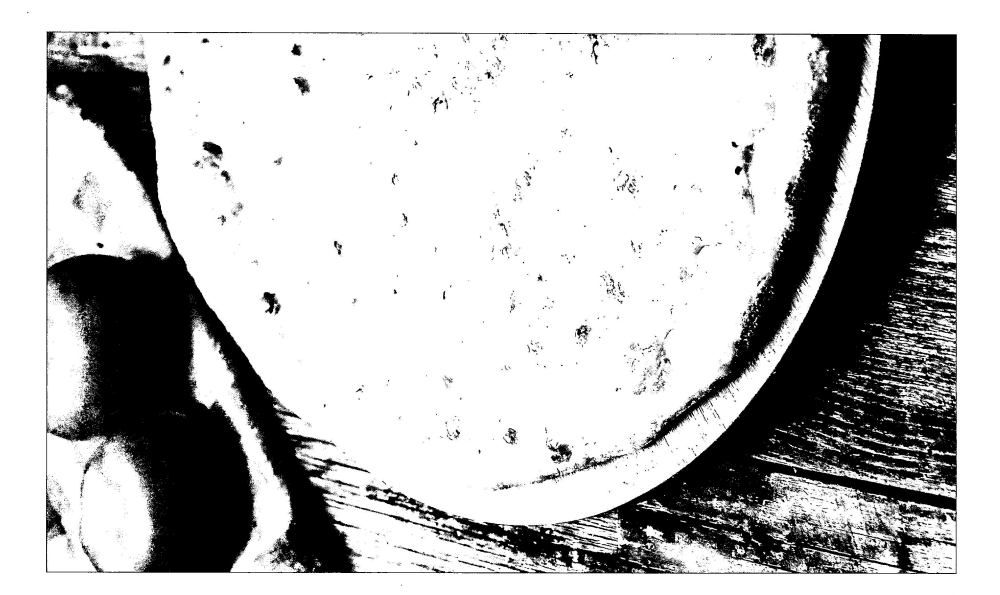

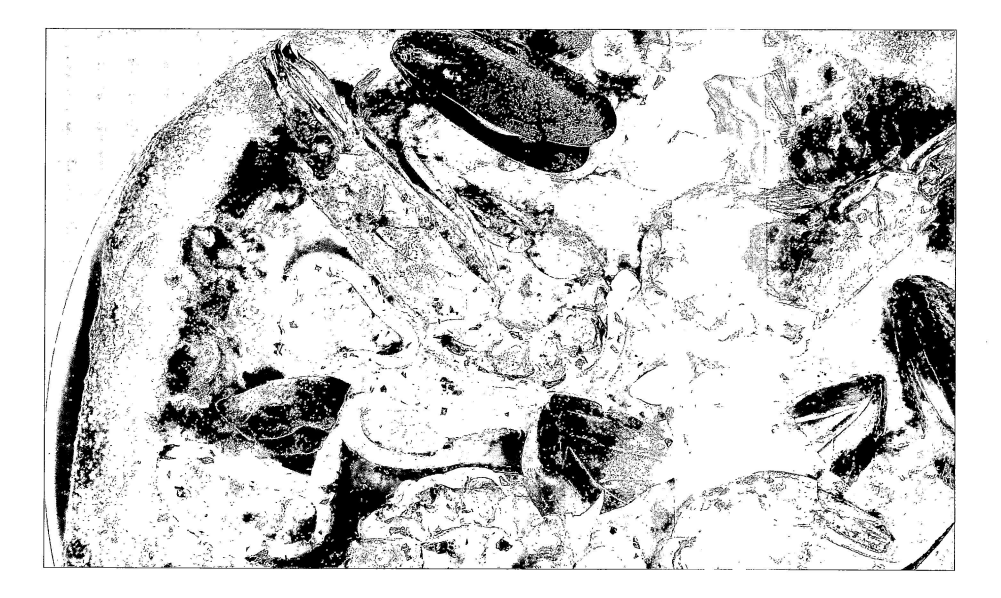

PESCATORA

YIELD: 1 PIZZA / **ACTIVE TIME:** 25 MINUTES / **TOTAL TIME:** 40 MINUTES

You can take the easy road and use a frozen and/or precooked mix of seafood or go the slightly more arduous—and much more delicious—route of using fresh seafood.

1. Place a baking stone or steel on the middle rack of the oven and preheat the oven to the maximum temperature. Coat the bottom of a skillet with olive oil and warm over medium-high heat. When the oil starts to shimmer, add all of the seafood and the garlic. Season with salt and red pepper flakes and cook until the mussels have opened and the rest of the seafood is just cooked through, about 5 minutes. Remove from heat, discard any mussels that do not open, and remove the meat from those that have opened.

2. Dust a work surface with the semolina flour, place the dough on the surface, and gently stretch it into a round. For more detailed instructions on properly stretching a ball of pizza dough see page 73. Cover the dough with the sauce and season with oregano and pepper.

3. Using a peel or a flat baking sheet, transfer the pizza to the heated baking implement in the oven. Bake for 5 to 8 minutes, until the crust starts to brown. Remove the pizza, distribute the seafood over the pizza, drizzle olive oil on top, and return the pizza to the oven. Bake for about 5 minutes, until the crust is golden brown and starting to char. Remove and let cool slightly before garnishing with the parsley, slicing, and serving.

INGREDIENTS:

OLIVE OIL, AS NEEDED

5 LARGE PRAWNS, PEELED

1 HANDFUL SQUID RINGS

6 MUSSELS, DEBEARDED AND RINSED WELL

1.4 OZ. | 40 GRAMS BABY OCTOPUS

½ GARLIC CLOVE, MINCED

SALT AND PEPPER, TO TASTE

RED PEPPER FLAKES, TO TASTE

SEMOLINA FLOUR, AS NEEDED

1 BALL PIZZA DOUGH

3.5 OZ. | 100 GRAMS RAW PIZZA SAUCE (SEE PAGE 103)

DRIED OREGANO, TO TASTE

FRESH PARSLEY LEAVES, FOR GARNISH

CAPRESE

YIELD: 1 PIZZA / **ACTIVE TIME:** 15 MINUTES / **TOTAL TIME:** 30 MINUTES

A variation on the margherita pizza that is inspired by the classic caprese salad. Perfect for a hot summer night.

1. Place a baking stone or steel on the middle rack of the oven and preheat the oven to the maximum temperature. Dust a work surface with semolina flour, place the dough on the surface, and gently stretch it into a round. For more detailed instructions on properly stretching a ball of pizza dough see page 73.

2. Cover the dough with the sauce and top with the mozzarella and tomatoes. Season the pizza with salt, pepper, and oregano and drizzle olive oil over the top.

3. Using a peel or a flat baking sheet, transfer the pizza to the heated baking implement in the oven. Bake for about 10 minutes, until the crust is golden brown and starting to char. Remove and let cool slightly before garnishing with the basil, slicing, and serving.

INGREDIENTS:

. . . .

CHEESE (FIOR DI LATTE OR BUFFALO), DRAINED AND SLICED

1 TOMATO, SLICED

SALT AND PEPPER, TO TASTE

DRIED OREGANO, TO TASTE

OLIVE OIL, TO TASTE

FRESH BASIL LEAVES, FOR GARNISH

MARI E MONTI

YIELD: 1 PIZZA / **ACTIVE TIME:** 35 MINUTES / **TOTAL TIME:** 55 MINUTES

Translated as "sea and mountains," this pizza does indeed combine *frutti di mare* with the mushrooms that grow in the mountain forests.

1. Place a baking stone or steel on the middle rack of the oven and preheat the oven to the maximum temperature. Place the mushrooms in a bowl, season with salt and pepper, and generously drizzle olive oil over them. Stir to combine and let the mixture sit for 10 minutes. Drain and set aside.

2. Coat the bottom of a skillet with olive oil and warm over medium-high heat. When the oil starts to shimmer, add the prawns, mussels, and garlic, season with salt and the red pepper flakes, and sauté until the prawns are cooked and the mussels have opened, about 5 minutes. Remove from heat, discard any mussels that do not open, and remove the meat from those that have opened.

3. Dust a work surface with the semolina flour, place the dough on the surface, and gently stretch it into a round. For more detailed instructions on properly stretching a ball of pizza dough see page 73. Cover the dough with the mozzarella and mushrooms, season with salt, and drizzle olive oil over the pizza.

4. Using a peel or a flat baking sheet, transfer the pizza to the heated baking implement in the oven. Bake for 5 to 8 minutes, until the crust starts to brown. Remove the pizza, distribute the seafood over the top, and return the pizza to the oven. Bake for about 5 minutes, until the crust is golden brown and starting to char. Remove and let cool slightly before garnishing with the parsley, slicing, and serving.

INGREDIENTS:

2.1 OZ. | 60 GRAMS MUSHROOMS, CHOPPED

SALT AND PEPPER, TO TASTE

OLIVE OIL, AS NEEDED

5 LARGE PRAWNS, PEELED

1 SMALL HANDFUL MUSSELS, DEBEARDED AND RINSED WELL

½ GARLIC CLOVE, MINCED

RED PEPPER FLAKES, TO TASTE

SEMOLINA FLOUR, AS NEEDED

1 BALL PIZZA DOUGH

2.8 OZ. | 80 GRAMS FRESH MOZZARELLA CHEESE, DRAINED AND CUT INTO SHORT STRIPS

FRESH PARSLEY, FOR GARNISH

ORTOLANA

As you may expect of a pizza that trumpets being "from the garden," the topping features no cheese—just tomato sauce and a selection of vegetables.

1. Place a baking stone or steel on the middle rack of the oven and preheat the oven to the maximum temperature. Place the mushrooms in a bowl, season with salt and pepper, and generously drizzle olive oil over them. Stir to combine and let the mixture sit for 10 minutes. Drain and set aside.

2. Place the bell pepper and eggplant on an aluminum foil–lined baking sheet, season with salt and pepper, drizzle olive oil over the vegetables, and place in the oven. Roast until they are tender and browned, about 25 minutes. Remove from the oven and let cool.

3. Dust a work surface with the semolina flour, place the dough on the surface, and gently stretch it into a round. For more detailed instructions on properly stretching a ball of pizza dough see page 73.

4. Cover the dough with the sauce and top with the mushrooms, peppers, eggplant, onion, basil leaves, and oregano. Season the pizza with salt and drizzle olive oil over the top.

5. Using a peel or a flat baking sheet, transfer the pizza to the heated baking implement in the oven. Bake for 10 to 15 minutes, until the crust is golden brown and starting to char. Remove and let cool slightly before slicing and serving.

INGREDIENTS:

1.5 OZ. | 40 GRAMS MUSHROOMS, CLEANED

SEMOLINA FLOUR, AS NEEDED

1 BALL PIZZA DOUGH

3.5 OZ. | 100 GRAMS RAW PIZZA SAUCE (SEE PAGE 103)

¼ ONION, SLICED

FRESH BASIL LEAVES, TO TASTE

DRIED OREGANO, TO TASTE

REGIONAL
AMERICAN PIZZA

Just as pizza developed in Italy based on what regional climates could yield in terms of ingredients, and also the cultures that inhabited those regions, when Italian immigrants settled in the United States, pizza entered a new phase based on location and availability of products. The following recipes describe how to make the essential American-style pizzas.

NEW YORK THIN-CRUST PIZZA

YIELD: 1 PIZZA / **ACTIVE TIME:** 15 MINUTES / **TOTAL TIME:** 30 MINUTES

The prototypical American pizza is this simple, pliable, thin-crust pie from New York City, typically served with a very simple topping of marinara sauce and mozzarella. For best results, shred the mozzarella yourself rather than buying it already shredded—it will melt better.

1. Place a baking stone or steel on the middle rack of the oven and preheat the oven to the maximum temperature. Dust a work surface with the semolina flour, place the dough on the surface, and gently stretch it into a round. For more detailed instructions on properly stretching a ball of pizza dough see page 73. Cover the dough with the sauce and top with the mozzarella and basil leaves. Season with the oregano and drizzle olive oil over the pizza.

2. Using a peel or a flat baking sheet, transfer the pizza to the heated baking implement in the oven. Bake for about 15 minutes, until the crust is golden brown and starting to char. Remove and let cool slightly before slicing and serving.

INGREDIENTS:

SEMOLINA FLOUR, AS NEEDED

1 BALL 24-HOUR PIZZA DOUGH WITH 62 PERCENT HYDRATION (SEE PAGE 111)

3.2 OZ. | 90 GRAMS RAW PIZZA SAUCE (SEE PAGE 103)

5.3 OZ. | 150 GRAMS LOW-MOISTURE MOZZARELLA CHEESE, SHREDDED

DRIED OREGANO, TO TASTE

OLIVE OIL, TO TASTE

NEW HAVEN TOMATO PIE

YIELD: 1 PIZZA / ACTIVE TIME: 15 MINUTES / TOTAL TIME: 30 MINUTES

In New Haven, pizza generally does not include a layer of melted mozzarella on top, allowing the tomato sauce to shine, completed by a good sprinkle of grated pecorino cheese and a generous drizzle of quality olive oil. When the mozzarella is present, it comes in smaller amounts than most American pies, functioning as a topping itself rather than a base for other toppings.

1. Place a baking stone or steel on the middle rack of the oven and preheat the oven to the maximum temperature. Dust a work surface with the semolina flour, place the dough on the surface, and gently stretch it into a round. For more detailed instructions on properly stretching a ball of pizza dough see page 73. Cover the dough with the sauce, top with the pecorino, and drizzle olive oil over the pizza. If desired, top with mozzarella and basil leaves.

2. Using a peel or a flat baking sheet, transfer the pizza to the heated baking implement in the oven. Bake for about 10 minutes, until the crust is golden brown and starting to char. Remove and let cool slightly before slicing and serving.

5.3 OZ. | 150 GRAMS RAW PIZZA SAUCE (SEE PAGE 103)

1 OZ. | 30 GRAMS PECORINO CHEESE, GRATED

1.75 OZ. | 50 GRAMS FRESH MOZZARELLA CHEESE, DRAINED AND CUT INTO SHORT STRIPS (OPTIONAL)

FRESH BASIL LEAVES, TO TASTE (OPTIONAL)

OLIVE OIL, TO TASTE

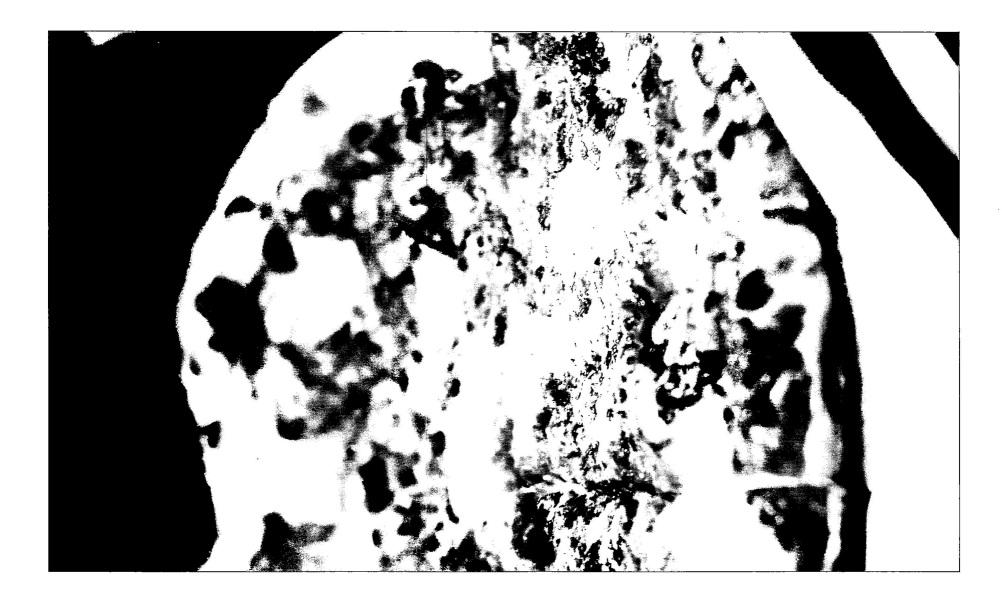

CHICAGO DEEP-DISH PIZZA

YIELD: 1 PIZZA / **ACTIVE TIME:** 45 MINUTES / **TOTAL TIME:** 3 HOURS

The classic pizza from Chicago is something between pizza and pie. It has the depth and flaky crust of a pie and is overflowing with cheese and tomato sauce. A delicious, decadent treat.

INGREDIENTS:

1⅓ TEASPOONS | 3.75 GRAMS ACTIVE DRY YEAST OR 1 TEASPOON | 3 GRAMS INSTANT YEAST

5.3 OZ. | 150 GRAMS WARM WATER (105°F | 40°C)

7 OZ. | 200 GRAMS ALL-PURPOSE FLOUR, PLUS MORE AS NEEDED

2.6 OZ. | 75 GRAMS YELLOW CORNMEAL

1 TEASPOON | 6 GRAMS SUGAR

¾ TEASPOON | 4.5 GRAMS TABLE SALT

2.1 OZ. | 60 GRAMS UNSALTED BUTTER, ½ MELTED AND ½ AT ROOM TEMPERATURE

OLIVE OIL, AS NEEDED

8.8 OZ. | 250 GRAMS LOW-MOISTURE MOZZARELLA CHEESE, SHREDDED

1 LB. | 450 GRAMS RAW PIZZA SAUCE (SEE PAGE 103)

1 OZ. | 30 GRAMS PARMESAN CHEESE, GRATED

⅓ RED BELL PEPPER, SLICED (OPTIONAL)

1. If using active dry yeast, warm 3½ tablespoons (1.75 oz./50 grams) of the water until it is about 105°F (40°C). Add the water and the yeast to a bowl and gently stir. Let sit for 5 to 10 minutes. Instant yeast does not need to be proofed.

2. In a large bowl, combine the flour, cornmeal, sugar, salt, melted butter, yeast, and water. Work the mixture until it just holds together. If kneading by hand, transfer it to a flour-dusted work surface . Work it until it is compact, smooth, and elastic. For further instructions on kneading dough see page 73. Form the dough into a ball and place it in an airtight container that has been greased with olive oil. Let rest in a warm spot until it has doubled in size, about 1 hour.

3. Place the dough on a flour-dusted work surface and roll it out to an approximately ¼-inch-thick rectangle (½ centimeter thick). Spread the softened butter over the rectangle and roll up the dough into a tight cylinder. Roll out the dough into a ¼-inch-thick rectangle (6 centimeters thick) and then fold it as you would a letter you were going to put into an envelope. Bring the edges toward the center and pinch to form a ball. Place the dough in a greased bowl, cover it with a damp kitchen towel, and let it rest at room temperature until it has doubled in size, about 45 minutes.

4. Preheat the oven to 425°F (220°C). Place the dough on a flour-dusted work surface and roll it out into an approximately ¼-inch-thick disk that is a bit larger than the dish you will use to bake it. Grease the dish with olive oil and carefully place the dough in it. A good technique to transfer the dough is to roll it loosely around the rolling pin and then unroll it into the pan.

5. Cover the dough with the mozzarella and top with the sauce, Parmesan, and pepper (if using). Place the pizza in the oven and bake for 25 to 30 minutes, until the crust is golden brown and the cheese is melted. Remove and let cool for 10 minutes before slicing and serving.

DETROIT-STYLE PIZZA

YIELD: 1 PIZZA / **ACTIVE TIME:** 25 MINUTES / **TOTAL TIME:** 1 HOUR AND 15 MINUTES

I n Detroit, pizza is not round but square, very much like traditional Italian focaccia, and, in the American tradition, it is loaded with gooey cheese.

1. Preheat the oven to the maximum temperature. Grease an 11 × 14–inch baking pan with olive oil, place the dough on it, and gently stretch it until it covers the pan, taking care to deflate the dough as little as possible. If time allows, stretch the dough in steps, letting it rest for 10 to 15 minutes before stretching it again.

2. Drizzle olive oil over the dough and cover it with the cheese. Spoon the sauce on top, making sure to leave some cheese-only spots. If desired, top with the pepperoni. Place the pizza on the lowest rack of the oven and bake for about 15 minutes, until the edges are crunchy and nearly charred. Remove and let cool briefly before slicing and serving.

INGREDIENTS:

OLIVE OIL, AS NEEDED

[illegible] DOUGH [illegible]

[illegible]

[illegible]

[illegible] PIZZA SAUCE
(SEE PAGE 165)

6 OZ. | 170 GRAMS PEPPERONI (OPTIONAL)

ST. LOUIS–STYLE PIZZA

YIELD: 1 PIZZA / **ACTIVE TIME:** 25 MINUTES / **TOTAL TIME:** 1 HOUR AND 15 MINUTES

There are two distinctive features of St. Louis pizza: the cracker-thin crust, which is not leavened and therefore quick to prepare, and the cheese, a local blend called Provel, which can be approximated at home by blending cheddar, Swiss, and provolone.

1. In a large bowl, combine the flour, baking powder, salt, olive oil, corn syrup, and water. Work the mixture until it is a very stiff dough. Form the dough into a ball, cover with a damp kitchen towel, and let it rest at room temperature for 30 minutes.

2. Place a baking stone or steel on the middle rack of the oven and preheat it to 450°F (230°C). Place a baking stone or steel on the middle rack of the oven and preheat the oven to the maximum temperature. Dust a work surface with semolina flour, place the dough on it, and roll it into a paper-thin disk, while letting it relax and become more extensible at regular intervals.

3. Dust a peel or a flat baking sheet with semolina flour, transfer the dough onto it, and cover with the sauce. Combine the cheeses in a bowl and top the pizza with the mixture. Distribute the sausage and pepperoni (if using) over the pizza, transfer it to the heated baking implement in the oven, and bake for about 10 minutes, until the crust is crispy and golden brown. Remove and let cool slightly before slicing and serving.

INGREDIENTS:

5.3 OZ. | 150 GRAMS ALL-PURPOSE FLOUR

½ TEASPOON | 2.5 GRAMS BAKING POWDER

½ TEASPOON | 3 GRAMS TABLE SALT

1½ TEASPOONS | 6 GRAMS OLIVE OIL

1½ TEASPOONS | 6 GRAMS DARK CORN SYRUP

2.6 OZ. | 75 GRAMS WATER

SEMOLINA FLOUR, TO TASTE

7 OZ. | 200 GRAMS RAW PIZZA SAUCE
(SEE PAGE 103)

1.75 OZ. | 50 GRAMS SHARP WHITE CHEDDAR
CHEESE, SHREDDED

1.75 OZ. | 50 GRAMS SWISS CHEESE, SHREDDED

1.75 OZ. | 50 GRAMS SMOKED PROVOLONE
CHEESE, SHREDDED

2.1 OZ. | 60 GRAMS ITALIAN SAUSAGE, CHOPPED
AND CASING REMOVED

1.75 OZ. | 50 GRAMS PEPPERONI (OPTIONAL)

CALIFORNIA-STYLE PIZZA

YIELD: 1 PIZZA / **ACTIVE TIME:** 25 MINUTES / **TOTAL TIME:** 40 MINUTES

In the 1980s, California's kitchens forever changed the "face" of pizza, creating the gourmet pizza that quickly influenced the rest of the world. The main concept behind Californian pizza is creativity. According to Ed LaDou, the main chef behind this new wave, toppings are akin to the artist's color palette: every combination is allowed, so long as it tastes good. The typical Californian pizza is white and features fresh, local produce. Here's a simple version with nettles

Place a baking stone or steel on the middle rack of the oven and preheat the oven to the maximum temperature. Dust a work surface with the semolina flour, place the dough on the surface, and gently stretch it into a round. For more detailed instructions on properly stretching a ball of pizza dough see page 73. Drizzle olive oil over the dough, cover it with the mozzarella (if using), and top with the nettles. Season with salt and pepper and drizzle olive oil over the pizza.

2. Using a peel or a flat baking sheet, transfer the pizza to the heated baking implement in the oven. Bake for about 10 minutes, until the crust is golden brown and starting to char. Remove, sprinkle the ricotta salata over the pizza, and let cool slightly before slicing and serving.

(SEE PAGE 108)

OLIVE OIL, TO TASTE

1.4 OZ. | 40 GRAMS LOW-MOISTURE MOZZARELLA CHEESE, SHREDDED (OPTIONAL)

3.5 OZ. | 100 GRAMS WILD NETTLES, BOILED, DRAINED, AND PATTED DRY

SALT AND PEPPER, TO TASTE

1.75 OZ. | 50 GRAMS RICOTTA SALATA CHEESE, GRATED

HAWAIIAN-STYLE PIZZA

YIELD: 1 PIZZA / **ACTIVE TIME:** 15 MINUTES / **TOTAL TIME:** 35 MINUTES

Whether you love it or hate it, you can't ignore it. Hawaiian pizza, which actually originated in Canada during the 1960s, has become one of the most popular, and divisive, pizzas out there.

1. Place a baking stone or steel on the middle rack of the oven and preheat the oven to the maximum temperature. Dust a work surface with the semolina flour, place the dough on the surface, and gently stretch it into a round. For more detailed instructions on properly stretching a ball of pizza dough see page 73. Cover the dough with the sauce and top with the mozzarella, Canadian bacon or ham, and pineapple. Season with salt and pepper and drizzle olive oil over the pizza.

2. Using a peel or a flat baking sheet, transfer the pizza to the heated baking implement in the oven. Bake for about 15 minutes, until the crust is golden brown and starting to char. Remove and let cool slightly before slicing and serving.

INGREDIENTS:

SEMOLINA FLOUR, AS NEEDED

1 BALL PIZZA DOUGH

2.8 OZ. | 80 GRAMS RAW PIZZA SAUCE (SEE PAGE 103)

5.3 OZ. | 150 GRAMS LOW-MOISTURE MOZZARELLA CHEESE, SHREDDED

3 SLICES CANADIAN BACON OR THICK-CUT HAM, CHOPPED

5 SLICES CANNED PINEAPPLE, DRAINED AND PATTED DRY

SALT AND PEPPER, TO TASTE

OLIVE OIL, TO TASTE

CLASSIC PEPPERONI PIZZA

YIELD: 1 PIZZA / **ACTIVE TIME:** 15 MINUTES / **TOTAL TIME:** 35 MINUTES

A national treasure. Born in New York at the beginning of the 1900s, it is based off of a locally produced salami made from beef and pork and seasoned with chili pepper and paprika.

1. Place a baking stone or steel on the middle rack of the oven and preheat the oven to the maximum temperature. Dust a work surface with the semolina flour, place the dough on the surface, and gently stretch it into a round. For more detailed instructions on properly stretching a ball of pizza dough see page 73. Cover the dough with the sauce, season with pepper, and top with one-third of the pepperoni. Distribute the mozzarella, top with the remaining pepperoni, and drizzle olive oil over the pizza.

2. Using a peel or a flat baking sheet, transfer the pizza to the heated baking implement in the oven. Bake for about 15 minutes, until the crust is golden brown and starting to char. Remove and let cool slightly before slicing and serving.

INGREDIENTS:

SEMOLINA FLOUR, AS NEEDED

12 TO 15 SLICES PEPPERONI

5.3 OZ. | 150 GRAMS LOW-MOISTURE MOZZARELLA CHEESE, SHREDDED

OLIVE OIL, TO TASTE

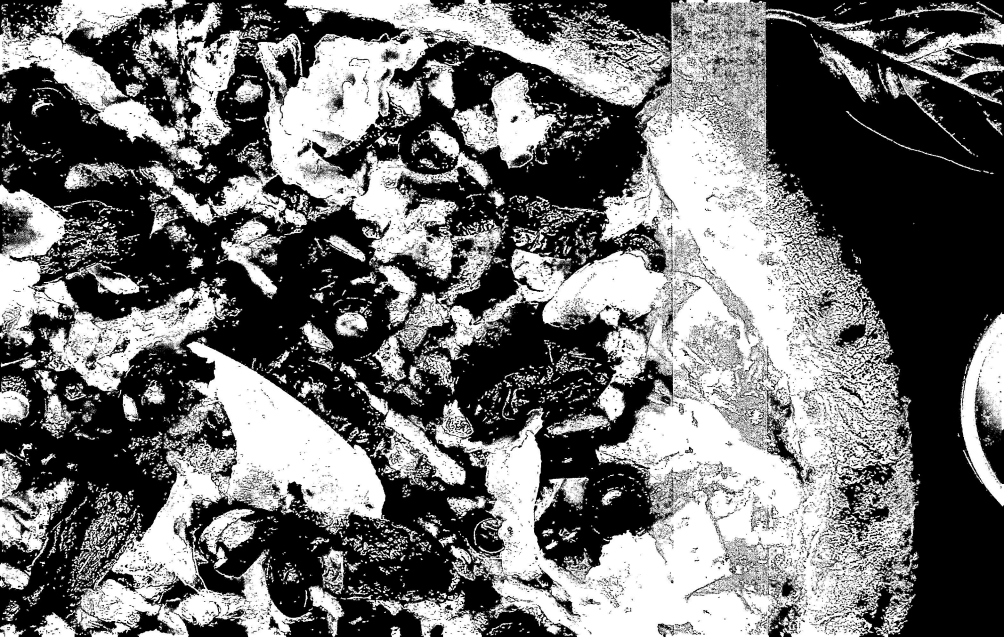

GLOBAL PIZZA

*P*izza is one of the most popular foods in the world. The international pizza scene is ever so lively with toppings that often represent daring culinary fusions that would please the most progressive chef, while other variations have been created as extensions of local comfort food. All of the recipes in this chapter are popular somewhere on the planet, and well worth tasting for yourself, no matter where you live.

TERIYAKI CHICKEN & MUSHROOM PIZZA

YIELD: 1 PIZZA / **ACTIVE TIME:** 20 MINUTES / **TOTAL TIME:** 1 HOUR

After first being introduced in the 1950s, pizza in Japan has undergone really interesting developments. Here is a typical contemporary topping.

1. Preheat the oven to the maximum temperature and place a baking stone or steel on the middle rack of the oven as it warms. Place the chicken, mushrooms, and spring onions in a bowl, generously drizzle olive oil over the mixture, season with salt and shichimi pepper, and let the mixture marinate for 10 minutes. Drain and set aside. Place the mayonnaise and the tablespoon of olive oil in another bowl, stir to combine, and set it aside.

2. Dust a work surface with the semolina flour, place the dough on the surface, and gently stretch it into a round. For more detailed instructions on properly stretching a ball of pizza dough see page 73. Cover the dough with the mayonnaise mixture and top with the chicken mixture and corn. Drizzle teriyaki sauce and olive oil over the pizza.

3. Using a peel or a flat baking sheet, transfer the pizza to the heated baking implement in the oven. Bake for about 5 minutes, until the crust starts to brown. Remove the pizza, distribute the mozzarella over the top, and return the pizza to the oven. Bake for about 10 minutes, until the crust is golden brown and starting to char. Remove and let cool slightly before garnishing with the seaweed, slicing, and serving.

INGREDIENTS:

2.8 OZ. | 80 GRAMS COOKED TERIYAKI CHICKEN, SHREDDED

1.75 OZ. | 50 GRAMS SHIITAKE MUSHROOMS

1.75 OZ. | 50 GRAMS SPRING ONIONS, SLICED THIN

1 TABLESPOONS | 14.4 GRAMS OLIVE OIL, PLUS MORE AS NEEDED

SALT AND SHICHIMI PEPPER, TO TASTE

1 OZ. | 30 GRAMS MAYONNAISE

SEMOLINA FLOUR, AS NEEDED

1 BALL PIZZA DOUGH

1 OZ. | 30 GRAMS SWEET CORN

TERIYAKI SAUCE, TO TASTE

3.5 OZ. | 100 GRAMS FRESH MOZZARELLA, DRAINED AND TORN

NORI, SHREDDED, FOR GARNISH

TERIYAKI SALMON PIZZA

YIELD: 1 PIZZA / **ACTIVE TIME:** 15 MINUTES / **TOTAL TIME:** 45 MINUTES

Teriyaki salmon pizza is a recent addition to the very lively Japanese pizza scene, but, as it is quite delicious, the bet here is that it will be around awhile.

1. Preheat the oven to the maximum temperature and place a baking stone or steel on the middle rack of the oven as it warms. Place the mayonnaise and the tablespoon of olive oil in another bowl, stir to combine, and set it aside.

Dust a work surface with the semolina flour, place the dough on the surface, and gently stretch it into a round. For more detailed instructions on properly stretching a ball of pizza dough see page 73. Cover the dough with the mayonnaise mixture and top with the salmon, cucumber, and bell pepper. Season with salt, drizzle olive oil over the pizza, and distribute the mozzarella over the top.

3. Using a peel or a flat baking sheet, transfer the pizza to the heated baking implement in the oven. Bake for about 15 minutes, until the crust is golden brown and starting to char. Remove, drizzle teriyaki sauce and additional mayonnaise over the top, and let cool slightly before slicing and serving.

INGREDIENTS:

1 BALL PIZZA DOUGH

2.8 OZ. | 80 GRAMS COOKED TERIYAKI SALMON

1 OZ. | 30 GRAMS CUCUMBER, SLICED

1 OZ. | 30 GRAMS BELL PEPPER, SLICED

SALT, TO TASTE

2.8 OZ. | 80 GRAMS LOW-MOISTURE MOZZARELLA CHEESE, SHREDDED

TERIYAKI SAUCE, TO TASTE

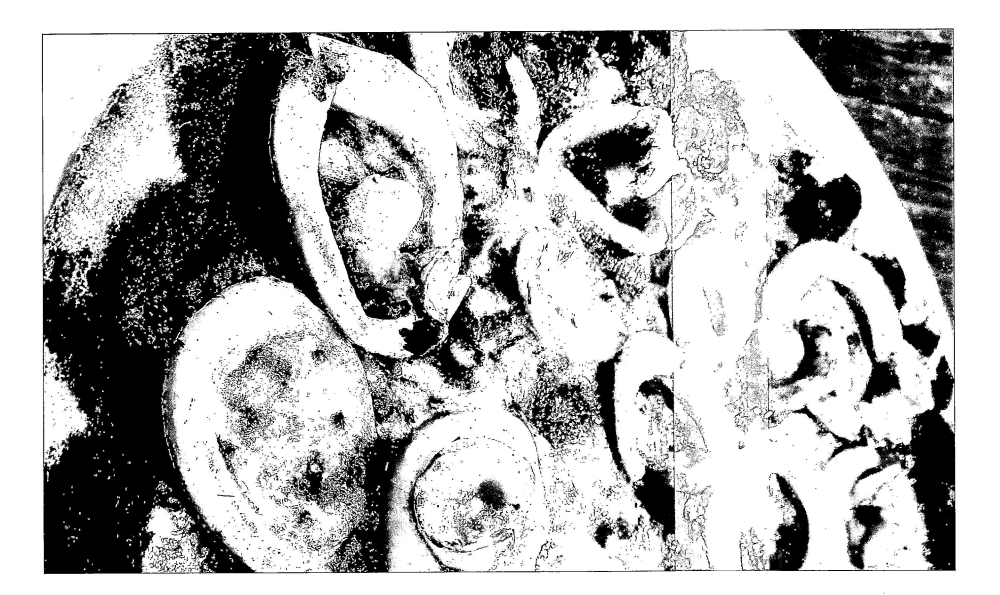

PIZZA WITH SQUID INK & SEAFOOD

YIELD: 1 PIZZA / **ACTIVE TIME:** 20 MINUTES / **TOTAL TIME:** 1 HOUR

Possibly the most eye-catching Japanese pizza is the one that uses squid ink mixed with pizza sauce as a base. While it may look odd, the taste is not as exotic as one would expect, as squid ink is a common ingredient in Italian cuisine.

1. Preheat the oven to the maximum temperature and place a baking stone or steel on the middle rack of the oven as it warms. Coat the bottom of a skillet with olive oil and warm over medium-high heat. When the oil starts to shimmer, add the seafood and sauté until cooked through, 2 to 3 minutes. Season with salt and shichimi pepper, remove the pan from heat, and let the mixture cool. Combine the squid ink and pizza sauce and set the mixture aside.

2. Dust a work surface with the semolina flour, place the dough on the surface, and gently stretch it into a round. For more detailed instructions on properly stretching a ball of pizza dough see page 73. Cover the dough with the sauce and top with the seafood. Season with salt and drizzle olive oil over the pizza.

3. Using a peel or a flat baking sheet, transfer the pizza to the heated baking implement in the oven. Bake for about 5 minutes, until the crust starts to brown. Remove the pizza, distribute the mozzarella over the top, and return the pizza to the oven. Bake for about 10 minutes, until the crust is golden brown and starting to char. Remove and let cool slightly before garnishing with the fish roe and parsley, slicing, and serving.

INGREDIENTS:

OLIVE OIL, AS NEEDED

5.3 OZ. | 150 GRAMS SQUID OR ASSORTED SEAFOOD, FRESH OR FROZEN

SALT AND SHICHIMI PEPPER, TO TASTE

1 PACKET SQUID INK

2.4 OZ. | 70 GRAMS RAW PIZZA SAUCE (SEE PAGE 103)

SEMOLINA FLOUR, AS NEEDED

1 BALL PIZZA DOUGH

3.5 OZ. | 100 GRAMS FRESH MOZZARELLA CHEESE, DRAINED AND TORN

1 OZ. | 30 GRAMS PREFERRED FISH ROE, FOR GARNISH

FRESH PARSLEY, FINELY CHOPPED, FOR GARNISH

OKONOMIYAKI PIZZA

YIELD: 1 PIZZA / **ACTIVE TIME:** 25 MINUTES / **TOTAL TIME:** 1 HOUR

O konomiyaki is sometimes referred to as "Japanese pizza," so it's only natural that its flavors would work well in a topping.

1. Preheat the oven to the maximum temperature and place a baking stone or steel on the middle rack of the oven as it warms. Dust a work surface with the semolina flour, place the dough on the surface, and gently stretch it into a round. For more detailed instructions on properly stretching a ball of pizza dough see page 73. Cover the dough with the cabbage and top with the seaweed, mayonnaise, soy sauce, sriracha, and gochujang.

2. Using a peel or a flat baking sheet, transfer the pizza to the heated baking implement in the oven. Bake for about 5 minutes, until the crust starts to brown. Remove the pizza, distribute the shrimp and pork belly over the top, drizzle vegetable oil over the toppings and return the pizza to the oven. Bake for about 10 minutes, until the crust is golden brown and starting to char. Remove and let cool slightly before slicing and serving.

INGREDIENTS:

SEMOLINA FLOUR, AS NEEDED

MORE TO TASTE

1 OZ. | 30 GRAMS SOY SAUCE

SRIRACHA, TO TASTE

GOCHUJANG, TO TASTE

1.75 OZ. | 50 GRAMS SHRIMP, PEELED, COOKED, AND MINCED

1.75 OZ. | 50 GRAMS PORK BELLY, COOKED AND SHREDDED

VEGETABLE OIL, AS NEEDED

NATTO & BACON PIZZA

YIELD: 1 PIZZA / **ACTIVE TIME:** 25 MINUTES / **TOTAL TIME:** 1 HOUR

N atto are fermented soybeans, one of those super-healthy Japanese ingredients that you can find in specialty stores. Using it on pizza is a new trend in Japan and makes a great way to transform this superfood into something yummy.

1. Preheat the oven to the maximum temperature and place a baking stone or steel on the middle rack of the oven as it warms. Coat the bottom of a skillet with olive oil and warm over medium-high heat. When the oil starts to shimmer, add the natto and bacon and cook until the bacon starts to get crispy, about 6 minutes. Remove the pan from heat, season with salt and shichimi pepper, and let the mixture cool.

2. Dust a work surface with the semolina flour, place the dough on the surface, and gently stretch it into a round. For more detailed instructions on properly stretching a ball of pizza dough see page 73. Distribute the natto mixture over the dough and top with the sweet corn and mozzarella.

3. Using a peel or a flat baking sheet, transfer the pizza to the heated baking implement in the oven. Bake for about 15 minutes, until the crust is golden brown and starting to char. Remove and let cool slightly before garnishing with the spring onion, slicing, and serving.

INGREDIENTS:

OLIVE OIL, AS NEEDED

5.3 OZ. | 150 GRAMS NATTO

1.75 OZ. | 50 GRAMS BACON, CHOPPED

SALT AND SHICHIMI PEPPER, TO TASTE

SEMOLINA FLOUR, AS NEEDED

1 BALL PIZZA DOUGH

2.4 OZ. | 70 GRAMS SWEET CORN

3.5 OZ. | 100 GRAMS LOW-MOISTURE MOZZARELLA CHEESE, SHREDDED

0.5 OZ. | 15 GRAMS SLICED SPRING ONION, FOR GARNISH

SEAFOOD & MAYONNAISE PIZZA

YIELD: 1 PIZZA / **ACTIVE TIME:** 15 MINUTES / **TOTAL TIME:** 1 HOUR

This pizza combines two of the most beloved ingredients in contemporary Japanese cuisine: seafood and mayonnaise. This match works just fine on pizza, and the addition of soy sauce provides an extra burst of that umami flavor Asian cuisines are known for.

1. Preheat the oven to the maximum temperature and place a baking stone or steel on the middle rack of the oven as it warms. Place the seafood in a bowl, drizzle the seafood with soy sauce, toss well, and set aside.

2. Dust a work surface with the semolina flour, place the dough on the surface, and gently stretch it into a round. For more detailed instructions on properly stretching a ball of pizza dough see page 73. Cover the dough with the mayonnaise and top with the seafood.

3. Using a peel or a flat baking sheet, transfer the pizza to the heated baking implement in the oven. Bake for about 15 minutes, until the crust is golden brown and starting to char and the seafood is cooked through. Remove, drizzle additional mayonnaise over the pizza, and let it cool slightly before slicing and serving.

INGREDIENTS:

1 BALL PIZZA DOUGH

1.5 OZ. | 45 GRAMS MAYONNAISE, PLUS MORE AS NEEDED

BALADO & CHICKEN PIZZA

YIELD: 1 PIZZA / **ACTIVE TIME:** 25 MINUTES / **TOTAL TIME:** 1 HOUR

Pizza is very popular in Indonesia, and some very interesting toppings have originated from the lively local food scene. Balado sauce may be hard to find, but as you'll see, you can whip up your own in no time.

1. Preheat the oven to the maximum temperature and place a baking stone or steel on the middle rack of the oven as it warms. Coat the bottom of a skillet with olive oil and warm over medium-high heat. When the oil starts to shimmer, add the chicken and onion and sauté until the chicken is cooked through, about 10 minutes. Remove from heat, season with salt, and let the mixture cool.

2. Dust a work surface with the semolina flour, place the dough on the surface, and gently stretch it into a round. For more detailed instructions on properly stretching a ball of pizza dough see page 73. Brush the pizza with an emulsion of vegetable oil and water.

3. Using a peel or a flat baking sheet, transfer the pizza to the heated baking implement in the oven. Bake for about 7 minutes, until the crust starts to brown. Remove the pizza, spread the Balado Sauce over it, distribute the mozzarella, slices of egg, and the chicken mixture over the top, and return the pizza to the oven. Bake for about 5 minutes, until the crust is golden brown and starting to char. Remove and let cool slightly before garnishing with the basil and Parmesan, slicing, and serving.

BALADO SAUCE

1. Coat the bottom of a skillet with the vegetable oil and warm over medium-high heat. When the oil starts to shimmer, add the shallots, chilies, and tomato and stir-fry until the shallots have softened, about 4 minutes.

2. Stir in the lime juice, sugar, and salt, then transfer the mixture to a blender and blitz until pureed. If the sauce is too watery, place it in a saucepan and cook over low heat until it has reduced to the desired consistency.

INGREDIENTS:

VEGETABLE OIL, AS NEEDED

3.5 OZ. | 100 GRAMS CHICKEN, MINCED

½ SMALL ONION, CHOPPED

SALT, TO TASTE

SEMOLINA FLOUR, AS NEEDED

1 BALL PIZZA DOUGH

1.5 OZ. | 45 GRAMS BALADO SAUCE (SEE RECIPE)

2.7 GRAMS | 80 GRAMS LOW-MOISTURE MOZZARELLA CHEESE, SHREDDED

2 HARD-BOILED QUAIL EGGS OR 1 CHICKEN EGG, SLICED

FRESH BASIL LEAVES, FOR GARNISH

PARMESAN CHEESE, GRATED, FOR GARNISH

BALADO SAUCE

VEGETABLE OIL, AS NEEDED

5.3 OZ. | 150 GRAMS SHALLOTS, CHOPPED

4.4 OZ. | 250 GRAMS MILD RED CHILI PEPPERS, STEMMED, SEEDED, CHOPPED

1 LARGE TOMATO, CHOPPED

JUICE OF 1 LIME

1 TABLESPOON | 12.5 GRAMS SUGAR

SALT, TO TASTE

PIZZA WITH RENDANG & MUSHROOMS

YIELD: 1 PIZZA / **ACTIVE TIME:** 15 MINUTES / **TOTAL TIME:** 45 MINUTES

Rendang is an Indonesian stew that works surprisingly well on pizza. This is a perfect excuse to learn a new beef stew, knowing that you can save the leftovers to use on a delicious pizza.

1. Preheat the oven to the maximum temperature and place a baking stone or steel on the middle rack of the oven as it warms. Dust a work surface with the semolina flour, place the dough on the surface, and gently stretch it into a round. For more detailed instructions on properly stretching a ball of pizza dough see page 73. Cover the dough with the sauce and top with the Beef Rendang and mushrooms. Season with salt and dried parsley, distribute the mozzarella over the pizza, and drizzle vegetable oil on top.

2. Using a peel or a flat baking sheet, transfer the pizza to the heated baking implement in the oven. Bake for about 10 minutes, until the crust is golden brown and starting to char. Remove and let cool slightly before garnishing with the fresh parsley and Parmesan, slicing, and serving.

BEEF RENDANG

1. Place the shallots, 3 of the lemongrass stalks, the galangal, garlic, ginger, and chilies in a food processor and blitz until finely chopped.

2. Coat the bottom of a Dutch oven with olive oil and warm over medium-high heat. When the oil starts to shimmer, add the chili mixture, cinnamon stick, cloves, star anise, and cardamom and stir-fry until aromatic, about 1 minute. Add the short ribs and the remaining lemongrass and cook, stirring continuously for 5 minutes. Add the coconut milk, water, and tamarind and simmer, stirring frequently, until the meat is nearly cooked through, about 10 minutes.

3. Stir in the remaining ingredients, reduce heat to low, cover the Dutch oven, and cook until the short ribs are very tender, about 1 hour.

INGREDIENTS:

SEMOLINA FLOUR, AS NEEDED

SALT, TO TASTE

DRIED PARSLEY, TO TASTE

2.8 OZ. | 80 GRAMS LOW-MOISTURE MOZZARELLA CHEESE, SHREDDED

VEGETABLE OIL, TO TASTE

FRESH PARSLEY, FINELY CHOPPED, FOR GARNISH

PARMESAN CHEESE, GRATED, FOR GARNISH

BEEF RENDANG

5 SHALLOTS, CHOPPED

4 LEMONGRASS STALKS, BASHED

1-INCH PIECE GALANGAL, PEELED AND MINCED

5 GARLIC CLOVES

1-INCH PIECE FRESH GINGER, PEELED AND MINCED

10 DRIED CHILIES

OLIVE OIL, AS NEEDED

1 CINNAMON STICK

3 WHOLE CLOVES

3 STAR ANISE PODS

3 CARDAMOM PODS

1.5 LBS. | 700 GRAMS BONELESS BEEF SHORT RIBS, CUBED

8 OZ. | 225 GRAMS COCONUT MILK

8 OZ. | 225 GRAMS WATER

TAMARIND PULP, TO TASTE

6 MAKRUT LIME LEAVES, SLICED THIN

0.8 OZ. | 40 GRAMS COCONUT, TOASTED

1 TABLESPOON | 12.5 GRAMS SUGAR

SALT, TO TASTE

TOM YUM PIZZA WITH SHRIMP

YIELD: 1 PIZZA / **ACTIVE TIME:** 15 MINUTES / **TOTAL TIME:** 45 MINUTES

Inspired by the ingredients of the famously delicious soup, this is truly a slice of Thailand.

1. Preheat the oven to the maximum temperature and place a baking stone or steel on the middle rack of the oven as it warms. Combine the Tom Yum Paste and the pizza sauce in a small bowl and set it aside.

2. Dust a work surface with the semolina flour, place the dough on the surface, and gently stretch it into a round. For more detailed instructions on properly stretching a ball of pizza dough see page 73. Cover the dough with the sauce and top with the mushrooms and shrimp. Season with salt and drizzle vegetable oil over the pizza.

3. Using a peel or a flat baking sheet, transfer the pizza to the heated baking implement in the oven. Bake for about 7 minutes, until the crust starts to brown. Remove the pizza, distribute the mozzarella over the top, and return the pizza to the oven. Bake for about 5 minutes, until the crust is golden brown and starting to char. Remove and let cool slightly before garnishing with the cilantro, slicing, and serving.

TOM YUM PASTE

1. Place all of the ingredients in a food processor or blender and blitz until the mixture is a smooth paste. It will keep in the refrigerator for 3 weeks.

INGREDIENTS:

1 OZ. | 30 GRAMS TOM YUM PASTE (SEE RECIPE)

1 OZ. | 30 GRAMS RAW PIZZA SAUCE (SEE PAGE 103)

SEMOLINA FLOUR, AS NEEDED

1 BALL PIZZA DOUGH

2.4 OZ. | 70 GRAMS OYSTER MUSHROOMS, SLICED THIN

6 LARGE SHRIMP (KING PRAWNS PREFERRED)

SALT, TO TASTE

VEGETABLE OIL, TO TASTE

3.5 OZ. | 100 GRAMS FRESH MOZZARELLA CHEESE, DRAINED AND SLICED

FRESH CILANTRO LEAVES, FOR GARNISH

TOM YUM PASTE

1 LEMONGRASS STALK, PEELED

2-INCH PIECE FRESH GALANGAL OR GINGER, PEELED AND MINCED

3 MAKRUT LIME LEAVES, SLICED THIN

0.5 OZ. | 15 GRAMS THAI CHILI PASTE

4 RED CHILI PEPPERS, STEMMED AND SEEDED

1 OZ. | 30 GRAMS FISH SAUCE

JUICE OF 2 LIMES

2 SHALLOTS, CHOPPED

2 TEASPOONS | 8.3 GRAMS SUGAR

FRESH CILANTRO, FINELY CHOPPED, TO TASTE

BULGOGI PIZZA

YIELD: 1 PIZZA / **ACTIVE TIME:** 25 MINUTES / **TOTAL TIME:** 1 HOUR

This version of South Korean pizza features bulgogi both as a sauce and as a meat topping. It's best to use leftover bulgogi, but if that is not possible, one can quickly fix some while the dough rises.

1 Preheat the oven to the maximum temperature and place a baking stone or steel on the middle rack of the oven as it warms. Coat the bottom of a skillet with vegetable oil and warm over medium-high heat. When the oil starts to shimmer, add the beef and cook until it is browned and cooked through, about 8 minutes.

2. Dust a work surface with the semolina flour, place the dough on the surface, and gently stretch it into a round. For more detailed instructions on properly stretching a ball of pizza dough see page 73. Cover the dough with the Bulgogi Sauce and top with the mozzarella, mushrooms, bell pepper, beef, olives, onion, and corn. Drizzle vegetable oil over the pizza.

3. Using a peel or a flat baking sheet, transfer the pizza to the heated baking implement in the oven. Bake for about 15 minutes, until the crust is golden brown and starting to char. Remove and let cool slightly before slicing and serving.

BULGOGI SAUCE

1. Combine the potato starch and water and set aside.

2. Combine the remaining ingredients and place the mixture in a saucepan. Stir in the potato starch mixture and cook over medium heat until the sauce has reduced to the desired consistency. Taste and add more water if the flavor is too strong for your liking.

INGREDIENTS

1 BALL PIZZA DOUGH

2.8 OZ. | 80 GRAMS BULGOGI SAUCE (SEE RECIPE)

2.8 OZ. | 80 GRAMS LOW-MOISTURE MOZZARELLA CHEESE, SHREDDED

2 SMALL MUSHROOMS, SLICED THIN

⅓ GREEN BELL PEPPER, DICED

0.5 OZ. | 15 GRAMS SLICED BLACK OLIVES

0.5 OZ. | 15 GRAMS YELLOW ONION, SLICED THIN

0.5 OZ. | 15 GRAMS CANNED SWEET CORN, DRAINED

BULGOGI SAUCE

0.75 OZ. | 22.5 GRAMS POTATO STARCH

0.75 OZ. | 22.5 GRAMS WATER, PLUS MORE AS NEEDED

1 OZ. | 30 GRAMS BROWN SUGAR

2.1 OZ. | 60 GRAMS SOY SAUCE

1 OZ. | 30 GRAMS RICE VINEGAR

1 TEASPOON | 5 GRAMS OYSTER SAUCE

1 GARLIC CLOVE, MINCED

1 TEASPOON | 4.4 GRAMS SESAME OIL

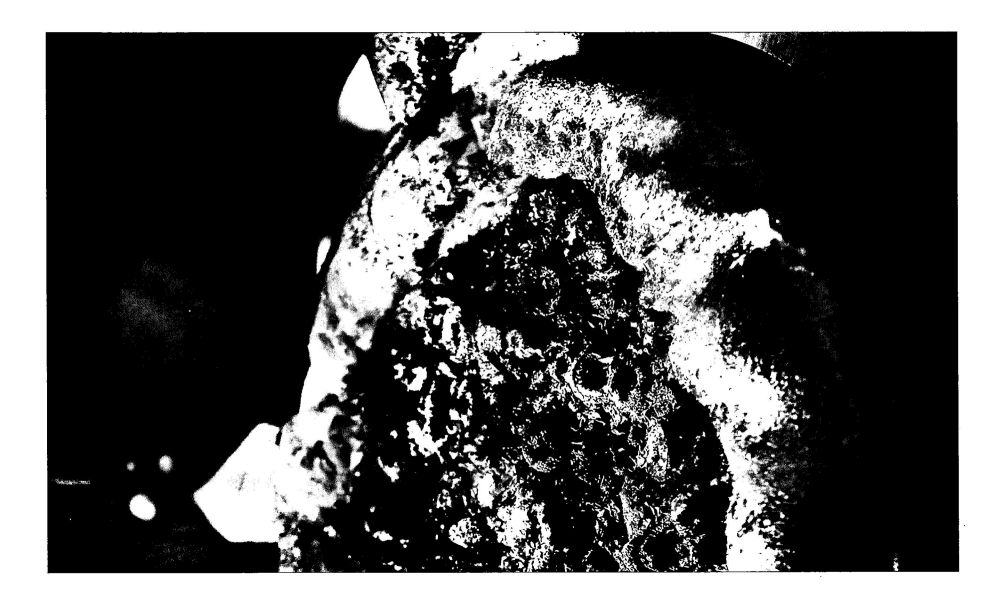

PIZZA WITH KIMCHI

YIELD: 1 PIZZA / **ACTIVE TIME:** 15 MINUTES / **TOTAL TIME:** 45 MINUTES

An elegant and simple white pizza featuring Korea's favorite funky topping.

1. Preheat the oven to the maximum temperature and place a baking stone or steel on the middle rack of the oven as it warms. Place the vegetable oil, dried parsley, garlic, and sugar in a bowl, stir to combine, and set aside.

2. Dust a work surface with the semolina flour, place the dough on the surface, and gently stretch it into a round. For more detailed instructions on properly stretching a ball of pizza dough see page 73. Cover the dough with the seasoned oil and kimchi.

3. Using a peel or a flat baking sheet, transfer the pizza to the heated baking implement in the oven. Bake for about 7 minutes, until the crust starts to brown. Remove the pizza, distribute the mozzarella over the top, and return the pizza to the oven. Bake for about 5 minutes, until the crust is golden brown and starting to char. Remove from the oven and let cool slightly before garnishing with the cilantro, slicing, and serving.

INGREDIENTS:

1 OZ. | 30 GRAMS VEGETABLE OIL

DRIED PARSLEY, TO TASTE

1 GARLIC CLOVE, SLICED THIN

1 TEASPOON | 4.1 GRAMS GRANULATED SUGAR

SEMOLINA FLOUR, AS NEEDED

1 BALL PIZZA DOUGH

5.3 OZ. | 150 GRAMS SPICY KIMCHI, DRAINED AND CHOPPED

4.4 OZ. | 125 GRAMS FRESH MOZZARELLA CHEESE, DRAINED AND SLICED

FRESH CILANTRO, FINELY CHOPPED, FOR GARNISH

PIZZA WITH PEKING DUCK

YIELD: 1 PIZZA / **ACTIVE TIME:** 15 MINUTES / **TOTAL TIME:** 45 MINUTES

Pizza in China is often stuffed, but in the US, several scrumptious Chinese-inspired toppings are regularly used.

1. Preheat the oven to the maximum temperature and place a baking stone or steel on the middle rack of the oven as it warms. Dust a work surface with the semolina flour, place the dough on the surface, and gently stretch it into a round. For more detailed instructions on properly stretching a ball of pizza dough see page 73. Drizzle vegetable oil over the dough, cover with half of the mozzarella, and top with the duck, mushrooms, and scallion. Drizzle hoisin sauce over the pizza and sprinkle the remaining mozzarella on top.

2. Using a peel or a flat baking sheet, transfer the pizza to the heated baking implement in the oven. Bake for about 15 minutes, until the crust is golden brown and starting to char. Remove and let cool slightly before garnishing with the sesame seeds (if using), slicing, and serving.

INGREDIENTS:

SEMOLINA FLOUR, AS NEEDED

3.5 OZ. | 100 GRAMS COOKED DUCK MEAT, SHREDDED

2.4 OZ. | 70 GRAMS SHIITAKE MUSHROOMS, SLICED THIN

1 SCALLION, TRIMMED AND SLICED THIN

HOISIN SAUCE, TO TASTE

SESAME SEEDS, FOR GARNISH (OPTIONAL)

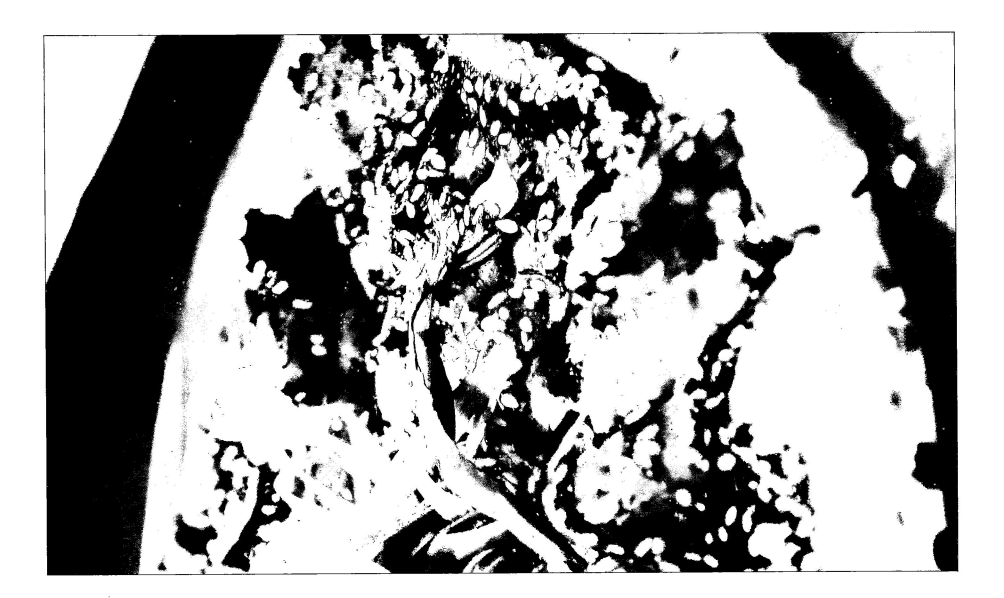

TIKKA MASALA PIZZA

YIELD: 1 PIZZA / **ACTIVE TIME:** 15 MINUTES / **TOTAL TIME:** 1 HOUR

Indian pizza is mostly a US phenomenon, but it is conquering both Indian and non-Indian tastebuds alike. The concept is quite simple: place your favorite Indian food on a well-prepared crust, and you can't go wrong.

1. Preheat the oven to the maximum temperature and place a baking stone or steel on the middle rack of the oven as it warms. Combine the sour cream and the sauce in a small bowl and set it aside. Coat the bottom of a skillet with olive oil and warm over medium-high heat. When the oil starts to shimmer, add the chicken and cook until it is cooked through, about 8 minutes. Remove the pan from heat and let the chicken cool.

2. Dust a work surface with the semolina flour, place the dough on the surface, and gently stretch it into a round. For more detailed instructions on properly stretching a ball of pizza dough see page 73. Cover the dough with the sour cream mixture and top with the chicken, onion, and mozzarella.

3. Using a peel or a flat baking sheet, transfer the pizza to the heated baking implement in the oven. Bake for about 15 minutes, until the crust is golden brown and starting to char. Remove and let cool slightly before garnishing with the cilantro, slicing, and serving.

INGREDIENTS:

1 OZ. | 30 GRAMS SOUR CREAM

1.6 OZ. | 45 GRAMS TIKKA MASALA SAUCE

OLIVE OIL, AS NEEDED

5.3 OZ. | 150 GRAMS CHICKEN MARINATED IN TIKKA MASALA SAUCE, CUBED OR SLICED

SEMOLINA FLOUR, AS NEEDED

1 BALL PIZZA DOUGH

3.5 OZ. | 100 GRAMS LOW-MOISTURE MOZZARELLA CHEESE, SHREDDED

1 OZ. | 30 GRAMS ONION, SLICED THIN

FRESH CILANTRO, FINELY CHOPPED, FOR GARNISH

PIZZA WITH ALOO GOBI

YIELD: 1 PIZZA / **ACTIVE TIME:** 15 MINUTES / **TOTAL TIME:** 1 HOUR AND 30 MINUTES

Vegetarian Indian food is out-of-this-world delicious. Here is a popular match for pizza crust that is based on aloo gobi, potato, and cauliflower, marinated in spices and yogurt and then roasted.

1. Preheat the oven to the maximum temperature and place a baking stone or steel on the middle rack of the oven as it warms. Place the potato, cauliflower, and 2 tablespoons of the marinade in a bowl, season with salt, stir to combine, and let the mixture rest for 1 hour. Combine the pizza sauce and the remaining marinade in a separate bowl and set it aside.

2. Dust a work surface with the semolina flour, place the dough on the surface, and gently stretch it into a round. For more detailed instructions on properly stretching a ball of pizza dough see page 73. Cover the dough with the sauce mixture and top with the cauliflower mixture, chili pepper, onion, and bell pepper. Season with salt and drizzle vegetable oil over the pizza.

3. Using a peel or a flat baking sheet, transfer the pizza to the heated baking implement in the oven. Bake for about 15 minutes, until the crust is golden brown and starting to char. Remove and let cool slightly before slicing and serving.

ALOO GOBI MARINADE

1. Place all of the ingredients in a small bowl and stir until combined.

INGREDIENTS:

SALT, TO TASTE

1.75 OZ. | 50 GRAMS RAW PIZZA SAUCE (SEE PAGE 103)

SEMOLINA FLOUR, AS NEEDED

1 BALL PIZZA DOUGH

½ GREEN CHILI PEPPER, SLICED THIN

¼ SMALL ONION, SLICED THIN

3 SLICES BELL PEPPER

VEGETABLE OIL, AS NEEDED

ALOO GOBI MARINADE

5.3 OZ. | 150 GRAMS PLAIN YOGURT

½ TEASPOON | 5.4 GRAMS CHILI POWDER

½ TEASPOON | 5.4 GRAMS CHAAT MASALA POWDER

½ TEASPOON | 2 GRAMS CRUSHED CUMIN SEEDS

½ TEASPOON | 5.4 GRAMS TURMERIC POWDER

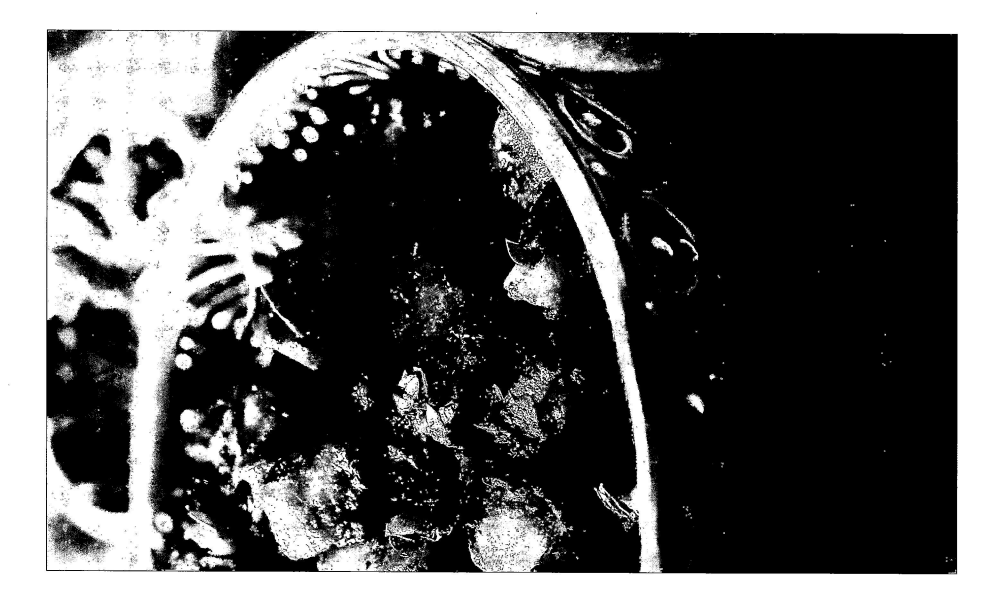

CHICKEN SATAY & MANGO PIZZA

YIELD: 1 PIZZA / **ACTIVE TIME:** 20 MINUTES / **TOTAL TIME:** 1 HOUR

Australia has a very lively food scene, and pizza is not an exception. Here is one of the country's most popular contemporary toppings.

1. Preheat the oven to the maximum temperature and place a baking stone or steel on the middle rack of the oven the oven as it warms. Place the chicken, curry powder, salt, and a generous amount of olive oil in a bowl and stir to combine. Place the peanut butter, coconut cream, and red pepper flakes in a separate bowl and stir to combine.

2. Dust a work surface with the semolina flour, place the dough on the surface, and gently stretch it into a round. For more detailed instructions on properly stretching a ball of pizza dough see page 73. Cover with the peanut sauce and top with the curry chicken, bell pepper, and mango. Season with salt and drizzle olive oil over the pizza.

3. Using a peel or a flat baking sheet, transfer the pizza to the heated baking implement in the oven. Bake for about 15 minutes, until the crust is golden brown and starting to char. Remove and let cool slightly before slicing and serving.

INGREDIENTS:

2.8 OZ. | 80 GRAMS COOKED CHICKEN BREAST, SLICED

½ TEASPOON | 5.4 GRAMS CURRY POWDER

SALT, TO TASTE

OLIVE OIL, AS NEEDED

0.5 OZ. | 15 GRAMS CRUNCHY PEANUT BUTTER

1 OZ. | 30 GRAMS COCONUT CREAM

1 PINCH RED PEPPER FLAKES

SEMOLINA FLOUR, AS NEEDED

1 BALL PIZZA DOUGH

½ RED BELL PEPPER, SLICED

FLESH OF ½ SMALL MANGO, SLICED THIN

CHICKEN & CATUPIRY PIZZA

YIELD: 1 PIZZA / **ACTIVE TIME:** 15 MINUTES / **TOTAL TIME:** 45 MINUTES

I n Brazil, it is typical to replace tomato sauce with a local cream cheese called *catupiry*. You can imitate its taste by blending equal parts cream cheese and melted Muenster cheese.

1. Preheat the oven to the maximum temperature and place a baking stone or steel on the middle rack of the oven as it warms. Dust a work surface with the semolina flour, place the dough on the surface, and gently stretch it into a round. For more detailed instructions on properly stretching a ball of pizza dough see page 73. Cover the dough with ⅔ of the catupiry and top with the chicken, tomato, and onion. Season with salt and drizzle olive oil over the pizza.

2. Using a peel or a flat baking sheet, transfer the pizza to the heated baking implement in the oven. Bake for about 7 minutes, until the crust starts to brown. Remove pizza from the oven and top with the rest of the cheese, making a lattice pattern. Return to the oven and bake for about 5 more minutes, until the crust is golden brown and starting to char. Remove and let cool slightly before drizzling ketchup over the pizza (if using), slicing, and serving.

INGREDIENTS:

SEMOLINA FLOUR, AS NEEDED

1 TOMATO, SLICED

⅓ SMALL ONION, SLICED

SALT, TO TASTE

OLIVE OIL, TO TASTE

KETCHUP, TO TASTE (OPTIONAL)

PIZZA À LA PORTUGUESA

YIELD: 1 PIZZA / **ACTIVE TIME:** 15 MINUTES / **TOTAL TIME:** 45 MINUTES

If you happen to hear about a "Portuguese" pizza, chances are good that it is Brazilian and has little to do with how pizza is made in Portugal. There are many variations on these toppings; this is one of the most typical.

1. Preheat the oven to the maximum temperature and place a baking stone or steel on the middle rack of the oven as it warms. Dust a work surface with the semolina flour, place the dough on the surface, and gently stretch it into a round. For more detailed instructions on properly stretching a ball of pizza dough see page 73. Cover the dough with the sauce and top with the mozzarella, onion, ham, and olives.

2. Using a peel or a flat baking sheet, transfer the pizza to the heated baking implement in the oven. Bake for about 15 minutes, until the crust is golden brown and starting to char. Remove, top with the eggs, season with oregano, and drizzle olive oil over the pizza. Let cool slightly before slicing and serving.

INGREDIENTS:

SEMOLINA FLOUR, AS NEEDED

1 BALL PIZZA DOUGH

2.8 OZ. | 80 GRAMS RAW PIZZA SAUCE (SEE PAGE 103)

3.5 OZ. | 100 GRAMS LOW-MOISTURE MOZZARELLA CHEESE, SHREDDED

¼ SMALL ONION, SLICED THIN

2 SLICES THICK-CUT HAM, CHOPPED

1 HANDFUL GREEN OLIVES, PITTED

2 HARD-BOILED EGGS, SLICED

DRIED OREGANO, TO TASTE

OLIVE OIL, TO TASTE

GLOBAL PIZZA | 315

THICK-CRUST PIZZA WITH ONIONS

YIELD: 1 PIZZA / **ACTIVE TIME:** 20 MINUTES / **TOTAL TIME:** 1 HOUR

Locally called *fugazza* due to the influence of Ligurian immigrants in Argentina, the typical Argentinian pie is as thick as a focaccia, but topped with mozzarella cheese like a pizza. The most popular version, *fugazza con queso*, is loaded with onions. Suffice to say, Ligurians would approve.

Preheat the oven to 480°F (250°C) and place a baking stone or steel on the middle rack of the oven as it warms. Coat the bottom of a skillet with olive oil and warm over medium-high heat. When the oil starts to shimmer, add the onions and sauté until they are soft, about 10 minutes. Remove the pan from heat, season the onions with salt, and let cool completely.

2. Grease a round baking dish with olive oil, place the dough in it, and spread it until it is approximately ½ inch thick (1.5 centimeters). Place the dish in the oven and bake for about 10 minutes, until the crust starts to brown. Remove the pizza, distribute the mozzarella and onions over the top, and return the pizza to the oven. Bake for about 10 minutes, until the crust is golden brown and starting to char. Remove and let cool slightly before garnishing with dried oregano, slicing, and serving.

SALT, TO TASTE

⅓ BATCH QUICK FOCACCIA DOUGH (SEE PAGE 83)

8.8 OZ. | 250 GRAMS FRESH MOZZARELLA CHEESE, DRAINED AND SLICED

DRIED OREGANO, TO TASTE

CHORIZO & JALAPEÑO PIZZA

YIELD: 1 PIZZA / **ACTIVE TIME:** 15 MINUTES / **TOTAL TIME:** 45 MINUTES

Surprisingly, Mexico is one of the countries with the biggest consumption of pizza, second only to the US. Turns out, the earthy flavors of Mexican cuisine are a perfect match for an Italian flatbread.

1. Preheat the oven to the maximum temperature and place a baking stone or steel on the middle rack of the oven as it warms. Dust a work surface with the semolina flour, place the dough on the surface, and gently stretch it into a round. For more detailed instructions on properly stretching a ball of pizza dough see page 73. Cover the pizza with the mozzarella and top with the onion, chorizo, and pickled jalapeño. Season with salt and drizzle olive oil over the pizza.

2. Using a peel or a flat baking sheet, transfer the pizza to the heated baking implement in the oven. Bake for about 15 minutes, until the crust is golden brown and starting to char. Remove and let cool slightly before slicing and serving.

INGREDIENTS:

SEMOLINA FLOUR, AS NEEDED

1 BALL PIZZA DOUGH

2.8 OZ. | 80 GRAMS LOW-MOISTURE MOZZARELLA CHEESE, SHREDDED

½ WHITE OR RED ONION, SLICED THIN

1 LINK CHORIZO, CHOPPED

0.5 OZ. | 15 GRAMS SLICED PICKLED JALAPEÑO PEPPERS

SALT, TO TASTE

OLIVE OIL, TO TASTE

MINCEMEAT & VEGETABLE PIZZA

YIELD: 1 PIZZA / **ACTIVE TIME:** 25 MINUTES / **TOTAL TIME:** 1 HOUR

Pizza has become a popular street food in Iran, and this pie showcases just one of several interesting toppings popular in the country. As one would expect, Iranians' favorites have been influenced by the flavors of the local cuisine.

1. Preheat the oven to the maximum temperature and place a baking stone or steel on the middle rack of the oven as it warms. Coat the bottom of a skillet with olive oil and warm over medium-high heat. When the oil starts to shimmer, add the onion and sauté until it has softened, about 10 minutes. Add the ground beef, advieh, bell pepper, and mushrooms, season with salt, and cook, breaking up the ground beef with a wooden spoon, until it is browned, about 8 minutes. Remove from heat and let the mixture cool completely.

2. Dust a work surface with the semolina flour, place the dough on the surface, and gently stretch it into a round. For more detailed instructions on properly stretching a ball of pizza dough see page 73. Cover the dough with half of the mozzarella and top with the ground beef mixture and the corn. Sprinkle the remaining mozzarella over the pizza.

3. Using a peel or a flat baking sheet, transfer the pizza to the heated baking implement in the oven. Bake for about 15 minutes, until the crust is golden brown and starting to char. Remove and let cool slightly before garnishing with the ketchup and mustard (if using), slicing, and serving.

INGREDIENTS:

SPICE MIX)

½ SMALL RED BELL PEPPER, CHOPPED

2.4 OZ. | 70 GRAMS MUSHROOMS, CHOPPED

SALT, TO TASTE

SEMOLINA FLOUR, AS NEEDED

1 BALL PIZZA DOUGH

3.5 OZ. | 100 GRAMS LOW-MOISTURE MOZZARELLA CHEESE, SHREDDED

0.5 OZ. | 15 GRAMS SWEET CORN

KETCHUP, TO TASTE (OPTIONAL)

MUSTARD, TO TASTE (OPTIONAL)

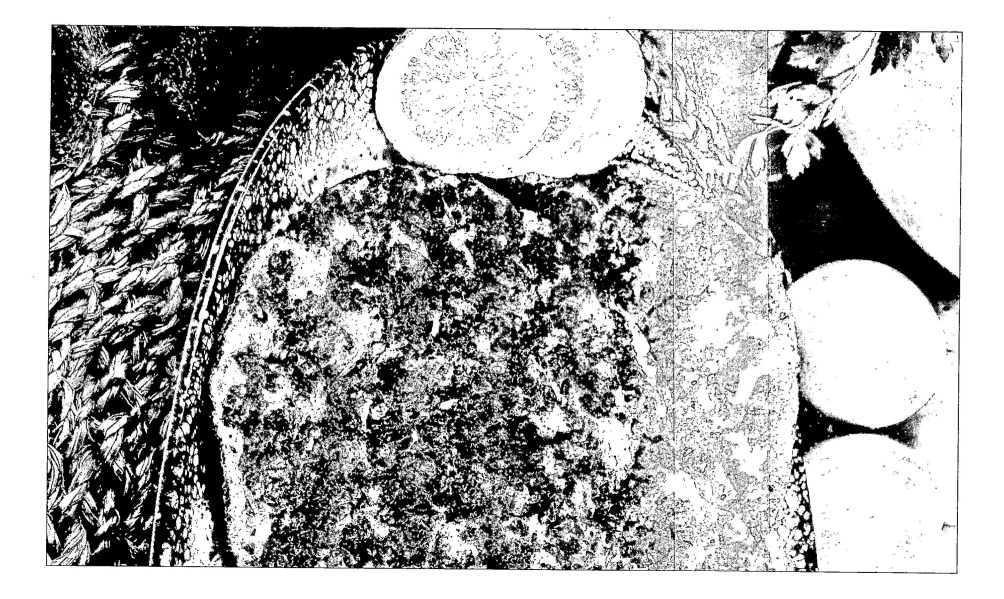

LAHMACUN

In Turkey, pizza is not really pizza—instead, it is a local flatbread called *lahmacun*. *Lahmacun* means "dough with meat," and the bread consists of a thin layer of flattened dough covered by a spicy paste containing raw meat. This is then baked together. With this one, it is important to bake the "pizza" at a lower temperature than usual, as this will allow the meat to be fully cooked.

1. Preheat the oven to 410°F (210°C) and place a baking stone or steel on the middle rack of the oven as it warms. Place the dough on a piece of parchment paper and gently stretch it into a very thin round. For more detailed instructions on properly stretching a ball of pizza dough see page 73. Spread the Lahmacun over the dough.

2. Using a peel or a flat baking sheet, transfer the pizza to the heated baking implement in the oven. Bake for about 10 minutes, until the crust is golden brown and starting to char. Remove and top with the lemon juice, sumac powder, onion, tomato, cucumber, and feta. Drizzle olive oil over the top and garnish with fresh mint leaves.

LAHMACUN

1. Place all of the ingredients in a food processor or blender and blitz until the mixture is a smooth paste.

INGREDIENTS:

1 BALL PIZZA DOUGH (24-HOUR PIZZA DOUGH WITH 62 PERCENT HYDRATION RECOMMENDED, SEE PAGE 111)

3 TABLESPOONS LAHMACUN (SEE RECIPE)

JUICE OF 1 LEMON WEDGE

SUMAC POWDER, TO TASTE

¼ SMALL RED ONION, SLICED

⅓ TOMATO, SLICED

1.4 OZ. | 40 GRAMS CUCUMBER, JULIENNED

0.5 OZ. | 15 GRAMS CRUMBLED FETA CHEESE

OLIVE OIL, TO TASTE

FRESH MINT LEAVES, FOR GARNISH

LAHMACUN

12.3 OZ. | 350 GRAMS GROUND BEEF

½ LARGE ONION, CHOPPED

½ GREEN BELL PEPPER

1 TOMATO, CHOPPED

1 BUNCH FRESH PARSLEY

1½ TEASPOONS | 7.5 GRAMS TAHINI

0.5 OZ. | 15 GRAMS TOMATO PASTE

¼ TEASPOON | 0.6 GRAMS RED PEPPER FLAKES

¼ TEASPOON | 0.6 GRAMS BLACK PEPPER

¼ TEASPOON | 0.6 GRAMS GROUND NUTMEG

½ TEASPOON | 1.3 GRAMS CINNAMON

½ TEASPOON | 1.3 GRAMS GROUND ALLSPICE

½ TEASPOON | 1.3 GRAMS SUMAC POWDER

½ TEASPOON | 1.3 GRAMS DRIED THYME

½ TEASPOON | 2.9 GRAMS TABLE SALT

JUICE OF 1 LEMON WEDGE

PIZZA WITH ZA'ATAR

YIELD: 1 PIZZA / **ACTIVE TIME:** 10 MINUTES / **TOTAL TIME:** 30 MINUTES

The Middle East has many pizza restaurants that offer a variety of classic, gourmet, and fusion pizza toppings. Here, we use pizza dough to make *manaquish fi za'atar*, a popular flatbread throughout the region.

1. Preheat the oven to 400°F (205°C) and place a baking stone or steel on the middle rack of the oven as it warms. Place the dough on a piece of parchment paper and gently stretch it into a very thin round. For more detailed instructions on properly stretching a ball of pizza dough see page 73. Spread the Za'atar over the dough.

2. Using a peel or a flat baking sheet, transfer the pizza to the heated baking implement in the oven. Bake for about 10 minutes, until the crust is golden brown and starting to char. Remove and top with the onion, tomato, cucumber, feta, and olives.

ZA'ATAR

1. Place the ingredients in a bowl and stir until they are combined into a paste.

INGREDIENTS·

¼ SMALL RED ONION, SLICED

⅓ TOMATO, SLICED

1.4 OZ. | 40 GRAMS CUCUMBER, JULIENNED

0.5 OZ. | 15 GRAMS FETA CHEESE, CRUMBLED

1 HANDFUL GREEN OLIVES, PITTED

ZA'ATAR
½ CUP ZA'ATAR SEASONING

3.5 OZ. | 100 GRAMS OLIVE OIL

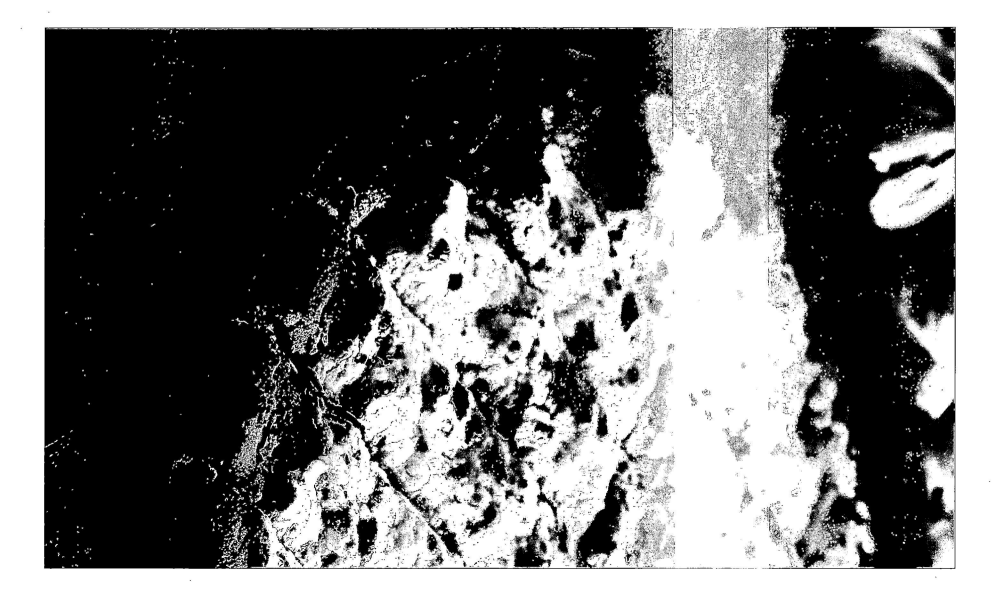

GARLIC FINGERS

YIELD: 1 PIZZA / **ACTIVE TIME:** 15 MINUTES / **TOTAL TIME:** 45 MINUTES

In Canada, one can find a pizza that is a bit like garlic bread smothered in mozzarella cheese and dipped in a local sauce called "donair." This is probably more of a flatbread than a pizza, but it's undeniably intriguing.

1. Preheat the oven to the maximum temperature and place a baking stone or steel on the middle rack of the oven as it warms. Dust a work surface with the semolina flour, place the dough on the surface, and gently stretch it into a round. For more detailed instructions on properly stretching a ball of pizza dough see page 73. Cover the dough with the Garlic Butter and top with the mozzarella.

2. Using a peel or a flat baking sheet, transfer the pizza to the heated baking implement in the oven. Bake for about 15 minutes, until the crust is golden brown and starting to char. Remove and let cool slightly before slicing into thin strips and serving with the Donair Sauce.

GARLIC BUTTER

1. Combine all of the ingredients and use as desired.

DONAIR SAUCE

1. Combine all of the ingredients and use as desired.

INGREDIENTS:

1 TABLESPOON | 14.2 GRAMS GARLIC BUTTER (SEE RECIPE), AT ROOM TEMPERATURE

SEMOLINA FLOUR, AS NEEDED

1 BALL PIZZA DOUGH

5.3 OZ. | 150 GRAMS LOW-MOISTURE MOZZARELLA CHEESE, SHREDDED

DONAIR SAUCE (SEE RECIPE), FOR SERVING

GARLIC BUTTER

3.5 OZ. | 100 GRAMS SALTED BUTTER, AT ROOM TEMPERATURE

1 GARLIC CLOVE, MINCED

1 TABLESPOON | 3.8 GRAMS FINELY CHOPPED FRESH PARSLEY

1½ TEASPOONS | 1.5 GRAMS SLICED FRESH CHIVES

1 OZ. | 30 GRAMS FRESH LEMON JUICE

DONAIR SAUCE

7 OZ. | 200 GRAMS SWEETENED CONDENSED MILK

2.1 OZ. | 60 GRAMS WHITE VINEGAR

½ TEASPOON | 1.6 GRAMS GARLIC POWDER

PIZZA WITH BANANA CURRY

YIELD: 1 PIZZA / **ACTIVE TIME:** 15 MINUTES / **TOTAL TIME:** 45 MINUTES

S weden has become known for some very unorthodox pizza toppings, and this one has elicited reactions of astonishment and sometimes disgust all over the world. Being an Italian living in Sweden, I have first-hand impressions and, against all odds, I have to admit that I like this topping. Curry just goes so well with bananas that it feels all right even on a pizza crust. Due to Middle Eastern influences, Swedish pizza crust is often more like Turkish flatbread—paper thin

Preheat the oven to the maximum temperature and place a baking stone or steel on the middle rack of the oven as it warms. Dust a work surface with the semolina flour, place the dough on the surface, and gently stretch it into a very thin round. It may be easier to use a rolling pin to get it thin enough.

2. Combine the sauce and the tomato paste and spread the mixture over the dough. Top with the banana, pineapple (if desired), chicken, and mozzarella. Generously sprinkle curry over the pizza.

3. Using a peel or a flat baking sheet, transfer the pizza to the heated baking implement in the oven. Bake for about 15 minutes, until the crust is golden brown and starting to char. Remove and let cool slightly before slicing and serving.

1 OZ. | 30 GRAMS RAW PIZZA SAUCE (SEE PAGE 103)

1 TABLESPOON | 16.6 GRAMS TOMATO PASTE

½ LARGE OR 1 SMALL BANANA, SLICED

2 SLICES CANNED PINEAPPLE RINGS, CHOPPED (OPTIONAL)

½ COOKED CHICKEN BREAST, CHOPPED

3.5 OZ. | 100 GRAMS LOW-MOISTURE MOZZARELLA CHEESE, SHREDDED

CURRY POWDER, TO TASTE

MUSHROOM & GHERKIN PIZZA

YIELD: 1 PIZZA / **ACTIVE TIME:** 15 MINUTES / **TOTAL TIME:** 45 MINUTES

Don't be so quick to scrunch up your nose at this pizza—the beguiling sweet-and-tart flavor of the gherkin makes for a memorable experience.

1. Preheat the oven to the maximum temperature and place a baking stone or steel on the middle rack of the oven as it warms. Dust a work surface with the semolina flour, place the dough on the surface, and gently stretch it into a round. For more detailed instructions on properly stretching a ball of pizza dough see page 73. Cover the dough with half of the mozzarella and distribute the mushrooms and gherkins on top. Sprinkle the remaining mozzarella over the pizza.

2. Using a peel or a flat baking sheet, transfer the pizza to the heated baking implement in the oven. Bake for about 15 minutes, until the crust is golden brown and starting to char. Remove and let cool slightly before slicing and serving.

INGREDIENTS:

SEMOLINA FLOUR, AS NEEDED

1 BALL PIZZA DOUGH

3.5 OZ. | 100 GRAMS LOW-MOISTURE MOZZARELLA CHEESE, SHREDDED

2.4 OZ. | 70 GRAMS BUTTON MUSHROOMS, SLICED

3 GHERKINS, SLICED

PIZZA TODAY

*S*ome pizzaiolos contend that for pizza to be authentic it must adhere to the very strict guidelines established by the Associazone Verace Pizza Napoletana. But authenticity is in the eye of the beholder, and, as the following recipes make clear, pizza's most authentic quality is its ability to accommodate a truly global and contemporary range of flavors.

ROASTED FENNEL & SAUSAGE PIZZA

YIELD: 1 PIZZA / **ACTIVE TIME:** 25 MINUTES / **TOTAL TIME:** 1 HOUR AND 15 MINUTES

An elegant combination of muscular flavors. Roasted fennel complements Italian sausage (*salsiccia*) very well, as the meat is often flavored with fennel seed.

1. Preheat the oven to 430°F (220°C). Place the fennel in a baking dish, season with salt, drizzle olive oil over the fennel, and place on the middle rack. Roast until it is tender and just starting to caramelize, 30 to 35 minutes. Remove from the oven and let cool completely.

2. Preheat the oven to the maximum temperature and place a baking stone or steel in the oven as it warms. Dust a work surface with the semolina flour, place the dough on the surface, and gently stretch it into a round. For more detailed instructions on properly stretching a ball of pizza dough see page 73. Cover the dough with the sauce and top with the sausage, roasted fennel, and onion, and the pizza with salt and pepper and drizzle olive oil over the top.

3. Using a peel or a flat baking sheet, transfer the pizza to the heated baking implement surface in the oven. Bake for about 7 minutes, until the crust starts to brown. Remove the pizza, distribute the mozzarella over the top, and return the pizza to the oven. Bake for about 5 minutes, until the crust is golden brown and starting to char. Remove and let cool slightly before slicing and serving.

INGREDIENTS:

2.8 OZ. | 80 GRAMS RAW PIZZA SAUCE (SEE PAGE 103)

2.1 OZ. | 60 GRAMS ITALIAN SAUSAGE, CHOPPED

½ ONION, SLICED

3.5 OZ. | 100 GRAMS FRESH MOZZARELLA CHEESE, DRAINED AND TORN

PIZZA WITH ROMANESCO BROCCOLI CREAM, ANCHOVIES & BURRATA

YIELD: 1 PIZZA / **ACTIVE TIME:** 15 MINUTES / **TOTAL TIME:** 45 MINUTES

There are a few vegetables I like more than Romanesco broccoli. It pairs naturally with anchovies, and of course it is to die for when we add burrata to the already delicious combo.

1. Preheat the oven to the maximum temperature and place a baking stone or steel on the middle rack of the oven as it warms. Dust a work surface with the semolina flour, place the dough on the surface, and gently stretch it into a round. For more detailed instructions on properly stretching a ball of pizza dough see page 73. Cover the dough with the Romanesco Broccoli Cream, top with the anchovies, season the pizza with salt, and drizzle olive oil over the top.

2. Using a peel or a flat baking sheet, transfer the pizza to the heated baking implement in the oven. Bake for about 15 minutes, until the crust is golden brown and starting to char. Remove, top with the burrata, season with salt and pepper, and drizzle olive oil over the top.

ROMANESCO BROCCOLI CREAM

1. Bring salted water to a boil and add the broccoli. Cook until it starts to feel tender, drain, and pat dry.

2. Coat the bottom of a skillet with olive oil and warm over medium-high heat. When the oil starts to shimmer, add the onion and broccoli and cook until the onion starts to soften, about 5 minutes. Transfer the mixture to a blender or food processor, add the remaining ingredients, and blitz until smooth.

3. If the sauce is not as thick as you would like, place it in a saucepan and cook over medium-high heat until it has reduced to the desired consistency.

INGREDIENTS:

SEMOLINA FLOUR, AS NEEDED

1 BALL PIZZA DOUGH

3 TABLESPOONS ROMANESCO BROCCOLI CREAM (SEE RECIPE)

4 ANCHOVIES IN OLIVE OIL

SALT AND PEPPER, TO TASTE

OLIVE OIL, TO TASTE

4.4 OZ. | 125 GRAMS BURRATA CHEESE, TORN

ROMANESCO BROCCOLI CREAM

SALT AND PEPPER, TO TASTE

17.6 OZ. | 500 GRAMS ROMANESCO BROCCOLI FLORETS

1 TABLESPOON | 13.3 GRAMS OLIVE OIL, PLUS MORE AS NEEDED

½ SMALL ONION, SLICED THIN

1 OZ. | 30 GRAMS PARMESAN CHEESE, GRATED

3 FRESH BASIL LEAVES (OPTIONAL)

PIZZA WITH PROSCIUTTO, ARUGULA & PARMESAN

YIELD: 1 PIZZA / **ACTIVE TIME:** 15 MINUTES / **TOTAL TIME:** 45 MINUTES

For all the lovers of prosciutto, here it is paired with its perfect partners, arugula and Parmesan.

1. Preheat the oven to the maximum temperature and place a baking stone or steel on the middle rack as it warms. Dust a work surface with the semolina flour, place the dough on the surface, and gently stretch it into a round. For more detailed instructions on properly stretching a ball of pizza dough see page 73. Cover the dough with the sauce, season with salt and pepper, and drizzle olive oil over the top.

2. Using a peel or a flat baking sheet, transfer the pizza to the heated baking implement in the oven. Bake for about 7 minutes, until the crust starts to brown. Remove the pizza, distribute the mozzarella over the top, and return the pizza to the oven. Bake for about 5 minutes, until the crust is golden brown and starting to char. Remove and top with the prosciutto slices, the arugula, and the shaved Parmesan. Season with salt and pepper, drizzle olive oil over the pizza, and serve.

INGREDIENTS:

SEMOLINA FLOUR, AS NEEDED

1 BALL PIZZA DOUGH

2.8 OZ. | 80 GRAMS RAW PIZZA SAUCE (SEE PAGE 103)

SALT AND PEPPER, TO TASTE

OLIVE OIL, TO TASTE

3.5 OZ. | 100 GRAMS FRESH MOZZARELLA CHEESE, DRAINED AND TORN

2.8 OZ. | 80 GRAMS PROSCIUTTO, SLICED THIN

1 GENEROUS HANDFUL ARUGULA

1.75 OZ. | 50 GRAMS PARMESAN CHEESE, SHAVED

TUNA & ORANGE-MARINATED FENNEL PIZZA

YIELD: 1 PIZZA / **ACTIVE TIME:** 20 MINUTES / **TOTAL TIME:** 1 HOUR

Inspired by the flavors of Sicilian cuisine, this pizza is a wonderful Mediterranean explosion of flavors that will surely impress.

1. Preheat the oven to the maximum temperature and place a baking stone or steel on the middle rack as it warms. Place the fennel, olive oil, and orange juice in a bowl, season with salt and pepper, and stir to combine. Let the mixture marinate for 25 minutes, then drain and pat dry.

2. Dust a work surface with the semolina flour, place the dough on the surface, and gently stretch it into a round. For more detailed instructions on properly stretching a ball of pizza dough see page 73. Generously drizzle olive oil over the top, cover the pizza with the mozzarella, and distribute the tuna and fennel over the cheese.

3. Using a peel or a flat baking sheet, transfer the pizza to the heated baking implement in the oven. Bake for about 15 minutes, until the crust is golden brown and starting to char. Remove, sprinkle the orange zest over the pizza, and drizzle more olive oil on top. Let cool slightly before slicing and serving.

INGREDIENTS:

SEMOLINA FLOUR, AS NEEDED

1 BALL PIZZA DOUGH

1.75 OZ. | 50 GRAMS FRESH, LOW-MOISTURE MOZZARELLA CHEESE, SLICED

2.8 OZ. | 80 GRAMS CANNED TUNA, DRAINED

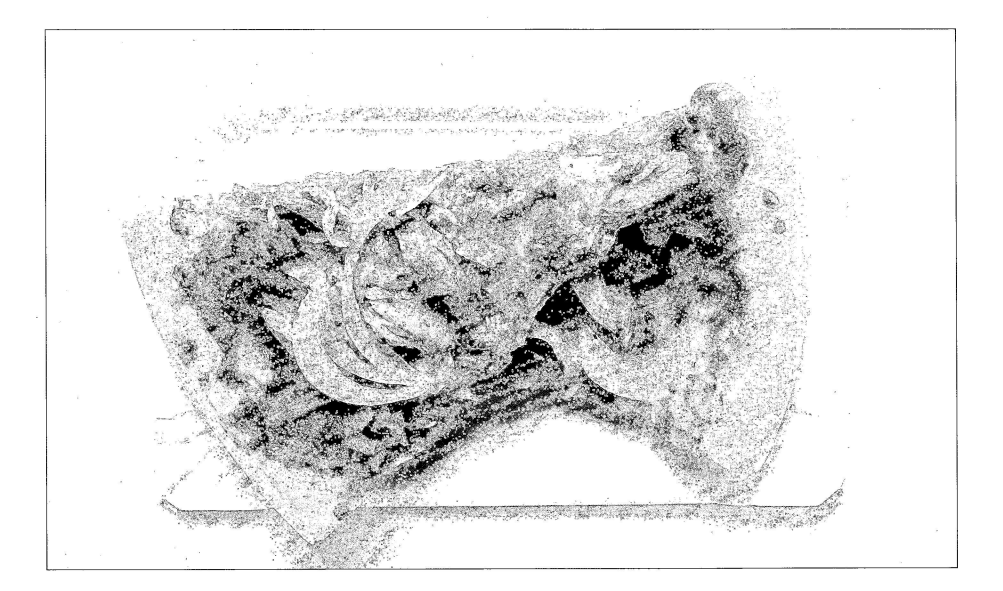

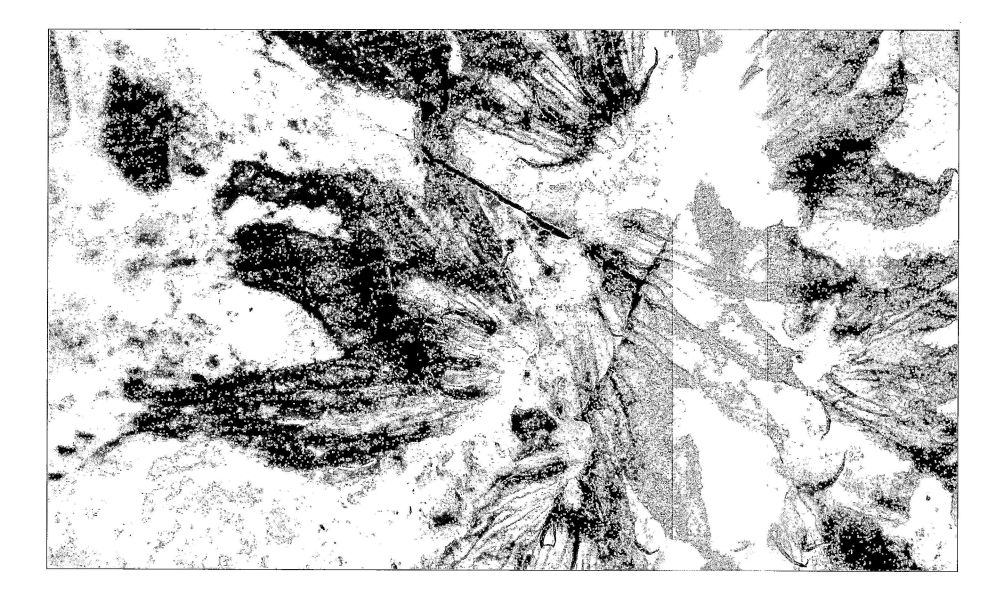

SQUASH BLOSSOM & RICOTTA PIZZA

YIELD: 1 PIZZA / **ACTIVE TIME:** 15 MINUTES / **TOTAL TIME:** 45 MINUTES

A summery bianca that makes good use of seasonal delicacies. If you have a green thumb, this is a great way to use your squash blossoms and mint leaves.

1. Preheat the oven to the maximum temperature and place a baking stone or steel on the middle rack as it warms. Dust a work surface with the semolina flour, place the dough on the surface, and gently stretch it into a round. For more detailed instructions on properly stretching a ball of pizza dough see page 73.

2. Drizzle olive oil over the dough, cover with the shredded mozzarella, and distribute the squash blossoms over the cheese. You want to open the squash blossoms up so that they cover as much of the pizza as possible. Distribute the anchovies and dollops of the ricotta over the pizza, season with salt and pepper, and drizzle more olive oil over the top.

3. Using a peel or a flat baking sheet, transfer the pizza to the heated baking implement in the oven. Bake for about 15 minutes, until the crust is golden brown and starting to char. Remove from the oven, sprinkle the lemon zest and mint over the pizza, and let it cool slightly before serving.

INGREDIENTS:

SEMOLINA FLOUR, AS NEEDED

1 BALL PIZZA DOUGH

OLIVE OIL, TO TASTE

3.5 OZ. | 100 GRAMS LOW-MOISTURE MOZZARELLA CHEESE, SHREDDED

3 SQUASH BLOSSOMS, SLICED LENGTHWISE

2 TO 3 ANCHOVIES, DRAINED

3.5 OZ. | 100 GRAMS RICOTTA CHEESE

SALT AND PEPPER, TO TASTE

ZEST OF 1 LEMON

FRESH MINT LEAVES, TO TASTE

EGGPLANT PARMIGIANA PIZZA

YIELD: 1 PIZZA / **ACTIVE TIME:** 25 MINUTES / **TOTAL TIME:** 1 HOUR AND 15 MINUTES

My grandma was from the deep south of Italy and her parmigiana was so rich that it verged on the epic. One thing she liked to do was to hide boiled eggs within the layers of fried eggplant, and I still think that is quite a good idea. Here's a pizza with a slightly lighter version of her speciality.

1. Preheat the oven to the maximum temperature and place a baking stone or steel on the middle rack as it warms. Place the eggplant in a baking dish, drizzle olive oil over the slices, and season with salt. Roast the eggplant in the warming oven until the slices are fork-tender, about 25 minutes. Remove and let cool completely.

2. Dust a work surface with the semolina flour, place the dough on the surface, and gently stretch it into a round. For more detailed instructions on properly stretching a ball of pizza dough see page 73. Cover the dough with the sauce and distribute the roasted eggplant on top. Season with salt and pepper and drizzle olive oil over the pizza.

3. Using a peel or a flat baking sheet, transfer the pizza to the heated baking implement in the oven. Bake for about 7 minutes, until the crust starts to brown. Remove the pizza and distribute the mozzarella, hard-boiled egg (if using), and Parmesan over the top. Return the pizza to the oven and bake for about 5 minutes, until the crust is golden brown and starting to char. Remove from the oven, sprinkle shaved Parmesan and the basil over the pizza, and drizzle more olive oil on top. Let cool slightly before slicing and serving.

SEMOLINA FLOUR, AS NEEDED

1 BALL PIZZA DOUGH

3.5 OZ. | 100 GRAMS RAW PIZZA SAUCE (SEE PAGE 103)

3.5 OZ. | 100 GRAMS FRESH MOZZARELLA CHEESE, DRAINED AND TORN

1 HARD-BOILED EGG, SLICED (OPTIONAL)

1.75 OZ. | 50 GRAMS PARMESAN CHEESE, GRATED, PLUS MORE FOR GARNISH

FRESH BASIL LEAVES, TO TASTE

PIZZA WITH MUSHROOMS, CARAMELIZED ONIONS & CACIOCAVALLO

YIELD: 1 PIZZA / **ACTIVE TIME:** 20 MINUTES / **TOTAL TIME:** 1 HOUR

Perfect for a cold winter night, this white pizza brings the classic mushroom topping to a whole new level. If you can't locate caciocavallo, substitute any medium-hard cheese that melts well.

INGREDIENTS:

3.5 OZ. | 100 GRAMS MIXED MUSHROOMS (PORCINI, SHIITAKE, CREMINI, OYSTER, CHANTERELLE), CHOPPED

½ GARLIC CLOVE, MINCED

FRESH PARSLEY, FINELY CHOPPED, TO TASTE

SALT AND PEPPER, TO TASTE

OLIVE OIL, AS NEEDED

½ ONION, SLICED THIN

SEMOLINA FLOUR, AS NEEDED

1 BALL PIZZA DOUGH

3.5 OZ. | 100 GRAMS LOW-MOISTURE MOZZARELLA CHEESE, SHREDDED

2.8 OZ. | 80 GRAMS CACIOCAVALLO CHEESE, CUBED

1. Preheat the oven to the maximum temperature and place a baking stone or steel on the middle rack as it warms. Place the mushrooms, garlic, parsley, salt, and a generous amount of olive oil in a bowl, stir to combine, and let the mixture marinate for 10 minutes. Drain and set aside.

2. Coat the bottom of a skillet with olive oil and warm it over medium-high heat. When the oil starts to shimmer, add the onion and sauté until it is soft, about 10 minutes. Remove from heat and let cool.

3. Dust a work surface with the semolina flour, place the dough on the surface, and gently stretch it into a round. For more detailed instructions on properly stretching a ball of pizza dough see page 73. Drizzle olive oil over the dough and cover with the mozzarella. Sprinkle the mushrooms over the cheese. Distribute the onion over the pizza, season with salt and pepper, drizzle olive oil over the top, and layer the caciocavallo on top.

4. Using a peel or a flat baking sheet, transfer the pizza to the heated baking implement in the oven. Bake for about 15 minutes, until the crust is golden brown and starting to char. Remove from the oven, sprinkle more parsley on top, and drizzle with olive oil. Let the pizza cool slightly before slicing and serving.

PIZZA WITH ASPARAGUS, PINE NUTS & BUFALA

YIELD: 1 PIZZA / **ACTIVE TIME:** 20 MINUTES / **TOTAL TIME:** 1 HOUR

A delicate combination that makes good use of fresh and delicious Mediterranean ingredients.

1. Preheat the oven to the maximum temperature and place a baking stone or steel on the middle rack as it warms. Bring a pot of salted water to a boil and prepare an ice bath. Add the asparagus to the boiling water and cook for 2 minutes. Drain, transfer the asparagus to the ice bath, and let sit until completely cool. Drain well, pat dry, and halve each spear lengthwise.

2. Dust a work surface with the semolina flour, place the dough on the surface, and gently stretch it into a round. For more detailed instructions on properly stretching a ball of pizza dough see page 73. Drizzle olive oil over the dough, cover with the shredded mozzarella, and distribute the asparagus and pine nuts on top of the cheese. Season with salt and pepper and drizzle olive oil over the pizza.

3. Using a peel or a flat baking sheet, transfer the pizza to the heated baking implement in the oven. Bake for about 15 minutes, until the crust is golden brown and starting to char. Remove from the oven and top with the buffalo mozzarella. Sprinkle the lemon zest and drizzle olive oil over the pizza and let it cool slightly before slicing and serving.

INGREDIENTS:

SALT AND PEPPER, TO TASTE

MOZZARELLA CHEESE, SHREDDED

1 HANDFUL PINE NUTS

2.4 OZ. | 70 GRAMS BUFFALO MOZZARELLA CHEESE, DRAINED AND TORN

ZEST OF ½ LEMON

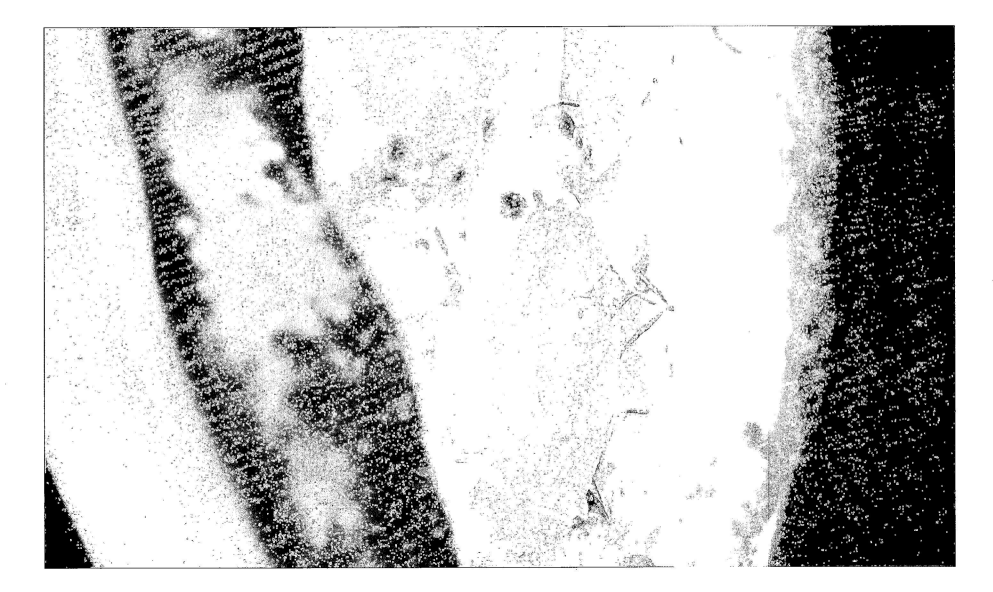

ARTICHOKE & POTATO PIZZA

YIELD: 1 PIZZA / **ACTIVE TIME:** 20 MINUTES / **TOTAL TIME:** 1 HOUR

An earthy pizza where the rich flavor of the artichokes is balanced by the smoothness of the potatoes.

INGREDIENTS:

SALT AND PEPPER, TO TASTE

1 POTATO, PEELED AND SLICED THIN

SEMOLINA FLOUR, AS NEEDED

1 BALL PIZZA DOUGH

OLIVE OIL, TO TASTE

2.8 OZ. | 80 GRAMS LOW-MOISTURE MOZZARELLA CHEESE, SHREDDED

3 TO 4 ARTICHOKE HEARTS IN OLIVE OIL, CHOPPED

FRESH ROSEMARY, TO TASTE

1. Preheat the oven to the maximum temperature and place a baking stone or steel on the middle rack as it warms. Bring a pot of salted water to a boil and prepare an ice bath. Add the potato to the boiling water and cook until it is translucent, 1 to 2 minutes. Drain, transfer the potato to the ice bath, and let sit for 2 minutes. Drain well and pat dry.

2. Dust a work surface with the semolina flour, place the dough on the surface, and gently stretch it into a round. For more detailed instructions on properly stretching a ball of pizza dough see page 73. Drizzle olive oil over the dough, cover with the shredded mozzarella, and distribute the potato and artichoke over the cheese. Season with salt and pepper, drizzle olive oil over the pizza, and sprinkle a generous amount of rosemary on top.

3. Using a peel or a flat baking sheet, transfer the pizza to the heated baking implement in the oven. Bake for about 15 minutes, until the crust is golden brown and starting to char. Remove and let the pizza cool slightly before slicing and serving.

PIZZA WITH SICILIAN-STYLE TUNA & BELL PEPPERS

YIELD: 1 PIZZA / **ACTIVE TIME:** 25 MINUTES / **TOTAL TIME:** 1 HOUR AND 15 MINUTES

My Roman grandmother had a Sicilian neighbor who taught her how to make tuna fish–stuffed bell peppers, and that became a favorite dish of my youth. Here's a topping inspired by that lovely memory.

1. Preheat the oven to the maximum temperature and place a baking stone or steel on the middle rack as it warms. Place the bell pepper in a baking dish, drizzle olive oil over it, and season with salt. Place the pepper in the warming oven and roast for 25 to 30 minutes, until it is tender and starting to char. Remove and let cool completely.

2. Place the tomatoes in a bowl and add the olives, capers, garlic, and parsley. Season with salt, pepper, and olive oil, stir to combine, and set aside.

3. Dust a work surface with the semolina flour, place the dough on the surface, and gently stretch it into a round. For more detailed instructions on properly stretching a ball of pizza dough see page 73. Cover the dough with the tomato sauce and distribute the tuna and roasted pepper over the sauce. Season with salt and pepper and drizzle olive oil over the pizza.

4. Using a peel or a flat baking sheet, transfer the pizza to the heated baking implement in the oven. Bake for about 15 minutes, until the crust is golden brown and starting to char. Remove and sprinkle the pecorino and basil on top. Let the pizza cool slightly before slicing and serving.

INGREDIENTS:

3.5 OZ. | 100 GRAMS WHOLE CANNED TOMATOES, MASHED

1 TABLESPOON | 11.2 GRAMS CHOPPED GREEN OLIVES

1 TABLESPOON | 7.5 GRAMS CAPERS

1 GARLIC CLOVE, MINCED

1 SMALL HANDFUL FRESH PARSLEY, FINELY CHOPPED

SEMOLINA FLOUR, AS NEEDED

1 BALL PIZZA DOUGH

2.8 OZ. | 80 GRAMS CANNED TUNA IN OLIVE OIL, DRAINED

1 TABLESPOON | 14 GRAMS PECORINO CHEESE, GRATED

FRESH BASIL LEAVES, TO TASTE

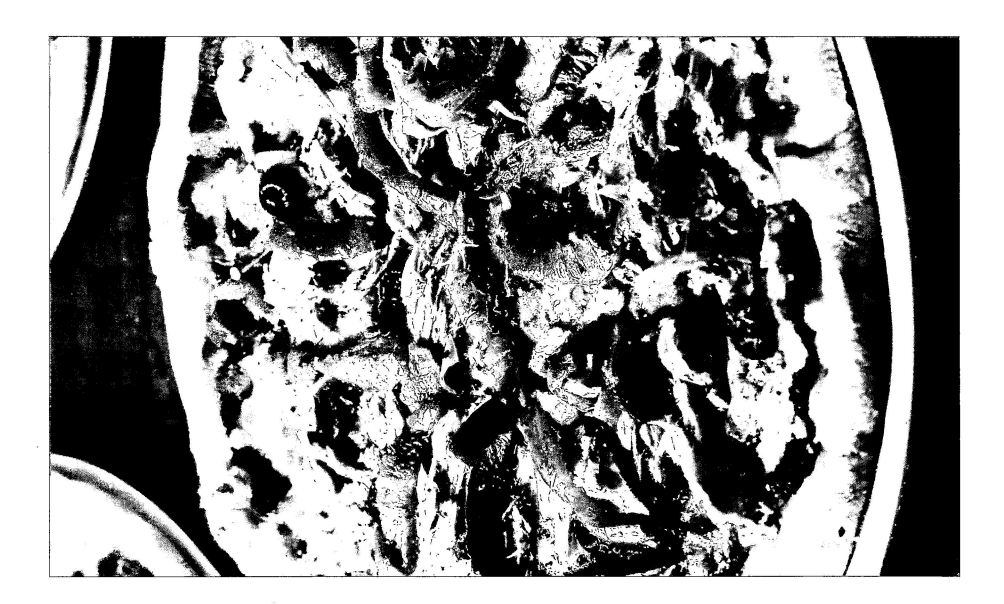

HAM & MUSHROOM PIZZA

YIELD: 1 PIZZA / **ACTIVE TIME:** 15 MINUTES / **TOTAL TIME:** 45 MINUTES

A real comfort food. Very simple ingredients, and plenty of taste.

1. Preheat the oven to the maximum temperature and place a baking stone or steel on the middle rack as it warms. Place the mushrooms and garlic in a bowl, season with salt, and drizzle olive oil over the mixture. Stir to combine and let the mushrooms marinate for 10 minutes.

2. Dust a work surface with the semolina flour, place the dough on the surface, and gently stretch it into a round. For more detailed instructions on properly stretching a ball of pizza dough see page 73. Cover the dough with the sauce, drain the mushrooms, and distribute them on top. Season the pizza with salt and pepper and drizzle olive oil over the top.

3. Using a peel or a flat baking sheet, transfer the pizza to the heated baking implement in the oven. Bake for about 7 minutes, until the crust starts to brown. Remove, distribute the mozzarella and ham over the top, and return the pizza to the oven. Bake for about 5 minutes, until the crust is golden brown and starting to char. Remove and let cool slightly before slicing and serving.

INGREDIENTS:

2.8 OZ. | 80 GRAMS BUTTON MUSHROOMS, SLICED

½ GARLIC CLOVE, MINCED

SALT AND PEPPER, TO TASTE

OLIVE OIL, AS NEEDED

SEMOLINA FLOUR, AS NEEDED

1 BALL PIZZA DOUGH

2.8 OZ. | 80 GRAMS RAW PIZZA SAUCE (SEE PAGE 103)

3.5 OZ. | 100 GRAMS FRESH MOZZARELLA CHEESE, DRAINED AND TORN

2.4 OZ. | 70 GRAMS HAM, CHOPPED

RICOTTA & BRESAOLA PIZZA

YIELD: 1 PIZZA / **ACTIVE TIME:** 15 MINUTES / **TOTAL TIME:** 45 MINUTES

The delicate flavor and creamy consistency of ricotta cheese match perfectly with lean and salty bresaola in this delicious white pizza.

1. Preheat the oven to the maximum temperature and place a baking stone or steel on the middle rack as it warms. Dust a work surface with the semolina flour, place the dough on the surface, and gently stretch it into a round. For more detailed instructions on properly stretching a ball of pizza dough see page 73. Drizzle olive oil over the dough, top with the mozzarella, and season with salt and pepper.

2. Using a peel or a flat baking sheet, transfer the pizza to the heated baking implement in the oven. Bake for about 15 minutes, until the crust is golden brown and starting to char. Remove the pizza from the oven, distribute the ricotta, bresaola, and Parmesan over it, and drizzle olive oil on top. Let cool slightly before slicing and serving.

INGREDIENTS:

SEMOLINA FLOUR, AS NEEDED

SALT AND PEPPER, TO TASTE

3.5 OZ. | 100 GRAMS RICOTTA CHEESE

1.4 OZ. | 40 GRAMS BRESAOLA, SLICED

1 OZ. | 30 GRAMS PARMESAN CHEESE, SHAVED

PIZZA WITH MUSSELS & ARTICHOKES

YIELD: 1 PIZZA / **ACTIVE TIME:** 15 MINUTES / **TOTAL TIME:** 45 MINUTES

A seafood topping enriched by the unique flavor of artichokes, which perfectly balances out the other ingredients.

1. Preheat the oven to the maximum temperature and place a baking stone or steel on the middle rack as it warms. Dust a work surface with the semolina flour, place the dough on the surface, and gently stretch it into a round. For more detailed instructions on properly stretching a ball of pizza dough see page 73.

2. Cover the dough with the sauce and distribute the anchovies over the pizza. Season the pizza with salt and drizzle olive oil over the top.

3. Using a peel or a flat baking sheet, transfer the pizza to the heated baking implement in the oven. Bake for about 5 minutes, until the crust starts to brown. Remove the pizza, distribute the artichokes, mussels, mozzarella, and parsley over the top, and season with salt and pepper. Drizzle olive oil over the pizza and return it to the oven. Bake for about 10 minutes, until the crust is golden brown and starting to char. Remove and let cool slightly before slicing and serving.

INGREDIENTS:

SEMOLINA FLOUR, AS NEEDED

1 BALL PIZZA DOUGH

2.4 OZ. | 70 GRAMS RAW PIZZA SAUCE (SEE PAGE 103)

4 ANCHOVIES IN OLIVE OIL, DRAINED

SALT AND PEPPER, TO TASTE

OLIVE OIL, AS NEEDED

2.8 OZ. | 80 GRAMS ARTICHOKE HEARTS IN OLIVE OIL, CHOPPED

1.4 OZ. | 40 GRAMS COOKED AND SHELLED MUSSELS

2.8 OZ. | 80 GRAMS FRESH MOZZARELLA CHEESE, DRAINED AND SLICED

FRESH PARSLEY, FINELY CHOPPED, FOR GARNISH

ROASTED ASPARAGUS & CHERRY TOMATO PIZZA

YIELD: 1 PIZZA / **ACTIVE TIME:** 20 MINUTES / **TOTAL TIME:** 1 HOUR AND 15 MINUTES

A classic Italian topping featuring the king of spring, asparagus, and a bit of sweetness from the roasted cherry tomatoes.

1. Preheat the oven to the maximum temperature and place a baking stone or steel on the middle rack as it warms. Place the asparagus in a bowl, drizzle olive oil over it, and season with salt and pepper. Toss to combine, place the asparagus on a baking sheet, and place in the warming oven. Roast for about 18 minutes, until just tender. Remove from the oven and let cool completely.

2. Dust a work surface with the semolina flour, place the dough on the surface, and gently stretch it into a round. For more detailed instructions on properly stretching a ball of pizza dough see page 73. Drizzle olive oil over the dough and top with the mozzarella and provolone. Distribute the asparagus and cherry tomatoes over the cheese, season with salt and pepper, and drizzle more olive oil over the pizza.

3. Using a peel or a flat baking sheet, transfer the pizza to the heated baking implement in the oven. Bake for about 15 minutes, until the crust is golden brown and starting to char. Remove and let cool slightly before slicing and serving.

INGREDIENTS:

1.75 OZ. | 50 GRAMS FRESH MOZZARELLA CHEESE, DRAINED AND TORN

1 OZ. | 30 GRAMS PROVOLONE CHEESE, SHREDDED

6 CHERRY TOMATOES, HALVED

RADICCHIO & GARDEN VEGETABLE PIZZA

YIELD: 1 PIZZA / **ACTIVE TIME:** 25 MINUTES / **TOTAL TIME:** 1 HOUR AND 15 MINUTES

With the bitter touch of the radicchio, the sweetness of the garden vegetables, and the umami present in the olives and capers, this is a bianca with character.

INGREDIENTS:

SALT, TO TASTE

3.5 OZ. | 100 GRAMS RADICCHIO

1 HANDFUL PITTED BLACK OLIVES

2 TEASPOONS | 6 GRAMS CAPERS, DRAINED

RED PEPPER FLAKES, TO TASTE (OPTIONAL)

OLIVE OIL, AS NEEDED

⅓ SMALL ZUCCHINI, SLICED

⅓ SMALL BELL PEPPER, SLICED

⅓ SMALL RED ONION, SLICED

SEMOLINA FLOUR, AS NEEDED

1 BALL PIZZA DOUGH

1. Preheat the oven to the maximum temperature and place a baking stone or steel on the middle rack as it warms. Bring salted water to a boil in a saucepan and add the radicchio. Cook until tender, drain, and pat dry with paper towels. Place the radicchio in a bowl, add the olives and capers, season with salt and red pepper flakes (if using), and generously drizzle olive oil over the mixture. Let it marinate for 10 minutes, drain, and set aside.

2. Place the zucchini and bell pepper in another bowl, season with salt, and drizzle olive oil over the vegetables. Toss to combine, place the mixture on a baking sheet, and place it in the oven. Roast for 12 to 15 minutes, until the vegetables are just starting to soften. Remove from the warming oven and let cool completely. Place the onion in a bowl of cold water and let it sit as the zucchini and pepper cool. When the vegetables are cool, drain the onion and pat it dry with paper towels.

3. Dust a work surface with the semolina flour, place the dough on the surface, and gently stretch it into a round. For more detailed instructions on properly stretching a ball of pizza dough see page 73. Drizzle olive oil over the dough and distribute the radicchio on top, making sure to spread the leaves open as much as possible. Arrange the zucchini and bell pepper over the radicchio, sprinkle the olives and capers on top, and cover the pizza with the onion. Season with salt and drizzle olive oil over the pizza.

4. Using a peel or a flat baking sheet, transfer the pizza to the heated baking implement in the oven. Bake for about 15 minutes, until the crust is golden brown and starting to char. Remove and let cool slightly before slicing and serving.

SPICY SALAMI & PROVOLONE PIZZA

YIELD: 1 PIZZA / **ACTIVE TIME:** 15 MINUTES / **TOTAL TIME:** 45 MINUTES

A simple but delicious combination, Italian spicy salami and provolone really need no other accompaniment to make a perfectly earthy pizza.

1. Preheat the oven to the maximum temperature and place a baking stone or steel on the middle rack as it warms. Dust a work surface with the semolina flour, place the dough on the surface, and gently stretch it into a round. For more detailed instructions on properly stretching a ball of pizza dough see page 73. Cover the dough with the sauce and drizzle olive oil over the top.

2. Using a peel or a flat baking sheet, transfer the pizza to the heated baking implement in the oven. Bake for about 7 minutes, until the crust starts to brown. Remove the pizza, drizzle olive oil over it, and then top with the provolone and salami. Return the pizza to the oven and bake for about 5 minutes, until the crust is golden brown and starting to char. Remove from the oven and let cool slightly before slicing and serving.

INGREDIENTS:

SEMOLINA FLOUR, FOR DUSTING

1.75 OZ. | 50 GRAMS PROVOLONE CHEESE, SLICED

1.75 OZ. | 50 GRAMS SPICY SALAMI, SLICED

PESTO, TOMATO & BUFALA PIZZA

YIELD: 1 PIZZA / **ACTIVE TIME:** 15 MINUTES / **TOTAL TIME:** 45 MINUTES

How can you go wrong with pesto, fresh buffalo mozzarella, and tomatoes? Well-tuned ingredients make for a classic and light Italian topping.

1. Preheat the oven to the maximum temperature and place a baking stone or steel on the middle rack as it warms. Dust a work surface with the semolina flour, place the dough on the surface, and gently stretch it into a round. For more detailed instructions on properly stretching a ball of pizza dough see page 73.

2. Cover the dough with the pizza sauce and top with the tomato. Season the pizza with salt and pepper and drizzle olive oil over the top.

3. Using a peel or a flat baking sheet, transfer the pizza to the heated baking implement in the oven. Bake for about 7 minutes, until the crust starts to brown. Remove the pizza, distribute the Basil Pesto and mozzarella over the top, and return the pizza to the oven. Bake for about 5 minutes, until the crust is golden brown and starting to char. Remove and let cool slightly before garnishing with the basil, slicing, and serving.

BASIL PESTO

1. Combine all of the ingredients, except for the salt, in a food processor and puree. Season with salt and use as desired. The pesto will keep in the refrigerator for up to 4 days and in the freezer for up to 3 months.

INGREDIENTS:

SEMOLINA FLOUR, AS NEEDED

1 BALL PIZZA DOUGH

2.8 OZ. | 80 GRAMS RAW PIZZA SAUCE (SEE PAGE 103)

1 TOMATO, SLICED

SALT AND PEPPER, TO TASTE

OLIVE OIL, TO TASTE

1 OZ. | 30 GRAMS BASIL PESTO (SEE RECIPE)

4.4 OZ. | 125 GRAMS BUFFALO MOZZARELLA CHEESE, DRAINED AND TORN

FRESH BASIL LEAVES, FOR GARNISH

BASIL PESTO

1 OZ. | 30 GRAMS FRESH BASIL LEAVES

1.75 OZ. | 50 GRAMS OLIVE OIL

2.8 OZ. | 80 GRAMS PINE NUTS

1 OZ. | 30 GRAMS PARMESAN CHEESE, GRATED

0.7 OZ. | 20 GRAMS PECORINO CHEESE, GRATED

SALT, TO TASTE

SPINACH & RICOTTA PIZZA

YIELD: 1 PIZZA / ACTIVE TIME: 20 MINUTES / TOTAL TIME: 1 HOUR

Spinach and ricotta cheese are a typical combo in Italian cooking, used to fill ravioli and cannelloni and to make vegetarian lasagna. As you'll find, it also makes for a good bianca topping.

INGREDIENTS:

SALT AND PEPPER, TO TASTE

SEMOLINA FLOUR, AS NEEDED

1 BALL PIZZA DOUGH

1.75 OZ. | 50 GRAMS LOW-MOISTURE MOZZARELLA CHEESE, SHREDDED

3.5 OZ. | 100 GRAMS RICOTTA CHEESE

1 OZ. | 30 GRAMS PROVOLONE CHEESE, GRATED

* Preheat the oven to the maximum temperature and place a baking stone or steel on the middle rack as it warms. Coat the bottom of a skillet with olive oil and warm over medium heat. When the oil starts to shimmer, add the spinach and garlic, cover the pan, and cook until the spinach has wilted, about 3 minutes. Uncover the pan, add the nutmeg, and season with salt and pepper. Raise the heat to medium-high and cook the spinach until all of the liquid has evaporated. Remove from heat and let cool.

2. Dust a work surface with the semolina flour, place the dough on the surface, and gently stretch it into a round. For more detailed instructions on properly stretching a ball of pizza dough see page 73. Drizzle olive oil over the dough and distribute the mozzarella over it.

3. Using a peel or a flat baking sheet, transfer the pizza to the heated baking implement in the oven. Bake for about 7 minutes, until the crust starts to brown. Remove from the oven and distribute the spinach and dollops of the ricotta over the pizza. Drizzle olive oil over the top and sprinkle the provolone over the pizza. Return the pizza to the oven and bake for about 5 minutes, until the crust is golden brown and starting to char. Remove and let cool slightly before slicing and serving.

PIZZA WITH MUSHROOMS, ASPARAGUS & PESTO

YIELD: 1 PIZZA / ACTIVE TIME: 20 MINUTES / TOTAL TIME: 1 HOUR

As mushrooms cook quickly in the oven, they do not need to be cooked before being placed on top of a pizza.

1. Preheat the oven to the maximum temperature and place a baking stone or steel on the middle rack as it warms. Place the mushrooms and garlic in a bowl, generously drizzle olive oil over the top, and season with salt and pepper. Let the mixture marinate for 10 minutes, drain, and set aside.

2. Bring salted water to a boil in a saucepan and add the asparagus. Cook for 1 minute, drain, run under cold water, and set aside.

3. Place the Basil Pesto and olive oil in a bowl and stir to combine. You want the pesto to become a bit more runny than it is on its own.

4. Dust a work surface with the semolina flour, place the dough on the surface, and gently stretch it into a round. For more detailed instructions on properly stretching a ball of pizza dough see page 73. Cover the dough with the pesto, the asparagus, the mushroom mixture, and the pine nuts. Season with salt and pepper, drizzle with olive oil, and sprinkle the Parmesan cheese on top of the pizza.

5. Using a peel or a flat baking sheet, transfer the pizza to the heated baking implement in the oven. Bake for about 15 minutes, until the crust is golden brown and starting to char. Remove, top with the Parmesan and pine nuts, and let cool slightly before slicing and serving.

INGREDIENTS:

2.8 OZ. | 80 GRAMS PORCINI MUSHROOMS, CHOPPED

½ GARLIC CLOVE, CHOPPED

1 TABLESPOON | 13.3 GRAMS OLIVE OIL, PLUS MORE AS NEEDED

SALT AND PEPPER, TO TASTE

4 ASPARAGUS STALKS, TRIMMED

0.75 OZ. | 22.5 GRAMS BASIL PESTO (SEE PAGE 365)

SEMOLINA FLOUR, AS NEEDED

1 BALL PIZZA DOUGH

1 TABLESPOON | 8.1 GRAMS PINE NUTS

0.5 OZ. | 15 GRAMS PARMESAN CHEESE, SHAVED

GARDEN VEGETABLE & RICOTTA PIZZA

YIELD: 1 PIZZA / ACTIVE TIME: 25 MINUTES / TOTAL TIME: 1 HOUR AND 15 MINUTES

This topping, freighted with fresh herbs, makes the most of summer produce.

1. Preheat the oven to the maximum temperature and place a baking stone or steel on the middle rack as it warms. Place the eggplant and zucchini on an aluminum foil–lined baking sheet, season with salt and pepper, drizzle olive oil over the vegetables, and place in the warming oven. Roast until they are tender and browned, about 20 minutes. Remove from the oven and let cool.

2. Place the sage, rosemary, and garlic in a small bowl, stir to combine, and set the mixture aside.

3. Dust a work surface with the semolina flour, place the dough on the surface, and gently stretch it into a round. For more detailed instructions on properly stretching a ball of pizza dough see page 73. Cover the dough with the sauce and distribute the zucchini, eggplant, garlic-and-herb mixture, and the olives on top. Season the pizza with salt and drizzle olive oil over the top.

4. Using a peel or a flat baking sheet, transfer the pizza to the heated baking implement in the oven. Bake for about 7 minutes, until the crust starts to brown. Remove the pizza, distribute the ricotta and Parmesan over the pizza, and drizzle olive oil on top. Return the pizza to the oven and bake for about 5 minutes, until the crust is golden brown and starting to char. Remove and let cool slightly before slicing and serving.

INGREDIENTS:

1.75 OZ. | 50 GRAMS EGGPLANT, SLICED

FRESH ROSEMARY

½ GARLIC CLOVE, CHOPPED

SEMOLINA FLOUR, AS NEEDED

1 BALL PIZZA DOUGH

2.8 OZ. | 80 GRAMS RAW PIZZA SAUCE (SEE PAGE 103)

0.5 OZ. | 15 GRAMS PITTED BLACK OLIVES, CHOPPED

3.5 OZ. | 100 GRAMS RICOTTA CHEESE

0.5 OZ. | 15 GRAMS PARMESAN CHEESE, GRATED

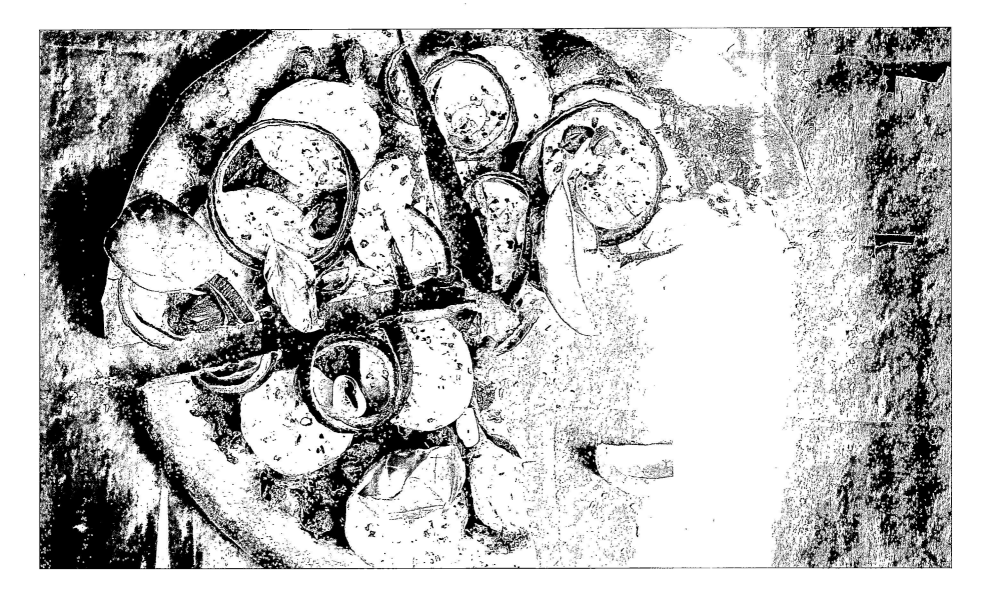

POTATO & PESTO PIZZA

YIELD: 1 PIZZA / **ACTIVE TIME:** 20 MINUTES / **TOTAL TIME:** 1 HOUR

A hard-and-fast rule: potatoes make a great addition to white pizzas. The Basil Pesto is there to add color and flavor to this simple, elegant topping.

1. Preheat the oven to the maximum temperature and place a baking stone or steel on the middle rack as it warms. Bring salted water to a boil in a saucepan and prepare an ice bath. Add the potato to the boiling water, cook for 1 minute, drain, and place it in the ice bath. Let it sit for 2 minutes, drain, and pat dry with paper towels.

2. Dust a work surface with the semolina flour, place the dough on the surface, and gently stretch it into a round. For more detailed instructions on properly stretching a ball of pizza dough see page 73. Distribute the cheese, Basil Pesto, and potato over the dough, season with salt and pepper, and drizzle olive oil over the pizza.

3. Using a peel or a flat baking sheet, transfer the pizza to the heated baking implement in the oven. Bake for about 15 minutes, until the crust is golden brown and starting to char. Remove and let cool slightly before slicing and serving.

INGREDIENTS:

SALT AND PEPPER, TO TASTE

1 SMALL POTATO, SLICED

SEMOLINA FLOUR, AS NEEDED

1 BALL PIZZA DOUGH

2.4 OZ. | 70 GRAMS CACIOCAVALLO CHEESE, SLICED

1 OZ. | 30 GRAMS BASIL PESTO (SEE PAGE 365)

OLIVE OIL, AS NEEDED

PANFRIED POTATO & SAUSAGE PIZZA

YIELD: 1 PIZZA / **ACTIVE TIME:** 25 MINUTES / **TOTAL TIME:** 1 HOUR

Panfrying the potatoes adds a bit more flavor than boiling them would, and that boost is necessary to compete with the savory, earthy sausage.

1. Preheat the oven to the maximum temperature and place a baking stone or steel on the middle rack as it warms. Coat the bottom of a skillet with olive oil and warm over medium-high heat. When the oil starts to shimmer, add the potato and garlic and sauté until the potato starts to soften, about 6 minutes. Remove from heat, season with salt and pepper, and let cool completely.

2. Dust a work surface with the semolina flour, place the dough on the surface, and gently stretch it into a round. For more detailed instructions on properly stretching a ball of pizza dough see page 73.

3. Drizzle olive oil generously over the dough and top with the potato, sausage, mozzarella, and rosemary. Season the pizza with salt and pepper and drizzle olive oil over the top.

4. Using a peel or a flat baking sheet, transfer the pizza to the heated baking implement in the oven. Bake for about 15 minutes, until the crust is golden brown and starting to char. Remove and let cool slightly before slicing and serving.

INGREDIENTS:

OLIVE OIL, AS NEEDED

1 BALL PIZZA DOUGH

2.4 OZ. | 70 GRAMS GROUND ITALIAN SAUSAGE

2.4 OZ. | 70 GRAMS FRESH MOZZARELLA CHEESE, DRAINED AND CUBED

FRESH ROSEMARY, TO TASTE

PISTACHIO PESTO & MOZZARELLA PIZZA

YIELD: 1 PIZZA / **ACTIVE TIME:** 15 MINUTES / **TOTAL TIME:** 45 MINUTES

A simple and elegant topping that uses both crumbled pistachios and Pistachio Pesto to complement a gooey mozzarella-and-Parmesan layer. Leftover pesto is great to use on pasta, too.

1. Preheat the oven to the maximum temperature and place a baking stone or steel on the middle rack as it warms. Dust a work surface with the semolina flour, place the dough on the surface, and gently stretch it into a round. For more detailed instructions on properly stretching a ball of pizza dough see page 73.

2. Cover the dough with two-thirds of the mozzarella. Season the pizza with salt and drizzle olive oil over the top.

3. Using a peel or a flat baking sheet, transfer the pizza to the heated baking implement in the oven. Bake for about 7 minutes, until the crust is golden brown and almost done. Remove, top with the remaining mozzarella, the Pistachio Pesto, the pistachios, and the Parmesan, and drizzle olive oil over the pizza. Return to the oven and bake bake for about 5 minutes, the crust is golden brown and just starting to char. Remove from the oven and let cool briefly before slicing and serving.

PISTACHIO PESTO

1. Place the pistachios in a food processor or blender and pulse until coarsely ground. Add the remaining ingredients and pulse until the mixture is a slightly chunky paste.

INGREDIENTS:

SEMOLINA FLOUR, AS NEEDED

1 BALL PIZZA DOUGH

4.4 OZ. | 125 GRAMS FRESH MOZZARELLA CHEESE, DRAINED AND SLICED

SALT AND PEPPER, TO TASTE

OLIVE OIL, AS NEEDED

1 OZ. | 30 GRAMS PISTACHIO PESTO (SEE RECIPE)

0.5 OZ. | 15 GRAMS SALTED PISTACHIOS, CRUSHED

0.5 OZ. | 15 GRAMS GRATED PARMESAN CHEESE

PISTACHIO PESTO

7 OZ. | 200 GRAMS UNSALTED PISTACHIOS, SHELLED

1.75 OZ. | 50 GRAMS PARMESAN CHEESE, GRATED

ZEST OF ½ LEMON

½ GARLIC CLOVE

3.5 OZ. | 100 GRAMS WATER

1 GENEROUS HANDFUL FRESH BASIL LEAVES

SALT AND PEPPER, TO TASTE

3.5 OZ. | 100 GRAMS OLIVE OIL

PIZZA WITH SAUSAGE, CIME DI RAPA & CHERRY TOMATOES

YIELD: 1 PIZZA / **ACTIVE TIME:** 25 MINUTES / **TOTAL TIME:** 1 HOUR

Possibly one of the earthiest Italian pizza toppings, featuring broccoli rabe (*cime di rapa*) and sausage. This typical winter pairing is brightened up just enough by the cherry tomatoes.

1. Preheat the oven to the maximum temperature and place a baking stone or steel on the middle rack as it warms. Coat the bottom of a skillet with olive oil and warm over medium-high heat. When the oil starts to shimmer, add the broccoli rabe and garlic and sauté until the broccoli rabe has softened, about 8 minutes. Add the sausage to the pan and cook until it is browned and all of the liquid has evaporated, about 5 minutes. Remove the pan from heat, remove the garlic and discard it, season the mixture with salt and pepper, and let cool.

2. Dust a work surface with the semolina flour, place the dough on the surface, and gently stretch it into a round. For more detailed instructions on properly stretching a ball of pizza dough see page 73. Drizzle olive oil over the dough and distribute the mozzarella over it. Top with the sausage mixture and cherry tomatoes. Season the pizza with salt and drizzle olive oil over the top.

3. Using a peel or a flat baking sheet, transfer the pizza to the heated baking implement in the oven. Bake for about 15 minutes, until the crust is golden brown and starting to char. Remove and let cool slightly before slicing and serving.

INGREDIENTS

OLIVE OIL, AS NEEDED

7.7 OZ. | 100 GRAMS BROCCOLI RABE, TRIMMED

1 GARLIC CLOVE

3.5 OZ. | 100 GRAMS ITALIAN SAUSAGE, SLICED

SALT AND PEPPER, TO TASTE

SEMOLINA FLOUR, AS NEEDED

1 BALL PIZZA DOUGH

2.8 OZ. | 80 GRAMS FRESH MOZZARELLA CHEESE, DRAINED AND TORN

1 HANDFUL CHERRY TOMATOES

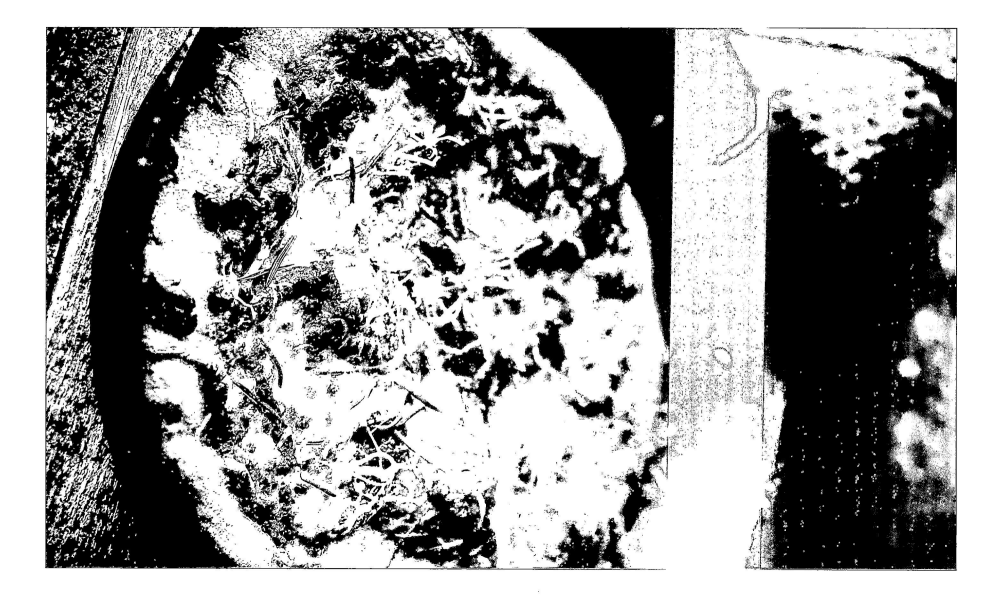

PIZZA WITH SUN-DRIED TOMATOES & ZUCCHINI CREAM

YIELD: 1 PIZZA / **ACTIVE TIME:** 15 MINUTES / **TOTAL TIME:** 45 MINUTES

Replacing tomato sauce with Zucchini Cream adds a touch of class to this bianca.

1. Preheat the oven to the maximum temperature and place a baking stone or steel on the middle rack as it warms. Dust a work surface with the semolina flour, place the dough on the surface, and gently stretch it into a round. For more detailed instructions on properly stretching a ball of pizza dough see page 73.

2. Cover the dough with the Zucchini Cream and top with the mozzarella and sun-dried tomatoes. Season the pizza with salt, drizzle olive oil over the top, and sprinkle the Parmesan over the pizza.

3. Using a peel or a flat baking sheet, transfer the pizza to the heated baking implement in the oven. Bake for about 15 minutes, until the crust is golden brown and starting to char. Remove and let cool slightly before slicing and serving.

ZUCCHINI CREAM

1. Coat the bottom of a skillet with olive oil and warm over medium heat. When the oil starts to shimmer, add the zucchini and onion and sauté until they have softened, about 10 minutes. Season with salt and pepper, raise the heat to medium-high, and cook until all of the liquid in the pan has evaporated.

2. Place the sautéed vegetables in a blender or food processor, add the remaining ingredients, and blitz until smooth.

INGREDIENTS:

SEMOLINA FLOUR, AS NEEDED

1 BALL PIZZA DOUGH

1.75 OZ. | 50 GRAMS ZUCCHINI CREAM (SEE RECIPE)

3.5 OZ. | 100 GRAMS FRESH MOZZARELLA CHEESE, DRAINED AND TORN

4 SUN-DRIED TOMATOES, SLICED

SALT AND PEPPER, TO TASTE

OLIVE OIL, AS NEEDED

0.5 OZ. | 15 GRAMS PARMESAN CHEESE, GRATED

ZUCCHINI CREAM
1 ZUCCHINI, CHOPPED

½ SMALL ONION, CHOPPED

SALT AND PEPPER, TO TASTE

1 OZ. | 30 GRAMS PARMESAN CHEESE, GRATED

1 TABLESPOON | 13.3 GRAMS OLIVE OIL, PLUS MORE AS NEEDED

4 FRESH MINT LEAVES (OPTIONAL)

SAUSAGE & SPINACH PIZZA

YIELD: 1 PIZZA / **ACTIVE TIME:** 25 MINUTES / **TOTAL TIME:** 1 HOUR

A variation of the "greens and sausage" theme that is so wonderful in winter, when we need to make sure to get tons of nutrients in our pizza slice.

1. Preheat the oven to the maximum temperature and place a baking stone or steel on the middle rack as it warms. Coat the bottom of a skillet with olive oil and warm over medium-high heat. When the oil starts to shimmer, add the spinach and sauté until it has wilted, about 3 minutes. Add the sausage and cook until it is browned and all of the liquid in the pan has evaporated, about 5 minutes. Remove the pan from heat, season with the nutmeg, salt, and pepper, and let the mixture cool.

2. Dust a work surface with the semolina flour, place the dough on the surface, and gently stretch it into a round. For more detailed instructions on properly stretching a ball of pizza dough see page 73.

3. Drizzle olive oil over the dough and top with the mozzarella and spinach-and-sausage mixture. Season the pizza with salt and pepper and drizzle olive oil over the top.

4. Using a peel or a flat baking sheet, transfer the pizza to the heated baking implement in the oven. Bake for about 15 minutes, until the crust is golden brown and starting to char. Remove and let cool slightly before slicing and serving.

INGREDIENTS:

OLIVE OIL, AS NEEDED

SALT AND PEPPER, TO TASTE

SEMOLINA FLOUR, AS NEEDED

1 BALL PIZZA DOUGH

2.8 OZ. | 80 GRAMS FRESH MOZZARELLA CHEESE, DRAINED AND TORN

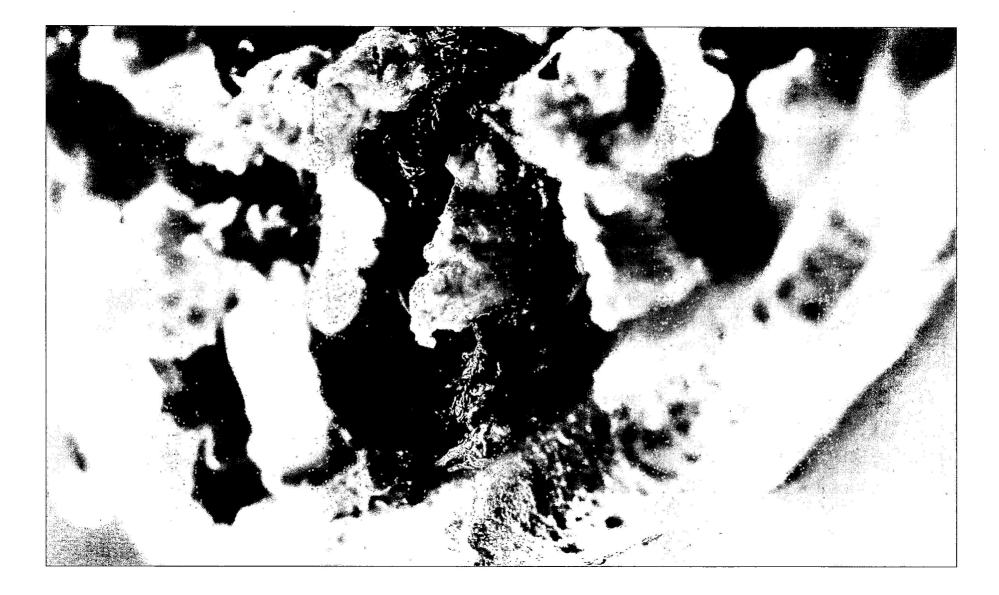

SAUSAGE & BROCCOLI PIZZA

YIELD: 1 PIZZA / **ACTIVE TIME:** 20 MINUTES / **TOTAL TIME:** 1 HOUR

By enriching a classic margherita base with broccoli and sausage, you get a simple, tasty, and nutritious pizza that is the perfect representation of all that authentic Italian food is about.

1. Preheat the oven to the maximum temperature and place a baking stone or steel on the middle rack as it warms. Bring salted water to a boil in a saucepan and prepare an ice bath. Add the broccoli, cook for 1 minute, and transfer to the ice bath. Let it sit for 2 minutes, drain, and pat dry with paper towels.

2. Dust a work surface with the semolina flour, place the dough on the surface, and gently stretch it into a round. For more detailed instructions on properly stretching a ball of pizza dough see page 73.

3. Cover the dough with the sauce and top with the sausage and broccoli. Season the pizza with salt and pepper and drizzle olive oil over the top.

4. Using a peel or a flat baking sheet, transfer the pizza to the heated baking implement in the oven. Bake for about 5 minutes, until the crust starts to brown. Remove the pizza, distribute the mozzarella over the top, and return the pizza to the oven. Bake for about 10 minutes, until the crust is golden brown and starting to char. Remove and let cool slightly before slicing and serving.

INGREDIENTS:

SALT AND PEPPER, TO TASTE

3.5 OZ. | 100 GRAMS BROCCOLI FLORETS

SEMOLINA FLOUR, AS NEEDED

1 BALL PIZZA DOUGH

2.8 OZ. | 80 GRAMS RAW PIZZA SAUCE
(SEE PAGE 103)

1 LINK ITALIAN SAUSAGE, CASING REMOVED
AND CRUMBLED

OLIVE OIL, AS NEEDED

4.4 OZ. | 125 GRAMS FRESH MOZZARELLA
CHEESE, DRAINED AND TORN

PIZZA WITH RICOTTA & CREMINI MUSHROOMS

YIELD: 1 PIZZA / **ACTIVE TIME:** 20 MINUTES / **TOTAL TIME:** 1 HOUR

The umami imparted by the mushrooms is perfectly balanced by the mild and slightly sweet flavor of ricotta.

1. Preheat the oven to the maximum temperature and place a baking stone or steel on the middle rack as it warms. Place the mushrooms and garlic in a bowl, season with salt and pepper, generously drizzle olive oil over the mixture, stir to combine, and set aside.

2. Dust a work surface with the semolina flour, place the dough on the surface, and gently stretch it into a round. For more detailed instructions on properly stretching a ball of pizza dough see page 73. Cover the dough with the mozzarella and mushrooms.

3. Drain the mushrooms. Cover the dough with the mozzarella and the mushrooms. Season with salt and drizzle olive oil over the pizza.

4. Using a peel or a flat baking sheet, transfer the pizza to the heated baking implement in the oven. Bake for about 15 minutes, until the crust is golden brown and starting to char. Remove and distribute the ricotta and arugula over the pizza. Drizzle olive oil over the pizza and let it cool slightly before slicing and serving.

INGREDIENTS:

SEMOLINA FLOUR, AS NEEDED

1 BALL PIZZA DOUGH

1.75 OZ. | 50 GRAMS LOW-MOISTURE MOZZARELLA CHEESE, SHREDDED

3.5 OZ. | 100 GRAMS RICOTTA CHEESE

1 HANDFUL ARUGULA

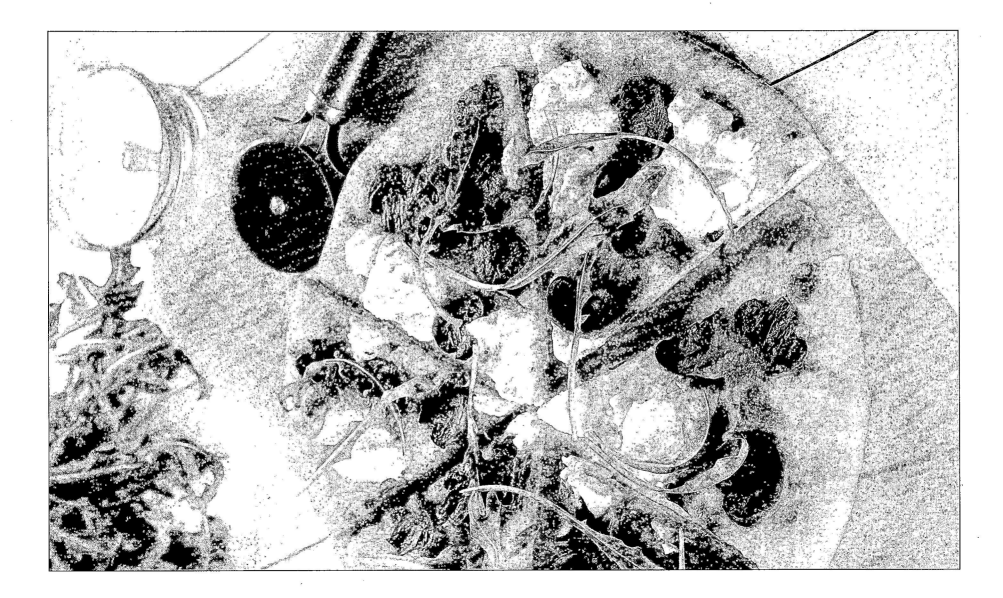

PIZZA WITH GARDEN VEGETABLES, ARTICHOKES & SALAMI

YIELD: 1 PIZZA / **ACTIVE TIME:** 15 MINUTES / **TOTAL TIME:** 1 HOUR AND 15 MINUTES

For the lovers of an all-in-one slice, this pizza is loaded with a bit of everything from a plate of antipasti.

1. Preheat the oven to the maximum temperature and place a baking stone or steel on the middle rack as it warms. Place the eggplant and bell pepper on an aluminum foil–lined baking sheet, season with salt and pepper, drizzle olive oil over the vegetables, and place in the warming oven. Roast until they are tender, about 20 minutes. Remove from the oven and let cool.

2. Dust a work surface with the semolina flour, place the dough on the surface, and gently stretch it into a round. For more detailed instructions on properly stretching a ball of pizza dough see page 73.

3. Cover the dough with the sauce and top with the artichokes, eggplant, bell pepper, salami, and mozzarella. Season the pizza with salt and drizzle olive oil over the top.

4. Using a peel or a flat baking sheet, transfer the pizza to the heated baking implement in the oven. Bake for about 15 minutes, until the crust is golden brown and starting to char. Remove and let cool slightly before slicing and serving.

INGREDIENTS:

1.75 OZ. | 50 GRAMS EGGPLANT, AND SLICED

1.75 OZ. | 50 GRAMS BELL PEPPERS, STEMMED, SEEDED, AND SLICED

SALT AND PEPPER, TO TASTE

OLIVE OIL, AS NEEDED

SEMOLINA FLOUR, AS NEEDED

1 BALL PIZZA DOUGH

2.4 OZ. | 70 GRAMS RAW PIZZA SAUCE (SEE PAGE 103)

2.8 OZ. | 80 GRAMS ARTICHOKE HEARTS IN OLIVE OIL, CHOPPED

1.4 OZ. | 40 GRAMS SALAMI

2.4 OZ. | 70 GRAMS FRESH MOZZARELLA CHEESE, DRAINED AND SLICED

PIZZA WITH ASPARAGUS, GUANCIALE & BOTTARGA

YIELD: 1 PIZZA / **ACTIVE TIME:** 15 MINUTES / **TOTAL TIME:** 45 MINUTES

B ottarga is salted, cured fish roe, a delicacy from the Italian islands. If you manage to get hold of some, this pizza is a great landing spot for it.

1. Preheat the oven to the maximum temperature and place a baking stone or steel on the middle rack as it warms. Dust a work surface with the semolina flour, place the dough on the surface, and gently stretch it into a round. For more detailed instructions on properly stretching a ball of pizza dough see page 73.

2. Cover the dough with the cheeses, asparagus, and guanciale. Season the pizza with salt and pepper and drizzle olive oil over the top.

3. Using a peel or a flat baking sheet, transfer the pizza to the heated baking implement in the oven. Bake for about 15 minutes, until the crust is golden brown and starting to char. Remove, top with the bottarga and more olive oil, and let cool slightly before slicing and serving.

INGREDIENTS:

SEMOLINA FLOUR, AS NEEDED

1 FRESH PIZZA DOUGH BALL

3 OZ. . . . .

. . . .

. . . .
CHEESE, SHREDDED

1.75 OZ. | 50 GRAMS ASPARAGUS, TRIMMED, BLANCHED, AND HALVED

1.4 OZ. | 40 GRAMS GUANCIALE, FINELY SLICED

SALT AND PEPPER, TO TASTE

OLIVE OIL, TO TASTE

1 OZ. | 30 GRAMS BOTTARGA, SHAVED

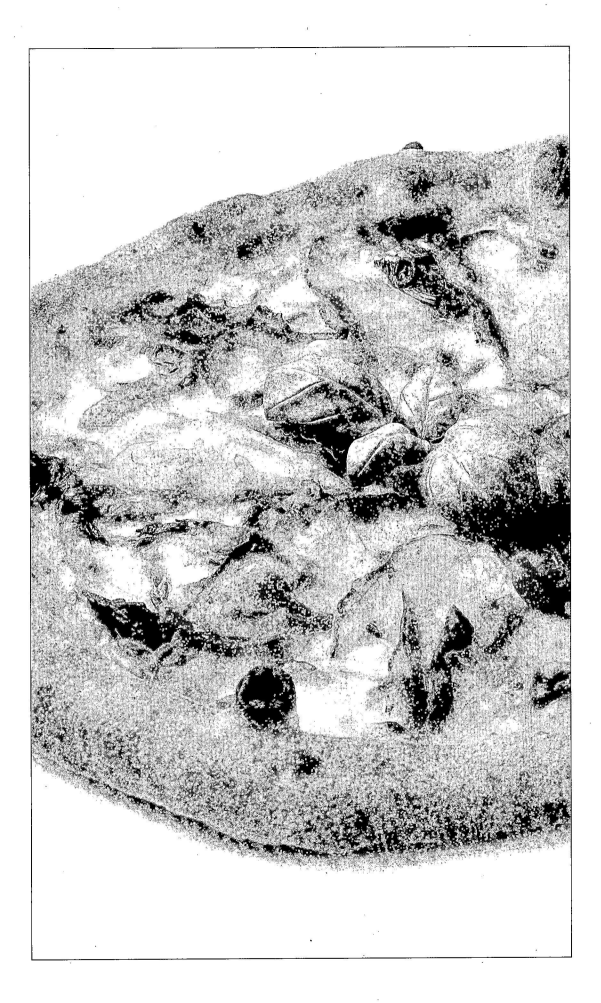

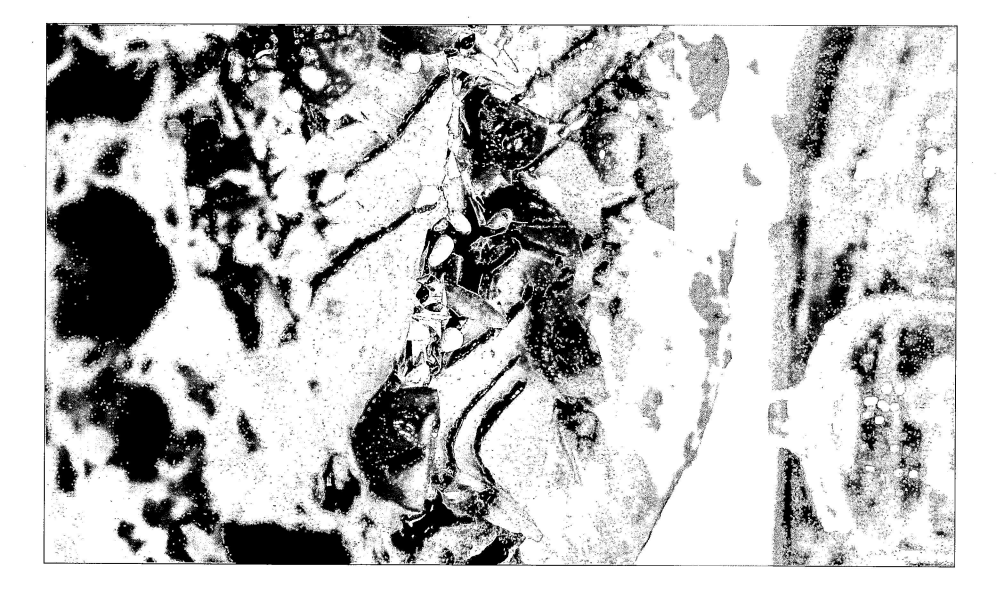

PIZZA WITH SWORDFISH, PINE NUTS & CHERRY TOMATOES

YIELD: 1 PIZZA / **ACTIVE TIME:** 15 MINUTES / **TOTAL TIME:** 45 MINUTES

For me, swordfish carpaccio will always evoke memories of sunny Sicily, where small, fresh swordfish was often the catch of the day.

1. Preheat the oven to the maximum temperature and place a baking stone or steel on the middle rack as it warms. Dust a work surface with the semolina flour, place the dough on the surface, and gently stretch it into a round. For more detailed instructions on properly stretching a ball of pizza dough see page 73.

2. Drizzle olive oil over the dough and top with the mozzarella. Season the pizza with salt and drizzle olive oil over the top.

3. Using a peel or a flat baking sheet, transfer the pizza to the heated baking implement in the oven. Bake for about 15 minutes, until the crust is golden brown and starting to char. Remove and top with the arugula, Swordfish Carpaccio, pine nuts, and cherry tomatoes. Season with salt and pepper and drizzle olive oil and balsamic glaze over the pizza.

SWORDFISH CARPACCIO

1. Make sure your freezer is set to the coldest possible temperature and freeze the swordfish for at least 24 hours.

2. Cut the swordfish into very thin slices, drizzle olive oil over them, cover with lemon juice, and season with salt and pepper. Refrigerate for 15 minutes before serving.

INGREDIENTS:

SEMOLINA FLOUR, AS NEEDED

1 BALL PIZZA DOUGH

OLIVE OIL, TO TASTE

1 OZ. | 30 GRAMS LOW-MOISTURE MOZZARELLA CHEESE, SHREDDED

SALT AND PEPPER, TO TASTE

1 HANDFUL ARUGULA

1.75 OZ. | 50 GRAMS SWORDFISH CARPACCIO (SEE RECIPE)

1 TABLESPOON | 8.1 GRAMS PINE NUTS

1 HANDFUL CHERRY TOMATOES, QUARTERED

BALSAMIC GLAZE, TO TASTE

SWORDFISH CARPACCIO

8 OZ. | 225 GRAMS SWORDFISH FILLET

OLIVE OIL, TO TASTE

FRESH LEMON JUICE, TO TASTE

SALT AND PEPPER, TO TASTE

MARGHERITA WITH PROSCIUTTO & ASPARAGUS

YIELD: 1 PIZZA / **ACTIVE TIME:** 20 MINUTES / **TOTAL TIME:** 1 HOUR

There are nearly infinite variations on the classic Neapolitan margherita. This one, featuring asparagus and prosciutto, is both rich and light.

1. Preheat the oven to the maximum temperature and place a baking stone or steel on the middle rack as it warms. Bring salted water to a boil in a saucepan and add the asparagus. Cook until just tender, drain, and pat dry. Chop the asparagus into large pieces and set it aside.

2. Dust a work surface with the semolina flour, place the dough on the surface, and gently stretch it into a round. For more detailed instructions on properly stretching a ball of pizza dough see page 73. Cover the dough with the sauce, top it with the mozzarella, season with salt and pepper, and drizzle olive oil over the pizza.

3. Using a peel or a flat baking sheet, transfer the pizza to the heated baking implement in the oven. Bake for about 15 minutes, until the crust is golden brown and starting to char. Remove, top with the prosciutto and asparagus, and drizzle olive oil and balsamic glaze over the pizza.

INGREDIENTS:

SALT AND PEPPER, TO TASTE

1.4 OZ. | 40 GRAMS ASPARAGUS, TRIMMED

SEMOLINA FLOUR, AS NEEDED

1 BALL OF PIZZA DOUGH

7 OZ. | 200 GRAMS BASIC PIZZA SAUCE (SEE PAGE 103)

2.4 OZ. | 70 GRAMS FRESH MOZZARELLA CHEESE, SLICED

OLIVE OIL, AS NEEDED

2.4 OZ. | 70 GRAMS PROSCIUTTO

BALSAMIC GLAZE, FOR GARNISH

POTATO & OLIVE PIZZA

YIELD: 1 PIZZA / **ACTIVE TIME:** 20 MINUTES / **TOTAL TIME:** 1 HOUR

Potatoes on pizza is one of my favorite things. Here's a version that complements their creaminess with the pungent saltiness of olives.

1. Preheat the oven to the maximum temperature and place a baking stone or steel on the middle rack as it warms. Bring salted water to a boil in a saucepan and prepare an ice bath. Place the potatoes in the water and cook until they turn translucent, 1 to 2 minutes. Transfer to the ice bath and let sit until cool. Drain, pat dry, and set aside.

2. Dust a work surface with the semolina flour, place the dough on the surface, and gently stretch it into a round. For more detailed instructions on properly stretching a ball of pizza dough see page 73.

3. Drizzle olive oil over the dough and top with the potato, mozzarella, and olives. Season the pizza with salt and drizzle olive oil over the top.

4. Using a peel or a flat baking sheet, transfer the pizza to the heated baking implement in the oven. Bake for about 15 minutes, until the crust is golden brown and starting to char. Remove and let cool slightly before sprinkling the thyme on top, slicing, and serving.

INGREDIENTS:

SALT AND PEPPER, TO TASTE

1 SMALL POTATO, UNPEELED AND SLICED THIN

SEMOLINA FLOUR, AS NEEDED

1 BALL PIZZA DOUGH

OLIVE OIL, TO TASTE

1.4 OZ. | 40 GRAMS LOW-MOISTURE MOZZARELLA CHEESE, SHREDDED

1 OZ. | 30 GRAMS PITTED OLIVES

FRESH THYME, FINELY CHOPPED, TO TASTE

MARGHERITA WITH PANFRIED ZUCCHINI

YIELD: 1 PIZZA / **ACTIVE TIME:** 25 MINUTES / **TOTAL TIME:** 1 HOUR AND 15 MINUTES

When making Italian-style pizza, it is important to remember to properly cook the vegetables you're using for toppings. Panfried, almost caramelized, zucchini turns a simple margherita into something special.

1. Preheat the oven to the maximum temperature and place a baking stone or steel on the middle rack as it warms. Coat the bottom of a skillet with olive oil and warm over medium-high heat. When the oil starts to shimmer, add the zucchini and the onion, season with salt and pepper, and sauté until all of the liquid has evaporated and the zucchini is browned, about 15 minutes. Remove the pan from heat and let cool.

2. Dust a work surface with the semolina flour, place the dough on the surface, and gently stretch it into a round. For more detailed instructions on properly stretching a ball of pizza dough see page 73. Cover the dough with the sauce, season with salt and pepper, and drizzle olive oil over the pizza.

3. Using a peel or a flat baking sheet, transfer the pizza to the heated baking implement in the oven. Bake for about 7 minutes, until the crust starts to brown. Remove the pizza, distribute the mozzarella and the zucchini mixture over the top, and return the pizza to the oven. Bake for about 5 minutes, until the crust is golden brown and starting to char. Remove and let cool slightly before garnishing with the basil, slicing, and serving.

INGREDIENTS:

SEMOLINA FLOUR, AS NEEDED

1 BALL PIZZA DOUGH

2.8 OZ. | 80 GRAMS RAW PIZZA SAUCE (SEE PAGE 103)

3.5 OZ. | 100 GRAMS FRESH MOZZARELLA CHEESE, DRAINED AND TORN

FRESH BASIL LEAVES, FOR GARNISH

PIZZA WITH SMOKED HAM, PEARS & PECORINO

YIELD: 1 PIZZA / **ACTIVE TIME:** 15 MINUTES / **TOTAL TIME:** 45 MINUTES

The always-underrated pear has myriad talents, and one of them just happens to be the creamy, sweet, and fresh element it can add to a pizza.

1. Preheat the oven to the maximum temperature and place a baking stone or steel on the middle rack as it warms. Dust a work surface with the semolina flour, place the dough on the surface, and gently stretch it into a round. For more detailed instructions on properly stretching a ball of pizza dough see page 73. Drizzle olive oil over the dough and sprinkle half of the pecorino on top. Top with the ham, pear, and ricotta, season with salt, and drizzle olive oil over the top.

2. Using a peel or a flat baking sheet, transfer the pizza to the heated baking implement in the oven. Bake for about 15 minutes, until the crust is golden brown and starting to char. Remove from the oven and sprinkle the rest of the pecorino on top. Let cool slightly before slicing and serving.

INGREDIENTS:

SEMOLINA FLOUR, AS NEEDED

1 BALL PIZZA DOUGH

OLIVE OIL, TO TASTE

2.4 OZ. | 70 GRAMS PECORINO CHEESE, GRATED

1.4 OZ. | 40 GRAMS SMOKED, CURED HAM (SUCH AS SPECK)

½ SMALL PEAR, SLICED

2.1 OZ. | 60 GRAMS RICOTTA CHEESE

SALT AND PEPPER, TO TASTE

PIZZA WITH PARMESAN, BRESAOLA & TRUFFLES

YIELD: 1 PIZZA / ACTIVE TIME: 15 MINUTES / TOTAL TIME: 45 MINUTES

I f you are looking for a pizza topping for a special occasion, look no further. The truffle—king of all mushrooms—gives this simple pizza a luxurious touch. Plus, it matches so well with the musty and slightly sweet flavor of bresaola.

1. Preheat the oven to the maximum temperature and place a baking stone or steel on the middle rack as it warms. Dust a work surface with the semolina flour, place the dough on the surface, and gently stretch it into a round. For more detailed instructions on shaping the dough from a ball of pizza dough see page 73.

2. Cover the dough with the sauce and top with the mozzarella and basil. Season the pizza with salt and pepper and drizzle olive oil over the top.

3. Using a peel or a flat baking sheet, transfer the pizza to the heated baking implement in the oven. Bake for about 15 minutes, until the crust is golden brown and starting to char. Remove and distribute the bresaola, Parmesan, and truffle over the pizza. Season with pepper, drizzle more olive oil on top, and let the pizza cool slightly before slicing and serving.

INGREDIENTS:

2.1 OZ. | 6 GRAMS FRESH MOZZARELLA CHEESE, DRAINED AND TORN

FRESH BASIL LEAVES, TO TASTE

SALT AND PEPPER, TO TASTE

OLIVE OIL, AS NEEDED

1.4 OZ. | 40 GRAMS BRESAOLA

1 OZ. | 30 GRAMS PARMESAN CHEESE, SHAVED

2 TO 3 THIN SLICES BLACK TRUFFLE

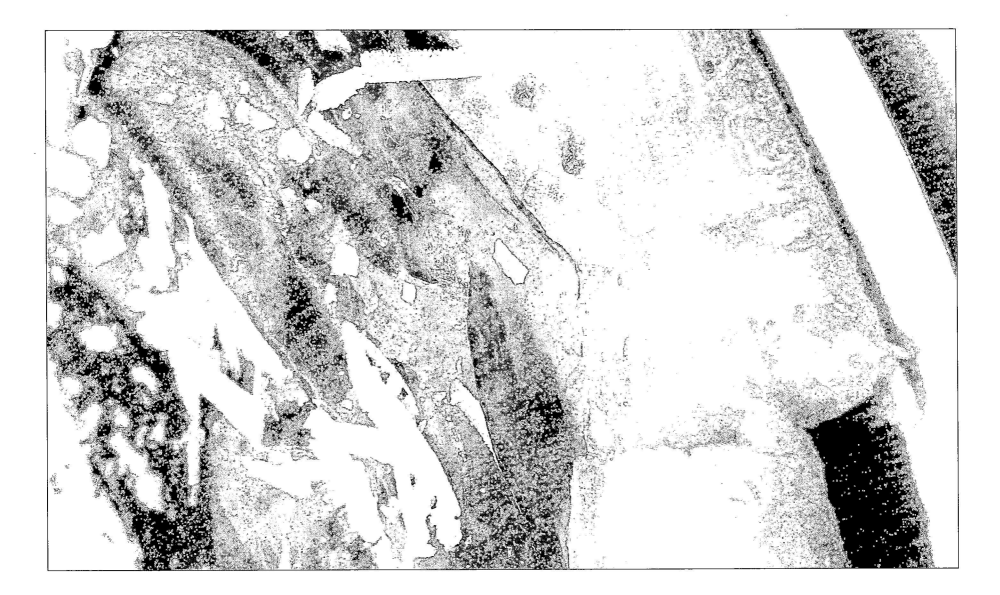

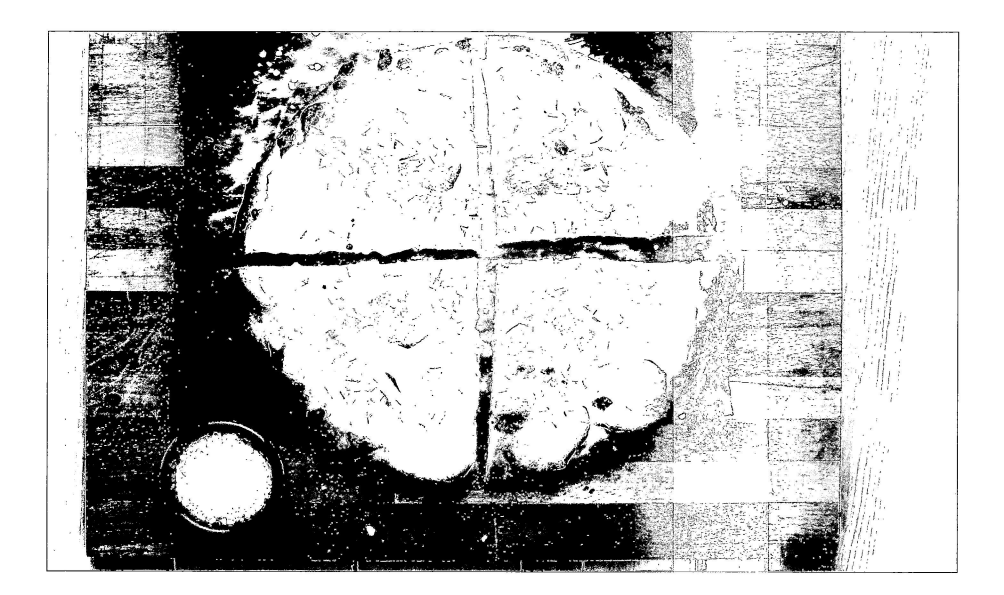

ROSEMARY & POTATO PIZZA

YIELD: 1 PIZZA / **ACTIVE TIME:** 20 MINUTES / **TOTAL TIME:** 1 HOUR

There are many versions of pizza topped with potatoes. This one is inspired by the classic Roman potato pizza bianca, with the welcome addition of mozzarella cheese.

1. Preheat the oven to the maximum temperature and place a baking stone or steel on the middle rack as it warms. Bring salted water to a boil in a saucepan and prepare an ice bath. Place the potatoes in the water and cook until they turn translucent, 1 minute. Transfer to the ice bath and let sit until cool. Drain, pat dry, and set aside.

2. Dust a work surface with the semolina flour, place the dough on the surface, and gently stretch it into a round. For more detailed instructions on properly stretching a ball of pizza dough see page 73. Drizzle olive oil over the dough and top with the mozzarella and potato. Sprinkle the coarse-grained salt and rosemary on top and generously drizzle olive oil over the pizza.

3. Using a peel or a flat baking sheet, transfer the pizza to the heated baking implement in the oven. Bake for about 15 minutes, until the crust is golden brown and starting to char. Remove and let cool slightly before slicing and serving.

INGREDIENTS:

SALT, TO TASTE

1 POTATO, PEELED AND SLICED THIN

SEMOLINA FLOUR, AS NEEDED

1 BALL PIZZA DOUGH

OLIVE OIL, TO TASTE

1.75 OZ. | 50 GRAMS LOW-MOISTURE MOZZARELLA CHEESE, SHREDDED

COARSE SEA SALT, TO TASTE

FRESH ROSEMARY, TO TASTE

TUNA & ONION PIZZA

YIELD: 1 PIZZA / **ACTIVE TIME:** 20 MINUTES / **TOTAL TIME:** 1 HOUR

This is a delicious yet unassuming pizza topping that you should be able to fix with ingredients typically present in your pantry.

1. Preheat the oven to the maximum temperature and place a baking stone or steel on the middle rack as it warms. Coat the bottom of a skillet with olive oil and warm over medium-high heat. When the oil starts to shimmer, add the onion and cook until it starts to soften, about 5 minutes. Add the tuna, cook for another minute, and remove from heat. Season with salt and pepper and set the mixture aside.

2. Dust a work surface with the semolina flour, place the dough on the surface, and gently stretch it into a round. For more detailed instructions on properly stretching a ball of pizza dough see page 73.

3. Cover the dough with the sauce and top with the mozzarella. Season the pizza with salt, pepper, and oregano and drizzle olive oil over the top.

4. Using a peel or a flat baking sheet, transfer the pizza to the heated baking implement in the oven. Bake for about 7 minutes, until the crust starts to brown. Remove the pizza, distribute the onion-and-tuna mixture over the top, and return the pizza to the oven. Bake for about 5 minutes, until the crust is golden brown and starting to char. Remove and let cool slightly before slicing and serving.

INGREDIENTS:

OLIVE OIL, AS NEEDED

1 BALL PIZZA DOUGH

2.8 OZ. | 80 GRAMS RAW PIZZA SAUCE (SEE PAGE 103)

1.75 OZ. | 50 GRAMS LOW-MOISTURE MOZZARELLA CHEESE, SHREDDED

DRIED OREGANO, TO TASTE

PIZZA WITH 'NDUJA, SUN-DRIED TOMATOES & CACIOCAVALLO

YIELD: 1 PIZZA / **ACTIVE TIME:** 15 MINUTES / **TOTAL TIME:** 45 MINUTES

In the southern Italian region of Calabria, bold flavors are a requisite. One of the most typical ingredients called upon to meet this charge is 'nduja, a spicy salami paste that one can put on virtually anything. Here, it makes for a great topping.

1. Preheat the oven to the maximum temperature and place a baking stone or steel on the middle rack as it warms. Dust a work surface with the semolina flour, place the dough on the surface, and gently stretch it into a round. For more detailed instructions on properly stretching a ball of pizza dough see page 73. Cover the dough with the sauce and top with the 'nduja and sun-dried tomatoes. Drizzle olive oil over the pizza, season with salt, and distribute the cacio-cavallo on top.

2. Using a peel or a flat baking sheet, transfer the pizza to the heated baking implement in the oven. Bake for about 15 minutes, until the crust is golden brown and starting to char. Remove and let cool slightly before slicing and serving.

INGREDIENTS

(SEE PAGE 103)

0.5 OZ. | 15 GRAMS 'NDUJA, OR TO TASTE

4 SUN-DRIED TOMATOES, SLICED

OLIVE OIL, TO TASTE

SALT, TO TASTE

1.75 OZ. | 50 GRAMS CACIOCAVALLO CHEESE, SLICED

RED CABBAGE, RICOTTA & WALNUT PIZZA

YIELD: 1 PIZZA / **ACTIVE TIME:** 25 MINUTES / **TOTAL TIME:** 1 HOUR AND 15 MINUTES

Red cabbage is becoming more and more common as an ingredient in Italian dishes. Here the savory ham balances its slight bitterness, and the creamy ricotta is a great contrast with the cabbage's crunch.

1. Preheat the oven to the maximum temperature and place a baking stone or steel on the middle rack as it warms. Coat the bottom of a skillet with olive oil and warm over medium-high heat. When the oil starts to shimmer, add the onion and cook until it starts to soften, about 5 minutes. Add the cabbage and a few tablespoons of water, cover the pan, reduce the heat to low, and cook, stirring frequently, until the cabbage is tender. Add more water if the pan starts to look dry before the cabbage is ready. Remove the lid and cook until all of the liquid has evaporated. Remove the pan from heat, season with salt and pepper, and let the mixture cool.

2. Dust a work surface with the semolina flour, place the dough on the surface, and gently stretch it into a round. For more detailed instructions on properly stretching a ball of pizza dough see page 73. Cover the dough with the mozzarella and top with the cabbage mixture.

3. Using a peel or a flat baking sheet, transfer the pizza to the heated baking implement in the oven. Bake for about 7 minutes, until the crust starts to brown. Remove the pizza, distribute the ricotta, walnuts, and Parmesan over the top, and return the pizza to the oven. Bake for about 5 minutes, until the crust is golden brown and starting to char. Remove and let cool slightly before slicing and serving.

INGREDIENTS:

OLIVE OIL, AS NEEDED

¼ ONION, MINCED

3.5 OZ. | 100 GRAMS RED CABBAGE, SLICED THIN

WATER, AS NEEDED

SALT AND PEPPER, TO TASTE

SEMOLINA FLOUR, AS NEEDED

1 BALL PIZZA DOUGH

2.8 OZ. | 80 GRAMS LOW-MOISTURE MOZZARELLA CHEESE, SHREDDED

1 OZ. | 30 GRAMS RICOTTA CHEESE

1 OZ. | 30 GRAMS WALNUTS, CHOPPED

1 OZ. | 30 GRAMS PARMESAN CHEESE, GRATED

BBQ CHICKEN PIZZA

YIELD: 1 PIZZA / **ACTIVE TIME:** 15 MINUTES / **TOTAL TIME:** 45 MINUTES

Topping pizza with this savory staple has become hugely popular in the last few years, and once you find the ideal BBQ sauce for it, you'll see why.

1. Preheat the oven to the maximum temperature and place a baking stone or steel on the middle rack as it warms. Dust a work surface with the semolina flour, place the dough on the surface, and gently stretch it into a round. For more detailed instructions on properly stretching a ball of pizza dough see page 73. Spread the barbeque sauce over the dough and top with the chicken, pepperoncini, and onion. Season with red pepper flakes and salt, drizzle olive oil over the top, and then sprinkle the cheese over the pizza.

2. Using a peel or a flat baking sheet, transfer the pizza to the heated baking implement in the oven. Bake for about 15 minutes, until the crust is golden brown and starting to char. Remove and let cool slightly before garnishing with the cilantro, slicing, and serving.

INGREDIENTS:

SEMOLINA FLOUR, AS NEEDED

1 BALL PIZZA DOUGH

2.8 OZ. | 80 GRAMS SPICY BARBEQUE SAUCE

3.5 OZ. | 100 GRAMS COOKED CHICKEN BREAST, CHOPPED

1 OZ. | 30 GRAMS PEPPERONCINI, SLICED

½ SMALL RED ONION, SLICED THIN

RED PEPPER FLAKES, TO TASTE

SALT, TO TASTE

OLIVE OIL, TO TASTE

3.5 OZ. | 100 GRAMS GOUDA OR MONTEREY JACK CHEESE, SHREDDED

FRESH CILANTRO, FINELY CHOPPED, FOR GARNISH

CAULIFLOWER & BROCCOLI PIZZA

YIELD: 1 PIZZA / **ACTIVE TIME:** 15 MINUTES / **TOTAL TIME:** 50 MINUTES

You can use frozen broccoli and cauliflower for this pizza, just so long as you don't boil them before-hand—and if you're OK with the less-than-ideal crunch that frozen vegetables will provide.

1. Preheat the oven to the maximum temperature and place a baking stone or steel on the middle rack as it warms. Bring sliced water to a boil in a saucepan and add the broccoli and cauliflower. Cook until just tender, drain, remove, then set aside.

Then, work the dough on a lightly floured surface. Place the dough on the surface, and gently stretch it into a round. For more detailed instructions on properly stretching a ball of pizza dough see page 73. Cover the dough with the sauce and top with the broccoli, cauliflower, and olives. Season with salt and pepper, drizzle olive oil over the top, and then sprinkle the cheeses over the pizza.

3. Using a peel or a flat baking sheet, transfer the pizza to the heated baking implement in the oven. Bake for about 15 minutes, until the crust is golden brown and starting to char. Remove and let cool slightly before slicing and serving.

INGREDIENTS:

SALT AND PEPPER, TO TASTE

1 BALL PIZZA DOUGH

2.8 OZ. | 80 GRAMS RAW PIZZA SAUCE (SEE PAGE 103)

1 HANDFUL PITTED BLACK OLIVES

OLIVE OIL, TO TASTE

1.75 OZ. | 50 GRAMS LOW-MOISTURE MOZZARELLA CHEESE, SHREDDED

1.75 OZ. | 50 GRAMS CHEDDAR CHEESE, SHREDDED

PESTO & VEGGIE PIZZA

YIELD: 1 PIZZA / **ACTIVE TIME:** 15 MINUTES / **TOTAL TIME:** 45 MINUTES

Not cooking the vegetables before placing them atop the pizza amplifies the fresh flavor of this heavenly vegetarian pie.

1. Preheat the oven to the maximum temperature and place a baking stone or steel on the middle rack as it warms. Dust a work surface with the semolina flour, place the dough on the surface, and gently stretch it into a round. For more detailed instructions on properly stretching a ball of pizza dough see page 73. Cover the dough with the sauce and top with the peppers, mushrooms, and onion. Season with salt and drizzle olive oil over the pizza. Sprinkle the mozzarella on top and then distribute dollops of the Basil Pesto over the pizza.

2. Using a peel or a flat baking sheet, transfer the pizza to the heated baking implement in the oven. Bake for about 15 minutes, until the crust is golden brown and starting to char. Remove and let cool slightly before slicing and serving.

INGREDIENTS:

SEMOLINA FLOUR, AS NEEDED

1 BALL PIZZA DOUGH

2.8 OZ. | 80 GRAMS RAW PIZZA SAUCE (SEE PAGE 103)

⅓ SMALL RED BELL PEPPER, SLICED THIN

⅓ SMALL GREEN BELL PEPPER, SLICED THIN

2 BUTTON MUSHROOMS, SLICED THIN

¼ WHITE ONION, SLICED THIN

SALT, TO TASTE

OLIVE OIL, AS NEEDED

3.5 OZ. | 100 GRAMS LOW-MOISTURE MOZZARELLA CHEESE, SHREDDED

1 OZ. | 30 GRAMS BASIL PESTO (SEE PAGE 365)

PIZZA WITH BROCCOLI & BACON

YIELD: 1 PIZZA / **ACTIVE TIME:** 15 MINUTES / **TOTAL TIME:** 50 MINUTES

As lovers of broccoli salad know, the nutty taste of broccoli was made for the do-it-all flavor of bacon.

1. Preheat the oven to the maximum temperature and place a baking stone or steel on the middle rack as it warms. Bring salted water to a boil in a saucepan and add the broccoli. Cook for no more than 3 minutes, drain, and set aside.

Dust a work surface with the semolina flour, place the dough on the surface, and gently stretch it into a round. For more detailed instructions on properly stretching a ball of pizza dough see page 73. Sprinkle half of the mozzarella over the dough and top with the broccoli, bacon, and sun-dried tomatoes. Season with salt and pepper, drizzle olive oil over the pizza, and sprinkle the rest of the mozzarella on top.

3. Using a peel or a flat baking sheet, transfer the pizza to the heated baking implement in the oven. Bake for about 15 minutes, until the crust is golden brown and starting to char. Remove and let cool slightly before slicing and serving.

INGREDIENTS:

SALT AND PEPPER, TO TASTE

MOZZARELLA CHEESE, SHREDDED

1.75 OZ. | 50 GRAMS BACON, CHOPPED

4 SUN-DRIED TOMATOES, HALVED

OLIVE OIL, TO TASTE

PIZZA WITH SEAFOOD & BROCCOLI

YIELD: 1 PIZZA / **ACTIVE TIME:** 20 MINUTES / **TOTAL TIME:** 50 MINUTES

Shrimp and squid are recommended considering the rest of the ingredients, but don't hesitate to try your favorite fruits of the sea on this pizza.

1. Preheat the oven to the maximum temperature and place a baking stone or steel on the middle rack as it warms. Dust a work surface with the semolina flour, place the dough on the surface, and gently stretch it into a round. For more detailed instructions on properly stretching a ball of pizza dough see page 73. Cover the dough with the sauce and top with the mozzarella and broccoli. Season with salt and drizzle olive oil over the pizza.

2. Using a peel or a flat baking sheet, transfer the pizza to the heated baking implement in the oven. Bake for about 7 minutes, until the crust starts to brown. Remove the pizza, distribute the shrimp and squid over the top, drizzle olive oil over the pizza, and return the pizza to the oven. Bake for about 5 minutes, until the crust is golden brown and starting to char. Remove and let cool slightly before slicing and serving.

INGREDIENTS:

SEMOLINA FLOUR, AS NEEDED

1 BALL PIZZA DOUGH

2.4 OZ. | 70 GRAMS RAW PIZZA SAUCE (SEE PAGE 103)

4.2 OZ. | 120 GRAMS LOW-MOISTURE MOZZARELLA CHEESE, SHREDDED

1 OZ. | 30 GRAMS BROCCOLI FLORETS, COOKED

SALT, TO TASTE

OLIVE OIL, TO TASTE

1.4 OZ. | 40 GRAMS SHRIMP, PEELED AND COOKED

1.4 OZ. | 40 GRAMS SQUID RINGS, COOKED

PEPPER & EGG PIZZA

YIELD: 1 PIZZA / **ACTIVE TIME:** 15 MINUTES / **TOTAL TIME:** 45 MINUTES

The crunch supplied by the peppers provides a lovely contrast to the cheese and egg on this pie.

1. Preheat the oven to the maximum temperature and place a baking stone or steel on the middle rack as it warms. Dust a work surface with the semolina flour, place the dough on the surface, and gently stretch it into a round. For more detailed instructions on properly stretching a ball of pizza dough see page 73. Cover the dough with the sauce and top with half of the mozzarella.

2. Using a peel or a flat baking sheet, transfer the pizza to the heated baking implement in the oven. Bake for about 7 minutes, until the crust starts to brown. Remove the pizza, distribute the peppers, onion, corn, pepperoni, and egg over the top, season with salt, and drizzle olive oil over everything. Sprinkle the rest of the mozzarella on top and return the pizza to the oven. Bake for about 5 minutes, until the crust is golden brown and starting to char. Remove and let cool slightly before slicing and serving.

INGREDIENTS:

SEMOLINA FLOUR, AS NEEDED

MOZZARELLA CHEESE, SHREDDED

⅓ SMALL RED BELL PEPPER, SLICED

⅓ SMALL GREEN BELL PEPPER, SLICED

½ RED CHILI PEPPER, SLICED

¼ SMALL RED ONION, SLICED THIN

1 OZ. | 30 GRAMS CANNED CORN

5 SLICES PEPPERONI

1 HARD-BOILED EGG, SLICED

SALT, TO TASTE

OLIVE OIL, AS NEEDED

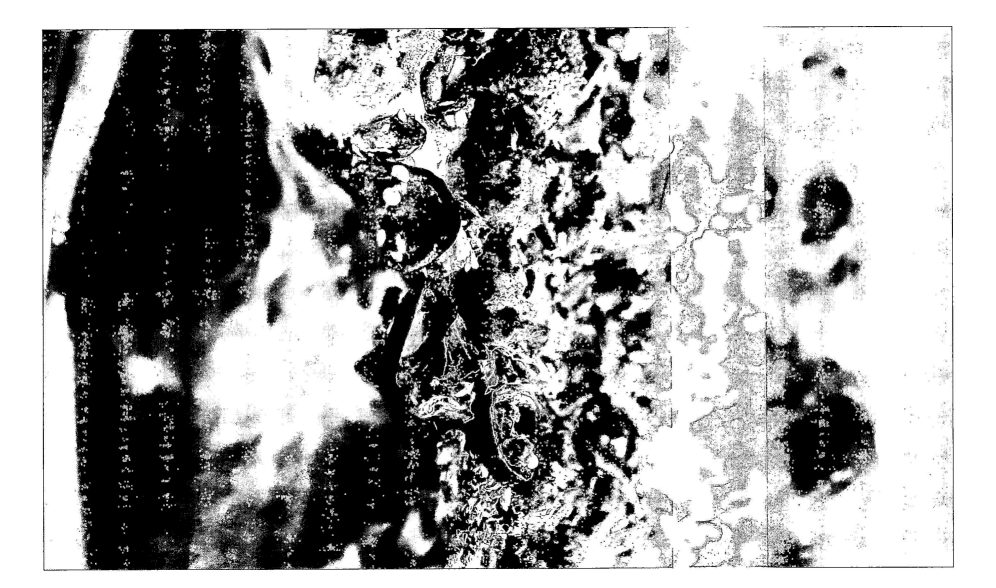

BROCCOLI, CHORIZO & CHILI PEPPER PIZZA

YIELD: 1 PIZZA / **ACTIVE TIME:** 15 MINUTES / **TOTAL TIME:** 45 MINUTES

The chorizo can be swapped out for pepperoni, but the former's unique flavor was made to sit beside the chili pepper here.

1. Preheat the oven to the maximum temperature and place a baking stone or steel on the middle rack as it warms. Dust a work surface with the semolina flour, place the dough on the surface, and gently stretch it into a round. For more detailed instructions on properly stretching a ball of pizza dough see page 73. Cover the dough with the mozzarella and top with the broccoli, chili pepper, chorizo, and onion. Season with salt and drizzle olive oil over the pizza.

2. Using a peel or a flat baking sheet, transfer the pizza to the heated baking implement in the oven. Bake for about 15 minutes, until the crust is golden brown and starting to char. Remove and let cool slightly before slicing and serving.

INGREDIENTS:

SEMOLINA FLOUR, AS NEEDED

1 BALL PIZZA DOUGH

2.8 OZ. | 80 GRAMS LOW-MOISTURE MOZZARELLA CHEESE, SHREDDED

2.4 OZ. | 70 GRAMS BROCCOLI FLORETS, MINCED

½ RED CHILI PEPPER, SLICED

½ LINK CHORIZO SAUSAGE, CASING REMOVED AND CRUMBLED

¼ SMALL RED ONION, SLICED THIN

SALT, TO TASTE

OLIVE OIL, TO TASTE

TWO CHEESE & BACON PIZZA

YIELD: 1 PIZZA / **ACTIVE TIME:** 15 MINUTES / **TOTAL TIME:** 45 MINUTES

t's all about the bacon here, as the rest of the ingredients are here only to amplify its universally loved flavor.

1. Preheat the oven to the maximum temperature and place a baking stone or steel on the middle rack as it warms. Dust a work surface with the semolina flour, place the dough on the surface, and gently stretch it into a round. For more detailed instructions on preparing and stretching a pizza dough see page 73. Cover the dough with the cheeses, peppers, and bacon. Season with oregano and drizzle olive oil over the pizza.

2. Using a peel or a flat baking sheet, transfer the pizza to the heated baking implement in the oven. Bake for about 15 minutes, until the crust is golden brown and starting to char. Remove and let cool slightly before slicing and serving.

INGREDIENTS:

MOZZARELLA CHEESE, SHREDDED

4 SMALL MILD CHILI PEPPERS, CHOPPED

1.75 OZ. | 50 GRAMS BACON, COOKED AND CHOPPED

FRESH OREGANO, FINELY CHOPPED, TO TASTE

OLIVE OIL, TO TASTE

PIZZA WITH EGGS & BACON

YIELD: 1 PIZZA / **ACTIVE TIME:** 15 MINUTES / **TOTAL TIME:** 45 MINUTES

Cold leftover pizza is always a great breakfast option, but this pie does it one better.

1. Preheat the oven to the maximum temperature and place a baking stone or steel on the middle rack as it warms. Dust a work surface with the semolina flour, place the dough on the surface, and gently stretch it into a round. For more detailed instructions on properly stretching a ball of pizza dough see page 73. Cover the dough with the mozzarella and top with the bacon. Crack the eggs open onto the center of the pizza, season with salt and pepper, and drizzle olive oil over the top.

2. Using a peel or a flat baking sheet, transfer the pizza to the heated baking implement in the oven. Bake for about 15 minutes, until the crust is golden brown and starting to char. Remove and let cool slightly before slicing and serving.

INGREDIENTS:

SEMOLINA FLOUR, AS NEEDED

1 BALL PIZZA DOUGH

3.5 OZ. | 100 GRAMS LOW-MOISTURE MOZZARELLA CHEESE, SHREDDED

2.4 OZ. | 70 GRAMS BACON, COOKED AND CHOPPED

2 EGGS

SALT AND PEPPER, TO TASTE

OLIVE OIL, AS NEEDED

VEGETABLE & MUSHROOM PIZZA

YIELD: 1 PIZZA / **TOTAL TIME:** 15 MINUTES / **ACTIVE TIME:** 45 MINUTES

The best bits of a summer garden are gathered on this delightful pizza, which benefits tremendously from the slight blistering the cherry tomatoes acquire in the oven.

1. Preheat the oven to the maximum temperature and place a baking stone or steel on the middle rack as it warms. Dust a work surface with the semolina flour, place the dough on the surface, and gently stretch it into a round. For more detailed instructions on properly stretching a ball of pizza dough see page 73. Cover the dough with the sauce and top with the mozzarella, zucchini, tomatoes, mushrooms, onion, and ham, if using. Season with salt and drizzle olive oil over the pizza.

2. Using a peel or a flat baking sheet, transfer the pizza to the heated baking implement in the oven. Bake for about 15 minutes, until the crust is golden brown and starting to char. Remove and let cool slightly before garnishing with the chives, slicing, and serving.

INGREDIENTS:

SEMOLINA FLOUR, TO TASTE

1 BALL OF PIZZA DOUGH

3 ⅛ OZ. | 90 GRAMS SAN MARZANO TOMATO SAUCE

3 ½ OZ. | 100 GRAMS FRESH MOZZARELLA, TORN, SHREDDED

1.75 OZ. | 50 GRAMS ZUCCHINI, DICED

1.75 OZ. | 50 GRAMS CHERRY TOMATOES, CUT INTO WEDGES

1.4 OZ. | 40 GRAMS BUTTON MUSHROOMS, SLICED

¼ SMALL RED ONION, SLICED THIN

1 SLICE HAM, CHOPPED (OPTIONAL)

SALT, TO TASTE

OLIVE OIL, TO TASTE

FRESH CHIVES, FINELY CHOPPED, FOR GARNISH

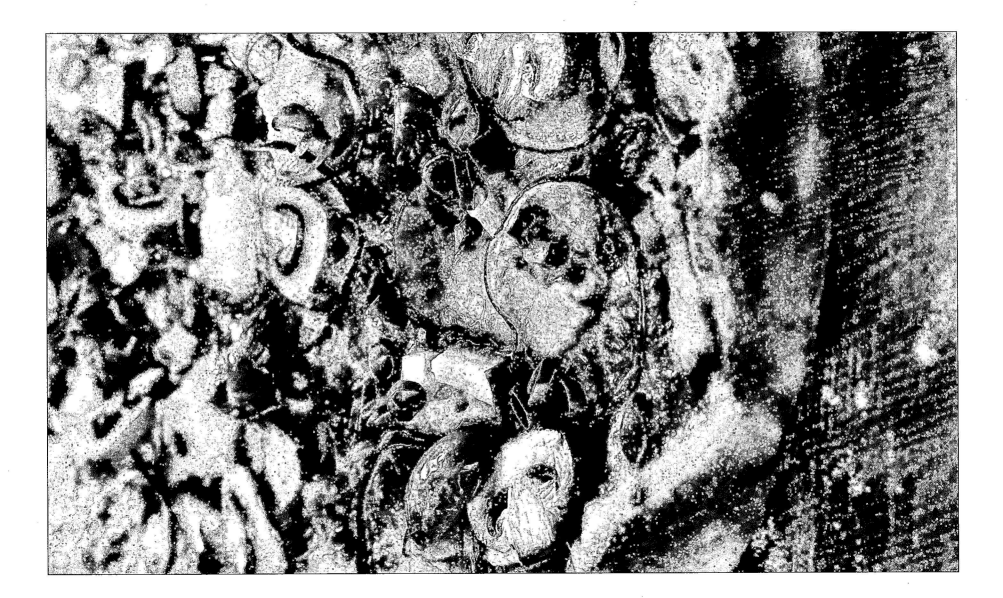

TWO CHEESE & MUSHROOM PIZZA

YIELD: 1 PIZZA / **ACTIVE TIME:** 15 MINUTES / **TOTAL TIME:** 45 MINUTES

A simple yet delicious gooey topping with lots of umami from the cremini mushrooms and the thyme leaves.

1. Preheat the oven to the maximum temperature and place a baking stone or steel on the middle rack as it warms. Dust a work surface with the semolina flour, place the dough on the surface, and gently stretch it into a round. For more detailed instructions on properly stretching a ball of pizza dough see page 73. Cover the dough with the sauce and top with the cheeses and mushrooms. Season with salt and drizzle olive oil over the pizza.

2. Using a peel or a flat baking sheet, transfer the pizza to the heated baking implement in the oven. Bake for about 15 minutes, until the crust is golden brown and starting to char. Remove and let cool slightly before garnishing with the thyme, slicing, and serving.

INGREDIENTS:

SEMOLINA FLOUR, AS NEEDED

1 BALL PIZZA DOUGH

1.75 OZ. | 50 GRAMS RAW PIZZA SAUCE (SEE PAGE 103)

1.75 OZ. | 50 GRAMS PROVOLONE CHEESE, SHREDDED

1.75 OZ. | 50 GRAMS LOW-MOISTURE MOZZARELLA CHEESE, SHREDDED

2.4 OZ. | 70 GRAMS CREMINI MUSHROOMS, SLICED

SALT, TO TASTE

OLIVE OIL, TO TASTE

1 HANDFUL FRESH THYME LEAVES, FOR GARNISH

CHORIZO & OLIVE PIZZA

YIELD: 1 PIZZA / **ACTIVE TIME:** 15 MINUTES / **TOTAL TIME:** 45 MINUTES

I f you're in the mood for something super-savory, the combination of chorizo and olives is tough to beat.

1. Preheat the oven to the maximum temperature and place a baking stone or steel on the middle rack as it warms. Dust a work surface with the semolina flour, place the dough on the surface, and gently stretch it into a round. For more detailed instructions on properly stretching a ball of pizza dough see page 73. Cover the dough with the sauce and top with the mozzarella, chorizo, and olives. Season with salt and pepper and drizzle olive oil over the pizza.

2. Using a peel or a flat baking sheet, transfer the pizza to the heated baking implement in the oven. Bake for about 15 minutes, until the crust is golden brown and starting to char. Remove, sprinkle the Parmesan over the pizza, and let cool slightly before slicing and serving.

INGREDIENTS:

SEMOLINA FLOUR, AS NEEDED

3.5 OZ. | 100 GRAMS CHORIZO, SLICED

1.75 OZ. | 50 GRAMS BLACK OLIVES, PITTED AND SLICED

SALT AND PEPPER, TO TASTE

OLIVE OIL, TO TASTE

1 OZ. | 30 GRAMS PARMESAN CHEESE, GRATED

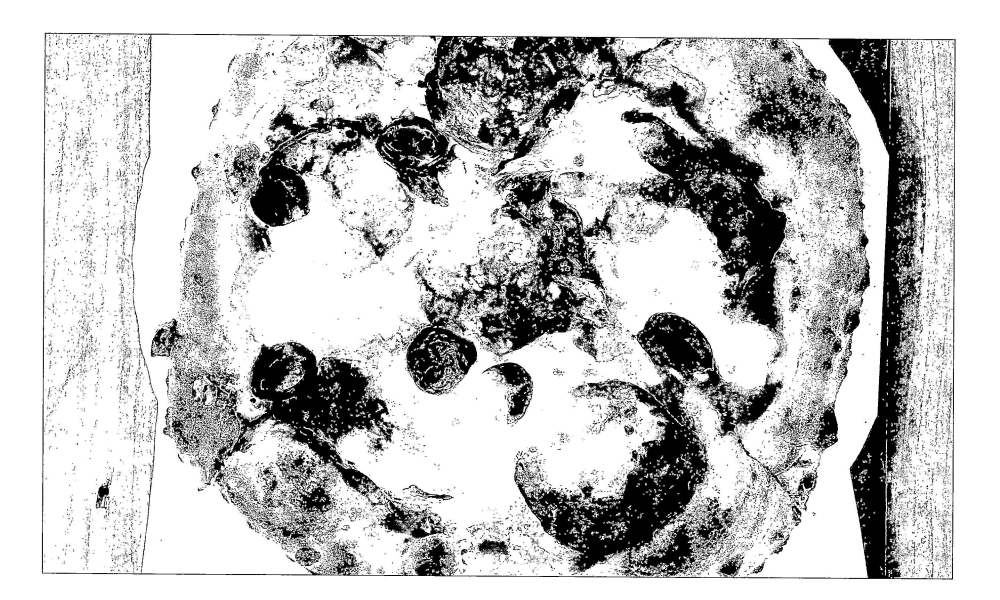

DOUBLE MOZZARELLA & HAM PIZZA

YIELD: 1 PIZZA / **ACTIVE TIME:** 15 MINUTES / **TOTAL TIME:** 45 MINUTES

Adding a layer of fresh mozzarella right in the middle of baking this pie gives it that festive, decadent feel that we all crave.

1. Preheat the oven to the maximum temperature and place a baking stone or steel on the middle rack as it warms. Dust a work surface with the semolina flour, place the dough on the surface, and gently stretch it into a round. For more detailed instructions on properly stretching a ball of pizza dough see page 73. Cover the dough with the sauce and top with the shredded mozzarella, ham, and onion. Season with salt and pepper and drizzle olive oil over the pizza.

2. Using a peel or a flat baking sheet, transfer the pizza to the heated baking implement in the oven. Bake for about 7 minutes, until the crust starts to brown. Remove the pizza, distribute the fresh mozzarella and oregano over the top, and return the pizza to the oven. Bake for about 5 minutes, until the crust is golden brown and starting to char. Remove and let cool slightly before slicing and serving.

INGREDIENTS:

SEMOLINA FLOUR, AS NEEDED

1 BALL PIZZA DOUGH

2.8 OZ. | 80 GRAMS RAW PIZZA SAUCE (SEE PAGE 103)

1.75 OZ. | 50 GRAMS LOW-MOISTURE MOZZARELLA CHEESE, SHREDDED

2.4 OZ. | 70 GRAMS HAM, CUT INTO SHORT STRIPS

¼ SMALL WHITE ONION, SLICED

SALT AND PEPPER, TO TASTE

OLIVE OIL, TO TASTE

2.4 OZ. | 70 GRAMS FRESH MOZZARELLA CHEESE, DRAINED AND CUT INTO SHORT STRIPS

FRESH OREGANO, FINELY CHOPPED, TO TASTE

HAM & VEGGIE PIZZA

YIELD: 1 PIZZA / **ACTIVE TIME:** 15 MINUTES / **TOTAL TIME:** 45 MINUTES

The slightly sweet taste of ham is precisely what the potent flavor of olives cries out for.

1. Preheat the oven to the maximum temperature and place a baking stone or steel on the middle rack as it warms. Dust a work surface with the semolina flour, place the dough on the surface, and gently stretch it into a round. For more detailed instructions on properly stretching a ball of pizza dough see page 73. Cover the dough with the sauce and top with half of the mozzarella, the mushrooms, ham, onion, and olives. Season with salt and pepper, drizzle olive oil over the pizza, and sprinkle the remaining mozzarella on top.

2. Using a peel or a flat baking sheet, transfer the pizza to the heated baking implement in the oven. Bake for about 15 minutes, until the crust is golden brown and starting to char. Remove and let cool slightly before garnishing with the tomatoes and basil, slicing, and serving.

INGREDIENTS:

SEMOLINA FLOUR, AS NEEDED

1 BALL PIZZA DOUGH

1/2 CUP | 80 GRAMS RAW PIZZA SAUCE (SEE PAGE 3 TRAY)

... MOZZARELLA ... STRIPS OR MOZZARELLA CHEESE, SHREDDED

1.75 OZ. | 50 GRAMS BUTTON MUSHROOMS, SLICED

1.75 OZ. | 50 GRAMS HAM, CUT INTO SHORT STRIPS

¼ SMALL RED ONION, SLICED

1 HANDFUL PITTED BLACK OLIVES

SALT AND PEPPER, TO TASTE

OLIVE OIL, TO TASTE

4 CHERRY TOMATOES, HALVED, FOR GARNISH

FRESH BASIL LEAVES, FOR GARNISH

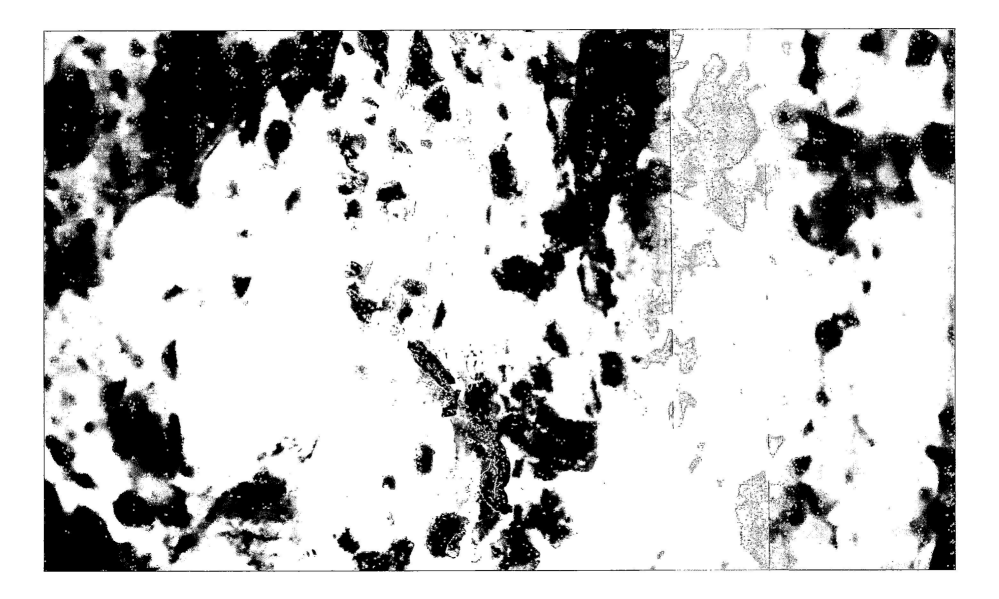

PIZZA WITH ZUCCHINI CREAM, BACON & BUFALA

YIELD: 1 PIZZA / **ACTIVE TIME:** 15 MINUTES / **TOTAL TIME:** 45 MINUTES

The texture provided by the Zucchini Cream and the buffalo mozzarella makes this pizza more than enough for anyone, while the bacon takes it over the top.

1. Preheat the oven to the maximum temperature and place a baking stone or steel on the middle rack as it warms. Dust a work surface with the semolina flour, place the dough on the surface, and gently stretch it into a round. For more detailed instructions on properly stretching a ball of pizza dough see page 73. Cover the dough with the Zucchini Cream, distribute the mozzarella over it, and drizzle olive oil on top.

2. Using a peel or a flat baking sheet, transfer the pizza to the heated baking implement in the oven. Bake for about 15 minutes, until the crust is golden brown and starting to char. Remove and let cool slightly before sprinkling the bacon over the pizza, slicing, and serving.

INGREDIENTS:

SEMOLINA FLOUR, AS NEEDED

1 BALL PIZZA DOUGH

1.5 OZ. | 45 GRAMS ZUCCHINI CREAM (SEE PAGE 379)

3.5 OZ. | 100 GRAMS BUFFALO MOZZARELLA CHEESE, DRAINED AND TORN

OLIVE OIL, TO TASTE

2 SLICES BACON, COOKED AND CRUMBLED

GARLIC POTATO & ZUCCHINI PIZZA

YIELD: 1 PIZZA / **ACTIVE TIME:** 20 MINUTES / **TOTAL TIME:** 1 HOUR

Save this one for the spring, when baby potatoes are at their peak.

1. Preheat oven to maximum temperature and place a baking stone or steel on the middle rack as it warms. Coat the bottom of a skillet with olive oil and warm over medium-high heat. When the oil starts to shimmer, add the potatoes and garlic, season with salt and pepper, and cook until the potatoes are tender, about 10 minutes. Remove from heat and let cool.

2. Dust a work surface with the semolina flour, place the dough on the surface, and gently stretch it into a round. For more detailed instructions on properly stretching a ball of pizza dough see page 73. Cover the dough with the mozzarella and top with the potato-and-garlic mixture, zucchini, tomatoes, and rosemary. Season with salt and pepper and drizzle olive oil over the pizza.

3. Using a peel or a flat baking sheet, transfer the pizza to the heated baking implement in the oven. Bake for about 15 minutes, until the crust is golden brown and starting to char. Remove and let cool slightly before slicing and serving.

INGREDIENTS:

OLIVE OIL, AS NEEDED

1 BALL PIZZA DOUGH

2.1 OZ. | 60 GRAMS LOW-MOISTURE MOZZARELLA CHEESE, SHREDDED

⅓ SMALL ZUCCHINI, SLICED VERY THIN WITH MANDOLINE

3 CHERRY TOMATOES, CHOPPED

FRESH ROSEMARY, TO TASTE

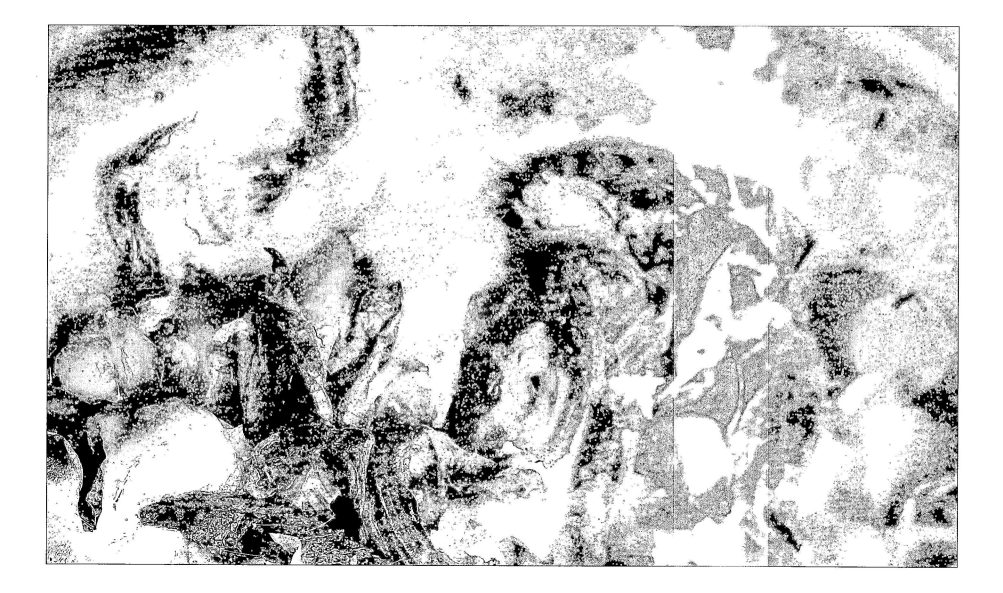

ZUCCHINI BLOSSOM & CHERRY TOMATO PIZZA

YIELD: 1 PIZZA / **ACTIVE TIME:** 15 MINUTES / **TOTAL TIME:** 45 MINUTES

This pizza owes its charm to the subtle freshness and velvety texture of zucchini blossom, a staple of Roman cuisine. The addition of yellow cherry tomatoes beautifully matches the colors and flavors of this elegant bianca.

1. Preheat the oven to the maximum temperature and place a baking stone or steel on the middle rack as it warms. Dust a work surface with the semolina flour, place the dough on the surface, and gently stretch it into a round. For more detailed instructions on properly stretching a ball of pizza dough see page 73. Cover the dough with the mozzarella and top with the zucchini blossoms, cherry tomatoes, and basil. Season with salt and drizzle olive oil over the pizza.

2. Using a peel or a flat baking sheet, transfer the pizza to the heated baking implement in the oven. Bake for about 15 minutes, until the crust is golden brown and starting to char. Remove, sprinkle the Parmesan over the top, and let cool slightly before slicing and serving.

INGREDIENTS:

SEMOLINA FLOUR, AS NEEDED

1 BALL PIZZA DOUGH

2.4 OZ. | 70 GRAMS LOW-MOISTURE MOZZARELLA CHEESE, SHREDDED

3 ZUCCHINI BLOSSOMS, CLEANED AND CUT INTO WEDGES

1 HANDFUL YELLOW CHERRY TOMATOES, HALVED

FRESH BASIL LEAVES, TO TASTE

SALT, TO TASTE

OLIVE OIL, TO TASTE

PARMESAN CHEESE, GRATED, TO TASTE

PIZZA WITH FETA, OLIVES & PEPPERS

YIELD: 1 PIZZA / **ACTIVE TIME:** 15 MINUTES / **TOTAL TIME:** 45 MINUTES

Take the best parts of a Greek salad, place them on a pizza, and voila! The mushrooms and bell pepper manage to temper the considerable flavor provided by the feta and olives.

1. Preheat the oven to the maximum temperature and place a baking stone or steel on the middle rack as it warms. Dust a work surface with the semolina flour, place the dough on the surface, and gently stretch it into a round. For more detailed instructions on properly stretching a ball of pizza dough see page 73. Cover the dough with the sauce and top with the mozzarella, bell pepper, olives, and mushrooms. Season with salt and pepper and drizzle olive oil over the pizza.

2. Using a peel or a flat baking sheet, transfer the pizza to the heated baking implement in the oven. Bake for about 7 minutes, until the crust starts to brown. Remove the pizza, distribute the feta on top, drizzle olive oil over the pizza, and return it to the oven. Bake for about 5 minutes, until the crust is golden brown and starting to char. Remove and let cool slightly before slicing and serving.

INGREDIENTS:

SEMOLINA FLOUR, AS NEEDED

¼ BELL PEPPER, SLICED

1 HANDFUL PITTED KALAMATA OLIVES

1 OZ. | 30 GRAMS BUTTON MUSHROOMS, SLICED

SALT AND PEPPER, TO TASTE

OLIVE OIL, TO TASTE

1.75 OZ. | 50 GRAMS FETA CHEESE, CRUMBLED

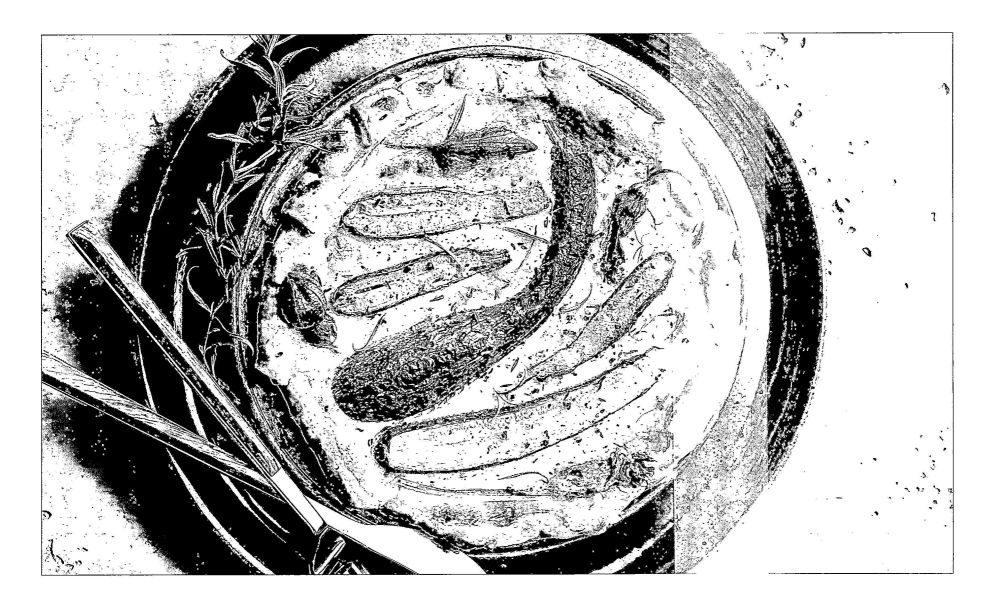

ROASTED ZUCCHINI, BÉCHAMEL & ROSEMARY PIZZA

YIELD: 1 PIZZA / **ACTIVE TIME:** 20 MINUTES / **TOTAL TIME:** 1 HOUR AND 15 MINUTES

Béchamel Sauce is generally found on savory pies, but not on pizza pies. Here you will be surprised by how much flair this sauce gives to a simple zucchini bianca.

1. Preheat the oven to the maximum temperature and place a baking stone or steel on the middle rack as it warms. Place the zucchini in a baking dish, season with salt and pepper, and drizzle olive oil over the top. Toss to combine, place it in the warming oven, and roast until it softens slightly, about 20 minutes. Remove and let cool.

2. Dust a work surface with the semolina flour, place the dough on the surface, and gently stretch it into a round. For more detailed instructions on properly stretching a ball of pizza dough see page 73. Cover the dough with the Béchamel Sauce and top with the mozzarella and zucchini. Season with salt and pepper, drizzle olive oil over the pizza, and sprinkle the rosemary on top.

3. Using a peel or a flat baking sheet, transfer the pizza to the heated baking implement in the oven. Bake for about 15 minutes, until the crust is golden brown and starting to char. Remove and let cool slightly before slicing and serving.

BÉCHAMEL SAUCE

1. Place the unsalted butter in a saucepan and melt it over low heat. Add the flour, whisk to combine, and cook for 1 minute.

2. Gradually add the warm milk, whisking constantly to prevent lumps from forming. Continue whisking until the sauce has thickened, about 5 minutes.

3. Season with salt and pepper, stir in the nutmeg, and use as desired.

INGREDIENTS:

1 SMALL ZUCCHINI, SLICED LENGTHWISE

SALT AND PEPPER, TO TASTE

OLIVE OIL, TO TASTE

SEMOLINA FLOUR, AS NEEDED

1 BALL PIZZA DOUGH

2.4 OZ. | 70 GRAMS BÉCHAMEL SAUCE (SEE RECIPE)

1.75 OZ. | 50 GRAMS LOW-MOISTURE MOZZARELLA CHEESE, SHREDDED

FRESH ROSEMARY, TO TASTE

BÉCHAMEL SAUCE

1 OZ. | 30 GRAMS UNSALTED BUTTER

1 OZ. | 30 GRAMS ALL-PURPOSE FLOUR

10.6 OZ. | 300 GRAMS MILK, WARMED

SALT AND PEPPER, TO TASTE

1 PINCH GROUND NUTMEG

CAULIFLOWER, PROVOLONE & SMOKED HAM PIZZA

YIELD: 1 PIZZA / **ACTIVE TIME:** 15 MINUTES / **TOTAL TIME:** 45 MINUTES

When working with an ingredient with a unique flavor like smoked ham, you want to do as little as possible to stand in its way. The mild provolone and cauliflower do just that.

1. Preheat the oven to the maximum temperature and place a baking stone or steel on the middle rack as it warms. Dust a work surface with the semolina flour, place the dough on the surface, and gently stretch it into a round. For more detailed instructions on properly stretching a ball of pizza dough see page 73. Cover the dough with the provolone and top with the ham and cauliflower. Season with pepper and drizzle olive oil over the pizza.

2. Using a peel or a flat baking sheet, transfer the pizza to the heated baking implement in the oven. Bake for about 15 minutes, until the crust is golden brown and starting to char. Remove and let cool slightly before slicing and serving.

INGREDIENTS:

· · ·   · ·   · ·   ·   · · · ·   ·

SMOKED SERVES

2.4 OZ. | 70 GRAMS CAULIFLOWER FLORETS, COOKED

BLACK PEPPER, TO TASTE

OLIVE OIL, TO TASTE

PIZZA WITH GARDEN VEGETABLES & BUFALA

YIELD: 1 PIZZA / **ACTIVE TIME:** 15 MINUTES / **TOTAL TIME:** 45 MINUTES

Celery gets short shrift in the culinary world, but its ability to tie together wide-ranging groups of ingredients is on display on this pizza.

1. Preheat the oven to the maximum temperature and place a baking stone or steel on the middle rack as it warms. Dust a work surface with the semolina flour, place the dough on the surface, and gently stretch it into a round. For more detailed instructions on properly stretching a ball of pizza dough see page 73. Cover the dough with the sauce and top with the vegetables. Season with salt and pepper and drizzle olive oil over the pizza.

2. Using a peel or a flat baking sheet, transfer the pizza to the heated baking implement in the oven. Bake for about 7 minutes, until the crust starts to brown. Remove the pizza, top it with the mozzarella, season with salt, drizzle olive oil over the pizza, and return it to the oven. Bake for about 5 minutes, until the crust is golden brown and starting to char. Remove and let cool slightly before slicing and serving.

INGREDIENTS:

SEMOLINA FLOUR, AS NEEDED

1 BALL PIZZA DOUGH

2.8 OZ. | 80 GRAMS RAW PIZZA SAUCE (SEE PAGE 103)

1 OZ. | 30 GRAMS CELERY, CHOPPED

1 OZ. | 30 GRAMS BELL PEPPER, CHOPPED

1 OZ. | 30 GRAMS LEEKS, CHOPPED

1 HANDFUL GREEN OLIVES, CHOPPED

¼ RED ONION, SLICED

5 CHERRY TOMATOES

SALT AND PEPPER, TO TASTE

OLIVE OIL, TO TASTE

2.8 OZ. | 80 GRAMS BUFFALO MOZZARELLA CHEESE, DRAINED AND TORN

SPICY BEEF & ZUCCHINI PIZZA

YIELD: 1 PIZZA / **ACTIVE TIME:** 20 MINUTES / **TOTAL TIME:** 1 HOUR

A bit of Tabasco makes what could be a humble topping a real eye-opener.

1. Preheat the oven to the maximum temperature and place a baking stone or steel on the middle rack as it warms. Coat the bottom of a skillet with olive oil and warm over medium-high heat. When the oil starts to shimmer, add the ground beef and cook, while breaking it up with a fork, until it is browned, about 8 minutes. Season with Tabasco and salt, remove from heat, and set aside.

2. Dust a work surface with the semolina flour, place the dough on the surface, and gently stretch it into a round. For more detailed instructions on properly stretching a ball of pizza dough see page 73. Cover the dough with the sauce and top with the mozzarella, zucchini, and ground beef. Season with salt and drizzle olive oil over the pizza.

3. Using a peel or a flat baking sheet, transfer the pizza to the heated baking implement in the oven. Bake for about 15 minutes, until the crust is golden brown and starting to char. Remove and let cool slightly before slicing and serving.

INGREDIENTS:

OLIVE OIL, AS NEEDED

2.8 OZ. | 80 GRAMS RAW PIZZA SAUCE (SEE PAGE 103)

2.8 OZ. | 80 GRAMS LOW-MOISTURE MOZZARELLA CHEESE, SHREDDED

⅓ SMALL ZUCCHINI, SLICED

GRILLED ZUCCHINI & EGGPLANT PIZZA

YIELD: 1 PIZZA / **ACTIVE TIME:** 20 MINUTES / **TOTAL TIME:** 55 MINUTES

No meat, no problem. The meaty taste and texture of eggplant add some heft to this all-veggie pie.

1. Preheat a grill to medium heat. Preheat the oven to the maximum temperature and place a baking stone or steel in the oven as it warms. Place the vegetables in a bowl, season with salt and pepper, and drizzle olive oil over them. Place them on the grill and cook until charred all over and softened slightly, about 5 minutes. Remove from the grill and let cool.

2. Dust a work surface with the semolina flour, place the dough on the surface, and gently stretch it into a round. For more detailed instructions on properly stretching a ball of pizza dough see page 73. Cover the dough with the sauce and top with the mozzarella and grilled vegetables. Season with salt and pepper and drizzle olive oil over the pizza.

3. Using a peel or a flat baking sheet, transfer the pizza to the heated baking implement in the oven. Bake for about 15 minutes, until the crust is golden brown and starting to char. Remove, sprinkle the Parmesan over the pizza, drizzle olive oil over the top, and let the pizza cool slightly before slicing and serving.

INGREDIENTS:

⅓ SMALL EGGPLANT, SLICED LENGTHWISE

⅓ ZUCCHINI, SLICED LENGTHWISE

¼ BELL PEPPER, SLICED

SALT AND PEPPER, TO TASTE

OLIVE OIL, AS NEEDED

SEMOLINA FLOUR, AS NEEDED

1 BALL PIZZA DOUGH

2.8 OZ. | 80 GRAMS RAW PIZZA SAUCE (SEE PAGE 103)

2.8 OZ. | 80 GRAMS LOW-MOISTURE MOZZARELLA CHEESE, SHREDDED

PARMESAN CHEESE, GRATED, TO TASTE

CAPER & OLIVE PIZZA

YIELD: 1 PIZZA / **ACTIVE TIME:** 15 MINUTES / **TOTAL TIME:** 45 MINUTES

Capers, olives, and the peppery taste of arugula mean that you can employ a light hand with the seasonings here.

1. Preheat the oven to the maximum temperature and place a baking stone or steel on the middle rack as it warms. Dust a work surface with the semolina flour, place the dough on the surface, and gently stretch it into a round. For more detailed instructions on properly stretching a ball of pizza dough see page 73. Cover the dough with the sauce and top with the olives and capers. Season with salt and pepper and drizzle olive oil over the pizza.

2. Using a peel or a flat baking sheet, transfer the pizza to the heated baking implement in the oven. Bake for about 15 minutes, until the crust is golden brown and starting to char. Remove, top with the arugula, and let the pizza cool slightly before slicing and serving.

INGREDIENTS:

SEMOLINA FLOUR, AS NEEDED

1 OZ. | 30 GRAMS CAPERS

SALT AND PEPPER, TO TASTE

OLIVE OIL, TO TASTE

1 HANDFUL ARUGULA

PIZZA WITH SHELLFISH & BELL PEPPERS

YIELD: 1 PIZZA / **ACTIVE TIME:** 15 MINUTES / **TOTAL TIME:** 45 MINUTES

Loaded with seafood and peppers, pizza just doesn't get any fresher than this.

1. Preheat the oven to the maximum temperature and place a baking stone or steel on the middle rack as it warms. Dust a work surface with the semolina flour, place the dough on the surface, and gently stretch it into a round. For more detailed instructions on properly stretching a ball of pizza dough see page 73. Cover the dough with the sauce and top with the mozzarella and bell pepper. Season with salt and pepper and drizzle olive oil over the pizza.

2. Using a peel or a flat baking sheet, transfer the pizza to the heated baking implement in the oven. Bake for about 7 minutes, until the crust starts to brown. Remove the pizza, distribute the shrimp and mussels over it, season with salt and pepper, drizzle olive oil over the pizza, and return it to the oven. Bake for about 5 minutes, until the crust is golden brown and starting to char. Remove, sprinkle the olives over the top, and let cool slightly before slicing and serving.

INGREDIENTS:

SEMOLINA FLOUR, AS NEEDED

1 BALL PIZZA DOUGH

2.8 OZ. | 80 GRAMS RAW PIZZA SAUCE (SEE PAGE 103)

2.1 OZ. | 60 GRAMS LOW-MOISTURE MOZZARELLA CHEESE, SHREDDED

½ BELL PEPPER, SLICED

SALT AND PEPPER, TO TASTE

OLIVE OIL, AS NEEDED

2.4 OZ. | 70 GRAMS SHRIMP, PEELED AND COOKED

2.4 OZ. | 70 GRAMS MUSSELS, COOKED AND SHELLED

5 BLACK OLIVES, SLICED

PIZZA WITH TUNA & CORN

YIELD: 1 PIZZA / **ACTIVE TIME:** 15 MINUTES / **TOTAL TIME:** 45 MINUTES

Make sure you use a high-quality canned corn here, as this pizza lays every shortcut bare.

1. Preheat the oven to the maximum temperature and place a baking stone or steel on the middle rack as it warms. Dust a work surface with the semolina flour, place the dough on the surface, and gently stretch it into a round. For more detailed instructions on properly stretching a ball of pizza dough see page 73. Cover the dough with the sauce and top with the mozzarella, tuna, corn, and onion. Season with salt and pepper and drizzle olive oil over the pizza.

2. Using a peel or a flat baking sheet, transfer the pizza to the heated baking implement in the oven. Bake for about 15 minutes, until the crust is golden brown and starting to char. Remove and let cool slightly before slicing and serving.

INGREDIENTS:

SEMOLINA FLOUR, TO TASTE

[illegible]

[illegible] RAW PIZZA SAUCE

[illegible]

[illegible]

[illegible] SHREDDED

3.5 OZ. | 100 GRAMS TUNA IN OLIVE OIL, DRAINED

2.4 OZ. | 70 GRAMS CANNED SWEET CORN

¼ SMALL RED ONION, SLICED

SALT AND PEPPER, TO TASTE

OLIVE OIL, TO TASTE

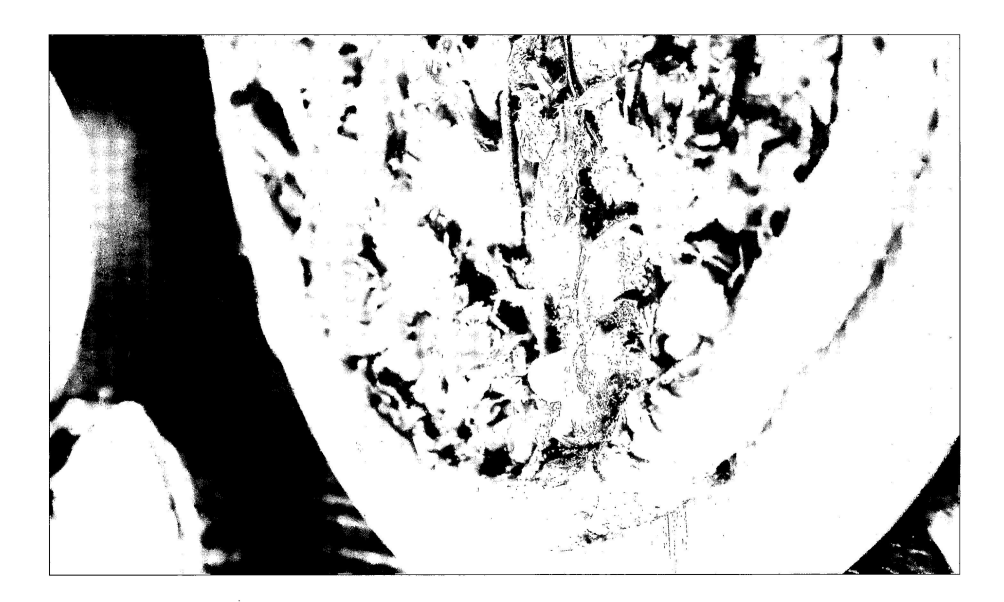

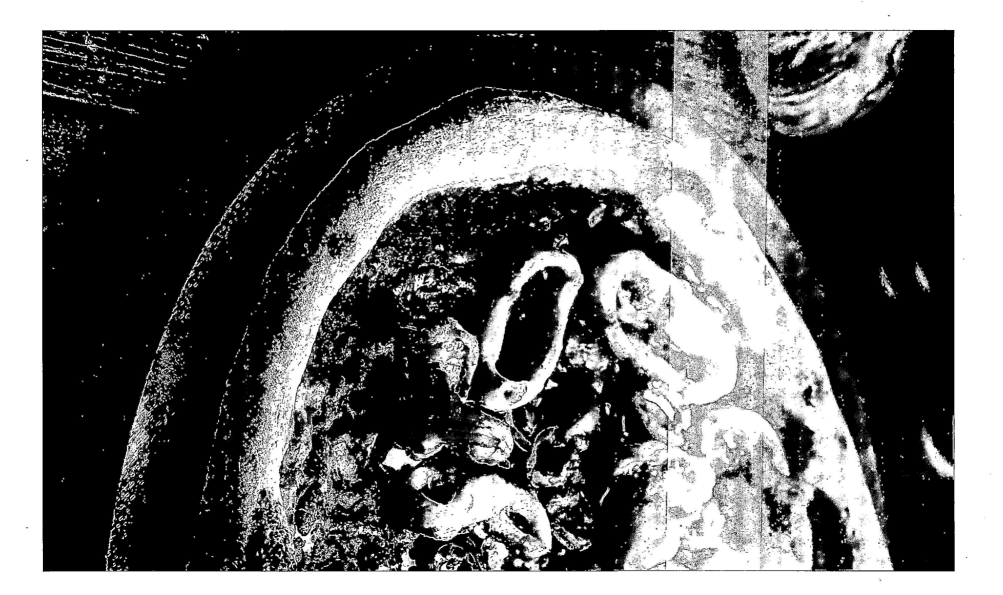

CALAMARI, SHRIMP & PESTO PIZZA

YIELD: 1 PIZZA / **ACTIVE TIME:** 15 MINUTES / **TOTAL TIME:** 45 MINUTES

S eafood and pesto have such a long tradition as a winning combination that putting it on a pizza is a no-brainer.

1. Preheat the oven to the maximum temperature and place a baking stone or steel on the middle rack as it warms. Dust a work surface with the semolina flour, place the dough on the surface, and gently stretch it into a round. For more detailed instructions on properly stretching a ball of pizza dough see page 73. Cover the dough with the sauce and top with the olives. Season with salt and pepper and drizzle olive oil over the pizza.

2. Using a peel or a flat baking sheet, transfer the pizza to the heated baking implement in the oven. Bake for about 7 minutes, until the crust starts to brown. Remove the pizza, distribute the calamari, shrimp, and Basil Pesto over the top, and return the pizza to the oven. Bake for about 5 minutes, until the crust is golden brown and starting to char. Remove and let cool slightly before slicing and serving.

INGREDIENTS:

SEMOLINA FLOUR, AS NEEDED

1 BALL PIZZA DOUGH

3.5 OZ. | 100 GRAMS RAW PIZZA SAUCE (SEE PAGE 103)

1 HANDFUL BLACK AND GREEN OLIVES, PITTED AND HALVED

SALT AND PEPPER, TO TASTE

OLIVE OIL, TO TASTE

3.5 OZ. | 100 GRAMS CALAMARI RINGS, COOKED

3.5 OZ. | 100 GRAMS SHRIMP, PEELED AND COOKED

1 OZ. | 30 GRAMS BASIL PESTO (SEE PAGE 365)

PIZZA WITH SHRIMP, CHILI PEPPERS & BUFALA

YIELD: 1 PIZZA / **ACTIVE TIME:** 15 MINUTES / **TOTAL TIME:** 45 MINUTES

As anyone who has had the good fortune to enjoy spicy shrimp at a first-class seafood restaurant knows, this pizza is positively divine.

1. Preheat the oven to the maximum temperature and place a baking stone or steel on the middle rack as it warms. Dust a work surface with the semolina flour, place the dough on the surface, and gently stretch it into a round. For more detailed instructions on properly stretching a ball of pizza dough see page 73. Cover the dough with the sauce and top with the mozzarella, chili peppers, and basil. Season with salt and pepper and drizzle olive oil over the pizza.

2. Using a peel or a flat baking sheet, transfer the pizza to the heated baking implement in the oven. Bake for about 7 minutes, until the crust starts to brown. Remove the pizza, top with the shrimp, drizzle olive oil over the pizza, and return the pizza to the oven. Bake for about 5 minutes, until the crust is golden brown and starting to char. Remove and let cool slightly before slicing and serving.

INGREDIENTS:

SEMOLINA FLOUR, AS NEEDED

[illegible]

[illegible]

[illegible]

2 SMALL MILD CHILI PEPPERS, SEEDED AND SLICED

FRESH BASIL LEAVES, TO TASTE

SALT AND PEPPER, TO TASTE

OLIVE OIL, TO TASTE

3.5 OZ. | 100 GRAMS SHRIMP, PEELED AND COOKED

SPICY SALAMI, SMOKED HAM & PEPPER PIZZA

YIELD: 1 PIZZA / **ACTIVE TIME:** 15 MINUTES / **TOTAL TIME:** 45 MINUTES

The spiciest salami you can stand will serve you well on this loaded pizza.

1. Preheat the oven to the maximum temperature and place a baking stone or steel on the middle rack as it warms. Dust a work surface with the semolina flour, place the dough on the surface, and gently stretch it into a round. For more detailed instructions on properly stretching a ball of pizza dough see page 73. Cover the dough with the sauce and top with the mozzarella, salami, ham, and bell pepper. Season with salt and pepper and drizzle olive oil over the top.

2. Using a peel or a flat baking sheet, transfer the pizza to the heated baking implement in the oven. Bake for about 15 minutes, until the crust is golden brown and starting to char. Remove and let cool slightly before slicing and serving.

INGREDIENTS:

SEMOLINA FLOUR, AS NEEDED

1 BALL PIZZA DOUGH

2.8 OZ. | 80 GRAMS RAW PIZZA SAUCE (SEE PAGE 103)

2.4 OZ. | 70 GRAMS LOW-MOISTURE MOZZARELLA CHEESE, SHREDDED

1.4 OZ. | 40 GRAMS SPICY SALAMI, SLICED

1.4 OZ. | 40 GRAMS SMOKED HAM, CUT IN SHORT STRIPS

¼ BELL PEPPER, SLICED

SALT AND PEPPER, TO TASTE

OLIVE OIL, TO TASTE

PIZZA WITH PUMPKIN, FETA & ARUGULA

YIELD: 1 PIZZA / **ACTIVE TIME:** 15 MINUTES / **TOTAL TIME:** 45 MINUTES

Pumpkin's earthy and sweet flavor is the perfect bridge between the peppery arugula and the salty feta.

1. Preheat the oven to the maximum temperature and place a baking stone or steel on the middle rack as it warms. Dust a work surface with the semolina flour, place the dough on the surface, and gently stretch it into a round. For more detailed instructions on properly stretching a ball of pizza dough see page 73. Cover the dough with the mozzarella and top with the pumpkin. Season with salt and pepper and drizzle olive oil over the pizza.

2. Using a peel or a flat baking sheet, transfer the pizza to the heated baking implement in the oven. Bake for about 7 minutes, until the crust starts to brown. Remove the pizza, top with the feta, arugula, and Parmesan, drizzle olive oil over the pizza, and return it to the oven. Bake for about 5 minutes, until the crust is golden brown and starting to char. Remove and let cool slightly before slicing and serving.

INGREDIENTS:

SEMOLINA FLOUR, AS NEEDED

1 BALL PIZZA DOUGH

2.8 OZ. | 80 GRAMS LOW-MOISTURE MOZZARELLA CHEESE, SHREDDED

3.5 OZ. | 100 GRAMS ROASTED PUMPKIN, DICED

SALT AND PEPPER, TO TASTE

OLIVE OIL, TO TASTE

2.8 OZ. | 80 GRAMS FETA CHEESE, CRUMBLED

1.75 OZ. | 50 GRAMS ARUGULA

PARMESAN CHEESE, GRATED, TO TASTE

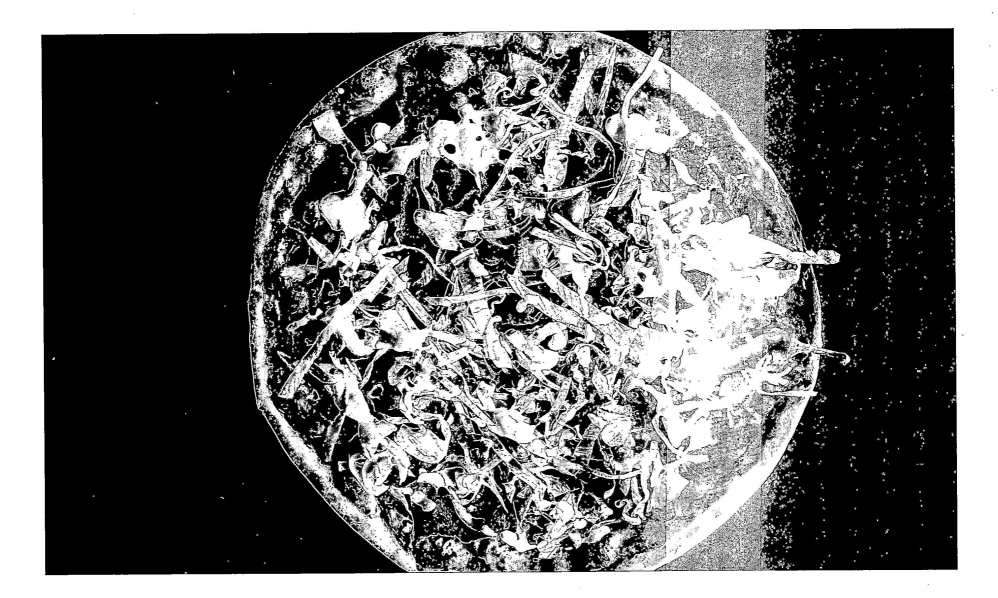

KEBAB PIZZA

YIELD: 1 PIZZA / **ACTIVE TIME:** 30 MINUTES / **TOTAL TIME:** 1 HOUR AND 30 MINUTES

Feferoni peppers are a very popular chili pepper in the Mediterranean and Balkan regions. Here, they lend their mild spice and crunch to this elevated take on the kebab wrap.

1. Preheat the oven to the maximum temperature and place a baking stone or steel on the middle rack as it warms. Dust a work surface with the semolina flour, place the dough on the surface, and gently stretch it into a round. For more detailed instructions on properly stretching a ball of pizza dough see page 73. Cover the dough with the sauce and top with the mozzarella.

2. Using a peel or a flat baking sheet, transfer the pizza to the heated baking implement in the oven. Bake for about 7 minutes, until the crust starts to brown. Remove the pizza, top with the Chicken Kebab, peppers, onion, and lettuce, season with salt and pepper, and return the pizza to the oven. Bake for about 5 minutes, until the crust is golden brown and starting to char. Remove and let cool while combining the yogurt and lemon juice. Drizzle the mixture over the pizza before slicing and serving.

CHICKEN KEBAB

1. Place the paprika, turmeric, onion powder, garlic powder, oregano, olive oil, vinegar, yogurt, and salt in a large bowl and whisk to combine. Add the chicken pieces and stir until they are coated. Cover the bowl, place it in the refrigerator, and let the chicken marinate for at least 2 hours. If time allows, let the chicken marinate overnight.

2. Remove the chicken from the refrigerator and let it sit at room temperature for about 30 minutes. Preheat a gas or charcoal grill to medium-high heat and warm for 10 minutes. While the grill or the pan is heating up, thread the chicken onto skewers and season with salt and pepper.

3. Brush the grill or the pan with a light coating of olive oil and then add the chicken kebabs. Cook, turning occasionally, until the chicken is well browned and cooked through, approximately 10 minutes.

INGREDIENTS:

SEMOLINA FLOUR, AS NEEDED

1 BALL PIZZA DOUGH

2.4 OZ. | 70 GRAMS RAW PIZZA SAUCE (SEE PAGE 103)

1.75 OZ. | 50 GRAMS LOW-MOISTURE MOZZARELLA CHEESE, SHREDDED

2.8 OZ. | 80 GRAMS CHICKEN KEBAB (SEE RECIPE)

5 FEFERONI PEPPERS

¼ WHITE ONION, SLICED

1.75 OZ. | 50 GRAMS ICEBERG LETTUCE, SLICED

SALT AND PEPPER, TO TASTE

1 OZ. | 30 GRAMS YOGURT

FRESH LEMON JUICE, TO TASTE

CHICKEN KEBAB

1½ TEASPOONS | 3.4 GRAMS PAPRIKA

¼ TEASPOON | 0.6 GRAMS TURMERIC

¼ TEASPOON | 0.6 GRAMS ONION POWDER

¼ TEASPOON | 0.6 GRAMS GARLIC POWDER

1¼ TEASPOONS | 1.25 GRAMS DRIED OREGANO

1 OZ. | 30 GRAMS OLIVE OIL, PLUS MORE AS NEEDED

2 TEASPOONS | 9.6 GRAMS WHITE WINE VINEGAR

2.1 OZ. | 60 GRAMS PLAIN GREEK YOGURT

1 PINCH TABLE SALT, PLUS MORE TO TASTE

12 OZ. | 340 GRAMS BONELESS, SKINLESS CHICKEN THIGHS, CUT INTO BITE-SIZED PIECES

BLACK PEPPER, TO TASTE

MEAT LOVER'S PIZZA

YIELD: 1 PIZZA / **ACTIVE TIME:** 25 MINUTES / **TOTAL TIME:** 45 MINUTES

The name says it all, but the chicken is the key to this pie, as its neutral flavor balances out the trio of flavor-packed pork-based offerings.

1. Preheat the oven to the maximum temperature and place a baking stone or steel on the middle rack as it warms. Dust a work surface with the semolina flour, place the dough on the surface, and gently stretch it into a round. For more detailed instructions on properly stretching a ball of pizza dough see page 73. Cover the dough with the sauce and top with the mozzarella, chicken, ham, sausage, and salami. Season with salt and pepper and drizzle olive oil over the pizza.

2. Using a peel or a flat baking sheet, transfer the pizza to the heated baking implement in the oven. Bake for about 15 minutes, until the crust is golden brown and starting to char. Remove and let cool slightly before slicing and serving.

INGREDIENTS:

SEMOLINA FLOUR, AS NEEDED

1.75 OZ. | 50 GRAMS COOKED CHICKEN BREAST, SHREDDED

1 OZ. | 30 GRAMS SLICED HAM, CHOPPED

1.4 OZ. | 40 GRAMS ITALIAN SAUSAGE, SLICED AND COOKED

1 OZ. | 30 GRAMS SPICY SALAMI, SLICED

SALT AND PEPPER, TO TASTE

OLIVE OIL, TO TASTE

SPINACH, EGG & CHEESE PIZZA

YIELD: 1 PIZZA / **ACTIVE TIME:** 20 MINUTES / **TOTAL TIME:** 50 MINUTES

Eggs Florentine, but you also get to eat the plate—and it's as delicious as what's served on it, if not more.

1. Preheat the oven to the maximum temperature and place a baking stone or steel on the middle rack as it warms. Coat the bottom of a skillet with olive oil and warm over medium-high heat. When the oil starts to shimmer, add the spinach and cook until it starts to wilt, about 2 minutes. Remove the pan from heat and let the spinach cool slightly.

2. Dust a work surface with the semolina flour, place the dough on the surface, and gently stretch it into a round. For more detailed instructions on properly stretching a ball of pizza dough see page 73. Cover the dough with half of the mozzarella and the spinach. Top with the rest of the mozzarella and crack the eggs in the center of the pizza. Season with salt and pepper and drizzle with olive oil.

3. Using a peel or a flat baking sheet, transfer the pizza to the heated baking implement in the oven. Bake for about 15 minutes, until the crust is golden brown and starting to char. Remove, sprinkle the Parmesan over the pizza, and let cool slightly before slicing and serving.

INGREDIENTS:

OLIVE OIL, AS NEEDED

3.5 OZ. | 100 GRAMS SPINACH

SEMOLINA FLOUR, AS NEEDED

1 BALL PIZZA DOUGH

3.5 OZ. | 100 GRAMS LOW-MOISTURE MOZZARELLA CHEESE, SHREDDED

2 EGGS

SALT AND PEPPER, TO TASTE

1 OZ. | 30 GRAMS PARMESAN CHEESE, GRATED

ARUGULA, EGG & MUSHROOM PIZZA

YIELD: 1 PIZZA / **ACTIVE TIME:** 15 MINUTES / **TOTAL TIME:** 45 MINUTES

This trio of toppings would make for a pretty standard omelet, but having creamy, runny eggs on top of a pizza is anything but ho-hum.

1. Preheat the oven to the maximum temperature and place a baking stone or steel on the middle rack as it warms. Dust a work surface with the semolina flour, place the dough on the surface, and gently stretch it into a round. For more detailed instructions on properly stretching a ball of pizza dough see page 73. Cover the dough with the mozzarella and top with the arugula, mushrooms, and prosciutto. Crack the eggs over the center of the pizza, season with salt and pepper, and drizzle olive oil over the top.

2. Using a peel or a flat baking sheet, transfer the pizza to the heated baking implement in the oven. Bake for about 15 minutes, until the crust is golden brown and starting to char. Remove, sprinkle the Parmesan over the pizza, and let cool slightly before slicing and serving.

INGREDIENTS:

SEMOLINA FLOUR, AS NEEDED

1.4 OZ. | 40 GRAMS BUTTON MUSHROOMS, SLICED

2 SLICES PROSCIUTTO, CUT INTO SHORT STRIPS

2 EGGS

SALT AND PEPPER, TO TASTE

OLIVE OIL, TO TASTE

1 OZ. | 30 GRAMS PARMESAN CHEESE, GRATED

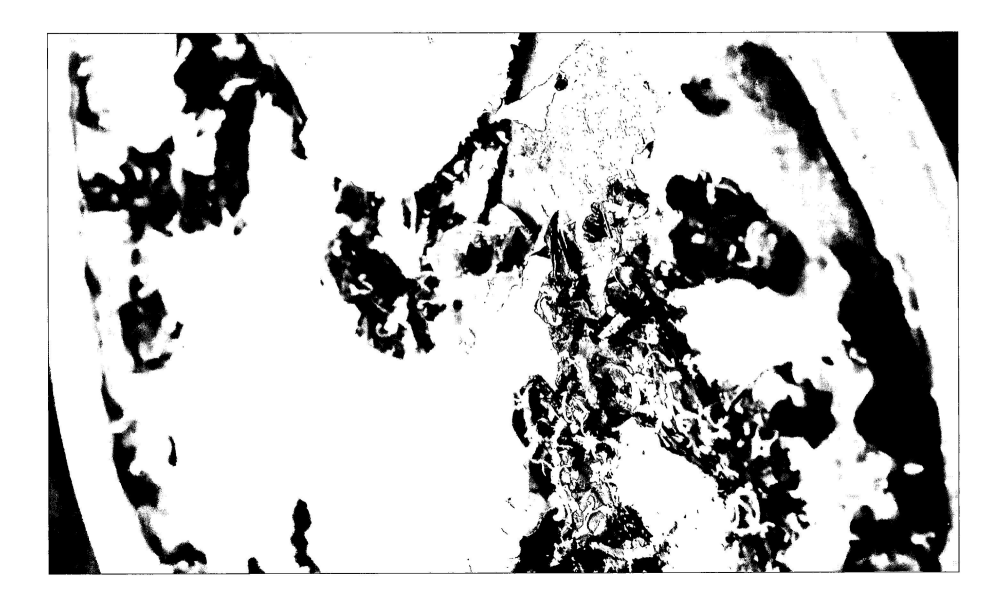

PIZZA WITH ROSE SAUCE, SAUSAGE & POTATO

YIELD: 1 PIZZA / **ACTIVE TIME:** 25 MINUTES / **TOTAL TIME:** 1 HOUR

Thick, creamy, and comforting, this pizza will entrance all who encounter it, thanks in large part to the sauce.

1. Preheat the oven to the maximum temperature and place a baking stone or steel on the middle rack as it warms. Coat the bottom of a skillet with olive oil and warm over medium-high heat. When the oil starts to shimmer, add the potato and sausage and cook until the sausage is browned and the potato is just tender, about 8 minutes. Remove the pan from heat and let cool.

2. Dust a work surface with the semolina flour, place the dough on the surface, and gently stretch it into a round. For more detailed instructions on properly stretching a ball of pizza dough see page 73. Cover the dough with the Rose Sauce and top with the sausage-and-potato mixture and rosemary. Season with salt and drizzle olive oil over the pizza.

3. Using a peel or a flat baking sheet, transfer the pizza to the heated baking implement in the oven. Bake for about 7 minutes. Remove the pizza, top with the mozzarella, return the pizza to the oven. Bake for about 5 minutes, until the crust is golden brown and starting to char. Remove and let cool slightly before slicing and serving.

ROSE SAUCE

1. Place the tomatoes in a food processor or blender and blitz until smooth. Place the butter in a saucepan and melt over medium heat. Add the onion and a pinch of salt and stir. When the onion begins to gently sizzle, adjust the heat to low, cover, and cook, stirring occasionally, until the onion has softened and is starting to brown, about 10 minutes.

2. Add the pureed tomatoes and a couple pinches of salt. Bring to a boil, then reduce the heat to low and simmer for 20 minutes.

3. As the tomato sauce cooks, place the cream in a small saucepan and cook over low heat until it has reduced by about half. Once the tomato sauce has thickened, add the reduced cream and season the sauce with salt.

INGREDIENTS:

OLIVE OIL, AS NEEDED

½ POTATO, PEELED AND CHOPPED

1 LINK FENNEL SAUSAGE, CASING REMOVED AND CRUMBLED

SEMOLINA FLOUR, TO TASTE

1 BALL PIZZA DOUGH

3.5 OZ. | 100 GRAMS ROSE SAUCE (SEE RECIPE)

LEAVES FROM 2 SPRIGS FRESH ROSEMARY

3.5 OZ. | 100 GRAMS FRESH MOZZARELLA CHEESE, DRAINED AND TORN

SALT, TO TASTE

ROSE SAUCE

1 LB. | 450 GRAMS CANNED TOMATOES

1 TABLESPOON | 14.2 GRAMS UNSALTED BUTTER

1 OZ. | 30 GRAMS WHITE ONION, CHOPPED

SALT AND PEPPER, TO TASTE

4 OZ. | 113.4 GRAMS HEAVY CREAM

TACO PIZZA

YIELD: 1 PIZZA / ACTIVE TIME: 25 MINUTES / TOTAL TIME: 1 HOUR

The toppings listed here are the bare minimum. Don't hesitate to try out any of your typical taco accompaniments on this pizza.

1. Preheat the oven to the maximum temperature and place a baking stone or steel on the middle rack as it warms. Place the ground beef in a skillet, season with the taco seasoning, and cook, while breaking the meat up with a fork, until it is browned, about 8 minutes. Remove from heat and set aside.

2. Dust a work surface with the semolina flour, place the dough on the surface, and gently stretch it into a round. For more detailed instructions on properly stretching a ball of pizza dough see page 73. Cover the dough with the sauce, top with the mozzarella, ground beef, peppers, corn, and onion, and season with salt and pepper.

3. Using a peel or a flat baking sheet, transfer the pizza to the heated baking implement in the oven. Bake for about 15 minutes, until the crust is golden brown and starting to char. Remove and let cool slightly before garnishing with the cilantro, slicing, and serving.

INGREDIENTS:

3.5 OZ. | 100 GRAMS GROUND BEEF

(SEE PAGE 103)

2.4 OZ. | 70 GRAMS LOW-MOISTURE MOZZARELLA CHEESE, SHREDDED

2 CHILI PEPPERS, SEEDED AND SLICED

1.75 OZ. | 50 GRAMS CANNED CORN

¼ RED ONION, SLICED

SALT AND PEPPER, TO TASTE

FRESH CILANTRO, FINELY CHOPPED, FOR GARNISH

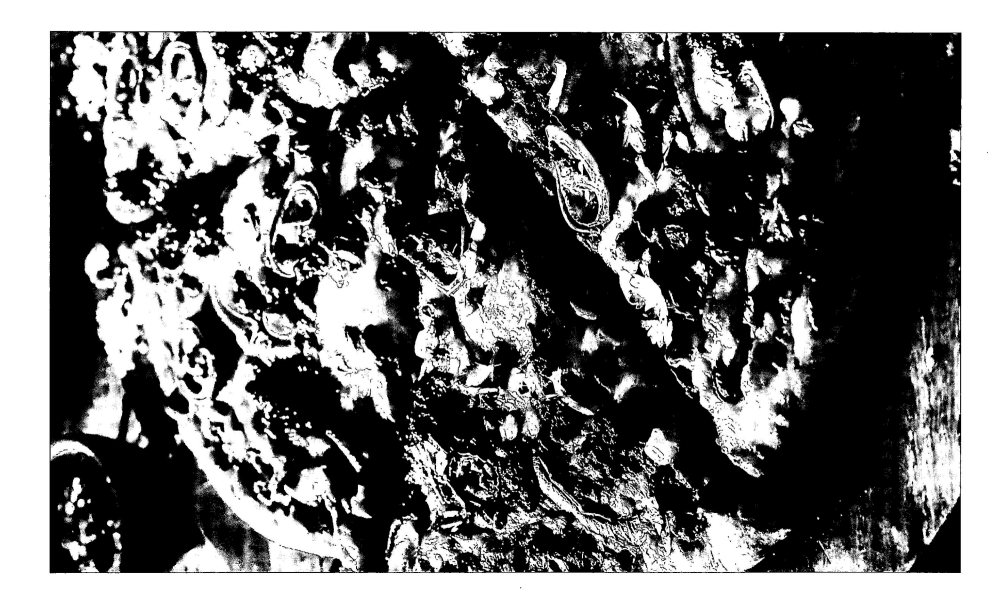

SMOKED COD & CHEDDAR PIZZA

YIELD: 1 PIZZA / **ACTIVE TIME:** 15 MINUTES / **TOTAL TIME:** 45 MINUTES

When you see a pizza that is this straightforward, you can be confident that you're in for something special.

1. Preheat the oven to the maximum temperature and place a baking stone or steel on the middle rack as it warms. Dust a work surface with the semolina flour, place the dough on the surface, and gently stretch it into a round. For more detailed instructions on properly stretching a ball of pizza dough see page 73. Cover the dough with the mozzarella, top with the cod, and then sprinkle the cheddar over the pizza.

2. Using a peel or a flat baking sheet, transfer the pizza to the heated baking implement in the oven. Bake for about 15 minutes, until the crust is golden brown and starting to char. Remove and let cool slightly before slicing and serving.

INGREDIENTS:

SEMOLINA FLOUR, AS NEEDED

1 BALL PIZZA DOUGH

1.75 OZ. | 50 GRAMS LOW-MOISTURE MOZZARELLA CHEESE, SHREDDED

3.5 OZ. | 100 GRAMS SMOKED COD, CUBED

1.75 OZ. | 50 GRAMS CHEDDAR CHEESE, SHREDDED

SMOKED SALMON & CHIVE PIZZA

YIELD: 1 PIZZA / **ACTIVE TIME:** 15 MINUTES / **TOTAL TIME:** 45 MINUTES

A combo that would traditionally rest atop some cream cheese and a bagel is just as wonderful atop a pizza crust and mozzarella.

1. Preheat the oven to the maximum temperature and place a baking stone or steel on the middle rack as it warms. Dust a work surface with the semolina flour, place the dough on the surface, and gently stretch it into a round. For more detailed instructions on properly stretching a ball of pizza dough see page 73. Cover the dough with the mozzarella and onion and drizzle olive oil over the pizza.

2. Using a peel or a flat baking sheet, transfer the pizza to the heated baking implement in the oven. Bake for about 7 minutes, until the crust starts to brown. Remove the pizza, top with the salmon and chives, season with pepper, drizzle olive oil over the top, and return the pizza to the oven. Bake for about 5 minutes, until the crust is golden brown and starting to char. Remove and let cool slightly before slicing and serving.

INGREDIENTS:

SEMOLINA FLOUR, AS NEEDED

1 ( ) PIZZA DOUGH

OLIVE OIL, TO TASTE

3.5 OZ. | 100 GRAMS SMOKED SALMON, SLICED

FRESH CHIVES, FINELY CHOPPED, TO TASTE

BLACK PEPPER, TO TASTE

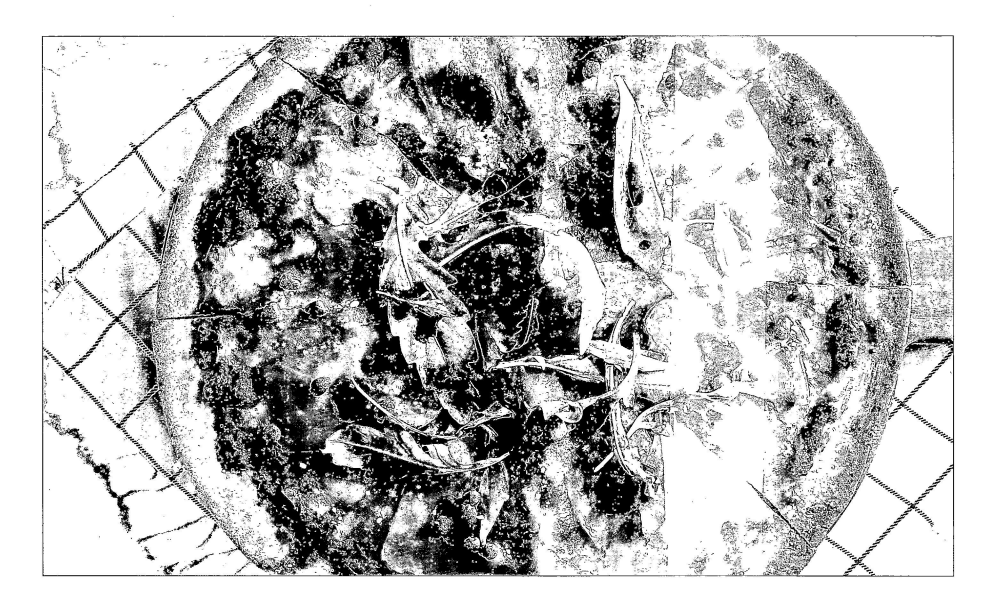

PIZZA WITH SMOKED SALMON & CAPERS

YIELD: 1 PIZZA / **ACTIVE TIME:** 15 MINUTES / **TOTAL TIME:** 45 MINUTES

With a taste that resides somewhere between the tartness of lemons and the famed brininess of an olive, a few capers make every bite of this pizza explode.

1. Preheat the oven to the maximum temperature and place a baking stone or steel on the middle rack as it warms. Dust a work surface with the semolina flour, place the dough on the surface, and gently stretch it into a round. For more detailed instructions on properly stretching a ball of pizza dough see page 73. Cover the dough with the sauce, top with the mozzarella, and drizzle olive oil over the pizza.

2. Using a peel or a flat baking sheet, transfer the pizza to the heated baking implement in the oven. Bake for about 7 minutes, until the crust starts to brown. Remove the pizza, top with the salmon and capers, season with pepper, drizzle olive oil over the pizza, and return it to the oven. Bake for about 5 minutes, until the crust is golden brown and starting to char. Remove and let cool slightly before topping with the arugula, Parmesan, and balsamic glaze, slicing, and serving.

INGREDIENTS:

SEMOLINA FLOUR, AS NEEDED

1 BALL PIZZA DOUGH

2.4 OZ. | 70 GRAMS RAW PIZZA SAUCE (SEE PAGE 103)

2.4 OZ. | 70 GRAMS LOW-MOISTURE MOZZARELLA CHEESE, SHREDDED

OLIVE OIL, TO TASTE

3.5 OZ. | 100 GRAMS SMOKED SALMON, SLICED

1½ TABLESPOONS | 11 GRAMS CAPERS

BLACK PEPPER, TO TASTE

1 HANDFUL ARUGULA

PARMESAN CHEESE, GRATED, FOR GARNISH

BALSAMIC GLAZE, TO TASTE

SALMON & PEPPER PIZZA

YIELD: 1 PIZZA / **ACTIVE TIME:** 15 MINUTES / **TOTAL TIME:** 45 MINUTES

The bit of crunch provided by the pepper is all the flaky salmon needs to set it apart as a pizza topping.

1. Preheat the oven to the maximum temperature and place a baking stone or steel on the middle rack as it warms. Dust a work surface with the semolina flour, place the dough on the surface, and gently stretch it into a round. For more detailed instructions on properly stretching a ball of pizza dough see page 73. Cover the dough with the sauce, top with the bell pepper and mozzarella, and drizzle olive oil over the top.

2. Using a peel or a flat baking sheet, transfer the pizza to the heated baking implement in the oven. Bake for about 7 minutes, until the crust starts to brown. Remove the pizza, top with the salmon, season with salt and pepper, drizzle olive oil over the pizza, and return it to the oven. Bake for about 5 minutes, until the crust is golden brown and starting to char. Remove and let cool slightly before topping the pizza with the arugula and Parmesan, slicing, and serving.

INGREDIENTS:

SEMOLINA FLOUR, AS NEEDED

2.4 OZ. | 70 GRAMS LOW-MOISTURE MOZZARELLA CHEESE, SHREDDED

OLIVE OIL, TO TASTE

3.5 OZ. | 100 GRAMS BAKED SALMON, SHREDDED

SALT AND PEPPER, TO TASTE

1 HANDFUL ARUGULA

PARMESAN CHEESE, GRATED, FOR GARNISH

PIZZA WITH PARSLEY PESTO & CAVIAR

YIELD: 1 PIZZA / **ACTIVE TIME:** 20 MINUTES / **TOTAL TIME:** 50 MINUTES

There's no reason to hold back with this one—spring for the best caviar that fits within your budget, and you'll be rewarded with a pie that carries a flavor and texture beyond the bounds of the imagination.

1. Preheat the oven to the maximum temperature and place a baking stone or steel on the middle rack as it warms. Dust a work surface with the semolina flour, place the dough on the surface, and gently stretch it into a round. For more detailed instructions on properly stretching a ball of pizza dough see page 73. Cover the dough with the Parsley Pesto, top with the mozzarella, and drizzle olive oil over the pizza.

2. Using a peel or a flat baking sheet, transfer the pizza to the heated baking implement in the oven. Bake for about 15 minutes, until the crust is golden brown and starting to char. Remove, top with the remaining ingredients, and let cool slightly before slicing and serving.

PARSLEY PESTO

1. Place all of the ingredients in a food processor and blitz until combined.

INGREDIENTS:

SEMOLINA FLOUR, AS NEEDED

1 BALL PIZZA DOUGH

1 OZ. | 30 GRAMS PARSLEY PESTO (SEE RECIPE)

2.8 OZ. | 80 GRAMS LOW-MOISTURE MOZZARELLA CHEESE, SHREDDED

OLIVE OIL, TO TASTE

1 OZ. | 30 GRAMS RED CAVIAR

1 HANDFUL ARUGULA

PARMESAN CHEESE, GRATED, TO TASTE

PARSLEY PESTO

3.5 OZ. | 100 GRAMS FRESH PARSLEY

1.75 OZ. | 50 GRAMS BREAD CRUMBS

2.8 OZ. | 80 GRAMS OLIVE OIL, PLUS MORE TO TASTE

1 DASH WATER

3 ANCHOVIES

SALT, TO TASTE

PIZZA WITH BRIE & PEAR

YIELD: 1 PIZZA / **ACTIVE TIME:** 15 MINUTES / **TOTAL TIME:** 45 MINUTES

The always underrated pear shows how its subtle sweetness and soft vanilla notes fit in just about anywhere.

1. Preheat the oven to the maximum temperature and place a baking stone or steel on the middle rack as it warms. Dust a work surface with the semolina flour, place the dough on the surface, and gently stretch it into a round. For more detailed instructions on properly stretching a ball of pizza dough see page 73. Cover the dough with the mozzarella, top with the brie and the pear, and drizzle olive oil over the pizza.

2. Using a peel or a flat baking sheet, transfer the pizza to the heated baking implement in the oven. Bake for about 15 minutes, until the crust is golden brown and starting to char. Remove and let cool slightly before garnishing with the thyme, slicing, and serving.

INGREDIENTS:

SEMOLINA FLOUR, AS NEEDED

1 (8) PIZZA DOUGH

[illegible]

½ SMALL PEAR, CUBED

OLIVE OIL, TO TASTE

FRESH THYME, FOR GARNISH

FIG, PROSCIUTTO & BALSAMIC PIZZA

YIELD: 1 PIZZA / **ACTIVE TIME:** 15 MINUTES / **TOTAL TIME:** 45 MINUTES

The burst of freshness provided by the pesto is what keeps the rest of these heavy hitters from trampling each other.

1. Preheat the oven to the maximum temperature and place a baking stone or steel on the middle rack as it warms. Dust a work surface with the semolina flour, place the dough on the surface, and gently stretch it into a round. For more detailed instructions on properly stretching a ball of pizza dough see page 73. Cover the dough with the mozzarella, pesto, and Gorgonzola and drizzle olive oil over the pizza.

2. Using a peel or a flat baking sheet, transfer the pizza to the heated baking implement in the oven. Bake for about 7 minutes, until the crust starts to brown. Remove the pizza, top with the figs and prosciutto, and return the pizza to the oven. Bake for about 5 minutes, until the crust is golden brown and starting to char. Remove and let cool slightly before topping with the arugula, Parmesan, and balsamic glaze, slicing, and serving.

INGREDIENTS:

SEMOLINA FLOUR, AS NEEDED

1 BALL PIZZA DOUGH

2.4 OZ. | 70 GRAMS LOW-MOISTURE MOZZARELLA CHEESE, SHREDDED

0.5 OZ. | 15 GRAMS BASIL PESTO (SEE PAGE 365)

1.75 OZ. | 50 GRAMS GORGONZOLA CHEESE, TORN

OLIVE OIL, TO TASTE

3 FIGS, CHOPPED

3 SLICES PROSCIUTTO, TORN

1 HANDFUL ARUGULA

PARMESAN CHEESE, GRATED, TO TASTE

BALSAMIC GLAZE, TO TASTE

PIZZA WITH PROSCIUTTO, CACIOCAVALLO, WILD MUSHROOMS & NUTS

YIELD: 1 PIZZA / **ACTIVE TIME:** 25 MINUTES / **TOTAL TIME:** 1 HOUR

You may be surprised by just how welcome the added bit of crunch provided by the pistachios and walnuts is.

1. Preheat the oven to the maximum temperature and place a baking stone or steel on the middle rack as it warms. Coat the bottom of a skillet with olive oil and warm over medium-high heat. When the oil starts to shimmer, add the mushrooms and sauté until they start to brown, about 8 minutes. Remove from heat and let cool slightly.

2. Dust a work surface with the semolina flour, place the dough on the surface, and gently stretch it into a round. For more detailed instructions on properly stretching a ball of pizza dough see page 73. Cover the dough with the mozzarella, mushrooms, and caciocavallo and drizzle olive oil over the pizza.

3. Using a peel or a flat baking sheet, transfer the pizza to the heated baking implement in the oven. Bake for about 7 minutes, until the crust starts to brown. Remove the pizza, distribute the prosciutto, pistachios, and walnuts over the top, and return the pizza to the oven. Bake for about 5 minutes, until the crust is golden brown and starting to char. Remove and let cool slightly before garnishing with the basil, drizzling olive oil over the pizza, slicing, and serving.

INGREDIENTS:

OLIVE OIL, AS NEEDED

1.75 OZ. | 50 GRAMS WILD MUSHROOMS

SEMOLINA FLOUR, AS NEEDED

1 BALL PIZZA DOUGH

1.4 OZ. | 40 GRAMS LOW-MOISTURE MOZZARELLA CHEESE, SHREDDED

1.75 OZ. | 50 GRAMS CACIOCAVALLO CHEESE, SLICED

3 SLICES PROSCIUTTO, TORN

1 OZ. | 30 GRAMS PISTACHIOS, MINCED

1 OZ. | 30 GRAMS WALNUTS, MINCED

FRESH BASIL LEAVES, FOR GARNISH

PIZZA WITH HAM, GORGONZOLA, PEARS & WALNUTS

YIELD: 1 PIZZA / **ACTIVE TIME:** 15 MINUTES / **TOTAL TIME:** 45 MINUTES

Should you prefer another blue cheese to gorgonzola, don't hesitate to swap it in.

1. Preheat the oven to the maximum temperature and place a baking stone or steel on the middle rack as it warms. Dust a work surface with the semolina flour, place the dough on the surface, and gently stretch it into a round. For more detailed instructions on properly stretching a ball of pizza dough see page 73. Cover the dough with the mozzarella, pear, and Gorgonzola and drizzle olive oil over the pizza.

2. Using a peel or a flat baking sheet, transfer the pizza to the heated baking implement in the oven. Bake for about 7 minutes, until the crust starts to brown. Remove the pizza, top with the ham and walnuts, season with pepper, drizzle olive oil over the top, and return the pizza to the oven. Bake for about 5 minutes, until the crust is golden brown and starting to char. Remove and let cool slightly before slicing and serving.

INGREDIENTS:

SEMOLINA FLOUR, AS NEEDED

1 BALL PIZZA DOUGH

1.75 OZ. | 50 GRAMS LOW-MOISTURE MOZZARELLA CHEESE, SHREDDED

½ SMALL PEAR, SLICED THIN

1.75 OZ. | 50 GRAMS GORGONZOLA CHEESE, CRUMBLED

OLIVE OIL, TO TASTE

3 SLICES SERRANO HAM, TORN

1 OZ. | 30 GRAMS WALNUTS, CHOPPED

BLACK PEPPER, TO TASTE

PIZZA WITH FIGS, SPECK, ASIAGO & GORGONZOLA

YIELD: 1 PIZZA / **ACTIVE TIME:** 15 MINUTES / **TOTAL TIME:** 45 MINUTES

With a taste that is milder and simpler than its older sibling, young Asiago is able to elevate all the ingredients it shares this pie with.

1. Preheat the oven to the maximum temperature and place a baking stone or steel on the middle rack as it warms. Dust a work surface with the semolina flour, place the dough on the surface, and gently stretch it into a round. For more detailed instructions on properly stretching a ball of pizza dough see page 73. Cover the dough with the mozzarella and Asiago and drizzle olive oil over the top.

2. Using a peel or a flat baking sheet, transfer the pizza to the heated baking implement in the oven. Bake for about 7 minutes, until the crust starts to brown. Remove the pizza, top with the Gorgonzola, figs, and speck, drizzle olive oil over the pizza, and return it to the oven. Bake for about 5 minutes, until the crust is golden brown and starting to char. Remove and let cool slightly before slicing and serving.

INGREDIENTS:

SEMOLINA FLOUR, AS NEEDED

1 BALL PIZZA DOUGH

4 OZ. | 110 GRAMS LOW-MOISTURE MOZZARELLA CHEESE, SHREDDED

2.5 OZ. | 70 GRAMS YOUNG ASIAGO CHEESE, SLICED THIN

OLIVE OIL, TO TASTE

1.4 OZ. | 40 GRAMS SWEET GORGONZOLA CHEESE, CRUMBLED

3 FIGS, CHOPPED

3 SLICES SPECK, TORN

EGGPLANT, BUFALA & ARUGULA PIZZA

YIELD: 1 PIZZA / **ACTIVE TIME:** 20 MINUTES / **TOTAL TIME:** 1 HOUR AND 15 MINUTES

The recipe calls for roasting the eggplant in the oven, but if you want a little more oomph, the char and smoke provided by a spell on the grill is a good option.

INGREDIENTS:

⅓ EGGPLANT, SLICED

SALT AND PEPPER, TO TASTE

OLIVE OIL, AS NEEDED

SEMOLINA FLOUR, AS NEEDED

1 BALL PIZZA DOUGH

2.8 OZ. | 80 GRAMS RAW PIZZA SAUCE (SEE PAGE 103)

3.5 OZ. | 100 GRAMS BUFFALO MOZZARELLA CHEESE, DRAINED AND TORN

1 HANDFUL ARUGULA

PARMESAN CHEESE, GRATED, TO TASTE

BALSAMIC VINEGAR, TO TASTE

1. Preheat the oven to the maximum temperature and place a baking stone or steel on the middle rack as it warms. Place the eggplant in a baking dish, season with salt and pepper, and drizzle olive oil over the top. Place in the warming oven and roast until it starts to become tender, about 15 minutes. Remove from the oven and let cool.

2. Dust a work surface with the semolina flour, place the dough on the surface, and gently stretch it into a round. For more detailed instructions on properly stretching a ball of pizza dough see page 73. Cover the dough with the sauce, top with the eggplant, and drizzle olive oil over the pizza.

3. Using a peel or a flat baking sheet, transfer the pizza to the heated baking implement in the oven. Bake for about 7 minutes, until the crust starts to brown. Remove the pizza, top with the mozzarella, season with salt and pepper, drizzle olive oil over the pizza, and return it to the oven. Bake for about 5 minutes, until the crust is golden brown and starting to char. Remove and let cool slightly before topping with the arugula, Parmesan, and balsamic vinegar, slicing, and serving.

THREE CHEESE & SPINACH PIZZA

YIELD: 1 PIZZA / **ACTIVE TIME:** 15 MINUTES / **TOTAL TIME:** 45 MINUTES

All the cheese and fresh greens make this pizza the ultimate version of creamed spinach.

1. Preheat the oven to the maximum temperature and place a baking stone or steel on the middle rack as it warms. Dust a work surface with the semolina flour, place the dough on the surface, and gently stretch it into a round. For more detailed instructions on properly stretching a ball of pizza dough see page 73. Cover the dough with the provolone and top with the spinach. Season with salt and drizzle with olive oil.

2. Using a peel or a flat baking sheet, transfer the pizza to the heated baking implement in the oven. Bake for about 7 minutes, until the crust starts to brown. Remove the pizza, top with the mozzarella and Parmesan, and return the pizza to the oven. Bake for about 5 minutes, until the crust is golden brown and starting to char. Remove and let cool slightly before slicing and serving.

INGREDIENTS:

SEMOLINA FLOUR, AS NEEDED

1 BALL PIZZA DOUGH

1.75 OZ. | 50 GRAMS PROVOLONE CHEESE, SHREDDED

2.5 OZ. | 80 GRAMS SPINACH

SALT, TO TASTE

OLIVE OIL, TO TASTE

1.75 OZ. | 50 GRAMS BUFFALO MOZZARELLA CHEESE, DRAINED AND TORN

1 OZ. | 30 GRAMS PARMESAN CHEESE, GRATED

CHICKEN, SPINACH & PINE NUT PIZZA

YIELD: 1 PIZZA / **ACTIVE TIME:** 20 MINUTES / **TOTAL TIME:** 50 MINUTES

Pine nuts' considerable price tag means that one has to be choosy with where to deploy them. This pizza is one of those instances where you can feel confident about the expenditure.

1. Preheat the oven to the maximum temperature and place a baking stone or steel on the middle rack as it warms. Coat the bottom of a skillet with olive oil and warm over medium-high heat. When the oil starts to shimmer, add the spinach, season with salt and pepper, and cook until it is wilted, about 2 minutes. Remove the pan from heat and set it aside.

2. Dust a work surface with the semolina flour, place the dough on the surface, and gently stretch it into a round. For more detailed instructions on properly stretching a ball of pizza dough see page 73. Cover the dough with half of the mozzarella and top with the chicken, pine nuts, and spinach. Season with salt and pepper, drizzle olive oil over the pizza, and distribute the remaining mozzarella over the top.

3. Using a peel or a flat baking sheet, transfer the pizza to the heated baking implement in the oven. Bake for about 15 minutes, until the crust is golden brown and starting to char. Remove and let cool slightly before slicing and serving.

INGREDIENTS:

OLIVE OIL, TO TASTE

2.8 OZ. | 80 GRAMS BABY SPINACH

SALT AND PEPPER, TO TASTE

SEMOLINA FLOUR, AS NEEDED

1 BALL PIZZA DOUGH

2.8 OZ. | 80 GRAMS LOW-MOISTURE MOZZARELLA CHEESE, SHREDDED

2.8 OZ. | 80 GRAMS COOKED CHICKEN BREAST, CUBED

1 OZ. | 30 GRAMS PINE NUTS

PIZZA WITH GOAT CHEESE, SPINACH, HONEY & HAZELNUTS

YIELD: 1 PIZZA / **ACTIVE TIME:** 15 MINUTES / **TOTAL TIME:** 45 MINUTES

The delightful trio of honey, nuts, and goat cheese leaps off the serving board and onto this flavorful pizza.

1 Preheat the oven to the maximum temperature and place a baking stone or steel on the middle rack as it warms. Dust a work surface with the semolina flour, place the dough on the surface, and gently stretch it into a round. For more detailed instructions on properly stretching a ball of pizza dough see page 73. Distribute the spinach over the dough, season with salt, and drizzle olive oil over the pizza. Top the pizza with the goat cheese, hazelnuts, rosemary, and honey.

2. Using a peel or a flat baking sheet, transfer the pizza to the heated baking implement in the oven. Bake for about 15 minutes, until the crust is golden brown and starting to char. Remove and let cool slightly before slicing and serving.

INGREDIENTS:

SEMOLINA FLOUR, AS NEEDED

1 BALL OF PIZZA DOUGH

1 CUP FRESH BABY SPINACH

SALT, TO TASTE

OLIVE OIL, TO TASTE

3 SLICES GOAT CHEESE

1 HANDFUL HAZELNUTS, CHOPPED

FRESH ROSEMARY, TO TASTE

1 TABLESPOON | 21 GRAMS HONEY

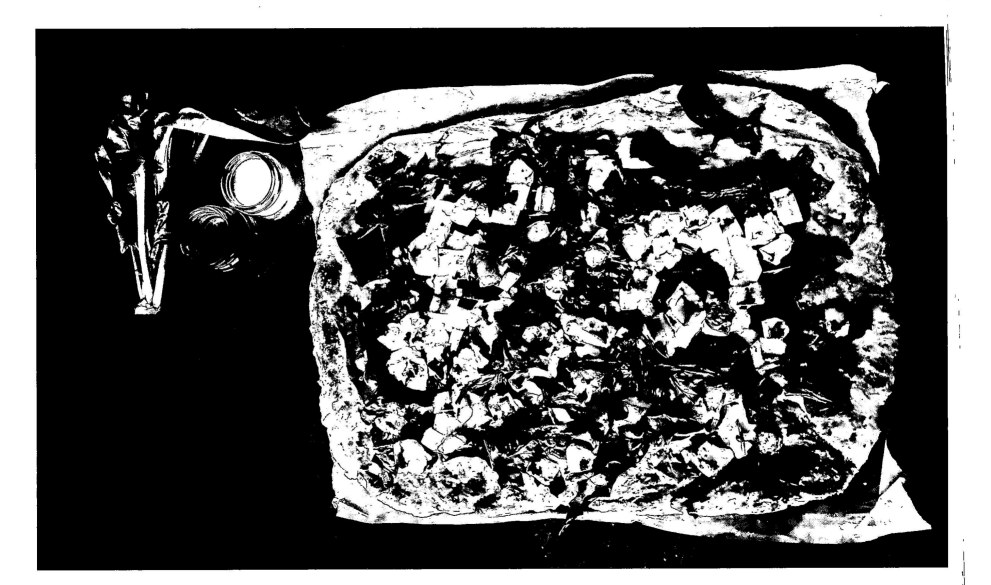

TURKEY HAM, ARTICHOKE & CREAM CHEESE PIZZA

YIELD: 1 PIZZA / ACTIVE TIME: 15 MINUTES / TOTAL TIME: 45 MINUTES

Turkey ham is the smoked and cured thigh of a turkey. If you can't track it down, use smoked or honeyed turkey breast in its stead.

1. Preheat the oven to the maximum temperature and place a baking stone or steel on the middle rack as it warms. Dust a work surface with the semolina flour, place the dough on the surface, and gently stretch it into a round. For more detailed instructions on properly stretching a ball of pizza dough see page 73. Cover the dough with the sauce and top with the olives and artichokes. Season with salt and drizzle olive oil over the pizza.

2. Using a peel or a flat baking sheet, transfer the pizza to the heated baking implement in the oven. Bake for about 7 minutes, until the crust starts to brown. Remove the pizza, top with the turkey ham and cream cheese, drizzle olive oil over the pizza, and return it to the oven. Bake for about 5 minutes, until the crust is golden brown and starting to char. Remove and let cool slightly before garnishing with the basil, slicing, and serving.

INGREDIENTS:

SEMOLINA FLOUR, AS NEEDED

1 BALL PIZZA DOUGH

2.8 OZ. | 80 GRAMS RAW PIZZA SAUCE
(SEE PAGE 103)

1 HANDFUL BLACK OLIVES, PITTED AND
SLICED

2 ARTICHOKE HEARTS IN OLIVE OIL, CHOPPED

SALT, TO TASTE

OLIVE OIL, TO TASTE

4 SLICES SMOKED TURKEY HAM

1.5 OZ. | 42 GRAMS CREAM CHEESE

FRESH BASIL LEAVES, FOR GARNISH

WILD GARLIC & SAUSAGE PIZZA

YIELD: 1 PIZZA / **ACTIVE TIME:** 25 MINUTES / **TOTAL TIME:** 1 HOUR

Wild garlic, also known as ramson or buckram, carries the taste of garlic without the pungent aroma. If you can't find it, a few chard leaves are an acceptable stand-in.

1. Preheat the oven to the maximum temperature and place a baking stone or steel on the middle rack as it warms. Coat the bottom of a skillet with olive oil and warm over medium-high heat. When the oil starts to shimmer, add the sausage and cook until it is browned all over, about 8 minutes. Remove the pan from heat and set it aside.

2. Dust a work surface with the semolina flour, place the dough on the surface, and gently stretch it into a round. For more detailed instructions on properly stretching a ball of pizza dough see page 73. Cover the dough with the mozzarella and top with the wild garlic and sausage. Season with pepper and drizzle olive oil over the pizza.

3. Using a peel or a flat baking sheet, transfer the pizza to the heated baking implement in the oven. Bake for about 15 minutes, until the crust is golden brown and starting to char. Remove and let cool slightly before slicing and serving.

INGREDIENTS:

OLIVE OIL, AS NEEDED

2.8 OZ. | 80 GRAMS LOW-MOISTURE MOZZARELLA CHEESE, SHREDDED

1 HANDFUL WILD GARLIC

BLACK PEPPER, TO TASTE

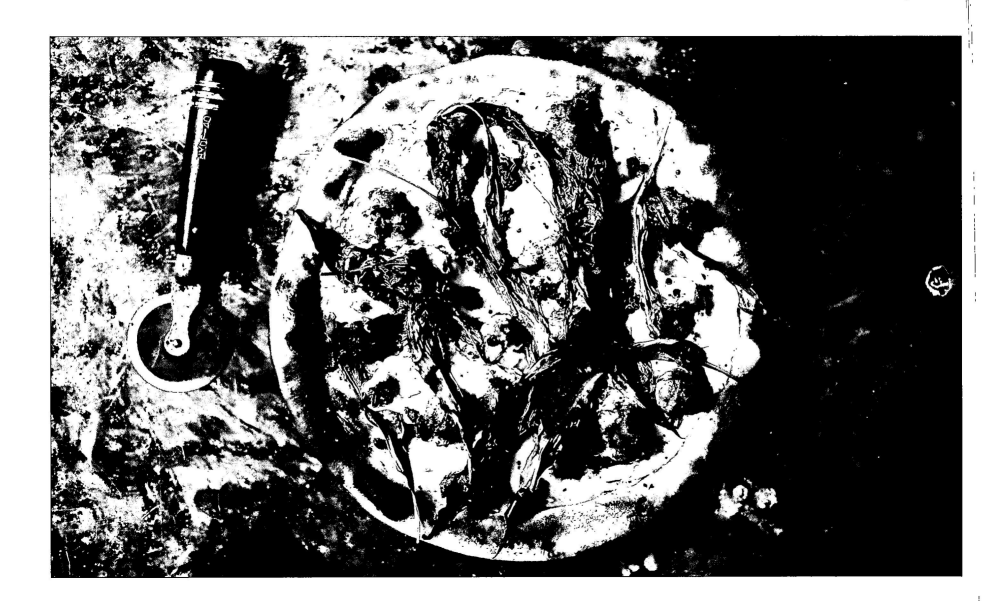

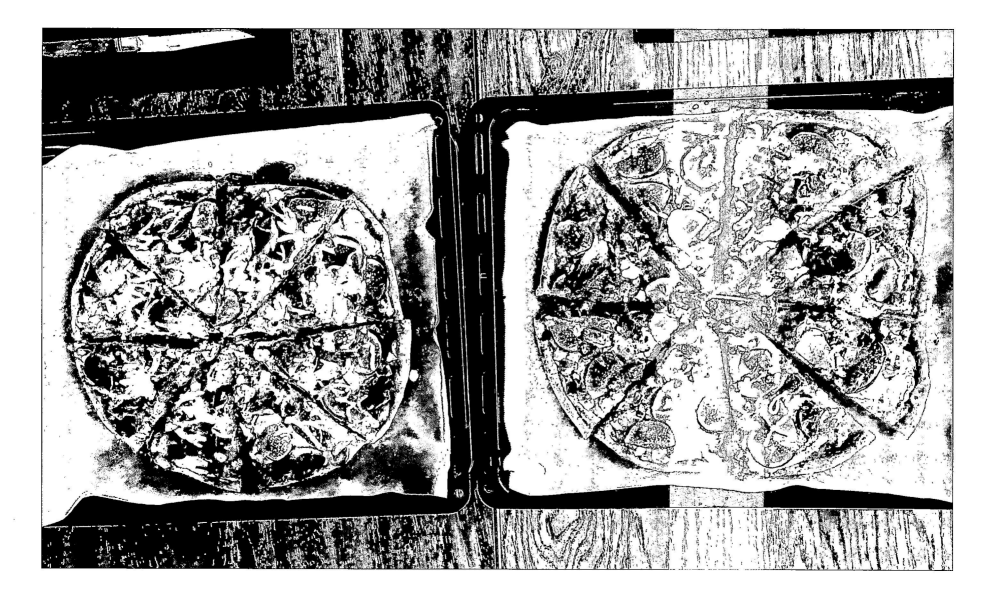

PIZZA WITH GOAT CHEESE, FIGS & WALNUTS

YIELD: 1 PIZZA / **ACTIVE TIME:** 15 MINUTES / **TOTAL TIME:** 45 MINUTES

B alsamic glaze is available at the store, but it's also easy to make at home. Just place balsamic vinegar in a saucepan and reduce over medium heat until it is syrupy.

1. Preheat the oven to the maximum temperature and place a baking stone or steel on the middle rack as it warms. Dust a work surface with the semolina flour, place the dough on the surface, and gently stretch it into a round. For more detailed instructions on properly stretching a ball of pizza dough see page 73. Cover the dough with the mozzarella and top with the goat cheese, figs, and walnuts. Season with pepper and drizzle olive oil over the pizza.

2. Using a peel or a flat baking sheet, transfer the pizza to the heated baking implement in the oven. Bake for about 15 minutes, until the crust is golden brown and starting to char. Remove and let cool slightly before drizzling the balsamic glaze over the pizza, slicing, and serving.

INGREDIENTS:

SEMOLINA FLOUR, AS NEEDED

1 BALL PIZZA DOUGH

1.75 OZ. | 50 GRAMS LOW-MOISTURE MOZZARELLA CHEESE, SHREDDED

3 SLICES GOAT CHEESE

3 FRESH FIGS, CHOPPED

1 HANDFUL WALNUTS

BLACK PEPPER, TO TASTE

OLIVE OIL, TO TASTE

BALSAMIC GLAZE, FOR GARNISH

COPPA, PROSCIUTTO & SAUSAGE PIZZA

YIELD: 1 PIZZA / **ACTIVE TIME:** 25 MINUTES / **TOTAL TIME:** 1 HOUR

Coppa, also known as capicola and "gabagool," is made from the pork shoulder. Even when flanked by two other flavorful meats, its rich taste is sure to stand out.

1. Preheat the oven to the maximum temperature and place a baking stone or steel on the middle rack as it warms. Coat the bottom of a skillet with olive oil and warm over medium-high heat. When the oil starts to shimmer, add the sausage and cook until it is browned, about 8 minutes. Remove the pan from heat and set it aside.

2. Dust a work surface with the semolina flour, place the dough on the surface, and gently stretch it into a round. For more detailed instructions on properly stretching a ball of pizza dough see page 73. Cover the dough with the sauce and top with the mozzarella and sausage. Season with pepper and drizzle olive oil over the pizza.

3. Using a peel or a flat baking sheet, transfer the pizza to the heated baking implement in the oven. Bake for about 7 minutes, until the crust starts to brown. Remove the pizza, top it with the coppa and prosciutto, drizzle olive oil over the pizza, and return it to the oven. Bake for about 5 minutes, until the crust is golden brown and starting to char. Remove and let cool slightly before slicing and serving.

INGREDIENTS:

OLIVE OIL, AS NEEDED

2.4 OZ. | 70 GRAMS RAW PIZZA SAUCE (SEE PAGE 103)

1.75 OZ. | 50 GRAMS LOW-MOISTURE MOZZARELLA CHEESE, SHREDDED

BLACK PEPPER, TO TASTE

3 SLICES COPPA

2 SLICES PROSCIUTTO

PIZZA WITH SMOKED TROUT, POACHED EGGS & CAPERS

YIELD: 1 PIZZA / **ACTIVE TIME:** 20 MINUTES / **TOTAL TIME:** 50 MINUTES

The delicate texture of the smoked trout is the ideal complement to the creaminess provided by the cheese and poached eggs.

1. Preheat the oven to the maximum temperature and place a baking stone or steel on the middle rack as it warms. Bring salted water to a boil in a saucepan and add the eggs. Poach until the whites are set, about 5 minutes, remove with a slotted spoon, and set them aside.

2. Dust a work surface with the semolina flour, place the dough on the surface, and gently stretch it into a round. For more detailed instructions on properly stretching a ball of pizza dough see page 73. Cover the dough with the sauce and top with the mozzarella. Season with salt and pepper and drizzle olive oil over the pizza.

3. Using a peel or a flat baking sheet, transfer the pizza to the heated baking implement in the oven. Bake for about 7 minutes, until the crust is just about to turn golden brown. Remove the pizza, top it with the caciocavallo, trout, capers, and poached eggs, drizzle olive oil over the pizza, and return it to the oven. Bake for about 5 minutes, until the crust is golden brown and starting to char. Remove and let cool slightly before slicing and serving.

INGREDIENTS:

SALT AND PEPPER, TO TASTE

2 EGGS

SEMOLINA FLOUR, AS NEEDED

1 BALL PIZZA DOUGH

2.4 OZ. | 70 GRAMS RAW PIZZA SAUCE (SEE PAGE 103)

1.75 OZ. | 50 GRAMS LOW-MOISTURE MOZZARELLA CHEESE, SHREDDED

OLIVE OIL, TO TASTE

1.4 OZ. | 40 GRAMS CACIOCAVALLO CHEESE, SLICED

1.75 OZ. | 50 GRAMS SMOKED TROUT, SLICED THIN

1 HANDFUL CAPERS

PEACH, PINEAPPLE & PEPPERONI PIZZA

YIELD: 1 PIZZA / **ACTIVE TIME:** 15 MINUTES / **TOTAL TIME:** 45 MINUTES

Fruit over pizza is an acquired taste, either you love it or hate it. Here, spicy pepperoni serves as a complementary contrast to sweet fruit.

1. Preheat the oven to the maximum temperature and place a baking stone or steel on the middle rack as it warms. Dust a work surface with the semolina flour, place the dough on the surface, and gently stretch it into a round. For more detailed instructions on properly stretching a ball of pizza dough see page 73. Cover the dough with the sauce, top with the mozzarella, pepperoni, pineapple, and peaches, and drizzle olive oil over the pizza.

2. Using a peel or a flat baking sheet, transfer the pizza to the heated baking implement in the oven. Bake for about 15 minutes, until the crust is golden brown and starting to char. Remove and let cool slightly before slicing and serving.

INGREDIENTS:

. . . .

MOZZARELLA CHEESE, SHREDDED

1.4 OZ. | 40 GRAMS PEPPERONI

1.4 OZ. | 40 GRAMS CANNED PINEAPPLE, DRAINED AND DICED

1.4 OZ. | 40 GRAMS CANNED PEACHES, DRAINED AND DICED

OLIVE OIL, TO TASTE

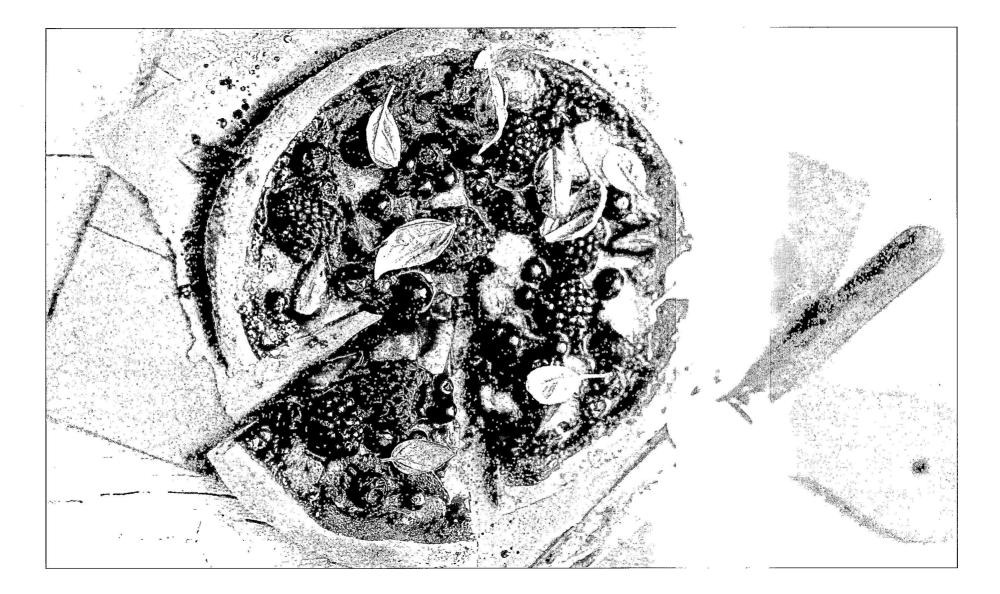

MIXED BERRY PIZZA

YIELD: 1 PIZZA / **ACTIVE TIME:** 15 MINUTES / **TOTAL TIME:** 45 MINUTES

This is not a dessert pizza. The strawberry puree stands in for tomato sauce, pairing surprisingly well with the cheese and making for a sweet, sour, and savory flavor experience.

1. Preheat the oven to the maximum temperature and place a baking stone or steel on the middle rack as it warms. Place the strawberries in a blender and blitz until smooth. Strain the puree to remove the seeds and set aside.

2. Dust a work surface with the semolina flour, place the dough on the surface, and gently stretch it into a round. For more detailed instructions on properly stretching a ball of pizza dough see page 73. Cover the dough with the strawberry puree and top with the mozzarella, raspberries, blackberries, and blueberries.

3. Using a peel or a flat baking sheet, transfer the pizza to the heated baking implement in the oven. Bake for about 15 minutes, until the crust is golden brown and starting to char. Remove and let cool slightly before garnishing with the basil, slicing, and serving.

INGREDIENTS:

1.75 OZ. | 50 GRAMS STRAWBERRIES

SEMOLINA FLOUR, AS NEEDED

1 BALL PIZZA DOUGH

2.1 OZ. | 60 GRAMS LOW-MOISTURE MOZZARELLA CHEESE, SHREDDED

1 OZ. | 30 GRAMS RASPBERRIES

1 OZ. | 30 GRAMS BLACKBERRIES

1 OZ. | 30 GRAMS BLUEBERRIES

FRESH BASIL LEAVES, FOR GARNISH

GREEN TOMATO PIZZA

YIELD: 1 PIZZA / **ACTIVE TIME:** 15 MINUTES / **TOTAL TIME:** 45 MINUTES

If you've never tasted the complex flavors of a grilled or baked green tomato, here's your chance.

1. Preheat the oven to the maximum temperature and place a baking stone or steel on the middle rack as it warms. Dust a work surface with the semolina flour, place the dough on the surface, and gently stretch it into a round. For more detailed instructions on properly stretching a ball of pizza dough see page 73. Cover the dough with the mozzarella and top with the caciocavallo and green tomato. Season with salt and pepper and drizzle olive oil over the pizza.

2. Using a peel or a flat baking sheet, transfer the pizza to the heated baking implement in the oven. Bake for about 15 minutes, until the crust is golden brown and starting to char. Remove and let cool slightly before slicing and serving.

INGREDIENTS:

SEMOLINA FLOUR, AS NEEDED

1 GREEN TOMATO, SLICED

SALT AND PEPPER, TO TASTE

OLIVE OIL, TO TASTE

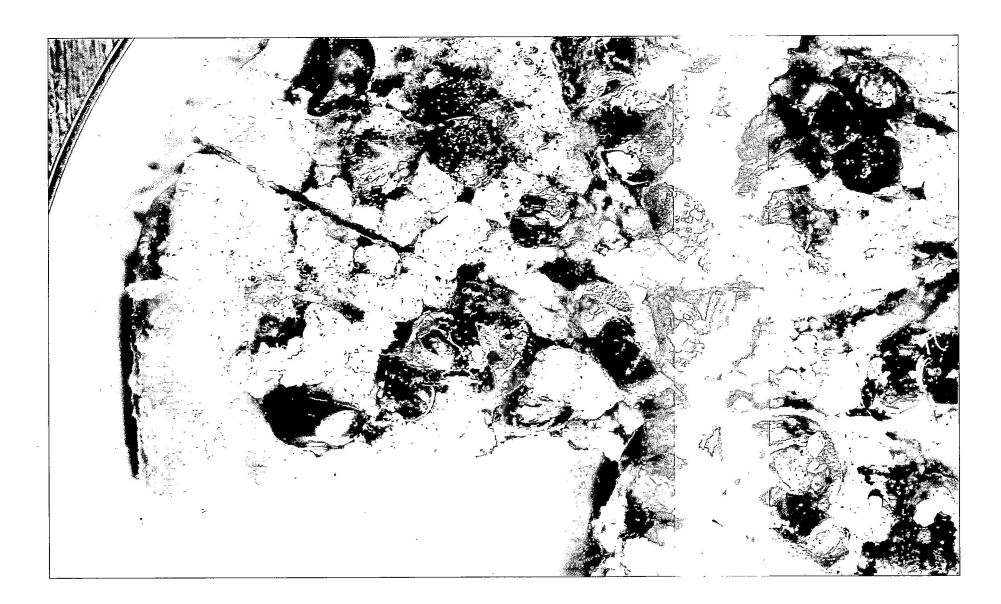

AVOCADO, TOMATO & FETA PIZZA

YIELD: 1 PIZZA / **ACTIVE TIME:** 15 MINUTES / **TOTAL TIME:** 45 MINUTES

Creamy avocado and salty feta are perfect company for a tomato-dotted pie during the height of the summer.

1. Preheat the oven to the maximum temperature and place a baking stone or steel on the middle rack as it warms. Dust a work surface with the semolina flour, place the dough on the surface, and gently stretch it into a round. For more detailed instructions on properly stretching a ball of pizza dough see page 73. Cover the dough with the mozzarella and drizzle olive oil over the pizza.

2. Using a peel or a flat baking sheet, transfer the pizza to the heated baking implement in the oven. Bake for about 15 minutes, until the crust is golden brown and starting to char. Remove and let cool slightly before topping with the avocado, tomato, and feta and seasoning with salt, pepper, and a drizzle of olive oil.

INGREDIENTS:

SEMOLINA FLOUR, AS NEEDED

1 BALL PIZZA DOUGH

1.4 OZ. | 40 GRAMS LOW-MOISTURE MOZZARELLA CHEESE, SHREDDED

OLIVE OIL, TO TASTE

FLESH OF ½ AVOCADO, MASHED

½ TOMATO, DICED

1.75 OZ. | 50 GRAMS FETA CHEESE, CRUMBLED

SALT AND PEPPER, TO TASTE

PIZZA WITH RICOTTA, FIGS & BACON

YIELD: 1 PIZZA / **ACTIVE TIME:** 25 MINUTES / **TOTAL TIME:** 1 HOUR

Figs are always a merry pairing with cured meats and the addition of ricotta makes for a somewhat refined, yet filling pizza.

1. Preheat the oven to the maximum temperature and place a baking stone or steel on the middle rack as it warms. Place the bacon in a skillet and cook over medium heat until it is browned and crispy, about 8 minutes. Transfer to a paper towel–lined plate to drain. When the bacon has cooled slightly, crumble it into bite-sized pieces.

2. Dust a work surface with the semolina flour, place the dough on the surface, and gently stretch it into a round. For more detailed instructions on properly stretching a ball of pizza dough see page 73. Drizzle olive oil over the dough and top with the ricotta, figs, and bacon. Season with pepper and drizzle olive oil over the pizza.

3. Using a peel or a flat baking sheet, transfer the pizza to the heated baking implement in the oven. Bake for about 15 minutes, until the crust is golden brown and starting to char. Remove and let cool slightly before garnishing with the sage, slicing, and serving.

INGREDIENTS:

2 STRIPS BACON

3 FIGS, SLICED

BLACK PEPPER, TO TASTE

FRESH SAGE, FOR GARNISH

BEET & GOAT CHEESE PIZZA

YIELD: 1 PIZZA / **ACTIVE TIME:** 15 MINUTES / **TOTAL TIME:** 45 MINUTES

Perfect on a salad, beets and goat cheese will also shine on a pizza.

1. Preheat the oven to the maximum temperature and place a baking stone or steel on the middle rack as it warms. Dust a work surface with the semolina flour, place the dough on the surface, and gently stretch it into a round. For more detailed instructions on properly stretching a ball of pizza dough see page 73. Cover the dough with the sauce and top with the beet puree and onion. Season with pepper and drizzle olive oil over the pizza.

2. Using a peel or a flat baking sheet, transfer the pizza to the heated baking implement in the oven. Bake for about 7 minutes, until the crust starts to brown. Remove the pizza, top it with the goat cheese, drizzle olive oil over the pizza, season it with salt, and return the pizza to the oven. Bake for about 5 minutes, until the crust is golden brown and starting to char. Remove, top with the arugula and Parmesan, and let the pizza cool slightly before slicing and serving.

INGREDIENTS:

SEMOLINA FLOUR, AS NEEDED

1 BALL PIZZA DOUGH

2.4 OZ. | 70 GRAMS RAW PIZZA SAUCE (SEE PAGE 103)

2.1 OZ. | 60 GRAMS ROASTED BEET, PUREED

⅓ SMALL RED ONION, SLICED

SALT AND PEPPER, TO TASTE

OLIVE OIL, TO TASTE

1.75 OZ. | 50 GRAMS GOAT CHEESE, CRUMBLED

1 HANDFUL FRESH ARUGULA

PARMESAN CHEESE, GRATED, FOR GARNISH

PIZZA WITH LAMB, EGGPLANT & BURRATA

YIELD: 1 PIZZA / **ACTIVE TIME:** 30 MINUTES / **TOTAL TIME:** 1 HOUR AND 15 MINUTES

This rich Mediterranean combination of flavors will impress with its earthy lusciousness.

1. Preheat the oven to the maximum temperature and place a baking stone or steel on the middle rack as it warms. Place the eggplant in a baking dish, season with salt and pepper, and drizzle olive oil over it. Roast the eggplant in the warming oven until it is tender, about 15 minutes. Remove and let cool.

While the eggplant is roasting, coat the bottom of a skillet with olive oil and warm over medium-high heat. When the oil starts to shimmer, add the lamb and cook, while breaking it up with a fork, until it is browned, about 8 minutes. Remove the pan from heat and set it aside.

3. Dust a work surface with the semolina flour, place the dough on the surface, and gently stretch it into a round. For more detailed instructions on properly stretching a ball of pizza dough see page 73. Cover the dough with the sauce and top with the eggplant and lamb. Season with salt and pepper and drizzle olive oil over the pizza.

4. Using a peel or a flat baking sheet, transfer the pizza to the heated baking implement in the oven. Bake for about 15 minutes, until the crust is golden brown and starting to char. Remove, top with the burrata, basil, and a drizzle of olive oil, and let the pizza cool slightly before slicing and serving.

INGREDIENTS:

½ EGGPLANT, SLICED

SALT AND PEPPER, TO TASTE

2.4 OZ. | 70 GRAMS RAW PIZZA SAUCE (SEE PAGE 103)

3.5 OZ. | 100 GRAMS BURRATA CHEESE, TORN

FRESH BASIL LEAVES, FOR GARNISH

BROCCOLI RABE, TOMATO & OLIVE PIZZA

YIELD: 1 PIZZA / **ACTIVE TIME:** 20 MINUTES / **TOTAL TIME:** 50 MINUTES

I f you're not a fan of olives, try using some capers in their place. Their slightly toned-down briny flavor will still give this pizza its desired effect.

1. Preheat the oven to the maximum temperature and place a baking stone or steel on the middle rack as it warms. Coat the bottom of a skillet with olive oil and warm over medium-high heat. When the oil starts to shimmer, add the broccoli rabe and cook until it is browned and tender, about 6 minutes. Remove the pan from heat and set it aside.

2. Dust a work surface with the semolina flour, place the dough on the surface, and gently stretch it into a round. For more detailed instructions on properly stretching a ball of pizza dough see page 73. Cover the dough with the mozzarella and top with the tomatoes, olives, garlic, and broccoli rabe. Season with salt and pepper and drizzle olive oil over the pizza.

3. Using a peel or a flat baking sheet, transfer the pizza to the heated baking implement in the oven. Bake for about 15 minutes, until the crust is golden brown and starting to char. Remove and let cool slightly before slicing and serving.

INGREDIENTS:

OLIVE OIL, AS NEEDED

2.8 OZ. | 80 GRAMS BROCCOLI RABE

SEMOLINA FLOUR, AS NEEDED

1 BALL PIZZA DOUGH

1.4 OZ. | 40 GRAMS LOW-MOISTURE MOZZARELLA CHEESE, SHREDDED

2.8 OZ. | 80 GRAMS CHERRY TOMATOES

1 HANDFUL PITTED BLACK OLIVES

1 GARLIC CLOVE, CHOPPED

SALT AND PEPPER, TO TASTE

SPINACH, ZUCCHINI & PISTACHIO PESTO PIZZA

YIELD: 1 PIZZA / **ACTIVE TIME:** 15 MINUTES / **TOTAL TIME:** 45 MINUTES

A vegetarian pizza that delivers plenty of flavor thanks to the delicate but distinctive note of the Pistachio Pesto.

1. Preheat the oven to the maximum temperature and place a baking stone or steel on the middle rack as it warms. Dust a work surface with the semolina flour, place the dough on the surface, and gently stretch it into a round. For more detailed instructions on properly stretching a ball of pizza dough see page 73. Cover the dough with the sauce, top with the spinach, zucchini, mushrooms, and Pistachio Pesto, and drizzle olive oil over the pizza.

2. Using a peel or a flat baking sheet, transfer the pizza to the heated baking implement in the oven. Bake for about 15 minutes, until the crust is golden brown and starting to char. Remove, sprinkle the Parmesan over the pizza, and let cool slightly before slicing and serving.

INGREDIENTS:

SEMOLINA FLOUR, AS NEEDED

⅓ SMALL ZUCCHINI, SLICED

2 BUTTON MUSHROOMS, SLICED

1 OZ. | 30 GRAMS PISTACHIO PESTO (SEE PAGE 375)

OLIVE OIL, TO TASTE

1 OZ. | 30 GRAMS PARMESAN CHEESE, GRATED

PIZZA WITH SEAFOOD, AVOCADO & MANGO

YIELD: 1 PIZZA / **ACTIVE TIME:** 15 MINUTES / **TOTAL TIME:** 45 MINUTES

Fresh mango and avocado paired with seafood evoke Peruvian ceviche. If you prefer clams or mussels to squid, don't hesitate to make the substitution—this pizza is sumptuous enough to take on all comers.

1. Preheat the oven to the maximum temperature and place a baking stone or steel on the middle rack as it warms. Dust a work surface with the semolina flour, place the dough on the surface, and gently stretch it into a round. For more detailed instructions on properly stretching a ball of pizza dough see page 73. Cover the dough with the sauce, top with the mozzarella, and drizzle olive oil over the pizza.

2. Using a peel or a flat baking sheet, transfer the pizza to the heated baking implement in the oven. Bake for about 15 minutes, until the crust is golden brown and starting to char. Remove, top with the squid, salmon, mango, and avocado, and season with salt and pepper. Let the pizza cool slightly before garnishing with the basil, slicing, and serving.

INGREDIENTS:

SEMOLINA FLOUR, AS NEEDED

1 BALL PIZZA DOUGH

2.8 OZ. | 80 GRAMS RAW PIZZA SAUCE (SEE PAGE 103)

2.4 OZ. | 70 GRAMS FRESH MOZZARELLA CHEESE, DRAINED AND CUT INTO SHORT STRIPS

OLIVE OIL, TO TASTE

2.4 OZ. | 70 GRAMS COOKED SQUID

1.4 OZ. | 40 GRAMS SMOKED SALMON

1.4 OZ. | 40 GRAMS MANGO, CHOPPED

1.4 OZ. | 40 GRAMS AVOCADO, SLICED

SALT AND PEPPER, TO TASTE

FRESH BASIL LEAVES, FOR GARNISH

PIZZA WITH POTATO, RED ONION & BÉCHAMEL

YIELD: 1 PIZZA / **ACTIVE TIME:** 15 MINUTES / **TOTAL TIME:** 45 MINUTES

The sharp flavor of red onion is necessary to cut through all the creaminess supplied by the Béchamel and potato.

1. Preheat the oven to the maximum temperature and place a baking stone or steel on the middle rack as it warms. Dust a work surface with the semolina flour, place the dough on the surface, and gently stretch it into a round. For more detailed instructions on properly stretching a ball of pizza dough see page 73. Cover the dough with the Béchamel Sauce and top with the potato and onion. Season with salt, pepper, and rosemary and drizzle olive oil over the pizza.

2. Using a peel or a flat baking sheet, transfer the pizza to the heated baking implement in the oven. Bake for about 15 minutes, until the crust is golden brown and starting to char. Remove and let cool slightly before slicing and serving.

INGREDIENTS:

SEMOLINA FLOUR, AS NEEDED

½ RED ONION, SLICED THIN

SALT AND PEPPER, TO TASTE

DRIED ROSEMARY, TO TASTE

OLIVE OIL, TO TASTE

SAUSAGE, MUSHROOM & PROVOLONE PIZZA

YIELD: 1 PIZZA / **ACTIVE TIME:** 25 MINUTES / **TOTAL TIME:** 1 HOUR

The mildly smoky quality of provolone stands out on this earthy white pie.

1. Preheat the oven to the maximum temperature and place a baking stone or steel on the middle rack as it warms. Coat the bottom of a skillet with olive oil and warm over medium-high heat. When the oil starts to shimmer, add the sausage, onion, and mushrooms and cook until the sausage is browned all over, about 8 minutes. Remove the pan from heat and set it aside.

2. Dust a work surface with the semolina flour, place the dough on the surface, and gently stretch it into a round. For more detailed instructions on properly stretching a ball of pizza dough see page 73. Cover the dough with the provolone and top with the sausage, onion, and mushrooms. Season with salt and pepper and drizzle olive oil over the pizza.

3. Using a peel or a flat baking sheet, transfer the pizza to the heated baking implement in the oven. Bake for about 15 minutes, until the crust is golden brown and starting to char. Remove and let cool slightly before slicing and serving.

INGREDIENTS:

OLIVE OIL, AS NEEDED

½ LINK ITALIAN SAUSAGE, CASING REMOVED AND CRUMBLED

⅓ WHITE ONION, SLICED THIN

3 BUTTON MUSHROOMS, SLICED

SEMOLINA FLOUR, AS NEEDED

1 BALL PIZZA DOUGH

2.8 OZ. | 80 GRAMS PROVOLONE CHEESE, SHREDDED

SALT AND PEPPER, TO TASTE

ENDIVE & CHERRY TOMATO PIZZA

YIELD: 1 PIZZA / **ACTIVE TIME:** 15 MINUTES / **TOTAL TIME:** 45 MINUTES

With this pizza you can enjoy your salad right over your favorite carb. If you don't like the faint bitterness of curly endive, feel free to use a different salad green.

1. Preheat the oven to the maximum temperature and place a baking stone or steel on the middle rack as it warms. Dust a work surface with the semolina flour, place the dough on the surface, and gently stretch it into a round. For more detailed instructions on properly stretching a ball of pizza dough see page 73. Cover the dough with the mozzarella and drizzle olive oil over the top.

2. Using a peel or a flat baking sheet, transfer the pizza to the heated baking implement in the oven. Bake for about 15 minutes, until the crust is golden brown and starting to char. Remove and top with the endive and cherry tomatoes. Drizzle olive oil and white balsamic vinegar glaze over the pizza, season with salt and pepper, and let cool slightly before slicing and serving.

INGREDIENTS:

SEMOLINA FLOUR, AS NEEDED

1.75 OZ. | 50 GRAMS CURLY ENDIVE

1.75 OZ. | 50 GRAMS CHERRY TOMATOES, HALVED

WHITE BALSAMIC VINEGAR GLAZE, TO TASTE

SALT AND PEPPER, TO TASTE

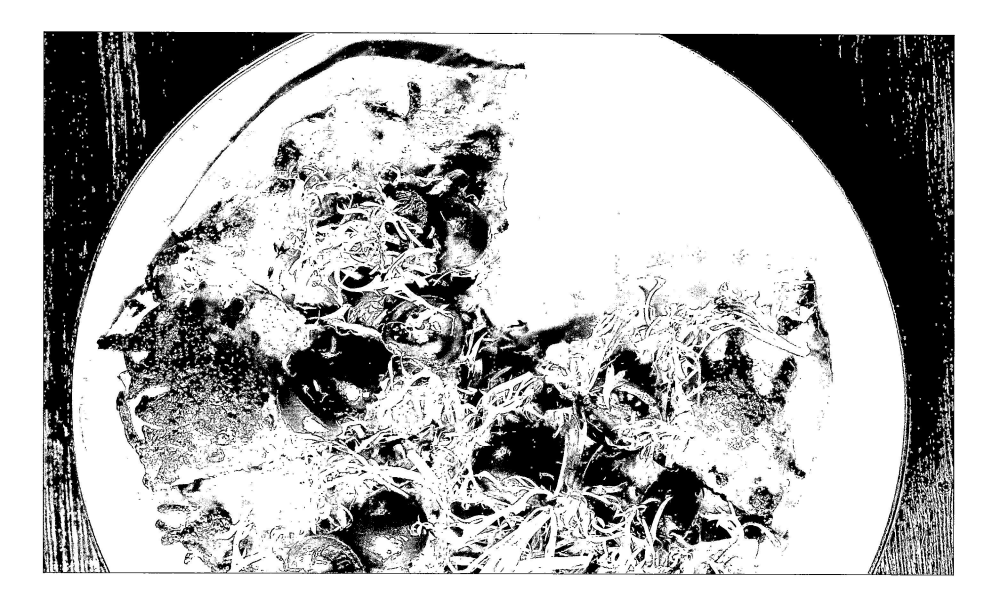

PIZZA WITH CHANTERELLES, BÉCHAMEL & PARMESAN

YIELD: 1 PIZZA / **ACTIVE TIME:** 25 MINUTES / **TOTAL TIME:** 1 HOUR

Should you have the good fortune to come across some chanterelles, this pizza is a great spot for some of that haul.

1. Preheat the oven to the maximum temperature and place a baking stone or steel on the middle rack as it warms. Coat the bottom of a skillet with olive oil and warm over medium-high heat. When the oil starts to shimmer, add the mushrooms, season with salt and pepper, and cook until they start to brown, about 8 minutes. Remove the pan from heat and set it aside.

2. Place the Béchamel Sauce and the Parmesan in a small bowl and stir to combine. Dust a work surface with the semolina flour, place the dough on the surface, and gently stretch it into a round. For more detailed instructions on properly stretching a ball of pizza dough see page 73. Cover the dough with the sauce-and-cheese mixture and top with the mozzarella and mushrooms. Season with salt and pepper and drizzle olive oil over the pizza.

3. Using a peel or a flat baking sheet, transfer the pizza to the heated baking implement in the oven. Bake for about 15 minutes, until the crust is golden brown and starting to char. Remove, top with the arugula and a drizzle of olive oil, and let the pizza cool slightly before slicing and serving.

INGREDIENTS:

OLIVE OIL, AS NEEDED

2.4 OZ. | 70 GRAMS CHANTERELLE MUSHROOMS

SALT AND PEPPER, TO TASTE

2.8 OZ. | 80 GRAMS BÉCHAMEL SAUCE (SEE PAGE 445)

1 OZ. | 30 GRAMS PARMESAN CHEESE, GRATED

SEMOLINA FLOUR, AS NEEDED

1 BALL PIZZA DOUGH

2.4 OZ. | 70 GRAMS FRESH MOZZARELLA CHEESE, DRAINED AND CUT INTO SHORT STRIPS

1 HANDFUL ARUGULA

PISTACHIO & ONION PIZZA

YIELD: 1 PIZZA / **ACTIVE TIME:** 15 MINUTES / **TOTAL TIME:** 45 MINUTES

An elegant and mild pizza bianca that is perked up by the contrast between red onions and pistachios.

1. Preheat the oven to the maximum temperature and place a baking stone or steel on the middle rack as it warms. Dust a work surface with the semolina flour, place the dough on the surface, and gently stretch it into a round. For more detailed instructions on properly stretching a ball of pizza dough see page 73. Cover the dough with the mozzarella and top with the caciocavallo, onion, and pistachios. Season with pepper and drizzle olive oil over the pizza.

2. Using a peel or a flat baking sheet, transfer the pizza to the heated baking implement in the oven. Bake for about 15 minutes, until the crust is golden brown and starting to char. Remove and let cool slightly before slicing and serving.

INGREDIENTS:

SEMOLINA FLOUR, AS NEEDED

⅓ RED ONION, SLICED

1 HANDFUL PISTACHIOS, CHOPPED

BLACK PEPPER, TO TASTE

OLIVE OIL, TO TASTE

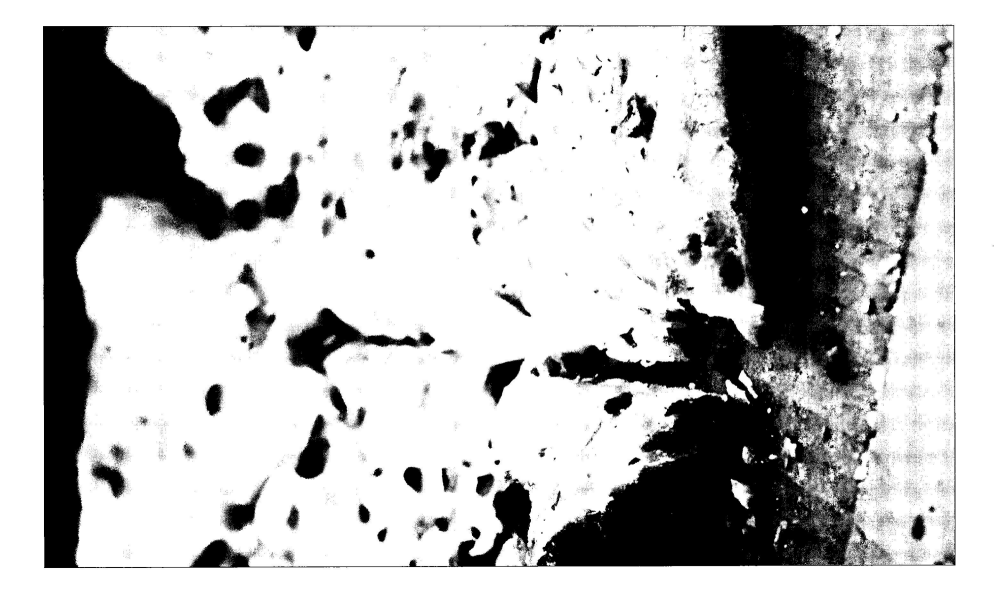

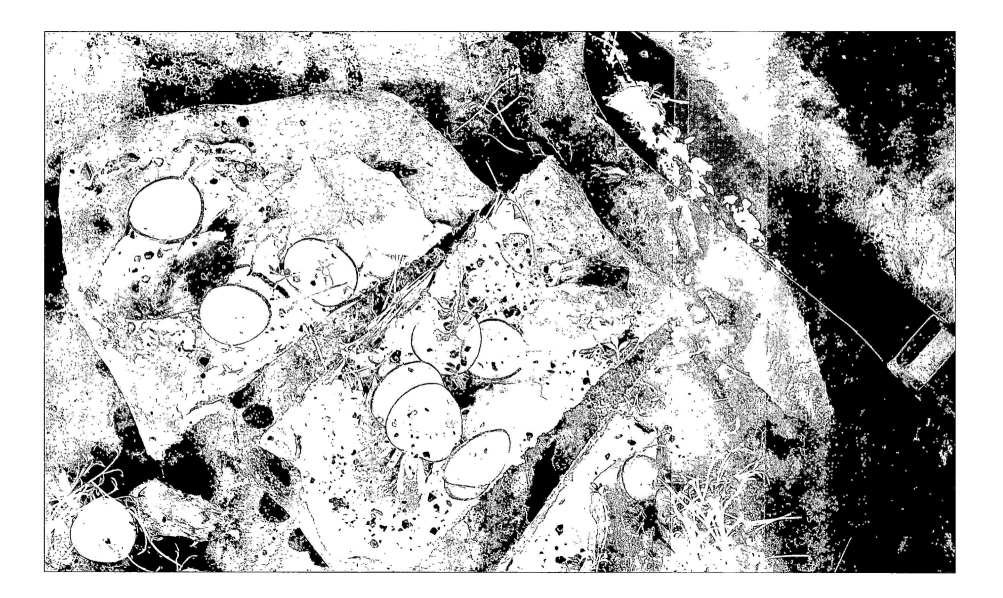

PIZZA WITH SMOKED HERRING, RADISH & CREAM CHEESE

YIELD: 1 PIZZA / **ACTIVE TIME:** 15 MINUTES / **TOTAL TIME:** 45 MINUTES

Simple, yet daring, the pairing of smoked herring with peppery radish is tempered by the cream cheese. A pizza no foodie should pass up trying.

1. Preheat the oven to the maximum temperature and place a baking stone or steel on the middle rack as it warms. Dust a work surface with the semolina flour, place the dough on the surface, and gently stretch it into a round. For more detailed instructions on properly stretching a ball of pizza dough see page 73. Cover the dough with the mozzarella and drizzle olive oil over the top.

2. Using a peel or a flat baking sheet, transfer the pizza to the heated baking implement in the oven. Bake for about 7 minutes, until the crust starts to brown. Remove the pizza, top it with the herring and cream cheese, and return the pizza to the oven. Bake for about 5 minutes, until the crust is golden brown and starting to char. Remove, top with the radish and sprouts, and season with pepper. Drizzle olive oil over the pizza and let cool slightly before slicing and serving.

INGREDIENTS:

SEMOLINA FLOUR, AS NEEDED

1 BALL PIZZA DOUGH

1.4 OZ. | 40 GRAMS LOW-MOISTURE MOZZARELLA CHEESE, SHREDDED

OLIVE OIL, TO TASTE

2.1 OZ. | 60 GRAMS SMOKED HERRING, TORN

1 OZ. | 30 GRAMS CREAM CHEESE

1 RADISH, SLICED THIN

1 HANDFUL ALFALFA OR BROCCOLI SPROUTS

BLACK PEPPER, TO TASTE

CHICKEN & ESCAROLE PIZZA

YIELD: 1 PIZZA / **ACTIVE TIME:** 15 MINUTES / **TOTAL TIME:** 45 MINUTES

When you've got some leftover chicken and a hankering for pizza, try this simple yet delectable bianca.

1. Preheat the oven to the maximum temperature and place a baking stone or steel on the middle rack as it warms. Dust a work surface with the semolina flour, place the dough on the surface, and gently stretch it into a round. For more detailed instructions on properly stretching a ball of pizza dough see page 73. Cover the dough with the mozzarella and top with the chicken, escarole, and garlic. Season with salt and pepper and drizzle olive oil over the pizza.

2. Using a peel or a flat baking sheet, transfer the pizza to the heated baking implement in the oven. Bake for about 15 minutes, until the crust is golden brown and starting to char. Remove and let cool slightly before slicing and serving.

INGREDIENTS:

SEMOLINA FLOUR, AS NEEDED

2.5 OZ. | 70 GRAMS COOKED CHICKEN BREAST, SHREDDED

1.75 OZ. | 50 GRAMS ESCAROLE, TORN

2 GARLIC CLOVES, HALVED

SALT AND PEPPER, TO TASTE

OLIVE OIL, TO TASTE

PIZZA WITH GOAT CHEESE, FENNEL & WALNUTS

YIELD: 1 PIZZA / **ACTIVE TIME:** 15 MINUTES / **TOTAL TIME:** 45 MINUTES

A woodsy, earthy pizza that would work wonderfully on a summer evening when a tinge of fall has entered the air.

1. Preheat the oven to the maximum temperature and place a baking stone or steel on the middle rack as it warms. Dust a work surface with the semolina flour, place the dough on the surface, and gently stretch it into a round. For more detailed instructions on properly stretching a ball of pizza dough see page 73. Cover the dough with the mozzarella and top with the fennel, goat cheese, sun-dried tomatoes, and walnuts. Season with salt and pepper and drizzle olive oil over the pizza.

2. Using a peel or a flat baking sheet, transfer the pizza to the heated baking implement in the oven. Bake for about 15 minutes, until the crust is golden brown and starting to char. Remove, top with the arugula or spinach, and let the pizza cool slightly before slicing and serving.

INGREDIENTS:

SEMOLINA FLOUR, AS NEEDED

1 BALL PIZZA DOUGH

1.75 OZ. | 50 GRAMS LOW-MOISTURE MOZZARELLA CHEESE, SHREDDED

2.4 OZ. | 70 GRAMS FENNEL, SLICED THIN

1.4 OZ. | 40 GRAMS GOAT CHEESE, CRUMBLED

2 SUN-DRIED TOMATOES, SLICED THIN

1 HANDFUL WALNUTS

SALT AND PEPPER, TO TASTE

OLIVE OIL, TO TASTE

1 HANDFUL ARUGULA OR SPINACH, FOR GARNISH

CAJUN SHRIMP & SALAMI PIZZA

YIELD: 1 PIZZA / **ACTIVE TIME:** 20 MINUTES / **TOTAL TIME:** 50 MINUTES

For the lovers of Cajun seasoning, this pizza combines fruit from the sea and from the land.

1. Preheat the oven to the maximum temperature and place a baking stone or steel on the middle rack as it warms. Place the shrimp and olive oil in a bowl, season with Cajun seasoning, and toss to combine. Place the shrimp in a skillet and cook over medium-high heat until they are cooked through, about 2 minutes. Remove the pan from heat and set it aside.

2. Dust a work surface with the semolina flour, place the dough on the surface, and gently stretch it into a round. For more detailed instructions on properly stretching a ball of pizza dough see page 73. Cover the dough with the sauce, top with the mozzarella, and drizzle olive oil over the pizza.

3. Using a peel or a flat baking sheet, transfer the pizza to the heated baking implement in the oven. Bake for about 7 minutes, until the crust starts to brown. Remove the pizza, top it with the salami and shrimp, drizzle olive oil over the pizza, and return it to the oven. Bake for about 5 minutes, until the crust is golden brown and starting to char. Remove and let cool slightly before slicing and serving.

INGREDIENTS:

3.5 OZ. | 100 GRAMS JUMBO SHRIMP, PEELED

(SEE PAGE 103)

2.8 OZ. | 80 GRAMS FRESH MOZZARELLA CHEESE, DRAINED AND CUT INTO SHORT STRIPS

1.4 OZ. | 40 GRAMS SPICY SALAMI, SLICED

BOK CHOY, PINE NUT & RAISIN PIZZA

YIELD: 1 PIZZA / **ACTIVE TIME:** 15 MINUTES / **TOTAL TIME:** 45 MINUTES

This is a modern take on a classic Sicilian pairing, where the bok choy replaces escarole, giving this pizza a milder and sweeter bite.

1. Preheat the oven to the maximum temperature and place a baking stone or steel on the middle rack as it warms. Coat the bottom of a skillet with olive oil and warm over medium-high heat. When the oil starts to shimmer, add the bok choy and garlic, season with salt, and cook until the bok choy has wilted, about 5 minutes. Remove the pan from heat and set it aside.

2. Dust a work surface with the semolina flour, place the dough on the surface, and gently stretch it into a round. For more detailed instructions on properly stretching a ball of pizza dough see page 73. Cover the dough with the sauce and top with the raisins, pine nuts, and bok choy mixture. Season with salt and drizzle olive oil over the pizza.

3. Using a peel or a flat baking sheet, transfer the pizza to the heated baking implement in the oven. Bake for about 15 minutes, until the crust is golden brown and starting to char. Remove and let cool slightly before slicing and serving.

INGREDIENTS:

OLIVE OIL, AS NEEDED

2.1 OZ. | 60 GRAMS BOK CHOY, CHOPPED

1 GARLIC CLOVE, MINCED

SALT, TO TASTE

2.4 OZ. | 70 GRAMS RAW PIZZA SAUCE (SEE PAGE 103)

1 OZ. | 30 GRAMS RAISINS

SEMOLINA FLOUR, AS NEEDED

1 BALL PIZZA DOUGH

1 HANDFUL PINE NUTS

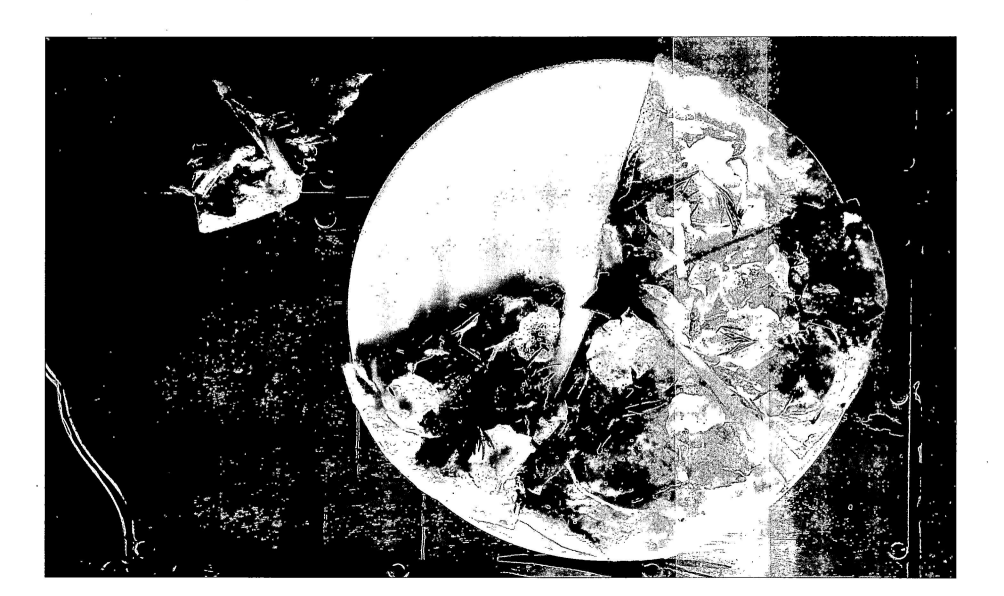

PIZZA WITH POTATO, PARSNIP & PROSCIUTTO

YIELD: 1 PIZZA / **ACTIVE TIME:** 20 MINUTES / **TOTAL TIME:** 55 MINUTES

The delicate sweetness of parsnips is finally gaining a wider audience and popping up in all sorts of unexpected places: ice creams, latkes, and, now, pizzas.

1. Preheat the oven to the maximum temperature and place a baking stone or steel on the middle rack as it warms. Bring salted water to a boil in a saucepan and cook the potato and the parsnip for no more than 1 minute. Drain, pat the vegetables dry, and set aside.

2. Dust a work surface with the semolina flour, place the dough on the surface, and gently stretch it into a round. For more detailed instructions on properly stretching a ball of pizza dough see page 73. Drizzle olive oil over the dough and top with the mozzarella, prosciutto, potato, and parsnip. Season with salt, pepper, and rosemary and drizzle olive oil over the pizza.

3. Using a peel or a flat baking sheet, transfer the pizza to the heated baking implement in the oven. Bake for about 15 minutes, until the crust is golden brown and starting to char. Remove and let cool slightly before slicing and serving.

INGREDIENTS:

SALT AND PEPPER, TO TASTE

½ POTATO, SLICED THIN WITH MANDOLINE

½ PARSNIP, SLICED THIN WITH MANDOLINE

SEMOLINA FLOUR, AS NEEDED

1 BALL PIZZA DOUGH

OLIVE OIL, TO TASTE

2.4 OZ. | 70 GRAMS FRESH MOZZARELLA CHEESE, DRAINED AND CUT INTO SHORT STRIPS

3 SLICES PROSCIUTTO, TORN

FRESH ROSEMARY, TO TASTE

PIZZA WITH PEAS & CAVIAR

YIELD: 1 PIZZA / **ACTIVE TIME:** 15 MINUTES / **TOTAL TIME:** 45 MINUTES

A pizza that is positively bursting with freshness.

INGREDIENTS:

2.4 OZ. | 70 GRAMS PEAS

1. Preheat the oven to the maximum temperature and place a baking stone or steel on the middle rack as it warms. Place the peas and basil in a food processor and blitz until smooth and creamy, adding olive oil as needed to achieve the desired consistency. Season the puree with salt and pepper and set it aside.

Dust a work surface with the semolina flour, place the dough on the surface, and gently stretch it into a round. For more detailed instructions on properly stretching a ball of pizza dough see page 73. Cover the dough with the puree and top with the mozzarella. Season with salt and pepper and drizzle olive oil over the pizza.

2.4 OZ. | 70 GRAMS FRESH MOZZARELLA CHEESE, DRAINED AND CUT INTO SHORT STRIPS

0.75 OZ. | 22.5 GRAMS CAVIAR

1 HANDFUL ARUGULA OR SPINACH, FOR GARNISH

3. Using a peel or a flat baking sheet, transfer the pizza to the heated baking implement in the oven. Bake for about 15 minutes, until the crust is golden brown and starting to char. Remove, distribute the caviar and arugula or spinach over the pizza, and let it cool slightly before slicing and serving.

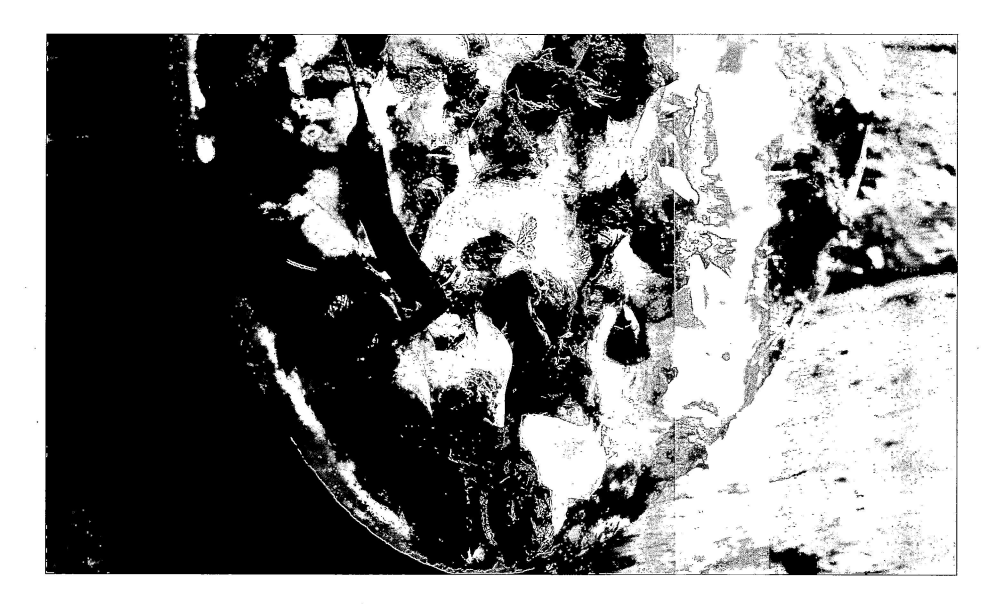

PULLED PORK PIZZA

YIELD: 1 PIZZA / **ACTIVE TIME:** 15 MINUTES / **TOTAL TIME:** 45 MINUTES

The unsurpassed flavor and molten texture of pulled pork ensure that this simple pizza is a memorable meal.

1. Preheat the oven to the maximum temperature and place a baking stone or steel on the middle rack as it warms. Dust a work surface with the semolina flour, place the dough on the surface, and gently stretch it into a round. For more detailed instructions on properly stretching a ball of pizza dough see page 73. Spread the barbeque sauce over the dough and top with the pork, chilies, and onion. Season with salt, drizzle olive oil over the top, and then sprinkle the Gouda over the pizza.

2. Using a peel or a flat baking sheet, transfer the pizza to the heated baking implement in the oven. Bake for about 15 minutes, until the crust is golden brown and starting to char. Remove and let cool slightly before garnishing with the cilantro, slicing, and serving.

INGREDIENTS:

SEMOLINA FLOUR, AS NEEDED

1 BALL PIZZA DOUGH

1.6 OZ | 45 GRAMS SPICY BARBEQUE SAUCE

3.5 OZ. | 100 GRAMS COOKED PULLED PORK

3 RED CHILI PEPPERS, STEMMED, SEEDED, AND SLICED

⅓ SMALL RED ONION, SLICED THIN

SALT, TO TASTE

OLIVE OIL, TO TASTE

3.5 OZ. | 100 GRAMS GOUDA CHEESE, SHREDDED

FRESH CILANTRO, FINELY CHOPPED, FOR GARNISH

PIZZA WITH ANCHOVIES

YIELD: 1 PIZZA / **ACTIVE TIME:** 15 MINUTES / **TOTAL TIME:** 45 MINUTES

Anchovies on pizza have historically gotten a bad rap, to the point that it was a running joke in the early 1990s. Luckily, increased appreciation for umami has rehabbed that image.

1. Preheat the oven to the maximum temperature and place a baking stone or steel on the middle rack as it warms. Dust a work surface with the semolina flour, place the dough on the surface, and gently stretch it into a round. For more detailed instructions on properly stretching a ball of pizza dough see page 73. Cover the dough with the sauce and top with the mozzarella and anchovies. Season with salt and oregano and drizzle olive oil over the pizza.

2. Using a peel or a flat baking sheet, transfer the pizza to the heated baking implement in the oven. Bake for about 15 minutes, until the crust is golden brown and starting to char. Remove, sprinkle the Parmesan over the pizza, and let cool slightly before slicing and serving.

INGREDIENTS:

SEMOLINA FLOUR, AS NEEDED

6 ANCHOVY FILLETS, HALVED

SALT, TO TASTE

FRESH OREGANO, FINELY CHOPPED, TO TASTE

OLIVE OIL, AS NEEDED

1 OZ. | 30 GRAMS PARMESAN CHEESE, GRATED

PIZZA WITH JALAPEÑOS, RED PEPPERS & ONIONS

YIELD: 1 PIZZA / **ACTIVE TIME:** 15 MINUTES / **TOTAL TIME:** 45 MINUTES

If you're looking for the jalapeños to make an outsized impact, try making this pizza without sauce—without its sweetness, there's nothing to mask the spice.

1. Preheat the oven to the maximum temperature and place a baking stone or steel on the middle rack as it warms. Dust a work surface with the semolina flour, place the dough on the surface, and gently stretch it into a round. For more detailed instructions on properly stretching a ball of pizza dough see page 73. Cover the dough with the sauce and top with the mozzarella, garlic, peppers, and onion. Season with salt and pepper and drizzle olive oil over the pizza.

2. Using a peel or a flat baking sheet, transfer the pizza to the heated baking implement in the oven. Bake for about 15 minutes, until the crust is golden brown and starting to char. Remove, sprinkle the Parmesan and basil over the pizza, and let cool slightly before slicing and serving.

INGREDIENTS:

SEMOLINA FLOUR, AS NEEDED

1 BALL PIZZA DOUGH

3.5 OZ. | 100 GRAMS RAW PIZZA SAUCE (SEE PAGE 103)

3.5 OZ. | 100 GRAMS LOW-MOISTURE MOZZARELLA CHEESE, SHREDDED

1 GARLIC CLOVE, MINCED

½ RED BELL PEPPER, STEMMED, SEEDED, AND SLICED

2 JALAPEÑO PEPPERS, STEMMED, SEEDED, AND SLICED

½ ONION, SLICED

SALT AND PEPPER, TO TASTE

OLIVE OIL, AS NEEDED

1 OZ. | 30 GRAMS PARMESAN CHEESE, GRATED

FRESH BASIL LEAVES, FOR GARNISH

PIZZA WITH GRILLED VEGETABLES
& TOFU CREAM CHEESE

YIELD: 1 PIZZA / **ACTIVE TIME:** 15 MINUTES / **TOTAL TIME:** 45 MINUTES

While making a successful vegan pizza can seem daunting, this easy recipe will keep you and all the vegans in your life happy. Dollops of Basil Pesto (see page 365) would be a lovely addition if you happen to have some laying around, and don't need to keep this pizza vegan.

1. Preheat the oven to the maximum temperature and place a baking stone or steel on the middle rack as it warms. Preheat a gas or charcoal grill to high heat. Place the zucchini, pepper, and onion on the grill and cook for 5 to 6 minutes, until tender. Remove from the grill, transfer to a cutting board, and chop into bite-sized pieces. Place the vegetables in a bowl, drizzle olive oil over them, season with salt, and toss to coat.

2. Dust a work surface with the semolina flour, place the dough on the surface, and gently stretch it into a round. For more detailed instructions on properly stretching a ball of pizza dough see page 73. Cover the dough with the tofu cream cheese, grilled vegetables, and mushrooms. Season with salt and pepper and drizzle olive oil over the pizza.

3. Using a peel or a flat baking sheet, transfer the pizza to the heated baking implement in the oven. Bake for about 15 minutes, until the crust is golden brown and starting to char. Remove and let cool slightly before garnishing with the fennel fronds, slicing, and serving.

INGREDIENTS

SALT AND PEPPER, TO TASTE

OLIVE OIL, AS NEEDED

SEMOLINA FLOUR, AS NEEDED

1 BALL PIZZA DOUGH

1.75 OZ. | 50 GRAMS TOFU CREAM CHEESE

3 BUTTON MUSHROOMS, SLICED

1 HANDFUL FRESH FENNEL FRONDS, FOR GARNISH

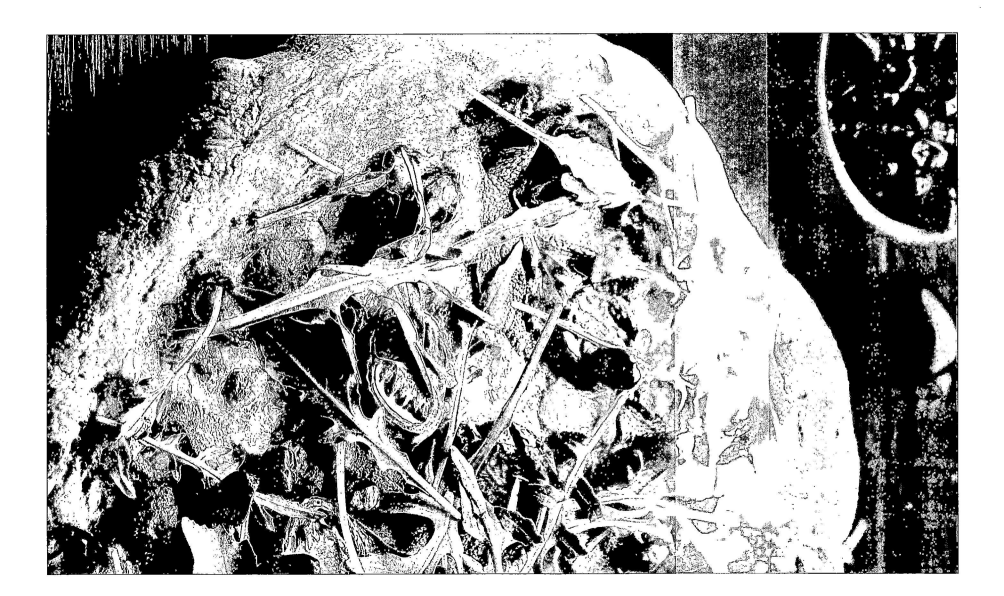

ARUGULA, POMEGRANATE & CHERRY TOMATO PIZZA

YIELD: 1 PIZZA / **ACTIVE TIME:** 15 MINUTES / **TOTAL TIME:** 45 MINUTES

A stunning pizza with an outstanding balance of flavors: peppery arugula, sweet tomatoes, and slightly sour pomegranate seeds.

1. Preheat the oven to the maximum temperature and place a baking stone or steel on the middle rack as it warms. Dust a work surface with the semolina flour, place the dough on the surface, and gently stretch it into a round. For more detailed instructions on properly stretching a ball of pizza dough see page 73. Cover the dough with the mozzarella, drizzle olive oil over the pizza, and season it with salt.

2. Using a peel or a flat baking sheet, transfer the pizza to the heated baking implement in the oven. Bake for about 15 minutes, until the crust is golden brown and starting to char. Remove, top with the arugula, pomegranate seeds, and cherry tomatoes, and let cool slightly before slicing and serving.

INGREDIENTS:

SEMOLINA FLOUR, AS NEEDED

1 BALL PIZZA DOUGH

3.5 OZ. | 100 GRAMS LOW-MOISTURE MOZZARELLA CHEESE, SHREDDED

OLIVE OIL, TO TASTE

SALT, TO TASTE

1 HANDFUL ARUGULA

1 OZ. | 30 GRAMS POMEGRANATE SEEDS

1 OZ. | 30 GRAMS CHERRY TOMATOES, HALVED

MUSHROOM & ARTICHOKE PAN PIZZA

YIELD: 1 PIZZA / **ACTIVE TIME:** 30 MINUTES / **TOTAL TIME:** 1 HOUR AND 45 MINUTES

Any mushroom will work on this pizza, but do your best to track down some chanterelles.

1. Grease a 9 × 13–inch baking pan with olive oil and place the pizza dough in it. Gradually stretch the dough to cover the pan, making sure to let it rest from time to time so that it doesn't deflate. Cover the dough with plastic wrap and let rest for 1 hour.

Coat the bottom of a skillet with olive oil and warm over medium-high heat. When the oil starts to shimmer, add the mushrooms and garlic and sauté until the mushrooms begin to release their liquid, about 3 minutes. Remove from heat and set aside.

3. Preheat the oven to the maximum temperature. Place the dough on the bottom rack of the oven, bake for 10 minutes, and remove it from the oven. Lower the oven's temperature to 430°F (220°C). Distribute the mozzarella, mushrooms, and half of the artichokes over the dough. Season with salt, return to the oven, and bake for about 15 minutes, until the crust is crispy and golden brown. Remove from the oven, top with the remaining artichokes and the buffalo mozzarella, and let the pizza cool slightly before slicing and serving.

INGREDIENTS:

OLIVE OIL, AS NEEDED

1 BALL PIZZA DOUGH

[...]

[...] OZ. | 130 GRAMS FRESH MOZZARELLA CHEESE, DRAINED AND CUT INTO SHORT STRIPS

3.5 OZ. | 100 GRAMS ARTICHOKE HEARTS, CHOPPED

SALT, TO TASTE

1 OZ. | 30 GRAMS BUFFALO MOZZARELLA, DRAINED AND TORN

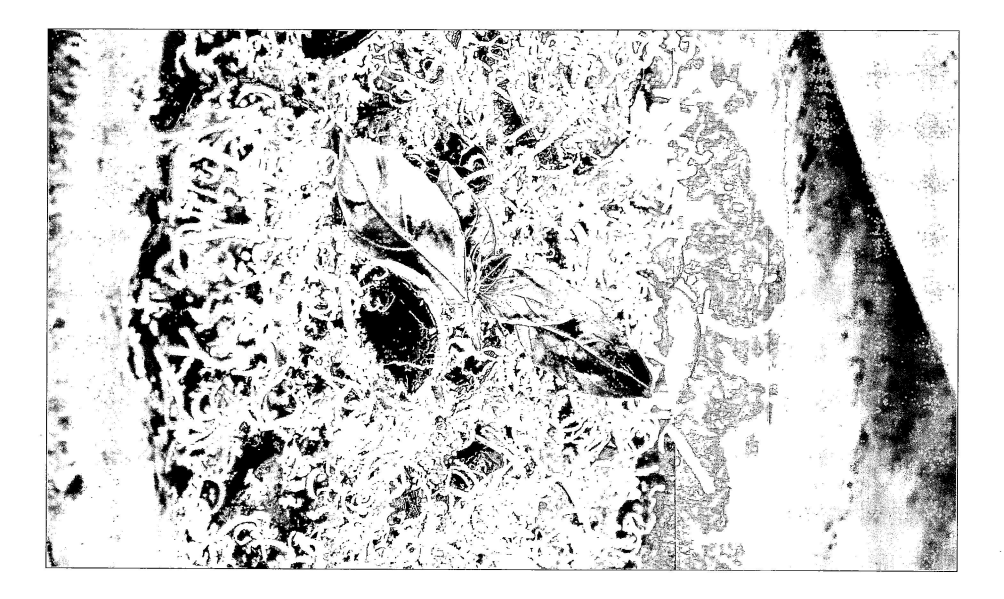

ARRABBIATA, EGGPLANT & PEPPER PIZZA

YIELD: 4 SERVINGS / **ACTIVE TIME:** 10 MINUTES / **TOTAL TIME:** 25 MINUTES

Arrabbiata translates to "angry," and this spicy sauce is sure to get your taste buds agitated—in a good way.

1. Preheat the oven to the maximum temperature and place a baking stone or steel on the middle rack as it warms. Place the eggplant in a baking dish, drizzle olive oil over it, and season with salt. Roast the eggplant in the warming oven for about 15 minutes, until it is tender. Remove from the oven and let cool slightly.

2. Dust a work surface with the semolina flour, place the dough on the surface, and gently stretch it into a round. For more detailed instructions on properly stretching a ball of pizza dough see page 73. Cover the dough with the Arrabbiata Sauce and top with the mozzarella, pepper, and roasted eggplant. Season with salt and drizzle olive oil over the pizza.

3. Using a peel or a flat baking sheet, transfer the pizza to the heated baking implement in the oven. Bake for about 15 minutes, until the crust is golden brown and starting to char. Remove, top the pizza with the Parmesan and basil, and let cool slightly before slicing and serving.

ARRABBIATA SAUCE

1. Place the olive oil and red pepper flakes in a saucepan and warm over medium-high heat. When the oil starts to shimmer, add the onion and garlic and cook until the onion is translucent, about 3 minutes.

2. Stir in the tomatoes, reduce the heat to medium, and simmer the sauce until the flavor has developed to your liking, about 25 minutes. Stir in the basil, season with salt and pepper, and use as desired.

INGREDIENTS:

½ EGGPLANT, SLICED LENGTHWISE

OLIVE OIL, AS NEEDED

SALT, TO TASTE

SEMOLINA FLOUR, AS NEEDED

1 BALL PIZZA DOUGH

3.5 OZ. | 100 GRAMS ARRABBIATA SAUCE (SEE RECIPE)

3.5 OZ. | 100 GRAMS LOW-MOISTURE MOZZARELLA CHEESE, SHREDDED

⅓ RED PEPPER, SLICED

1 OZ. | 30 GRAMS PARMESAN CHEESE, GRATED

FRESH BASIL LEAVES, FOR GARNISH

ARRABBIATA SAUCE

1 OZ. | 30 GRAMS OLIVE OIL

RED PEPPER FLAKES, TO TASTE

1 ONION, SLICED

3 GARLIC CLOVES, MINCED

28.2 OZ. | 800 GRAMS CANNED WHOLE TOMATOES, CRUSHED

2.1 OZ. | 60 GRAMS FRESH BASIL LEAVES

SALT AND PEPPER, TO TASTE

PIZZA WITH BACON, BLUE CHEESE, ONION & PICKLES

YIELD: 1 PIZZA / **ACTIVE TIME:** 15 MINUTES / **TOTAL TIME:** 45 MINUTES

Four potent flavors join forces to bring you this decadent pie.

1. Preheat the oven to the maximum temperature and place a baking stone or steel on the middle rack as it warms. Dust a work surface with the semolina flour, place the dough on the surface, and gently stretch it into a round. For more detailed instructions on properly stretching a ball of pizza dough see page 73. Cover the dough with the mozzarella, top with the bacon, blue cheese, and onion, and drizzle olive oil over the pizza.

2. Using a peel or a flat baking sheet, transfer the pizza to the heated baking implement in the oven. Bake for about 7 minutes, until the crust starts to brown. Remove the pizza, top with the pickles, drizzle olive oil over the pizza, and return it to the oven. Bake for about 5 minutes, until the crust is golden brown and starting to char. Remove and let cool slightly before slicing and serving.

INGREDIENTS:

SEMOLINA FLOUR, AS NEEDED

1 OZ. | 30 GRAMS BLUE CHEESE, CRUMBLED

⅓ RED ONION, SLICED

OLIVE OIL, TO TASTE

1 OZ. | 30 GRAMS DILL PICKLES

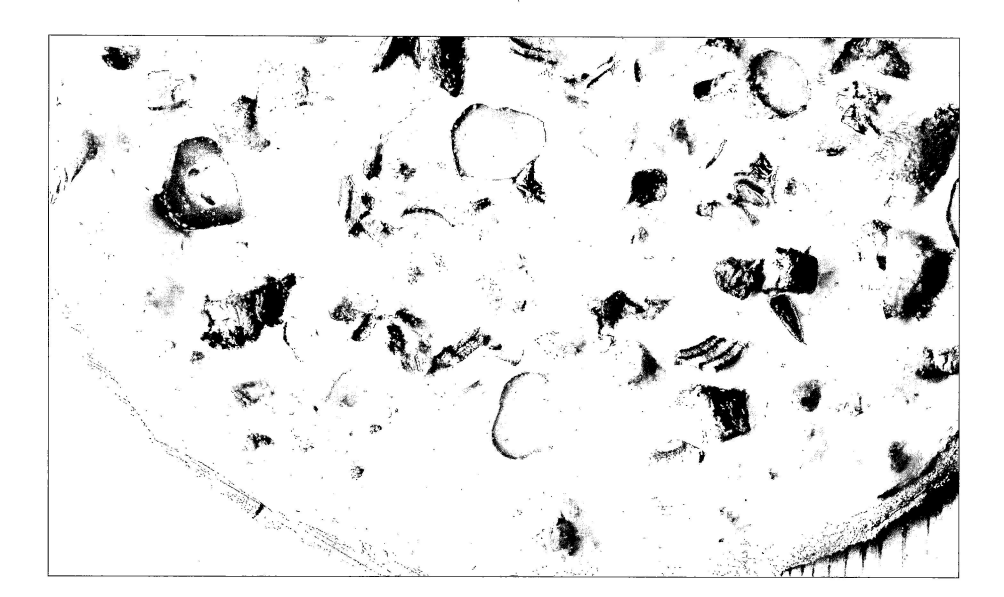

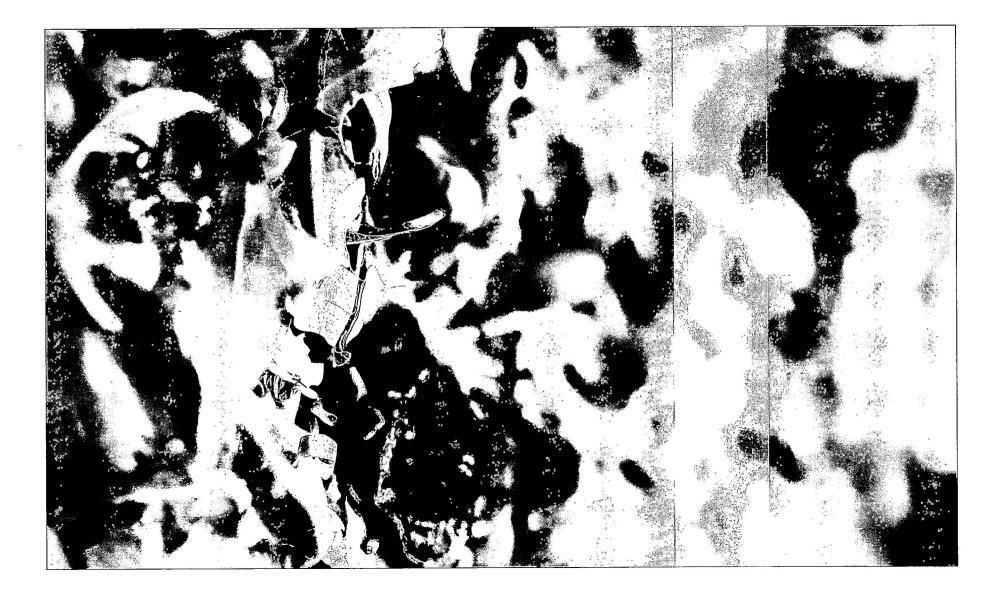

PIZZA WITH PRUNES, GOAT CHEESE & TOMATOES

YIELD: 1 PIZZA / **ACTIVE TIME:** 15 MINUTES / **TOTAL TIME:** 45 MINUTES

The standard trio of goat cheese, greens, and tomatoes gets a shot in the arm from the rich sweetness of prunes.

1. Preheat the oven to the maximum temperature and place a baking stone or steel on the middle rack as it warms. Dust a work surface with the semolina flour, place the dough on the surface, and gently stretch it into a round. For more detailed instructions on properly stretching a ball of pizza dough see page 73. Cover the dough with the mozzarella and drizzle olive oil over the pizza.

2. Using a peel or a flat baking sheet, transfer the pizza to the heated baking implement in the oven. Bake for about 7 minutes, until the crust starts to brown. Remove the pizza, top it with the prunes and tomatoes, drizzle olive oil over the pizza, and return it to the oven. Bake for about 5 minutes, until the crust is golden brown and starting to char. Remove, top with the arugula, goat cheese, and a drizzle of olive oil, and let cool slightly before slicing and serving.

INGREDIENTS:

SEMOLINA FLOUR, AS NEEDED

1 BALL PIZZA DOUGH

2.8 OZ. | 80 GRAMS LOW-MOISTURE MOZZARELLA CHEESE, SHREDDED

OLIVE OIL, TO TASTE

2.1 OZ. | 60 GRAMS PRUNES, HALVED

2.1 OZ. | 60 GRAMS CHERRY TOMATOES, HALVED

2 HANDFULS ARUGULA

1 OZ. | 30 GRAMS GOAT CHEESE, CRUMBLED

ROMESCO & LEEK PIZZA

YIELD: 1 PIZZA / **ACTIVE TIME:** 25 MINUTES / **TOTAL TIME:** 1 HOUR

his zippy Spanish sauce was made to pair with the creamy and mild leek, and to provide you with the full measure of this accord, we recommend grilling the leeks before placing them on the pizza.

1. Preheat the oven to the maximum temperature and place a baking stone or steel on the middle rack as it warms. Preheat a gas or charcoal grill to medium-high heat. Place the leeks on the grill and cook, turning occasionally, until they are charred all over, about 10 minutes. Remove the leeks from the grill and let them cool slightly. When the leeks are cool enough to handle, slice them thin.

2. Dust a work surface with the semolina flour, place the dough on the surface, and gently stretch it into a round. For more detailed instructions on properly stretching a ball of pizza dough see page 73. Cover the dough with the Romesco Sauce and top with the mozzarella, mushrooms, onion, and leeks. Season with salt and pepper and drizzle olive oil over the pizza.

3. Using a peel or a flat baking sheet, transfer the pizza to the heated baking implement in the oven. Bake for about 15 minutes, until the crust is golden brown and starting to char. Remove and let cool slightly before slicing and serving.

ROMESCO SAUCE

1. Place all of the ingredients, except for the olive oil, in a blender or food processor and blitz until the mixture is smooth.

2. Add the olive oil in a steady stream and blitz until emulsified. Adjust the seasoning as necessary and use as desired.

INGREDIENTS:

2.8 OZ. | 80 GRAMS ROMESCO SAUCE (SEE RECIPE)

3.5 OZ. | 100 GRAMS FRESH MOZZARELLA CHEESE, DRAINED AND TORN

2.1 OZ. | 60 GRAMS BUTTON MUSHROOMS, SLICED

⅓ RED ONION, SLICED THIN

SALT AND PEPPER, TO TASTE

OLIVE OIL, TO TASTE

ROMESCO SAUCE
2 LARGE RED BELL PEPPERS, ROASTED

1 GARLIC CLOVE, SMASHED

1.75 OZ. | 50 GRAMS SLIVERED ALMONDS

2.1 OZ. | 60 GRAMS TOMATOES, PUREED

1 HANDFUL FRESH PARSLEY

1 OZ. | 30 GRAMS SHERRY VINEGAR

SMOKED PAPRIKA, TO TASTE

4 OZ. | 113.4 GRAMS OLIVE OIL

SALT AND PEPPER, TO TASTE

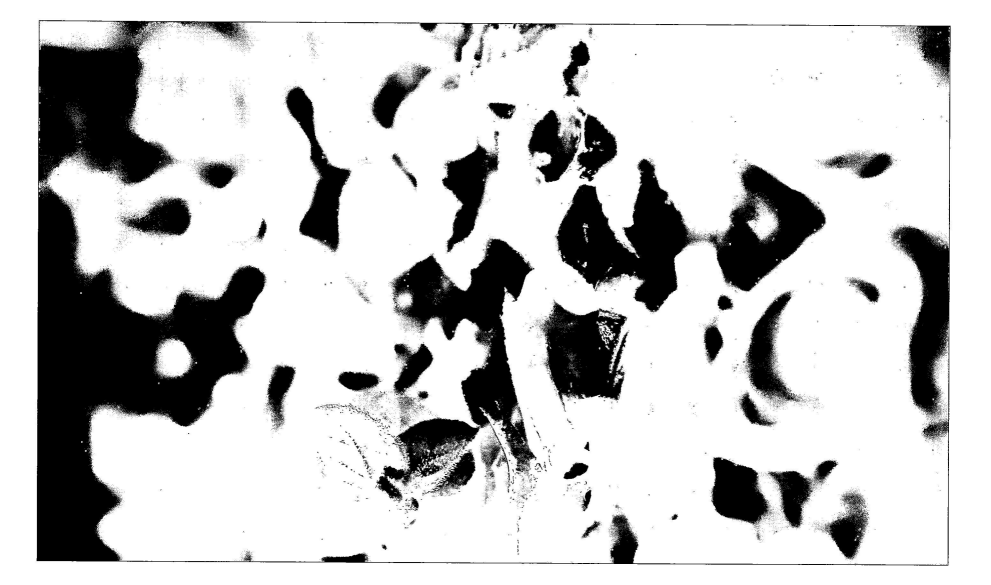

CUCUMBER, TOMATO & CHICKEN PIZZA

YIELD: 1 PIZZA / **ACTIVE TIME:** 15 MINUTES / **TOTAL TIME:** 45 MINUTES

The fresh crunch of cucumbers is a wonderful way to change things up when your old standbys start to get a bit well-worn.

1. Preheat the oven to the maximum temperature and place a baking stone or steel on the middle rack as it warms. Dust a work surface with the semolina flour, place the dough on the surface, and gently stretch it into a round. For more detailed instructions on properly stretching a ball of pizza dough see page 73. Cover the dough with the sauce and top with the mozzarella and chicken. Season with salt and pepper and drizzle olive oil over the pizza.

2. Using a peel or a flat baking sheet, transfer the pizza to the heated baking implement in the oven. Bake for about 7 minutes, until the crust starts to brown. Remove the pizza, top it with the tomatoes and cucumbers, drizzle olive oil over the pizza, and return it to the oven. Bake for about 5 minutes, until the crust is golden brown and starting to char. Remove and let cool slightly before slicing and serving.

INGREDIENTS:

SEMOLINA FLOUR, AS NEEDED

1 BALL PIZZA DOUGH

2.4 OZ. | 70 GRAMS RAW PIZZA SAUCE (SEE PAGE 103)

2.8 OZ. | 80 GRAMS FRESH MOZZARELLA CHEESE, DRAINED AND TORN

2.8 OZ. | 80 GRAMS COOKED CHICKEN BREAST, CHOPPED

SALT AND PEPPER, TO TASTE

OLIVE OIL, TO TASTE

2.1 OZ. | 60 GRAMS CHERRY TOMATOES, HALVED

2.1 OZ. | 60 GRAMS CUCUMBERS, CHOPPED

APPLE, ONION & BALSAMIC PIZZA

YIELD: 1 PIZZA / **ACTIVE TIME:** 25 MINUTES / **TOTAL TIME:** 1 HOUR

This is precisely the kind of inventive, produce-focused topping that Californian cuisine ushered in during the early '80s.

1. Preheat the oven to the maximum temperature and place a baking stone or steel on the middle rack as it warms. Coat the bottom of a skillet with olive oil and warm over medium-high heat. When the oil starts to shimmer, add the onion, season with salt and pepper, and cook until it is soft, about 8 minutes. Remove from heat and let cool.

2. Dust a work surface with the semolina flour, place the dough on the surface, and gently stretch it into a round. For more detailed instructions on properly stretching a ball of pizza dough see page 73. Cover the dough with the mozzarella and top with the apple and sautéed onion. Season with salt and pepper and drizzle olive oil over the pizza.

3. Using a peel or a flat baking sheet, transfer the pizza to the heated baking implement in the oven. Bake for about 15 minutes, until the crust is golden brown and starting to char. Remove, top with the balsamic vinegar and Parmesan, and let cool slightly before slicing and serving.

INGREDIENTS:

OLIVE OIL, AS NEEDED

[illegible]

[illegible]

[illegible]

[illegible]

2.8 OZ. | 80 GRAMS FRESH MOZZARELLA CHEESE, DRAINED AND TORN

1 GRANNY SMITH APPLE, CORED AND SLICED THIN

1 OZ. | 30 GRAMS BALSAMIC VINEGAR

1 OZ. | 30 GRAMS PARMESAN CHEESE, GRATED

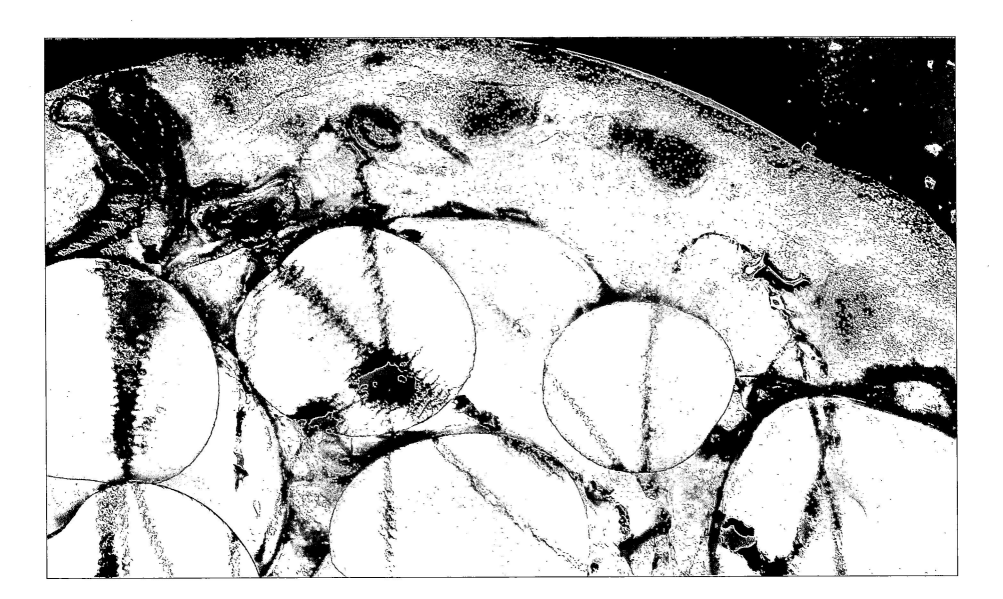

DANDELION & TOMATO PIZZA

YIELD: 1 PIZZA / **ACTIVE TIME:** 15 MINUTES / **TOTAL TIME:** 45 MINUTES

Earthy, nutty, and subtly bitter, dandelions are an incredibly underutilized ingredient, as this summery pie proves.

1. Preheat the oven to the maximum temperature and place a baking stone or steel on the middle rack as it warms. Dust a work surface with the semolina flour, place the dough on the surface, and gently stretch it into a round. For more detailed instructions on properly stretching a ball of pizza dough see page 73. Cover the dough with the sauce and top with the mozzarella. Season with salt and pepper and drizzle olive oil over the pizza.

2. Using a peel or a flat baking sheet, transfer the pizza to the heated baking implement in the oven. Bake for about 7 minutes, until the crust starts to brown. Remove the pizza, top it with the dandelion greens, ricotta, and tomato, drizzle olive oil over the pizza, and return it to the oven. Bake for about 5 minutes, until the crust is golden brown and starting to char. Remove and let cool slightly before slicing and serving.

INGREDIENTS:

SEMOLINA FLOUR, AS NEEDED

1 BALL PIZZA DOUGH

2.8 OZ. | 80 GRAMS RAW PIZZA SAUCE (SEE PAGE 103)

3.5 OZ. | 100 GRAMS FRESH MOZZARELLA CHEESE, DRAINED AND TORN

SALT AND PEPPER, TO TASTE

OLIVE OIL, TO TASTE

1 HANDFUL DANDELION GREENS

1.75 OZ. | 50 GRAMS RICOTTA CHEESE

½ TOMATO, CHOPPED

LAMB, EGGPLANT & TOMATO PIZZA

YIELD: 1 PIZZA / **ACTIVE TIME:** 30 MINUTES / **TOTAL TIME:** 1 HOUR AND 15 MINUTES

The most important constituents of moussaka, the Greek comfort classic, lend their talents to this delicious pizza.

1. Preheat the oven to the maximum temperature and place a baking stone or steel on the middle rack as it warms. Place the eggplant in a baking dish, drizzle olive oil over it, and season with salt and pepper. Roast the eggplant in the warming oven until it is tender, about 15 minutes. Remove and let cool.

2. While the eggplant is roasting, coat the bottom of a skillet with olive oil and warm over medium-high heat. When the oil starts to shimmer, add the ground lamb, season with salt and pepper, and cook, while breaking the meat up with a fork, until it is browned all over, about 8 minutes. Remove from heat and let cool.

3. Dust a work surface with the semolina flour, place the dough on the surface, and gently stretch it into a round. For more detailed instructions on properly stretching a ball of pizza dough see page 73. Cover the dough with the sauce and top with the lamb, mozzarella, tomatoes, and roasted eggplant. Season with salt and pepper and drizzle olive oil over the pizza.

4. Using a peel or a flat baking sheet, transfer the pizza to the heated baking implement in the oven. Bake for about 15 minutes, until the crust is golden brown and starting to char. Remove and let cool slightly before slicing and serving.

INGREDIENTS:

1 EGGPLANT, SLICED

1 BALL PIZZA DOUGH

2.8 OZ. | 80 GRAMS RAW PIZZA SAUCE (SEE PAGE 103)

3.5 OZ. | 100 GRAMS LOW-MOISTURE MOZZARELLA CHEESE, SHREDDED

2 TOMATOES, SLICED

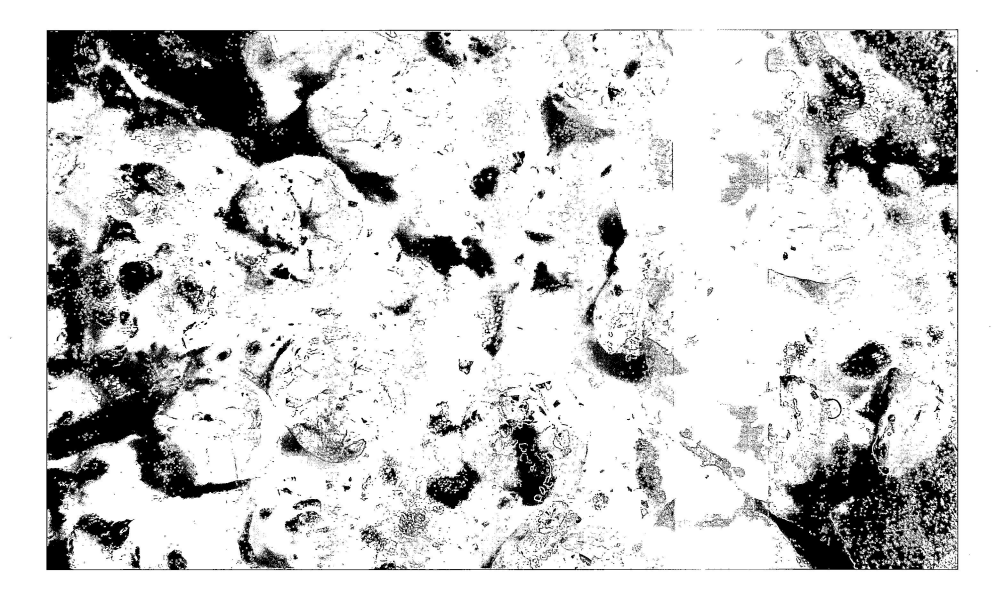

SHRIMP & PINEAPPLE PIZZA

YIELD: 1 PIZZA / **ACTIVE TIME:** 20 MINUTES / **TOTAL TIME:** 50 MINUTES

If you thought Hawaiian-style pizza was controversial, just imagine people's responses to this pie. Fortunately, you can be sure any naysayers aren't speaking from experience.

1. Preheat the oven to the maximum temperature and place a baking stone or steel on the middle rack as it warms. Coat the bottom of a skillet with olive oil and warm over medium-high heat. When the oil starts to shimmer, add the shrimp, season with salt, and sauté until the shrimp are cooked through, about 3 minutes. Remove from the pan and let cool.

2. Dust a work surface with the semolina flour, place the dough on the surface, and gently stretch it into a round. For more detailed instructions on properly stretching a ball of pizza dough see page 73. Cover the dough with the mozzarella and top with the pineapple. Season with salt and drizzle olive oil over the pizza.

3. Using a peel or a flat baking sheet, transfer the pizza to the heated baking implement in the oven. Bake for about 7 minutes, until the crust starts to brown. Remove the pizza, top it with the shrimp, drizzle olive oil over the pizza, and return it to the oven. Bake for about 5 minutes, until the crust is golden brown and starting to char. Remove and let cool slightly before slicing and serving.

INGREDIENTS:

OLIVE OIL, AS NEEDED

3.5 OZ. | 100 GRAMS SHRIMP, PEELED AND DEVEINED

SALT, TO TASTE

SEMOLINA FLOUR, AS NEEDED

1 BALL PIZZA DOUGH

3.5 OZ. | 100 GRAMS LOW-MOISTURE MOZZARELLA CHEESE, SHREDDED

2.4 OZ. | 70 GRAMS PINEAPPLE CHUNKS

QUARK & ZUCCHINI PIZZA

YIELD: 1 PIZZA / ACTIVE TIME: 25 MINUTES / TOTAL TIME: 50 MINUTES

Q .uark is a creamy, unripe cheese that is popular in Germany and Eastern Europe, and it is delightful when paired with fresh vegetables.

1. Preheat the oven to the maximum temperature and place a baking stone or steel on the middle rack as it warms. Coat the bottom of a skillet with olive oil and warm over medium-high heat. When the oil starts to shimmer, add the onion, season with salt and pepper, and sauté until the onion has softened, about 8 minutes. Remove from heat and let cool.

2. Dust a work surface with the semolina flour, place the dough on the surface, and gently stretch it into a round. For more detailed instructions on properly stretching a ball of pizza dough see page 73. Cover the dough with the mozzarella and top with dollops of the quark, the zucchini, and the onion. Season with salt and pepper and drizzle olive oil over the pizza.

3. Using a peel or a flat baking sheet, transfer the pizza to the heated baking implement in the oven. Bake for about 15 minutes, until the crust is golden brown and starting to char. Remove and let cool slightly before garnishing with the parsley, slicing, and serving.

INGREDIENTS:

OLIVE OIL, AS NEEDED

ONION, SEE PAGE THIN

[illegible]

[illegible]

[illegible]

2.1 OZ. | 60 GRAMS LOW-MOISTURE MOZZARELLA CHEESE, SHREDDED

1.75 OZ. | 50 GRAMS QUARK CHEESE

½ ZUCCHINI, SLICED THIN

FRESH PARSLEY, FINELY CHOPPED, FOR GARNISH

FOCACCIA TODAY

As seen in the Traditional Focaccia Recipes chapter, there is a wonderful and beautiful variety of focaccia throughout Italy, with this deep tradition shifting slightly depending on the character of specific regions. In recent times, a wider spectrum of toppings have started to be used, following the trend set by contemporary artisan pizza. And, compared to a normal-sized pizza, a focaccia has the advantage of feeding a whole horde with just one bake.

TOPPINGS

In the following pages we offer an essential selection of toppings for modern focaccia, but any of the toppings suggested in the Pizza Today chapter can be used.

To convert a pizza topping to the amounts needed for a large focaccia, simply multiply the amounts given in the pizza recipe by four (i.e., the 3.5 oz. | 100 grams of mozzarella cheese used on a pizza would become 14 oz. | 400 grams for a focaccia).

One general rule of thumb when making focaccia is to press some of the toppings into the dough before baking. This way the flavor will infuse the dough, making the end result even more delicious.

Another useful tip when adapting a pizza recipe to a focaccia is to use cheese that has been chopped into cubes rather than shredded. Using cubes of cheese will make it easier to press the cheese into the dough and ultimately, provide better results. It will also make the cheese slightly more heat-resistant, which is necessary for the longer baking times focaccia requires compared to pizza.

BAKING FOCACCIA

As focaccia has a thicker crust than pizza, it takes longer to bake. In terms of heat distribution, baking on a sheet pan or in a skillet is also less effective than baking directly on the stone. Therefore, the baking temperature for focaccia needs to be lower than that of pizza. The recommended oven temperature is around 445°F | 230°C, but if your oven is very efficient you may consider further reducing the temperature in order to ensure the focaccia gets baked evenly. (This also applies the other way around: a less effective oven may require higher temperatures.) The baking time is between 15 and 30 minutes depending on the thickness of the focaccia and the toppings. Thinner focaccias and white focaccias will cook faster than thicker focaccias and focaccias covered with tomato sauce or a thick layer of vegetables.

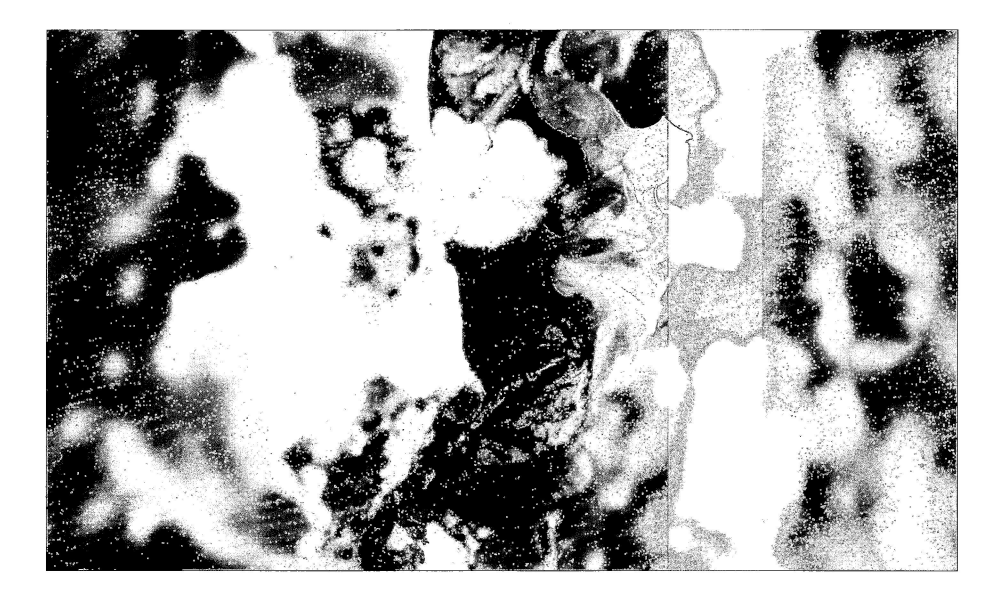

SMOKED CHICKEN, BUFALA & PESTO FOCACCIA

YIELD: 1 LARGE FOCACCIA / **ACTIVE TIME:** 45 MINUTES / **TOTAL TIME:** 3 HOURS

More a pan-pizza than a focaccia, these toppings are unconventional, but work really well together.

1. Once the dough has finished its initial rise, place it on a flour-dusted work surface and form it into a loose ball, making sure not to compress the core of the dough. Grease an 18 × 13–inch baking pan with olive oil, place the dough in the center, and gently stretch it into an oval. Brush the dough with olive oil, cover it with plastic wrap, and let rest at room temperature for 1 hour. Preheat the oven to 445°F (230°C).

2. Use your hands to flatten the dough and stretch it toward the edges of the pan. For more detailed instructions on properly stretching a ball of focaccia dough see page 73. When the dough is covering the pan, let it rest for 30 minutes.

3. In a small bowl, combine the pesto with the 2 tablespoons of olive oil and mix well. Cover the dough with the emulsion, distribute the cherry tomatoes over the top, press them into the dough, and drizzle olive oil over the focaccia.

4. Place the focaccia in the oven and bake for 15 to 20 minutes, until the focaccia starts to brown. Remove from the oven, top with the smoked chicken and mozzarella, drizzle olive oil over the focaccia, and return it to the oven. Bake for another 5 to 10 minutes, until the edges are crispy. Remove from the oven, top the focaccia with the arugula and balsamic glaze, and let it cool slightly before slicing and serving.

INGREDIENTS:

1 BATCH FOCACCIA DOUGH

ALL-PURPOSE FLOUR, AS NEEDED

3.5 OZ. | 100 GRAMS BASIL PESTO (SEE PAGE 365)

2 TABLESPOONS OLIVE OIL, PLUS MORE AS NEEDED

8.8 OZ. | 250 GRAMS CHERRY TOMATOES, HALVED

8.8 OZ. | 250 GRAMS SMOKED CHICKEN BREAST, TORN

13.2 OZ. | 375 GRAMS BUFFALO MOZZARELLA CHEESE, TORN

1.75 OZ. | 50 GRAMS ARUGULA

BALSAMIC GLAZE, TO TASTE

PEAR & RICOTTA FOCACCIA

YIELD: 1 LARGE FOCACCIA / **ACTIVE TIME:** 45 MINUTES / **TOTAL TIME:** 3 HOURS

An array of textures and flavors in this dish show focaccia doesn't necessarily need to take a backseat to pizza.

1. Once the dough has finished its initial rise, place it on a flour-dusted work surface and form it into a loose ball, making sure not to compress the core of the dough. Grease an 18 × 13–inch baking pan with olive oil, place the dough in the center, and gently stretch it into an oval. Brush the dough with olive oil, cover it with plastic wrap, and let rest at room temperature for 1 hour. Preheat the oven to 445°F (230°C).

2. Use your hands to flatten the dough and stretch it toward the edges of the pan. For more detailed instructions on properly stretching a ball of focaccia dough see page 73. When the dough is covering the pan, let it rest for 30 minutes.

3. Top the dough with the mozzarella, pressing the cheese partially into the dough. Season with salt and drizzle olive oil over the focaccia.

4. Place the focaccia in the oven and bake for 15 to 20 minutes, until the focaccia starts to brown. Remove from the oven, top with dollops of the ricotta, the walnuts, and the pears, drizzle olive oil over the focaccia, and return it to the oven. Bake for another 5 to 10 minutes, until the edges are crispy. Remove from the oven, top with the greens, drizzle honey over the top, and let the focaccia cool slightly before slicing and serving.

INGREDIENTS:

1 BATCH FOCACCIA DOUGH

ALL-PURPOSE FLOUR, AS NEEDED

OLIVE OIL, AS NEEDED

9 OZ. | 250 GRAMS FRESH MOZZARELLA CHEESE, CUBED

SALT, TO TASTE

8.8 OZ. | 250 GRAMS RICOTTA CHEESE

1.75 OZ. | 50 GRAMS WALNUTS, CHOPPED

1 LB. | 450 GRAMS PEARS, CORED AND SLICED

1.4 OZ. | 40 GRAMS ARUGULA OR OTHER GREENS

HONEY, WARMED, TO TASTE

FOCACCIA WITH PUMPKIN CREAM, ANCHOVIES & BURRATA

YIELD: 1 LARGE FOCACCIA / **ACTIVE TIME:** 1 HOUR / **TOTAL TIME:** 3 HOURS

A focaccia that will look as uniquely wonderful as it tastes.

INGREDIENTS:

1 BATCH FOCACCIA DOUGH

ALL-PURPOSE FLOUR, AS NEEDED

1 PUMPKIN, HALVED AND SEEDED

OLIVE OIL, AS NEEDED

SALT AND PEPPER, TO TASTE

FRESH THYME, TO TASTE

2.8 OZ. | 80 GRAMS ANCHOVIES

13.2 OZ. | 375 GRAMS BURRATA CHEESE, TORN

1. Once the dough has finished its initial rise, place it on a flour-dusted work surface and form it into a loose ball, making sure not to compress the core of the dough. Grease an 18 × 13–inch baking pan with olive oil, place the dough in the center, and gently stretch it into an oval. Brush the dough with olive oil, cover it with plastic wrap, and let rest at room temperature for 1 hour. Preheat the oven to 445°F (230°C).

2. Place the pumpkin halves cut-side up on a baking sheet, season with salt, and drizzle olive oil over them. Place in the oven and roast until the flesh is tender, about 30 minutes. Remove, let the pumpkin cool slightly, and then scrape 1 pound (450 grams) of the flesh into a food processor. Add olive oil, salt, and thyme to taste and blitz until the mixture is smooth and creamy. Set the pumpkin cream aside. Reserve any remaining pumpkin for another preparation.

3. Use your hands to flatten the dough and stretch it toward the edges of the pan. For more detailed instructions on properly stretching a ball of focaccia dough see page 73. When the dough is covering the pan, let it rest for 30 minutes.

4. Drizzle olive oil over the focaccia and season it with salt. Place it in the oven and bake for 15 to 20 minutes, until the focaccia starts to brown. Remove from the oven, top with the pumpkin cream and anchovies, drizzle olive oil over the top, and return the focaccia to the oven. Bake for another 5 to 10 minutes, until the edges are crispy. Remove from the oven, top the focaccia with the burrata, season it with pepper, and drizzle olive oil over the top. Let the focaccia cool slightly before slicing and serving.

SWEET POTATO & SAGE FOCACCIA

YIELD: 1 LARGE FOCACCIA / **ACTIVE TIME:** 1 HOUR / **TOTAL TIME:** 3 HOURS

The piney, citrus flavor of sage provides a lovely contrast to the sweet potatoes.

1. Once the dough has finished its initial rise, place it on a flour-dusted work surface and form it into a loose ball, making sure not to compress the core of the dough. Grease an 18 × 13–inch baking pan with olive oil, place the dough in the center, and gently stretch it into an oval. Brush the dough with olive oil, cover it with plastic wrap, and let rest at room temperature for 1 hour. Preheat the oven to 445°F (230°C).

2. Place the sweet potatoes on a baking sheet, season with salt, and drizzle olive oil over them. Place in the oven and roast until tender, about 40 minutes. Remove and let cool.

3. Use your hands to flatten the dough and stretch it toward the edges of the pan. For more detailed instructions on properly stretching a ball of focaccia dough see page 73. When the dough is covering the pan, let it rest for 30 minutes.

4. Top the dough with the roasted sweet potatoes, pressing the pieces into the dough. Season with the coarse-grained salt and drizzle olive oil generously over the focaccia.

5. Place the focaccia in the oven and bake for 20 to 25 minutes, until it is golden brown. Remove from the oven, top with the sage and goat cheese (if using), drizzle olive oil over the focaccia, and let cool slightly before slicing and serving.

INGREDIENTS:

1 BATCH FOCACCIA DOUGH

ALL-PURPOSE FLOUR, AS NEEDED

COARSE SEA SALT, TO TASTE

FRESH SAGE LEAVES, TO TASTE

12.3 OZ. | 350 GRAMS FRESH GOAT CHEESE, SLICED (OPTIONAL)

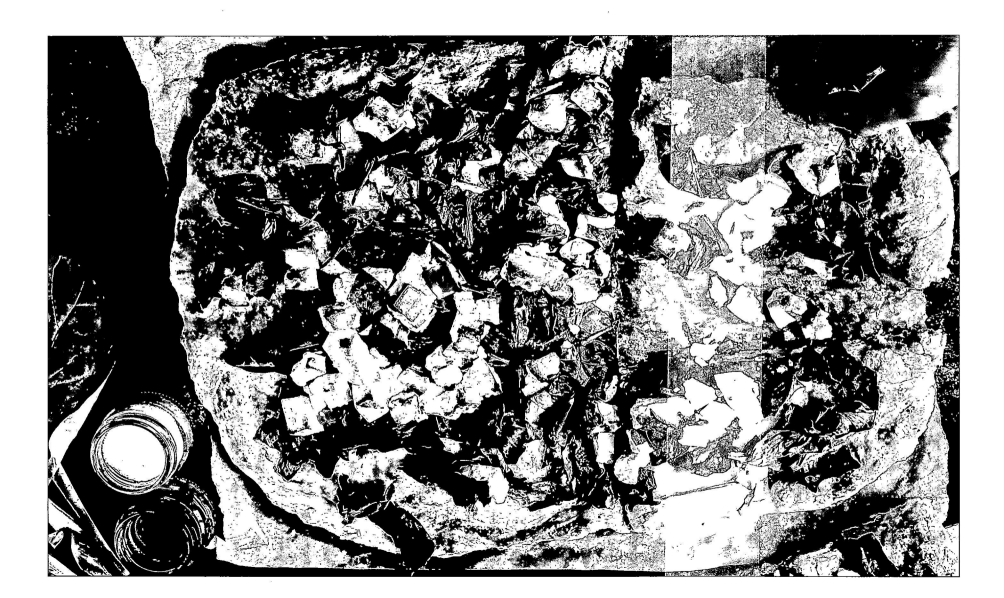

SPINACH & FETA FOCACCIA

YIELD: 1 LARGE FOCACCIA / **ACTIVE TIME:** 45 MINUTES / **TOTAL TIME:** 3 HOURS

Good on its own, but don't be afraid to pile additional toppings on this one, as spinach and feta make a great launching pad.

1. Once the dough has finished its initial rise, place it on a flour-dusted work surface and form it into a loose ball, making sure not to compress the core of the dough. Grease an 18 × 13–inch baking pan with olive oil, place the dough in the center, and gently stretch it into an oval. Brush the dough with olive oil, cover it with plastic wrap, and let rest at room temperature for 1 hour. Preheat the oven to 445°F (230°C).

2. Use your hands to flatten the dough and stretch it toward the edges of the pan. For more detailed instructions on properly stretching a ball of focaccia dough see page 73. When the dough is covering the pan, let it rest for 30 minutes.

3. Drizzle olive oil over the focaccia and season it with salt. Place the focaccia in the oven and bake for 15 to 20 minutes, until the focaccia starts to brown. Remove from the oven, top with the spinach and feta, season with salt and pepper, and drizzle olive oil over the focaccia.

4. Return to the oven and bake for another 5 to 10 minutes, until the edges are crispy. Remove from the oven and let the focaccia cool slightly before slicing and serving.

INGREDIENTS:

1 BATCH FOCACCIA DOUGH

ALL-PURPOSE FLOUR, AS NEEDED

OLIVE OIL, AS NEEDED

SALT AND PEPPER, TO TASTE

8.8 OZ. | 250 GRAMS FRESH SPINACH

12.3 OZ. | 350 GRAMS FETA CHEESE, CUBED

FOCACCIA WITH OLIVES & LEMON

YIELD: 1 LARGE FOCACCIA / **ACTIVE TIME:** 45 MINUTES / **TOTAL TIME:** 3 HOURS

Italy looks across the Mediterranean to Greece for the toppings on this focaccia.

1. Once the dough has finished its initial rise, place it on a flour-dusted work surface and form it into a loose ball, making sure not to compress the core of the dough. Grease an 18 × 13–inch baking pan with olive oil, place the dough in the center, and gently stretch it into an oval. Brush the dough with olive oil, cover it with plastic wrap, and let rest at room temperature for 1 hour. Preheat the oven to 445°F (230°C).

2. Use your hands to flatten the dough and stretch it toward the edges of the pan. For more detailed instructions on properly stretching a ball of focaccia dough see page 73. When the dough is covering the pan, let it rest for 30 minutes.

3. Drizzle olive oil over the focaccia and season with the coarse-grained salt. Press the olives into the dough and then top it with the lemon slices and rosemary.

4. Drizzle olive oil over the focaccia, place it in the oven, and bake for 20 to 25 minutes, until the focaccia is golden brown. Remove, season with salt and pepper, and let cool slightly before cutting and serving.

INGREDIENTS:

1 BATCH FOCACCIA DOUGH

ALL-PURPOSE FLOUR, AS NEEDED

1½ LEMONS, SLICED THIN

LEAVES FROM 6 SPRIGS FRESH ROSEMARY

BLACK PEPPER, TO TASTE

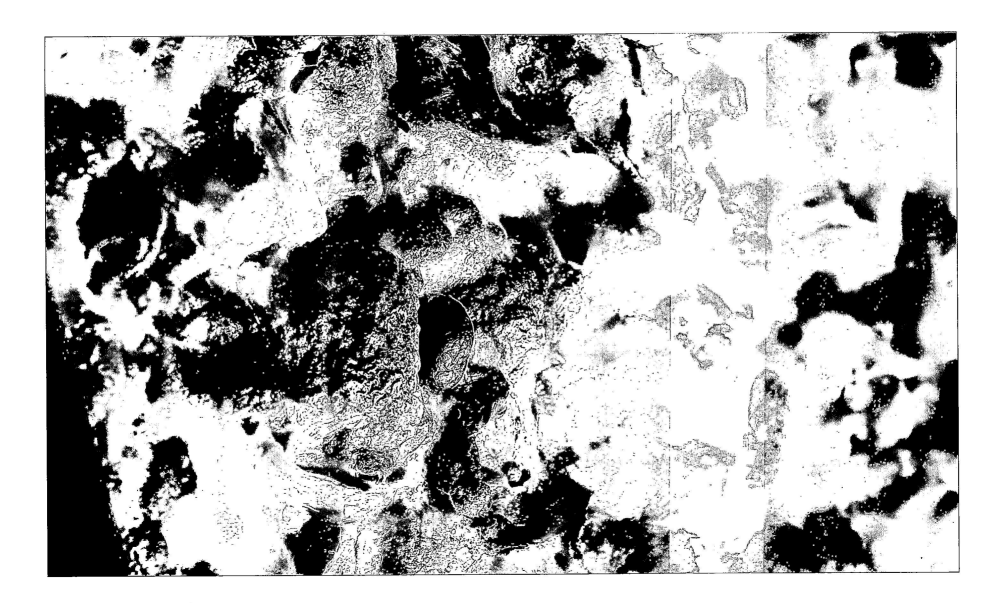

HAM & ARTICHOKE FOCACCIA

YIELD: 1 LARGE FOCACCIA / **ACTIVE TIME:** 45 MINUTES / **TOTAL TIME:** 3 HOURS

B y now, you're so used to liberally sprinkling salt over the preparations in this book that you're probably reaching for it as you read this. Refrain in this instance, as the ham, olives, and artichokes provide plenty.

1. Once the dough has finished its initial rise, place it on a flour-dusted work surface and form it into a loose ball, making sure not to compress the core of the dough. Grease an 18 × 13–inch baking pan with olive oil, place the dough in the center, and gently stretch it into an oval. Brush the dough with olive oil, cover it with plastic wrap, and let rest at room temperature for 1 hour. Preheat the oven to 445°F (230°C).

2. Use your hands to flatten the dough and stretch it toward the edges of the pan. For more detailed instructions on properly stretching a ball of focaccia dough see page 73. When the dough is covering the pan, let it rest for 30 minutes.

3. Drizzle olive oil over the focaccia and press the cubes of mozzarella into the dough. Top with the olives, ham, artichokes, and provolone and drizzle olive oil over the focaccia.

4. Place the focaccia in the oven and bake for 20 to 25 minutes, until the focaccia is golden brown. Remove from the oven and let the focaccia cool slightly before slicing and serving.

INGREDIENTS:

1 BATCH FOCACCIA DOUGH

ALL-PURPOSE FLOUR, AS NEEDED

OLIVE OIL, AS NEEDED

13.2 OZ. | 375 GRAMS LOW-MOISTURE MOZZARELLA CHEESE, CUBED

3.5 OZ. | 100 GRAMS PITTED BLACK OLIVES

7 OZ. | 200 GRAMS SLICED HAM, CHOPPED

10.6 OZ. | 300 GRAMS ARTICHOKE HEARTS, CHOPPED

2.8 OZ. | 80 GRAMS PROVOLONE CHEESE, SHREDDED

PIZZA AL TAGLIO

Pizza al taglio has ruled Rome since the 1970s. Nowadays, this "pizza on the go" is conquering new territo-
ries every day, as it is one of the hottest trends in the
pizza scene.

PIZZA AL TAGLIO WITH BUFALA, EGGPLANT & GARLIC

YIELD: 1 LARGE FOCACCIA / **ACTIVE TIME:** 1 HOUR / **TOTAL TIME:** 3 HOURS AND 30 MINUTES

For pizza al taglio, you can bake the toppings with the dough, as in most pizzas and traditional focaccias, or bake the dough before adding the toppings, which is becoming increasingly popular. By baking the dough ahead of time, the focaccia can support a larger amount of toppings.

INGREDIENTS:

BASIC FOCACCIA DOUGH (SEE PAGE 84)

ALL-PURPOSE FLOUR, AS NEEDED

OLIVE OIL, AS NEEDED

14 OZ. | 400 GRAMS EGGPLANT, SLICED

SALT, TO TASTE

6 GARLIC CLOVES, MINCED

RED PEPPER FLAKES, TO TASTE

13.2 OZ. | 375 GRAMS BUFFALO MOZZARELLA CHEESE, DRAINED AND TORN

1 OZ. | 30 GRAMS FRESH PARSLEY LEAVES, CHOPPED

1. Once the dough has finished its initial rise, place it on a flour-dusted work surface and form it into a loose ball, making sure not to compress the core of the dough. Grease an 18 × 13–inch baking pan with olive oil, place the dough in the center, and gently stretch it into an oval. Brush the dough with olive oil, cover it with plastic wrap, and let rest at room temperature for 1 hour. Preheat the oven to 445°F (230°C).

2. Preheat a gas or charcoal grill to medium heat. Place the eggplant in a mixing bowl, drizzle olive oil over it, and season it with salt. Toss to combine and place the eggplant on the grill. Cook until it is tender and charred all over, about 8 minutes. Remove and let cool.

3. Use your hands to flatten the dough and stretch it toward the edges of the pan. For more detailed instructions on properly stretching a ball of focaccia dough see page 73.

4. Drizzle olive oil over the focaccia and let rest at room temperature for another 30 minutes.

5. Season the focaccia with salt, place it in the oven, and bake for 20 to 25 minutes, until the edges of the focaccia are slightly crispy.

6. While the focaccia is in the oven, coat the bottom of a skillet with olive oil and warm it over medium-high heat. When it starts to shimmer, add the garlic, season with salt and red pepper flakes, and sauté until it just starts to brown, about 2 minutes. Remove from heat and set it aside.

7. Remove the focaccia from the oven and let it cool slightly. Top it with the buffalo mozzarella, parsley, eggplant, and garlic, drizzle olive oil over the top, slice, and serve.

PEPPER, PINE NUT & RAISIN PIZZA AL TAGLIO

YIELD: 1 LARGE FOCACCIA / **ACTIVE TIME:** 45 MINUTES / **TOTAL TIME:** 3 HOURS AND 30 MINUTES

Sweet raisins were made to complement roasted peppers and the buttery texture of pine nuts.

INGREDIENTS:

BASIC FOCACCIA DOUGH (SEE PAGE 84)

ALL-PURPOSE FLOUR, AS NEEDED

SALT, TO TASTE

1. Once the dough has finished its initial rise, place it on a flour-dusted work surface and form it into a loose ball, making sure not to compress the core of the dough. Grease an 18 × 13-inch baking pan with olive oil, place the dough in the center, and gently stretch it into an oval. Brush the dough with olive oil, cover it with plastic wrap, and let rest at room temperature for 1 hour. Preheat the oven to 445°F (230°C).

2. Use your hands to flatten the dough and stretch it toward the edges of the pan. For more detailed instructions on properly stretching a ball of focaccia dough see page 73.

3. Drizzle olive oil over the focaccia and let it rest at room temperature for another 30 minutes.

4. Place the raisins in a bowl, cover them with water, and let them soak for 30 minutes. Drain, pat dry, and set the raisins aside.

5. Place the focaccia in the oven and bake for 20 to 25 minutes, until the edges are slightly crispy. Remove the focaccia from the oven and let it cool slightly. Distribute the roasted peppers, pine nuts, and raisins over the top, season with salt and olive oil, slice, and serve.

PIZZA AL TAGLIO WITH WILD MUSHROOMS & TWO CHEESES

YIELD: 1 LARGE FOCACCIA / **ACTIVE TIME:** 1 HOUR / **TOTAL TIME:** 3 HOURS AND 30 MINUTES

This preparation suggests sautéing the mushrooms, but don't hesitate to roast them in the oven before adding them to the focaccia.

1. Once the dough has finished its initial rise, place it on a flour-dusted work surface and form it into a loose ball, making sure not to compress the core of the dough. Grease an 18 × 13–inch baking pan with olive oil, place the dough in the center, and gently stretch it into an oval. Brush the dough with olive oil, cover it with plastic wrap, and let rest at room temperature for 1 hour. Preheat the oven to 445°F (230°C).

2. Use your hands to flatten the dough and stretch it toward the edges of the pan. For more detailed instructions on properly stretching a ball of focaccia dough see page 73.

3. Drizzle olive oil over the focaccia and let it rest at room temperature for another 30 minutes.

4. Season the focaccia with salt, place it in the oven and bake for 20 to 25 minutes, until the edges are slightly crispy.

5. While the focaccia is in the oven, coat the bottom of a skillet with olive oil and warm it over medium-high heat. When it starts to shimmer, add the mushrooms, season with salt, and sauté until they start to brown, about 10 minutes. Remove from heat and let cool.

6. Remove the focaccia from the oven and let it cool slightly. Top with the caciocavallo, mozzarella, parsley, red pepper flakes, and sautéed mushrooms, slice, and serve.

INGREDIENTS:

BASIC FOCACCIA DOUGH (SEE PAGE 84)

ALL-PURPOSE FLOUR, AS NEEDED

OLIVE OIL, AS NEEDED

SALT, TO TASTE

14 OZ. | 400 GRAMS WILD MUSHROOMS

7 OZ. | 200 GRAMS CACIOCAVALLO CHEESE, SLICED

13.2 OZ. | 375 GRAMS BUFFALO MOZZARELLA CHEESE, DRAINED AND TORN

1 OZ. | 30 GRAMS FRESH PARSLEY LEAVES, CHOPPED

RED PEPPER FLAKES, TO TASTE

PIZZA AL TAGLIO WITH ROMAINE, SALAMI & PARMESAN

YIELD: 1 LARGE FOCACCIA / **ACTIVE TIME:** 45 MINUTES / **TOTAL TIME:** 3 HOURS

The famously fresh taste of romaine lettuce takes just enough of the edge off the salami and Parmesan.

1. Once the dough has finished its initial rise, place it on a flour-dusted work surface and form it into a loose ball, making sure not to compress the core of the dough. Grease an 18 × 13-inch baking pan with olive oil, place the dough in the center, and gently stretch it into an oval. Brush the dough with olive oil, cover it with plastic wrap, and let rest at room temperature for 1 hour. Preheat the oven to 445°F (230°C).

2. Use your hands to flatten the dough and stretch it toward the edges of the pan. For more detailed instructions on properly stretching a ball of focaccia dough see page 73.

3. Cover the dough with the sauce and drizzle olive oil over the top. Let the focaccia rest at room temperature for another 30 minutes.

4. Place the focaccia in the oven and bake for 20 to 25 minutes, until the edges are slightly crispy. Remove from the oven and let the focaccia cool slightly. Distribute the lettuce, salami, and Parmesan over the top, drizzle with olive oil, slice, and serve.

INGREDIENTS:

(SEE PAGE 103)

5.3 OZ. | 150 GRAMS ROMAINE LETTUCE, CHOPPED

11.3 OZ. | 320 GRAMS ITALIAN SALAMI, SLICED

3.5 OZ. | 100 GRAMS PARMESAN CHEESE, GRATED

PIZZA AL TAGLIO WITH PROSCIUTTO

YIELD: 1 LARGE FOCACCIA / **ACTIVE TIME:** 45 MINUTES / **TOTAL TIME:** 3 HOURS AND 30 MINUTES

A classic Roman pizza topping that is always in fashion.

1. Once the dough has finished its initial rise, place it on a flour-dusted work surface and form it into a loose ball, making sure not to compress the core of the dough. Grease an 18 × 13–inch baking pan with olive oil, place the dough in the center, and gently stretch it into an oval. Brush the dough with olive oil, cover it with plastic wrap, and let rest at room temperature for 1 hour. Preheat the oven to 445°F (230°C).

2. Use your hands to flatten the dough and stretch it toward the edges of the pan. For more detailed instructions on properly stretching a ball of focaccia dough see page 73.

3. Cover the dough with the sauce and drizzle olive oil over it. Let the focaccia rest at room temperature for another 30 minutes.

4. Place the focaccia in the oven and bake for 20 to 25 minutes, until the edges are slightly crispy. Remove the focaccia from the oven and let it cool slightly. Distribute the prosciutto and mozzarella over the focaccia, season with pepper and olive oil, and garnish with the basil.

INGREDIENTS:

BASIC FOCACCIA DOUGH (SEE PAGE 84)

ALL-PURPOSE FLOUR, AS NEEDED

OLIVE OIL, AS NEEDED

14 OZ. | 400 GRAMS RAW PIZZA SAUCE (SEE PAGE 103)

11.3 OZ. | 320 GRAMS PROSCIUTTO, SLICED THIN

8.8 OZ. | 250 GRAMS FRESH BOCCONCINI, HALVED

SALT AND PEPPER, TO TASTE

FRESH BASIL LEAVES, FOR GARNISH

SHRIMP, ARUGULA & OLIVE PIZZA AL TAGLIO

YIELD: 1 LARGE FOCACCIA / **ACTIVE TIME:** 50 MINUTES / **TOTAL TIME:** 3 HOURS AND 30 MINUTES

Y ou could just as easily go without the sauce here, as the mélange of flavors in the toppings is worth savoring in full.

1. Once the dough has finished its initial rise, place it on a flour-dusted work surface and form it into a loose ball, making sure not to compress the core of the dough. Grease an 18 × 13–inch baking pan with olive oil, place the dough in the center, and gently stretch it into an oval. Brush the dough with olive oil, cover it with plastic wrap, and let rest at room temperature for 1 hour. Preheat the oven to 445°F (230°C).

2. Use your hands to flatten the dough and stretch it toward the edges of the pan. For more detailed instructions on properly stretching a ball of focaccia dough see page 73.

3. Cover the dough with the sauce and drizzle olive oil over the top. Let the focaccia rest at room temperature for another 30 minutes.

4. Place the focaccia in the oven and bake for 20 to 25 minutes, until the edges are slightly crispy.

5. While the focaccia is in the oven, coat the bottom of a skillet with olive oil and warm it over medium-high heat. When it starts to shimmer, add the shrimp, season with salt, and cook until the shrimp are just cooked through, about 3 minutes. Remove from heat and set them aside.

6. Remove the focaccia from the oven and let it cool slightly. Distribute the arugula, olives, mozzarella, and shrimp over the focaccia, slice, and serve.

INGREDIENTS:

BASIC FOCACCIA DOUGH (SEE PAGE 84)

ALL-PURPOSE FLOUR, AS NEEDED

SEMOLINA, AS NEEDED

SALT, TO TASTE

1 CUP TOMATO BASIL PIZZA SAUCE (SEE PAGE 103)

14 OZ. | 400 GRAMS JUMBO SHRIMP, PEELED AND DEVEINED

3.5 OZ. | 100 GRAMS ARUGULA

3.5 OZ. | 100 GRAMS PITTED GREEN OLIVES, SLICED

11.3 OZ. | 320 GRAMS BUFFALO MOZZARELLA CHEESE, DRAINED AND TORN

PIZZA ALLA PALA

Pizza alla pala uses the crust of traditional pizza bianca and the toppings of pizza al taglio, making for a crunchier and somewhat more refined version of the latter.

PIZZA ALLA PALA WITH PROSCIUTTO & ENDIVE

YIELD: 1 MEDIUM FOCACCIA / **ACTIVE TIME:** 25 MINUTES / **TOTAL TIME:** 3 HOURS

The smoky bitterness of the grilled endive is perfectly balanced by the faint sweetness of the prosciutto and the mild tang of the buffalo mozzarella.

1. Prepare the Pizza Bianca Romana.

2. While preparing the focaccia, preheat a gas or charcoal grill to medium-high heat. Place the endive in a mixing bowl, drizzle olive oil over it, and season with salt and pepper. Toss to combine and place the endive on the grill. Cook until it is charred all over, about 5 minutes. Remove, let cool slightly, and then chop it. Set the endive aside.

3. Remove the focaccia from the oven and let it cool slightly. Distribute the endive over the focaccia, drizzle olive oil over the endive, and top with the mozzarella and the prosciutto. Slice and serve.

INGREDIENTS:

½ BATCH PIZZA BIANCA ROMANA (SEE PAGE 181)

8.8 OZ. | 250 GRAMS ENDIVE

OLIVE OIL, AS NEEDED

SALT AND PEPPER, TO TASTE

8.8 OZ. | 250 GRAMS BUFFALO MOZZARELLA CHEESE, TORN

7 OZ. | 200 GRAMS PROSCIUTTO, SLICED

PIZZA ALLA PALA WITH ZUCCHINI BLOSSOMS, ANCHOVIES & BURRATA

YIELD: 1 MEDIUM FOCACCIA / **ACTIVE TIME:** 25 MINUTES / **TOTAL TIME:** 3 HOURS

Don't wrinkle your nose up at the inclusion of anchovies. When matched with zucchini blossoms and mozzarella, or better burrata, the flavors are out of this world delicious.

1. Prepare the Pizza Bianca Romana.

2. While the focaccia is in the oven, coat the bottom of a skillet with olive oil and warm over medium-high heat. When it starts to shimmer, add the zucchini blossoms and sauté until they start to wilt, about 2 minutes. Remove from heat and let cool.

3. Remove the focaccia from the oven and let it cool slightly. Cover the focaccia with the zucchini blossoms, top with the anchovies and the burrata, drizzle olive oil over the toppings, slice, and serve.

INGREDIENTS:

2.8 OZ. | 80 GRAMS ANCHOVIES, HALVED

8.8 OZ. | 250 GRAMS BURRATA CHEESE, TORN

SALT, TO TASTE

MORTADELLA, RICOTTA & PISTACHIO PIZZA ALLA PALA

YIELD: 1 MEDIUM FOCACCIA / **ACTIVE TIME:** 25 MINUTES / **TOTAL TIME:** 3 MINUTES

This focaccia is elevated by mortadella, and its saltiness is perfectly balanced by a topping of pistachio-flavored ricotta cheese.

1. Prepare the Pizza Bianca Romana.

2. Remove the focaccia from the oven and let it cool slightly. Drizzle olive oil over the focaccia, cover with the mortadella, and top with dollops of ricotta. Sprinkle the pistachios over the ricotta, slice, and serve.

INGREDIENTS:

½ BATCH PIZZA BIANCA ROMANA
(SEE PAGE 181)

7 OZ. | 200 GRAMS RICOTTA CHEESE

8.5 OZ. | 240 GRAMS MORTADELLA, SLICED

3.5 OZ. | 100 GRAMS PISTACHIOS, COARSELY
GROUND

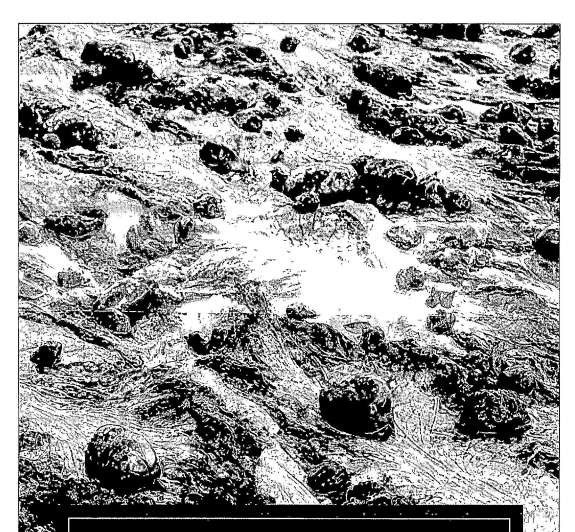

FOCACCIA ALLA SPIGAMADRE

In the Årsta neighborhood of Stockholm, Sweden, just around the corner from a beautiful park by the water, one can stumble in to my slightly off-the-beaten-path little Italian bakery. Since 2017, at Spigamadre we make bread, pastries, and focaccias based on one common denominator: long fermentation and carefully sourced ingredients. Our focaccias are light and soft, much like ones from the traditions of southern Italy. Our style, however, does not really adhere to any specific region but takes inspiration from all of them in different ways. Besides an incessant attention to fermentation, we emphasize the use of fresh but simple ingredients, with a special focus on vegetables. The most common ingredient, in fact, can gift us with an explosion of flavor so long as we prepare it with respect to its "essence." Here, to wrap up the focaccia recipes in this book, is a selection of some of our customers' favorites. I hope they will inspire you to experiment further and make your own focaccias "alla Spigamadre."

ENDIVE, OLIVE & CAPER ALLA SPIGAMADRE

YIELD: 1 LARGE FOCACCIA / **ACTIVE TIME:** 1 HOUR / **TOTAL TIME:** 3 HOURS AND 30 MINUTES

This is one of my all-time favorites, thanks to the escarole, which can create beautiful patterns when it is lovingly spread over a well-risen dough.

1. Once the dough has finished its initial rise, place it on a flour-dusted work surface and form it into a loose ball, making sure not to compress the core of the dough. Grease an 18 × 13–inch baking pan with olive oil, place the dough in the center, and gently stretch it into an oval. Brush the dough with olive oil, cover it with oiled plastic wrap, and let rest at room temperature for 1 hour. Preheat the oven to 445°F (230°C).

2. Use your hands to flatten the dough and stretch it toward the edges of the pan. For more detailed instructions on properly stretching a ball of focaccia dough see page 73.

3. Drizzle olive oil over the focaccia and let it rest at room temperature for another 30 minutes.

4. While the focaccia rests, blanch the endive leaves in salted boiling water. Drain almost immediately and rinse under cold water. Gently squeeze to remove any excess water and toss in a salad bowl with the olives, capers, and a generous drizzle of olive oil.

5. When the dough is ready, open the endive leaves and cover the focaccia. When all leaves are in place, drain the olives and capers and distribute them evenly over the endive, gently pressing the olives into the dough. Season with salt and drizzle the focaccia with olive oil.

6. Place the focaccia in the oven and bake for 20 to 25 minutes, until the edges are slightly crispy. Remove from the oven and let cool slightly before slicing and serving.

INGREDIENTS:

BASIC FOCACCIA DOUGH (SEE PAGE 84), OR PREFERRED FOCACCIA DOUGH

ALL-PURPOSE FLOUR, AS NEEDED

OLIVE OIL, AS NEEDED

SALT, TO TASTE

1 HEAD ENDIVE

7 OZ. | 200 GRAMS ITALIAN OR GREEK GREEN OLIVES, PITTED

3.5 OZ. | 100 GRAMS CAPERS

ZUCCHINI & FETA ALLA SPIGAMADRE

YIELD: 1 LARGE FOCACCIA / **ACTIVE TIME:** 1 HOUR / **TOTAL TIME:** 3 HOURS AND 30 MINUTES

My favorite Cretan dish, boureki, a lovely vegetarian casserole of zucchini and fresh local cheese flavored with mint, inspired this focaccia.

1. Once the dough has finished its initial rise, place it on a flour-dusted work surface and form it into a loose ball, making sure not to compress the core of the dough. Grease an 18 × 13–inch baking pan with olive oil, place the dough in the center, and gently stretch it into an oval. Brush the dough with olive oil, cover it with plastic wrap, and let rest at room temperature for 1 hour. Preheat the oven to 445°F (230°C).

2. Use your hands to flatten the dough and stretch it toward the edges of the pan. For more detailed instructions on properly stretching a ball of focaccia dough see page 73.

3. Drizzle olive oil over the focaccia and let it rest at room temperature for another 30 minutes.

4. Distribute the zucchini so that it covers the whole surface of the focaccia. Season with salt and generously drizzle with olive oil.

5. Place the focaccia in the oven and bake for 20 to 25 minutes, until the edges start to brown.

6. Remove the focaccia from the oven and top with the feta and mint leaves. Drizzle with olive oil, return to the oven, and bake for another 5 to 10 minutes, or until darker spots appear on the surface of the focaccia. Remove from the oven and let cool slightly before slicing and serving.

INGREDIENTS:

BASIC FOCACCIA DOUGH (SEE PAGE 84), OR
PREFERRED STORE-BOUGHT

ALL-PURPOSE FLOUR, AS NEEDED

OLIVE OIL, AS NEEDED

SALT, TO TASTE

2 ZUCCHINI, SLICED INTO THIN STRIPS LENGTHWISE

10.6 OZ. | 300 GRAMS FETA CHEESE, CRUMBLED

FRESH MINT LEAVES, TO TASTE

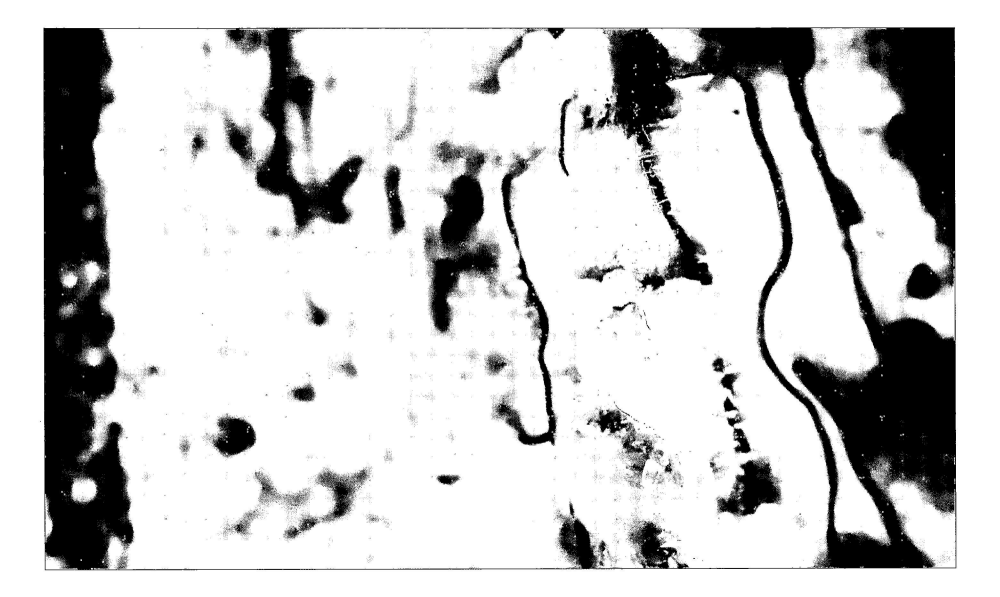

MARGHERITA ALLA SPIGAMADRE

YIELD: 1 LARGE FOCACCIA / **ACTIVE TIME:** 40 MINUTES / **TOTAL TIME:** 3 HOURS AND 30 MINUTES

At Spigamadre we call this focaccia "margherita delux," as it is inspired by the classic Neapolitan pizza topping, and made even more luscious by the addition of fresh greens and buffalo mozzarella before serving.

1. Once the dough has finished its initial rise, place it on a flour-dusted work surface and form it into a loose ball, making sure not to compress the core of the dough. Grease an 18 × 13–inch baking pan with olive oil, place the dough in the center, and gently stretch it into an oval. Brush the dough with olive oil, cover it with greased plastic wrap, and let rest at room temperature for 1 hour. Preheat the oven to 445°F (230°C).

2. Use your hands to flatten the dough and stretch it toward the edges of the pan. For more detailed instructions on properly stretching a ball of focaccia dough see page 73.

3. Drizzle olive oil over the focaccia and let it rest at room temperature for another 30 minutes.

4. Spread the sauce over the focaccia, distributing it with the tips of your fingers without deflating the dough. Drizzle with olive oil, place in the oven, and bake for about 20 to 25 minutes, until the edges start to brown.

5. Remove the focaccia from the oven and top with the mozzarella. Season with salt, drizzle with olive oil, return to the oven, and bake for another 5 to 10 minutes, or until the cheese is melted. Remove from the oven and let cool slightly.

6. Top with the salad greens, cherry tomatoes, and the buffalo mozzarella. Season with salt and drizzle with olive oil before slicing and serving.

INGREDIENTS:

BASIC FOCACCIA DOUGH (SEE PAGE 84), OR PREFERRED FOCACCIA DOUGH

ALL-PURPOSE FLOUR, AS NEEDED

OLIVE OIL, AS NEEDED

SALT, TO TASTE

21.1 OZ. | 600 GRAMS RAW PIZZA SAUCE (SEE PAGE 103)

OLIVE OIL, AS NEEDED

8.8 OZ. | 250 GRAMS LOW-MOISTURE MOZZARELLA CHEESE, TORN

2.1 OZ. | 60 GRAMS MIXED SALAD GREENS

7 OZ. | 200 GRAMS CHERRY TOMATOES, HALVED

8.8 OZ | 250 GRAMS BUFFALO MOZZARELLA CHEESE, TORN

SALT, TO TASTE

BROCCOLI & PINE NUT ALLA SPIGAMADRE

YIELD: 1 LARGE FOCACCIA / **ACTIVE TIME:** 1 HOUR / **TOTAL TIME:** 3 HOURS AND 30 MINUTES

Broccoli is one of the few vegetables always available in Sweden during the long winters, so we make the best of it by spicing it up with some pine nuts.

1. Once the dough has finished its initial rise, place it on a flour-dusted work surface and form it into a loose ball, making sure not to compress the core of the dough. Grease an 18 × 13–inch baking pan with olive oil, place the dough in the center, and gently stretch it into an oval. Brush the dough with olive oil, cover it with plastic wrap, and let rest at room temperature for 1 hour. Preheat the oven to 445°F (230°C).

2. Use your hands to flatten the dough and stretch it toward the edges of the pan. For more detailed instructions on properly stretching a ball of focaccia dough see page 73.

3. Drizzle olive oil over the focaccia and let it rest at room temperature for another 30 minutes.

4. Separate the individual broccoli florets and cut them in half. Distribute them over the focaccia, gently pressing them into the dough. Season with salt, generously drizzle with olive oil, and bake for about 20 to 25 minutes, until the edges start to brown.

5. Remove the focaccia from the oven and top with the pine nuts. Drizzle with olive oil, return to the oven, and bake for another 5 minutes, or until the crust looks to be evenly golden brown. Remove from the oven and let cool slightly before slicing and serving.

INGREDIENTS:

BASIC FOCACCIA DOUGH (SEE PAGE 84), OR [illegible] FOCACCIA DOUGH

[illegible]

[illegible]

[illegible]

[illegible] WATER

SALT, TO TASTE

3.5 OZ. | 100 GRAMS PINE NUTS

SALT, TO TASTE

POTATO & CACIOCAVALLO ALLA SPIGAMADRE

YIELD: 1 LARGE FOCACCIA / **ACTIVE TIME:** 1 HOUR / **TOTAL TIME:** 3 HOURS AND 30 MINUTES

Potatoes are among the most timeless toppings of Roman pizza. Here, in an homage to southern Italian focaccias, caciocavallo is added, making the potatoes even creamier.

1. Once the dough has finished its initial rise, place it on a flour-dusted work surface and form it into a loose ball, making sure not to compress the core of the dough. Grease an 18 × 13–inch baking pan with olive oil, place the dough in the center, and gently stretch it into an oval. Brush the dough with olive oil, cover it with greased plastic wrap, and let rest at room temperature for 1 hour. Preheat the oven to 445°F (230°C).

2. Use your hands to flatten the dough and stretch it toward the edges of the pan. For more detailed instructions on properly stretching a ball of focaccia dough see page 73.

3. Drizzle olive oil over the focaccia and let it rest at room temperature for another 30 minutes.

4. Distribute the potatoes so that they cover the whole surface of the focaccia. Season with salt, generously drizzle with olive oil, place in the oven, and bake for 20 to 25 minutes, until the edges start to brown.

5. Remove the focaccia from the oven and top with the caciocavallo. Drizzle with olive oil and return to the oven. Bake for another 5 to 10 minutes, or until the cheese is melted. Remove from the oven and let cool slightly before slicing and serving.

INGREDIENTS:

BASIC FOCACCIA DOUGH (SEE PAGE 84), OR PREFERRED FOCACCIA DOUGH

ALL-PURPOSE FLOUR, AS NEEDED

OLIVE OIL, AS NEEDED

SALT, TO TASTE

1 LB. | 450 GRAMS POTATOES, SLICED THIN AND BLANCHED IN SALTED WATER

8.8 OZ. | 250 GRAMS CACIOCAVALLO CHEESE, SLICED

SALADS AND SIDES

*P*izza on its own does make a meal. But it is also nice to balance out the richness of dough, sauce, cheese, and toppings with some crisp, citrusy, and sharp vegetal flavors and textures. Plus, the leftover dressings and sauces from these recipes are begging to be sopped up with a yummy crust.

Note: Because baking is about precision, the focaccia and pizza recipes in this book feature both imperial and metric measurements. The following recipes do not; see page 793 for the conversion chart.

ROASTED BABY BEET, RADISH & APPLE SALAD
WITH BLUE CHEESE MOUSSE

YIELD: 4 TO 6 SERVINGS / **ACTIVE TIME:** 30 MINUTES / **TOTAL TIME:** 1 HOUR AND 20 MINUTES

Baby beets are picked in the spring to thin the field and leave room for other beets to grow, an early harvest that results in a rich and delicate flavor. When you're working with something so uniquely delicious, it's important to keep it simple, and roasting these beets with a few aromatics is all they require.

Preheat the oven to 400°F.

Form three sheets of aluminum foil into pouches. Group the beets according to color and place each group into a pouch. Drizzle each with the olive oil and sprinkle with salt. Divide the whole sprigs of thyme, garlic, and water between the pouches and seal them. Place the pouches on a baking sheet, place in the oven, and cook until fork-tender, 45 minutes to 1 hour depending on the size of the beets. Remove the pouches from the oven and let cool. When cool enough to handle, peel the beets, cut into bite-sized pieces, and set aside.

3. Bring a pot of salted water to a boil and prepare an ice bath in a mixing bowl. Remove the greens from the radishes, wash them thoroughly, and set aside. Quarter the radishes.

4. Place the radishes in the boiling water, cook for 1 minute, and then transfer to the ice bath until completely cool. Drain and set aside.

5. Place the blue cheese, heavy cream, ricotta, and thyme leaves in a food processor and blitz until smooth. Set the mousse aside.

6. Place the beets, except for the red variety, in a salad bowl. Add the radishes, radish greens, and apples and toss to combine. Add half of the Honey Mustard Vinaigrette, season with salt and pepper, and toss to coat.

7. Spread the mousse on the serving dishes. Place the salad on top, sprinkle the red beets over the salad, drizzle with the remaining vinaigrette, and garnish with the honeycomb.

HONEY MUSTARD VINAIGRETTE

1. Place all of the ingredients, except for the olive oil, in a small mixing bowl and whisk to combine. Add the oil in a slow stream and whisk until incorporated.

INGREDIENTS

2 BABY BEETS, USE A MIX OF RED, GOLDEN, & PINK

3 TABLESPOONS OLIVE OIL

1 TABLESPOON KOSHER SALT, PLUS MORE TO TASTE

9 SPRIGS FRESH THYME, 6 LEFT WHOLE, LEAVES REMOVED FROM 3

6 GARLIC CLOVES

6 TABLESPOONS WATER

8 RADISHES WITH TOPS

¾ CUP BLUE CHEESE, AT ROOM TEMPERATURE

½ CUP HEAVY CREAM

½ CUP RICOTTA CHEESE, AT ROOM TEMPERATURE

2 APPLES, PEELED, CORED, AND DICED

¼ CUP HONEY MUSTARD VINAIGRETTE (SEE RECIPE)

BLACK PEPPER, TO TASTE

2 OZ. HONEYCOMB, FOR GARNISH

HONEY MUSTARD VINAIGRETTE
¼ CUP HONEY

2 TABLESPOONS WHOLE GRAIN MUSTARD

3 TABLESPOONS APPLE CIDER VINEGAR

1 TEASPOON KOSHER SALT

½ TEASPOON BLACK PEPPER

⅓ CUP OLIVE OIL

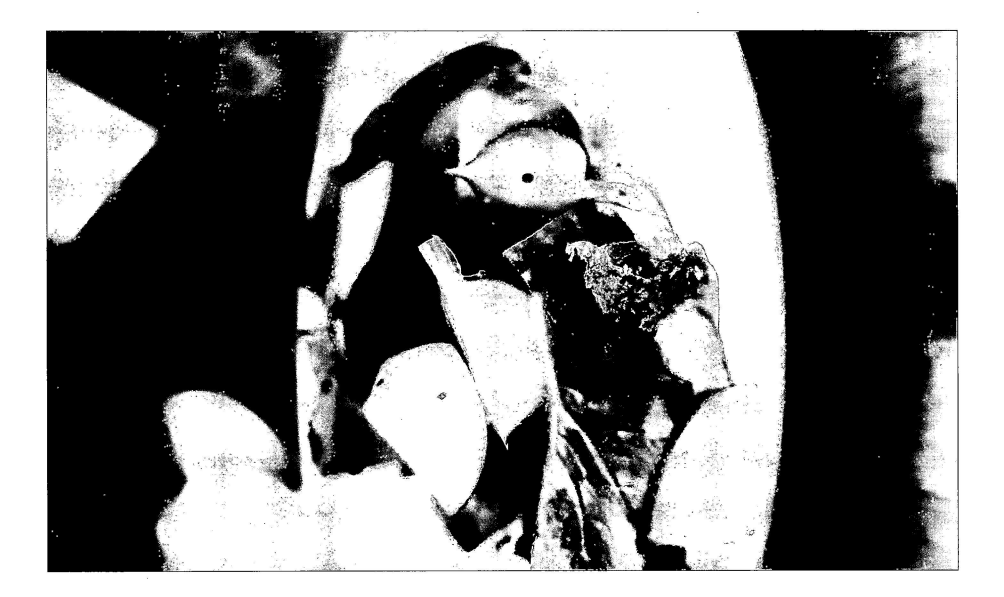

ARUGULA, NECTARINE, FARRO & GOAT CHEESE SALAD WITH WHITE BALSAMIC VINAIGRETTE

YIELD: 2 SERVINGS / **ACTIVE TIME:** 10 MINUTES / **TOTAL TIME:** 30 MINUTES

Arugula pairs beautifully with sweet fruit, and what better choice than a honey-sweet summer nectarine? I've topped this salad with a white balsamic dressing, which draws out the sweetness of the fruit. You can sub out the farro for wild rice with very good results.

In a medium-sized pot, bring 2 cups of water to a boil, add the farro, and then lower the heat and simmer for 15 minutes, or until all the liquid has been absorbed. Set aside to cool.

2. Whisk the vinegar, mustard, salt, pepper, and honey together in a mixing bowl. Once mixed, slowly drizzle in the olive oil to emulsify the vinaigrette. Set aside.

3. In a large bowl, gently toss the farro, nectarine, goat cheese, and cashews to combine. Add a few tablespoons of dressing to taste.

4. Put the arugula on a plate and top with the farro mixture. Add a little more vinaigrette to taste and serve.

½ TEASPOON KOSHER SALT

½ TEASPOON BLACK PEPPER

1 TEASPOON HONEY

½ CUP OLIVE OIL

1 RIPE NECTARINE, PITTED AND DICED

2 OZ. GOAT CHEESE, CRUMBLED

2 TABLESPOONS CHOPPED CASHEWS

2 HANDFULS OF ARUGULA

RED & GREEN CABBAGE SALAD
WITH GINGER & TAHINI DRESSING

YIELD: 2 SERVINGS / **ACTIVE TIME:** 15 MINUTES / **TOTAL TIME:** 15 MINUTES

This is a great recipe for the weekend after Thanksgiving, but it is also delicious enough to make anytime with sliced turkey from the deli. The zesty dressing pairs wonderfully with the cabbage, and the ginger notes tie it all together.

1. Place all of the ingredients, except for the Ginger & Tahini Dressing and the turkey, in a bowl and combine. Add the Ginger & Tahini Dressing and toss to coat. Taste and add more dressing if desired. Add the turkey, toss to evenly distribute, and serve.

GINGER & TAHINI DRESSING

1. Combine all of the ingredients in a bowl and whisk vigorously until combined.

INGREDIENTS:

2 CUPS THINLY SLICED GREEN CABBAGE

2 CUPS THINLY SLICED RED CABBAGE

3 TABLESPOONS CHOPPED PEANUTS

3 SCALLIONS, TRIMMED AND CHOPPED

½ CUP CHOPPED FRESH CILANTRO OR PARSLEY

¼ CUP GINGER & TAHINI DRESSING (SEE RECIPE), PLUS MORE TO TASTE

¼ LB. COOKED TURKEY, DICED

GINGER & TAHINI DRESSING

3 TABLESPOONS FRESH LEMON JUICE

2 TABLESPOONS SOY SAUCE

2 TABLESPOONS TAHINI

1 TEASPOON MAPLE SYRUP

1 TEASPOON GRATED GINGER

1 TEASPOON RICE VINEGAR

1 TEASPOON TOASTED SESAME OIL

½ CUP OLIVE OIL

RAW BEET SALAD WITH BLOOD ORANGE, JALAPEÑO & BRIE

YIELD: 4 TO 6 SERVINGS / **ACTIVE TIME:** 20 TO 30 MINUTES / **TOTAL TIME:** 2½ TO 24 HOURS

This salad riffs on the traditional beet-and-goat cheese salad by switching out the goat cheese for creamy Brie. Leaving the beets raw and grating and marinating them both tenderizes and flavors the roots.

1. Place the beet greens and stems in a bowl of ice water to remove any dirt.

2. Place the grated beets and the jalapeño in a salad bowl.

3. Remove the beet greens and stems from the ice water and dice the stems. Set the greens aside. Add the beet stems to the salad bowl. Add the salt and stir.

4. Take the blood orange segments and add to the salad bowl, being sure to remove any membranes from the fruit. Squeeze the juice from the remnants of the orange into the bowl.

5. In a separate small bowl, whisk the olive oil, honey, and vinegar together and pour over the beet mixture.

6. Cover the salad bowl and refrigerate for at least 2 hours. For best results, leave in the refrigerator overnight.

7. Combine the beet greens with the arugula and place them in the salad bowl with the grated beet mixture. Toss to combine, top with the Brie, and serve.

TIP: Beets, while delicious, stain everything they touch. Make sure that whatever bowl you grate the beets into is big enough to put a box grater inside. This will prevent the beets from spilling and staining everything. When cooking with beets, it is best to use stainless steel or glass cookware.

INGREDIENTS:

5 TO 7 RED BEETS, PEELED AND GRATED, STEMS AND GREENS RESERVED

1 JALAPEÑO PEPPER, STEMMED, SEEDED TO TASTE, AND MINCED

½ TEASPOON KOSHER SALT

ZEST, SEGMENTS, AND JUICE OF 1 BLOOD ORANGE

3 TABLESPOONS OLIVE OIL

3 TABLESPOONS HONEY

1 TABLESPOON RICE VINEGAR

2 LBS. ARUGULA

½ LB. BRIE CHEESE, SLICED AND AT ROOM TEMPERATURE

ROASTED BRASSICA SALAD WITH PICKLED RAMPS & BUTTERMILK CAESAR DRESSING

YIELD: 4 TO 6 SERVINGS / ACTIVE TIME: 20 MINUTES / TOTAL TIME: 35 MINUTES

Broccoli, Brussels sprouts, and cauliflower are only a few of the fine members of the brassica family. Charring them brings out their sweet side, which pairs wonderfully with the creamy and slightly acidic dressing.

Bring a large pot of salted water to a boil. Add the cauliflower, cook for 1 minute, remove with a slotted spoon, and transfer to a paper towel–lined plate. Wait for the water to return to a boil, add the broccoli, and cook for 30 seconds. Use a slotted spoon to remove the broccoli and let the water drip off before transferring it to the paper towel–lined plate.

2. Place the olive oil and Brussels sprouts, cut-side down, in a large cast-iron skillet. Add the broccoli and cauliflower, season with salt and pepper, and cook over high heat without moving the vegetables. Cook until charred, turn over, and cook until charred on that side. Remove and transfer to a bowl.

3. Add the Pickled Ramps and Buttermilk Caesar Dressing to the bowl and toss to evenly coat. Garnish with Parmesan and red pepper flakes and serve.

PICKLED RAMPS

1. Place all of the ingredients, except for the ramps, in a small saucepan and bring to a boil over medium heat.

2. Add the ramps, reduce heat, and simmer for 1 minute. Transfer to a mason jar, cover with aluminum foil, and let cool completely. Once cool, cover with a lid and store in the refrigerator for up to 1 week.

BUTTERMILK CAESAR DRESSING

1. Place all of the ingredients in a food processor and blitz until combined. Season to taste and serve.

¼ CUP OLIVE OIL

¼ LB. BRUSSELS SPROUTS, TRIMMED AND HALVED

SALT AND PEPPER, TO TASTE

10 PICKLED RAMPS (SEE RECIPE)

BUTTERMILK CAESAR DRESSING (SEE RECIPE)

PARMESAN CHEESE, GRATED, FOR GARNISH

RED PEPPER FLAKES, FOR GARNISH

PICKLED RAMPS
½ CUP CHAMPAGNE VINEGAR

½ CUP WATER

¼ CUP SUGAR

1½ TEASPOONS KOSHER SALT

¼ TEASPOON FENNEL SEEDS

¼ TEASPOON CORIANDER SEEDS

⅛ TEASPOON RED PEPPER FLAKES

10 SMALL RAMP BULBS

BUTTERMILK CAESAR DRESSING
1 LARGE GARLIC CLOVE, MINCED

2 ANCHOVY FILLETS

⅔ CUP MAYONNAISE

¼ CUP BUTTERMILK

¼ CUP GRATED PARMESAN CHEESE

ZEST OF 1 LEMON

1 TEASPOON WORCESTERSHIRE SAUCE

1 TEASPOON KOSHER SALT, PLUS MORE TO TASTE

½ TEASPOON BLACK PEPPER, PLUS MORE TO TASTE

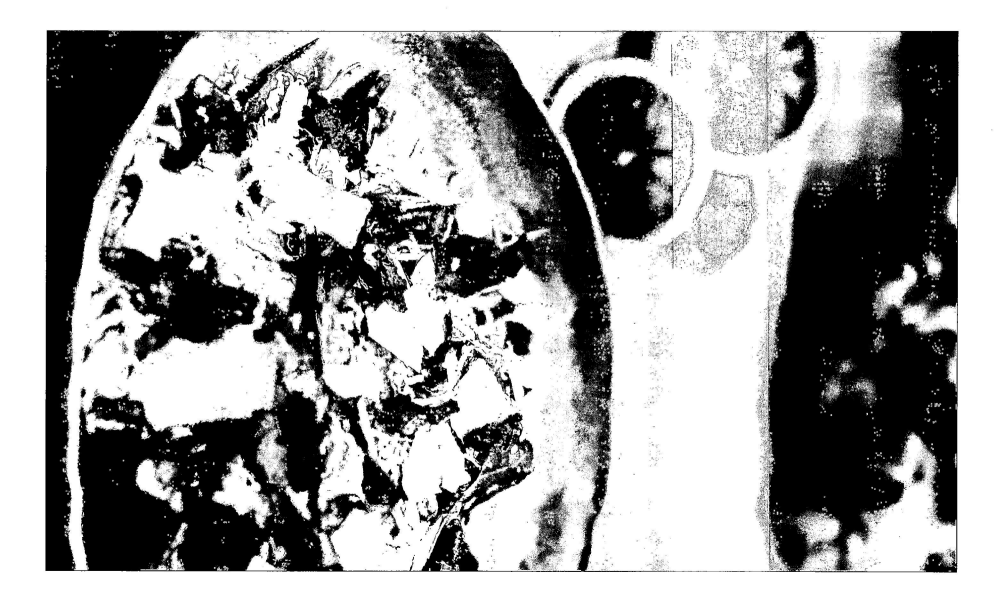

SHAVED BRUSSELS SPROUTS & KALE SALAD WITH BLOOD ORANGE VINAIGRETTE

YIELD: 4 TO 6 SERVINGS / **ACTIVE TIME:** 10 MINUTES / **TOTAL TIME:** 25 MINUTES

Brussels sprouts are as delicious raw as they are cooked, and pairing their robust, savory flavor with bright citrus is the perfect way to play up that attribute.

1. Place the bacon in a sauté pan and cook over medium heat until crisp, about 8 minutes. Transfer to a paper towel–lined plate to drain. When cool enough to handle, chop into bite-sized pieces.

2. Remove the skin from the segments of the blood orange and cut each segment in half. Place in a mixing bowl, add the Brussels sprouts and kale, season with salt and pepper, and toss to combine. Add the Blood Orange Vinaigrette, toss to evenly coat, and season to taste.

3. Plate the salad, top with the bacon, garnish with the toasted pecans and Parmesan, and serve with the remaining vinaigrette on the side.

BLOOD ORANGE VINAIGRETTE

1. Place all of the ingredients, except for the olive oil, in a blender. Blitz on high and add the oil in a slow stream. Blitz until the mixture has emulsified and season to taste.

INGREDIENTS:

½ LB. BACON, SLICED

3 BLOOD ORANGES, PEELED

1 LB. BRUSSELS SPROUTS, TRIMMED AND SLICED VERY THIN WITH A MANDOLINE

2 CUPS PACKED BABY KALE

SALT AND PEPPER, TO TASTE

⅔ CUP BLOOD ORANGE VINAIGRETTE (SEE RECIPE)

½ CUP TOASTED PECANS, FOR GARNISH

PARMESAN CHEESE, SHAVED, FOR GARNISH

BLOOD ORANGE VINAIGRETTE

½ CUP BLOOD ORANGE JUICE (ABOUT 2 BLOOD ORANGES)

½ TEASPOON KOSHER SALT

¼ TEASPOON BLACK PEPPER

1½ TABLESPOONS APPLE CIDER VINEGAR

1 TABLESPOON HONEY

1 ICE CUBE

1 CUP OLIVE OIL

MELON, CUCUMBER & PROSCIUTTO SALAD
WITH MINT VINAIGRETTE

YIELD: 4 TO 6 SERVINGS / **ACTIVE TIME:** 15 MINUTES / **TOTAL TIME:** 40 MINUTES

The versatile melon can comfortably straddle the sweet-savory divide. Here it pairs up with crispy cured prosciutto and creamy feta to carry this dynamic salad.

1 Preheat the oven to 350°F.

· Place the prosciutto on a parchment-lined baking sheet. Cover with another sheet of parchment paper and place another baking sheet that is the same size on top. Place in the oven and bake until the prosciutto is crisp, about 12 minutes. Remove from the oven and let cool. When the prosciutto is cool enough to handle, chop it into bite-sized pieces.

3. Place the cantaloupe, honeydew melon, and cucumber in a salad bowl, season with salt and pepper, and toss to combine. Add the jalapeño and Mint Vinaigrette and toss until evenly coated. Plate the salad, top with the chopped prosciutto and feta, and garnish with the mint leaves.

MINT VINAIGRETTE

1. Place all of the ingredients in a mixing bowl and whisk until thoroughly combined.

INGREDIENTS

[illegible]

[illegible]

[illegible]

[illegible]

SALT AND PEPPER, TO TASTE

1 JALAPEÑO PEPPER, STEMMED, SEEDED TO TASTE, AND SLICED

MINT VINAIGRETTE (SEE RECIPE), TO TASTE

⅔ CUP CRUMBLED FETA CHEESE

FRESH MINT LEAVES, CHOPPED, FOR GARNISH

MINT VINAIGRETTE
3 TABLESPOONS FINELY CHOPPED FRESH MINT

¼ CUP OLIVE OIL

3 TABLESPOONS APPLE CIDER VINEGAR

1 TABLESPOON HONEY

2 TEASPOONS DICED SHALLOT

1 TEASPOON KOSHER SALT

¼ TEASPOON BLACK PEPPER

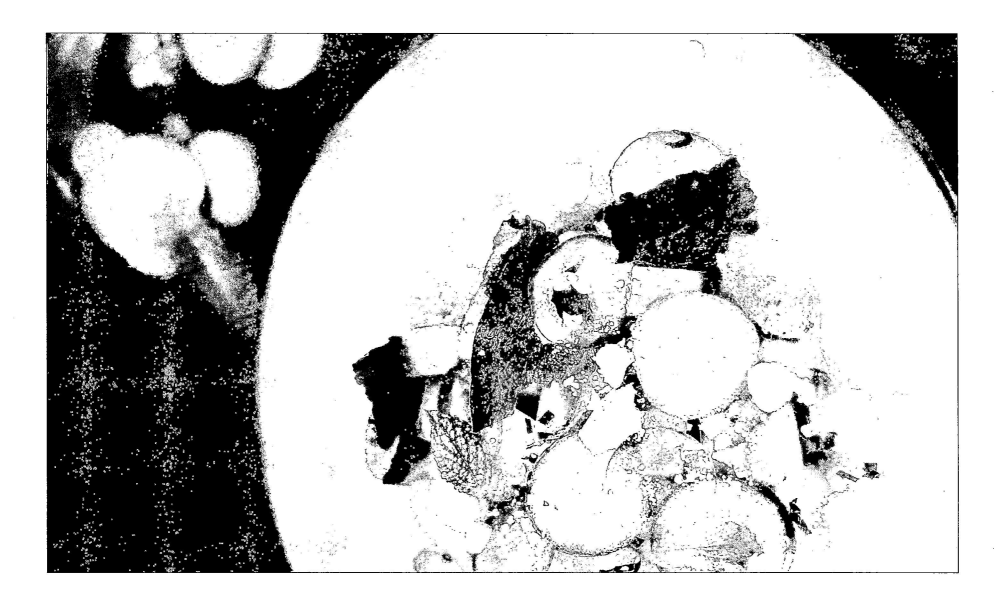

FENNEL, GRAPEFRUIT & PISTACHIO SALAD

YIELD: 2 SERVINGS / **ACTIVE TIME:** 10 MINUTES / **TOTAL TIME:** 10 MINUTES

While this may seem like an odd combination, the individual flavors meld together into a simple salad that was made for those days when you just don't feel like cooking.

1. Place the fennel and grapefruit in a bowl, drizzle with the olive oil, add the salt, season with pepper, and then add the pistachios. Toss to combine and serve.

To supreme a citrus fruit, trim the top and bottom from a piece of citrus and place it cut-side up. Cut along the contour of the fruit to remove the pith and peel. Cut one segment, lengthwise, between the pulp and the membrane. Make a similar slice on the other side of the segment and then remove the pulp. Set aside and repeat with the remaining segments.

INGREDIENTS:

½ LARGE FENNEL BULB, TRIMMED, CORED

BLACK PEPPER, TO TASTE

2 TABLESPOONS CHOPPED PISTACHIOS

LATE SUMMER SALAD WITH WILD MUSHROOMS, PARMESAN & PINE NUTS

YIELD: 2 TO 4 SERVINGS / **ACTIVE TIME:** 25 MINUTES / **TOTAL TIME:** 35 MINUTES

The trick to searing mushrooms is to give them plenty of room in the pan and not disturb them. This gets them nice and brown. Adding a light sprinkling of salt will help them release excess moisture as well, which further concentrates the flavor.

1. Coat the bottom of a saucepan with some of the olive oil and warm over medium-high heat. When the oil starts to shimmer, add the mushrooms, taking care not to crowd the pan. Sprinkle a pinch of salt over the mushrooms and then let them cook undisturbed until they release their liquid and begin to brown, about 6 minutes. Gently turn them over to sear the other side. When they are done, remove from the pan and set aside.

2. Place the onion and garlic in the pan, adding an additional splash of oil if the pan looks dry. Cook over medium heat until the onion has softened, about 5 minutes. Turn off heat and deglaze the pan with the vinegar, scraping off any browned bits from the bottom of the pan. Remove from heat and let the pan cool to room temperature.

3. Place the pine nuts in a dry skillet and toast over medium heat for 2 minutes, shaking the pan frequently so as not to burn the pine nuts. Transfer to a bowl and let cool.

4. Place the cooled onion-and-garlic mixture in a bowl and add the remaining oil. Whisk until combined and season with salt.

5. Arrange the greens on plates and top with the mushrooms, pine nuts, and a light sprinkling of Parmesan and dill. Top with the dressing and serve.

INGREDIENTS:

½ CUP OLIVE OIL, PLUS MORE AS NEEDED

½ LB. WILD MUSHROOMS, SLICED

SALT, TO TASTE

¼ CUP DICED RED ONION

1 GARLIC CLOVE, CHOPPED

¼ CUP BALSAMIC VINEGAR

1 TABLESPOON PINE NUTS

MESCLUN GREENS, FOR SERVING

2 TABLESPOONS GRATED PARMESAN CHEESE

CHOPPED DILL, TO TASTE

ROASTED RADICCHIO, PEAR & GORGONZOLA SALAD

YIELD: 4 SERVINGS / **ACTIVE TIME:** 15 MINUTES / **TOTAL TIME:** 40 MINUTES

Cooking radicchio mellows it considerably, and as long as you are roasting it, you may as well roast the pears, too. This recipe is really more of an outline, as you should assemble this salad to your taste.

1. Preheat the oven to 400°F. Place the radicchio and pear on a baking sheet and drizzle with olive oil. Place in the oven and roast until they start to brown, about 10 minutes. Remove from the oven and let cool.

Build the salad on individual plates by putting greens, arugula, radicchio, pear, and hazelnuts on each one. Top with Gorgonzola and drizzle with balsamic vinegar and olive oil. Season with salt and pepper and serve.

INGREDIENTS:

MESCLUN GREENS, AS NEEDED

ARUGULA, TO TASTE

¼ CUP CHOPPED HAZELNUTS

2 OZ. GORGONZOLA CHEESE

BALSAMIC VINEGAR, TO TASTE

SALT AND PEPPER, TO TASTE

RADICCHIO & RICOTTA SALATA SALAD WITH APPLE CIDER VINAIGRETTE

YIELD: 4 SERVINGS / **ACTIVE TIME:** 10 MINUTES / **TOTAL TIME:** 10 MINUTES

This is a salad designed to wake up the palate. The bitter radicchio counters the sweet apple and fennel. The key is to slice everything very fine, so all of the flavors can fit on the fork. The vinaigrette is the perfect sweet-tart topper, cutting through the smokiness of the grilled chicken for an irresistible finish.

1. Arrange the greens on four plates and top with equal amounts of radicchio, fennel, apple, and the ricotta salata. Top with the chicken, if using, and serve with the Apple Cider Vinaigrette.

APPLE CIDER VINAIGRETTE

1. Place all of the ingredients in a jar, shake until thoroughly combined, and serve.

INGREDIENTS:

3½ CUPS MESCLUN GREENS

½ HEAD RADICCHIO, CORED AND SLICED VERY THIN

½ LARGE FENNEL, TRIMMED AND SLICED VERY THIN

1 APPLE, CORED, SEEDED, AND SLICED THIN

2 OZ. RICOTTA SALATA CHEESE

2 CHICKEN BREASTS, GRILLED AND SLICED (OPTIONAL)

APPLE CIDER VINAIGRETTE (SEE RECIPE), FOR SERVING

APPLE CIDER VINAIGRETTE

3 TABLESPOONS APPLE CIDER VINEGAR

½ CUP OLIVE OIL

½ TEASPOON SEA SALT

½ TEASPOON BLACK PEPPER

1 TEASPOON HONEY

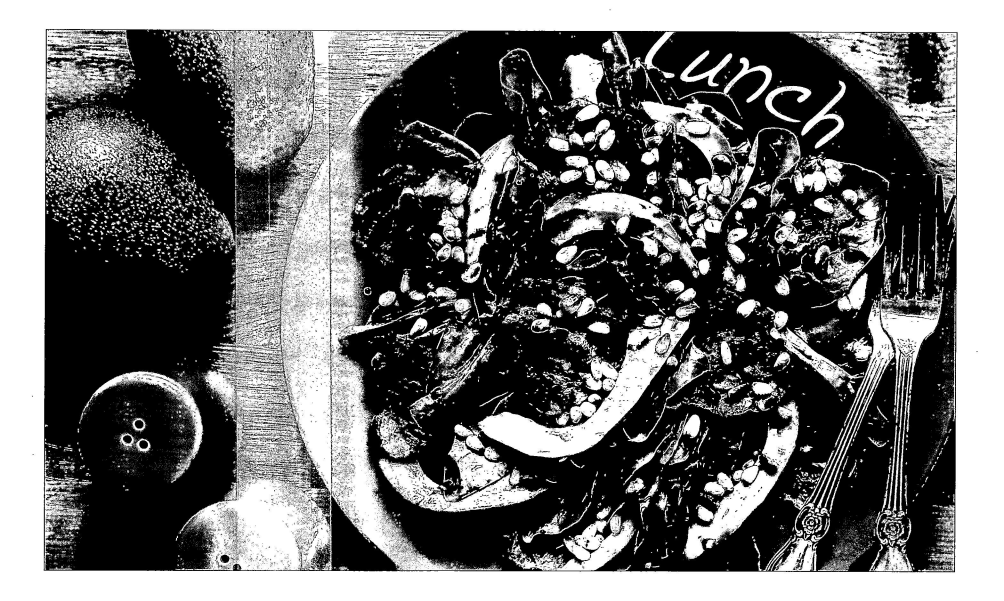

SPINACH, BACON, AVOCADO & ORANGE SALAD

YIELD: 4 SERVINGS / **ACTIVE TIME:** 15 MINUTES / **TOTAL TIME:** 15 MINUTES

Spinach-and-bacon salad is a classic preparation. In my house, I add segmented oranges, avocado, and sunflower seeds and toss it all in a moderately sweet dressing. If you want to make it vegetarian, switch out the bacon for sautéed shiitake mushrooms. There is enough going on in this salad to make a meal of it, perhaps with some leftover focaccia on the side.

1. Place the spinach in a large salad bowl. Add the supremed orange pieces to the salad bowl, reserving one piece.

2. Squeeze the reserved orange segment over the avocado slices to prevent browning and add the avocado to the salad bowl. Add the Red Wine & Maple Vinaigrette, toss to coat, and top the salad with the bacon and sunflower seeds before serving.

RED WINE & MAPLE VINAIGRETTE

1. Place all of the ingredients in a small jar and shake until combined.

INGREDIENTS:

5 OZ. BABY SPINACH

1 NAVEL ORANGE, SUPREMED (SEE PAGE 654)

FLESH FROM 1 AVOCADO, SLICED

RED WINE & MAPLE VINAIGRETTE (SEE RECIPE)

4 SLICES BACON, COOKED AND CRUMBLED

1 TABLESPOON SUNFLOWER SEEDS

RED WINE & MAPLE VINAIGRETTE
½ CUP OLIVE OIL

2 TABLESPOONS RED WINE VINEGAR

1 TEASPOON DIJON MUSTARD

1 TEASPOON MAPLE SYRUP

SALT AND PEPPER, TO TASTE

CHILLED CORN SALAD

YIELD: 4 TO 6 SERVINGS / **ACTIVE TIME:** 15 MINUTES / **TOTAL TIME:** 4 TO 24 HOURS

This recipe is a riff on the classic Mexican dish known as *esquites*.

1. Preheat the oven to 400°F.

2. Place the corn on a baking sheet and roast in the oven until it turns a light golden brown, about 35 minutes.

3. Remove the corn from the oven, let cool slightly, and then transfer to a large mixing bowl. Add the remaining ingredients and stir to combine.

4. Place the salad in the refrigerator for at least 3 hours, although letting it chill overnight is highly recommended.

TIP: The amount of jalapeño suggested in the ingredients is a safe amount of heat to accommodate a broad spectrum of tastes. If you and yours like things spicier, feel free to include the seeds or another jalapeño.

INGREDIENTS:

2 CUPS CORN KERNELS

2 TABLESPOONS UNSALTED BUTTER

[illegible]

[illegible]

2 TABLESPOONS MAYONNAISE

2 TEASPOONS GARLIC POWDER

3 TABLESPOONS SOUR CREAM OR MEXICAN CREMA

¼ TEASPOON CAYENNE PEPPER

¼ TEASPOON CHILI POWDER

2 TABLESPOONS FETA CHEESE

2 TABLESPOONS COTIJA CHEESE

2 TEASPOONS FRESH LIME JUICE

½ CUP CHOPPED FRESH CILANTRO

BLACK PEPPER, TO TASTE

ROASTED BRUSSELS SPROUTS WITH BACON, BLUE CHEESE & PICKLED RED ONION

YIELD: 4 TO 6 SERVINGS / **ACTIVE TIME:** 15 MINUTES / **TOTAL TIME:** 40 MINUTES

Brussels sprouts have a bad reputation with a lot of folks, but when seared and seasoned well, their savory, nutty flavor is a revelation, able to go toe-to-toe with rich ingredients like bacon and blue cheese.

1. Place the vinegar, water, sugar, and salt in a saucepan and bring to a boil. Place the onion in a bowl and pour the boiling liquid over the slices. Cover and allow to cool completely.

2. Place the bacon in a large sauté pan over medium heat and cook, stirring occasionally, until crisp, about 8 minutes. Transfer to a paper towel–lined plate and leave the rendered fat in the pan.

3. Place the Brussels sprouts in the pan cut-side down, season with salt and pepper, and cook over medium heat until they are a deep golden brown, about 7 minutes.

4. Transfer the Brussels sprouts to a platter, top with the pickled onions, bacon, and blue cheese, and serve.

INGREDIENTS:

1 CUP CHAMPAGNE VINEGAR

1 CUP WATER

½ CUP SUGAR

2 TEASPOONS KOSHER SALT, PLUS MORE TO TASTE

1 SMALL RED ONION, SLICED

½ LB. BACON, CUT INTO 1-INCH PIECES

1½ LBS. BRUSSELS SPROUTS, TRIMMED AND HALVED

BLACK PEPPER, TO TASTE

4 OZ. BLUE CHEESE, CRUMBLED

SAUTÉED RED CABBAGE WITH APPLES, FENNEL & BALSAMIC

YIELD: 4 SERVINGS / ACTIVE TIME: 25 MINUTES / TOTAL TIME: 30 MINUTES

This is a lovely dish for fall, when the weather cools. It is very easy to make vegan by substituting olive oil for the butter.

1. Place the cabbage in a large sauté pan with a tablespoon of the butter and the water. Bring to a boil and cover the pan. Let the cabbage steam until the thick ribs are tender, 5 to 8 minutes, then remove the lid and cook until the water has evaporated.

2. Add the remaining butter, the apple, fennel seeds, and pinches of salt and pepper. Reduce heat to medium-low and cook, stirring occasionally.

3. When the apples and cabbage have caramelized, add the vinegar, cook for another minute, and serve.

1 TEASPOON FENNEL SEEDS

SALT AND PEPPER, TO TASTE

1 TABLESPOONS BALSAMIC VINEGAR

SAUTÉED RADICCHIO
WITH BEANS, PARMESAN & BALSAMIC

YIELD: 4 SERVINGS / **ACTIVE TIME:** 1 HOUR / **TOTAL TIME:** 5 TO 24 HOURS

There are many good companions to radicchio, and among them are mild, creamy beans. You can use any type of dry bean in this dish, but I would choose a medium-sized one like Jacob's Cattle or Cannellini. The Parmesan and balsamic are considered condiments for this dish, so add as much or as little as you like. If you have a fun, infused balsamic, like fig or pear, this would be a good opportunity to use it.

1. Place the beans in a colander and rinse with cold water. Place them in a pot, cover with 1 inch of water, and leave to soak for at least 4 hours and ideally overnight.

2. Drain the beans, place them in a small saucepan, cover with water, and bring to a boil. Reduce to a simmer and cook for 30 minutes, checking every so often to make sure there is enough liquid in the pan. When the beans are tender but not mushy, remove from heat and let cool.

3. Place the olive oil in a sauté pan, warm over medium heat, and add the radicchio. Sauté until it starts to wilt and brown, about 3 minutes. Add the shallot and garlic and cook until everything is browned and the garlic is fragrant, about 5 minutes. Deglaze the pan with the wine and stock.

4. Drain the beans and add them to the radicchio mixture. Season with salt and pepper, stir in the thyme, and cook until most of the liquid has evaporated. Remove the pan from heat. Serve warm or at room temperature, topped with Parmesan and a splash of balsamic vinegar.

INGREDIENTS:

⅔ CUP DRIED BEANS

1 TABLESPOON OLIVE OIL

1 SMALL HEAD RADICCHIO, CORED AND SLICED THIN

1 SHALLOT, DICED

1 GARLIC CLOVE, MINCED

¼ CUP WHITE WINE

¼ CUP CHICKEN OR VEGETABLE STOCK

SALT AND PEPPER, TO TASTE

½ TEASPOON CHOPPED FRESH THYME

PARMESAN CHEESE, GRATED, FOR GARNISH

BALSAMIC VINEGAR, FOR GARNISH

STEAMED JAPANESE EGGPLANT
WITH BLACK BEAN GARLIC SAUCE & BASIL

YIELD: 4 SERVINGS / **ACTIVE TIME:** 30 MINUTES / **TOTAL TIME:** 45 MINUTES

This recipe is a great way to showcase the lovely, delicate flavor of steamed Japanese eggplant. The sauce is made from fermented black beans and garlic and is intense and salty. You can find a jarred version in the Asian section of the supermarket. Thai basil is the best accompaniment for this dish, but if you can't find any, Italian basil will work fine.

1. Place 1 inch of water in a saucepan, set a steaming tray above it, and bring the water to a boil.

2. Place the eggplant in the steaming tray and steam until tender, 5 to 8 minutes. Remove from heat and place on a serving plate.

3. Place the garlic and shallot in a small saucepan with enough olive oil to coat the bottom. Sauté over medium heat until the vegetables start to brown, about 5 minutes.

4. Add the black bean garlic sauce, soy sauce, and vinegar and stir until the sauce starts to thicken. If the sauce thickens so much that it becomes lumpy, add water 1 teaspoon at a time.

5. Taste, adjust the seasoning as needed, remove from heat, and pour the sauce over the eggplant. Garnish with the basil and serve.

INGREDIENTS

2 LBS. JAPANESE EGGPLANT, SLICED LENGTHWISE AND HALVED

1 GARLIC CLOVE, SLICED

1 TABLESPOON MINCED SHALLOT

OLIVE OIL, AS NEEDED

2 TABLESPOONS BLACK BEAN GARLIC SAUCE

2 TEASPOONS SOY SAUCE

2 TEASPOONS RICE VINEGAR

WATER, AS NEEDED

8 FRESH BASIL LEAVES, SHREDDED, FOR GARNISH

SOUTHERN COLLARD GREENS

YIELD: 4 TO 6 SERVINGS / **ACTIVE TIME:** 30 MINUTES / **TOTAL TIME:** 2 HOURS AND 30 MINUTES

The inspiration for this recipe, Phillip Barr, a celebrated restauranteur in Hilton Head, South Carolina, passed along some useful information regarding the long cook time: When you think they are done, just keep cooking them.

1. Place the olive oil in a large saucepan and warm over medium-high heat. When the oil starts to shimmer, add the onion and sauté until translucent, about 3 minutes. Add the ham, reduce heat to medium, and cook until the ham starts to brown, about 5 minutes.

2. Add the remaining ingredients, stir to combine, and cover the pan. Braise the collard greens until they are very tender, about 2 hours. Check on the collards every so often and add water if all of the liquid has evaporated.

INGREDIENTS:

3 LBS. COLLARD GREENS, STEMS REMOVED, CHOPPED

2 CUPS VEGETABLE STOCK

¼ CUP APPLE CIDER VINEGAR

1 TABLESPOON BROWN SUGAR

1 TEASPOON RED PEPPER FLAKES

KALE WITH GARLIC, RAISINS & LEMON

YIELD: 4 SERVINGS / **ACTIVE TIME:** 10 MINUTES / **TOTAL TIME:** 25 MINUTES

This is a quick, healthy, and delicious dish.

1. Place the olive oil in a wide sauté pan and warm over medium heat. Once it is shimmering, add the kale and cook, stirring occasionally, until it starts to wilt, about 5 minutes.

2. Add the garlic and cook until it starts to brown, about 2 minutes.

3. Add the raisins and deglaze the pan with the water, stirring constantly and scraping up any browned bits from the bottom of the pan. Cook until the water evaporates, about 5 minutes. Season with salt and pepper and serve with lemon wedges.

INGREDIENTS:

1 TABLESPOON OLIVE OIL

½ LB. LACINATO OR RED RUSSIAN KALE, STEMS REMOVED, CHOPPED

2 GARLIC CLOVES, MINCED

¼ CUP RAISINS

¼ CUP WATER

SALT AND PEPPER, TO TASTE

LEMON WEDGES, FOR SERVING

ROASTED PARSNIPS & CARROTS WITH RAS EL HANOUT & HONEY

YIELD: 4 SERVINGS / **ACTIVE TIME:** 20 MINUTES / **TOTAL TIME:** 40 MINUTES

Roasting brings out the best in parsnips and carrots, and adding honey and spice at the end only enhances the deep flavor already there. Ras el hanout is a North African spice blend. Much like Indian curry, there is no official recipe, but it often contains cardamom, cumin, nutmeg, mace, cinnamon, ginger, chilies, allspice, and salt. It's best to adjust your seasonings to taste as you go, to avoid oversalting.

1. Preheat the oven to 400°F. Place the parsnips and carrots in a roasting pan in one layer, add the olive oil and salt, and toss to coat. Place in the oven and roast for 20 minutes, or until browned.

2. Remove the pan from the oven and pile the vegetables in the center. Drizzle the honey over the top and toss to coat. Sprinkle the ras el hanout over the top and toss to coat.

3. Return the pan to the oven and roast for another 5 to 10 minutes, making sure the vegetables do not burn. Remove from the oven and serve immediately.

INGREDIENTS:

4 LARGE PARSNIPS, PEELED, TRIMMED, AND CORED

4 LARGE CARROTS, PEELED AND SLICED LENGTHWISE

2 TABLESPOONS OLIVE OIL

SALT, TO TASTE

2 TABLESPOONS HONEY

1 TABLESPOON RAS EL HANOUT

YU CHOY WITH GARLIC & SOY

YIELD: 4 SERVINGS / **ACTIVE TIME:** 10 MINUTES / **TOTAL TIME:** 15 MINUTES

S teaming yu choy keeps it tender and light. If the stalks are large, leave them to cook a little longer.

1. Place the yu choy in a sauté pan large enough to fit all of the stalks, cover with the water, cover the pan, and cook over high heat.

2 After about 5 minutes, check the thickest stalk to see if it is tender. If not, cook until it is. Once tender, add the olive oil and the garlic. Sauté until the garlic is fully cooked but not browned, about 2 minutes.

3. Add the vinegar and soy sauce, toss to combine, and serve.

INGREDIENTS:

½ TABLESPOON RICE VINEGAR

1 TABLESPOON SOY SAUCE

YU CHOY WITH BLACK BEAN GARLIC SAUCE & EXTRA GARLIC

YIELD: 4 SERVINGS / ACTIVE TIME: 15 MINUTES / TOTAL TIME: 20 MINUTES

Black bean garlic sauce is perfect with steamed yu choy because a spoonful makes for an intense, instant sauce.

Place the yu choy in a sauté pan large enough to fit all the greens, add the water, cover the pan, and cook over high heat.

After about 5 minutes, remove the lid and cook until most of the water cooks off.

3. Add the olive oil and garlic and stir-fry until the garlic is fragrant, about 2 minutes.

4. Add the black bean garlic sauce, stir to coat, and cook until heated through. Serve immediately.

1 GARLIC CLOVE, MINCED

1 TABLESPOON BLACK BEAN GARLIC SAUCE

ZUCCHINI WITH TOMATOES, FETA, GARLIC & LEMON

YIELD: 4 SERVINGS / **ACTIVE TIME:** 25 MINUTES / **TOTAL TIME:** 45 MINUTES

This is a great way of preparing zucchini fresh from the garden. The key is to not crowd the squash in the pan; otherwise, they will steam instead of brown. You can substitute yellow summer squash or pattypan squash; just cut them into pieces of a similar size so they cook at the same rate.

1. Place the olive oil in a large sauté pan and warm over medium-high heat. When it starts to shimmer, add the zucchini, making sure not to overcrowd the pan. Let the zucchini brown, turn them over, then brown on the other sides. Season with salt and pepper. If it is necessary to cook in batches, set the browned zucchini aside and repeat, adding oil if the pan starts to look dry.

2. Return any zucchini to the pan and add the garlic. Cook until the garlic starts to soften, about 3 minutes. Add the tomato, cook for 1 more minute to heat everything through, and transfer the mixture to a platter.

3. Sprinkle the feta and parsley on top, season with lemon juice, and serve.

INGREDIENTS:

1 TABLESPOON OLIVE OIL, PLUS MORE AS NEEDED

3 ZUCCHINI, CHOPPED

SALT AND PEPPER, TO TASTE

2 GARLIC CLOVES, CHOPPED

1 LARGE TOMATO, DICED

2 OZ. FETA CHEESE, CRUMBLED

2 TABLESPOONS CHOPPED FRESH PARSLEY

FRESH LEMON JUICE, TO TASTE

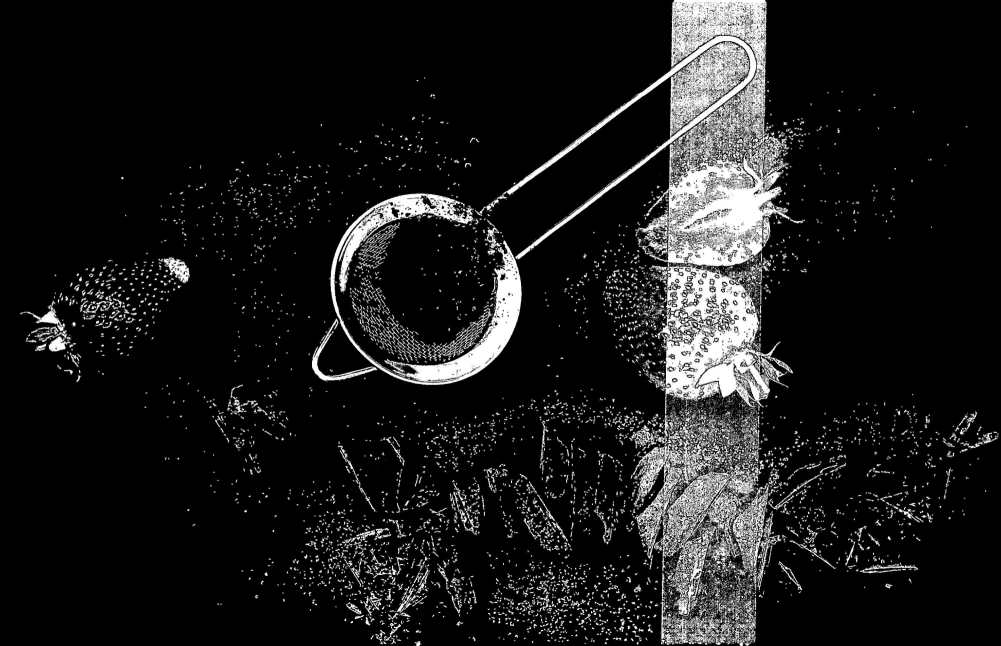

DESSERTS

*T*he dessert pizza is a novelty, but you'll find lots of familiar combinations in this chapter, like the Cinnamon Apple Pizza (see page 699). Think of these as deconstructed traditional desserts—and remember, there's nothing wrong with whimsy, especially when it tastes good and satisfies sweet-tooth cravings.

MARBLE PIZZA

YIELD: 1 PIZZA / **ACTIVE TIME:** 25 MINUTES / **TOTAL TIME:** 1 HOUR AND 30 MINUTES

This recipe is incredibly addictive, so make sure you're very fond of whoever you prepare it for. Chances are, they'll be coming around quite a bit.

1. Place the cream cheese, butter, and sugar in a mixing bowl and beat with a handheld mixer until the mixture is fluffy.

Place the pudding and milk in a separate bowl and stir until combined. Fold in the whipped cream and then stir the pudding mixture into the cream cheese mixture. Stir until thoroughly combined. Place the bowl in the refrigerator and chill for at least 1 hour.

3. Preheat the oven to the maximum temperature and place a baking stone or steel on the middle rack of the oven as it warms. Dust a work surface with the semolina flour, place the dough on the surface, and gently stretch it into a round. For more detailed instructions on properly stretching a ball of pizza dough see page 73.

4. Using a peel or a flat baking sheet, transfer the pizza to the heated baking implement in the oven. Bake for about 15 minutes, until the crust is golden brown and starting to char. Remove and let cool slightly before spreading the cream cheese-and-pudding mixture on top, slicing, and serving.

INGREDIENTS:

8 OZ. | 225 GRAMS CREAM CHEESE, AT ROOM

7 OZ. | 200 GRAMS WHIPPED CREAM

SEMOLINA FLOUR, AS NEEDED

1 BALL PIZZA DOUGH

BERRIES, CHERRIES & MASCARPONE PIZZA

YIELD: 1 PIZZA / **ACTIVE TIME:** 15 MINUTES / **TOTAL TIME:** 45 MINUTES

This is a wonderful dessert for a summer night, when all of the fruit is in season.

1. Preheat the oven to the maximum temperature and place a baking stone or steel on the middle rack of the oven as it warms. Dust a work surface with the semolina flour, place the dough on the surface, and gently stretch it into a round. For more detailed instructions on properly stretching a ball of pizza dough see page 73.

2. Using a peel or a flat baking sheet, transfer the pizza to the heated baking implement in the oven. Bake for about 15 minutes, until the crust is golden brown and starting to char. Remove and let cool slightly. Spread the mascarpone over the pizza, distribute the blueberries, raspberries, and cherries on top, and then sprinkle with confectioners' sugar.

INGREDIENTS:

SEMOLINA FLOUR, AS NEEDED

1 BALL PIZZA DOUGH

3.5 OZ. | 100 GRAMS MASCARPONE CHEESE

2.1 OZ. | 60 GRAMS FRESH BLUEBERRIES

2.1 OZ. | 60 GRAMS FRESH RASPBERRIES

2.1 OZ. | 60 GRAMS FRESH CHERRIES

CONFECTIONERS' SUGAR, FOR GARNISH

PIZZA WITH PEAR, THYME, BLUE CHEESE & WALNUTS

YIELD: 1 PIZZA / **ACTIVE TIME:** 15 MINUTES / **TOTAL TIME:** 45 MINUTES

This pizza is savory compared to the rest of the dessert pizzas, but it's still a very satisfying conclusion to a wonderful meal.

1. Preheat the oven to the maximum temperature and place a baking stone or steel on the middle rack of the oven as it warms. Dust a work surface with the semolina flour, place the dough on the surface, and gently stretch it into a round. For more detailed instructions on properly stretching a ball of pizza dough see page 73. Distribute the thyme, blue cheese, walnuts, and slices of pear over the pizza dough.

2. Using a peel or a flat baking sheet, transfer the pizza to the heated baking implement in the oven. Bake for about 15 minutes, until the crust is golden brown and starting to char. Remove and let cool slightly before drizzling honey over the top, slicing, and serving.

INGREDIENTS:

SEMOLINA FLOUR, AS NEEDED

1 PEAR, CORED AND SLICED

HONEY, TO TASTE

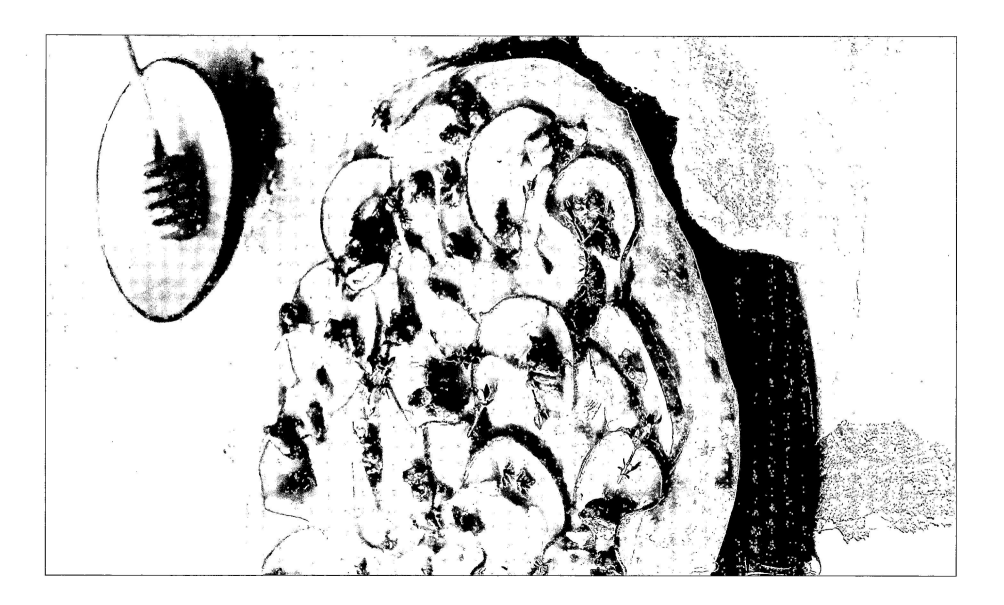

CHOCOLATE, HAZELNUT & STRAWBERRY PIZZA

YIELD: 1 PIZZA / **ACTIVE TIME:** 30 MINUTES / **TOTAL TIME:** 1 HOUR

This homemade version of Nutella is 100 times more flavorful and enchanting than the store-bought version. Pizza isn't the only place you'll end up using it.

1. Preheat the oven to the maximum temperature and place a baking stone or steel on the middle rack of the oven as it warms. Place the hazelnuts in a dry skillet and cook over medium heat until fragrant, approximately 3 minutes. Remove the hazelnuts from the pan and let them cool slightly. Place the hazelnuts in a food processor, add the sugar and salt, and pulse until the mixture is finely chopped.

2. Place the butter and the chocolate chips in a microwave-safe bowl and microwave on medium until melted, removing to stir every 10 seconds. Stir the cream into the mixture and then incorporate the hazelnut mixture.

3. Dust a work surface with the semolina flour, place the dough on the surface, and gently stretch it into a round. For more detailed instructions on properly stretching a ball of pizza dough see page 73.

4. Using a peel or a flat baking sheet, transfer the pizza to the heated baking implement in the oven. Bake for about 10 minutes, until the crust is just about to char. Remove the pizza, spread the chocolate-and-hazelnut mixture over it, and return the pizza to the oven. Bake for another 5 minutes, remove, and let cool slightly before distributing the strawberries on top, slicing, and serving.

INGREDIENTS:

8.8 OZ. | 250 GRAMS HAZELNUTS

2.1 OZ. | 60 GRAMS SUGAR

1 TEASPOON | 6 GRAMS TABLE SALT

1 STICK UNSALTED BUTTER

1 LB. | 450 GRAMS SEMISWEET CHOCOLATE CHIPS

8 OZ. | 225 GRAMS HEAVY CREAM

SEMOLINA FLOUR, AS NEEDED

1 BALL PIZZA DOUGH

16 STRAWBERRIES, HULLED AND HALVED

S'MORES PIZZA

YIELD: 1 PIZZA / **ACTIVE TIME:** 20 MINUTES / **TOTAL TIME:** 50 MINUTES

t's common to have a craving for s'mores without a campfire in sight. This delicious pizza allows you to get your fix.

1. Preheat the oven to the maximum temperature and place a baking stone or steel on the middle rack of the oven as it warms. Place the cream cheese, 2 tablespoons of the heavy cream, and the marshmallow creme in a bowl and beat until fluffy. Fold in the marshmallows and graham cracker crumbs and then set aside. Place the pudding and remaining cream in a separate bowl, stir until combined, and place in the refrigerator.

2. Dust a work surface with the semolina flour, place the dough on the surface, and gently stretch it into a round. For more detailed instructions on properly stretching a ball of pizza dough see page 73.

3. Using a peel or a flat baking sheet, transfer the pizza to the heated baking implement in the oven. Bake for about 10 minutes, until the crust is just starting to char. Remove, spread the pudding over the crust, and top with the cream cheese-and-marshmallow mixture. Return to the oven and bake for another 5 minutes, until the marshmallows are toasted. Remove and let cool slightly before slicing and serving.

INGREDIENTS:

3.5 OZ. | 100 GRAMS CREAM CHEESE

CRUMBS

1 OZ. | 30 GRAMS CONFECTIONERS' SUGAR

½ PACKAGE INSTANT CHOCOLATE PUDDING

SEMOLINA FLOUR, AS NEEDED

1 BALL QUICK PIZZA DOUGH (SEE PAGE 107)

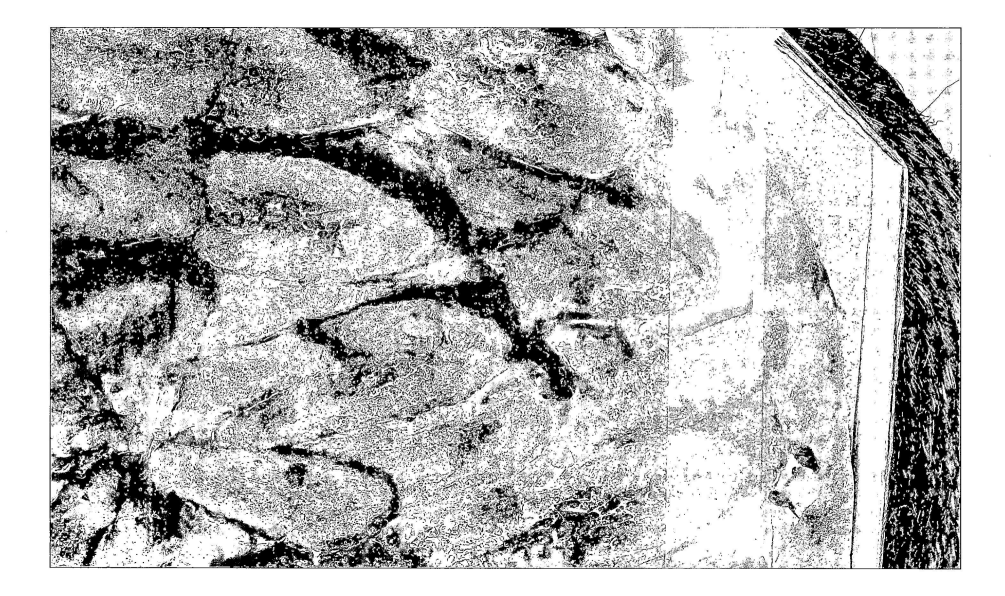

PIZZA WITH BANANA & CINNAMON

YIELD: 1 PIZZA / **ACTIVE TIME:** 15 MINUTES / **TOTAL TIME:** 40 MINUTES

S weet pizza, although not an exclusive specialty of the country, is very big in Brazil. This particular combination is a national favorite.

1. Preheat the oven to 410°F (210°C) and place a baking stone or steel on the middle rack of the oven as it warms. Combine the sugar, cinnamon, and hot water in a bowl and set it aside.

2. Place the dough on a piece of parchment paper and gently stretch it into a very thin round. For more detailed instructions on properly stretching a ball of pizza dough see page 73. Cover the dough with the cinnamon mixture and top with the bananas, butter, and mozzarella.

3. Using a peel or a flat baking sheet, transfer the pizza to the heated baking implement in the oven. Bake for about 10 minutes, until the crust is golden brown and starting to char. Remove and let cool slightly before slicing and serving.

INGREDIENTS:

0.5 OZ. | 15 GRAMS BROWN SUGAR

1 TEASPOON | 5.4 GRAMS CINNAMON

2 TEASPOONS | 9.8 GRAMS HOT WATER (125°F)

1 BALL PIZZA DOUGH (24-HOUR PIZZA DOUGH WITH 62 PERCENT HYDRATION RECOMMENDED, SEE PAGE 111)

7 OZ. | 200 GRAMS BANANAS, SLICED

2.1 OZ. | 60 GRAMS UNSALTED BUTTER, AT ROOM TEMPERATURE

3.5 OZ. | 100 GRAMS LOW-MOISTURE MOZZARELLA CHEESE, SHREDDED

BRIGADEIRO & STRAWBERRY PIZZA

YIELD: 1 PIZZA / **ACTIVE TIME:** 15 MINUTES / **TOTAL TIME:** 40 MINUTES

If banana can fit on a pizza, why not chocolate? In this interesting Brazilian topping, a local sweet sauce based on condensed milk and cocoa is matched with strawberries, resulting in an unusual but delicious dessert pizza.

1. Preheat the oven to 410°F (210°C) and place a baking stone or steel on the middle rack of the oven as it warms. Place the dough on a piece of parchment paper and gently stretch it into a very thin round. For more detailed instructions on properly stretching a ball of pizza dough see page 73. Cover the dough with a few spoonfuls of the Brigadeiro Sauce.

2. Using a peel or a flat baking sheet, transfer the pizza to the heated baking implement in the oven. Bake for about 10 minutes, until the crust is golden brown and starting to char. Remove and top with any remaining Brigadeiro Sauce, the chocolate sprinkles, and the strawberries. Let cool slightly before slicing and serving.

BRIGADEIRO SAUCE

1. Place all of the ingredients in a saucepan and cook over medium heat, while stirring, until the sauce has thickened slightly. Remove from heat and let cool.

INGREDIENTS:

8 STRAWBERRIES, CORED AND HALVED

BRIGADEIRO SAUCE

1 (14 OZ. | 400 GRAM) CAN CONDENSED MILK

1 OZ. | 30 GRAMS UNSWEETENED COCOA POWDER

1 TABLESPOON | 14.2 GRAMS UNSALTED BUTTER

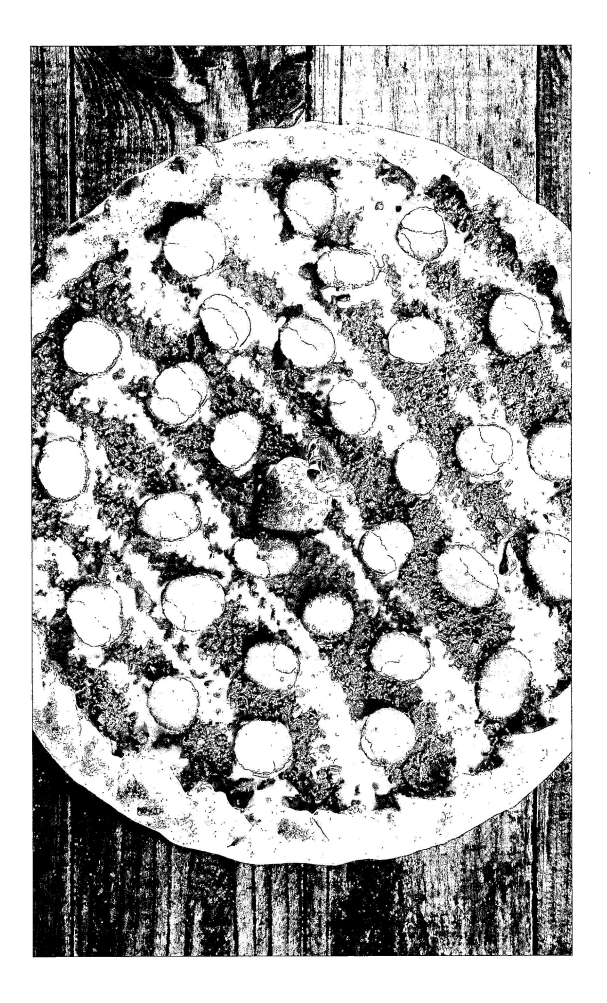

RASPBERRY & ALMOND PIZZA

YIELD: 1 PIZZA / **ACTIVE TIME:** 15 MINUTES / **TOTAL TIME:** 45 MINUTES

Tuck the recipe for this delicious almond paste away, as it will come in handy in a number of other preparations.

1. Preheat the oven to the maximum temperature and place a baking stone or steel on the middle rack of the oven as it warms. Place the almonds, butter, sugar, egg yolk, and vanilla extract in a food processor and blitz until the mixture is a smooth paste.

2. Dust a work surface with the semolina flour, place the dough on the surface, and gently stretch it into a round. For more detailed instructions on properly stretching a ball of pizza dough see page 73.

3. Using a peel or a flat baking sheet, transfer the pizza to the heated baking implement in the oven. Bake for about 15 minutes, until the crust is golden brown and starting to char. Remove, spread the almond paste over the pizza, distribute the raspberries on top, and let the pizza cool slightly before slicing and serving.

INGREDIENTS:

4 OZ. | 113.4 GRAMS SLICED ALMONDS

1 STICK UNSALTED BUTTER, MELTED

1.5 OZ. | 45 GRAMS CONFECTIONERS' SUGAR

1 EGG YOLK

½ TEASPOON | 2.1 GRAMS PURE VANILLA EXTRACT

SEMOLINA FLOUR, AS NEEDED

1 BALL PIZZA DOUGH

8 OZ. | 225 GRAMS RASPBERRIES

VANILLA CUSTARD PIZZA

YIELD: 1 PIZZA / **ACTIVE TIME:** 25 MINUTES / **TOTAL TIME:** 1 HOUR AND 30 MINUTES

After trying this twist on a classic pudding pie, you might just end up throwing out all of your pie plates.

1. Preheat the oven to the maximum temperature and place a baking stone or steel on the middle rack of the oven as it warms. In a small bowl, whisk together the sugar and cornstarch. Add the eggs and whisk until smooth and creamy.

2. Place the milk and butter in a small saucepan and bring to a simmer over medium heat. Pour half of the hot milk-and-butter mixture into the egg mixture and stir until all incorporated. Add the salt and vanilla extract and then pour this mixture back into the saucepan. Cook, stirring constantly, until the mixture is very thick and about to come to a boil. Remove from heat and pour the custard into a bowl. Place plastic wrap directly on top of the custard to prevent a skin from forming and transfer to the refrigerator until cool.

3. Dust a work surface with the semolina flour, place the dough on the surface, and gently stretch it into a round. For more detailed instructions on properly stretching a ball of pizza dough see page 73.

4. Using a peel or a flat baking sheet, transfer the pizza to the heated baking implement in the oven. Bake for about 12 minutes, until the crust is golden brown and starting to char. Remove and let cool slightly. Preheat the broiler on the oven.

5. Spread the custard over the pizza, place it under the broiler, and broil until the custard starts to caramelize, about 5 minutes. Remove and garnish with the slivered almonds.

INGREDIENTS:

4 OZ. | 113.4 GRAMS SUGAR

PINCH OF TABLE SALT

½ TEASPOON | 2.1 GRAMS PURE VANILLA EXTRACT

SEMOLINA FLOUR, AS NEEDED

1 BALL PIZZA DOUGH

SLIVERED ALMONDS, FOR GARNISH

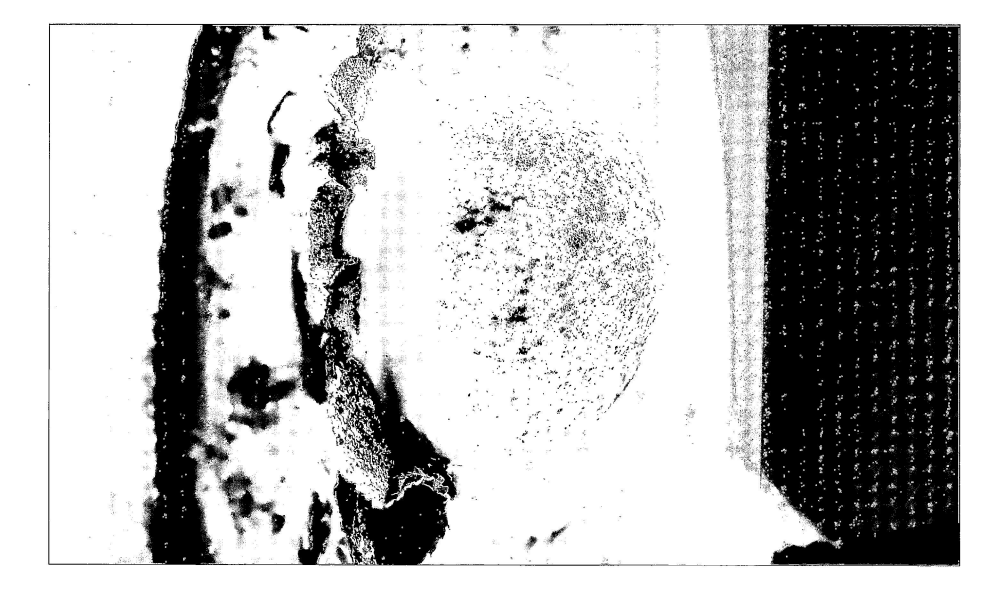

CINNAMON APPLE PIZZA

YIELD: 1 PIZZA / **ACTIVE TIME:** 25 MINUTES / **TOTAL TIME:** 1 HOUR

There are few better ways to celebrate the flavors of fall than this simple dessert pizza.

1. Preheat the oven to the maximum temperature and place a baking stone or steel on the middle rack of the oven as it warms. Place the butter in a skillet and melt over medium heat. Add the apples, sprinkle the brown sugar and cinnamon on top, and cook, turning the apples as they brown, until the apples are caramelized, about 8 minutes. Remove the pan from heat and let the apples cool.

2. Dust a work surface with the semolina flour, place the dough on the surface, and gently stretch it into a round. For more detailed instructions on properly stretching a ball of pizza dough see page 73.

3. Using a peel or a flat baking sheet, transfer the pizza to the heated baking implement in the oven. Bake for about 15 minutes, until the crust is golden brown and starting to char. Remove and drizzle the sauce in the pan over the crust. Distribute the apples over the pizza and serve with vanilla ice cream.

INGREDIENTS:

1 OZ. | 30 GRAMS UNSALTED BUTTER

3 APPLES, CORED AND SLICED

2.1 OZ. | 60 GRAMS BROWN SUGAR

0.5 OZ. | 15 GRAMS CINNAMON

SEMOLINA FLOUR, AS NEEDED

1 BALL PIZZA DOUGH

VANILLA ICE CREAM, FOR SERVING

LEMON CURD PIZZA

YIELD: 1 PIZZA / **ACTIVE TIME:** 25 MINUTES / **TOTAL TIME:** 1 HOUR

L emon makes for a shockingly good pizza topping. So good that you shouldn't hesitate to take this pie in a savory direction and top it with arugula and mushrooms.

1. Preheat the oven to the maximum temperature and place a baking stone or steel on the middle rack of the oven as it warms. Place the lemon juice, lemon zest, eggs, sugar, and butter in a bowl and stir until well combined. Pour the mixture into a saucepan and cook over low heat until it has thickened, approximately 10 minutes. Transfer to a bowl and chill in the refrigerator until it thickens further.

2. Dust a work surface with the semolina flour, place the dough on the surface, and gently stretch it into a round. For more detailed instructions on properly stretching a ball of pizza dough see page 73.

3. Using a peel or a flat baking sheet, transfer the pizza to the heated baking implement in the oven. Bake for about 5 minutes, until the crust starts to brown. Remove the pizza, spread the lemon curd over the top, and return the pizza to the oven. Bake for about 10 minutes, until the crust is golden brown and starting to char. Remove and let cool slightly before slicing and serving.

INGREDIENTS:

4 OZ. | 113.4 GRAMS FRESH LEMON JUICE

SEMOLINA FLOUR, AS NEEDED

1 BALL PIZZA DOUGH

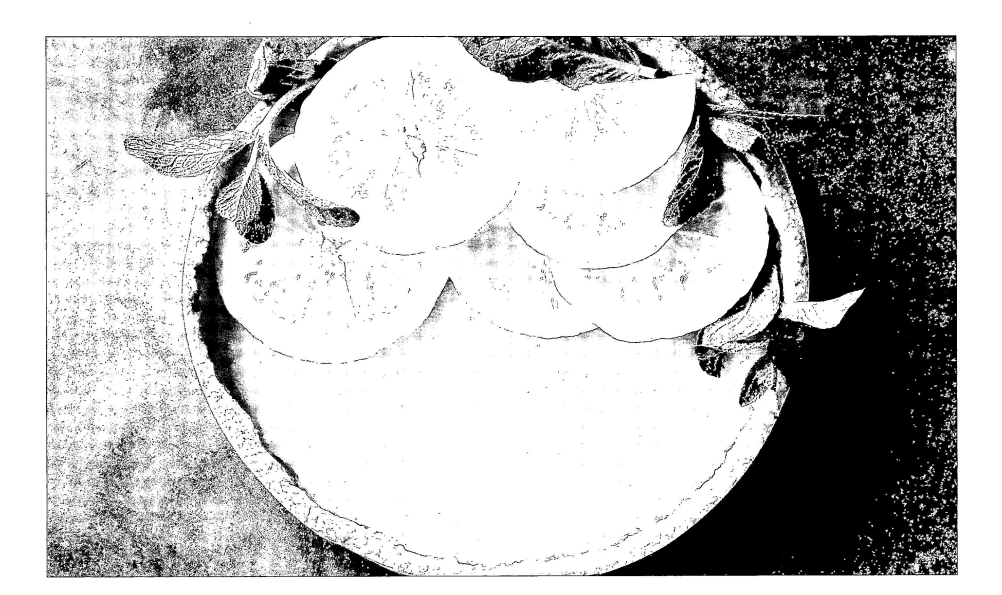

TIRAMISU PIZZA

YIELD: 1 PIZZA / ACTIVE TIME: 20 MINUTES / TOTAL TIME: 55 MINUTES

Combining these two beloved cornerstones of Italian cuisine makes for a very special treat.

1. Preheat the oven to the maximum temperature and place a baking stone or steel on the middle rack of the oven as it warms. Place the cheeses, sugar, vanilla extract, brewed espresso, espresso powder, and Kahlúa in a mixing bowl and beat with a handheld mixer until thoroughly combined. Fold in the chocolate chips and refrigerate for 20 minutes.

2. Dust a work surface with the semolina flour, place the dough on the surface, and gently stretch it into a round. For more detailed instructions on properly stretching a ball of pizza dough see page 73.

3. Using a peel or a flat baking sheet, transfer the pizza to the heated baking implement in the oven. Bake for about 15 minutes, until the crust is golden brown and starting to char. Remove, spread the chocolate chip-and-espresso mixture over the pizza, and sprinkle the cocoa powder on top. Let cool slightly before slicing and serving.

INGREDIENTS:

8 OZ. | 225 GRAMS MASCARPONE CHEESE

4 OZ. | 113.4 GRAMS RICOTTA CHEESE

2.1 OZ. | 60 GRAMS CONFECTIONERS' SUGAR

1 TEASPOON | 4.2 GRAMS PURE VANILLA EXTRACT

1 OZ. | 30 GRAMS BREWED ESPRESSO

1 TEASPOON | 2.4 GRAMS FINE ESPRESSO POWDER

1 OZ. | 30 GRAMS KAHLÚA

2.8 OZ. | 80 GRAMS SEMISWEET CHOCOLATE CHIPS

SEMOLINA FLOUR, AS NEEDED

1 BALL PIZZA DOUGH

2 TABLESPOONS | 14.4 GRAMS UNSWEETENED COCOA POWDER

CARAMEL APPLE PIZZA

YIELD: 1 PIZZA / **ACTIVE TIME:** 20 MINUTES / **TOTAL TIME:** 40 MINUTES

The glory of the county fair, the caramel apple, may work even better as a pizza topping.

1. Preheat the oven to the maximum temperature and place a baking stone or steel on the middle rack of the oven as it warms. Place the sugar, water, butter, and salt in a small saucepan and cook over medium-high heat until the mixture is light brown. Be sure not to stir the mixture; instead, swirl the pan a few times. Reduce heat to medium and cook until the mixture caramelizes, about 4 minutes. Stir the mixture once or twice to make sure it does not burn. Remove from heat and let cool slightly.

2. Dust a work surface with the semolina flour, place the dough on the surface, and gently stretch it into a round. For more detailed instructions on properly stretching a ball of pizza dough see page 73.

3. Using a peel or a flat baking sheet, transfer the pizza to the heated baking implement in the oven. Bake for about 15 minutes, until the crust is golden brown and starting to char. Remove and let cool slightly.

4. While the pizza is cooking, place the apple slices on a baking sheet, place them in the oven, and bake until they are browned, about 8 minutes.

5. Distribute the apples over the crust and then drizzle the caramel over the top of the pizza.

INGREDIENTS:

7 OZ. | 200 GRAMS SUGAR

2.1 OZ. | 60 GRAMS WATER

2 GRANNY SMITH APPLES, CORED AND SLICED

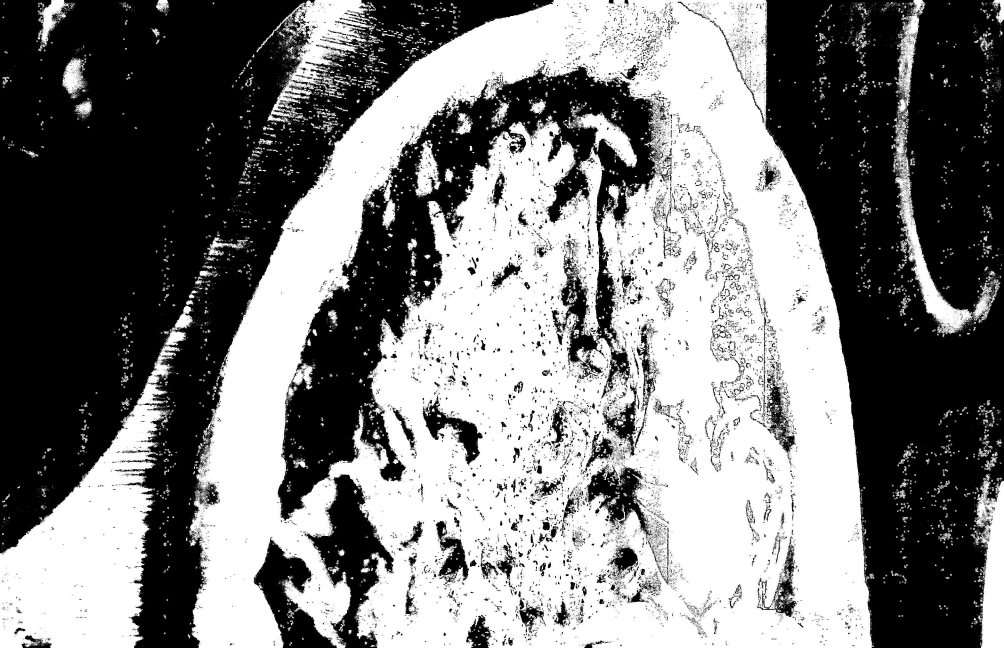

INDUSTRY INSIDERS

*E*veryone knows that pizza is celebrated the world over and that its popularity has inspired both preparations devoted to tradition as well as those that reflect where the pizzas are being crafted today. The following interviews and recipes feature expert pizza makers whose stories and experiences come through in their approaches to this culinary craft.

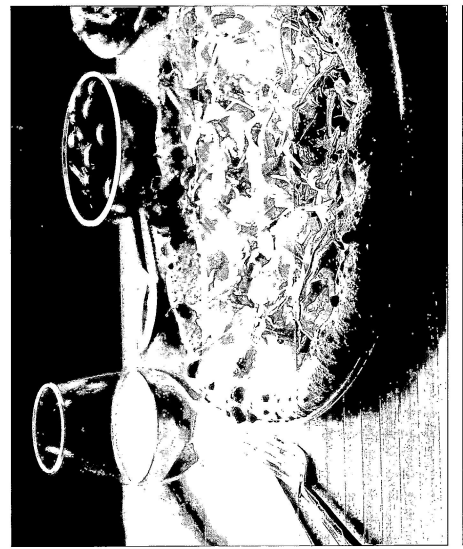

SPACCA NAPOLI PIZZERIA / CHICAGO

Chicago's Spacca Napoli Pizzeria produces not only some of the best Neapolitan pizza in that city, but some of the best in the world, thanks to certified pizzaiolo Jonathan Goldsmith. Recommended by the Michelin Guide and celebrated by local and international pizza aficionados, Goldsmith's reverence for tradition comes through in his team's commitment to turning out delicious uncut pies with beautifully blistered crusts. When he is not busy running the restaurant, Goldsmith is dedicated to educating aspiring pizza makers about why this culinary art form elicits so much passion.

What type of oven do you use to cook your pizzas? What temperature do you cook at?
We have two wood-burning ovens. Both built on-site by the Agliarulo family of Naples, fourth- and fifth-generation oven builders. The first oven built by the family is circa 1870 somewhere in Naples. The normal temperature range is 850 to 900°F (454 to 482°C).

If you use a wood-burning oven, what type of wood do you burn? Why?
We use locally kiln-dried oak. We have played with imported beech, as both give a clean, hot burn. Were we in Connecticut, we would be using beech. In Colorado or Arizona, something else.

What flour(s) do you use for your doughs?
Our principal flour producer is Molino Caputo of Naples. Our daily mix consists of Caputo Red, Caputo Blue, and a touch of *tipo uno*. We also use Caputo's gluten-free mix and one with a special selection of grains and seeds such as

sunflower, rye, flax, barley, sesame, and wheat for our *cuor di cereal* (heart of cereal) dough. Focaccia is new for us, but fun. A much wetter dough with 70 percent hydration; our usual hydration is 62.5 percent. We sometimes go out of the box, using a biga and incorporating quinoa, chia, and cracked wheat. Our usual method is more direct.

Do you primarily use locally sourced ingredients, or a combination of imported ingredients and local ones?
Produce is primarily local and from elsewhere around the US. During the warmer months in Chicago, we purchase as much as possible from the surrounding farms: tomatoes, peppers, beets, and squash blossoms come to mind. From Italy, we bring in tomatoes, olives, olive oils, vinegars, prosciutto, beans, anchovies, capers, salt, Vesuvian peaches and apricots, select beers and sodas, and all of our wines. The wines we offer are all from Campania, representing all of the region and all of its terroir. A few years back,

we let go of marinated white anchovies, as some products are best enjoyed where they are produced. There is no comparison between anchovies fresh out of the water and those packed in brine for six months.

A big move we made a few years back was our bringing in a mozzarella for our pizza (though not for our antipasti) that is working great. It's a blend of 85 percent cow's milk and 15 percent *bufala* milk. Less moisture, and lovely, gentle acidity. We are also making more use of a burrata we bring in from Puglia.

What's the most important factor to keep in mind when making pizza?
YOU HAVE TO MIND THE DOUGH. IF YOU HAVE NO DOUGH, YOU HAVE NO PIZZA! Some say the pizza maker is most important. Maybe so in a small shop where the pizza maker is doing everything—from making the dough, preparing ingredients, and opening, extending, and baking a pie. When you are a big operation, you are an ensemble with many moving parts—each one being important. I am the *arrangiatore*, the conductor, as well as

the dough maker, menu planner, visionary, etc. I would be lost without my pizza makers, salad station staff, runners, wait, bus, and dish staff, managers, hosts, and office administrator. Everyone is important!

Before you thought about being a pizza maker, and before you thought about entering the hospitality industry, you were fascinated by Italy. Why? What made you want to spend so much time in Italy?
Art brought my wife, Ginny, and me to Italy in 1988. We lived in Florence for 3½ years. My wife, who is a painter and mixed media artist, studied at the Cecil Graves atelier. I was the atelier's janitor in exchange for Ginny's tuition, and I was also dedicated to our daughter's care. Not a bad life, to be a househusband in Florence. Three of our four summers were in Puglia. There, I was a *bagnino* on the beach. Our daughter, 20 months old when we arrived, was our passport to goodwill. We were embraced by our local communities, we were not tourists passing through. We were lucky to have had this opportunity early in our adult years.

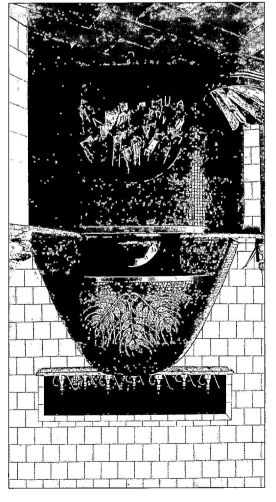

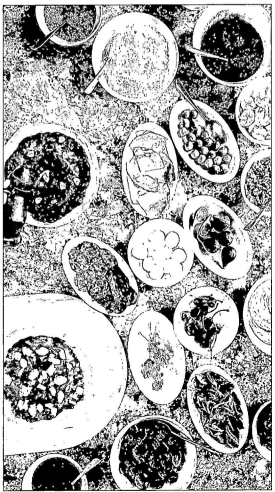

We enjoyed the rhythm of daily life, the local culture and customs, shopping in the neighborhood, the spontaneous generosity and hospitality of new friends as well as strangers, the magic of a simple tomato with good olive oil and salt. We were surrounded by art, architecture, fashion, the beautiful countryside, artisans, and *contadini* (farmers).

The transition home was not easy, it took many years to settle back in. I longed for Italy. Luckily, we were able to continue our summers in the south, in Rodi Garganico. By the grace of a chance encounter, the pizza idea was born, and that renewed my connection to Italy. Through pizza we try to share all of the joy, wonder, simplicity, and generosity we experienced in Italy. We are a *terzo posto*, a third place, somewhere between home and work, that nourishes the soul as well as the stomach.

You are very involved with educating others about making pizza. What about your craft inspires you to share your knowledge with others? So many restaurants keep certain recipes and techniques closely guarded, but it seems you are happy to share all your pizza making "secrets."

There are many who keep their craft close to their vest. Not me. I learned, and continue to learn, through others sharing with me. I did not invent this craft, but I can celebrate it. When we first opened, I would get nervous when I learned of a new place in town, but I soon realized that I would go crazy if I worried whether someone else's pizza was better than mine. I focus on my own work. More importantly, I realized that pizzerias can have the same formula, the same product, the same oven, but each one can produce a pizza and a culture that is unique unto itself, and that is a great thing for all of us.

CONSPIRACY PIZZA /
TORONTO, CANADA

Dan Rios opened Conspiracy Pizza in 2017. The name comes into focus with menu items like the Jimmy Hoffa and the Grassy Knoll. Everyone knows how a good conspiracy theory can get folks worked up, and these pizzas, defined by big, bold, and at times surprising flavor combinations, elicit the same kind of opinionated excitement. The two Toronto locations are local favorites, though they do not supply plastic utensils or paper plates because "climate change is not a conspiracy."

What type of oven do you use to cook your pizzas? What temperature do you cook at?
We use a PizzaMaster electric oven with three cooking decks. We do a two-stage cook with the pizzas, first going in at 400°C (750°F) for 1 to 2 minutes, and then finishing at 250°C (480°F) for 3 to 4 minutes.

If you use a wood-burning oven, what type of wood do you burn?
For the smokers we cook our meat in, we use a 50/50 mix of red or white oak and sugar maple. Oak is expensive but offers excellent flavor, and sugar maple is cheap and plentiful in Canada and burns well.

What flour(s) do you use for your dough?
We use Caputo Neapolitan pizza flour. We find it gives the best flavor and texture.

Do you primarily use locally sourced ingredients or a combination of imported ingredients and local ones?
We use local products as much as we are able, such as pork, beef, and produce, when in season.

Due to our short growing season in Canada, we end up using American or Mexican produce in the fall and winter months. We use Italian pizza flour and tomatoes, as we find they both taste and cook better than the local alternatives.

What's the most important factor to keep in mind when making pizza?
I think attention to detail is the most important factor. Paying attention to your dough and changing factors as needed—like temperature, moisture, and yeast—to ensure a consistent product is critical. Secondarily, focusing on quality of ingredients and toppings is necessary to ensure the final product is high quality and good value.

What are your signature pizzas? Why do you think they are so popular?
Our signature pizzas are the Cowspiracy and Halifax Explosion. The Cowspiracy features a creamy garlic-and-Parmesan white sauce as the base; Emmental cheese; smoked beef brisket; red onions; pickled jalapeños; and barbecue sauce. The smoky, buttery brisket carries this

pizza, and our tangy barbecue sauce cuts the richness.

Our Halifax Explosion is inspired by eastern Canada's donair pizza, and it is very popular. The base is tomato sauce and mozzarella, with donair-spiced ground beef, shredded pepperoni, and red onions, with fresh tomatoes added after cooking and a drizzle of sweet, tangy, and garlicky donair sauce. Transplants from Canada's east coast love that they can find a taste of home, and people who have never had it are blown away by the combination of ingredients and the very addictive donair sauce.

to happen in part because of the success of Adamson Barbecue? Barbecue is the art of low-and-slow cooking, while pizza is fired very quickly. Is there any crossover in terms of how to approach these two very different types of cuisine?
Conspiracy Pizza began as an offshoot of Adamson Barbecue and definitely benefited from the popularity of their top-quality smoked meats.

We are fully inspired by barbecue in its many forms and feature pickles, mustard, barbecue sauce, pork, and smoke in all that we do. We took the idea of "low and slow" to heart and began experimenting with longer proofing times for our dough. Currently, we age our dough 5 to 7 days, allowing for a richer flavor to develop and a crispier crust to result.

Who do you think your pizza appeals to, and why?

Our unique dough and toppings are the main selling points for us. There are not a lot of places in Toronto where you can get smoked meat on pizzas. We work hard to constantly come up with new and interesting pizzas to keep our customers interested. We aren't afraid to take chances and experiment with new flavor combinations, such as our French onion soup–inspired pizza, the Tour de France, or our nacho pizza, the Roswell. We take what we do very seriously and always aim to offer excellent value and service to our customers.

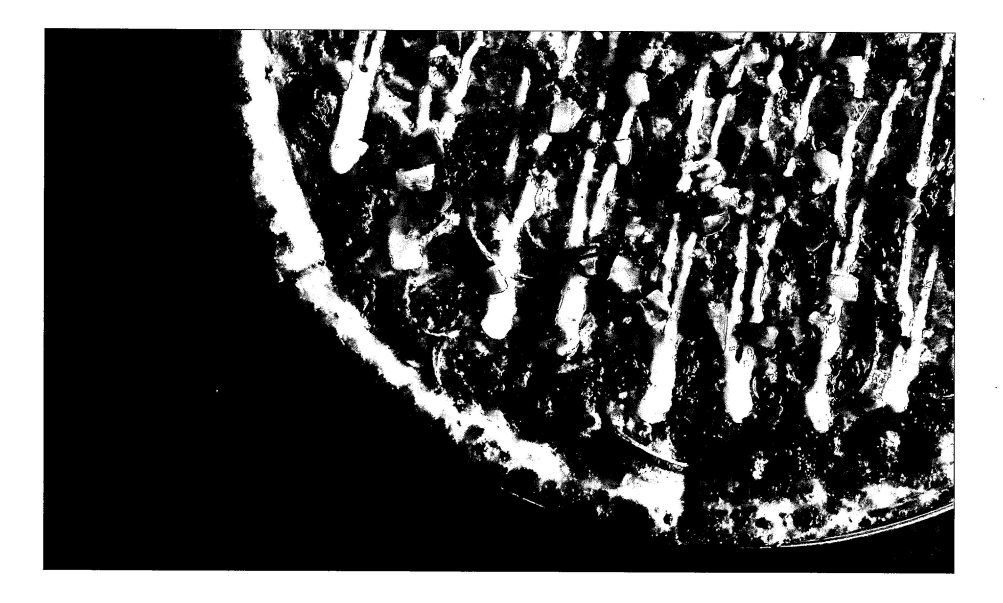

HALIFAX EXPLOSION

YIELD: 1 PIZZA / **ACTIVE TIME:** 1 HOUR / **TOTAL TIME:** 24 HOURS

O ne of Conspiracy Pizza's most notorious offerings.

1. In a large mixing bowl, combine the dry ingredients, then add the water and olive oil and work the mixture until it is a smooth and extensible dough; a stand mixer fitted with a dough hook or paddle works well for this. Let the dough proof in the refrigerator overnight.

Preheat the oven to the maximum temperature and place a baking stone or steel on the middle rack as it warms. To form a 10-inch round, dust a work surface with gluten-free flour. Weigh out 280 grams (9.9 oz) of dough, place it on the work surface, and gently stretch it into a round. For more detailed instructions on properly stretching a ball of pizza dough see page 73.

3. Transfer dough to a baking sheet or pizza peel and top with the tomato puree, mozzarella, ground beef, pepperoni, and onion.

4. Using a peel or a flat baking sheet, transfer the pizza to the heated baking implement in the oven. Bake for about 15 minutes, until the crust is golden brown and starting to char. Remove from the oven, top with the tomatoes and Donair Sauce, and let cool briefly before serving.

DONAIR-SPICED GROUND BEEF

1. Place all of the spices in a bowl and stir to combine.

2. Place the ground beef in the work bowl of a stand mixer fitted with the paddle attachment. Add the spice mixture and mix on low speed until thoroughly combined.

NOTE: A medium-lean ground beef provides the best results. Conspiracy Pizza uses ground-up brisket trimmings.

INGREDIENTS:

2.2 LBS. | 1 KILOGRAM CAPUTO GLUTEN-FREE FLOUR, PLUS MORE AS NEEDED

8 OZ. | 225 GRAMS TOMATO PUREE

10.6 OZ. | 300 GRAMS WHOLE MILK MOZZARELLA, SHREDDED

5.3 OZ. | 150 GRAMS DONAIR-SPICED GROUND BEEF (SEE RECIPE)

3.5 OZ. | 100 GRAMS PEPPERONI, SHREDDED

1.75 OZ. | 50 GRAMS RED ONION, SLICED THIN

1.75 OZ. | 50 GRAMS TOMATOES, DICED

1 OZ. | 30 GRAMS DONAIR SAUCE (SEE NEXT PAGE)

DONAIR-SPICED GROUND BEEF

2½ TEASPOONS | 12 GRAMS TABLE SALT

5 TEASPOONS | 5 GRAMS DRIED OREGANO

4 TEASPOONS | 10 GRAMS ONION POWDER

2 TEASPOONS | 5 GRAMS BLACK PEPPER

4 TEASPOONS | 10 GRAMS PAPRIKA

2.2 LBS. | 1 KILOGRAM GROUND BEEF

BUTTERMILK WHITE SAUCE

YIELD: 12 CUPS / ACTIVE TIME: 20 MINUTES / TOTAL TIME: 20 MINUTES

Here's a rich, tangy sauce from Conspiracy Pizza that you can use to add an intriguing twist drizzled over your favorite pies.

1. Place 1 stick of the butter in a large saucepan and melt over low heat. Add the flour and stir to combine. Add the seasonings, season with salt, and cook for 2 minutes.

2. Whisk the milk into the mixture 1 liter at a time. Wait until the mixture has thickened slightly before adding the next liter.

3. Add the buttermilk and the rest of the butter and cook until the mixture is warmed through and has thickened. Add the Parmesan and stir constantly until the sauce has reduced to the desired consistency. If you want a smooth sauce, strain through a fine sieve before using.

DONAIR SAUCE

1. Combine the condensed milk and garlic powder in a large bowl.

2. Gradually work in the vinegar with a large whisk. Taste as you go and add more vinegar if desired; the sauce should be equally sweet and tangy. This preparation will yield about 6 cups of sauce.

INGREDIENTS:

1 LB. (4 STICKS) | 450 GRAMS UNSALTED BUTTER

17.6 OZ. | 500 GRAMS GLUTEN-FREE ALL-PURPOSE FLOUR

1 TABLESPOON | 6 GRAMS DRIED OREGANO

1 TABLESPOON | 6 GRAMS DRIED BASIL

4 TEASPOONS | 10 GRAMS GARLIC POWDER

SALT, TO TASTE

101.4 OZ. | 3 LITERS WHOLE MILK

33.8 OZ. | 1 LITER BUTTERMILK

8.8 OZ. | 250 GRAMS PARMESAN CHEESE, GRATED

DONAIR SAUCE

3 (10 OZ. | 300 ML) CANS CONDENSED MILK

1 OZ. | 30 GRAMS GARLIC POWDER

5.3–7 OZ. | 150-200 GRAMS WHITE VINEGAR

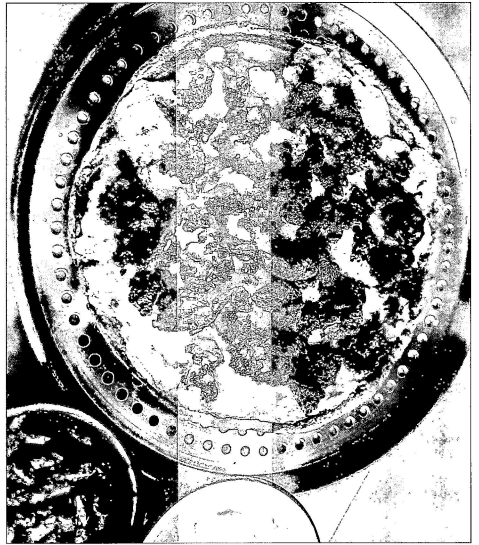

PIXZA /

MEXICO CITY, MEXICO

Declaring it "a social empowerment platform disguised as a pixzeria," founder Alejandro Souza started Pixza to help disadvantaged individuals and champion local ingredients, like blue corn, traditionally prepared meats, and grasshoppers.

What type of oven do you use to cook your pizzas? What temperature do you cook at?
A stone and gas oven, at 350°C (660°F).

What flour(s) do you use for your doughs?
High-protein flour and organic blue corn.

Do you primarily use locally sourced ingredients or a combination of imported ingredients and local ones?
Only locally sourced, 100 percent Mexican ingredients.

What's the most important factor to keep in mind when making pizza?
Getting the dough right.

Would you please explain the linguistic origin behind the name Pixza?
When Mexicans say *pizza*, they say "pixza." I am not sure why, or where this came from, but it is a cultural adaptation of the word that is uniquely Mexican. That being said, the *x* in the middle of the word is also representative and symbolic of the *x* in the middle of "Mexico." So

that has a nice ring to it also. For us this worked perfectly because we have a very Mexican name for a pizza that is 100 percent Mexican.

What came first, the pizza joint or the desire to create a food-centric social empowerment platform? And why pizza? Why not a Thai restaurant or a traditional Mexican restaurant?
Since day one, Pixza has operated as a social empowerment platform. The idea of creating a 100 percent Mexican pizza came to me while I was studying for my master's degree in New York City. I was with a friend of mine at a bar and we were doing what Mexicans abroad do: reminisce and dream of Mexican food. We were remembering a traditional Mexican dish called a *huarache*, which is made out of blue corn and has a bean sauce as a base, a variety of different ingredients on top, and cheese. The idea of the huarache made me think of a pizza and I said to my friend, "Why is there no such thing as a blue corn pizza? Maybe it isn't possible." But I kept dreaming of my blue corn pizza and thought out loud how, instead of having pepperoni or other traditional pizza ingredients,

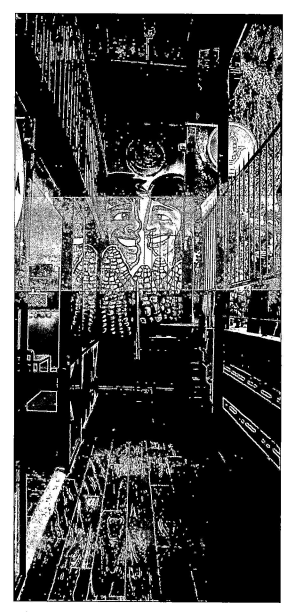

it would have grasshoppers and other purely Mexican ingredients. And that's how I decided to call it Pixza, to make it blue corn–based and 100 percent Mexican.

I've always been a social entrepreneur, so making it a social enterprise was an automatic calling. As a social empowerment platform, Pixza is dedicated to achieving the socioeconomically productive reintegration of young adults through a multidimensional empowerment program that drives them to achieve four objectives in 18 months. First, ensure and maintain formal employment and professional

development at Pixza. Second, establish and implement a personal and professional life plan. Third, move out of the shelter and into their own apartment. Finally, take ongoing practical and professional courses. We identify young adults between the ages of 17 and 27 who contend with any of the following challenges: homelessness, abandonment by their family, no formal education, history of drug abuse, a criminal record, or being a migrant or refugee. Since starting Pixza, over 70 such individuals have graduated from our program.

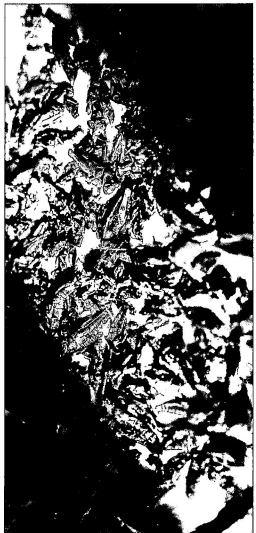

OTTO / MULTIPLE MAINE AND MASSACHUSETTS LOCATIONS

The pizza at OTTO is very good. So good, in fact, that it was dubbed one of the best slices in America by the Food Network's *50 Pizzas, 50 States*. But even if OTTO's pizza was just so-so, owners Mike Keon and Anthony Allen would still deserve a spotlight for their desire to give back. Allen started Nantucket's first-ever pizza joint at age 17—before his senior year of high school—because he knew how badly his fellow islanders were clamoring for it. In 2012, Keon and Allen traveled to New York City in the wake of Hurricane Sandy, armed only with 600 pizzas and a grill. They spent five days handing out free pizza and rations to storm victims, leaving only once their supplies were depleted. They've worked closely with local organizations to aid fundraising efforts in Maine and Massachusetts as well.

"We had talked for many years about working together and made steps toward larger restaurants in Boston. For many different reasons in many different locations, we never opened in Boston," says Allen. "Mike moved to Portland in '07 and was taken by the vibrant food culture. When a tiny space on Congress Street became available in '09, Mike called me and asked me to come up and take a look. We agreed that rather than open a big restaurant in a big city, maybe starting a very small slice shop that focused on one thing had its upsides. Having never worked together, it made sense to start small and see how it went as a team. It went remarkably well from the very start."

Who—or what—first inspired you to make pizza? Who inspires you now?

MK: We continue to inspire each other with the passion from which we began in 2009, searching for the perfect pie; a combination of the best ingredients we can source (or produce ourselves); the art of making a balanced pie; and focusing on the quality of the ingredients rather than the quantity. It's prepping the dough so it's just the right temperature and elasticity before being topped and baked. And it's about using the right equipment—the Marsal oven, a brick-lined cavity with consistently high, intense heat that bakes an unusually even pie with a golden crown and a crispy bottom. As a company, we're more inward looking, constantly asking how we can improve our consistency, our process, and delivery of our product. We make sure to remain current with all things pizza, but it's our commitment to ourselves, to constantly challenging what we do and how we do it, that enables us to produce our pie with consistency.

What is your golden rule for pizza making?
AA: "Golden" is the key word—it marks that the dough is perfectly proofed (62°F | 16.67°C) and ready for the oven, resulting in an airy, open cell–structured, crispy bake. The optimal point of doneness for our product is golden with slight blistering or char. If it's pulled too early, it can be bland, flaccid, and unremarkable. Left in too long, it can take on bitter and unwanted flavors.

AA: An interest in re-engineering a ubiquitous food. Our studied approach to pizza was one in which we transformed what is often blandly accepted into an exceptionally envisioned pie—one that ignites curiosity and a slow nod of approval as one begins to enjoy the often unusual combination of flavors, created and executed by a devoted and caring team.

What items should every pizza baker have?
MK: Cornmeal to create a gap between the dough and the stone.
AA: Cornmeal is absolutely essential. Essential equipment for the home pizza chef: a pizza stone and hopefully a gas-fired oven that cranks to 550°F (288°C). We use Marcel Ovens in all our shops; their brick-lined cavities allow for even heat distribution and recover exceptionally well.

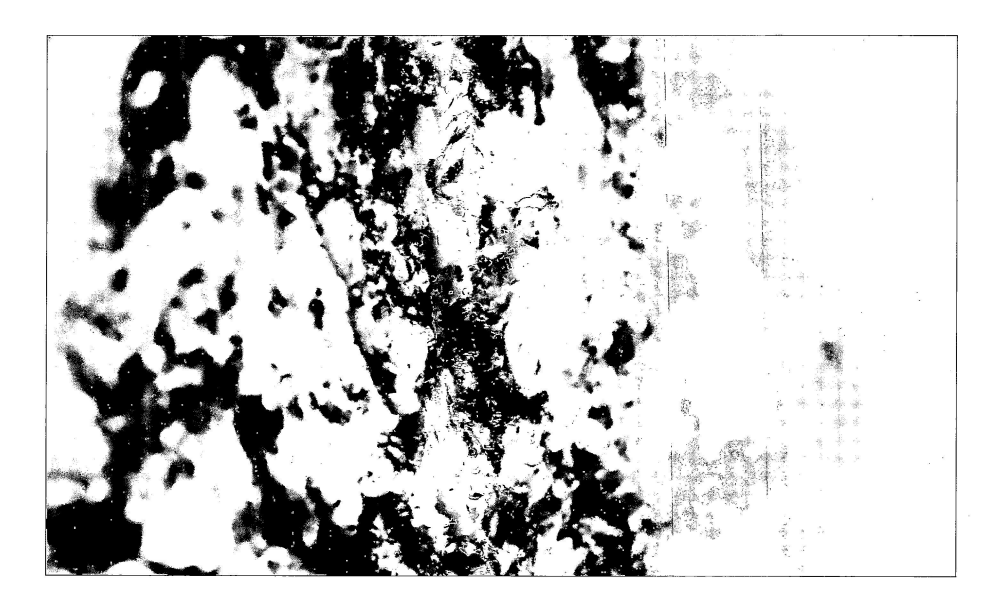

THE MASHER:
MASHED POTATO, BACON & SCALLION PIZZA

YIELD: 1 PIZZA / **ACTIVE TIME:** 25 MINUTES / **TOTAL TIME:** 45 MINUTES

Mike Keon says: "When we opened OTTO, we began with thinking about Maine. Kinda tough to put a lobster on a pie, so Maine potatoes it was; rich, creamy mashed potatoes, complemented with smoked bacon and scallion. We had to give these slices away at first, but once we started offering a money-back guarantee, we got 'em hooked, and the rest is history."

1. Preheat the oven to the maximum temperature and place a baking stone or steel on the middle rack as it warms. Dust a work surface with the cornmeal, place the dough on the surface, and gently stretch it into a round. For more detailed instructions on properly stretching a ball of pizza dough see page 73.

2. Brush the dough with the olive oil, season with black pepper, and sprinkle the Asiago on top. Spread the mashed potatoes over the pizza and top with the mozzarella. Drizzle generously with cream, sprinkle the bacon, scallions, and herb mixture on top, and season with salt.

3. Dust a peel or a flat baking sheet with cornmeal. Transfer the pizza to the heated baking implement in the oven. Bake for about 15 minutes, until the crust is golden brown and starting to char. Remove and let cool slightly before slicing and serving.

INGREDIENTS:

CORNMEAL, AS NEEDED

1 BALL PIZZA DOUGH

2 TABLESPOONS | 26.6 GRAMS OLIVE OIL

BLACK PEPPER, TO TASTE

1 OZ. | 30 GRAMS ASIAGO CHEESE, GRATED

11.4 OZ. | 325 GRAMS MASHED POTATOES (FOLLOW YOUR OWN RECIPE, BUT BE SURE TO USE LOTS OF CREAM AND BUTTER)

7 OZ. | 200 GRAMS LOW-MOISTURE MOZZARELLA CHEESE, SHREDDED

HEAVY CREAM, TO TASTE

4 OZ. | 113.4 GRAMS BACON, COOKED AND CHOPPED

2.6 OZ. | 75 GRAMS SCALLIONS, CUT ON A BIAS

1 TABLESPOON | 3 GRAMS FRESH PARSLEY, ROSEMARY, AND THYME MIXTURE

SALT, TO TASTE

DANTE'S PIZZERIA / AUCKLAND, NEW ZEALAND

How does pizzaiolo Kevin Morris (he of the Michelin-starred Dante's Pizzeria; host to prime ministers, advisor to celebrity chefs, and television star) make such a brilliant margherita? According to him, love. "The most important rule for me, before I start any recipe or idea, is that it has to come from the heart. Most bakers will tell you baking requires some luck. I choose to replace luck with love. When you put love and care into your baking, your finished dish will smile back at you with much more love when taken out from the oven."

Ah, if only it were so simple. But there's no denying Morris's passion, which has been cultivated over years of experience in Italy and elsewhere. What began with him watching his Italian mother bake focaccia in London and continued during frequent visits to his grandparents' home in Italy has led to him becoming one of the Southern Hemisphere's most respected authorities on pizza napoletana. And that's not just a platitude.

His was only the second pizza in the Southern Hemisphere to receive "La Vera Pizza Napoletana," a title that indicates his pizza (specifically, the margherita) is a legitimate member of the Naples pizza scene—as sanctioned by European law!

It is easy to lose track of the many achievements Morris has garnered in his career. Dante's has been awarded "Best Pizza in Auckland" by *Metro Magazine* four years in a row. In 2014, they also won "The Best Pizza in New Zealand" as chosen by Campionato Mondiale Della Pizza. He has appeared on New Zealand television to spread his gospel, and received countless write-ups in local and national publications.

For Kevin Morris, though, it all comes back to his mother's focaccia in the kitchen all those years ago. Without it, he would have never fallen in love with dough—and the world would never have gotten to enjoy his authentic pizza napoletana.

How did Dante's come to be? What are your most popular items?

One afternoon at a friend's barbecue, I was talking about pizza margherita and how I wished I could find one to eat. As a result, a friend suggested I open a pizzeria myself. So, I did. At this time, Auckland's restaurant scene was growing, so I started my first pizzeria in Kumeu, and Dante's Pizzeria Napoletana was born. Later on, we moved to Ponsonby, Auckland. We are most famous for our margherita, along with the sourdough *pannozzi* (a popular submarine sandwich in Naples) and our fried sourdough dressed in tomato sauce and mozzarella.

Who—or what—first inspired you to make pizza? Who inspires you now?

In 2008, I was invited by Associazione Verace Pizza Napoletana in Naples to experience their culture and advance my knowledge of pizza napoletana. During this time, I was honored to meet and work at Pizzeria Gaetano along with Gaetano [Genovesi] himself in Ischia. Even now, he is still the man who inspires me to uphold the art of the perfect *cornicione*—the perfect crust of the true pizza napoletana.

What does Dante's mean to you?

Dante was my Italian grandfather. Every Christmas as kids, we would fly to Italy to visit my grandparents. All my memories of that time were always about food. As a result, I wanted to use my grandfather's name to tie in my Italian side when opening my pizzeria.

What is your favorite pizza to make? Can you talk a bit about your process?

When it comes to food, I like simple dishes done well, with the best ingredients you can get. Therefore, the pizza margherita. It begins with the two-day sourdough base, after which the dough is stretched by hand. I then spread on hand-crushed San Marzano tomatoes imported from Italy, sprinkle with freshly picked basil, hand-broken buffalo mozzarella, and finish with a drizzle of extra virgin olive oil. It's important to remember that less is more. Finally, the pizza is cooked in a very hot wood-fired oven for just over a minute. During this time, I use the turning peel to turn the pizza in order to achieve an even cook. As the pizza arrives on the table, the aroma of the wood fire blended with the sourdough base and basil is what makes the margherita a Michelin star–winning dish.

The oven is the most important item. We imported our ovens from Naples and pizza tools from different parts of Italy. Every Naples oven has a dome shape, which allows a swirling effect of intense heat to create the pizza napoletana's signature blisters around the crust. In addition, a marble workbench is necessary to open (stretch) the pizza dough. Marble has a cool and even temperature all year, so the dough is always easy to work with. Last but not least, a good pizza peel and a turning peel are essential to place the pizza into the oven and help with even cooking. I also recommend a pizza stone for even cooking and to improve your crust.

What book(s) go on your required reading list for pizza makers?

One of my favorite books to read is *Bread* by Dean Brettschneider. Dean explains how simple baking can be as long as you prioritize the basic products and techniques. As we all say, practice makes perfect; once you have mastered the basics and understood the taste, texture, and feel of the dough, other baking will come easily.

Brag about yourself a bit. What are your proudest moments as a chef?

When I decided to open my own pizzeria, I started looking for the best pizza recipe. After days and days of trying different recipes, I made my mind up on pizza napoletana. However, I kept practicing and changing the recipe until I was able to achieve the light, fluffy, and chewy crust of the traditional pizza napoletana.

That was when Dante's Pizzeria was born. As I learned more about pizza napoletana, I found AVPN, an organization that protects the art and craft of the true Naples pizza. After contacting them and discussing what I do with them, they invited me to Naples to advance my knowledge of "opening the dough."

In early 2008, New Zealand Prime Minister and National Party leader John Key visited Dante's. He was not just happy enjoying his pizza, he also rolled up his sleeves and joined me in my kitchen for a one-on-one pizza-making lesson. Key also made a joke that the chance to swap politics for pizza could also be tempting.

I told him with a smile that if he ever wanted a part-time job, I'd happily employ him.

Favorite crust?
Napoletana crust is always the best. It's light, fluffy, crispy, and chewy, all at once. Since the dough is a two-day fermentation, the pizza base and crust can be digested easily and are light on your stomach, leaving room for your favorite dessert. Besides margherita, my other favorite pizza topping is hot Calabrese salami, another must-have in my pantry.

DANTE'S PERSONAL PIZZAS

YIELD: 4 SMALL PIZZAS / **ACTIVE TIME:** 1 HOUR / **TOTAL TIME:** 1 HOUR AND 30 MINUTES

These personal pizzas are packed with flavor and perfect for sharing with family and friends.

1. Place the olive oil in a saucepan and warm over medium heat. When the oil starts to shimmer, add the onion and garlic, season with salt, and cook until the onion starts to brown, about 10 minutes. Stir in the thyme and carrot and cook until the carrot is tender, about 5 minutes.

2. Add the tomatoes and their juices and bring to a boil, stirring often. Reduce heat so that the sauce simmers, crush the bouillon cube, and stir it in. Simmer until the sauce has reduced, about 30 minutes. Remove from heat and let cool.

3. Preheat the oven to the maximum temperature and place a baking stone or steel on the middle rack as it warms. Dust a work surface with the semolina flour. Divide the balls of dough in half, place the dough on the surface, and gently stretch them into rounds. For more detailed instructions on properly stretching a ball of pizza dough see page 73.

4. Using a peel or a flat baking sheet, transfer the pizzas to the heated baking implement in the oven. Bake for about 5 minutes, until the crusts start to brown. Remove the pizzas, cover them with the sauce, top with the mozzarella and basil, and return the pizzas to the oven. Bake for about 10 minutes, until the crusts are golden brown and starting to char. Remove and let cool slightly before slicing and serving.

INGREDIENTS:

2.1 OZ. | 60 GRAMS OLIVE OIL, PLUS MORE TO

LEAVES FROM 3 SPRIGS FRESH THYME

1 CARROT, PEELED AND GRATED

28.2 OZ. | 800 GRAMS WHOLE PEELED TOMATOES, CRUSHED BY HAND

1 CUBE CHICKEN OR VEGETABLE BOUILLON

SEMOLINA FLOUR, AS NEEDED

2 BALLS PIZZA DOUGH

7 OZ. | 200 GRAMS BUFFALO MOZZARELLA CHEESE, TORN

FRESH BASIL, FOR GARNISH

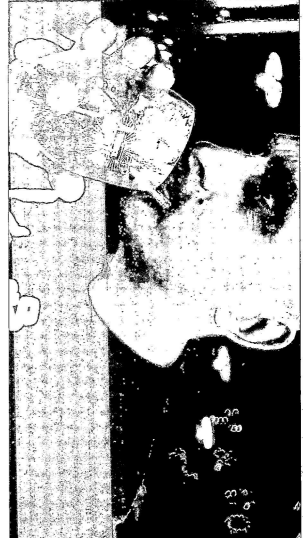

THEO & CO. /
PERTH, AUSTRALIA

When Theo Kalogeracos set out to become a pizza maker, it wasn't for fame. He just wanted to make fun pizzas. But that penchant for creative baking has made him famous all the same, as his big personality and out-of-the-box thinking have helped him become one of Australia's best-known pizzaiolos.

Walk into one of Theo & Co.'s two locations and the first thing you'll notice is the sheer number of pizzas. Starters, entrees, desserts—if you were so inclined, you could have a full meal consisting entirely of pizza. And the options are tempting. Stone-baked pizzas, skillet pizzas, and grandma-style pizzas made on fluffy focaccia are just three of the varieties Kalogeracos has mastered.

What's amazing about Theo & Co.'s success is how close it came to never even existing. Kalogeracos was already a star pizza maker in his own right when he worked at Little Caesars Pizzeria in Perth (unrelated to the popular American pizza chain). A dispute with management, however, led Kalogeracos to leave the restaurant and open his own pizzeria mere feet from his old employer.

"It came down to quality . . . I wasn't happy with what we were producing but the owners wanted to maximize their returns, and I don't blame them for that," he said in an interview with *WAtoday*. Neither do Theo & Co.'s customers, who have enjoyed his reliably fun and delicious pizzas ever since.

THEO & CO.'S BASIC PIZZA DOUGH

YIELD: DOUGH FOR 8 PIZZAS / **ACTIVE TIME:** 30 MINUTES / **TOTAL TIME:** 45 MINUTES

This is a great dough to develop your feel for making pizza. This dough is used on Theo & Co.'s Salt-N-Peppa Prawn, Farmer's Market, and Custom Royal pizzas.

1. Combine the flour, yeast, salt, and sugar, and make a well in the center. Add 20.9 oz. (590 grams) of the water and work the mixture until it just holds together. Add the remaining water only as needed. The gluten content of your flour will determine how much of the remaining water is needed.

Knead the dough until it is smooth, elastic, and extensible, about 10 minutes. Divide into eight pieces, shape them into rounds, and cover them with a damp kitchen towel. Let them rest for 10 to 15 minutes before stretching and using to make pizza. For detailed instructions on stretching a ball of pizza dough see page 73.

INGREDIENTS:

29.1 OZ. | 825 GRAMS STRONG BAKING FLOUR

29.2 OZ. | 830 GRAMS COLD WATER

THEO & CO.'S SKILLET PIZZA DOUGH

YIELD: 6 TO 8 BALLS OF DOUGH / **ACTIVE TIME:** 25 MINUTES / **TOTAL TIME:** 2 HOURS AND 15 MINUTES

Something of a combination between a quiche crust and a pizza crust. Use this dough if you have a desire for a thick crust, or even deep dish.

1. Combine the water, butter, and olive oil in a mixing bowl. Add half of the all-purpose flour, half of the semolina flour, the yeast, salt, and sugar and work the mixture until it is smooth, 3 to 4 minutes. Cover the bowl and let it rest for 20 minutes.

2. Add the remaining all-purpose flour and semolina flour and work the mixture until it is smooth, soft, and tacky. Form the dough into a round and rub it with olive oil. Place it in a large bowl, cover the bowl, and let the dough rest for 1 hour.

3. Place the dough in a large skillet and stretch it until it extends up the side of the pan. Cover the pan with a kitchen towel and let it rest for another 30 minutes before making pizza.

INGREDIENTS:

14.6 OZ. | 415 GRAMS WATER

3 TABLESPOONS | 43 GRAMS UNSALTED BUTTER

6 OZ. | 170 GRAMS OLIVE OIL, PLUS MORE AS NEEDED

18.4 OZ. | 523 GRAMS ALL-PURPOSE FLOUR (8 PERCENT PROTEIN RECOMMENDED)

3 OZ. | 85 GRAMS SEMOLINA FLOUR

2 TABLESPOONS PLUS 1 TEASPOON | 21 GRAMS ACTIVE DRY YEAST

1 TEASPOON | 5 GRAMS TABLE SALT

1 TEASPOON | 5 GRAMS SUGAR

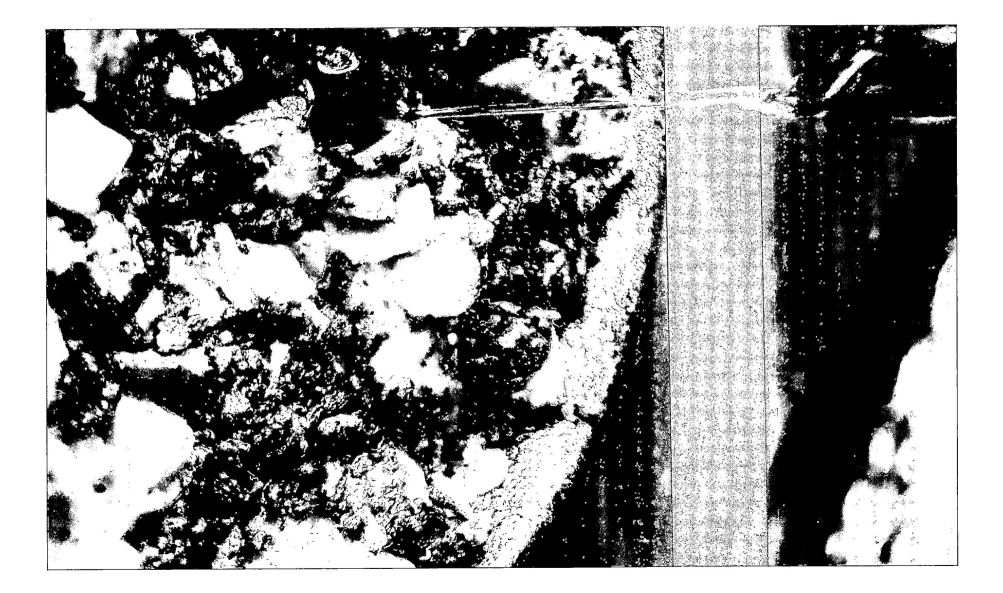

NOTORIOUS P.I.G. SKILLET PIZZA

YIELD: 1 PIZZA / **ACTIVE TIME:** 15 MINUTES / **TOTAL TIME:** 45 MINUTES

B reak out the cast-iron skillet and loosen your belt, because the Bacon Jam makes this deep-dish pie both decadent and irresistible.

1. Preheat the oven to the maximum temperature and generously grease a 12-inch cast-iron skillet with butter. Dust a work surface with the semolina flour, place the dough on the surface, and gently stretch it into a round that will fit inside the skillet. Place the dough in the skillet and cover it with half of the mozzarella. Distribute half of the bacon over the cheese and then top with the remaining mozzarella. Top with the remaining bacon and sprinkle the Parmesan over the pizza. Top with dollops of the Bacon Jam.

2. Place the pizza in the oven and cook until the crust is golden brown and the cheese is browned and bubbly, about 15 minutes. Remove the pizza from the oven, drizzle maple syrup over it, and let it cool slightly before slicing and serving.

BACON JAM

1. Place the vegetable oil and bacon in a medium saucepan and cook over medium-high heat until the bacon is browned, about 6 minutes. Stir in the tomatoes and onion and cook for another 10 minutes, stirring occasionally.

2. Stir in the remaining ingredients, reduce the heat to medium-low, and cook until the mixture has reduced to the desired consistency. Remove the pan from heat and let cool before using or storing.

INGREDIENTS:

UNSALTED BUTTER, AS NEEDED

SEMOLINA FLOUR, AS NEEDED

1 BALL PIZZA DOUGH

5.3 OZ. | 150 GRAMS LOW-MOISTURE MOZZARELLA CHEESE, SHREDDED

3.5 OZ. | 100 GRAMS BACON, COOKED AND CHOPPED

1 OZ. | 30 GRAMS PARMESAN CHEESE, GRATED

2 TABLESPOONS BACON JAM (SEE RECIPE)

MAPLE SYRUP, FOR GARNISH

BACON JAM

1 TABLESPOON | 13.3 GRAMS VEGETABLE OIL

5.3 OZ. | 150 GRAMS BACON, CHOPPED

3.5 OZ. | 100 GRAMS CHERRY TOMATOES, MINCED

3.5 OZ. | 100 GRAMS RED ONION, MINCED

8 OZ. | 225 GRAMS CHICKEN STOCK

7 OZ. | 200 GRAMS SUGAR

2.8 OZ. | 80 GRAMS MOLASSES

8 OZ. | 225 GRAMS WATER

½ TEASPOON | 2.8 GRAMS CAYENNE PEPPER

FARMERS MARKET

YIELDS: 1 PIZZA / **ACTIVE TIME:** 25 MINUTES / **TOTAL TIME:** 1 HOUR AND 15 MINUTES

66 **Y**ou can buy pretty much everything you need for this pizza from your local farmers market," says Theo Kalogeracos. "You will notice as you are eating the pizza that all the flavors of the vegetables stand out and the yogurt on top gives it a really light fresh zing."

1. Preheat the oven to the maximum temperature and place a baking stone or steel on the middle rack as it warms. Place the vegetables in a baking dish, season with salt and pepper, and drizzle olive oil over them. Place in the warming oven and roast until tender, about 30 minutes. Remove from the oven and let cool. Place the yogurt, chives, and lemon juice in a small bowl, stir to combine, and set aside.

2. Dust a work surface with the semolina flour and chia seeds, place the dough on the surface, and gently stretch it into a round. For more detailed instructions on properly stretching a ball of pizza dough see page 73. Cover the dough with the mozzarella and then top it with the roasted vegetables.

3. Using a peel or a flat baking sheet, transfer the pizza to the heated baking implement in the oven. Bake for about 15 minutes, until the crust is golden brown and starting to char. Remove, drizzle the yogurt sauce over the pizza, and let it cool slightly before slicing and serving.

INGREDIENTS:

2.8 OZ. | 80 GRAMS ZUCCHINI

1.4 OZ. | 40 GRAMS BEETS, PEELED AND CHOPPED

1 OZ. | 30 GRAMS GREEK YOGURT

FRESH CHIVES, FINELY CHOPPED, TO TASTE

JUICE OF 1 LEMON WEDGE

SEMOLINA FLOUR, AS NEEDED

1 TEASPOON CHIA SEEDS

1 BALL PIZZA DOUGH

3.5 OZ. | 100 GRAMS LOW-MOISTURE MOZZARELLA CHEESE, SHREDDED

SALT-N-PEPPA PRAWN PIZZA

YIELD: 1 PIZZA / **ACTIVE TIME:** 25 MINUTES / **TOTAL TIME:** 45 MINUTES

Theo Kalogeracos works culinary alchemy here with a pizza covered with shrimp and a healthy dose of "Srirachanaise."

1. Preheat the oven to the maximum temperature and place a baking stone or steel on the middle rack as it warms. Dust a work surface with the semolina flour, place the dough on the surface, and gently stretch it into a round. For more detailed instructions on properly stretching a ball of pizza dough see page 73. Cover the dough with the mozzarella and top with the arugula and garlic. Sprinkle sesame seeds over the pizza, season with salt and pepper, and drizzle olive oil over the top.

2. Using a peel or a flat baking sheet, transfer the pizza to the heated baking implement in the oven. Bake for about 5 minutes, until the crust starts to brown. Remove the pizza, distribute the prawns over the top, and return the pizza to the oven. Bake for about 10 minutes, until the crust is golden brown and starting to char. Remove, top with the Srirachanaise and Avocado Mousse, and let cool slightly before slicing and serving.

SRIRACHANAISE

1. Place all of the ingredients in a small bowl and whisk until combined.

AVOCADO MOUSSE

1. Place all of the ingredients in a blender and blitz until smooth.

INGREDIENTS:

SEMOLINA FLOUR, AS NEEDED

1 BALL PIZZA DOUGH

3.5 OZ. | 100 GRAMS LOW-MOISTURE MOZZARELLA CHEESE, SHREDDED

2.1 OZ. | 60 GRAMS ARUGULA

1 GARLIC CLOVE, MINCED

SESAME SEEDS, TO TASTE

SALT AND PEPPER, TO TASTE

OLIVE OIL, TO TASTE

10 LARGE PRAWNS, PEELED AND COOKED

1.75 OZ. | 50 GRAMS SRIRACHANAISE (SEE RECIPE)

1.75 OZ. | 50 GRAMS AVOCADO MOUSSE (SEE RECIPE)

SRIRACHANAISE
4 OZ. | 113.4 GRAMS SRIRACHA

4 OZ. | 113.4 GRAMS MAYONNAISE

JUICE OF 1 LEMON

SALT, TO TASTE

AVOCADO MOUSSE
FLESH OF 2 AVOCADOS

JUICE OF 1 LEMON

SALT, TO TASTE

CUSTOM ROYAL DESSERT PIZZA

YIELDS: 1 PIZZA / **ACTIVE TIME:** 25 MINUTES / **TOTAL TIME:** 1 HOUR

The only reason Theo Kalogeracos liked going to the Perth Royal Show (imagine a giant state fair) as a child was for a caramel apple. Here's his interpretation of that fond childhood memory.

1. Preheat the oven to the maximum temperature and place a baking stone or steel on the middle rack as it warms. Place the butter and sugar in the mixing bowl of a stand mixer fitted with the paddle attachment. Beat on medium for 1 minute, add the egg, and beat for another minute. Scrape the mixing bowl as needed. Add the flour and vanilla seeds, reduce the speed to low, and beat for 1 minute. Raise speed to medium and beat until the mixture is well combined.

2. Dust a work surface with the semolina flour, place the dough on the surface, and gently stretch it into a round. For more detailed instructions on properly stretching a ball of pizza dough see page 73. Cover the dough with the butter-and-sugar mixture and then spread the Pastry Cream on top. Distribute the apple slices over the pizza and sprinkle the brown sugar on top.

3. Using a peel or a flat baking sheet, transfer the pizza to the heated baking implement in the oven. Bake for about 15 minutes, until the crust is golden brown and starting to char. Remove, place the cotton candy in the center, and drizzle the caramel over the pizza. Let cool slightly before slicing and serving.

INGREDIENTS:

SEEDS OF ½ VANILLA BEAN

SEMOLINA FLOUR, AS NEEDED

1 BALL PIZZA DOUGH

2.1 OZ. | 60 GRAMS PASTRY CREAM (SEE RECIPE)

1 ROYAL GALA APPLE, CORED AND SLICED THIN

1 TABLESPOON | 12.5 GRAMS DARK BROWN SUGAR

1 HANDFUL COTTON CANDY

1 OZ. | 30 GRAMS CARAMEL, WARMED

PASTRY CREAM

2 CUPS | 450 ML WHOLE MILK

1 TABLESPOON | 14.2 GRAMS UNSALTED BUTTER

3.2 OZ. | 120 GRAMS SUGAR

0.75 OZ. | 22.5 GRAMS CORNSTARCH

2 LARGE EGGS

1 PINCH KOSHER SALT

½ TEASPOON | 2.1 GRAMS PURE VANILLA EXTRACT

PASTRY CREAM

1. Place the milk and butter in a saucepan and bring to a simmer over medium heat.

2. As the milk mixture is coming to a simmer, place the sugar and cornstarch in a small bowl and whisk to combine. Add the eggs and whisk until the mixture is smooth and creamy.

3. Pour half of the hot milk mixture into the egg mixture and stir until incorporated. Add the salt and vanilla extract, stir to incorporate, and pour the tempered eggs into the saucepan. Cook, stirring constantly, until the mixture is very thick.

4. Remove from heat and pour the mixture into a bowl. Place plastic wrap directly on the surface to prevent a skin from forming. Refrigerate until cool.

PIZZA PILGRIMS /
LONDON, ENGLAND

If Pizza Pilgrims strikes you as a fun, lighthearted name, you're not thinking literally enough. Thom and James Elliott's pizzeria was not named flippantly—the brothers had to live it before they could create it. One day in a London pub the brothers were thinking about the future when the idea for a three-wheeled van with a pizza oven on the back led to a trip to Sicily. While there they purchased a three-wheeled "tuk-tuk" and began what can only be called a "pizza pilgrimage." "We knew nothing when we set out," says James. "It took six weeks driving at 18 miles per hour, but we got to spend time working in the best pizzerias across the country."

Who—or what—first inspired you to make pizza? Who inspires you now?
My brother and I had much more normal jobs and hated them! The first pizzaiolo I worked with was Antonino Esposito from a pizzeria in Sorrento. He taught me the basics of pizza and we still use the dough recipe he taught us!

What is your golden rule for baking?
The wetter the better! We try to keep our dough at as high a hydration level as possible to ensure a gloriously soft crust.

What is your favorite pizza to make?
My favorite pizza to bake is with a 'nduja topping. It is a smoked and cured pork sausage with chili we found in Calabria. You bake it on the pizza and it melts, dressing the pizza in amazing smoky oils.

What type of ovens do you use?
Our ovens are actually produced in Dorset, UK. We work with this amazing company called Gozney Ovens who produce fantastic, Naples-style ovens.

What can you say about your baking process?
Our process is exactly the same as they do in Naples pizzerias. We make very simple dough from "00" Caputo blue flour, cold water, sea salt, and fresh baker's yeast. We mix it for a short time to not overdevelop the glutens, then roll it into individual balls. It proofs at room temperature for approximately 12 hours and then is stored in the fridge for an additional 24 hours to slow proof. We then bring the dough out and bring it back to room temperature, and it's ready to use.

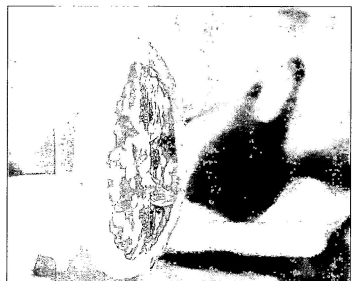

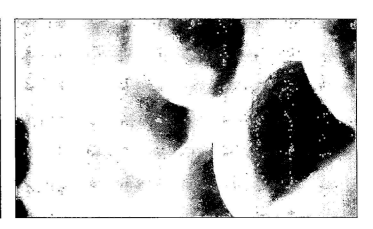

FRYING PAN MARGHERITA

YIELD: 1 PIZZA / **ACTIVE TIME:** 20 MINUTES / **TOTAL TIME:** ABOUT 25 MINUTES

The frying pan-and-grill combo replicates the intense heat you need to cook the pizza quickly and ensures that the dough does not dry out and become biscuit-y.

1. Preheat the grill to the maximum temperature. Place a dry cast-iron skillet over high heat until it is extremely hot.

2 Dust a work surface with the semolina flour, place the dough on the surface, and gently stretch it into a round. For more detailed instructions on properly stretching a ball of pizza dough see page 73. Place the dough in the hot cast-iron skillet.

3. Place the tomatoes and salt in a mixing bowl and stir to combine. Cover the dough with the sauce and distribute the Parmesan, basil, and mozzarella over the dough. Drizzle olive oil over the pizza and let it sit in the skillet until it has browned, 1 to 2 minutes.

4. Place the skillet on the grill, cover the grill, and let it cook until the crust is just turning golden brown, 1 to 2 minutes. Remove and let cool briefly before serving.

INGREDIENTS:

SEMOLINA FLOUR, AS NEEDED

1 BALL NEAPOLITAN PIZZA DOUGH
(SEE PAGE 19)

28 OZ. SAN MARZANO CANNED TOMATOES
AND SEEDS (SEE PAGE ...)

PINCH OF SALT

PARMESAN CHEESE, GRATED, TO TASTE

1 HANDFUL BASIL LEAVES

3.5 OZ. | 100 GRAMS FRESH MOZZARELLA CHEESE, DRAINED AND TORN

OLIVE OIL, TO TASTE

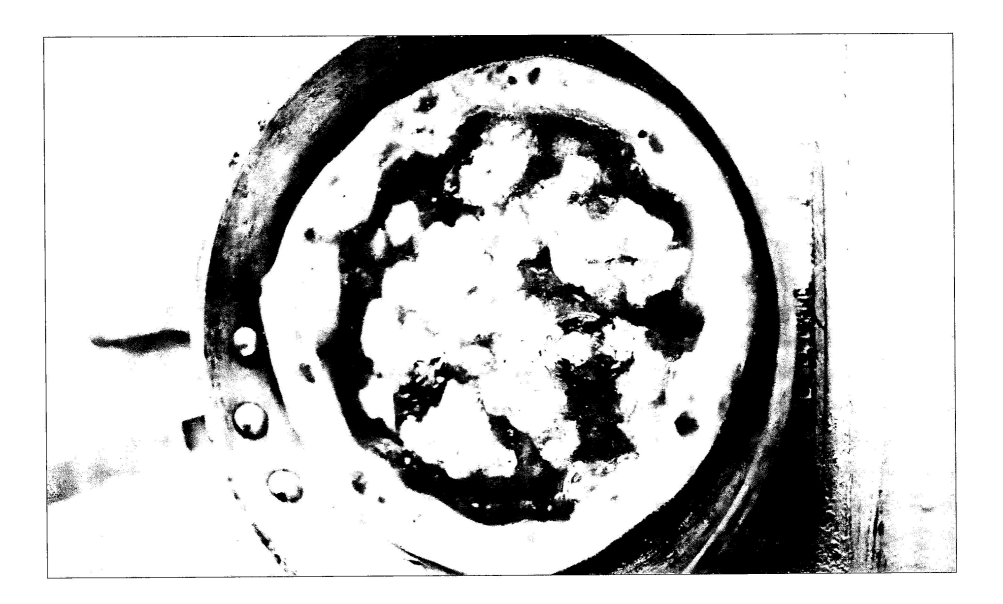

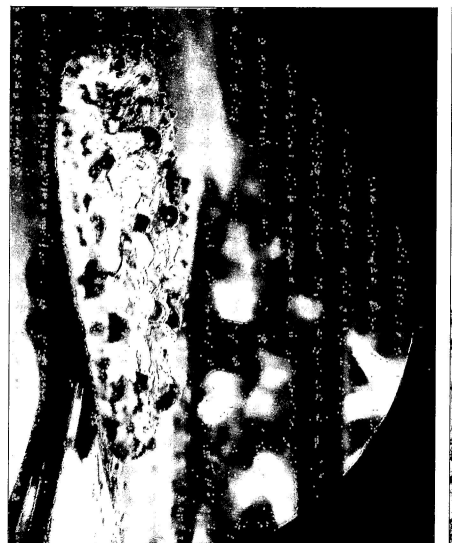
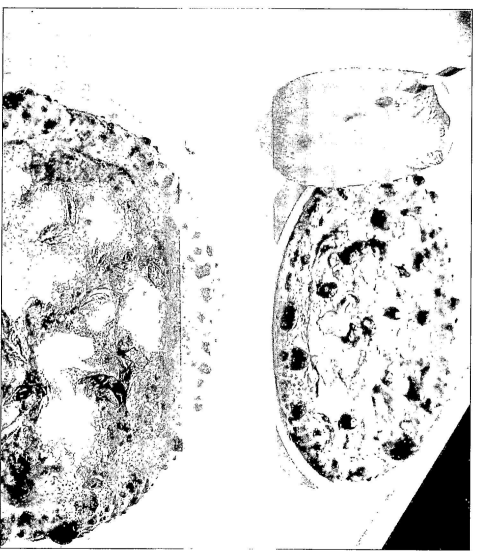

400 GRADI /
MELBOURNE, AUSTRALIA

Johnny Di Francesco has played a large role in putting Australia's pizza scene on the global map. In 2014, he took home top honors in the Pizza World Championship (Campionato Mondiale Della Pizza) in Parma, Italy, where he faced off against 600 competitors from 35 countries. It was a great honor, but for the Naples-descended pizzaiolo, success is nothing without family: "I'm inspired by a lot of chefs from around the world, the ones who are fusing tradition with trends, but I'm mostly inspired by my dad—his love of good food and family, and making sure the two came together often, is something I think about every time I cook."

How and when did you get your start baking?
As a true pizzaiolo, I'm not sure I'd call it baking—but I started making pizza when I was 12 years old, and I did it to buy myself a pair of sneakers. My family couldn't afford designer shoes, so I realized that if I wanted them, I had to buy them myself. I started working in a pizza shop, washing dishes, and literally worked my way up from there—it just found its way into my blood.

What is your golden rule for baking?
Your ingredients are the hero. The end result of any dish is only ever going to be as good as the ingredients in it. Traditional pizza napoletana uses very few, but very good, ingredients, and they each need to shine.

What makes your crust so special?
It's full of air, chewy, light, and a delight to eat!

TANO'S PIZZERIA /
CHICAGO

When you think of Chicago pizza, your mind probably jumps to deep dish. And for good reason—cheesy, thick, and gooey, deep dish has long been an iconic offering in the city. Which is why it's a surprise to find out that Tano's, which has been named on several best-of lists for its deep dish, makes more thin-crust pizza on a daily basis than any other kind.

"Our most popular item is a thin-crust pizza, which is not what you might expect in a deep-dish pizza town," says owner Tom Guagliardo. "But we cater to locals and neighborhood people and, truth be told, locals don't eat a lot of deep-dish pizza. Buffalo wings are our second-bestselling item, and those two go hand-in-hand. Both styles of pizza have had a lot of local recognition, so it's a good idea to go with a big group and an empty stomach to try each."

Tano's is a true neighborhood pizzeria, a descendent of the popular Manzo's down the street, which had been operated by Guagliardo's father for decades. "Tano's is part of the community—we help find lost dogs, serve as a meeting place for friends and families, and have a voice in the neighborhood's future. But my proudest moments come from the customers. We had a chef come from Africa to try our deep-dish pizza—that blows me away. More than anything, I am proud to have regulars; I've watched children grow up and I have mourned the loss of family members. I hear about bad first dates and I watch couples fall in love."

If pizza is family, then Tano's is the truest pizzeria going. Recipes passed down over half a century have remained largely unchanged, and Guagliardo still uses tools passed down from his father and grandfather. While Guagliardo's pizza speaks for itself, you would be crazy not to visit and experience a meal at Tano's in person. By the end, it might even start to feel like home.

How and when did you get your start in this industry?
I grew up in restaurants. My father started in this industry when he was 16. He learned the business, and eventually opened up his own restaurant with the help of his brother and father. As I grew up, I helped out in the kitchen, first making bread baskets and then salads. Soon, I was taking orders for delivery and rout-

ing delivery drivers. The real fun began when I learned the pizza station and then how to cook on the line.

Who—or what—first inspired you to begin pizza? Who inspires you now?
A restaurant kitchen is a magical place. It can be a hot, stress-laden environment, or it can be a beautiful dance of flying dough and sauté

pans. It's hard not to fall in love with it. When you're young in the kitchen, you get stuck doing boring tasks like slicing bread or making side salads, but it helps move the show along and can be a lifesaver when a server has five or six tables. Plus, you get to see what's going on in other stations. You get to watch flames fly from the sauté station and pizza sauce spiral out of the center of a pizza skin. It gives you a drive to "level up" in the kitchen. Nowadays, I get a lot of inspiration from the internet; viral videos of bakers giddy over yeasty, bubbly dough bins, and before-and-after shots of pizzas keep me excited about what I'm doing next.

What are your golden rules for baking pizza?
My golden rules are:

1. Never use water over 100°F. You don't want to kill the baby! Yeast is a living organism—you need to keep it alive so it can transform your dough into a beautiful product. If the water is too hot, it will kill the yeast.

2. Consistency is key. You have to do everything the same way each and every time. Baking is a science. Every batch of dough is an experiment; if you change one variable you will get a different outcome.

3. Time cooks the dough, temperature browns the cheese. This is great to remember when trying out new recipes or working on a new oven. You have to find the right temperature and time for a recipe. That little sentence will help you zero in on the perfect bake.

What does Tano's Pizzeria represent to you?
Tano's Pizzeria is my family legacy. My father and his lessons are the foundation of this place. Many recipes have remained the same for over 50 years. But we are also looking to the future, and always trying new things and updating others.

What is your favorite pizza to bake? Why?
Research and development for pizza is so much fun. Talk about a dream job! Who wouldn't want to make and eat pizza every day? When we have time, we test out new things. I'll hear about a new ingredient from a distributor or see something cool online. We jump on it and play around in the kitchen. It is a lot of fun.

What is your favorite type of pizza crust? Why? Least favorite crust? Why?
I have been into Neapolitan-style pizza for some time. I love the crispy exterior and the chewy interior of the crust. And, of course, the beautiful wood-fired ovens. I think it's great that they cook at such high temperatures—just 90 seconds and pizza is cooked! The blisters from the high heat give the pizza a great smokiness. I think it also has something to do with not being able to make it myself. My restaurant just doesn't have the right equipment for the job. My least favorite crust is something that's underdeveloped or overworked. Pizza dough needs time to ferment. The yeast does its thing, developing flavors and lightening the dough. Some places take shortcuts with fast rises or frozen dough, but nature cannot be rushed.

How did Tano's Pizzeria come to be? Why Chicago?
Tano's is a culmination of everything I have learned over the years. My father's last restaurant, Manzo's, was located only three blocks away from our location. That place raised my brother and me for 20 years. We celebrated and mourned inside those walls. The neighborhood was very good to my family and when my father decided to retire I knew I wanted to stay in the same neighborhood when I opened up Tano's.

Chicago is a world-class city, and the food here rivals that of anywhere else. We are lucky enough to have everything that makes a great pizza at our doorstep: flour from the Great Plains, Lake Michigan gives us the best water, and Wisconsin brings in the best cheese. Plus, Chicago is known as the sausage capital of the US, so it's no surprise we use a lot of it on our pizza. Our tomatoes take the longest trip—they come from California.

Where do you get your tools/materials? What items should every home pizza maker have?

Most of the tools of the trade can be found online or at our distributors. Luckily, I have some tools that are older than I am. I have a pizza peel that was made by my grandfather. And our oven, a beautiful, stainless steel carousel oven, is from the 1950s. The great thing about pizza is that you don't need many tools to create it. For the home cook, there are a few basic tools that can help, but nothing mandatory: Pizza stones are great for keeping a constant temperature in the oven and on the crust. A rolling pin is useful if you're making Chicago-style thin-crust pizza. Dark metal pans work the best for deep-dish pizza, as the dark finish brings more heat to the pizza.

Where did you learn to make pizza? Please tell me about your education and apprenticeships.

The restaurant business is in my blood. My father met my mother when she was waitress-ing at a restaurant; he used to close up shop and go out for breakfast, and that's where he met my mother. I learned everything from my father and, as his friends would say, you get the best education from the school of West Irving Park Road.

Tell me about your processes.

It all starts with the dough. Our dough is mixed and rests for 24 to 48 hours. It is rolled out to a thickness of about ¼ inch and placed in a dark, round baking pan that has been buttered. Any ingredients are placed directly on the dough and that is topped with our mozzarella blend. A thin layer of dough is placed on top of the cheese and our thick pizza sauce is ladled on over that. It is then baked in our oven at 450°F (232°C) for 35 minutes.

CHICAGO DEEP-DISH STUFFED PIZZA

YIELD: 1 PIZZA PLUS 1 CRUST / **ACTIVE TIME:** 1 HOUR / **TOTAL TIME:** 33 HOURS

A lmost more pie than pizza, this impressive stuffed deep dish is the ultimate version of the Chicago classic, coming courtesy of Tano's owner Tom Guagliardo.

1. Place the water, salt, and sugar in the work bowl of a stand mixer fitted with the dough hook. Add the flour and yeast and work the mixture at low speed. Gradually add the olive oil with the mixer running and mix for 5 minutes, until the dough holds together and is smooth. Cover the work bowl with plastic wrap and let the dough rise for 4 to 5 hours.

2. Place the dough on a flour-dusted work surface, divide it into three pieces, then form them into rounds. Place each ball in a separate container and oil them to keep them from drying out. Cover with plastic wrap and store the dough in the refrigerator for 24 hours. The dough will keep in the refrigerator for up to 48 hours.

3. Remove two balls of the dough from the refrigerator and let them sit at room temperature for 2½ hours.

4. Preheat the oven to 450°F (232°C). Stretch one ball of dough until it is a 10-inch round that is approximately ¼ inch (6 millimeters) thick. Grease a 10-inch round cake pan with butter and then lay the dough in it. Trim any excess dough if necessary, distribute the toppings over the dough, and sprinkle the mozzarella over them.

5. Roll the other piece of dough until it is a 9-inch circle that is about ⅛ inch thick (3 millimeters). Cut a few slits in the dough and lay it over the mozzarella, making sure to tuck it up against the other piece of dough.

6. Top the pizza with the sauce, place it in the oven, and bake for about 35 minutes, until the crust is golden brown. Remove and let cool briefly before slicing and serving.

INGREDIENTS:

FOR THE DOUGH

PLUS MORE AS NEEDED

¼ TEASPOON PLUS ⅛ TEASPOON | 1 GRAM ACTIVE DRY YEAST

2.8 OZ. | 80 GRAMS OLIVE OIL, PLUS MORE AS NEEDED

UNSALTED BUTTER, AS NEEDED

FOR THE FILLING & TOPPING
PREFERRED PIZZA TOPPINGS

4.9 OZ. | 140 GRAMS MOZZARELLA CHEESE, SHREDDED

2.8 OZ. | 80 GRAMS RAW PIZZA SAUCE (SEE PAGE 103)

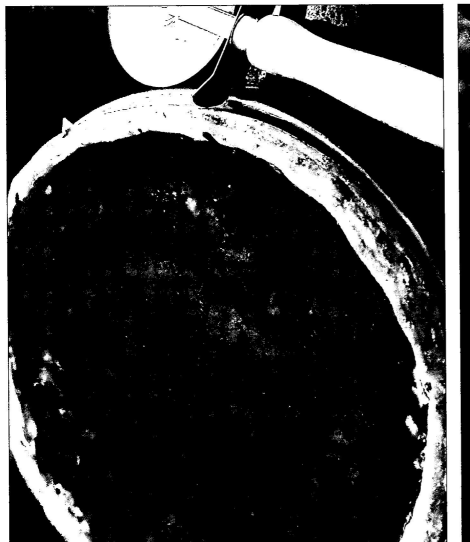
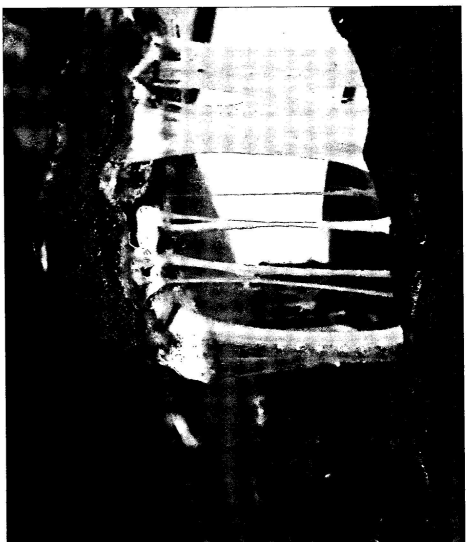

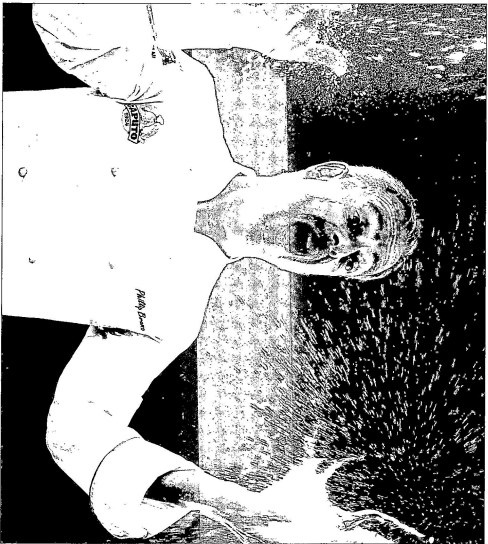

SCOOZI / VICTORIA, AUSTRALIA

Phillip Bruno is not your average pizza maker. Bruno is the president of the Associazione Pizzaiuoli Napoletani Australasia (or, as he calls it, the "Pizza Police"), where he oversees the accreditation of countless pizza chefs and pizzerias throughout the South Pacific. As a pizza judge, he's traveled the globe, visiting places like New York, Taipei, and Naples, where he helps crown the world's best pizza chef every year. And then there's Scoozi itself, awarded Best Pizza in Melbourne in 2014 and inducted into the Pizza Hall of Fame in 2017 by Melbourne's largest newspaper, the *Herald Sun*. The man lives and breathes pizza.

When Bruno is cooking, he says he likes to keep it simple. "I only have one golden rule: follow the traditional pizza napoletana recipe and have fun." His dough uses only four ingredients—flour, water, salt, and yeast—and cooks for 90 seconds, at most. But if you look a little closer you get a sense of the meticulous process he's managed to perfect over 35 years of making pizza. His oven is handmade—by Bruno himself. His dough's leavening process takes about 30 hours, in a temperature-controlled lab, where the dough builds flavor while using very little yeast. Talk to Bruno a little about making pizza, and it becomes clear that "simple" is far from simple. Of course, 35 years of practice will do that.

How and when did you get your start in this industry?
I started baking pizza in 1982, in my first pizza store.

What is your favorite pizza to make?
My favorite pizza to bake is the marinara (see page 234): well-rested dough baked to a Napoletano crust, quality San Marzano tomatoes, fragrant dried oregano, strong extra virgin olive oil, and some fresh, thinly sliced garlic. I always say pizza is a celebration of dough, and sim- plicity is always the best. We call this *marinara*, which translates to "sailor." Sailors were always in a rush before heading off to sea, so their pizza order would be, "Margherita, no cheese, just add a little garlic." I should add that this is also my favorite pizza to eat.

What items should every home pizza maker have?
The beauty of making pizza at home is you just need an oven—everything else is what you have at home. For a nonessential item, I recommend a terra-cotta tile pizza stone.

MELANZANE PIZZA

YIELD: 1 PIZZA / **ACTIVE TIME:** 25 MINUTES / **TOTAL TIME:** 1 HOUR AND 15 MINUTES

A simple way to enjoy two of Italy's favorite things: Neapolitan pizza crust and eggplant.

1. Place the eggplant in a colander and sprinkle salt on each piece. Let sit for 15 minutes.

2. Coat the bottom of a skillet with olive oil and warm over medium-high heat. When the oil starts to shimmer, add the eggplant (working in batches if necessary) and sauté until it is browned on both sides, about 2 minutes per side. Place the eggplant in a bowl and chill in the refrigerator until cool.

3. Preheat the oven to 480°F (250°C) and place a baking stone or steel on the middle rack as it warms. Dust a work surface with the semolina flour, place the dough on the surface, and gently stretch it into a round. For more detailed instructions on properly stretching a ball of pizza dough see page 73. Cover the dough with the sauce and distribute the mozzarella and eggplant over the pizza.

4. Using a peel or a flat baking sheet, transfer the pizza to the heated baking implement in the oven. Bake for about 15 minutes, until the crust is golden brown and starting to char. Remove and let cool slightly before distributing the Parmesan and basil over the pizza, slicing, and serving.

INGREDIENTS:

½ EGGPLANT, SLICED THIN

SALT AND PEPPER, TO TASTE

1.5 OZ. | 45 GRAMS RAW PIZZA SAUCE (SEE PAGE 103)

3.5 OZ. | 100 GRAMS FRESH MOZZARELLA CHEESE, DRAINED AND CUT INTO SHORT STRIPS

PARMESAN CHEESE, GRATED, TO TASTE

FRESH BASIL LEAVES, TO TASTE

SUD ITALIA / LONDON, ENGLAND

It's hard to miss Sud Italia at London's Old Spitalfields Market. The blue van and the blue-and-white mosaic-tiled pizza oven it houses are one of a kind, so it only stands to reason that the pizzas turned out by Silvestro Morlando are noteworthy. Using flours milled to Morlando's precise specifications, Sud Italia is a passion project that is tasted in every bite.

What type of oven do you use to cook your pizzas? What temperature do you cook at?
I use a traditional homemade Neapolitan wood-fired oven. We cook in the 450 to 500°C (840 to 930°F) range.

What type of wood do you burn?
A mix of beech and oak.

What flour(s) do you use for your doughs?
I use a mix of three different flours: "00" flour, organic whole-meal flour, and "0" flour. The dough rises for 24 to 48 hours at room temperature.

Do you primarily use locally sourced ingredients or a combination of imported ingredients and local ones?
We buy organic vegetables mostly from UK farmers. The rest of the products are coming from Italy. I'm really focused on researching the best that I can find.

What's the most important factor to keep in mind when making pizza?
For sure it is to understand that you can't make the pizza two or three hours before you want to eat it. You need to give time to the yeast to start its job, eat all the sugars.

So I advise to make the dough a day before. And don't forget to add the secret ingredient, the most important: a touch of love. It will make a huge different to the final result.

Is it common in Italy for pizza ovens to be found on the back of a truck?
No. There was no pizza truck in Italy before me, that's for sure. I don't know about elsewhere around the world. In another book about where to eat pizza all over the world, they called me "a pioneer of the pizza truck"!

Why do you think your pies are so often included on lists of the best in London?
I think that people just love my pizzas—sorry, but they are not pies—and they recognize the quality of the ingredients that we use and all the hard work that goes into making the pizzas.

PIZZA ALLA ZUCCA

YIELD: 4 PIZZAS / **ACTIVE TIME:** 45 MINUTES / **TOTAL TIME:** 24 HOURS

Silvestro Morlando insists that the dough be made at least one day in advance of when you want to make this pizza.

1. Place the water in a large bowl. Sprinkle the yeast over the water and mix in the flour. Let stand for 5 minutes and then add the honey.

2. Knead the pizza dough for 10 minutes, then add the salt and continue to knead for 5 more minutes.

3. Spread a thin layer of olive oil over the inside of a large bowl. Place the pizza dough in the bowl and cover it. Let the dough rise at room temperature for at least 18 hours.

4. Grease a baking sheet or pizza pans with olive oil.

5. Form 4 round balls of dough. Place each on its own baking sheet or pizza pan, cover with plastic wrap, and let rest for 5 hours at room temperature.

6. Preheat the oven to 400°F (205°C). Place the pumpkin pieces and garlic on a sheet pan, and coat with salt and olive oil. Roast in the oven for 30 minutes, or until they are tender. Remove from the oven, mash the pumpkin and garlic into a paste, and let the mixture cool.

7. After the dough has rested for 5 hours, preheat oven to 460°F (240°C). Working with one at a time, stretch a dough ball and flatten it with your hands on a lightly floured work surface. Starting at the center and working outward, use your fingertips to press the dough to a thickness of ½ inch. For more detailed instructions on properly stretching a ball of pizza dough see page 73.

8. Spread some of the pumpkin mixture over the dough and bake for 10 minutes. Remove the pizza from the oven, add the basil, Gorgonzola, mozzarella, and 'nduja and bake for another 8 minutes.

9. Remove from the oven, garnish with the Parmesan, and let cool briefly before slicing and serving.

INGREDIENTS:

21.1 OZ. | 600 GRAMS MINERAL WATER, AT ROOM TEMPERATURE

4 TEASPOONS | 10 GRAMS DRY YEAST

35.2 OZ. | 1 KILOGRAM "00" FLOUR

1 TEASPOON | 7 GRAMS ORGANIC HONEY

3½ TEASPOONS | 20 GRAMS SALT

OLIVE OIL, AS NEEDED

3 FIOR DI LATTE MOZZARELLA BALLS (12.3 OZ. | 350 GRAMS EACH), SLICED

1 SMALL PUMPKIN, CUT IN THICK CRESCENTS

3 GARLIC CLOVES

FRESH BASIL LEAVES, TO TASTE

GORGONZOLA PICCANTE, CRUMBLED, TO TASTE

'NDUJA, TO TASTE

GRATED PARMESAN CHEESE, TO TASTE

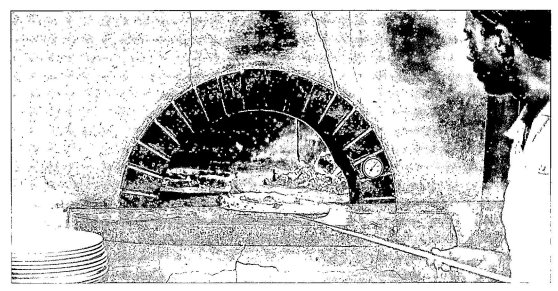

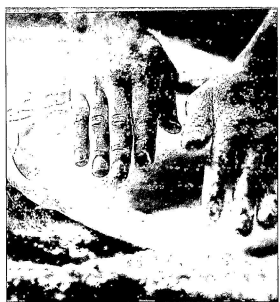
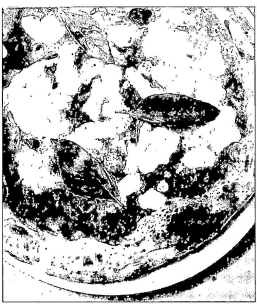

LA SVOLTA /
MELBOURNE, AUSTRALIA

La svolta literally translates to "the turning point," and for Valerio Calabro and Giueseppe "Pino" Russo, opening their Melbourne restaurant was a huge turning point in their lives. It's often said that the truest test of any pizzeria is their margherita pizza. If that's true, then La Svolta has nothing to worry about. Known for their simplicity and passion, owners Calabro and Russo consistently make one of the best margheritas available in the "Land Down Under."

How and when did you get your start baking? Why pizza over other breads or pastries?
Our passion has always been for making pizza—not baking! We began making pizza together in 2006 and opened La Svolta in 2010.

Who—or what—first inspired you to make pizza?
We were inspired by the art of cooking good, traditional Italian food, and pizza is a part of that tradition. And always our mothers in the kitchen, of course.

What is your golden rule for making pizza?
Cook the pizza for 60 to 90 seconds in a wood oven set at 400°C (750°F).

What is your favorite pizza to bake? Why? Least favorite pizza to bake? Why?
The classic margherita—it's a classic, and delicious! We don't have a least favorite.

What are your most popular items?
Our most popular pizzas are the Signor George (San Marzano tomato, fior di latte mozzarella, salami, olives, and chili peppers), the Linda (San Marzano tomato, bocconcini, cherry tomatoes, rocket, prosciutto di Parma, shaved Parmigiano), and the classic margherita.

How do you develop your recipes?
La Svolta is part of the Associazione Verace Pizza Napoletana. We prepare our pizzas based on the guidelines of the association, which has given us a global accreditation.

What should every pizza maker have?
A great set of hands!

SETTEBELLO PIZZERIA NAPOLETANA / AUCKLAND, NEW ZEALAND

For Francesco Acri, pizza is great—but the process is better. "Settebello is my way to communicate with people, telling them everything about pizza, but without using words—just baking." It is clear after only the briefest interaction that pizza is a labor of love for Acri. And while his exuberance for his Neapolitan heritage and his desire to see his culture represented in new areas are unmistakable, Acri also brings things back to his golden rule: "Take your time."

Opened in 2012, Settebello is a small pizzeria, tucked away in Auckland, but in its kitchen Acri is able to work magic. His approach—deliberate, passionate, locally focused—has made ripples that have reached as far as Italy. For a kid from Naples, that's a dream come true.

How and when did you get your start baking?
Baking has always been part of my life, but my professional baking career started when I moved to New Zealand in 2011. Why pizza? A few different reasons, but the most important is that pizza napoletana is part of my culture. I was inspired by Napoli, my native city and the birthplace of pizza.

How did Settebello come to be? Why Auckland?
When I moved to Auckland with my family, I wanted to start my own pizzeria and bring a touch of Napoli to the area.

What tools should every home pizza maker have?
It's very important to handle professional tools when you operate a pizzeria. It just makes life easier. It's always been hard to get good tools in New Zealand, so I get most of my tools from a company in Italy called Gi Metal.

Where did you learn to cook?
I've been making pizza since I came to New Zealand. During my time living here, I've also spent time in Napoli, where I trained with the master pizza makers of Associazione Verace Pizza Napoletana. From the association, I have to say: I learned a lot.

What's your favorite kind of pizza crust, your favorite toppings?
Clearly, my favorite is pizza napoletana, but the best part is the outer edge called *cornicione*—the frame of your topping. I love it because it's puffy and thick, crunchy on the outside, soft and chewy on the inside, and covered with leopard spots of char. I love to dip it into the tomato sauce and mozzarella. I really love margherita, which is just peeled tomatoes, mozzarella, basil, extra virgin olive oil, and a little bit of Parmigiano. And of course, you need to cook this pizza the right way! Otherwise don't call it margherita—just tomato and cheese! Plus, if you don't cook it properly, you will never appreciate the flavors of all these ingredients together.

BIANCA CON SALSICCIA DI FINOCCHIETTO

YIELD: 1 PIZZA / **ACTIVE TIME:** 25 MINUTES / **TOTAL TIME:** 1 HOUR

This savory white pizza with fennel sausage is so tasty that it's worth the extra heaviness. Francesco Acri warns: go easy on the truffle oil until you've tasted the pizza, as it can be very overpowering.

1. Preheat the oven to the maximum temperature and place a baking stone or steel on the middle rack as it warms. Coat the bottom of a skillet with olive oil and warm over medium-high heat. When the oil starts to shimmer, add the potato and sausage and cook until the sausage is browned and the potato is just tender. Remove the pan from heat and let cool.

2. Dust a work surface with the semolina flour, place the dough on the surface, and gently stretch it into a round. For more detailed instructions on properly stretching a ball of pizza dough see page 73. Cover the dough with the mozzarella and top with the sausage-and-potato mixture, onion, and rosemary. Season with salt and drizzle olive oil over the pizza.

3. Using a peel or a flat baking sheet, transfer the pizza to the heated baking implement in the oven. Bake for about 15 minutes, until the crust is golden brown and starting to char. Remove, drizzle truffle oil over the pizza, and let it cool slightly before slicing and serving.

INGREDIENTS:

1 BALL PIZZA DOUGH

3.5 OZ. | 100 GRAMS SMOKED MOZZARELLA CHEESE, CUT INTO SHORT STRIPS

¼ RED ONION, SLICED THIN

LEAVES FROM 2 SPRIGS FRESH ROSEMARY

SALT, TO TASTE

TRUFFLE OIL, TO TASTE

ROSSA CON FILETTI DI ACCIUGHE

YIELD: 1 PIZZA / **ACTIVE TIME:** 15 MINUTES / **TOTAL TIME:** 45 MINUTES

These classic Mediterranean flavors pair beautifully with Francesco Acri's tangy crust, creating a finished product that takes you straight to Naples.

1. Preheat the oven to the maximum temperature and place a baking stone or steel on the middle rack as it warms. Dust a work surface with the semolina flour, place the dough on the surface, and gently stretch it into a round. For more detailed instructions on properly stretching a ball of pizza dough see page 73. Cover the dough with the tomatoes and top with the mozzarella, anchovies, olives, and capers. Season with salt and oregano and drizzle olive oil over the pizza.

2. Using a peel or a flat baking sheet, transfer the pizza to the heated baking implement in the oven. Bake for about 15 minutes, until the crust is golden brown and starting to char. Remove and let cool slightly before slicing and serving.

INGREDIENTS:

SEMOLINA FLOUR, AS NEEDED

1 BALL PIZZA DOUGH

3.5 OZ. | 100 GRAMS WHOLE PEELED SAN MARZANO TOMATOES, CRUSHED BY HAND

3.5 OZ. | 100 GRAMS BUFFALO MOZZARELLA CHEESE, DRAINED AND TORN

8 ANCHOVY FILLETS

8 PITTED KALAMATA OLIVES

10 CAPERS

SALT, TO TASTE

DRIED OREGANO, TO TASTE

OLIVE OIL, TO TASTE

GLOSSARY

The following is a selective glossary that provides a bit more information about some of the less common ingredients utilized in this book. It also serves to explain the differences between various cheeses, cured meats, and flours.

"00" flour: super-fine white wheat flour with a protein content between 8 and 12 percent; this is the flour traditionally used in the Neapolitan tradition of pizza making.

Advieh: a mild Persian spice blend; ingredients vary regionally but often include cumin, cinnamon, cardamom, dried rose petals, coriander, black pepper, turmeric, and dried limes.

All-purpose flour: this versatile white flour is generally a combination of flour from hard (bronze-colored wheat that has a higher protein, and thus higher gluten, content) and soft wheat (wheat with a light golden color; also referred to as "white wheat"); it has a protein content between 10 and 12%.

Asiago cheese: a cow's milk cheese from the mountainous northeastern part of Italy; eaten fresh it is mild and semi-soft, while aged versions develop a sweet sharpness.

Baking powder: a mixture of acid, carbonate, and bicarbonate that is used as a leavening agent.

Baking soda: a salt composed of sodium and bicarbonate, this leavening agent responds to the acidic components in a recipe.

Black truffle: the catchall term for varieties of edible black truffles, including black winter truffle, burgundy truffle, and summer truffle; the flavors of each differ but all are earthy. Truffle oils are no substitute for fresh truffles.

Bottarga: the salted and cured roe sack of a fish, typically from grey mullet; it delivers savory umami flavor.

Bread flour: this white flour has a high protein content (between 12 and 13 percent) and is ideal for bread and pizza baking since the extra-elastic dough it produces can capture and hold more carbon dioxide than that yielded by other types of flour.

Bresaola: a lean, thin sliced dry-cured beef made from a single muscle from which any outer fat has been removed; it has a flavor reminiscent of pastrami.

Brie cheese: a French soft cheese that is creamy and quite dynamic in its flavor; brie exported outside of France has been stabilized, thus inhibiting the development of its flavor profile.

Broccoli rabe: also called rapini, this is not broccoli but rather a cruciferous vegetable with slightly bitter leaves and nutty buds that complement fatty cheeses and meats.

Buffalo mozzarella cheese: made from buffalo milk, which has twice the fat content of cow's milk, this cheese is delicately creamy and slightly sweet.

Burrata cheese: meaning "buttery" in Italian, this fresh cheese is formed into a globe, with a thin exterior layer of mozzarella (made from cow's or buffalo's milk) that is filled with a pillowy mixture of curd and cream, which

  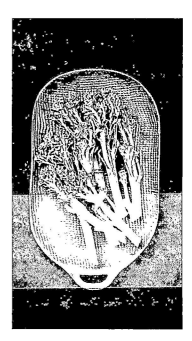

oozes out when the cheese is cut; because this is incredibly fresh cheese, it needs to be eaten immediately.

Caciocavallo cheese: pairs of gourd-shaped rounds of this cheese, made from pasteurized cow's milk, are hung over a board to age, which explains its literal name: "cheese on horseback"; the aging process results in a pungent aroma and a salty and sharp flavor.

Capers: the pickled bud of the caper bush, which is also referred to as Flinders rose.

Catupiry cheese: a mild, spreadable cow's milk cheese mixed with sour cream, salt, and cultures that is popular in Brazil.

Chaat masala: a peppery and floral Indian spice blend that typically contains cumin, coriander, dried ginger, black pepper, black salt, asafoetida, chili powder, and dried mango powder.

Cheddar cheese: probably the most popular cheese in the world, this semi hard cow's milk cheese can range from mild to sharp in flavor, depending on aging; it originated in England.

Chorizo: assertively seasoned with either sweet or hot smoked paprika (*pimentón*), this smoked Spanish pork sausage does not require addi-

tional cooking, unlike Mexican chorizo, which is made with raw pork.

Ciccioli: the byproduct of pressing, drying, and aging leftover cuts of fatty pork (often as a result of making lard), these fat-rich chunks of meat are often deep-fried as a snack.

Coppa: dry-cured meat derived from the whole muscle that runs from behind a pig's head to the shoulder; it is seasoned with wine, garlic, and spices that include paprika.

Cornmeal: made from dried, ground, and degerminated corn, it ranges in texture from fine to coarse.

Cream cheese: soft and mild cheese made from cream.

Diastatic malt: active enzymes in this powder help yeast grow and promote a good rise in doughs.

Feta cheese: made from sheep's or goat's milk, it is rich and salty; most of the feta that is made in North America and Greece has been pasteurized.

Fish roe: a catchall term for all fish eggs that are not harvested from sturgeon (the fish that is the source of caviar).

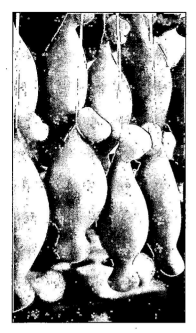 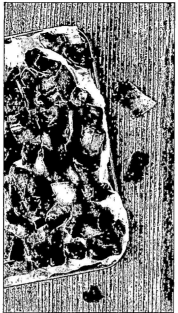 

Fish sauce: a regular seasoning in Asian cuisine, it is the product of fermented fish that is coated in salt and aged for up to two years. It has an extremely pungent smell and an intense flavor.

Goat cheese: a catchall term for all cheeses made from goat's milk; flavors and textures vary, but all styles have low lactose content. Younger goat cheese is soft and tangy; older varieties harden to the point of being crumbly and develop a nutty flavor.

Gorgonzola cheese: this veined Italian cow's milk blue cheese becomes more intensely flavored with age, developing from a buttery, slightly ashy flavor to a pungent and piquant one.

Guanciale: cured pork made from the jowl or cheek meat and typically seasoned with salt, pepper, garlic, sage, and rosemary.

High-gluten flour: a white wheat flour with a protein content between 13 and 14 percent; typically used for baked goods with a chew, like bagels, it can be used for pizza.

Hoisin sauce: a thick, salty, and tangy fermented soybean sauce commonly used in Chinese cuisine.

Italian sausage: a catchall term for pork sausage flavored with fennel or anise; versions with hot red pepper flakes are spicier.

Japanese mayonnaise: mostly commonly known by the brand Kewpie, this bottled condiment is creamier than other mayonnaises because it is made from only egg yolks; it has a tangier flavor, deriving from rice vinegar (instead of distilled vinegar) and MSG.

Lemongrass: used commonly in Thai cuisine, this herb has a citrus, ginger flavor.

Long-fermentation flour / pizza flour: also called "pizzeria" flour, this has a protein content of 12.5 percent and requires a long fermentation, yielding a light, elastic crust.

Low-moisture mozzarella cheese: sold in blocks or pre-grated, this cheese has a lower water content than fresh mozzarella as well as a tangier flavor.

Makrut lime leaves: a very aromatic herb common in Thai cuisine, often used like a bay leaf in Western cooking, with a bright, extremely citrus flavor.

Natto: these soybeans fermented by the bacteria Bacillus subtilis date to 10th century BCE Japan; they have a funky, ripe-cheese aroma and flavor and a slimy texture, all of which make them an acquired taste.

'Nduja: Calabrian chilis make this spreadable fermented pork red and spicy.

Nori: dried and pressed sheets of seaweed typically used for sushi rolls; used as seasoning, it adds a briny umami to any dish.

Nutmeg: native to Indonesia, this pungent spice is made from the seeds of a tropical evergreen tree; when possible, it is always preferable to grate your own.

a combination of caramelized oyster juice, salt, and sugar, among other ingredients, this syrupy sauce is sweet and salty.

Parmigiano reggiano: a regional hard cow's milk cheese that is strictly regulated (e.g., it can only be made using copper kettles), aged between 1 and 2 years; it has a nutty flavor.

Pecorino romano: a sheep's milk cheese typically aged for about a year; it has a sharp, salty flavor.

Pepperoni: this Italian American invention contains red peppers that give the sausage a bit of bite and its red hue.

Pine nuts: also called pignoli, these oily, almost buttery-tasting little nuts are seeds produced by one of twenty species of pine trees; the seeds are found within the pine cones and take approximately 18 months to mature.

Prosciutto: Italian dry-cured ham, made from the hind leg or thigh of a pig or wild boar.

Provolone cheese: made with either pasteurized or unpasteurized cow's milk, this is a mild and buttery cheese; the flavor becomes sharper with age.

smaller than chicken and duck eggs but with similar flavors, the most noticeable difference is that these eggs have a high yolk-to-egg ratio, making for a thicker, creamier egg.

Red caviar: brined roe from various types of salmon and trout that adds a salty, viscous mouthfeel to a dish.

Ricotta cheese: made from the whey yielded from the making of sheep, cow, goat, or buffalo cheeses, this is a smooth, sweet cheese that is firm but not solid.

Rye flour: milled from whole rye berries or rye grass grains, it imparts a distinctive flavor and provides greater nutritional value than wheat flour.

Salami: derived from the word *salame*, a reference to all salted meats, Italian salami is made with a mixture of pork, fat, and spices that is stuffed into casing (traditionally intestine) and then dried and cured.

Semolina flour: this golden, aromatic flour is made from durum wheat, and most often appears in Italian dishes.

Shichimi: a spicy Japanese blend of seven ingredients; typically sansho, dried orange peel, red chili pepper, nori, black sesame seeds, white poppy seeds, and garlic.

Speck: pork leg that has been rubbed with spices, including juniper berries and bay leaves, lightly smoked, and cured, yielding a deep, dense flavor.

Squash blossom: the delicate orange flower of a zucchini plant is a sign of summer in Italy and Mexico, and is traditionally stuffed and fried.

Sumac: a tart spice made from the dried red berries of the sumac bush.

Tahini: a slightly bitter and nutty Middle Eastern paste of ground sesame seeds.

Taleggio cheese: a pungent washed-rind soft cow's cheese with an edible rind that is shaped in rectangles; its aroma is much more pungent than the flavor, which is deeply creamy.

Tamarind pulp: a souring agent made from dried mature tamarinds that is an essential ingredient in Thai cuisine.

Teriyaki sauce: made with soy sauce, sake, ginger, and sugar, this sweet sauce is typically used as a marinade and glaze.

Thai chili paste: also known as *nam prik pao*, dried chilis, shrimp, and palm sugar give this condiment its signature briny, tangy, and spicy flavor.

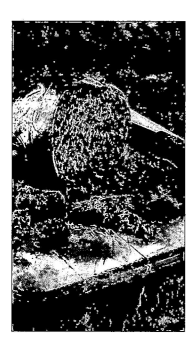

  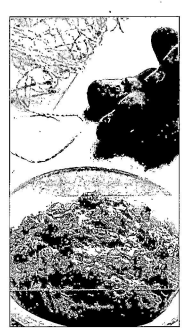

Tikka masala: a creamy Indian tomato sauce spiced with ginger, cumin, turmeric, and garam masala, among other ingredients, which determine the level of spiciness.

Whole-wheat flour: made from the entire grain—endosperm, wheat germ, and outer bran—this flour contains the most nutrients of any wheat flour; it has a protein content of about 13 to 14 percent.

Za'atar: a Middle Eastern spice blend of savory dried herbs that varies by region, but typically includes: sumac, sesame seed, coriander, cumin, marjoram, thyme, and oregano.

ACKNOWLEDGMENTS

I am deeply grateful to all the home bakers who helped create 2,500 years of focaccia tradition through methods learned from mothers and grandmothers and lovingly preserved them. I am also grateful to all the professional bakers who have developed pizza as we know it, mastering techniques and passing them down through generations.

On a more personal level, I am grateful to the Cider Mill Press editorial team for all the incredible work, and to Spigamadre's staff, especially the unbreakable Nora, who helped make everything go smoothly while I was busy with this project. A special thanks goes to my customers, the best supporters I could ever imagine and a constant source of inspiration.

I would not have made it through without the support of my fellow bakers from around the world: a big thank you goes to Sandra, Alessandra, Terry, Antonella, and Luigi from the recipe testing team and to Edgar and Augusto for the much needed discussions about baking.

And, finally, I want to thank my family. First and foremost my parents, my dad Salvatore for his passion for history and quality food, and my mom Maria Antonietta for having taught me since the crib about our food traditions. Thanks to my brothers Giancarlo and Massimo for having always been avid eaters of my creations, and my husband Larry for lovingly supporting me, especially when accompanying me on countless trips around the world, almost always without complaining. Lastly, I am forever grateful for my daughter Adina, such a gifted young baker and cook, who, I hope, will one day make good use of this book.

And thanks to all the future readers of *Pizza*. Your creations will make this story continue and keep the tradition stay alive for many more generations to come.

FURTHER READING

I never stop consulting these books – they are outstanding resources.

Bianco, Chris. *Bianco: Pizza, Pasta, and Other Food I Like*. Ecco, 2017.

Bjorstad, Asmund. *Our Daily Bread-A History of the Cereals*. Vidarforlaget AS, 2012

Bonci, Gabriele. *Il gioco della pizza. Le magnifiche ricette del re della pizza*. Rizzoli, 2012.

Boni, Ada. *Il Talismano della Felicità*. Colombo, 1927.

Boni, Ada. *Italian Regional Cooking*. Crescent, 1987.

Buehler, Emily. *Bread Science: The Chemistry and Craft of Making Bread*. Two Blue Books, 2006.

Dickie, John. *Delizia! The Epic History of the Italians and Their Food*. Sceptre, 2008.

Fioravanti, Ilaria & Venuti, Valentina. *Lievitati di Liguria. Dolci & Salati*. Sagep, 2017.

Geminiani, Tony. *The Pizza Bible*. Ten Speed Press, 2014.

Manca, Franco. *Artisan Pizza*. Kyle Books, 2013.

Molinari Pradelli, Alessandro. *La cucina regionale italiana in oltre 5000 ricette*. Newton Compton, 2013.

Padoan, Simone. *La Pizza Contemporanea*. Italian Gourmet, 2018.

Pane, Pizze, Focacce e Torte Salate. Giunti Demetra, 2010.

Pignataro, Luciano. *La Pizza. Una Storia Contemporanea*. Hoepli, 2018.

Pizzeria D'Italia 2019. Gambero Rosso, 2019.

Reinhart, Peter. *Perfect Pan Pizza: Square Pies to Make at Home, from Roman, Sicilian, and Detroit, to Grandma Pies and Focaccia*. Ten Speed Press, 2019.

Reinhart, Peter. *American Pie*. Ten Speed Press, 2003.

Stagnani, Vittorio. *La Luna e la Focaccia*. Progedit, 2011.

Tanga, Maria Ivana. *Il Grano e la Dea. Cereali e Pane del Mare Nostrum*. Aletti, 2018.

Vetri, Marc. *Mastering Pizza*. Ten Speed Press, 2018.

Whitson, Craig et al. *Passion for Pizza*. Surrey Books, 2014

ABOUT THE AUTHOR

Barbara Caracciolo is the founder and owner of Spigamadre, an Italian bakery in Årsta, Sweden. Born and raised in Rome, Italy, Caracciolo has baked since she can remember and she has been cultivating a passion for traditional Italian cuisine and food history since childhood. She earned a PhD in medicine and MSs in psychology and epidemiology, but today she spends her days either baking or writing about it in her quiet neighborhood in southern Stockholm.

IMAGE CREDITS

METRIC CONVERSIONS

WEIGHTS

1 oz. = 28 grams
2 oz. = 57 grams
4 oz. (¼ lb.) = 113 grams
8 oz. (½ lb.) = 227 grams
16 oz. (1 lb.) = 454 grams

VOLUME MEASURES

⅛ teaspoon = 0.6 ml
¼ teaspoon = 1.23 ml
½ teaspoon = 2.5 ml
1 teaspoon = 5 ml
1 tablespoon (3 teaspoons) = ½ fluid oz. = 15 ml
2 tablespoons = 1 fluid oz. = 29.5 ml
¼ cup (4 tablespoons) = 2 fluid oz. = 59 ml
⅓ cup (5 ⅓ tablespoons) = 2.7 fluid oz. = 80 ml
½ cup (8 tablespoons) = 4 fluid oz. = 120 ml
⅔ cup (10 ⅔ tablespoons) = 5.4 fluid oz. = 160 ml
¾ cup (12 tablespoons) = 6 fluid oz. = 180 ml
1 cup (16 tablespoons) = 8 fluid oz. = 240 ml

TEMPERATURE EQUIVALENTS

°F	°C	Gas Mark
225	110	¼
250	130	½
275	140	1
300	150	2
325	170	3
350	180	4
375	190	5
400	200	6
425	220	7
450	230	8
475	240	9
500	250	10

LENGTH MEASURES

1/16 inch = 1.6 mm
⅛ inch = 3 mm
¼ inch = 1.35 mm
½ inch = 1.25 cm
¾ inch = 2 cm
1 inch = 2.5 cm

INDEX

Abruzzi, 41

advieh, Mincemeat & Vegetable Pizza, 320

almonds
Raspberry & Almond Pizza, 695
Romesco Sauce, 578

Aloo Gobi Marinade, 308

Aloo Gobi, Pizza with, 308

American pizza pie
flours for, 67
history of, 61–63
recipes for, 261–276
See also pizza

American pizzerias, 56–57

anchovies
Buttermilk Caesar Dressing, 648
Calzone Pugliese, 208–209
Cavicione, 210
Chichiripieno, 177
Faccia di Vecchia, 216
Focaccia Messinese, 219
Focaccia with Pumpkin Cream, Anchovies & Burrata, 603
Grupariata, 199
Parsley Pesto, 489
Pissalandrea, 147
Pizza alla Pala with Zucchini Blossoms, Anchovies & Burrata, 624
Pizza with Anchovies, 562
Pizza with Mussels & Artichokes, 357
Pizza with Romanesco Broccoli Cream, Anchovies & Burrata, 337
Rianata, 220
Romana, 238
Rossa con Filetti di Acciughe, 779

Squash Blossom & Ricotta Pizza, 343

Aosta Valley, 32

Apple Cider Vinaigrette, 657

apples
Apple, Onion & Balsamic Vinegar Pizza, 582
Caramel Apple Pizza, 704
Cinnamon Apple Pizza, 699
Custom Royal Dessert Pizza, 748
Radicchio & Ricotta Salata Salad with Apple Cider Vinaigrette, 657
Roasted Baby Beet, Radish & Apple Salad with Blue Cheese Mousse, 642
Sautéed Red Cabbage with Apples, Fennel & Balsamic, 663

Apulia, 48–49

Arrabbiata, Eggplant & Pepper Pizza, 573

Arrabbiata Sauce, 573

artichokes and artichoke hearts
Artichoke & Potato Pizza, 351
Capricciosa, 241
Chichiripieno, 177
Ham & Artichoke Focaccia, 611
Mushroom & Artichoke Pan Pizza, 570
Pizza with Garden Vegetables, Artichokes & Salami, 387
Pizza with Mushrooms, Asparagus & Pesto, 369
Pizza with Mussels & Artichokes, 357
Quattro Stagioni, 249
Turkey Ham, Artichoke &

Cream Cheese Pizza, 509

arugula
Arugula, Egg & Mushroom Pizza, 474
Arugula, Nectarine, Farro & Goat Cheese Salad with White Balsamic Vinaigrette, 644
Arugula, Pomegranate & Cherry Tomato Pizza, 569
Beet & Goat Cheese Pizza, 529
Caper & Olive Pizza, 454
Eggplant, Bufala & Arugula Pizza, 501
Fig, Prosciutto & Balsamic Pizza, 493
Pear & Ricotta Focaccia, 600
Pizza with Chanterelles, Béchamel & Parmesan, 545
Pizza with Goat Cheese, Fennel & Walnuts, 553
Pizza with Parsley Pesto & Caviar, 489
Pizza with Peas & Caviar, 558
Pizza with Prosciutto, Arugula & Parmesan, 339
Pizza with Prunes, Goat Cheese & Tomatoes, 577
Pizza with Pumpkin, Feta & Arugula, 466
Pizza with Ricotta & Cremini Mushrooms, 384
Pizza with Smoked Salmon & Capers, 485
Pizza with Swordfish, Pine Nuts & Cherry Tomatoes, 391
Raw Beet Salad with Blood Orange, Jalapeño & Brie, 647
Salmon & Pepper Pizza, 486

Salt-n-Peppa Prawn Pizza, 747

Shrimp, Arugula & Olive Pizza al Taglio, 620

Smoked Chicken, Bufala & Pesto Focaccia, 599

asiago cheese

The Masher, 731

Pizza with Figs, Speck, Asiago & Gorgonzola, 498

asparagus

Margherita with Prosciutto & Asparagus, 392

Pizza with Asparagus, Guanciale & Bottarga, 388

Pizza with Asparagus, Pine Nuts & Bufala, 348

Roasted Asparagus & Cherry Tomato Pizza, 358

avocado

Avocado, Tomato & Feta Pizza, 525

Avocado Mousse, 747

Pizza with Seafood, Avocado & Mango, 537

Spinach, Bacon, Avocado & Orange Salad, 659

bacon

Bacon Jam, 743

The Masher, 731

Natto & Bacon Pizza, 291

Notorious P.I.G. Skillet Pizza, 743

Panuozzo, 191

Pinza onta Polesana, 130

Pizza with Bacon, Blue Cheese, Onion & Pickles, 574

Pizza with Broccoli & Bacon, 414

Pizza with Eggs & Bacon, 425

Pizza with Ricotta, Figs & Bacon, 526

Pizza with Zucchini Cream, Bacon & Bufala, 437

Roasted Brussels Sprouts with Bacon, Blue Cheese & Pickled Red Onion, 663

Shaved Brussels Sprouts & Kale Salad with Blood Orange

Vinaigrette, 651

Spinach, Bacon, Avocado & Orange Salad, 659

Torta al Testo con i Ciccioli, 169

Two Cheese & Bacon Pizza, 422

baking equipment, 74–79

baking peel, 77

baking sheet, 75

baking stone/steel, 76–77

Balado & Chicken Pizza, 295

Balado Sauce, 295

balsamic glaze/balsamic vinegar

Apple, Onion & Balsamic Vinegar Pizza, 582

Arugula, Nectarine, Farro & Goat Cheese Salad with White Balsamic Vinaigrette, 644

Beet & Goat Cheese Pizza, 529

Eggplant, Bufala & Arugula Pizza, 501

Endive & Cherry Tomato Pizza, 542

Fig, Prosciutto & Balsamic Pizza, 493

Late Summer Salad with Wild Mushrooms, Parmesan & Pine Nuts, 655

Margherita with Prosciutto & Asparagus, 392

Pizza with Chanterelles, Béchamel & Parmesan, 545

Pizza with Goat Cheese, Figs & Walnuts, 513

Pizza with Parsley Pesto & Caviar, 489

Pizza with Smoked Salmon & Capers, 485

Pizza with Swordfish, Pine Nuts & Cherry Tomatoes, 391

Roasted Radicchio, Pear & Gorgonzola Salad, 656

Sautéed Radicchio with Beans, Parmesan & Balsamic, 665

Sautéed Red Cabbage with Apples, Fennel & Balsamic, 664

Smoked Chicken, Bufala & Pesto Focaccia, 599

bananas

Pizza with Banana & Cinnamon, 691

Pizza with Banana Curry, 328

Basic Focaccia Dough, 84

basil

Basil Pesto, 365

Caprese, 254

Capricciosa, 241

Frying Pan Margherita, 754

Margherita, 237

New Haven Tomato Pie, 264

Ortolana, 258

Pistachio Pesto, 375

Pizza with Peas & Caviar, 558

Two Cheese & Mushroom Pizza, 429

Basil Pesto

Calamari, Shrimp & Pesto Pizza, 461

Fig, Prosciutto & Balsamic Pizza, 493

Pesto, Tomato & Bufala Pizza, 365

Pesto & Veggie Pizza, 413

Pizza with Mushrooms, Asparagus & Pesto, 369

Potato & Pesto Pizza, 373

recipe, 365

Smoked Chicken, Bufala & Pesto Focaccia, 599

Basilicata, 46

BBQ Chicken Pizza, 409

Beans, Parmesan & Balsamic, Sautéed Radicchio with, 665

Béchamel Sauce

Pizza with Chanterelles, Béchamel & Parmesan, 545

Pizza with Potato, Red Onion & Béchamel, 538

recipe, 445

Roasted Zucchini, Béchamel & Rosemary Pizza, 445

beef

Beef Rendang, 296

Bulgogi Pizza, 300

Donair-Spiced Ground Beef, 720

Halifax Explosion, 720

Lahmacun, 323
Mincemeat & Vegetable Pizza, 320
Pizza with Rendang & Mushrooms, 296
Spicy Beef & Zucchini Pizza, 450
Taco Pizza, 478
beets
 Beet & Goat Cheese Pizza, 529
 Farmers Market, 744
 Raw Beet Salad with Blood Orange, Jalapeño & Brie, 647
 Roasted Baby Beet, Radish & Apple Salad with Blue Cheese Mousse, 642
Berries, Cherries & Mascarpone Pizza, 683
Bianca con Salsiccia di Finocchietto, 776
biga
 Falia di Priverno, 182
 Focaccia Dough with Biga, 96
 Pizza Dough with Biga, 119
black bean garlic sauce
Steamed Japanese Eggplant with Black Bean Garlic Sauce & Basil, 666
Yu Choy with Black Bean Garlic Sauce & Extra Garlic, 674
blackberries, Mixed Berry Pizza, 521
Blood Orange Vinaigrette, 651
blue cheese
 Pizza with Bacon, Blue Cheese, Onion & Pickles, 574
 Pizza with Pear, Thyme, Blue Cheese & Walnuts, 684
 Roasted Baby Beet, Radish & Apple Salad with Blue Cheese Mousse, 642
 Roasted Brussels Sprouts with Bacon, Blue Cheese & Pickled Red Onion, 663
blueberries
 Berries, Cherries & Mascarpone Pizza, 683
 Mixed Berry Pizza, 521
Bok Choy, Pine Nut & Raisin

Pizza, 555
Boscaiola, 242
Bottarga, Pizza with Asparagus, Guanciale &, 388
brandy, Fugascina di Mergozzo, 135
bresaola
 Pizza with Parmesan, Bresaola & Truffles, 400
 Ricotta & Bresaola Pizza, 356
brick cheese, Detroit-Style Pizza, 268
brie cheese
 Pizza with Brie & Pear, 490
 Raw Beet Salad with Blood Orange, Jalapeño & Brie, 647
Brigadeiro & Strawberry Pizza, 692
Brigadeiro Sauce, 692
broccoli
 Broccoli, Chorizo & Chili Pepper Pizza, 421
 Broccoli & Pine Nut alla Spigamadre, 634
 Cauliflower & Broccoli Pizza, 410
 Pizza with Broccoli & Bacon, 414
 Pizza with Romanesco Broccoli Cream, Anchovies & Burrata, 337
 Pizza with Seafood & Broccoli, 417
 Roasted Brassica Salad with Pickled Ramps & Buttermilk Caesar Dressing, 648
 Sausage & Broccoli Pizza, 383
broccoli rabe
 Broccoli Rabe, Tomato & Olive Pizza, 533
 Carrettiera, 246
 Pizza with Sausage, Cime di Rapa & Cherry Tomatoes, 376
brusadela, 28
Brussels sprouts
 Roasted Brassica Salad with Pickled Ramps & Buttermilk Caesar Dressing, 648

Roasted Brussels Sprouts with Bacon, Blue Cheese & Pickled Red Onion, 663
 Shaved Brussels Sprouts & Kale Salad with Blood Orange Vinaigrette, 651
bufala
 Caprese, 254
 Eggplant, Bufala & Arugula Pizza, 501
 Pesto, Tomato & Bufala Pizza, 365
 Pizza al Taglio with Bufala, Eggplant & Garlic, 613
 Pizza with Asparagus, Pine Nuts & Bufala, 348
 Pizza with Garden Vegetables & Bufala, 449
 Pizza with Zucchini Cream, Bacon & Bufala, 437
 Smoked Chicken, Bufala & Pesto Focaccia, 599
 See also mozzarella cheese
Bulgogi Pizza, 300
Bulgogi Sauce, 300
burrata cheese
 Focaccia with Pumpkin Cream, Anchovies & Burrata, 603
 Pizza alla Pala with Zucchini Blossoms, Anchovies & Burrata, 624
 Pizza with Lamb, Eggplant & Burrata, 530
 Pizza with Romanesco Broccoli Cream, Anchovies & Burrata, 337
Buttermilk Caesar Dressing, 648
Buttermilk White Sauce, 721

cabbage
 Okonomiyaki Pizza, 288
 Red & Green Cabbage Salad with Ginger & Tahini Dressing, 645
 Red Cabbage, Ricotta & Walnut Pizza, 407
 Sautéed Red Cabbage with Apples, Fennel & Balsamic, 663

Cacciannanze, 39, 178
caciocavallo cheese
    Diavola, 245
    Faccia di Vecchia, 216
    Focaccia Messinese, 219
    Green Tomato Pizza, 522
    Parigina, 192
    Pistachio & Onion Pizza, 546
    Pizza al Taglio with Wild
        Mushrooms & Two Cheeses,
        617
    Pizza with Mushrooms,
        Caramelized Onions &
        Caciocavallo, 347
    Pizza with 'Ndjua, Sun-Dried
        Tomatoes & Caciocavallo,
        406
    Pizza with Prosciutto,
        Caciocavallo, Mushrooms &
        Nuts, 494
    Pizza with Smoked Trout,
        Poached Eggs & Capers, 517
    Potato & Caciocavallo alla
        Spigamadre, 637
    Potato & Pesto Pizza, 373
    Scaccia Ragusana, 224–225
    Sfincione Palermitano, 214–215
    Vastedda con Sambuco, 223
Cajun Shrimp & Salami Pizza, 554
Calabria, 46
Calamari, Shrimp & Pesto Pizza,
    461
California pizza, 63
California-Style Pizza, 272
Calzone Pugliese, 208–209
calzone pugliese, 49
Campania, 44–45
Canadian bacon, Hawaiian-Style
    Pizza, 275
cantaloupe, Melon, Cucumber &
    Prosciutto Salad with Mint
    Vinaigrette, 652
capers
    Calzone Pugliese, 208–209
    Caper & Olive Pizza, 454
    Chichiripieno, 177
    Endive, Olive & Caper alla
        Spigamadre, 629
    Pissalandrea, 147

Pizza with Smoked Salmon &
    Capers, 485
Pizza with Smoked Trout,
    Poached Eggs & Capers, 517
Puddica Salentina, 203
Radicchio & Garden Vegetable
    Pizza, 361
Romana, 238
Rossa con Filetti di Acciughe,
    779
Caprese, 254
Capricciosa, 241
Caramel Apple Pizza, 704
Caramelized Onions &
    Caciocavallo, Pizza with
    Mushrooms, 347
Carrettiera, 246
carrots
    Dante's Personal Pizzas, 736
    Roasted Parsnips & Carrots with
        Ras el Hanout & Honey, 671
cashews, Arugula, Nectarine, Farro
    & Goat Cheese Salad with
    White Balsamic Vinaigrette,
    644
cast-iron pizza pan, 75
cast-iron skillet, 75
Catupiry Pizza, Chicken &, 312
cauliflower
    Cauliflower, Provolone &
        Smoked Ham Pizza, 446
    Cauliflower & Broccoli Pizza,
        410
    Pizza with Aloo Gobi, 308
    Roasted Brassica Salad with
        Pickled Ramps & Buttermilk
        Caesar Dressing, 648
caviar
    Pizza with Parsley Pesto &
        Caviar, 489
    Pizza with Peas & Caviar, 558
Cavicione, 210
cecina, 36
celery, Pizza with Garden
    Vegetables & Bufala, 449
cheddar cheese
    Cauliflower & Broccoli Pizza, 410
    Smoked Cod & Cheddar Pizza,
        481

St. Louis–Style Pizza, 271
cheese. See individual cheese types
Cherries & Mascarpone Pizza,
    Berries, 683
Chicago Deep-Dish Pizza, 62, 267
Chicago Deep-Dish Stuffed Pizza,
    762
Chichiripieno, 39, 177
chicken
    Balado & Chicken Pizza, 295
    BBQ Chicken Pizza, 409
    Chicken, Sausage & Pine Nut
        Pizza, 505
    Chicken & Catupiry Pizza, 312
    Chicken & Escarole Pizza, 550
    Chicken Kebab, 469
    Chicken Satay & Mango Pizza,
        311
    Cucumber, Tomato & Chicken
        Pizza, 581
    Kebab Pizza, 469
    Meat Lover's Pizza, 470
    Radicchio & Ricotta Salata Salad
        with Apple Cider Vinaigrette,
        657
    Smoked Chicken, Bufala &
        Pesto Focaccia, 599
    Teriyaki Chicken & Mushroom
        Pizza, 283
    Tikka Masala Pizza, 307
chickpea flour, Farinata, 148
chili peppers/chilies
    Balado & Chicken Pizza, 295
    Beef Rendang, 296
    Broccoli, Chorizo & Chili
        Pepper Pizza, 421
    Kebab Pizza, 469
    Pepper & Egg Pizza, 418
    Pizza with Aloo Gobi, 308
    Pizza with Rendang &
        Mushrooms, 296
    Pizza with Shrimp, Chili Peppers
        & Bufala, 462
    Pulled Pork Pizza, 561
    Taco Pizza, 478
    Tom Yum Pizza with Shrimp,
        299
    Two Cheese & Bacon Pizza, 422
Chilled Corn Salad, 660

Chisola Piacentina, 36, 158
Chive Pizza, Smoked Salmon &, 482
chocolate
    Chocolate, Hazelnut & Strawberry Pizza, 687
    Tiramisu Pizza, 703
chocolate pudding
    Marble Pizza, 680
    S'mores Pizza, 688
chorizo
    Broccoli, Chorizo & Chili Pepper Pizza, 421
    Chorizo & Jalapeño Pizza, 319
    Chorizo & Olive Pizza, 430
    See also sausage
Ciaccino Senese, 36, 183
cilantro
    Chilled Corn Salad, 660
    Red & Green Cabbage Salad with Ginger & Tahini Dressing, 645
cinnamon
    Cinnamon Apple Pizza, 699
    Pizza with Banana & Cinnamon, 691
Classic Pepperoni Pizza, 276
cocoa powder
    Brigadeiro & Strawberry Pizza, 692
    Tiramisu Pizza, 703
coconut, Beef Rendang, 296
coconut cream
    Beef Rendang, 296
    Chicken Satay & Mango Pizza, 311
Cod & Cheddar Pizza, Smoked, 481
Collard Greens, Southern, 668
Conspiracy Pizza, 717–718
cookware, 75–77
Coppa, Prosciutto & Sausage Pizza, 514
corn
    Bulgogi Pizza, 300
    Chilled Corn Salad, 660
    Mincemeat & Vegetable Pizza, 320
    Natto & Bacon Pizza, 291

Pepper & Egg Pizza, 418
Pizza with Tuna & Corn, 458
Taco Pizza, 478
Teriyaki Chicken & Mushroom Pizza, 283
cotija cheese, Chilled Corn Salad, 660
cream cheese
    Marble Pizza, 680
    Pizza with Grilled Vegetables & Tofu Cream Cheese, 566
    Pizza with Smoked Herring, Radish & Cream Cheese, 549
    S'mores Pizza, 688
    Turkey Ham, Artichoke & Cream Cheese Pizza, 509
crescenta, 35
Crescenta Bolognese, 154–155
crescentine o tigelle, 36
crescenza, Focaccia di Recco, 151
Crescia Sfogliata, 39, 174
cucumber
    Cucumber, Tomato & Chicken Pizza, 581
    Lahmacun, 323
    Melon, Cucumber & Prosciutto Salad with Mint Vinaigrette, 652
    Pizza with Za'atar, 324
    Teriyaki Salmon Pizza, 284
Curry, Pizza with Banana, 328
Custom Royal Dessert Pizza, 748

Dandelion & Tomato Pizza, 585
Dante's Personal Pizzas, 736
Dante's Pizzeria, 733–735
desserts
    Berries, Cherries & Mascarpone Pizza, 683
    Brigadeiro & Strawberry Pizza, 692
    Caramel Apple Pizza, 704
    Chocolate, Hazelnut & Strawberry Pizza, 687
    Cinnamon Apple Pizza, 699
    Custom Royal Dessert Pizza, 748
    Lemon Curd Pizza, 700
    Marble Pizza, 680

Pizza with Pear, Thyme, Blue Cheese & Walnuts, 684
    Raspberry & Almond Pizza, 695
    S'mores Pizza, 688
    Tiramisu Pizza, 703
    Vanilla Custard Pizza, 696
Detroit-Style Pizza, 63, 268
diastatic malt
    Falia di Priverno, 182
    Pizza Bianca Romana, 181
Diavola, 245
Donair Sauce, 327, 720
Double Mozzarella & Ham Pizza, 433
dough
    Basic Focaccia Dough, 84
    basic methods for, 70–74
    Focaccia Dough with Biga, 96
    Focaccia with Old Dough, 99
    48-Hour Focaccia Dough, 92
    ingredients for, 65–69
    master focaccia doughs, 83–101
    master pizza doughs, 107–123
    Neapolitan Pizza Dough, 108
    No-Knead Focaccia Dough, 95
    No-Knead Pizza Dough, 116
    Pizza Dough with Biga, 119
    Pizza with Old Dough, 120
    Quick Focaccia Dough, 83
    Quick Pizza Dough, 107
    Sourdough Focaccia Dough, 100
    Sourdough Pizza Dough, 123
    Theo & Co.'s Basic Pizza Dough, 740
    Theo & Co.'s Skillet Pizza Dough, 741
    24-Hour Focaccia with 60 Percent Hydration, 87
    24-Hour Focaccia with 70 Percent Hydration, 88
    24-Hour Focaccia with 80 Percent Hydration, 91
    24-Hour Pizza Dough with 62 Percent Hydration, 111
    24-Hour Pizza Dough with 67 Percent Hydration, 112
    24-Hour Pizza Dough with 72 Percent Hydration, 115
Duck, Pizza with Peking, 304

eggplant

Arrabbiata, Eggplant & Pepper
Pizza, 573

Eggplant, Bufala & Arugula
Pizza, 501

Eggplant Parmigiana Pizza, 344

Garden Vegetable & Ricotta
Pizza, 370

Grilled Zucchini & Eggplant
Pizza, 453

Lamb, Eggplant & Tomato
Pizza, 586

Melanzane Pizza, 766

Ortolana, 258

Pizza al Taglio with Bufala,
Eggplant & Garlic, 613

Pizza with Garden Vegetables,
Artichokes & Salami, 387

Pizza with Lamb, Eggplant &
Burrata, 530

Steamed Japanese Eggplant with
Black Bean Garlic Sauce &
Basil, 666

eggs

Arugula, Egg & Mushroom
Pizza, 474

Balado & Chicken Pizza, 295

Eggplant Parmigiana Pizza, 344

Pepper & Egg Pizza, 418

Pizza à la Portuguesa, 315

Pizza with Eggs & Bacon, 425

Pizza with Smoked Trout,
Poached Eggs & Capers, 517

Spinach, Egg & Cheese Pizza,
473

elderflowers, Vastedda con
Sambuco, 223

electric pizza ovens, 79

Emilia Romagna, 35–36

endive

Endive & Cherry Tomato Pizza,
542

Endive, Olive & Caper alla
Spigamadre, 629

Pizza alla Pala with Prosciutto &
Endive, 623

Endive, Olive & Caper alla
Spigamadre, 629

escarole

Chicken & Escarole Pizza, 550

Focaccia Messinese, 219

espresso and espresso powder,
Tiramisu Pizza, 703

Faccia di Vecchia, 51, 216

fainè, 53

Falia di Priverno, 40, 182

Farinata, 34, 148

Farmers Market, 744

Farro & Goat Cheese Salad with
White Balsamic Vinaigrette,
Arugula, Nectarine, 644

fats, 68–69

fennel

Fennel, Grapefruit & Pistachio
Salad, 654

Pizza with Goat Cheese, Fennel
& Walnuts, 553

Pizza with Grilled Vegetables &
Tofu Cream Cheese, 566

Radicchio & Ricotta Salata Salad
with Apple Cider Vinaigrette,
657

Roasted Fennel & Sausage Pizza,
336

Sautéed Red Cabbage with
Apples, Fennel & Balsamic,
663

Tuna & Orange-Marinated
Fennel Pizza, 340

fermentation, 72, 74

feta cheese

Avocado, Tomato & Feta Pizza,
525

Chilled Corn Salad, 660

Lahmacun, 323

Melon, Cucumber & Prosciutto
Salad with Mint Vinaigrette,
652

Pizza with Feta, Olives &
Peppers, 442

Pizza with Pumpkin, Feta &
Arugula, 466

Pizza with Za'atar, 324

Spinach & Feta Focaccia, 607

Zucchini & Feta alla
Spigamadre, 630

Zucchini with Tomatoes, Feta,
Garlic & Lemon, 675

figs

Fig, Prosciutto & Balsamic
Pizza, 493

Pizza with Figs, Speck, Asiago &
Gorgonzola, 498

Pizza with Goat Cheese, Figs &
Walnuts, 513

Pizza with Ham, Gorgonzola,
Pears & Walnuts, 497

Pizza with Ricotta, Figs &
Bacon, 526

first fermentation, 72

fish

Chichiripieno, 177

Pizza with Seafood, Avocado &
Mango, 537

Pizza with Sicilian-Style Tuna &
Bell Peppers, 352

Pizza with Smoked Herring,
Radish & Cream Cheese, 549

Pizza with Smoked Salmon &
Capers, 485

Pizza with Smoked Trout,
Poached Eggs & Capers, 517

Pizza with Swordfish, Pine Nuts
& Cherry Tomatoes, 391

Pizza with Tuna & Corn, 458

Salmon & Pepper Pizza, 486

Smoked Cod & Cheddar Pizza,
481

Smoked Salmon & Chive Pizza,
482

Teriyaki Salmon Pizza, 284

Tuna & Onion Pizza, 404

Tuna & Orange-Marinated
Fennel Pizza, 340

See also seafood

fish sauce, Tom Yum Paste, 299

flour, 65–66

Focaccette di Aulla, 37, 161

focaccia

baking, 597

baking equipment for, 74–75

Basic Focaccia Dough, 84

Broccoli & Pine Nut alla
Spigamadre, 634

Endive, Olive & Caper alla
Spigamadre, 629

from Central Italy, 160–183

flours for, 66
focaccia alla Spigamadre, 628
Focaccia Barese, 48, 200
Focaccia con le Olive, 144
focaccia con le olive, 33
Focaccia di Altamura, 48, 202
Focaccia di Carnevale Salentina, 212
Focaccia di Giaveno, 31, 136
Focaccia di Recco, 34, 151
focaccia di susa, 30
focaccia di Voltri, 33
Focaccia Dough with Biga, 96
focaccia fioretto, 28
focaccia Genovese, 32, 33, 140
focaccia leva di Gallicano, 36, 37
Focaccia Messinese, 51, 219
Focaccia Portoscusese, 52, 227
Focaccia with Old Dough, 99
Focaccia with Olives & Lemon, 608
Focaccia with Pumpkin Cream, Anchovies & Burrata, 603
48-Hour Focaccia Dough, 92
Ham & Artichoke Focaccia, 611
history of, 19–23
Levain for Focaccia, 101
Margherita alla Spigamadre, 633
master focaccia doughs, 83–101
No-Knead Focaccia Dough, 95
from Northern Italy, 128–158
Pear & Ricotta Focaccia, 600
Potato & Caciocavallo alla Spigamadre, 637
Quick Focaccia Dough, 83
by region, 25–53
shaping, 73
Smoked Chicken, Bufala & Pesto Focaccia, 599
Sourdough Focaccia Dough, 100
from southern Italy, 185–228
Spinach & Feta Focaccia, 607
Sweet Potato & Sage Focaccia, 604
toppings, 596
24-Hour Focaccia with 60 Percent Hydration, 87
24-Hour Focaccia with 70 Percent Hydration, 88

24-Hour Focaccia with 80 Percent Hydration, 91
Zucchini & Feta alla Spigamadre, 630
fontina cheese, Quattro Formaggi, 250
48-Hour Focaccia Dough, 92
400 Gradi, 757
Friuli Venezia Giulia, 26
Frying Pan Margherita, 754
fucuazza, 46
Fugascina di Mergozzo, 30, 135
Fugàssa co a Ciòula, 33, 143
galangal
    Beef Rendang, 296
    Tom Yum Paste, 299
Garden Vegetable & Ricotta Pizza, 370
garlic
    Cacciannanze, 178
    Garlic Butter, 327
    Garlic Fingers, 327
    Garlic Potato & Zucchini Pizza, 438
    Kale with Garlic, Raisins & Lemon, 669
    Mustazzeddu, 228
    Pizza al Taglio with Bufala, Eggplant & Garlic, 613
    Wild Garlic & Sausage Pizza, 510
    Yu Choy with Black Bean Garlic Sauce & Extra Garlic, 674
    Yu Choy with Garlic & Soy, 672
    Zucchini with Tomatoes, Feta, Garlic & Lemon, 675
Gherkin Pizza, Mushroom &, 331
Ginger & Tahini Dressing, 645
goat cheese
    Arugula, Nectarine, Farro & Goat Cheese Salad with White Balsamic Vinaigrette, 644
    Beet & Goat Cheese Pizza, 529
    Pizza with Goat Cheese, Fennel & Walnuts, 553
    Pizza with Goat Cheese, Figs & Walnuts, 513
    Pizza with Goat Cheese,

Spinach, Honey & Hazelnuts, 506
    Pizza with Prunes, Goat Cheese & Tomatoes, 577
    Sweet Potato & Sage Focaccia, 604
gorgonzola cheese
    Fig, Prosciutto & Balsamic Pizza, 493
    Pizza with Figs, Speck, Asiago & Gorgonzola, 498
    Pizza with Ham, Gorgonzola, Pears & Walnuts, 497
    Quattro Formaggi, 250
    Roasted Radicchio, Pear & Gorgonzola Salad, 656
gouda cheese
    BBQ Chicken Pizza, 409
    Pulled Pork Pizza, 561
gourmet pizza, flours for, 67
grapefruit, Fennel, Grapefruit & Pistachio Salad, 654
grapes, Schiaccia All'uva, 165
grappa, Fugascina di Mergozzo, 135
Green Tomato Pizza, 522
Grilled Zucchini & Eggplant Pizza, 453
grills, 79
Grupariata, 46, 199
Guanciale & Bottarga, Pizza with Asparagus, 388
Halifax Explosion, 720
ham
    Cauliflower, Provolone & Smoked Ham Pizza, 446
    Ciaccino Senese, 183
    Double Mozzarella & Ham Pizza, 433
    Ham & Artichoke Focaccia, 611
    Ham & Mushroom Pizza, 355
    Ham & Veggie Pizza, 434
    Hawaiian-Style Pizza, 275
    Meat Lover's Pizza, 470
    Parigina, 192
    Pizza à la Portuguesa, 315
    Pizza with Banana Curry, 328
    Pizza with Ham, Gorgonzola, Pears & Walnuts, 497

Pizza with Smoked Ham, Pears
& Pecorino, 399
Southern Collard Greens, 668
Spicy Salami, Smoked Ham &
Pepper Pizza, 465
Turkey Ham, Artichoke &
Cream Cheese Pizza, 509
hand mixing, 70–71
Hawaiian-Style Pizza, 275
hazelnuts
Chocolate, Hazelnut &
Strawberry Pizza, 687
Pizza with Goat Cheese,
Spinach, Honey & Hazelnuts,
506
Roasted Radicchio, Pear &
Gorgonzola Salad, 656
heat sources, 75, 77, 79
Herring, Radish & Cream Cheese,
Pizza with Smoked, 549
home ovens, 77, 79
honey
Pizza with Goat Cheese,
Spinach, Honey & Hazelnuts,
506
Roasted Parsnips & Carrots with
Ras el Hanout & Honey, 671
Honey Mustard Vinaigrette
recipe, 642
Roasted Baby Beet, Radish &
Apple Salad with Blue Cheese
Mousse, 642
honeydew melon, Melon,
Cucumber & Prosciutto Salad
with Mint Vinaigrette, 652
ingredients, 65–67
jalapeños
Chilled Corn Salad, 660
Chorizo & Jalapeño Pizza, 319
Melon, Cucumber & Prosciutto
Salad with Mint Vinaigrette,
652
Pizza with Jalapeños, Red
Peppers & Onions, 565
Raw Beet Salad with Blood
Orange, Jalapeño & Brie,
647
See also peppers, hot
Kahlúa, Tiramisu Pizza, 703

kale
Kale with Garlic, Raisins &
Lemon, 669
Shaved Brussels Sprouts & Kale
Salad with Blood Orange
Vinaigrette, 651
Kebab Pizza, 469
Kimchi, Pizza with, 303
kizoa, 34
krese, 43
La Svolta, 773
Lahmacun, 323
lamb
Lamb, Eggplant & Tomato
Pizza, 586
Pizza with Lamb, Eggplant &
Burrata, 530
Late Summer Salad with Wild
Mushrooms, Parmesan &
Pine Nuts, 655
Lazio, 40
leeks
Pizza with Garden Vegetables &
Bufala, 449
Romesco & Leek Pizza, 578
lemon
Focaccia with Olives & Lemon,
608
Kale with Garlic, Raisins &
Lemon, 669
Lemon Curd Pizza, 700
Zucchini with Tomatoes, Feta,
Garlic & Lemon, 675
lemongrass stalks, Beef Rendang,
296
Lestopitta, 46, 196
lettuce/salad greens
Margherita alla Spigamadre,
633
Panuozzo, 191
Pizza al Taglio with Romaine,
Salami & Parmesan, 618
Levain for Focaccia
recipe, 100–101
Sourdough Focaccia Dough, 100
Levain for Pizza, 123
Liguria, 32–34
Lombardy, 28
long fermentation, 74

machine mixing, 70–72
makrut lime leaves, Beef Rendang,
296
mangoes
Chicken Satay & Mango Pizza,
311
Pizza with Seafood, Avocado &
Mango, 537
Marble Pizza, 680
Marche, 39
Margherita, 237
Margherita alla Spigamadre,
633
Margherita with Panfried
Zucchini, 396
Margherita with Prosciutto &
Asparagus, 392
Mari e Monti, 257
Marinara Sauce
Montanare, 195
recipe, 104
marshmallow creme, S'mores
Pizza, 688
mascarpone
Berries, Cherries & Mascarpone
Pizza, 683
Tiramisu Pizza, 703
Masher, The, 731
Mayonnaise Pizza, Seafood &, 292
Meat Lover's Pizza, 470
Melanzane Pizza, 766
Melon, Cucumber & Prosciutto
Salad with Mint Vinaigrette,
652
mesclun greens
Late Summer Salad with Wild
Mushrooms, Parmesan &
Pine Nuts, 655
Radicchio & Ricotta Salata Salad
with Apple Cider Vinaigrette,
657
Roasted Radicchio, Pear &
Gorgonzola Salad, 656
See also lettuce/salad greens
metric conversions, 790
miaccia, 31
miassa, 32
Mincemeat & Vegetable Pizza,
320

mint
 Melon, Cucumber & Prosciutto Salad with Mint Vinaigrette, 652
 Mint Vinaigrette, 652
Mixed Berry Pizza, 521
mixing, 70–72
Molise, 43
Montanare, 45, 195
Monterey Jack cheese, BBQ Chicken Pizza, 409
Mortadella, Ricotta & Pistachio Pizza alla Pala, 62?
mozzarella cheese
 Apple, Onion & Balsamic Vinegar Pizza, 58?
 Arrabbiata, Eggplant & Pepper Pizza, 573
 Artichoke & Potato Pizza, 351
 Arugula, Egg & Mushroom Pizza, 474
 Arugula, Pomegranate & Cherry Tomato Pizza, 569
 Avocado, Tomato & Feta Pizza, 525
 Balado & Chicken Pizza, 295
 Bianca con Salsiccia di Finocchietto, 776
 Boscaiola, 242
 Broccoli, Chorizo & Chili Pepper Pizza, 421
 Broccoli Rabe, Tomato & Olive Pizza, 533
 Bulgogi Pizza, 300
 Cajun Shrimp & Salami Pizza, 554
 California-Style Pizza, 272
 Caprese, 254
 Capricciosa, 241
 Carrettiera, 246
 Cauliflower & Broccoli Pizza, 410
 Chicago Deep-Dish Pizza, 267
 Chicago Deep-Dish Stuffed Pizza, 762
 Chicken, Sausage & Pine Nut Pizza, 505
 Chicken & Escarole Pizza, 550
 Chorizo & Jalapeño Pizza, 319

Chorizo & Olive Pizza, 430
Ciaccino Senese, 183
Classic Pepperoni Pizza, 276
Coppa, Prosciutto & Sausage Pizza, 514
Cucumber, Tomato & Chicken Pizza, 581
Dandelion & Tomato Pizza, 585
Dante's Personal Pizzas, 736
Double Mozzarella & Ham Pizza, 433
Eggplant, Bufala & Arugula Pizza, 501
Eggplant Parmigiana Pizza, 344
Endive & Cherry Tomato Pizza, 512
Farmers Market, 744
Fig, Prosciutto & Balsamic Pizza, 493
Focaccia di Carnevale Salentina, 212
Frying Pan Margherita, 754
Garlic Fingers, 327
Garlic Potato & Zucchini Pizza, 438
Green Tomato Pizza, 522
Grilled Zucchini & Eggplant Pizza, 453
Halifax Explosion, 720
Ham & Artichoke Focaccia, 611
Ham & Mushroom Pizza, 355
Ham & Veggie Pizza, 434
Hawaiian-Style Pizza, 275
Kebab Pizza, 469
Lamb, Eggplant & Tomato Pizza, 586
Margherita, 237
Margherita alla Spigamadre, 633
Margherita with Panfried Zucchini, 396
Margherita with Prosciutto & Asparagus, 392
Mari e Monti, 257
The Masher, 731
Meat Lover's Pizza, 470
Melanzane Pizza, 766
Mincemeat & Vegetable Pizza, 320
Mixed Berry Pizza, 521

Montanare, 195
Mushroom & Artichoke Pan Pizza, 570
Mushroom & Gherkin Pizza, 331
Natto & Bacon Pizza, 291
New Haven Tomato Pie, 264
New York Thin-Crust Pizza, 263
Notorious P.I.G. Skillet Pizza, 743
Panfried Potato & Sausage Pizza, 374
Panuozzo, 191
Parigina, 192
Peach, Pineapple & Pepperoni Pizza, 518
Pear & Ricotta Focaccia, 600
Pepper & Egg Pizza, 418
Pesto, Tomato & Bufala Pizza, 365
Pesto & Veggie Pizza, 413
Pistachio & Onion Pizza, 546
Pistachio Pesto & Mozzarella, 375
Pizza à la Portuguesa, 315
Pizza al Padellino, 139
Pizza al Taglio with Bufala, Eggplant & Garlic, 613
Pizza al Taglio with Prosciutto, 619
Pizza al Taglio with Wild Mushrooms & Two Cheeses, 617
Pizza alla Pala with Prosciutto & Endive, 623
Pizza alla Zucca, 771
Pizza with Anchovies, 562
Pizza with Asparagus, Guanciale & Bottarga, 388
Pizza with Asparagus, Pine Nuts & Bufala, 348
Pizza with Bacon, Blue Cheese, Onion & Pickles, 574
Pizza with Banana & Cinnamon, 691
Pizza with Banana Curry, 328
Pizza with Brie & Pear, 490
Pizza with Broccoli & Bacon, 414

Pizza with Chanterelles, Béchamel & Parmesan, 545

Pizza with Eggs & Bacon, 425

Pizza with Feta, Olives & Peppers, 442

Pizza with Figs, Speck, Asiago & Gorgonzola, 498

Pizza with Garden Vegetables & Bufala, 449

Pizza with Garden Vegetables, Artichokes & Salami, 387

Pizza with Goat Cheese, Fennel & Walnuts, 553

Pizza with Goat Cheese, Figs & Walnuts, 513

Pizza with Ham, Gorgonzola, Pears & Walnuts, 497

Pizza with Jalapeños, Red Peppers & Onions, 565

Pizza with Kimchi, 303

Pizza with Mushrooms, Caramelized Onions & Caciocavallo, 347

Pizza with Mussels & Artichokes, 357

Pizza with Parmesan, Bresaola & Truffles, 400

Pizza with Parsley Pesto & Caviar, 489

Pizza with Peas & Caviar, 558

Pizza with Peking Duck, 304

Pizza with Potato, Parsnip & Prosciutto, 557

Pizza with Prosciutto, Caciocavallo, Mushrooms & Nuts, 494

Pizza with Prunes, Goat Cheese & Tomatoes, 577

Pizza with Pumpkin, Feta & Arugula, 466

Pizza with Rendang & Mushrooms, 296

Pizza with Ricotta & Cremini Mushrooms, 384

Pizza with Romanesco Broccoli Cream, Anchovies & Burrata, 477

Pizza with Sausage, Cime di Rapa & Cherry Tomatoes, 376

Pizza with Seafood & Broccoli, 417

Pizza with Seafood, Avocado & Mango, 537

Pizza with Shellfish & Bell Peppers, 457

Pizza with Shrimp, Chili Peppers & Bufala, 462

Pizza with Smoked Herring, Radish & Cream Cheese, 549

Pizza with Smoked Salmon & Capers, 485

Pizza with Smoked Trout, Poached Eggs & Capers, 517

Pizza with Squid Ink & Seafood, 287

Pizza with Sun-Dried Tomatoes & Zucchini Cream, 379

Pizza with Swordfish, Pine Nuts & Cherry Tomatoes, 391

Pizza with Tuna & Corn, 458

Pizza with Zucchini Cream, Bacon & Bufala, 437

Potato & Olive Pizza, 395

Quark & Zucchini Pizza, 590

Quattro Formaggi, 250

Quattro Stagioni, 249

Red Cabbage, Ricotta & Walnut Pizza, 407

Ricotta & Bresaola Pizza, 356

Roasted Asparagus & Cherry Tomato Pizza, 358

Roasted Fennel & Sausage Pizza, 336

Roasted Zucchini, Béchamel & Rosemary Pizza, 445

Romana, 238

Romesco & Leek Pizza, 578

Rosemary & Potato Pizza, 403

Rossa con Filetti di Acciughe, 779

Salmon & Pepper Pizza, 486

Salt-n-Peppa Prawn Pizza, 747

Sausage & Broccoli Pizza, 383

Sausage & Spinach Pizza, 380

Shrimp, Arugula & Olive Pizza al Taglio, 620

Shrimp & Pineapple Pizza, 589

Smoked Chicken, Bufala & Pesto Focaccia, 599

Smoked Cod & Cheddar Pizza, 481

Smoked Salmon & Chive Pizza, 482

Spicy Beef & Zucchini Pizza, 450

Spicy Salami, Smoked Ham & Pepper Pizza, 465

Spinach, Egg & Cheese Pizza, 473

Squash Blossom & Ricotta Pizza, 343

Taco Pizza, 478

Teriyaki Chicken & Mushroom Pizza, 283

Teriyaki Salmon Pizza, 284

Thick-Crust Pizza with Onions, 316

Three Cheese & Spinach Pizza, 502

Tikka Masala Pizza, 307

Tom Yum Pizza with Shrimp, 299

Tuna & Onion Pizza, 404

Tuna & Orange-Marinated Fennel Pizza, 340

Two Cheese & Bacon Pizza, 422

Two Cheese & Mushroom Pizza, 429

Vegetable & Mushroom Pizza, 426

Wild Garlic & Sausage Pizza, 510

Zucchini Blossom & Cherry Tomato Pizza, 441

mushrooms

Arugula, Egg & Mushroom Pizza, 474

Boscaiola, 242

Bulgogi Pizza, 300

Capricciosa, 241

Ham & Mushroom Pizza, 355

Ham & Veggie Pizza, 434

Late Summer Salad with Wild Mushrooms, Parmesan & Pine Nuts, 655

Mari e Monti, 257

Mincemeat & Vegetable Pizza, 320

Mushroom & Artichoke Pan Pizza, 570

Mushroom & Gherkin Pizza, 331

Ortolana, 258

Pesto & Veggie Pizza, 413

Pizza al Taglio with Wild Mushrooms & Two Cheeses, 617

Pizza with Chanterelles, Béchamel & Parmesan, 545

Pizza with Feta, Olives & Peppers, 442

Pizza with Grilled Vegetables & Tofu Cream Cheese, 566

Pizza with Mushrooms, Asparagus & Pesto, 369

Pizza with Mushrooms, Caramelized Onions & Caciocavallo, 347

Pizza with Peking Duck, 304

Pizza with Prosciutto, Caciocavallo, Wild Mushrooms & Nuts, 494

Pizza with Rendang & Mushrooms, 296

Pizza with Ricotta & Cremini Mushrooms, 384

Quattro Stagioni, 249

Romesco & Leek Pizza, 578

Sausage, Mushroom & Provolone Pizza, 541

Spinach, Zucchini & Pistachio Pesto Pizza, 534

Teriyaki Chicken & Mushroom Pizza, 283

Tom Yum Pizza with Shrimp, 299

Two Cheese & Mushroom Pizza, 429

Vegetable & Mushroom Pizza, 426

mussels

Mari e Monti, 257

Pescatora, 253

Pizza with Mussels & Artichokes, 357

Pizza with Shellfish & Bell Peppers, 457

Mustazzeddu, 52–53, 228

Natto & Bacon Pizza, 291

'Ndjua, Sun-Dried Tomatoes & Caciocavallo, Pizza with, 406

Neapolitan pizza

flours for, 66–67

history of, 55–58

Neapolitan Pizza Dough, 108

Nectarine, Farro & Goat Cheese Salad with White Balsamic Vinaigrette, Arugula, 644

nettles, California-Style Pizza, 272

New Haven pizza, 62

New Haven Tomato Pie, 264

New York pizza, 61–62

New York Thin-Crust Pizza, 263

No-Knead Focaccia Dough, 95

no-knead mixing, 72

No-Knead Pizza Dough, 116

Notorious P.I.G. Skillet Pizza, 743

nuts. See individual nuts

octopus, Pescatora, 253

Okonomiyaki Pizza, 288

old dough

about, 68

Focaccia with Old Dough, 99

Pizza with Old Dough, 120

olives

Broccoli Rabe, Tomato & Olive Pizza, 533

Bulgogi Pizza, 300

Calamari, Shrimp & Pesto Pizza, 461

Calzone Pugliese, 208–209

Caper & Olive Pizza, 454

Capricciosa, 241

Cauliflower & Broccoli Pizza, 410

Cavicione, 210

Chichiripieno, 177

Chorizo & Olive Pizza, 430

Endive, Olive & Caper alla Spigamadre, 629

Focaccia Barese, 200

Focaccia con le Olive, 144

Focaccia with Olives & Lemon, 608

Garden Vegetable & Ricotta Pizza, 370

Ham & Artichoke Focaccia, 611

Ham & Veggie Pizza, 434

Pissalandrea, 147

Pizza à la Portuguesa, 315

Pizza with Feta, Olives & Peppers, 442

Pizza with Garden Vegetables & Bufala, 449

Pizza with Shellfish & Bell Peppers, 457

Pizza with Za'atar, 324

Potato & Olive Pizza, 395

Quattro Stagioni, 249

Radicchio & Garden Vegetable Pizza, 361

Rossa con Filetti di Acciughe, 779

Sceblasti & Pizzo Leccese, 205

Shrimp, Arugula & Olive Pizza al Taglio, 620

Turkey Ham, Artichoke & Cream Cheese Pizza, 509

onions

Apple, Onion & Balsamic Vinegar Pizza, 582

Balado & Chicken Pizza, 295

Bulgogi Pizza, 300

Calzone Pugliese, 208–209

Cavicione, 210

Chorizo & Jalapeño Pizza, 319

Faccia di Vecchia, 216

Focaccia di Altamura, 202

Focaccia di Carnevale Salentina, 212

Focaccia Portoscusese, 227

Fugàssa co a Çiòula, 143

Lahmacun, 323

Mincemeat & Vegetable Pizza, 320

Ortolana, 258

Pissalandrea, 147

Pistachio & Onion Pizza, 546

Pizza with Bacon, Blue Cheese, Onion & Pickles, 574

Pizza with Jalapeños, Red Peppers & Onions, 565

Pizza with Mushrooms, Caramelized Onions & Caciocavallo, 347

Pizza with Potato, Red Onion & Béchamel, 538

Roasted Brussels Sprouts with Bacon, Blue Cheese & Pickled Red Onion, 663

Scaccia Ragusana, 224–225

Sceblasti & Pizzo Leccese, 205

Schiacciata con Cipolla & Salvia, 166, 168

Sfincione Palermitano, 214–215

Thick-Crust Pizza with Onions, 316

Tikka Masala Pizza, 307

Tirot, 133

Tuna & Onion Pizza, 404

See also spring onions

oranges
  Raw Beet Salad with Blood Orange, Jalapeño & Brie, 647
  Spinach, Bacon, Avocado & Orange Salad, 659
  Tuna & Orange-Marinated Fennel Pizza, 340

Ortolana, 258

OTTO, 727–728

outdoor gas and wood-fired ovens, 79

ovens, 77, 79

pan pizzas, flours for, 66

pancetta
  Chisola Piacentina, 158
  Crescenta Bolognese, 154–155
  Panuozzo, 191
  Pinza onta Polesana, 130
  Torta al Testo con i Ciccioli, 169

Panfried Potato & Sausage Pizza, 374

Panuozzo, 44, 191

Paposcia del Gargano, 49, 206

Parigina, 44–45, 192

Parmesan cheese
  Apple, Onion & Balsamic Vinegar Pizza, 582

Arrabbiata, Eggplant & Pepper Pizza, 573

Arugula, Egg & Mushroom Pizza, 474

Basil Pesto, 365

Buttermilk Caesar Dressing, 648

Buttermilk White Sauce, 721

Chicago Deep-Dish Pizza, 267

Chorizo & Olive Pizza, 430

Eggplant Parmigiana Pizza, 344

Frying Pan Margherita, 754

Garden Vegetable & Ricotta Pizza, 370

Late Summer Salad with Wild Mushrooms, Parmesan & Pine Nuts, 655

Notorious P.I.G. Skillet Pizza, 743

Pistachio Pesto, 375

Pistachio Pesto & Mozzarella, 375

Pizza al Taglio with Romaine, Salami & Parmesan, 618

Pizza with Anchovies, 562

Pizza with Chanterelles, Béchamel & Parmesan, 545

Pizza with Jalapeños, Red Peppers & Onions, 565

Pizza with Mushrooms, Asparagus & Pesto, 369

Pizza with Parmesan, Bresaola & Truffles, 400

Pizza with Prosciutto, Arugula & Parmesan, 339

Pizza with Romanesco Broccoli Cream, Anchovies & Burrata, 337

Pizza with Sun-Dried Tomatoes & Zucchini Cream, 379

Quattro Formaggi, 250

Red Cabbage, Ricotta & Walnut Pizza, 407

Ricotta & Bresaola Pizza, 356

Sautéed Radicchio with Beans, Parmesan & Balsamic, 665

Spinach, Egg & Cheese Pizza, 473

Spinach, Zucchini & Pistachio Pesto Pizza, 534

Three Cheese & Spinach Pizza, 502

Zucchini Cream, 379

parsley
  Lahmacun, 323
  Parsley Pesto, 489
  Pizza al Taglio with Bufala, Eggplant & Garlic, 613
  Pizza al Taglio with Wild Mushrooms & Two Cheeses, 617
  Red & Green Cabbage Salad with Ginger & Tahini Dressing, 645
  Romesco Sauce, 578

Parsley Pesto
  Pizza with Parsley Pesto & Caviar, 489
  recipe, 489

parsnips
  Pizza with Potato, Parsnip & Prosciutto, 557
  Roasted Parsnips & Carrots with Ras el Hanout & Honey, 671

Pastry Cream
  Custom Royal Dessert Pizza, 748
  recipe, 748–749

Peach, Pineapple & Pepperoni Pizza, 518

peanut butter, Chicken Satay & Mango Pizza, 311

peanuts, Red & Green Cabbage Salad with Ginger & Tahini Dressing, 645

pears
  Pear & Ricotta Focaccia, 600
  Pizza with Brie & Pear, 490
  Pizza with Ham, Gorgonzola, Pears & Walnuts, 497
  Pizza with Pear, Thyme, Blue Cheese & Walnuts, 684
  Pizza with Smoked Ham, Pears & Pecorino, 399
  Roasted Radicchio, Pear & Gorgonzola Salad, 656

Peas & Caviar, Pizza with, 558

Pecorino cheese
  Basil Pesto, 365

Focaccia di Carnevale Salentina, 212
Focaccia Portoscusese, 227
Montanare, 195
New Haven Tomato Pie, 264
Pizza with Sicilian-Style Tuna & Bell Peppers, 352
Pizza with Smoked Ham, Pears & Pecorino, 399
Quattro Formaggi, 250
Rianata, 220
Peking Duck, Pizza with, 304
pepperoncini, BBQ Chicken Pizza, 409
pepperoni
    Classic Pepperoni Pizza, 246
    Detroit-Style Pizza, 268
    Halifax Explosion, 720
    Peach, Pineapple & Pepperoni Pizza, 518
    Pepper & Egg Pizza, 418
    St. Louis–Style Pizza, 271
peppers, bell
    Arrabbiata, Eggplant & Pepper Pizza, 573
    Bulgogi Pizza, 300
    Chicago Deep-Dish Pizza, 267
    Chicken Satay & Mango Pizza, 311
    Farmers Market, 744
    Grilled Zucchini & Eggplant Pizza, 453
    Lahmacun, 323
    Mincemeat & Vegetable Pizza, 320
    Ortolana, 258
    Pepper, Pine Nut & Raisin Pizza al Taglio, 614
    Pepper & Egg Pizza, 418
    Pesto & Veggie Pizza, 413
    Pizza with Aloo Gobi, 308
    Pizza with Feta, Olives & Peppers, 442
    Pizza with Garden Vegetables & Bufala, 449
    Pizza with Garden Vegetables, Artichokes & Salami, 387
    Pizza with Grilled Vegetables & Tofu Cream Cheese, 566

Pizza with Jalapeños, Red Peppers & Onions, 565
Pizza with Shellfish & Bell Peppers, 457
Pizza with Sicilian-Style Tuna & Bell Peppers, 352
Radicchio & Garden Vegetable Pizza, 361
Romesco Sauce, 578
Salmon & Pepper Pizza, 486
Spicy Salami, Smoked Ham & Pepper Pizza, 405
Teriyaki Salmon Pizza, 284
peppers, hot
    Balado Sauce, 295
    Broccoli, Chorizo & Chili Pepper Pizza, 421
    Chilled Corn Salad, 660
    Chorizo & Jalapeño Pizza, 319
    Kebab Pizza, 469
    Melon, Cucumber & Prosciutto Salad with Mint Vinaigrette, 652
    Pepper & Egg Pizza, 418
    Pizza with Aloo Gobi, 308
    Pizza with Jalapeños, Red Peppers & Onions, 565
    Pizza with Shrimp, Chili Peppers & Bufala, 462
    Pulled Pork Pizza, 561
    Raw Beet Salad with Blood Orange, Jalapeño & Brie, 647
    Taco Pizza, 478
    Tom Yum Paste, 299
    Two Cheese & Bacon Pizza, 422
Pescatora, 253
pesto
    Basil Pesto, 365
    Calamari, Shrimp & Pesto Pizza, 461
    Fig, Prosciutto & Balsamic Pizza, 493
    Parsley Pesto, 489
    Pesto, Tomato & Bufala Pizza, 365
    Pesto & Veggie Pizza, 413
    Pistachio Pesto, 375
    Pistachio Pesto & Mozzarella, 375

Pizza with Mushrooms, Asparagus & Pesto, 369
Pizza with Parsley Pesto & Caviar, 489
Potato & Pesto Pizza, 373
Smoked Chicken, Bufala & Pesto Focaccia, 599
Spinach, Zucchini & Pistachio Pesto Pizza, 534
Piadina, 35
    Arrabbiata, Eggplant & Pepper Pizza, 573
    recipe, 152
Pickled Ramps, Roasted Brassica Salad with Pickled Ramps & Buttermilk Caesar Dressing, 648
Pickles, Pizza with Bacon, Blue Cheese, Onion &, 574
Piedmont, 30–31
pine nuts
    Bok Choy, Pine Nut & Raisin Pizza, 555
    Broccoli & Pine Nut alla Spigamadre, 634
    Chicken, Sausage & Pine Nut Pizza, 505
    Late Summer Salad with Wild Mushrooms, Parmesan & Pine Nuts, 655
    Pepper, Pine Nut & Raisin Pizza al Taglio, 614
    Pizza with Asparagus, Pine Nuts & Bufala, 348
    Pizza with Mushrooms, Asparagus & Pesto, 369
    Pizza with Swordfish, Pine Nuts & Cherry Tomatoes, 391
pineapple
    Hawaiian-Style Pizza, 275
    Peach, Pineapple & Pepperoni Pizza, 518
    Pizza with Banana Curry, 328
    Shrimp & Pineapple Pizza, 589
pinza munara, 27
Pinza onta Polesana, 27, 130
pinza romana, 61
pinzone ferrarese, 36
Pissalandrea, 34, 147

Pistachio Pesto
Pistachio Pesto & Mozzarella, 375
recipe, 375
Spinach, Zucchini & Pistachio Pesto Pizza, 534
pistachios
Fennel, Grapefruit & Pistachio Salad, 654
Mortadella, Ricotta & Pistachio Pizza alla Pala, 627
Pistachio & Onion Pizza, 546
Pistachio Pesto, 375
Pizza with Prosciutto, Caciocavallo, Wild Mushrooms & Nuts, 494
Pixza, 723–724
pizza
Apple, Onion & Balsamic Vinegar Pizza, 582
Artichoke & Potato Pizza, 351
Arugula, Egg & Mushroom Pizza, 474
Arugula, Pomegranate & Cherry Tomato Pizza, 569
Avocado, Tomato & Feta Pizza, 525
baking equipment for, 75–77, 79
Balado & Chicken Pizza, 295
BBQ Chicken Pizza, 409
Beet & Goat Cheese Pizza, 529
Berries, Cherries & Mascarpone Pizza, 683
Bianca con Salsiccia di Finocchietto, 776
Bok Choy, Pine Nut & Raisin Pizza, 555
Boscaiola, 242
Brigadeiro & Strawberry Pizza, 692
Broccoli, Chorizo & Chili Pepper Pizza, 421
Broccoli Rabe, Tomato & Olive Pizza, 533
Bulgogi Pizza, 300
Cajun Shrimp & Salami Pizza, 554

Calamari, Shrimp & Pesto Pizza, 461
California-Style Pizza, 272
Caper & Olive Pizza, 454
Caprese, 254
Capricciosa, 241
Caramel Apple Pizza, 704
Carrettiera, 246
Cauliflower, Provolone & Smoked Ham Pizza, 446
Cauliflower & Broccoli Pizza, 410
Chicago Deep-Dish Pizza, 267
Chicago Deep-Dish Stuffed Pizza, 762
Chicken, Sausage & Pine Nut Pizza, 505
Chicken & Escarole Pizza, 550
Chocolate, Hazelnut & Strawberry Pizza, 687
Chorizo & Jalapeño Pizza, 319
Chorizo & Olive Pizza, 430
Cinnamon Apple Pizza, 699
Classic Pepperoni Pizza, 276
Coppa, Prosciutto & Sausage Pizza, 514
Cucumber, Tomato & Chicken Pizza, 581
Custom Royal Dessert Pizza, 748
Dandelion & Tomato Pizza, 585
Dante's Personal Pizzas, 736
Detroit-Style Pizza, 268
Diavola, 245
Double Mozzarella & Ham Pizza, 433
Eggplant, Bufala & Arugula Pizza, 501
Eggplant Parmigiana Pizza, 344
Endive & Cherry Tomato Pizza, 542
Farmers Market, 744
Fig, Prosciutto & Balsamic Pizza, 493
Frying Pan Margherita, 754
Garden Vegetable & Ricotta Pizza, 370
Garlic Potato & Zucchini Pizza, 438

global, 281–331
Green Tomato Pizza, 522
Grilled Zucchini & Eggplant Pizza, 453
Halifax Explosion, 720
Ham & Mushroom Pizza, 355
Ham & Veggie Pizza, 434
Hawaiian-Style Pizza, 275
history of, 55–63
Kebab Pizza, 469
Lahmacun, 323
Lemon Curd Pizza, 700
Marble Pizza, 680
Margherita, 237
Margherita with Prosciutto & Asparagus, 392
The Masher, 731
master pizza doughs, 107–123
Meat Lover's Pizza, 470
Melanzane Pizza, 766
Mincemeat & Vegetable Pizza, 320
Mixed Berry Pizza, 521
Mortadella, Ricotta & Pistachio Pizza alla Pala, 627
Mushroom & Artichoke Pan Pizza, 570
Natto & Bacon Pizza, 291
Neapolitan Pizza Dough, 108
New Haven Tomato Pie, 264
New York Thin-Crust Pizza, 263
No-Knead Pizza Dough, 116
Notorious P.I.G. Skillet Pizza, 743
Okonomiyaki Pizza, 288
Panfried Potato & Sausage Pizza, 374
Peach, Pineapple & Pepperoni Pizza, 518
Pepper, Pine Nut & Raisin Pizza al Taglio, 614
Pepper & Egg Pizza, 418
Pescatora, 253
Pesto, Tomato & Bufala Pizza, 365
Pesto & Veggie Pizza, 413
Pistachio & Onion Pizza, 546
Pizza à la Portuguesa, 315
Pizza al Padellino, 139

pizza al piatto romana, 61

pizza al taglio, 60, 612

Pizza al Taglio with Bufala, Eggplant & Garlic, 613

Pizza al Taglio with Prosciutto, 619

Pizza al Taglio with Romaine, Salami & Parmesan, 618

Pizza al Taglio with Wild Mushrooms & Two Cheeses, 617

pizza alla pala, 60, 622

Pizza alla Pala with Prosciutto & Indive, 623

Pizza alla Pala with Zucchini Blossoms, Anchovies & Burrata, 624

Pizza alla Zucca, 771

Pizza Assettata, 43, 188

Pizza Bianca Romana, 181

Pizza di Granoturco, 185

Pizza Dough with Biga, 119

Pizza Marinara, 234

Pizza Scima, 187

Pizza with Aloo Gobi, 308

Pizza with Anchovies, 562

Pizza with Asparagus, Guanciale & Bottarga, 388

Pizza with Asparagus, Pine Nuts & Bufala, 348

Pizza with Bacon, Blue Cheese, Onion & Pickles, 574

Pizza with Banana & Cinnamon, 691

Pizza with Banana Curry, 328

Pizza with Brie & Pear, 490

Pizza with Broccoli & Bacon, 414

Pizza with Chanterelles, Béchamel & Parmesan, 545

Pizza with Eggs & Bacon, 425

Pizza with Feta, Olives & Peppers, 442

Pizza with Figs, Speck, Asiago & Gorgonzola, 498

Pizza with Garden Vegetables & Bufala, 449

Pizza with Garden Vegetables, Artichokes & Salami, 387

Pizza with Goat Cheese, Fennel & Walnuts, 553

Pizza with Goat Cheese, Figs & Walnuts, 513

Pizza with Goat Cheese, Spinach, Honey & Hazelnuts, 506

Pizza with Grilled Vegetables & Tofu Cream Cheese, 566

Pizza with Ham, Gorgonzola, Pears & Walnuts, 497

Pizza with Jalapeños, Red Peppers & Onions, 565

Pizza with Kimchi, 303

Pizza with Lamb, Eggplant & Burrata, 530

Pizza with Mushrooms, Asparagus & Pesto, 369

Pizza with Mussels & Artichokes, 357

Pizza with 'Ndjua, Sun-Dried Tomatoes & Caciocavallo, 406

Pizza with Old Dough, 120

Pizza with Parmesan, Bresaola & Truffles, 400

Pizza with Parsley Pesto & Caviar, 489

Pizza with Pear, Thyme, Blue Cheese & Walnuts, 684

Pizza with Peas & Caviar, 558

Pizza with Peking Duck, 304

Pizza with Potato, Parsnip & Prosciutto, 557

Pizza with Potato, Red Onion & Béchamel, 538

Pizza with Prosciutto, Arugula & Parmesan, 339

Pizza with Prosciutto, Caciocavallo, Wild Mushrooms & Nuts, 494

Pizza with Prunes, Goat Cheese & Tomatoes, 577

Pizza with Pumpkin, Feta & Arugula, 466

Pizza with Rendang & Mushrooms, 296

Pizza with Ricotta & Cremini Mushrooms, 384

Pizza with Ricotta, Figs & Bacon, 526

Pizza with Romanesco Broccoli Cream, Anchovies & Burrata, 337

Pizza with Rose Sauce, Sausage & Potato, 477

Pizza with Sausage, Cime di Rapa & Cherry Tomatoes, 376

Pizza with Seafood & Broccoli, 417

Pizza with Seafood, Avocado & Mango, 537

Pizza with Shellfish & Bell Peppers, 457

Pizza with Shrimp, Chili Peppers & Bufala, 462

Pizza with Sicilian-Style Tuna & Bell Peppers, 352

Pizza with Smoked Ham, Pears & Pecorino, 399

Pizza with Smoked Herring, Radish & Cream Cheese, 549

Pizza with Smoked Salmon & Capers, 485

Pizza with Smoked Trout, Poached Eggs & Capers, 517

Pizza with Squid Ink & Seafood, 287

Pizza with Sun-Dried Tomatoes & Zucchini Cream, 379

Pizza with Swordfish, Pine Nuts & Cherry Tomatoes, 391

Pizza with Tuna & Corn, 458

Pizza with Wild Mushrooms, Caramelized Onions & Caciocavallo, 347

Pizza with Za'atar, 324

Pizza with Zucchini Cream, Bacon & Bufala, 437

Potato & Olive Pizza, 395

Potato & Pesto Pizza, 373

Pulled Pork Pizza, 561

Quark & Zucchini Pizza, 590

Quattro Formaggi, 250

Quattro Stagioni, 249

Quick Pizza Dough, 107

Radicchio & Garden Vegetable Pizza, 361

Raspberry & Almond Pizza, 695

Red Cabbage, Ricotta & Walnut Pizza, 407

regional American, 261–276

Ricotta & Bresaola Pizza, 356

Roasted Asparagus & Cherry Tomato Pizza, 358

Roasted Fennel & Sausage Pizza, 336

Roasted Zucchini, Béchamel & Rosemary Pizza, 445

Romana, 238

Romesco & Leek Pizza, 578

Rosemary & Potato Pizza, 403

Rossa con Filetti di Acciughe, 779

Salmon & Pepper Pizza, 486

Salt-n-Peppa Prawn Pizza, 747

Sausage, Mushroom & Provolone Pizza, 541

Sausage & Broccoli Pizza, 383

Sausage & Spinach Pizza, 380

Seafood & Mayonnaise Pizza, 292

shaping, 73

Smoked Cod & Cheddar Pizza, 481

Smoked Salmon & Chive Pizza, 482

S'mores Pizza, 688

Sourdough Pizza Dough, 123

Spicy Beef & Zucchini Pizza, 450

Spicy Salami & Provolone Pizza, 362

Spinach, Egg & Cheese Pizza, 473

Spinach, Zucchini & Pistachio Pesto Pizza, 534

Spinach & Ricotta Pizza, 366

Squash Blossom & Ricotta Pizza, 343

St. Louis–Style Pizza, 271

Taco Pizza, 478

Teriyaki Chicken & Mushroom Pizza, 283

Teriyaki Salmon Pizza, 284

Thick-Crust Pizza with Onions, 316

Three Cheese & Spinach Pizza, 502

Tikka Masala Pizza, 307

Tiramisu Pizza, 703

Tom Yum Pizza with Shrimp, 299

Tuna & Onion Pizza, 404

Tuna & Orange-Marinated Fennel Pizza, 340

24-Hour Pizza Dough with 62 Percent Hydration, 111

24-Hour Pizza Dough with 67 Percent Hydration, 112

24-Hour Pizza Dough with 72 Percent Hydration, 115

Two Cheese & Bacon Pizza, 422

Two Cheese & Mushroom Pizza, 429

Vanilla Custard Pizza, 696

Vegetable & Mushroom Pizza, 426

Wild Garlic & Sausage Pizza, 510

Zucchini Blossom & Cherry Tomato Pizza, 441

Pizza Bianca Romana

   Mortadella, Ricotta & Pistachio Pizza alla Pala, 627

   Pizza alla Pala with Prosciutto & Endive, 623

   Pizza alla Pala with Zucchini Blossoms, Anchovies & Burrata, 624

pizza bianca Romana, 40

pizza con le sfrigole, 41

pizza di Granoturco, 43

Pizza Pilgrims, 751

pizza scima, 41

Pizz'onta, 41, 186

Pomegranate & Cherry Tomato Pizza, Arugula, 569

pork belly, Okonomiyaki Pizza, 288

Pork Pizza, Pulled, 561

potatoes

   Artichoke & Potato Pizza, 351

Bianca con Salsiccia di Finocchietto, 776

Focaccia Barese, 200

Focaccia Portoscusese, 227

Garlic Potato & Zucchini Pizza, 438

The Masher, 731

Panfried Potato & Sausage Pizza, 374

Pizza with Aloo Gobi, 308

Pizza with Potato, Parsnip & Prosciutto, 557

Pizza with Potato, Red Onion & Béchamel, 538

Pizza with Rose Sauce, Sausage & Potato, 477

Potato & Caciocavallo alla Spigamadre, 637

Potato & Olive Pizza, 395

Potato & Pesto Pizza, 373

Rosemary & Potato Pizza, 403

prawns/shrimp

   Cajun Shrimp & Salami Pizza, 554

   Calamari, Shrimp & Pesto Pizza, 461

   Mari e Monti, 257

   Okonomiyaki Pizza, 288

   Pescatora, 253

   Pizza with Seafood & Broccoli, 417

   Pizza with Shellfish & Bell Peppers, 457

   Pizza with Shrimp, Chili Peppers & Bufala, 462

   Salt-n-Peppa Prawn Pizza, 747

   Shrimp, Arugula & Olive Pizza al Taglio, 620

   Shrimp & Pineapple Pizza, 589

   Tom Yum Pizza with Shrimp, 299

pre-ferments, 68, 72, 97, 118–120

proofing, 74

prosciutto

   Arugula, Egg & Mushroom Pizza, 474

   Capricciosa, 241

   Ciaccino Senese, 183

Coppa, Prosciutto & Sausage Pizza, 514
Crescenta Bolognese, 154–155
Fig, Prosciutto & Balsamic Pizza, 493
Margherita with Prosciutto & Asparagus, 392
Melon, Cucumber & Prosciutto Salad with Mint Vinaigrette, 652
Pizza al Taglio with Prosciutto, 619
Pizza alla Pala with Prosciutto & Endive, 623
Pizza with Potato, Parsnip & Prosciutto, 557
Pizza with Prosciutto, Arugula & Parmesan, 339
Pizza with Prosciutto, Caciocavallo, Wild Mushrooms & Nuts, 494
Quattro Stagioni, 249
provola cheese, Diavola, 245
provolone cheese
Cauliflower, Provolone & Smoked Ham Pizza, 446
Ham & Artichoke Focaccia, 611
Quattro Formaggi, 250
Roasted Asparagus & Cherry Tomato Pizza, 358
Sausage, Mushroom & Provolone Pizza, 541
Spicy Salami & Provolone Pizza, 362
Spinach & Ricotta Pizza, 366
St. Louis–Style Pizza, 271
Three Cheese & Spinach Pizza, 502
Two Cheese & Bacon Pizza, 422
Two Cheese & Mushroom Pizza, 429
Prunes, Goat Cheese & Tomatoes, Pizza with, 577
Puddica Salentina, 48, 203
puff pastry, Parigina, 192
Pulled Pork Pizza, 561
pumpkin
Focaccia with Pumpkin Cream, Anchovies & Burrata, 603

Pizza alla Zucca, 771
Pizza with Pumpkin, Feta & Arugula, 466
Sceblasti & Pizzo Leccese, 205
Quark & Zucchini Pizza, 590
Quattro Formaggi, 250
Quattro Stagioni, 249
Quick Focaccia Dough, 83
Quick Pizza Dough, 107
radicchio
Radicchio & Garden Vegetable Pizza, 361
Radicchio & Ricotta Salata Salad with Apple Cider Vinaigrette, 657
Roasted Radicchio, Pear & Gorgonzola Salad, 656
Sautéed Radicchio with Beans, Parmesan & Balsamic, 665
radishes
Pizza with Smoked Herring, Radish & Cream Cheese, 549
Roasted Baby Beet, Radish & Apple Salad with Blue Cheese Mousse, 642
raisins
Bok Choy, Pine Nut & Raisin Pizza, 555
Kale with Garlic, Raisins & Lemon, 669
Pepper, Pine Nut & Raisin Pizza al Taglio, 614
ramps
Pickled Ramps, 648
Roasted Brassica Salad with Pickled Ramps & Buttermilk Caesar Dressing, 648
Ras el Hanout & Honey, Roasted Parsnips & Carrots with, 671
raspberries
Berries, Cherries & Mascarpone Pizza, 683
Mixed Berry Pizza, 521
Raspberry & Almond Pizza, 695
Raw Beet Salad with Blood Orange, Jalapeño & Brie, 647
Raw Pizza Sauce
Beet & Goat Cheese Pizza, 529

Bok Choy, Pine Nut & Raisin Pizza, 555
Boscaiola, 242
Cajun Shrimp & Salami Pizza, 554
Calamari, Shrimp & Pesto Pizza, 461
Caper & Olive Pizza, 454
Caprese, 254
Capricciosa, 241
Cauliflower & Broccoli Pizza, 410
Chicago Deep-Dish Pizza, 267
Chicago Deep-Dish Stuffed Pizza, 762
Chorizo & Olive Pizza, 430
Classic Pepperoni Pizza, 276
Coppa, Prosciutto & Sausage Pizza, 514
Cucumber, Tomato & Chicken Pizza, 581
Dandelion & Tomato Pizza, 585
Detroit-Style Pizza, 268
Diavola, 245
Double Mozzarella & Ham Pizza, 433
Eggplant, Bufala & Arugula Pizza, 501
Eggplant Parmigiana Pizza, 344
Garden Vegetable & Ricotta Pizza, 370
Grilled Zucchini & Eggplant Pizza, 453
Ham & Mushroom Pizza, 355
Ham & Veggie Pizza, 434
Hawaiian-Style Pizza, 275
Kebab Pizza, 469
Lamb, Eggplant & Tomato Pizza, 586
Margherita, 237
Margherita alla Spigamadre, 633
Margherita with Panfried Zucchini, 396
Meat Lover's Pizza, 470
Melanzane Pizza, 766
New Haven Tomato Pie, 264
New York Thin-Crust Pizza, 263
Ortolana, 258

Peach, Pineapple & Pepperoni Pizza, 518

Pepper & Egg Pizza, 418

Pescatora, 253

Pesto, Tomato & Bufala Pizza, 365

Pesto & Veggie Pizza, 413

Pizza à la Portuguesa, 315

Pizza al Taglio with Prosciutto, 619

Pizza al Taglio with Romaine, Salami & Parmesan, 618

Pizza Marinara, 234

Pizza with Aloo Gobi, 308

Pizza with Banana Curry, 328

Pizza with Feta, Olives & Peppers, 442

Pizza with Garden Vegetables & Bufala, 449

Pizza with Garden Vegetables, Artichokes & Salami, 387

Pizza with Jalapeños, Red Peppers & Onions, 565

Pizza with Lamb, Eggplant & Burrata, 530

Pizza with Mussels & Artichokes, 357

Pizza with 'Ndjua, Sun-Dried Tomatoes & Caciocavallo, 406

Pizza with Parmesan, Bresaola & Truffles, 400

Pizza with Rendang & Mushrooms, 296

Pizza with Seafood & Broccoli, 417

Pizza with Seafood, Avocado & Mango, 537

Pizza with Shellfish & Bell Peppers, 457

Pizza with Shrimp, Chili Peppers & Bufala, 462

Pizza with Smoked Salmon & Capers, 485

Pizza with Smoked Trout, Poached Eggs & Capers, 517

Pizza with Squid Ink & Seafood, 287

Pizza with Tuna & Corn, 458

Quattro Stagioni, 249

recipe, 103

Roasted Fennel & Sausage Pizza, 336

Romana, 238

Salmon & Pepper Pizza, 486

Sausage & Broccoli Pizza, 383

Shrimp, Arugula & Olive Pizza al Taglio, 620

Spicy Beef & Zucchini Pizza, 450

Spicy Salami & Provolone Pizza, 362

Spicy Salami, Smoked Ham & Pepper Pizza, 465

Spinach, Zucchini & Pistachio Pesto Pizza, 534

St. Louis–Style Pizza, 271

Taco Pizza, 478

Tom Yum Pizza with Shrimp, 299

Tuna & Onion Pizza, 404

Turkey Ham, Artichoke & Cream Cheese Pizza, 509

Two Cheese & Mushroom Pizza, 429

Vegetable & Mushroom Pizza, 426

Red & Green Cabbage Salad with Ginger & Tahini Dressing, 645

Red Cabbage, Ricotta & Walnut Pizza, 407

Red Wine & Maple Vinaigrette, 659

Rendang & Mushrooms, Pizza with, 296

revzora, 34

Rianata, 220

rianata trapanese, 51–52

ricotta cheese

Dandelion & Tomato Pizza, 585

Garden Vegetable & Ricotta Pizza, 370

Mortadella, Ricotta & Pistachio Pizza alla Pala, 627

Pear & Ricotta Focaccia, 600

Pizza with Ricotta & Cremini Mushrooms, 384

Pizza with Ricotta, Figs & Bacon, 526

Red Cabbage, Ricotta & Walnut Pizza, 407

Ricotta & Bresaola Pizza, 356

Roasted Baby Beet, Radish & Apple Salad with Blue Cheese Mousse, 642

Spinach & Ricotta Pizza, 366

Squash Blossom & Ricotta Pizza, 343

Tiramisu Pizza, 703

ricotta salata cheese

California-Style Pizza, 272

Radicchio & Ricotta Salata Salad with Apple Cider Vinaigrette, 657

Roasted Asparagus & Cherry Tomato Pizza, 358

Roasted Brassica Salad with Pickled Ramps & Buttermilk Caesar Dressing, 648

Roasted Brussels Sprouts with Bacon, Blue Cheese & Pickled Red Onion, 663

Roasted Fennel & Sausage Pizza, 336

Roasted Parsnips & Carrots with Ras el Hanout & Honey, 671

Roasted Radicchio, Pear & Gorgonzola Salad, 656

Roasted Zucchini, Béchamel & Rosemary Pizza, 445

Romaine, Salami & Parmesan, Pizza al Taglio with, 618

Roman pizza

flours for, 67

history of, 58–61

Romana, 238

Romanesco Broccoli Cream, 337

Romesco Sauce

recipe, 578

Romesco & Leek Pizza, 578

Rose Sauce

Pizza with Rose Sauce, Sausage & Potato, 477

recipe, 477

rosemary

Cacciannanze, 178

Focaccia with Olives & Lemon, 608
Grupariata, 199
Roasted Zucchini, Béchamel & Rosemary Pizza, 445
Rosemary & Potato Pizza, 403
Rossa con Filetti di Acciughe, 779
sage
Schiacciata con Cipolla & Salvia, 166, 168
Sweet Potato & Sage Focaccia, 604
salad greens/lettuce
Margherita alla Spigamadre, 633
Pannozzo, 191
Pizza al Taglio with Romaine, Salami & Parmesan, 618
salads
Arugula, Nectarine, Farro & Goat Cheese Salad with White Balsamic Vinaigrette, 644
Chilled Corn Salad, 660
Fennel, Grapefruit & Pistachio Salad, 654
Late Summer Salad with Wild Mushrooms, Parmesan & Pine Nuts, 655
Radicchio & Ricotta Salata Salad with Apple Cider Vinaigrette, 657
Raw Beet Salad with Blood Orange, Jalapeño & Brie, 647
Red & Green Cabbage Salad with Ginger & Tahini Dressing, 645
Roasted Baby Beet, Radish & Apple Salad with Blue Cheese Mousse, 642
Roasted Brassica Salad with Pickled Ramps & Buttermilk Caesar Dressing, 648
Roasted Radicchio, Pear & Gorgonzola Salad, 656
Shaved Brussels Sprouts & Kale Salad with Blood Orange Vinaigrette, 651
Spinach, Bacon, Avocado & Orange Salad, 659

salami
Cajun Shrimp & Salami Pizza, 554
Diavola, 245
Meat Lover's Pizza, 470
Pizza al Taglio with Romaine, Salami & Parmesan, 618
Pizza with Garden Vegetables, Artichokes & Salami, 387
Spicy Salami & Provolone Pizza, 362
Spicy Salami, Smoked Ham & Pepper Pizza, 465
Vasteddi con Sambuco, 223
salmon
Pizza with Seafood, Avocado & Mango, 537
Pizza with Smoked Salmon & Capers, 485
Salmon & Pepper Pizza, 486
Smoked Salmon & Chive Pizza, 482
Teriyaki Salmon Pizza, 284
salt, 67–68
Salt-n-Peppa Prawn Pizza, 747
salvia leaves, Garden Vegetable & Ricotta Pizza, 370
Sardinia, 52–53
sauces
about, 69
Balado Sauce, 295
Bulgogi Sauce, 300
Donair Sauce, 327, 721
Marinara Sauce, 104
Raw Pizza Sauce, 103
Romanesco Broccoli Cream, 337
sausage
Bianca con Salsiccia di Finocchietto, 776
Boscaiola, 242
Broccoli, Chorizo & Chili Pepper Pizza, 421
Carrettiera, 246
Chicken, Sausage & Pine Nut Pizza, 505
Chorizo & Jalapeño Pizza, 319
Chorizo & Olive Pizza, 430
Coppa, Prosciutto & Sausage Pizza, 514

Focaccia di Carnevale Salentina, 212
Meat Lover's Pizza, 470
Panfried Potato & Sausage Pizza, 374
Pizza with Rose Sauce, Sausage & Potato, 477
Pizza with Sausage, Cime di Rapa & Cherry Tomatoes, 376
Roasted Fennel & Sausage Pizza, 336
Sausage, Mushroom & Provolone Pizza, 541
Sausage & Broccoli Pizza, 383
Sausage & Spinach Pizza, 380
Smacafam, 129
St. Louis–Style Pizza, 271
Wild Garlic & Sausage Pizza, 510
Sautéed Radicchio with Beans, Parmesan & Balsamic, 665
Sautéed Red Cabbage with Apples, Fennel & Balsamic, 664
Scaccia Ragusana, 52, 224–225
scale, 79
scallion
The Masher, 731
Pizza with Peking Duck, 304
Red & Green Cabbage Salad with Ginger & Tahini Dressing, 645
sceblasti, 48–49
Sceblasti & Pizzo Leccese, 205
schiaccia, 37
Schiaccia All'uva, 165
schiaccia con l'uva, 37
Schiaccia Toscana, 162
Schiacciata con Cipolla & Salvia, 38, 166, 168
Schizoto, 27, 134
Scoozi, 765
seafood
Cajun Shrimp & Salami Pizza, 554
Calamari, Shrimp & Pesto Pizza, 461
Mari e Monti, 257
Okonomiyaki Pizza, 288

Pescatora, 253
Pizza with Mussels & Artichokes, 357
Pizza with Parsley Pesto & Caviar, 489
Pizza with Peas & Caviar, 558
Pizza with Seafood & Broccoli, 417
Pizza with Seafood, Avocado & Mango, 537
Pizza with Shellfish & Bell Peppers, 457
Pizza with Shrimp, Chili Peppers & Bufala, 462
Pizza with Squid Ink & Seafood, 287
Pizza with Swordfish, Pine Nuts & Cherry Tomatoes, 391
Salt-n-Peppa Prawn Pizza, 747
Seafood & Mayonnaise Pizza, 292
Shrimp, Arugula & Olive Pizza al Taglio, 620
Shrimp & Pineapple Pizza, 589
Smoked Cod & Cheddar Pizza, 481
Smoked Salmon & Chive Pizza, 482
Tom Yum Pizza with Shrimp, 299
See also fish
seaweed, Okonomiyaki Pizza, 288
second fermentation, 74
Settebello Pizzeria Napoletana, 775
Sfincione Palermitano, 50–51, 214–215
shallots
Balado Sauce, 295
Beef Rendang, 296
Melon, Cucumber & Prosciutto Salad with Mint Vinaigrette, 652
Sautéed Radicchio with Beans, Parmesan & Balsamic, 665
Steamed Japanese Eggplant with Black Bean Garlic Sauce & Basil, 666
Tom Yum Paste, 299
shallow skillet, 75

Shaved Brussels Sprouts & Kale Salad with Blood Orange Vinaigrette, 651
shellfish, Pizza with Shellfish & Bell Peppers, 457
short fermentation, 74
shrimp/prawns
Cajun Shrimp & Salami Pizza, 554
Calamari, Shrimp & Pesto Pizza, 461
Mari e Monti, 257
Okonomiyaki Pizza, 288
Pescatora, 253
Pizza with Seafood & Broccoli, 417
Pizza with Shellfish & Bell Peppers, 457
Pizza with Shrimp, Chili Peppers & Bufala, 462
Salt-n-Peppa Prawn Pizza, 747
Shrimp, Arugula & Olive Pizza al Taglio, 620
Shrimp & Pineapple Pizza, 589
Tom Yum Pizza with Shrimp, 299
Sicilia, 50–52
Smacafam, 26, 129
Smoked Chicken, Bufala & Pesto Focaccia, 599
Smoked Cod & Cheddar Pizza, 481
smoked salmon
Pizza with Smoked Salmon & Capers, 485
Smoked Salmon & Chive Pizza, 482
S'mores Pizza, 688
sourdough
about, 68
Sourdough Focaccia Dough, 100
Sourdough Pizza Dough, 123
Sourdough Starter, 101
Southern Collard Greens, 668
Spacca Napoli Pizzeria, 711–712, 715
Speck, Asiago & Gorgonzola, Pizza with Figs, 498

Spicy Barbeque Sauce
BBQ Chicken Pizza, 409
Pulled Pork Pizza, 561
Spicy Beef & Zucchini Pizza, 450
Spicy Salami & Provolone Pizza, 362
Spicy Salami, Smoked Ham & Pepper Pizza, 465
spinach
Pizza with Goat Cheese, Fennel & Walnuts, 553
Pizza with Goat Cheese, Spinach, Honey & Hazelnuts, 506
Pizza with Peas & Caviar, 558
Sausage & Spinach Pizza, 380
Spinach, Bacon, Avocado & Orange Salad, 659
Spinach, Egg & Cheese Pizza, 473
Spinach, Zucchini & Pistachio Pesto Pizza, 534
Spinach & Feta Focaccia, 607
Spinach & Ricotta Pizza, 366
Three Cheese & Spinach Pizza, 502
spring onions
Cavicione, 210
Natto & Bacon Pizza, 291
Teriyaki Chicken & Mushroom Pizza, 283
sprouts, Pizza with Smoked Herring, Radish & Cream Cheese, 549
squash
Farmers Market, 744
Squash Blossom & Ricotta Pizza, 343
squid
Pescatora, 253
Pizza with Seafood & Broccoli, 417
Pizza with Seafood, Avocado & Mango, 537
Pizza with Squid Ink & Seafood, 287
Srirachanaise, 747
St. Louis pizza, 63
St. Louis–Style Pizza, 271

stand mixers, 79

Steamed Japanese Eggplant with Black Bean Garlic Sauce & Basil, 666

stracchino, Focaccia di Recco, 151

strawberries

Brigadeiro & Strawberry Pizza, 692

Chocolate, Hazelnut & Strawberry Pizza, 687

Mixed Berry Pizza, 521

strazzata, 46

Sud Italia, 769

sun-dried tomatoes

Pizza with Broccoli & Bacon, 414

Pizza with Goat Cheese, Fennel & Walnuts, 553

Pizza with 'Ndjua, Sun-Dried Tomatoes & Caciocavallo, 406

Pizza with Sun-Dried Tomatoes & Zucchini Cream, 379

Sweet Potato & Sage Focaccia, 604

Swiss cheese, St. Louis–Style Pizza, 271

Swordfish Carpaccio

Pizza with Swordfish, Pine Nuts & Cherry Tomatoes, 391

recipe, 391

Taco Pizza, 478

tahini

Ginger & Tahini Dressing, 645

Lahmacun, 323

taleggio cheese

Focaccia di Recco, 151

tamarind pulp, Beef Rendang, 296

Tano's Pizzeria, 759–761

Teriyaki Chicken & Mushroom Pizza, 283

Teriyaki Salmon Pizza, 284

Thai chili paste; Tom Yum Paste, 299

Theo & Co., 739

Theo & Co.'s Basic Pizza Dough, 740

Theo & Co.'s Skillet Pizza Dough, 741

Thick-Crust Pizza with Onions, 316

Three Cheese & Spinach Pizza, 502

Thyme, Blue Cheese & Walnuts, Pizza with Pear, 684

Tigelle, 157

Tikka Masala Pizza, 307

Tiramisu Pizza, 703

Tirot, 28, 133

Tofu Cream Cheese, Pizza with Grilled Vegetables &, 566

Tom Yum Paste, 299

Tom Yum Pizza with Shrimp, 299

tomatoes

Arugula, Pomegranate & Cherry Tomato Pizza, 569

Avocado, Tomato & Feta Pizza, 525

Balado Sauce, 295

Broccoli Rabe, Tomato & Olive Pizza, 533

Calzone Pugliese, 208–209

Caprese, 254

Chicken & Catupiry Pizza, 312

Cucumber, Tomato & Chicken Pizza, 581

Dandelion & Tomato Pizza, 585

Dante's Personal Pizzas, 736

Endive & Cherry Tomato Pizza, 542

Faccia di Vecchia, 216

Focaccia Barese, 200

Focaccia di Altamura, 202

Focaccia di Carnevale Salentina, 212

Focaccia Messinese, 219

Focaccia Portoscusese, 227

Frying Pan Margherita, 754

Garlic Potato & Zucchini Pizza, 438

Green Tomato Pizza, 522

Grupariata, 199

Halifax Explosion, 720

Ham & Veggie Pizza, 434

Lahmacun, 323

Lamb, Eggplant & Tomato Pizza, 586

Margherita alla Spigamadre, 633

Mustazzeddu, 228

Panuozzo, 191

Parigina, 192

Pesto, Tomato & Bufala Pizza, 365

Pissalandrea, 147

Pizza al Padellino, 139

Pizza with Broccoli & Bacon, 414

Pizza with Garden Vegetables & Bufala, 449

Pizza with Goat Cheese, Fennel & Walnuts, 553

Pizza with 'Ndjua, Sun-Dried Tomatoes & Caciocavallo, 406

Pizza with Prunes, Goat Cheese & Tomatoes, 577

Pizza with Sausage, Cime di Rapa & Cherry Tomatoes, 376

Pizza with Sicilian-Style Tuna & Bell Peppers, 352

Pizza with Sun-Dried Tomatoes & Zucchini Cream, 379

Pizza with Swordfish, Pine Nuts & Cherry Tomatoes, 391

Puddica Salentina, 203

Rianata, 220

Roasted Asparagus & Cherry Tomato Pizza, 358

Romesco Sauce, 578

Rose Sauce, 477

Rossa con Filetti di Acciughe, 779

Scaccia Ragusana, 224–225

Sceblasti & Pizzo Leccese, 205

Sfincione Palermitano, 214–215

Smoked Chicken, Bufala & Pesto Focaccia, 599

Vegetable & Mushroom Pizza, 426

Zucchini Blossom & Cherry Tomato Pizza, 441

Zucchini with Tomatoes, Feta, Garlic & Lemon, 675

See also sauces

Torta al Testo, 38, 170

ABOUT CIDER MILL PRESS BOOK PUBLISHERS

Good ideas ripen with time. From seed to harvest, Cider Mill Press brings fine reading, information, and entertainment together between the covers of its creatively crafted books. Our Cider Mill bears fruit twice a year, publishing a new crop of titles each spring and fall.

"Where Good Books Are Ready for Press"

501 Nelson Place
Nashville, Tennessee 37214
cidermillpress.com

Torta al Testo con Farina di Mais, 173

Torta al Testo con i Ciccioli, 169

torta coi ciccioli, 38

Toscana, 36–37

Trentino Alto Adige, 26

Trout, Poached Eggs & Capers, Pizza with Smoked, 517

Truffles, Pizza with Parmesan, Bresaola &, 400

tuma cheese, Vastedda con Sambuco, 223

tuna
  Chichiripieno, 177
  Pizza with Sicilian-Style Tuna & Bell Peppers, 352
  Pizza with Tuna & Corn, 458
  Tuna & Onion Pizza, 404
  Tuna & Orange-Marinated Fennel Pizza, 340

turkey
  Red & Green Cabbage Salad with Ginger & Tahini Dressing, 645
  Turkey Ham, Artichoke & Cream Cheese Pizza, 509

24-Hour Focaccia with 60 Percent Hydration, 87

24-Hour Focaccia with 70 Percent Hydration, 88

24-Hour Focaccia with 80 Percent Hydration, 91

24-Hour Pizza Dough with 62 Percent Hydration, 111

24-Hour Pizza Dough with 67 Percent Hydration, 112

24-Hour Pizza Dough with 72 Percent Hydration, 115

Two Cheese & Bacon Pizza, 422

Two Cheese & Mushroom Pizza, 429

Umbria, 38

Vanilla Custard Pizza, 696

Vastedda con Sambuco, 52, 223

Vegetable & Mushroom Pizza, 426

Veneto, 27

walnuts
  Basil Pesto, 365
  Pear & Ricotta Focaccia, 600
  Pizza with Goat Cheese, Fennel & Walnuts, 553
  Pizza with Goat Cheese, Figs & Walnuts, 513
  Pizza with Ham, Gorgonzola, Pears & Walnuts, 497
  Pizza with Pear, Thyme, Blue Cheese & Walnuts, 684
  Pizza with Prosciutto, Caciocavallo, Wild Mushrooms & Nuts, 494
  Red Cabbage, Ricotta & Walnut Pizza, 407

water, 67

Wild Garlic & Sausage Pizza, 510

wine, white
  Chisola Piacentina, 158
  Pizza Scima, 187
  Schiaccia Toscana, 162

yeast, 68

yogurt
  Aloo Gobi Marinade, 308
  Farmers Market, 744
  Kebab Pizza, 469

yu choy
  Yu Choy with Black Bean Garlic Sauce & Extra Garlic, 674
  Yu Choy with Garlic & Soy, 672

Za'atar, 324

zucchini
  Farmers Market, 744
  Garden Vegetable & Ricotta Pizza, 370

Garlic Potato & Zucchini Pizza, 438

Grilled Zucchini & Eggplant Pizza, 453

Margherita with Panfried Zucchini, 396

Pizza alla Pala with Zucchini Blossoms, Anchovies & Burrata, 624

Pizza with Grilled Vegetables & Tofu Cream Cheese, 566

Pizza with Sun-Dried Tomatoes & Zucchini Cream, 379

Quark & Zucchini Pizza, 590

Radicchio & Garden Vegetable Pizza, 361

Roasted Zucchini, Béchamel & Rosemary Pizza, 445

Sceblasti & Pizzo Leccese, 205

Spicy Beef & Zucchini Pizza, 450

Spinach, Zucchini & Pistachio Pesto Pizza, 534

Vegetable & Mushroom Pizza, 426

Zucchini & Feta alla Spigamadre, 630

Zucchini Blossom & Cherry Tomato Pizza, 441

Zucchini with Tomatoes, Feta, Garlic & Lemon, 675

Zucchini Cream
  Pizza with Sun-Dried Tomatoes & Zucchini Cream, 379
  Pizza with Zucchini Cream, Bacon & Bufala, 437
  recipe, 379